BLACK GENIUS

Inspirational Portraits of America's

Black Leaders

DICK RUSSELL

Foreword by
Alvin F. Poussaint, M.D.

A Herman Graf Book
SKYHORSE PUBLISHING

Skyhorse Publishing books may be purchased in bulk at special discounts for sales promotion, corporate gifts, fund-raising, or educational purposes. Special editions can also be created to specifications. For details, contact the Special Sales Department, Skyhorse Publishing, 555 Eighth Avenue, Suite 903, New York, NY 10018 or info@skyhorsepublishing.com.

www.skyhorsepublishing.com

10 9 8 7 6 5 4 3 2 1

Library of Congress Cataloging-in-Publication Data

Russell, Dick.
Black genius : inspirational portraits of America's black leaders / Dick Russell ; foreword by Alvin F. Poussaint.—Large print ed.
p. cm.
Includes bibliographical references and index.
ISBN 978-1-60239-369-1 (alk. paper)
1. African Americans—Biography. 2. African American leadership.
I. Title.
E185.96.R89 2009
920'.009296073—dc22
2008045975

Printed in the United States of America

Contents

Part 3. BUILDERS OF AMERICA:
Science, Invention, Mathematics and Architecture 287

Part 4. HEALERS OF BODY AND SPIRIT 373

Prologue

BARACK OBAMA: "AN ABIDING FAITH IN THE POSSIBILITIES OF THIS NATION"

"I stand here knowing that my story is part of the larger American story, that I owe a debt to all of those who came before me, and that, in no other country on earth is my story even possible."

> —*Barack Obama, in his keynote address to the Democratic National Convention, 2004.*

It was twelve degrees outside, and he was wearing a dark suit with a black overcoat (and long johns underneath). Behind him stood the Old State Capitol in Springfield, Illinois, with its pillars of sandstone. Here, in 1858, a little-known politician named Abraham Lincoln had accepted his party's nomination for the U.S. Senate by saying: "A house divided against itself cannot stand. I believe this government cannot endure, permanently half slave and half free."

Now, facing Lincoln's law office, Barack Obama speaks of how "the life of a tall, gangly, self-made Springfield lawyer tells us that a different future is possible. He tells us that there is power in words. He tells us that there is power in conviction. That beneath all the differences of race and region, faith and station, we are one people. He tells us that there is power in hope." His words rising in wisps of steam, this descendant of an African warrior and a Southern slave-holder, this man in his mid-forties whose extended family was spread across several continents, told a crowd estimated at 17,000 that he had gathered with them "to transform a nation." It was February 10, 2007, and recently-elected U.S. Senator Barack Obama was announcing his "improbable quest" for the presidency of the United States.

Almost a year later, at the invitation of the Ebenezer Baptist Church in Atlanta where Martin Luther King, Jr. initiated his ministry and his civil rights crusade, Obama began his speech by recalling King's rallying cry on the eve of the Montgomery bus boycotts: "Unity is the great need of the hour." This was true today, Obama said, in order to overcome "a moral

deficit. . . .an empathy deficit. . . .an inability to recognize ourselves in one
another. . . . Dr. King understood that unity cannot be won on the cheap;
that we would have to earn it through great effort and determination."

On the 45th anniversary of King's "I have a dream" speech in front
of the Lincoln Memorial, after the "great effort and determination" that
secured him the Democratic nomination, Obama told 80,000 people
gathered in a Denver stadium: ". . . it is that American spirit, that American
promise, that pushes us forward even when the path is uncertain; that
binds us together in spite of our differences; that makes us fix our eye not
on what is seen, but what is unseen." The promise that had also led Dr.
King to say, "We cannot walk alone."

The journey of Barack Obama is a quintessentially American one, and
much in keeping with the themes that are emphasized in this book: the
importance of family, ancestors, mentors, and tradition. It seems fitting,
then, that a number of the individuals profiled in these pages have been
cited by Obama among his most important influences. He has called
Professor Cornel West one of his heroes. He has listed Toni Morrison's
Song of Solomon, along with the tragedies of Shakespeare, as his favorite
literary works. He has said of Frederick Douglass that nobody speaks so
eloquently anymore, admiring above all his "collective voice that embraced
white and black concerns." He has read widely in James Baldwin, Ralph
Ellison, and W. E. B. Du Bois, and has listened deeply to Wynton Marsalis
(a personal friend of Obama's), as well as John Coltrane and other giants
of jazz.

The resonance and respect are mutual. Venerable author Albert Murray
proudly calls Obama "an American phenomenon." Cornel West, asked
whether he saw a line going from Jesse Jackson to Obama or two separate
traditions, responded: "Obama is a qualitative leap forward—a leap that
has to do primarily with the white electorate's openness to his political
genius."

Nobel Prize-winning author Toni Morrison wrote to Obama in
an open letter in January 2008: "I stunned myself when I came to the
following conclusion: that in addition to keen intelligence, integrity and a
rare authenticity, you exhibit something that has nothing to do with age,
experience, race or gender . . . a creative imagination which coupled with
brilliance equals wisdom."

Morrison went on: "When, I wondered, was the last time this
country was guided by such a leader? Someone whose moral center
was un-embargoed? Someone with courage instead of mere ambition?
Someone who truly thinks of his country's citizens as 'we,' not 'they'?

Someone who understands what it will take to help America realize the virtues it fancies about itself, what it desperately needs to become in the world?"

That "we" seems to have been engrained in the very blood that runs through Obama's veins. His immediate heritage is about more than a Caucasian mother who grew up in Kansas and an African father from Kenya. "What is a family?" he wondered in his first book, *Dreams From My Father*. "Is it just a genetic chain, parents and offspring, people like me? Or is it a social construct, an economic unit, optimal for child rearing and divisions of labor? Or is it something else entirely: a store of shared memories, say? An ambit of love? A reach across the void?"

On his mother's side, if we reach back ten generations to seventeenth-century Massachusetts and the Hinckley family that emigrated from England, it turns out that Obama and George W. Bush are eleventh cousins who share the same ancestors. One of the Hinckley sons, Thomas, became Governor of the Plymouth Colony. Nine generations ago, a French Protestant fleeing religious persecution "became one of the most successful merchants and planters" in colonial Maryland; Mareen DuVall and his wife Susannah were, besides being Obama's forbears, also the ninth-great-grandparents of Harry Truman and the eighth-great-grandparents of none other than Dick Cheney. (Another descendant is the actor Robert DuVall).

Over the course of the next three centuries, Obama's maternal heritage would come to include immigrants from Ireland, Scotland, Germany, and the Netherlands, as well as a full-blooded Cherokee. They would serve in the Revolutionary War and the Civil War. They would be killed by pirates, Indians, and Quantrill's Raiders. They would be farmers and pharmacists, restaurant owners and tobacconists, shoemakers and blacksmiths. They would manage oil leases and work in the new field of aviation. One, who accused another man of witchcraft in colonial Massachusetts, later changed his name to Dunham, Obama's mother's maiden name. Another was apparently a second cousin of Confederate leader Jefferson Davis.

On his father's side, his step-grandmother Sarah Obama tracked the ancestral line back twelve generations in Africa but, as she told Obama, "The women who bore them, their names are forgotten, for that was the way of our people." The first known ancestor, eight generations earlier, was known as Owiny. He was "a great warrior and leader of his people. He helped to defeat the Bantu armies," according to Sarah, "but the Bantu were allowed to stay on and marry Luo, and taught us many things about farming and the new land." Much of this region of Kenya would come to be called "Land of the Obama."

His paternal grandfather was Hussein Onyango Obama, "a prominent farmer, an elder of the tribe, a medicine man with healing powers," Barack Hussein Obama would write in his autobiography. An herbalist who learned to use plants to cure the sick, he worked for wealthy whites on their estates in colonial Kenya and is said to have been the first person in his region to wear Western clothes instead of just a loincloth. Saving enough wages to buy his own land and livestock, he served as an officer's cook while traveling widely with British regiments during World War II. He converted first to Christianity and later to Islam, altogether taking four wives.

Long after, making his first journey to Kenya, his grandson would learn of how the elder Obama had once chased a "night runner" in the guise of a leopard carrying off one of his goats. And the grandson would have a dream about running along a village road: "Panting for breath, I turned around to see the day turned night, and a giant figure looming as tall as the trees, wearing only a loincloth and a ghostly mask. The lifeless eyes bored into me, and I heard a thunderous voice saying only that it was time, and my entire body began to shake violently with the sound. . . ." Obama awoke in a sweat and slept no more that night.

His encounter with Africa came as an adult, part of a quest to learn more about the father who left home when Obama was only two. The boy had spent his formative teenaged years under the care of his white maternal grandparents, who had ended up living in Hawaii. Stanley Dunham, at the age of eight had discovered his own mother's body after she committed suicide in Wichita, Kansas, and had hopped freights and gotten involved in "moonshine, cards and women," before eventually becoming a furniture salesman. "His was an American character, one typical of men of his generation, men who embraced the notion of freedom and individualism and the open road without always knowing its price." Many would recall seeing Obama in the company of "Gramps," recalled by one reporter as "a loving soul inclined toward tall tales and unrealistic dreams." He used to tell tourists that Obama was the great-grandson of Hawaii's first monarch, King Kamehameha. Taking his grandson to see the returning Apollo astronauts, he would swear that one waved directly at the boy. Obama would write in his second book, *The Audacity of Hope*: "it was in my relationship with my grandfather that I think I first internalized the full meaning of empathy." He died shortly before Obama married, and the grandson would bring the wedding reception to tears recalling how Stanley Dunham "made a little boy with an absent father feel as though he was never alone."

His grandmother, Madelyne Durham, was affectionately called "Toot" by Obama and others ("Tutu" is the Hawaiian word for grandma). "Her dogged practicality kept the family afloat," Obama wrote; she was "suspicious of overwrought sentiments or overblown claims, content with common sense . . . a trailblazer of sorts, the first woman vice-president of a local bank." It was Madelyne, according to Obama biographer David Mendell, who bequeathed his "practical and pragmatic side." Traveling through southern Illinois during his campaign for the U. S. Senate, Obama revealed that "these mostly white, middle-class, down-to-earth Midwestern people reminded him of his grandparents and he felt completely comfortable in their midst." A feeling that was reciprocated.

Both his white grandmother and African step-grandmother were still alive to observe his run for the presidency. This was not the case for either of his parents, both of whom died while still in their early fifties (as did his Indonesian stepfather). The rise of Barack Obama Sr., not unlike that of his namesake, had been meteoric, "from being a goat herder in a small village in Africa to getting a scholarship to the University of Hawaii to going to Harvard," as the son once described it. It was John F. Kennedy, then chairman of a Senate subcommittee on Africa, who arranged a grant through his family's foundation that airlifted the first young Kenyans— including Obama's father—to receive scholarships in America. In Hawaii Obama Sr. met Ann Dunham, and their only child was born in 1961. Obama and his mother would be on food stamps for a time after the father soon left her and returned to Africa. There he would have two more children, while working for an American oil company and as a Kenyan government economist, before his political career "turned in on itself. . . .because of problems of tribalism and nepotism in Kenya and partly his own failures," his son would recall. Eventually his passport was revoked, and he would die in a car accident. Obama knew his father mainly through stories and letters, meeting him only once as a teenager. The image young Obama had carried of "the brilliant scholar, the generous friend, the upstanding leader" would take on darker characteristics as he learned more about him: "A bitter drunk? An abusive husband? A defeated, lonely bureaucrat? To think that all my life I had been wrestling with nothing more than a ghost!"

Obama came to believe that his own "fierce ambitions" were fueled by his father ("Every man is trying to live up to his father's expectations or make up for his mistakes. In my case, both things might be true.") Yet it was his mother's "fundamental faith—in the goodness of people and in the ultimate value of this brief life we've each been given—that channeled these ambitions." She was "the single constant in my life . . . the kindest, most generous spirit I have ever known. . . .what is best in me I owe to her." Biographer Mendell notes, "this is also the central message that Obama imparts in his political speeches—that all of us are bound together as one, and if we are to prosper as a country and, indeed, as a species, that we must focus on the good we see in others."

Ann Dunham, a cultural anthropologist, seemed born to wander. Obama wrote of her in recalling his youthful years in Indonesia, "It was as if, by traveling halfway around the globe, away from the smugness and hypocrisy that familiarity had disclosed, my mother could give voice to the virtues of her Midwestern past and offer them up in distilled form." She introduced her son to books about King and the Civil Rights movement, played him recordings of Mahalia Jackson, and filled him with stories of African-American heroes such as Thurgood Marshall and Sidney Poitier. She also sought to provide him "a working knowledge of the world's great religions. . . . In our household the Bible, the Koran, and the Bhagavad Gita sat on the shelf alongside books of Greek and Norse and African mythology." She was as likely to "drag" him to a Buddhist temple or ancient Hawaiian burial sites as a Christian church. His stepfather, Lolo Soetoro, who worked for the Indonesian government and an American oil company, "followed a brand of Islam that could make room for the remnants of more ancient animist and Hindu faiths."

Thus Obama was "raised as an Indonesian child and a Hawaiian child and as a black child and as a white child. And so what I benefited from is a multiplicity of cultures that all fed me." He came to "believe that part of America's genius has always been its ability to absorb newcomers, to forge a national identity out of the disparate lot that arrived on our shores."

But the realizations, like those about his father, did not come easily. While still a boy, "I began to notice that [Bill] Cosby never got the girl on *I Spy*, that the black man on *Mission Impossible* spent all his time underground. I noticed that there was nobody like me in the Sears, Roebuck Christmas catalog that Toot and Gramps sent us, and that Santa was a white man." By the time he reached adolescence and was living with his grandparents in Hawaii, he was immersing himself in books by Baldwin, Ellison, Du Bois, Richard Wright, and Langston Hughes. In his room at night, pretending to do his homework, "there I would sit and wrestle with words, locked in suddenly desperate argument, trying to reconcile the world as I'd found it with the terms of my birth. But there was no escape to be had. In every page of every book, in Bigger Thomas and invisible men, I kept finding the same anguish, the same doubt. . . . Only Malcolm X's autobiography seemed to offer something different. His repeated acts of self-creation spoke to me; the blunt poetry of his words, his unadorned insistence on respect, promised a new and uncompromising order, martial in its discipline, forged through sheer will."

At the same time Obama's militancy grew, he knew intrinsically "that traveling down the road to self-respect my own white blood would never recede into mere abstraction. I was left to wonder what else I would be severing if and when I left my mother and my grandparents at some uncharted border. . . . My identity might begin with the fact of my race, but it didn't, couldn't, end there."

He came to find, while attending Occidental College in California, that "what I needed was a community. . . .a community that cut deeper than the common despair that black friends and I shared when reading the latest crime statistics, or the high fives I might exchange on a basketball court. A place where I could put down stakes and test my commitments." He was deeply influenced by a professor named Roger Boesche, who taught courses in American and Modern Political Thought and whose personal hero was Jefferson.

At 20, Obama went on to Columbia University in New York, where he lived "an ascetic existence. I did a lot of spiritual exploration [and] withdrew from the world in a fairly deliberate way." Obama fasted, often going for days without speaking to another human being. He absorbed Nietzche, Melville, and Toni Morrison along with St. Augustine and the Bible. Professor Boesche would recall that Obama "went through a whole reasoning process in which he reevaluated all the core beliefs that he had—and then came out on the other side." Sometimes he would wander into a Harlem church on Sundays and find tears welling up as he listened to the choir. Always a seeker drawn to life's larger questions, "wandering the streets or reading books," Obama "decided that the meaning I found in my life, the values that were most important to me, the sense of wonder that I had, the sense of tragedy that I had—all these things were captured in the Christian story." Yet his strongest religious influences extended to the Founding Fathers, and to Lincoln, "men driven by reason [who] were full of skepticism and doubt."

New York was also where Obama "began to chronicle the day-to-day events of his life on a pad of lined white paper that he toted around," according to biographer Mendell, with thoughts of perhaps being a short-story writer. Organizing called him instead, through a Chicago activist Obama encountered named Jerry Kellman. Chicago's South Side constituted the biggest single aggregation of blacks anywhere in America. And community organizing would teach Obama, writes Mendell, "that idealism must be coupled with pragmatism and hard realism." Obama learned amid "the boarded-up homes, the decaying storefronts . . . all of it whispered painful truths."

He would also write of meeting these everyday people: "They'd offer a story to match or confound mine, a knot to bind our experiences together—a lost father, an adolescent brush with crime, a wandering heart, a moment of simple grace. As time passed, I found that these stories, taken together, had helped me bind my world together, that they gave me the sense of place and purpose I'd been looking for. . . . There was always a community there if you dug deep enough. . . . There was poetry as well—a luminous world always present beneath the surface, a world that people might offer up as a gift to me, if I only remembered to ask."

In Chicago, too, Obama found a church (Trinity) and a pastor, Reverend Jeremiah Wright. Listening to a sermon that Wright called "The Audacity of Hope" stirred Obama. Biblical stories merged in his imagination with those "of ordinary black people. . . . Our trials and triumphs became at once unique and universal. . . ." He was "drawn to the power of the African-American religious tradition to spur social change. Out of necessity, the black church had to minister to the whole person. Out of necessity, the black church rarely had the luxury of separating individual salvation from collective salvation. It had to serve as the center of the community's political, economic, and social as well as spiritual life; it understood in an intimate way the biblical call to feed the hungry and clothe the naked and challenge powers and principalities."

Obama's first trip to Kenya, in the early 1990s, brought him full circle. He would learn from "Granny" of his family's long history in Africa (using an interpreter, because she spoke only Luo). Afterward, sitting and weeping between the graves of his father and grandfather, Obama "realized that who I was, what I cared about, was no longer just a matter of intellect or obligation, no longer a construct of words. I saw that my life in America—the black life, the white life, the sense of abandonment I'd felt as a boy, the frustration and hope I'd witnessed in Chicago—all of it was connected with this small plot of earth an ocean away, connected by more than the accident of a name or the color of my skin."

Not long thereafter, Obama moved on to Harvard Law School, where one classmate described him as "mature beyond his years in being able to approach issues in the way that he did." Although he remained a liberal in his thinking, conservatives found him open to their viewpoints. He became the first African-American President of the Harvard Law Review. It was during a summer internship in Chicago that he met his future wife, the no-nonsense Michelle Robinson, also a Harvard Law graduate. "Beyond Obama's keen intellect and personal charm," writes biographer Mendell, "what sealed Michelle's love for him was his civility and human compassion."

After a four-year courtship, they married and the couple settled in Chicago's Hyde Park section, while Obama took a job at Miner, Barnhill & Galland, a civil rights law firm, and a professorship at the University of Chicago Law School. It had almost no black faculty, and its emphasis was on economics. One of Obama's three courses was on racism and the law, improvising his own textbook that contained essays by Douglass, Du Bois, King and Malcolm X. As he built a reputation for open and exciting discussions, student enrollment soared in his classes. At the same time, Obama was elected to the Illinois state legislature, then lost in his first bid for election to the U.S. Congress. When he decided to run for the Senate in 2003, he was forced to cancel his course load.

What introduced Obama to a national audience was the keynote speech that John Kerry invited him to give at the 2004 Democratic Convention in Boston. Obama wrote it out in long-hand, in hotel rooms, and his personal story electrified the country. Paraphrasing his pastor's sermon, he spoke of "The audacity of hope! In the end, that is God's greatest gift to us, the bedrock of this nation. A belief in things not seen. A belief that there are better days ahead."

His memoir, *Dreams From My Father*, first published in 1995, suddenly soared to the top of the best-seller list. It was written, of course, before he entered politics; its candor was raw and refreshing about what he'd experimented with and been through as a younger man. In that sense, it contained some of the qualities of *The Autobiography of Malcolm X* and the autobiographical essays of James Baldwin. Indeed, the book was highly literary, drawing upon influences from Ernest Hemingway to Toni Morrison. Here is a portion of his description of being on a safari in the land of the Masai: "There in the dusk, over that hill, I imagined the first man stepping forward, naked and rough-skinned, grasping a chunk of flint in his clumsy hand, no words yet for the fear, the anticipation, the awe he feels at the sky, the glimmering knowledge of his own death. If only we could remember that first common step, that first common word—that time before Babel."

No doubt with fear, anticipation, and considerable awe, Obama succeeded in becoming only the fifth African-American elected to the

U.S. Senate since Reconstruction. His second book, *The Audacity of Hope*, opens with a revealingly candid description of his introduction to the Senate chamber: "In the world's greatest deliberative body," Obama concludes, "no one is listening."

He is as forthright about the pitfalls of being a politician as he was about his earlier struggles in *Dreams*. "I know that as a consequence of my fund-raising I became more like the wealthy donors I met," Obama writes, "in the very particular sense that I spent more and more of my time above the fray, outside the world of immediate hunger, disappointment, fear, irrationality, and frequent hardship of the other 99 percent of the population—that is, the people that I'd entered public life to serve. . . . You learn to rationalize the changes as a matter of realism, of compromise, of learning the ropes. The problems of ordinary people, the voices of the Rust Belt town or the dwindling heartland, become a distant echo other than a palpable reality, abstractions to be managed rather than battles to be fought."

But if one is aware of such an inherent dilemma, and willing to admit it publicly, this is at least the first step in seeking to remedy it. For there is no doubt how aggrieved and angered Obama is by, as he also writes, "black men filling our prisons, black children unable to read or caught in a gangland shooting, the black homeless sleeping on grates and in the park of our nation's capital—we take these things for granted, as part of the natural order, a tragic situation, perhaps, but not one for which we are culpable, and certainly not something subject to change."

Above all, Obama was a man willing to question—both his society, and himself. Sometimes he would feel as though he was meeting his goal of "leaving behind a legacy that will make our children's lives more hopeful than our own. . . . At other times, it seems as if the goal recedes from me, and all the activity I engage in—the hearings and speeches and press conferences and position papers—are an exercise in vanity, useful to no one."

His wife, Michelle, has a large role in keeping him grounded. In a telling description of their being backstage together before the 2004 keynote speech that put him on the national map, he recalls Michelle saying: "Just don't screw it up, buddy!" As he walked out there, thinking of the family saga he was about to tell, he thought to himself, "Lord, let me tell their stories right."

Obama gave readers a revealing glimpse of his particular "human condition" with this passage in *Audacity* about his arrival in the nation's capital after the Senate election. ". . . After thirteen years of marriage,

I found myself to be fully domesticated, soft and helpless. My first morning in Washington, I realized I'd forgotten to buy a shower curtain and had to scrunch up against the shower wall in order to avoid flooding the bathroom floor. The next night, watching the game and having a beer, I fell asleep at halftime, and woke up on the couch two hours later with a bad crick in my neck."

The couple has two children, and both parents have spoken of the family strain resulting from his constant traveling. A close friend tells of approaching Obama, whose head was down, shortly before being elected to the Senate, and asking what was wrong. "When he lifted his head to answer, a tear rolled down his cheek. 'I'm really going to miss those two little girls,' he said."

How far Obama had come, and how quickly! In 2000, in the midst of a first campaign for Congress that failed dismally, he'd found a cheap flight to the Democratic Convention only to see his credit card rejected by the rental-car agency, then been unable to even obtain a convention floor pass and headed home early. Four years later came the keynote speech, followed by his election to the Senate, then the decision to run for the presidency.

Once, Obama told a reporter that the three men he most admired were Gandhi, Lincoln, and King—"men who were able to bring about extraordinary changes and place themselves in a difficult historical moment and be a moral center." It was beyond a question of ambition or of will. The times demanded him; the nation needed him.

Was he tough enough? In Obama's cluttered private office in Chicago, right behind his desk he keeps a large framed photograph of Muhammad Ali, glove raised and hollering down at a prone Sonny Liston lying on the canvas after a first-round knockdown in 1965. Obama bought the picture on the spot from a street vendor. Perhaps, in moments of doubt, the image would serve as a reminder of what it takes and what can happen.

He is, assuredly, not a man without his peccadilloes and vices. He was a secret smoker for years, agreeing to quit (at his wife's insistence) only when he announced his candidacy for president. His nature can be mercurial and some black leaders, including Cornel West, initially found Obama too idealistic in his approach. But, after West criticized him publicly for this, Obama telephoned him soon after announcing his presidential bid. "We talked for several hours," West remembers, "and had just a wonderful open, robust, uninhibited conversation, a beautiful dialogue. He laid it out, gave me his whole history and formation, the community organizing, what the freedom movement meant to him." West realized their backgrounds and callings were different, telling Obama that "your calling is one of progressive governance." Not long after this, Obama invited West to come to Washington, "so we could meet and talk face-to-face. After that I was on the bandwagon."

While West campaigned for Obama, he continued to issue critiques where he felt they were warranted. And Obama has referred to the Princeton professor's leaving phone messages for him as "the oracle, the voice of wisdom." For his part, West adds: "I think that he's actually a very introspective person. He's got a real kind of quiet dignity, juxtaposed with the public eloquence, and that's rare among politicians. Of course, Lincoln had it more than any other president."

Obama has said of Lincoln that he "starts off, as far as we can tell, a deeply skeptical but powerfully moral person who, as he finds himself in the midst of history and potential cataclysm, feels it necessary to hang on to a more explicit belief in providence and faith. And so that resonates with me."

The spirit that Obama carries—or perhaps the spirit that is carrying him—also harkens to other leaders, other times. No presidential candidate since Franklin D. Roosevelt had seen so many songs written about him by a grassroots following. There were echoes of the Kennedys as well. "I wouldn't be here if, time and again, the torch had not been passed to a new generation," Obama said in one campaign speech, echoing JFK's inaugural address. Like Kennedy, Obama went from being a rather introverted campaigner—considered by some to be a condescending elitist—to a skilled orator capable of connecting to people with an "everyman" quality. (Obama would speak of "a certain rhythm that you feel from the audience" that necessitated varying patterns of speech.) In the Senate, his desk would turn out to be the same one that Robert Kennedy had, and his chief political adviser David Axelrod had gotten his start passing out leaflets for RFK's 1968 campaign at the age of eight.

As Bruce Reed of the Democratic Leadership Council put it: "People don't come to Obama for what he's done. They come because of what they hope he can be." This was much evident during the final two months of the 2008 campaign, on a rainy evening in Concord, New Hampshire. Along with thousands of others, I went there to see Obama up close and personal. The banners were ubiquitous in the gymnasium of the New Hampshire Institute of Technology: CHANGE. CHANGE WE NEED. CHANGE WE CAN BELIEVE IN. I found a seat in the third row of the bleachers. "Why do you like Obama?" I asked an elderly lady next to me.

"I'm interested in education," she replied. "And it's about my grandchild, I don't want to see him fight in any more wars. I also like my children to be hopeful about their country, not cynical. So I'm not going to stand by this time. I'm doing whatever I possibly can to get this man elected." After a few minutes, she turned to me with another thought. "There's something else: he has a wonderful ability to speak to a person in close proximity, without seeming to invade their space. Yet this has been used against him, as if somehow it's wrong to have that ability." She contrasted this to watching Republican candidate John McCain introduce his running mate, Sarah Palin, at the convention, and seeming so awkward, uncertain of where to stand.

The crowd filtered in slowly past the security checkpoint, men in Red Sox caps, women wearing I'M A HEALTH CARE VOTER T-shirts, Seniors for Obama, pregnant women, veterans in wheelchairs. Many nationalities were present—women draped in the native dress of India, a man and his young son each wearing African *kente* cloths. By five PM, the bleachers were full and more people began packing the basketball court, standing and waiting and listening to "Born in the USA" and other songs coming over a loudspeaker. They sang along to the lyrics—"Get ready 'cause here I come. . . . We won't be fooled again." It was taking on the air of a festival.

I asked the white-haired man on the other side of me what had drawn him to Obama. "There's just something about him," he said. "We can't have what we've got now, and he offers us a new vision. And to see the young people so involved gives me hope."

It was after 7 PM now, and the chant was rising: "O-Bam-A! O-Bam-A!" I glimpsed his tall, thin frame behind the stage curtain. The chant intensified: "O-Bam-A! O-Bam-A!" There was something transcendent in the joined voices of this overwhelmingly white audience, their chorus intoning again and again the rhythmic African name.

After being introduced by a local school teacher, Obama ran up onto the stage to a thunderous standing ovation. He wore a white shirt and striped tie, but no jacket. In the course of his half-hour-long speech, he used no notes or teleprompter, and walked back-and-forth with microphone in hand, reaching out an index finger to make his strongest points.

His words for his Republican opponents were sharper than they'd been, and he pledged a series of reforms that would benefit a majority of Americans. "I may not have the lobbyists," he said, "but I've got you!" The audience believed him. And they loved him for it.

When it was over, I thought of those two burly guys who'd walked past me wearing yellow BOILERMAKERS FOR OBAMA T-shirts. I thought of how far Americans had come, when they were willing to trust their future to a man with that name. And I remembered what Obama had written in the epilogue of his latest book:

".... I think about America and those who built it. This nation's founders, who somehow rose above petty ambitions and narrow calculations to imagine a nation unfurling across a continent. And those like Lincoln and King, who ultimately laid down their lives in the service of perfecting an imperfect union. And all the faceless, nameless men and women, slaves and soldiers and tailors and butchers, constructing lives for themselves and their children and grandchildren, brick by brick, rail by rail, calloused hand by calloused hand, to fill in the landscape of our collective dreams."

FOR FURTHER READING:

Dreams From My Father: A Story of Race and Inheritance, by Barack Obama (New York: Random House, 1995).

The Audacity of Hope: Thoughts on Reclaiming the American Dream, by Barack Obama (New York: Crown Publishing Group, 2006).

Obama: From Promise to Power, by David Mendell (New York: Amistad, 2007).

Foreword

If asked to name noted African-Americans—noted African-Americans who are not entertainment or sports figures—the average black child might answer "Martin Luther King, Jr.; Malcolm X; and the Reverend Jesse Jackson." To the same question a white child might answer "Martin Luther King." A broadly educated child might add "Rosa Parks, Harriet Tubman, and George Washington Carver." It's a sad fact: Most of us, black or white, child or adult, know little of the richness that Africans have brought to America.

Now we have *Black Genius*. The collection of narratives presented by author Dick Russell offers a panorama of American life in these stories of extraordinary African-Americans. And though some of the names will be familiar to the reader, most of these geniuses, their fame confined to a small circle of people in their specific fields, have not been described in other biographical or historical works. The stories told here, many in first-person voice, document important lives that might otherwise have been lost to history. Social and political movements typically are linked to a handful of celebrated leaders, yet they result from the coming together of countless dedicated individuals, individuals who may be heroes only to their friends and neighbors. The civil rights movement, for example, succeeded because of thousands of committed activists. Martin Luther King, Jr., and other leaders would not have prevailed without them. Those souls, and thousands like them past and present, have made profound contributions to our lives. While we may never know their names, the geniuses in Russell's work represent them well.

In offering us the opportunity to broaden our knowledge beyond the standard presentations on black heroes like Martin Luther King, Jr., and Malcolm X, *Black Genius* is a valuable resource for people of all ages and races who wish to celebrate black history, though only a small sample of black geniuses could be included within the space of this collection. As the author notes, many names are missing. Marian Wright Edelman, William Julius Wilson, Derrick Bell, Bill Cosby, Maya Angelou, Henry Louis Gates, John Hope Franklin, Gwendolyn Brooks, Stokely Carmichael, Roy Wilkins, Bayard Rustin, Alice Walker, and hundreds of others belong here.

Books on important black Americans may eventually fill dozens of shelves; biographies are already available for notables such as Martin Luther King, Jr., Malcolm X, Langston Hughes, Arthur Ashe, Andrew Young, Jackie Robinson, Ralph Bunche, and the Reverend Jesse Jackson. But *Black Genius* is unique in its thoughtful selection of less publicly celebrated individuals. And these are not privileged men and women who attended the finest schools, with their family's wealth to support them, and went on to achieve the great success expected by all around them. Instead, these are men and women who triumphed in spite of racism, poverty, and countless other barriers. The greatness of the African-American people is that despite physical oppression and psychological assaults, many still manage to create a "way out of no way" when their goals seem unreachable. *Black Genius* celebrates a number of such successes.

Such celebrations are important, as many Americans continue to live in a segregated world, psychologically if not physically. Segregation creates ignorance, and the ignorance creates fear; both are compounded by the skewed but powerful impressions of blacks that Americans of all races receive from the media, where negative images often outweigh the positive. At the induction ceremony for the Academy of Television Arts and Sciences Hall of Fame in 1992, Bill Cosby excoriated the television industry for spewing out "drive-by images" that reinforce shallow stereotypes.[1] Camille Cosby also has spoken of her deep concern for young television viewers inundated with programs depicting African-Americans as "clownish figures or savage brutes who are inept, corrupt, prone to misfortune, and unable to solve their own problems."[2] These demeaning characterizations, coupled with news programming that includes an overrepresentation of black criminals, leaves viewers with images of blacks as comics, athletes, entertainers, and criminals—a limited and distorted perspective.

The dearth of positive images to counteract these distortions has serious consequences. For nonblack Americans, ignorance of the rich and brilliant African-American history leaves a void easily filled by damaging misinformation such as pseudo-scientific claims that blacks, on average, are less intelligent than whites. If more people were aware of the tremendous contributions African-Americans have made, and are making, to all aspects of American life, it would be harder for them to succumb to simplistic and stereotypical notions of Africans as less talented than Europeans.

While the need to educate nonblacks is undeniable, the need to educate blacks may be even more pressing. Far too many of us still don't know enough about our own history despite efforts in recent decades to develop African-American studies in universities and even secondary schools; it's important to take advantage of Black History Month and other opportunities to draw public attention to the heterogeneity of the black experience as well as the common cultural and political ties shaping the African-American perspective.

The experience of African-Americans is unique compared to other ethnic groups in America: Native African cultures and traditions could not take root in the new nation because slave family groups were deliberately separated. Although Africans were forced to assimilate European ways, they were a culturally rich people with their own views and values, and black culture has blended with and shaped the larger American culture in significant ways. (The blues and jazz come immediately to mind: We owe these distinctly American musical traditions to African-Americans.) But students receive only a smattering of black history at school, and that history often covers only a handful of black icons. While many students learn of the civil rights movement, for example, the lesson is oversimplified. They learn to applaud Martin Luther King, Jr., and Rosa Parks but are taught little about the circumstances and community dynamics that led to their emergence.

Consequently, some African-Americans accept the negative images surrounding them, especially in the media. As Jannette Dates and William Barlow note in *Split Image,* "The black images mass produced by [whites] . . . have been filtered through the racial misconceptions and fantasies of the dominant white culture, which has tended to deny the existence of a rich and resilient black culture of equal worth."[3] This denial has left too many blacks feeling that they are a minority not just in numbers, but in substance.

The word "minority" connotes lesser, smaller, lower: *minor.* Many of us have thought of ourselves as "minor" for so long, we have absorbed that characterization into our personalities without recognizing it. And so we acquiesce all too readily to "staying in our place" or otherwise accommodating to racist perspectives, often unaware of how we are circumscribing our options. In our own communities we often feel incapable even of running our own small businesses; a minority mind-set can deter us from being leaders and entrepreneurs. Having been told repeatedly that we are inferior, many of us have come to believe that we *are* inferior. Even persons regarded by the rest of the world as successful—lawyers, doctors, scientists—question their qualifications to compete and rise to the top of their chosen fields solely because of their minority status.

Black children raised in such an atmosphere develop self-doubt, not self-confidence. They come to feel incapable of taking charge of their own fate; they begin to act like victims. At worst, victims refuse to

take responsibility for themselves, always blaming others for their pre-
dicaments and failures, like the black student who fails her physics
exam and blames the professor's racism instead of her insufficient
study. In their power essay "Rumors of Inferiority," Jeff Howard and
Ray Hammond explain what happens:

*The need to avoid intellectual competition is a psychological reaction
to an image of black intellectual inferiority that has been projected by
the larger society, and to a less than conscious process of internaliza-
tion of that image by black people over the generations.*[4]

In a creative response to the problems stemming from "rumors of inferiority," incidentally, Howard and others established efficacy programs to develop techniques for promoting black achievement in
education and employment.

As the stories in *Black Genius* illustrate, many African-Americans
have demonstrated black efficacy to excel against the odds. The narratives offer a variety of successful models with whom the reader can
identify: educators, scientists, philosophers, architects, physicians, artists. What these geniuses have in common is their passion and commitment. They did not allow the self-negation often associated with
oppression to shackle their vision. They made things happen.

I was filled with poignant memories as I read the story of Elma
Lewis, an astonishing woman whom I have known and worked with
for years. Her dedication to making the arts an integral part of life for
children in Boston is unique, yet her name is virtually unknown outside
of that city. Bob Moses, another long-time friend profiled in *Black
Genius,* is noted for his work in the civil rights movement, but few
people are aware that he remained steadfast in his dedication to community empowerment long after the marches and voter registration
drives in the South had ceased. His narrative reveals an enduring commitment to children's education, exemplified by his creation of the Algebra Project. The stories of heroic African-Americans like Elma Lewis
and Bob Moses are important reading now—and they should be read
for generations to come.

Marian Wright Edelman, president of the Children's Defense Fund,
exhorts young people to "remember your roots, your history, and the
forebears' shoulders on which you stand." She further emphasizes that
"our Black children need the rightful pride of a great people . . . second
to none in helping transform America from a theoretic to a more living
democracy."[5] As *Black Genius* profiles particular individuals, it inevitably celebrates whole communities. Every narrative refers to other

pioneers, and *their* stories would refer to others still. The biographies are powerful illustrations of the proverb "It takes a village to raise a child." Each of the lives presented here is interwoven with the lives of other significant individuals, and the richness of the connections is striking. While our black geniuses are strong people, they didn't succeed by going it alone. The author describes, with eloquence, the threads of multiple lives and influences that encouraged each of these geniuses in their development. These great people were nurtured by families and neighbors, encouraged by teachers, and mentored by those who came before, either in person or through historical example. One cannot read about these heroes without hearing the echoes of the communities that raised them. Their stories describe a web of influences, black and white, that brought them to success.

Describing the multicultural influences on his own development, W. E. B. Du Bois wrote:

I sit with Shakespeare and he winces not. Across the color line I move arm in arm with Balzac and Dumas, where smiling men and welcoming women glide in gilded halls. From the caves of evening that swing between the strong-limbed earth and the tracery of the stars, I summon Aristotle and Aurelius and what soul I will, and they come all graciously with no scorn nor condescension.[6]

Du Bois would have appreciated the value of the stories in *Black Genius,* especially for young people, because of what they convey about the communities of African-Americans who have added so much to the texture of American culture and politics.

Black Genius inspires: Readers can expect to feel their own hopes raised. And while this rich work teaches African-Americans that with community we can fulfill our dreams, its lessons extend to all. Ultimately, *Black Genius* is about the best America has to offer.

—Alvin F. Poussaint, M.D.

[1]Joshua Hammer, "Must Blacks Be Buffoons?" *Newsweek,* October 26, 1992, pp. 70–71.

[2]Jannette L. Dates and Camille O. Cosby, "Quantity, Not Quality, Suffices for Our TV Images?" *The City Sun,* (New York City), September 30–October 6, 1992, p. 8.

[3]Jannette Dates and William Barlow, eds., *Split Image* (Washington, D.C.: Howard University Press 1993), p. 523.

[4]Jeff Howard and Ray Hammond, "Rumors of Inferiority," *The New Republic,* September 9, 1985, pp. 17–21.

[5]Marian Wright Edelman, "Beating the Odds," commencement address at Howard University, Washington, D.C., published in *Vital Issues: The Journal of African American Speeches,* Vol. VII, No. 1, 1997, p. 44.

[6]W. E. B. Du Bois, *Souls of Black Folk* (New York: Penguin Books, 1903).

This book is dedicated to the men and women I have written about who have been so gracious with their time; and to the younger generation, including my son Franklin, in hopes they will find inspiration in its pages.

". . . once in a while the veil which shrouds the details of our unwritten history is thrown back, and not only do the deserving find belated recognition, but sometimes marvelous interconnections between the past and the present spring to light."

—RALPH ELLISON

"You learn, yet you're empowered finally by someone else's testimony; to reach back and claim what has always been yours. Yet with that same gesture, you're empowered to move forward. So the chain, in effect, is never broken."

—JAMES BALDWIN

"Genius hovers with his sunshine and music close by the darkest and deafest of eras."

—RALPH WALDO EMERSON

INTRODUCTION:
BEARING WITNESS

My long voyage begins at home, gazing out my window at the hill-top park that fronts it. Here on Roxbury's Fort Hill, two revolution-aries once looked out across Boston from among the city's highest vantage points. George Washington came to examine the fortifications against the British at the onset of the Revolutionary War. Almost two centuries later, Malcolm X stood beneath a monolithic white tower that once served as a water standpipe for all of Boston. One was a slave-owner, the other a warrior against all that would perpetuate such a legacy. In my mind's eye, I see them reaching towards one another across the bridge of time.

My neighborhood teems with history. Right down the hill stands the white wood-frame house where the abolitionist leader William Lloyd Garrison moved soon after Lincoln's Emancipation Proclamation. A little further away is the Greek revival home of another abolitionist, the writer Edward Everett Hale, author of *Man without a Country*. A few blocks from there is Eliot Square, where the original First Church was built in 1630 and the Reverend John Eliot's translation of the Old and New Testaments into the Algonquian language became the first Bible printed in America.

In greater Boston, few know the rich lore of this particular area; it is off the beaten path and not part of the Freedom Trail. For, since the end of the Second World War, the neighborhood has been pre-dominantly black. I have lived here for some years with an extended family of close friends, and we are predominantly white. My teenaged son is of mixed race, of both worlds. It was, in part, for what I might be able to learn and pass along to him that I made the remarkable journey that became this book. For the majority of people you will find in these pages have been omitted from most of white America's history books.

As a product of this society, my own education was sorely lacking. I knew little about and, in some cases, had never even heard of the individuals I came to research and often had the great privilege to meet in the course of writing this work. I was, in a word, ignorant. Yes, I had read and been strongly moved by Ralph Ellison's classic *Invisible Man* and *The Autobiography of Malcolm X*; had watched stirring documentaries about Martin Luther King, Jr.; had been deeply affected listening to the music of Ray Charles and Duke Ellington. Still, I had no idea how much I did not know about the black tradition and experience in America, half of my son's ancestral heritage.

Was I a fool to attempt this immersion? That is a question I have asked myself many times over the course of the past two years. Another initial impetus had been *The Bell Curve*, the 1994 best-seller which revived the idea of a racially inherited basis of intelligence. I was outraged by the book and its refueling of stereotypes that ought to have died at Appomattox. It was basically telling us that equality and opportunity were reducible to the alleged "evidence" of one's genes and IQ scores. In a society polarized by the divides of poverty, crime, and drugs, what was *The Bell Curve* controversy if not another impediment to understanding?

I felt it was pointless, at least for me, to try to refute *The Bell Curve*'s insidious message. Yet the national debate over its content set me thinking: What about the other side? What about the true potential of African-Americans? How has it manifested? And, as I began to look into the subject, did I dare to seek such examples? I realized that there were many African-American scholars with far more qualifications than I possessed. Was I not being presumptuous, opening myself up to charges of being a white elitist simply focusing upon the "exceptional"? Was it possible for me to explore this realm and have something valid to offer?

I cannot say that I have fully answered any of those questions. I have struggled with them. In the process, I believe I have made some discoveries—about myself, my country, and a number of extraordinary people whose lives are bound together in a revealing way. These people have quite a story to tell. In spite of their lack of equal opportunity compared to the mainstream of society, they came to represent the least isolated of Americans. While many of them have been largely written out of conventional American history, they have forged a living history that not only merits greater recognition but is intrinsic to understanding the national experience.

Even grappling with how to explore the subject of "genius" is a task fraught with pitfalls. I think it can safely be said that neither race nor class limits the potential of an individual. People who are gifted with unusual intellectual ability or creativity—and who work diligently to make those talents a reality—we often call geniuses. This applies equally to Albert Einstein, and to Louis Armstrong.

In the ancient Roman religion, however, genius had a broader meaning. The word itself derives from "genii," implying an inner or attendant spirit. This conception of a kind of invisible illumination is a poetic one, but it seems to me an appropriate metaphor for what might be said to constitute "Black Genius" in terms of American culture. It brings to mind Ralph Ellison's nameless "Invisible Man," whose last words in the novel are these: "Who knows but that, on the lower frequencies, I speak for you?" The universality of that phrase echoes something else that Ellison wrote, about "the mystery which haunts American experience, and that is the mystery of how we are many and yet one." In this context, I believe, the exceptional individual accomplishments of African-Americans are representative of an invaluable lesson for the larger society. This has to do with acknowledging merit, beyond the artificial barriers of race and ethnicity.

At the same time, one must examine the cultural styles and traditions—linguistic, musical, perceptional, and spiritual—of the sensibility that black men and women brought with them when removed from Africa. Different versions came to exist in Brazil, Jamaica, Cuba, Haiti, and within the African-American community. In each place, characteristics of brilliance take on the particularities and detail of the new cultural experience and language, whether mediated by French, Spanish or English. They also take on the particular experience of displacement, exile, racism, and economic development in those various locations.

Intrinsic in this situation is a sense of continuity, of what is passed on from one generation to the next. For people uprooted from ancient tribal cultures, this became a necessity in order to survive. Forced exile required communal kinship, an essential legacy of ancestral connections. This was also true, to some degree, for American immigrants of Irish, Jewish, and Italian descent. But their village and family relations were not severed in the same way. Slavery tore the past asunder—but the inner need remained. It harkened back to an African culture where religion, industry, government, education and art, as W. E. B. Du Bois wrote, "were bred as integral inter-related things." White America, so geared to the idea of progress in the present through individual achievement, often lost touch with the more inclusive way of life that African-Americans recreated. And white America remained largely oblivious to their remarkable achievements engendered in its midst.

Very early in my research, when all I knew was that I wanted to shed light on an American story focusing upon important relationships within this country's racial amalgam and among its different groups, I had a memorable conversation with Edmund Barry Gaither. He is the director of the National Center of Afro-American Artists in Roxbury, about a mile from my home, and my son had spent a spring break from school helping him put up a new exhibit. A tall, broad-shouldered, handsome man in his fifties, Gaither sat me down in a folding chair just around the corner from the museum's ancient Nubian tomb. I described to him my misgivings concerning how to go about this project, and I turned on my tape recorder as he said:

"Take a look at how people are heroic, people who in the process of living respond to the encounters that come to them. They don't usually achieve anything perfect, because there isn't anything perfect in history. But they achieve places where there is sufficient consensus that the whole thing manages to stick together, to move forward. The point is not to have a society without tension. The point is to have a society in which there are creative solutions to the problems of living together. If this country only had white people, there would be class issues and regional issues, another whole set of stresses. The proposition that makes America unusual is that we have posited you can have a multicultural, multilayered society—and what makes it stick together can be stronger than what makes it come apart."

So, Gaither suggested, I should explore the question of mentors, relationships between generations, how bridges to significant public achievement are built. Because in examining these matters, he went on, "They say something useful. They say something about trust. They say something about the ability to muster a larger vision, even if it's a partial vision, and to act on it."

On an afternoon not long after that, I had a discussion with the eminent Harvard scholar Cornel West, whose life and ideas will be looked at in detail later in this book. At one point he stood up and walked to the overflowing bookshelf in his office, and picked out a volume titled *Genius—Romantic Ideology*. "This is very interesting," Professor West said, "because it's about where the construct of genius comes from. Sophocles didn't think of himself as a genius, nor did Euripides. Augustine didn't, Aquinas didn't, Erasmus didn't. But in the modern period, we have a construct of genius that has to do with a highly individualistic conception of concentrated artistic power, which manifests itself in creating monuments out of people. It's linked to a Romantic movement for the most part."

West continued: "But I think one of the things we must recognize—you especially see this in jazz—is that there *is* no great achievement without community. There's no John Coltrane at his highest level without Dizzy Gillespie, without Thelonius Monk, without Miles Davis—creating a context under which he could be affirmed, supported, encouraged, define his voice and then take off. So it becomes a community apprenticeship, various sets of ties and bonds that enable and equip people to be the best they can be. That doesn't mean that Coltrane's not Coltrane. In that sense, we can still use notions like genius. I still use the term. But I realize it's an ideological construct. And I try to resist that. Even though I believe that individuals play an important role in terms of their discipline and their sacrifice, it's within this larger historical backdrop of community."

I raised the point with West that I had been observing through my research, that African-American culture seemed to have given more of a sense of community to the country. "I think so," he responded. "There is something about democratic individuality, which is very different than rugged, ragged, rapacious individual*ism*, something that doesn't reduce individuals solely to community but doesn't view the individual as independent of community either. That individuality versus individualism, I think, is so crucial in terms of how a downtrodden, hated and hunted people have been able to preserve individuality, but also to be deeply rooted in a community for survival, sanity and health—spiritual as well as social and political."

In selecting whom to profile in this book, I have sought to emphasize what Edmund Barry Gaither and Cornel West described: the connections between people that serve to educate and thereby accentuate someone else's gifts. These linkages may be direct, or they may intersect across time. For example, the musical traditions that Pulitzer Prize-winning composer/trumpeter Wynton Marsalis draws upon to forge his own path are consciously derived from Duke Ellington and Louis Armstrong. Yet Marsalis has learned about the grand jazz heritage primarily from the venerable author Albert Murray, who in turn was strongly influenced by his friendships with Ralph Ellison and the artist Romare Bearden. Murray proceeded to put Marsalis in touch with his own circle, and thus created a continually expanding spiral.

At the same time, Duke Ellington's sense of composition gained considerable measure from his early meetings with Will Marion Cook, a musical master little known today. Cook then is an "Ancestor," both for Ellington and for Marsalis. The painter Loïs Mailou Jones would not have been who she became without the inspiration of the sculptor Meta Warrick Fuller. Paying homage to the ancestors is, of course, a crucial part of the African tradition. To this day, libations to the gods are poured in honor of those who have gone before, a moving ceremony that I witnessed personally while traveling through West Africa many years ago. So it is not surprising that this sensibility would be perpetuated among African-Americans. It is not an idea, but a reality that lives in the blood. It is enabling, and ennobling.

Thus, periodically through this book, I have interwoven various "Ancestors," whose lives often hold a mirror to those that followed them. What Mary McLeod Bethune began in a little Southern school-house, Elma Lewis rekindled in a little Roxbury schoolhouse fifty years later. What Lewis Latimer ignited with his invention of the carbon filament for electric light, Earl Shaw carried forward with his invention of a laser device one hundred years later. The echo of what Sojourner Truth offered of the gospel's social activism during her mid-nineteenth-century wanderings can be found in the Black Church of the civil rights movement.

Sometimes I found the parallels so striking that they seemed worthy of entire comparative chapters. This was true in looking at the legacy of philosophical thought that passes from W. E. B. Du Bois and Alain Locke to Cornel West. It was true in studying the lives of Ira Aldridge and Paul Robeson, protean figures far beyond the theater stages they walked a century apart. And it was evident in the writings of Frederick Douglass and James Baldwin. Also separated by a century of time, their common struggles and uncommon impact become timeless, etching across the American landscape a message that does not know boundaries. Prescient in their eras, they continue to resonate in our own.

So this book does not follow a linear form, but rather one of lineage. That is the book's central theme, weaving back and forth across time. Certain people play a predominant role in a number of others' lives. One is Frederick Douglass, who escaped from slavery to become the great abolitionist leader of the nineteenth century. Without Douglass's intervention in rescuing George Latimer from bondage, his son Lewis Latimer surely would not appear in the annals of invention. Douglass is central not only to his contemporaries, but as an inspiration for twentieth-century artists like Jacob Lawrence, and writers such as Baldwin and Murray. In more recent times, W. E. B. Du Bois and Paul Robeson merge similarly—in each other's histories, as well as influences upon many more individuals, including sculptor Meta Fuller, photographer/filmmaker Gordon Parks, teacher Elma Lewis, philosopher Cornel West, and physician Louis Tompkins Wright.

Alongside mentors, family emerges as crucial to the development of innate abilities. Parks, West, and Lewis all cite their parents as the people they admire most. Some of the accounts in this book offer direct instances where children follow their fathers into the same or similar fields of endeavor: scientist Earl Shaw and his son Alan, architect Charles McAfee and two of his daughters, physician Louis Tompkins Wright and his two daughters. In many other instances, a father is absent, often due to an early death. Here the mother's strength is abundantly evident. Grandparents, too, prove vital sources of wisdom. It is not accidental that "brother" and "sister" were, and remain, everyday expressions of the African-American lexicon. In these pages, the lives of historical figures are often viewed through descendants who have devoted themselves to keeping alive their memory: Latimer's granddaughter, Robeson's son, Wright's daughter.

Family values, a phrase whose meaning has become trivialized in the '90s, are utterly tangible in these stories. We find an emphasis on education, in some cases self-taught. We find a highly disciplined work ethic, a self-applied perseverance. The *genius* only emerges through intense desire to master one's craft. Also, the Christian Church is a constant presence. It is striking how many of these people come from backgrounds where a father or grandfather served in the ministry. Inherent in the African-American Church, no matter which denomination, is social activism. And this theme is accented whether we are looking at musicians and writers, artists and actors, philosophers and educators, or scientists and architects, doctors, or ministers. It is realized in a capability for organization, exemplified by Byllye Avery's pioneering work in healthcare, and by Bob Moses in the civil rights movement and subsequently with his educational Algebra Project. It is an aspect of African-American genius that has been a primary force of conscience, a spur to the ideals that formed America.

At least from the moment that Benjamin Banneker wrote a letter to Thomas Jefferson questioning how the author of the Declaration of Independence justified his slaveholding, the African-American challenged the nation to match substance to its words. In this book, we will examine how was forged, during the Civil War, the remarkable relationship between Frederick Douglass and Abraham Lincoln; during the Great Depression and World War II, the deep friendship between Mary McLeod Bethune and Eleanor Roosevelt; during the civil rights era, a "fire next time" in Robert Kennedy by James Baldwin. We will also look at pivotal interracial friendships: Baldwin and novelist William Styron, Parks and the editors of *Life* magazine. None of these encounters were easy, requiring an openness, a give-and-take. Yet through each of them, there appeared the possibility for greater understanding of the inner world of the human soul.

The destiny of the American Republic, at its core, has always been about the ways in which individuals of different backgrounds and ethnicities might work together. My own ancestors left Europe because they were looking for fulfillment beyond religious intolerance and separate nation-states. In the course of settlement and expansion across a largely empty, untamed continent, a phenomenon occurred unlike any in the history of man's urge for dominion and power over other men. It was inherent in the terrible system of slavery. Europe colonized Africa and India, but maintained its oppression at a distance. England took part in the slave trade, but put the problem elsewhere, in the

West Indies, out of sight for the majority of its population. Not so in America, where people taken from Africa were placed right in the bosom of the family. Their enforced servitude was ultimately inescapable for the Anglo-Saxon because it was a daily reality. You could turn your head, you could harden your heart, you could use all available means of justification—but the African-American was not going away.

It was an unprecedented kind of "wedding," as James Baldwin has said. Here Europeans could not remain as they were, nor could Africans. After all, every non-English-speaking immigrant abandoned his or her native tongue. Albert Murray has pointed out in his book *The Omni-Americans* that the African conception of time and continuity (or permanence and change) was vastly different from the European. The African orientation to culture was less structured and more geared to improvisation. Murray writes: "The traditional African disposition to refine all movement into dance-like elegance survived in the United States as work rhythms (and playful syncopation) in spite of the fact that African rituals were prohibited and the ceremonial drums were taken away." From this emanated the spirituals, the blues, jazz, swing, rhythm-and-blues, rock-and-roll—the essence of American music, the underlying blues affirming "life in America in all of its infinite confusions." In so many respects, the subjects of this book are quintessentially American.

The classical traditions in literature, music, and art also loom large in their development. The work of Nobel Prize-winning author Toni Morrison draws as much upon D. H. Lawrence as it does on Baldwin. Bach and Picasso find themselves at home in Harlem or Atlanta. While voyages to Africa are important linkages for a number of those profiled, more crucial were the formative years that many of them spent in Europe. In pilgrimages to the continent that white Americans had left behind, they often found their voices. With the exception of Ira Aldridge, they felt compelled to return to a United States which offered them far less dignity as human beings. And they were willing to fight for their acceptance.

Struggle is another central theme of this book. The anthem of the civil rights movement, *We Shall Overcome*, finds expression in all of the people I have selected to write about. Loneliness is implicit in the life of anyone of genius. For such individuals are possessed of a particular kind of determination and courage, willing to pursue their own path and attend to a guiding light. Such beacons of humanity may not be understood in their time, even by those closest to them. Yet they seem to have no choice but to embark upon an often rocky road toward their own destiny. The fact that the subjects of this book are African-Americans is of consequence because they had to transcend the added burden of bigotry to become who they were and are. Thus was their loneliness accentuated, their struggle exacerbated. Thus does what they overcame take on an additional quality.

The greatest difficulty with assembling this book is not that there are too few, but too many, individuals who could readily fit the category of genius in its various forms. I will doubtless be faulted for those I have omitted, or mentioned only in passing. I made the decision not to write about athletes or titans of finance. In the cases of people who have already been the subject of numerous biographies—such as Martin Luther King, Jr., Malcolm X, or Booker T. Washington—anything I might have to say would be redundant. I felt it would be more valuable to examine King's life through two of his mentors—Benjamin Mays and Howard Thurman—and through his ministerial legacy.

My choice was to focus in on twenty-four men and nine women as representatives of a tradition of brilliance among African-Americans. Some are well known, and many are not; for the most part, their achievements have gone underrecognized. My presence in telling their stories is that of a witness. Therefore, beyond this introduction, I have chosen to remain largely in the background of these pages. With historical figures, I have sought quotations by and about them which describe who they were and what they accomplished. With contemporary figures, most of whom I have interviewed, I provide a narrative thread but allow them to describe their life and times in their own words. It is, after all, their voices that matter. And many of these voices have not been heard, at least not within the broader context which I am attempting to convey.

I believe that this approach is warranted, too, because of the living vitality of an oral tradition that runs through African-American culture. This dates back to the tribal lore of such African cultures as the Ibo and the Ashanti, onward through enslavement, where learning to read and write was generally prohibited, and ultimately to finding prose-voice in the autobiographical narratives of such towering figures as Douglass, Du Bois, and Baldwin. Most of the people I have visited personally for this book are wonderful storytellers who articulate so well their histories, ideas, and values that they need little authorial elaboration.

My task has been to weave together the voices in a way that emphasizes the overarching themes I have briefly outlined here: family and intergenerational continuity, spirituality and diligence, activism and struggle. Often to my surprise, I found that these themes emerged through the process of writing the chapters. I set out with no particular modus operandi. I was not interested in ideology or political labels. I merely embarked upon a voyage of discovery, following a thread that led me from one remarkable person to another, in all walks of life. I traveled from my home base in the Boston area along the Eastern seaboard to Rhode Island, New York, New Jersey, Philadelphia, and Washington; then outward to the Midwest and Atlanta, from whence so many had migrated northward. Early on, when the majority of my time was spent in Harlem's Schomburg Center for Research in Black Culture figuring out whom I might write about, I thought of structuring the book chronologically. Over time, I came to realize that this was far less interesting than the parallels of confluence—how lives intertwine and overlap, how the circle is unbroken.

This came to seem equally true of my own quest. It was a writer acquaintance, Jack Newfield, who first told me about his own writer friend, Stanley Crouch. Through seeing Crouch about Ralph Ellison, I was led to seek out Crouch's and Ellison's mutual friend, Albert Murray. In turn, Murray informed me about his painter friend Romare Bearden. Wynton Marsalis, whom I then interviewed on two occasions, proved to be someone through whom the wisdom of numerous elders had room to flow. In so many instances, people I had considered describing in isolated circumstances suddenly swam in a wide sea. It became a piecing together of a kind of marvelous human puzzle.

Let us advance then through this web of creation with an epigraph from a sermon by Martin Luther King, Jr.:

"It really boils down to this: that all life is interrelated. We are all caught in an inescapable network of mutuality, tied into a single garment of destiny. Whatever affects one directly, affects all indirectly. We are made to live together because of the interrelated structure of reality."

Part 1

A CERTAIN HERITAGE

I contend that the Negro is the creative voice of America, is creative America, and it was a happy day in America when the first unhappy slave was landed on its shores.

There, in our tortured induction into this "land of liberty," we built its most graceful civilization. Its wealth, its flowering fields and handsome homes; its pretty traditions; its guarded leisure and its music, were all our creations.

We stirred in our shackles and our unrest awakened Justice in the hearts of a courageous few, and we recreated in America the desire for true democracy, freedom for all, the brotherhood of man, principles on which the country had been founded.

We were freed and as before, we fought America's wars, provided her labor, gave her music, kept alive her flickering conscience, prodded her on toward the yet unachieved goal, democracy—until we became more than a part of America! We—this kicking, yelling, touchy, sensitive, scupulously-demanding minority—are the personification of the ideal begun by the Pilgrims almost 350 years ago.

It is our voice that sang "America" when America grew too lazy, satisfied and confident to sing. . . .

We are more than a few isolated instances of courage, valor, achievement. We're the injection, the shot in the arm, that has kept America and its forgotten principles alive in the fat and corrupt years intervening between our divine conception and our near tragic present.

—DUKE ELLINGTON, *from a talk before black churchgoers in Los Angeles in February 1941, nine months before America's entry into World War II.*

Ancestors—Ellington's Mentor:
Will Marion Cook

Go out and up! Our souls and eyes
Shall follow thy continuous rise
Our ears shall list thy story
From bards who from thy root shall spring
And proudly tune their lyres to sing
Of Ethiopia's glory.
　　　　　　　—Paul Laurence Dunbar,
　　　　　　　"An Ode to Ethiopia"

It was 1893, thirty years since Lincoln's Emancipation Proclamation. The World's Columbian Exposition, a celebration to commemorate the 400th anniversary of the discovery of America, was being held in Chicago. Before it was over that summer, nearly twenty-eight million people would attend. Among them was Frederick Douglass, the onetime escaped slave whose great oratory had inspired the Abolitionist movement. Now, at seventy-five, he was a gray eminence.

Accompanying Douglass was his twenty-two-year-old grandson Joseph. While both his father and grandfather played amateur violin, Joseph was well on his way to classical mastery of the instrument. Also at the Exposition was another violin prodigy, twenty-four-year-old Will Marion Cook. He and Joseph were close friends. Born on January 27, 1869, Cook had displayed early musical talent and begun studying violin at Ohio's Oberlin College when he was only fifteen. Frederick Douglass, Cook's hero, had later sponsored him at a church concert in their mutual hometown of Washington, D.C. The affair had generated enough funds for Cook to complete his schooling. For two years he had studied in Berlin under the world-renowned violinist Josef Joachim. Then he had directed a chamber orchestra which toured the Eastern seaboard.

Something appeared to be stirring in the country since the Civil War. True, black minstrel troupes remained the vogue for white audiences. But the nation's most popular railroad song was a ballad about a black, 220-pound, "steel driving" man named John Henry. The Fisk and Hampton Jubilee Singers, groups of black university students, had been acclaimed on American and European tours that introduced the spirituals and folksongs of their people. Black concert singers and instrumentalists were beginning to appear on numerous stages. At the Chicago World's Fair, there would be something else: a lively new syncopated piano music called ragtime.

Still, the hopes that came with the post-Civil War constitutional amendments granting African-Americans full equality of citizenship and voting rights had been dashed. The Compromise of 1877 withdrew federal troops from the South and returned power to the states. By the time of the 1893 exposition, "Jim Crow" laws in the South enforced segregation in the areas of education, housing, transportation, and recreation.

So Frederick Douglass had considerable misgivings about the "Colored American Day" that Will Marion Cook had successfully convinced the Chicago fair to promote as a showcase for young African-American talent. Still, Douglass agreed to preside at a formal program. While his grandson Joseph and Cook stood alongside another of their friends, the poet Paul Laurence Dunbar, Douglass began reading from a prepared text on "The Race Problem in America." A sizeable crowd was gathered in Festival Hall. When some white men in the back began interrupting Douglass with derisive comments, he finally tossed his papers aside and launched into an impromptu speech.

"Men talk of the Negro problem," Douglass told the assembled. "There is no Negro problem. The problem is whether the American people have loyalty enough, honor enough, patriotism enough, to live up to their own Constitution. . . . We Negroes love our country. We fought for it. We ask only that we be treated as well as those who fought against it."

When Douglass concluded his hour-long oration, his grandson and Cook performed a duet of Cook's first composition. Their friend Dunbar read from his poetry. The event was a success. Joseph Douglass would go on to tour for over three decades around the country and, in 1914, become the first violinist to make recordings for the Victor Talking Machine Company. Paul Laurence Dunbar would be lauded by scholar/activist W. E. B. Du Bois as "the undoubted laureate of the race."

Fate had something else in mind for Will Marion Cook. In 1895, he was invited to play a concert at New York's Carnegie Hall. One press review described him as "the greatest colored violinist in the world." Cook took offense.

Author and music historian Albert Murray recounts what happened: "The story that Duke Ellington heard, and told me, was that Cook went down to the newspaper and said, 'Who's the music critic? You say I'm the greatest *colored* violinist. I'm the greatest violinist.' Cook figured, if that's how they're going to label him, he'd put his violin away. He just wouldn't play anymore."

Instead, Cook turned to composing and later conducting. He would soon fuse his classical training with a whole new sound that reverberates to this day. After the Chicago exposition, Cook had studied for two years at New York's National Conservatory of Music, the Juilliard School of its time. The Conservatory's Director during that period was the famed Bohemian composer Anton Dvořák. Through Cook and another student, Harry T. Burleigh, Dvořák was introduced to African-American music. His next three symphonies would employ themes based upon Negro spirituals and folksongs.

"These beautiful and varied themes are the product of the soil," Dvořák stated. "They are American. They are the folksongs of America, and your composers must turn to them. In the Negro melodies of America I discover all that is needed for a great and noble school of music."

Dvořák's influence extended to a Jewish student, Rubin Goldmark, who later headed the department of composition at Juilliard between 1924 and 1936. Goldmark's best-known composition was *A Negro Rhapsody*. His own students included George Gershwin. Among other works, Gershwin's *Rhapsody in Blue* and *Porgy and Bess* bear clear derivations from black folk music.

Cook later wrote of these pivotal years with Dvořák in the 1890s: "A few earnest Negro music students felt as did Dvořák. They studied the man, so broad, genial and human, carefully and thoroughly." The challenge taken up by Cook and Harry T. Burleigh was to propel Dvořák's counsel a step further.

Burleigh set out to preserve the spirituals, as he put it, "in harmonies that belong to modern methods of tonal progression without robbing the melodies of their racial flavor." He became the first arranger of spirituals as art songs for the solo voice. These included *Deep River*, *My Lord What a Morning*, *There's a Balm in Gilead*, *Were You There When They Crucified My Lord*, *Every Time I Feel the Spirit*, and *Joshua Fit the Battle of Jericho*. Blessed with a marvelous voice himself, Burleigh was a renowned church soloist for fifty years.

Meanwhile, Will Marion Cook became passionate about exploring and developing the possibilities of the African-American vernacular sound. He would write: "There was a good reason for the instantaneous hit made by 'ragtime.' The public was tired of sing-song, samey, monotonous, mother, sister, father sentimental songs. 'Ragtime' offered unique rhythms, curious groupings of words and melodies which gave the zest of unexpectedness. Many Negroes . . . wrote some of the most celebrated songs of the day."

Inspired by Dvořák and ragtime's ascendancy, Cook got together with Paul Laurence Dunbar. They teamed to tell the story of how a dance craze called the Cakewalk—as popular in its day as the Charleston or the Twist would later be—had originated in Louisiana during the 1880s.

Cook remembered: "We had two dozen bottles of beer, a quart of whiskey, and we took my brother's porterhouse steak, cut it up with onions and red peppers and ate it raw. Without a piano or anything but the kitchen table, we finished all the songs, all the libretto and all but a few bars of the ensembles by four o'clock the next morning."

Their musical comedy, *Clorindy, or the Origin of the Cakewalk*, was ready for the stage in 1898. They were told by New York promoters that audiences wouldn't listen to "Negroes singing Negro opera." Finally they got a spot at Broadway's Casino Roof Garden as an afterpiece for the main show. "When I entered the orchestra pit, there were only about fifty people on the Roof," Cook recalled. "When we finished the opening chorus, the house was packed to suffocation. What had happened was that the show downstairs in the Casino Theatre was just letting out. The big audience heard those heavenly Negro voices and took to the elevators. At the finish of the opening chorus, the applause and cheering were so tumultuous that I simply stood there transfixed."

With the final chorus, the crowd cheered the twenty-six participants for more than ten minutes. Cook rejoiced: "Negroes were at last on Broadway, and there to stay. Gone was the uff-dah of the minstrel! Gone the Massa Linkum stuff! We were artists and we were going a long, long way. . . ."

Cook's composition from the show, *Darktown Is Out Tonight*, swept the country. The doors to all the music publishers opened. When two young brothers from Florida showed up in the city, Cook helped get published their *Under the Bamboo Tree*. They were James Weldon Johnson and John Rosamond Johnson. Among their many accomplishments together, they would produce two successful operettas with all-black casts on Broadway and edit the first anthologies of Negro spirituals. They were but the first of many discoveries made by Will Marion Cook.

For several years, Cook served as composer-in-chief and musical director for the George Walker and Bert Williams vaudeville comedy team. Their performance of Cook's piece *In Dahomey* made King Edward VII laugh so hard that they became overnight the most popular comedians ever to tour the British Isles. Some years later, a Broadway producer told Cook that the public wouldn't stand for seeing Bert Williams appear in a play alongside the white actress Fanny Brice. Cook persisted. A year later, it was standing-room-only when the pair appeared in the Ziegfeld Follies.

In 1905, Cook started his own band, originally known as the Southern Syncopated Orchestra. It became the first of its kind ever to tour the country. "His ambition," says Albert Murray, "was to use the music indigenous to him as a basis for the nation's music. Cook was processing folk-level idiomatic expression to a more sophisticated level. Doing what Dvořák said to do. What Dvořák did not point out was the possibility that Americans would develop their own vocabulary, grammar and syntax for stylizing everyday raw experience into aesthetic musical statement. When Cook's orchestra came up with a syncopated sound, some called it jazz."

Where did the word come from? One legend tells of a wandering black musician in the Mississippi River Valley, whose name was Jasbo Brown. He made his trombone "talk" by putting a derby hat and later a tin can at its mouth. Whenever he played the honky-tonk cafés, the crowd would shout: "More, Jasbo! More, Jas, more!"

As James A. Rogers wrote in 1925 in an anthology called *The New Negro*: "In its elementals, jazz has always existed. It is in the Indian war-dance, the Highland fling, the Irish jig, the Cossack dance, the Spanish fandango, the Brazilian *maxixe*, the dance of the whirling dervish, the hula hula of the South Seas, the *danse du ventre* of the Orient, the *carmagnole* of the French Revolution, the strains of Gypsy music, and the ragtime of the Negro. Jazz proper, however, is something more than all these. It is a release of all the suppressed emotions at once, a blowing off of the lid, as it were. . . .

"The true spirit of jazz is a joyous revolt from convention, custom, authority, boredom, even sorrow—from everything that would confine the soul of man and hinder its riding free on the air. The Negroes who invented it called their songs the 'Blues,' and they weren't capable of satire or deception. Jazz was their explosive attempt to cast off the blues and be happy, carefree happy, even in the midst of sordidness and sorrow. And that is why it has been such a balm for modern ennui, and has become a safety valve for modern machine-ridden and convention-bound society. . . ."

In the autumn of 1918, Cook organized the New York Syncopated Orchestra. He had made a scouting tour in search of the finest possible musicians. Cook found one member in a restaurant in Chicago. This was Sidney Bechet, who would soon be acclaimed as jazz's greatest soprano saxophone player.

"Developed Negro music has just begun in America," Cook wrote in 1918. "The colored American is finding himself. He has thrown aside puerile imitations of the white man. He has learned that a thorough study of the masters gives knowledge of what is good and how to create. From the Russian he has learned to get his inspiration from within; that his inexhaustible wealth of folklore legends and songs furnish him with material for compositions that will establish a great school of music and enrich musical literature."

Nobody had ever before combined so many varieties of instruments, singers and styles. Cook's orchestra toured some of the biggest concert halls in America for four months. Then it took Europe by storm, doing a command performance at Buckingham Palace for England's King George V. Everywhere the forty-piece ensemble went, Cook combined standard concert pieces with music by black composers and spirituals sung a cappella. They did everything from Brahms to W. C. Handy's new *St. Louis Blues* and *Memphis Blues*.

Back in New York, in 1922 Cook created a new Clef Club Orchestra. It showcased Cook's arrangements on some of the earliest live broadcasts on the new medium of radio. The orchestra also formed the basis of a touring musical-show company. Two of its young members—Paul Robeson and Richard B. Harrison—would go on to become world-famous. In later years, Robeson recorded several numbers that he first performed with Cook.

W. C. Handy, known as "The Father of the Blues," said of Cook: "I had emulated our greatest conductors in the use of the baton, but when I saw Cook conducting the Clef Club of a hundred musicians and singers with no baton, when I saw him set the tempo with the sway of his body and develop perfect crescendos without a baton by the use of his opened and extended palms, he again was my ideal."

It is astonishing how many artists, white and black, received their baptism under Will Marion Cook. He took under his wing Harold Arlen, later the composer of *Stormy Weather*, *Over the Rainbow*, and many more popular standards. Cook so believed in the artistry of Ethel Waters that he persuaded stage producer Otto Kahn to back her show *Africana*. When a woman came looking to cast a "Negro revue" for a European tour, Cook insisted that she take on an unknown chorus girl. Within two months, all of Paris was at the feet of Josephine Baker.

Cook's son Mercer told this story in a memorial piece published shortly after his father's death:

"He found [Al] Jolson one evening playing in a third-rate vaudeville house.

" 'What are you doing here, boy?' Dad asked. 'You're great! You belong on Broadway.'

"Then, according to Dad, Jolson's eyes filled with tears as he said, 'They won't give me a chance.'

"The next day, Dad had raved so much about his 'find,' that the Shuberts [theatrical producers in New York] looked Jolson over and signed him up, thus beginning a successful association which lasted more than a decade."

In 1927, *The Jazz Singer*, featuring Al Jolson in blackface, became the first sound motion picture.

Sitting in the Harlem apartment where he wrote such works as *Stomping the Blues* and *Good Morning Blues: The Autobiography of Count Basie*, Albert Murray is looking back on his early years on the outskirts of Mobile, Alabama. "I grew up singing Cook's songs," he says. "Our glee club used to do his *Swing Along* in assembly. It was a part of the high school education in the South. That's probably the first time I ever heard anything about swing."

Murray, now in his early eighties, reflects and continues: "A hundred years after Cook's time with Dvořák, Wynton [Marsalis] and I are sitting up in Avery Fisher Hall setting up this first lecture about 'What Is Jazz.' I'm reading to Wynton what Dvořák said, and we're talking about Cook. Of course, Wynton had started out making a name for himself as a European concert hall-type musician. From the day we met, I had the impression he could relate to what I was saying. He could see the actual dynamics of extension, elaboration, and refinement—and see how Duke [Ellington] had done it.

"Duke was a guy who was always searching. You can see the transition in some of his pieces, from pop to fine art. Depends on how they play it. He could do *Sophisticated Lady* as a magnificent pop vocal, or take it as an instrumental to another level of artistic subtlety and profundity. That's what Cook was interested in. He took the time to tell Duke about that. And Duke was very responsive."

It was 1923 when Duke Ellington moved from Washington to New York, as Cook had so many years before. Already a promising bandleader, Ellington was thirty years younger than Cook. Precisely when and where they first met is not known. Most likely, it was around the time Ellington's band began a five-year stint at Harlem's Cotton Club in 1927. Cook befriended Ellington. They commenced lengthy discussions about composition techniques.

Ellington later said: "Will never wore a hat and when people asked him why, he'd say because he didn't have the money to buy one. They'd give him five dollars and then he and I would get in a taxi and ride around Central Park and he'd give me lectures in music. I'd sing a melody in its simplest form and he'd stop me and say, 'Reverse your figures.' He was a brief but strong influence. His language had to be pretty straight for me to know what he was talking about. Some of the things he used to tell me I never got a chance to use until years later, when I wrote the tone poem, *Black, Brown, and Beige*."

In *The Making of Jazz*, James Lincoln Collier writes: "It is apparent that Cook was teaching Ellington some of the fundamentals of melody-writing, the common devices a conservatory student learns as a matter of course. These include playing a melody upside down, or backward, repeating it lower or higher, turning it inside out, and so forth. . . . When we come to consider Ellington's music, he made frequent use of these devices in adapting to his purposes the themes he found around him."

Ellington also recalled receiving this advice from Cook: "First you find the logical way, and when you find it, avoid it, and let your inner self break through and guide you. Don't try to be anybody else but yourself."

Will Marion Cook died of cancer in 1944 at Harlem Hospital, at the age of seventy-five. His son Mercer remembered his father's influence in this way: "He found a publisher for many an unknown composer, or an opening for many a deserving performer. I have seen him, with less than fifty cents in his pocket, enter the offices of the Shapiro, Bernstein Music Corporation to get twenty dollars to send an ailing Negro singer to the country—a singer whom he scarcely knew. I have seen him, after an unprofitable week at the old Lafayette, pay out every cent to his men and go to his furnished room without his own rent."

In future years, Duke Ellington referred to Cook as "my conservatory . . . the master of all the masters of our people." Ellington would name his son Mercer after Cook's son. In 1966, while making his first tour of Africa, Ellington insisted he play for a party at the American Ambassador's residence in Senegal. The Ambassador was Mercer Cook.

"We, the colored people of America, have a glorious future in Art—especially and most likely, the vivid imagination, the courage, the dogged persistence and above all the ingratiating Smile. . . ."
—WILL MARION COOK, 1927

FOR FURTHER READING:

James Lincoln Collier, *The Making of Jazz: A Comprehensive History* (New York: Delta, 1978, paperback).

Eileen Southern, *The Music of Black Americans: A History* (New York and London: W. W. Norton & Co., 1983, paperback).

Albert Murray and Louis Armstrong

Perhaps in the swift change of American society in which the meanings of one's origin are so quickly lost, one of the chief values of living with music lies in its power to give us an orientation in time. In doing so, it gives significance to all those indefinable aspects of experience which nevertheless help to make us what we are. In the swift whirl of time music is a constant, reminding us of what we were and of that toward which we aspire. Art thou troubled? Music will not only calm, it will ennoble thee.

—RALPH ELLISON, 1955

Wynton Marsalis was not yet twenty-one the night he first walked into Albert Murray's apartment. From the picture window, the young trumpet player from New Orleans gazed out across Harlem toward the midtown Manhattan skyline. Thousands of jazz recordings and hundreds of books lined the shelves behind him: first editions of Hemingway, Faulkner, Mann, Malraux, saved and savored for nearly half a century. Along the wall beside Albert Murray's writing desk were large photographs of Duke Ellington composing and Louis Armstrong blowing his trumpet. Numerous paintings by the artist Romare Bearden hung on the walls.

The older man beckoned Marsalis to a couch and invited him to examine his photo albums. There were many pictures of Murray's close friend Ralph Ellison, whose novel *Invisible Man* became one of the classics of American literature. Here was the pianist/bandleader Count Basie, who had Murray put together his autobiography. There stood a handsome crew of the Tuskegee Airmen, the remarkable all-black World War II squadron which Murray helped to train. Here were the Spanish Steps in Rome, and the entryway to Jefferson's Monticello. "From Albert Murray," Marsalis would say years later, "I learned to envision things on a grand scale."

It was an auspicious night, one that not only changed Marsalis's life but eventually the direction of American music. For there is probably no more inspired example in our time of the continuity of tradition, of genius begetting genius, than we find in the evolutionary saga of Wynton Marsalis. Predominantly under Murray's tutelage, he came to know the musical heritage that he has so assiduously incorporated into his trumpet-playing, bandleading, composing, and educational programs for young people. Still only in his mid-thirties, Marsalis became the first jazz musician to receive a Pulitzer Prize for Music in 1997, for his composition *Blood on the Fields*. He is considered one of the greatest trumpeters since Louis Armstrong. Now an octogenarian, Murray is only today starting to be recognized as a writer of influence comparable to Ellison. The relationship between Marsalis and Murray is one that resonates across America's cultural history.

Albert Murray did not publish his first book until he was fifty-four. Since then, he has poured forth a diverse tapestry—nine books of essays, history, autobiography, and a fictional trilogy. In 1997, Murray was inducted into the American Academy of Arts and Letters and received a lifetime achievement award from the National Book Critics Circle. At a gathering to celebrate the publication of the *Norton Anthology of African American Literature*, he was introduced as "the dean of African-American letters."

Born on May 12, 1916, Murray was given up for adoption to a working-class family by his single mother. He had grown up in Magazine Point on the outskirts of Mobile, Alabama. His heroes were blues musicians at local joints like Gin's Alley, and the famed Negro League baseball pitcher Satchel Paige. Quarterback of his high school football team and captain of the basketball squad, he was voted the best all-around student at the Mobile County Training School. In 1935, he received a scholarship to Tuskegee Institute, the black college founded by Booker T. Washington. That is where Murray first ran into an upperclassman named Ralph Ellison.

After college, Murray was in the Air Force for more than twenty years—serving during World War II and Korea, and retiring in 1962 as Major Murray. Starting in 1968, he taught at numerous universities, including Columbia, Colgate, Brandeis, and Emory. All the while, he cultivated friendships within a vast artistic network: a man whom Duke Ellington called "an authority on soul from the days of old . . . the unsquarest person I know."

When Murray's first book, *The Omni-Americans*, appeared in 1970, the Southern writer Walker Percy wrote that it "well may be the most important book on black-white relations in the United States, indeed on American culture, published in this generation." It was a long essay that argued for the vitality that exists in the stylistic differences between the races, within a culture that "even in its most rigidly segregated precincts, is patently and irrevocably composite."

As Murray sees it, African-Americans are the country's truest representatives. "Essentially, they were becoming Americans before any-body else simply because everybody else still had something from the old country to live in terms of," he has said. "That's very fascinating stuff, and that's what we ought to have this generation be ready to come to terms with. The people freest to make an all-American syn-thesis were those who ironically are thought of as being the most ig-norant. It simply meant that they were coming in with less baggage."

Murray viewed the degradation of slavery and the subsequent op-pression of African-Americans as actually having forged something he-roic and life-enhancing. This, he felt, was best exemplified in jazz and the blues. His 1978 study, *Stomping the Blues,* was called by critic Stanley Crouch "the most eloquent book ever written about African-American music." When Count Basie selected Murray to collaborate on his life story, he said, "I wanted him because that's the way I would talk, if I could talk."

Murray's prose was highly musical, influenced as much by Kansas City Swing as by Joyce, Faulkner and Hemingway. He loved the idea that Germany's Thomas Mann had used Wagner's compositions as a literary model. Coming from his own tradition, Murray fashioned a style that one reviewer describes as "replete with shouts and squalls and snickers . . . a gorgeous, flaunting, rumbustious, rhythm-a-ning prose that curls and sprawls and edges sideways."

"Albert Murray has been an inspiration to a whole generation of writers," John Edgar Wideman was saying in the living room of his home in Amherst, Massachusetts. Wideman, the author of *Fathera-long, Brothers and Keepers,* and other widely acclaimed books, is him-self one of the best of that new generation. "Murray is a seminal thinker, a fine artist and, like Ralph Ellison, a genius in the vernacular. Also, as with Ellison, he's one of those people who maintains his stan-dards. Simply to go for a clear perspective.

"Murray is a national resource, because of his long career and the consistency of his thinking—just the people he knows and has stored up information about. Then, of course, the books, the great variety of his writing. He's the kind of person I would use the phrase 'public intellectual' for. Not because he gets a big public every time he goes out or is popular, but because he foregrounds the life of the mind in a consistent and sophisticated way, making it accessible to those of us who want to spend some time and discipline picking up on currents of thought of writers, artists, and musicians."

Then Wideman smiled and, with a sudden laugh, offered this cau-tionary note: "But he'll wear you out! Half the time, you have to take what he's saying on faith—because there's nobody alive who would remember in the same detail Albert Murray does. If that's what those guys were talking about on June 12, 1942, in Small's Paradise, well okay, yup!"

In the high-rise apartment building across from the A.M.E. Church in the heart of Harlem, Albert Murray is sitting in a comfortable chair, framed by his overflowing bookshelf. He is a lean, wiry man of medium height. His hair is close-cropped and he sports a pencil-thin gray mustache. He is wearing a light-blue turtleneck shirt and tan slacks. Slightly hard of hearing and plagued with an arthritic knee, he requires a walker to maneuver across the room. The light in Murray's eyes belies the physical difficulties. And when he smiles, it instantly brings to mind the wondrous raspy voice of Louis Armstrong singing: "The whole world smiles with you."

"You don't know how many choruses you have," Murray is saying, "so all you can do is swing as many of 'em as you can. How much elegance can you achieve? I want to write what I like about being American, and about being a brown-skinned American."

Murray's history lesson commences: From the beginnings of the evolution of consciousness, art forms always reenacted the survival techniques of given groups of people, through communication. Cultures arose from there. Underneath all the more complex formulas, the same dynamic was in operation. Extension, elaboration and refinement overlay the same basic rituals.

It ultimately had nothing to do with black and white. "Race is an ideological concept," Murray says. "It has to do with manipulating people, and with power, and with controlling people in a certain way. It has no basis in reality." The actual reality was fundamental—an identification through the human element. The only way to get there, however, was through the idiomatic. It was as ridiculous for American blacks to try to be African—"because they can't deal with African nuances and idiom"—as for the blues to be sung in an Irish, Italian, or New England accent. "We're talking about *culture*, not race. In the United States, they love to confuse the two. See, culture is what you live in *terms* of." And there were certain conventions involved; you would never see a "blues idiom person" snapping their fingers in church. Within the convention lies the idiom, a given way that people use language.

The blues idiom, Murray had told an interviewer for *American Heritage* magazine, was "an attitude of affirmation in the face of difficulty, of improvisation in the face of challenge. It means you acknowledge that life is a low-down dirty shame yet confront that fact with perseverance, with humor, and, above all, with elegance." The art form which encapsulates that, Murray is saying now, is jazz. Which is really an "attitude toward experience" that also defines the United States; the aesthetic statement made in the jam session being equivalent to the frontier scout finding his way across the wilderness.

But Murray notes that jazz did not originate with African tribes. In their painful amalgamation, they achieved their identity as Americans and then synthesized music from the other immigrant traditions: the Irish, the Germans, the British, the Scandinavians. "All the captive Africans from these various places," Murray continues, his words gathering momentum, "what they had in common was a *disposition* to make dance-oriented music. To move the whole body, to get a total response to music. So they approached musical instruments in terms of percussive statement. They heard Christmas carols and Gregorian chants and Protestant hymns and Catholic liturgies—and they made an American mix out of it." Their sense of rhythm and beat created a specific new musical form.

Murray offers the example of the Irish jig dances, which the African-Americans on the flatboats of the Ohio and the Mississippi witnessed and said, "Hell, we can do that." It was the same with "buck dancing," which originated with the Native Americans' flat-footed shuffle dance. From such elements, the American synthesis began to emerge. "The same metaphysical feeling you get from the stained-glass windows and the great Gothic cathedrals of Europe is in the American spirituals, no drop in aesthetic quality at all," as Murray says.

Then came the blues. Murray's character of Louisiana Charlie in his first novel, *Train Whistle Guitar*, was based on two blues folksingers: the legendary Leadbelly and a fellow Murray knew in his youth as "Old Choicy." "For me, he became 'Old Chaucer.' He used to come by my house all the time, come up out of the railroad bottom, and head for the juke joints around where I lived."

Murray calls this American fusion into the spirituals, the blues, and jazz a "down-home, brown-skinned idiom." The Japanese, he notes, love it but they can't loosen up and *do* it. "They've got what I'd call 'industrial swing'—because their thing is turning mechanical precision into miniaturization. Makes great microchips. But there's another type of precision that has to do with *elegant flow*. This reasserts the human element. That's why it's so universally appealing and cuts across other cultural divides. And that's what the average guy on the street probably means when he says, 'Soul.'

"Now someone like Wynton," Murray adds, "is very sensitive to realize those types of intellectual resonances beneath the surface of the music."

He begins talking about Marsalis. Stanley Crouch had originally brought Wynton up to meet him in 1982. Marsalis had just signed with Columbia Records and recorded his first solo album. He had already heard about Murray, through a young woman he'd known in New Orleans who had taken a creative writing class from him at Barnard College. Most of the young people who dropped in on Murray came and went. "To me it's fine if they don't come back, then I don't have to be bothered," Murray chuckles. Marsalis was different. Not only did he return regularly, he began sending others over. "Wynton'd say, 'You oughta talk to him, have him tell you what books to read,'" Murray recalls.

He would spend hours discussing literature with Marsalis. There was William Faulkner, a Southern writer "steeped in the folklore and wisdom of Uncle Remus" who nonetheless gave his black characters "a greater humanity. . . . You've got to come through Faulkner," Murray explained of the man's influence on his own work. "You've got to do something so that if you're in a jam session with Faulkner he would say, 'Hey, that was a good solo.' . . . From Faulkner, I got the challenge of dealing with time. But the *economy* I got from Hemingway. See, he was the master of epic style. Hemingway's a genius for simplicity, Faulkner's a genius for convolution."

He would read aloud to Marsalis from the poetry and essays of W. H. Auden: "Shit, Auden's like Thelonius Monk, I can't live without Auden." He would loan Marsalis the novels of Thomas Mann. "From Mann, I got the idea that you could find an aesthetic model in your [own] idiom for literature. So when he started talking about dialectic orchestration and leitmotifs and things like that, I started thinking about riffs, breaks. . . ."

Murray spoke to Marsalis of his belief "in a kind of Whitmanesque nationalism that Bessie Smith and Fats Waller are a part of." He showed Wynton his dozens of books on the Civil War—"How could you be a colored guy in the United States and talk about your position and not know anything about the Civil War?" And he offered historical perspectives: "You don't have a better prototype for the self-created American than Harriet Tubman, Frederick Douglass, or Louis Armstrong picking up that horn."

He would offer anecdotal lessons from his own youth: "There was a sort of convention that you recognized when you came up in a segregated time. We didn't dislike white people. There was just a special etiquette that was involved in a relationship with some of them, given the circumstances. Of course with those hobo guys on the railroad coming by asking for food—we didn't have any reason to feel inferior to white people. Just because they put that status stuff out there didn't mean we were going to go along with it."

Of Marsalis's response to all this, Murray says: "See, Wynton, being

in effect a prodigy, went through the formal courses faster. So he realized his education was lacking. But he has a sense of the richness of
the context that you're talking about. He asks questions and he thinks
about it." Each time Marsalis made his Harlem pilgrimage, it was with
more questions about something Murray had touched on before, something Wynton needed to understand before he could move on. "So
what makes him smart," Murray says, "is that he's aware of what he
doesn't know."

*"In the face of spelling out a tale of woe, you move from a purifi-
cation ritual into a celebration of life. . . . Now it's not by force alone
that one conquers chaos—that one conquers the dragon. It's style that
one uses to do that."*

—ALBERT MURRAY

Around the corner from Lincoln Center, next door to the Juilliard
School of Music where Marsalis first studied in New York, is the musician's penthouse apartment. A trio of trumpets rests atop a grand
piano. A fourth—a mysterious-looking one that looks almost like a
sculpture—is alongside Wynton on the couch. Against a wall stands
an old Victrola with a silver horn. Under a print of Duke Ellington
sits a well-worn trumpet case covered with travel stickers. In the bedroom, alongside pictures of his three sons, are detailed drawings of
railroad trains.

Marsalis seemed to be everywhere these days. He had just completed
a twenty-four-city American and European tour with his long original
work about the era of slavery, *Blood on the Fields*. He had performed
trumpet solos for President Clinton and conducted an orchestra at the
'96 Olympics, also serving as artistic director for the Jazz at Lincoln
Center program, doing educational workshops for schoolchildren, and
making top-of-the-charts recordings in both jazz and classical venues.
He had become the foremost spokesman in regenerating a musical
form that had gone largely dormant during the 1970s. "Jazz is a music
of conversation," he has said, "and that's what you need in a democracy."

For all his worldwide fame, there is a distinct lack of pretense about
the soft-spoken Marsalis, a sense of humility to a grand tradition that
he feels compelled to carry forward. It was in the ethers of the New
Orleans of Buddy Bolden, King Oliver, Jelly Roll Morton, Sidney Bechet and Louis Armstrong, where Marsalis grew up. He was nurtured
by a family, in which his father Ellis remains a prominent jazz pianist.
Three of Wynton's brothers also took up various instruments and be-

came professional musicians. He was nurtured, too, by hard times in the Deep South of the civil rights era.

Marsalis, born on October 18, 1961, remembers:

"As a little boy I was always around musicians, my daddy's friends. I remember the feeling of what they had when they would talk, how they were as men. What influenced me the most was the way they struggled. And they never made it. Nat Perelette died of a drug overdose. James Black was damn near crazy. My father, he was the sanest one. Because he wasn't gonna let the hurt of it all make him lose his mind. He wasn't out there as alone as they were, I don't think. I remember once, my daddy was down to like his last twenty dollars. I was maybe eleven or twelve. He was trying to determine whether he wanted to drive a cab, give up trying to play music. In my house there was always strife about money. So the perception I had was that my momma didn't want my daddy to be a musician. But then when he was gonna take a day job, she said no, he should keep playing.

"That struck me. My momma has real aesthetic understanding. Not that she ever had any real engagement with jazz, but she understood something of what this music was about, in terms of what it represents. I think I got a lot of that from her. She has an understanding of what integrity is, too. My mother, she would take us all to music lessons. My father's more purely a musician, he's not gonna *make* you play. I started playing trumpet real young with a couple of teachers, but I didn't practice.

"I was twelve when I began to get serious, after I started listening to music. *Giant Steps* by John Coltrane, I put that record on and liked it. There were only three or four such records, I never really knew about jazz from a student standpoint. Nobody I knew ever listened to it. What my daddy and his friends played I thought was old jazz, because funk and fusion were popular with *my* friends. We all loved that. But it always seemed more for synthesizers and guitars, not for a horn player. Plus the expression of it, I couldn't put it into words at that time, but it just seemed like there was something more. Then I stumbled onto classical music. A guy gave me a record of Maurice André and I wanted to play like that. But even then, I always longed to play jazz, to be like my father and his musician friends.

"Sometime in there, my daddy told me: 'The only way you can be different from other people is to do some shit they don't want to do. Get up at six in the morning and shed for an hour. After school, stay up late and deal with your horn. Do that every day for six or seven years. Don't miss no days.' I still didn't feel like doing it. At all. But I realized that if you practice you get better. When you're working, the spirit understands that you are serious and that you are preparing yourself to receive that information. Stay in the state of preparedness. Coltrane said that."

By the time Marsalis was ready for high school, his father had been invited to help found a New Orleans Center for the Creative Arts. Wynton and his brother Branford, today a renowned saxophonist, both attended. At only sixteen, Wynton performed the Haydn Trumpet Concerto with the city's Civic Orchestra. Simultaneously he and Branford played together in a funk band called The Creators. "In New Orleans," Marsalis says, "I could play with the symphony, a jazz quartet, a funk group, or at a parade. In most other cities I'd never have had all those chances."

In the summer of 1978, Marsalis journeyed to New York to audition for the Tanglewood Music Center. After playing his Haydn, Marsalis told the artistic director, Gunther Schuller, that he wanted to try Bach's very difficult Second Brandenburg Concerto. "While he was warming up," Schuller would remember, "he concealed himself behind a pillar, so I leaned over to see what he was doing. He was pumping the valves and talking to his trumpet, saying, 'Now don't let me down.' He knocked off the first three phrases flawlessly. We were overwhelmed by his talent."

Marsalis received a scholarship to Juilliard. He had been at the music school a year when he discovered Art Blakey's Jazz Messengers at an uptown Manhattan night-spot called Mickel's. Blakey, who died in 1990, is considered by many critics to have been the greatest jazz drummer ever. There was a long tradition of mentoring in jazz—Will Marion Cook's lessons to Duke Ellington, later Miles Davis being brought along by Charlie Parker and Dizzy Gillespie, and Davis in turn helping John Coltrane. Art Blakey was very much a part of this; such now-famous jazzmen as pianist Keith Jarrett and saxophonist Wayne Shorter got their start with the Jazz Messengers. Marsalis was eighteen when he asked to join the band. Blakey took him in, and he dropped out of Juilliard.

It was shortly thereafter that Stanley Crouch first heard Marsalis playing with Blakey's group. Today a highly regarded essayist of such titles as *Notes of a Hanging Judge* and *The All-American Skin Game*, Crouch was then in his mid-thirties. He had been a jazz drummer, actor, poet and college professor in California. Arriving in New York a few years before Marsalis, he became a jazz promoter and critic. Astounded at Marsalis's prowess, Crouch invited him for dinner and was equally taken aback with how little Wynton knew about jazz. "I mean, he didn't know much about Armstrong or Ellington or Monk or Ornette Coleman," Crouch recalls. "So I started loaning him records and making suggestions about things I thought he might want to look into."

Marsalis says that Crouch represented a phenomenon to him, with a thirst for knowledge and a penchant for asking probing questions. "Just a citizen who's constantly learning something? That was a very abstract concept for somebody like me. You didn't think about people knowing anything outside of school, not in the circles I was in."

Eventually, the man Marsalis now calls "the professor of connection" hooked him up with his own mentor, Albert Murray. Crouch had been only slightly older than Marsalis when he first met Murray ten years earlier. What so intrigued Wynton that first night in Harlem was the respect Crouch clearly possessed for Murray, "another whole new thing" to witness.

And so it began, the transcendent stage in the education of Wynton Marsalis. There were museums to visit, books to read, the dinner-table conversations that ranged from Homer to Galileo and from commedia dell'arte to Faulkner and Neruda. Wynton would sit on Murray's couch and watch him "just pull any of those books down off the wall and start reading from a specific page. That was mind-boggling, I'd never been around *nothin'* like that!" Asked which works Murray turned him onto, the list ripples rapid-fire from Marsalis like a trumpet riff: "Thomas Mann—*Joseph and His Brothers, The Coming Victory of Democracy, Doctor Faustus.* Heinrich Zimmer—*The King and the Corpse.* Joseph Campbell, all his books. William Faulkner—*Absalom Absalom, The Sound and the Fury, Intruder in the Dust, As I Lay Dying, Light in August.* Ernest Hemingway—*In Our Time.* I could just keep naming them, really.

"The most amazing thing about Mr. Murray is his incredible enthusiasm. He's my mentor, but it's more than that. His book *Stomping the Blues* had a profound impact on me in terms of understanding the context of the art form, and the society. I guess you'd say I'm a Murrayite."

Today it is hard to imagine that, before he came in contact with Crouch and Murray, Marsalis was so unaware of the jazz heritage. "When I was growing up, I always equated Louis Armstrong with being an Uncle Tom," Marsalis was saying, remembering how his father tried in vain to get him to listen to Armstrong's recordings. "I said, that's handkerchief-head [music]—you know, the way he waved that handkerchief around—mainly for white folks, tourists. All I knew really was *Hello Dolly.* The rest was just history."

Now, as a thick afternoon fog closed over the Hudson River just beyond his picture window, Marsalis nodded and said: "Yeah, Pops"—

as he fondly referred to Armstrong—"his sound is both the most modern and the most ancient, like somebody playing outside the walls of Jericho." The only comparison he could make was to Merlin the magician, able to pass through time and come out anywhere, thus belonging to *all* time. "It's like a circle. He was there in the beginning, too. Yeah, that's what Pops is.

"He brought back a real joy to music. Armstrong loosens up everybody's phrasing, their concept of where to place the beat. You get bass players trying to sound like him, and trombone and saxophone sections, and arrangers writing Louis Armstrong licks. Because more than any other musician's, his sound carries the feeling and the meaning of jazz. Anything you want, he has it—warmth and intelligence, worldly and provincial, spiritual and tawdry, down-home but sophisticated. The most complex player there's ever been, yet he can still sound like a country boy."

Wynton remembered trying to play Armstrong's solo on *Jubilee* when he was nineteen. "It was *tough*, man! It doesn't sound that high or hard, because he has such command of his instrument that he doesn't seem like he's straining. But it's deceptive. You see the scars and abrasions around his chops, and you know he didn't achieve those effects without paying a price."

The price went back to his youth. Born soon after the new century dawned, Armstrong was abandoned by his father shortly afterwards. He was raised by his grandmother, then his mother, in the New Orleans red-light district known as Storyville. As one of the birthplaces of jazz, Armstrong would recall, "on every corner I could hear music."

He stole from produce barrels to get food. At twelve, he got arrested for illegally firing off a .38 pistol on New Year's Eve. He spent three years in the city's Colored Waifs' Home for Boys. There Armstrong was invited into the brass band by the music teacher, and soon displayed an unusual grasp of harmony. At the Home, he learned to play several instruments, including the cornet. The band he came to lead played for social gatherings and funerals and marched in parades.

When he returned to Storyville at sixteen, Armstrong supported his family by delivering coal for seventy-five cents a day and playing cornet in the bars by night. The local musician who held him "spellbound" was Joe "King" Oliver—who "was so powerful he used to blow a cornet out of tune every two or three months," Armstrong wrote in his autobiography, *Swing That Music*. Oliver befriended and began teaching trumpet to the young Armstrong. When Oliver struck out for new horizons in Chicago, Louis took his place as cornetist in the city's hottest band, Kid Ory's Jazz Orchestra. Armstrong's reputation began to spread. In 1922, Oliver sent for him to join his Creole Jazz Band.

Albert Murray tells a wonderful story that Armstrong's second wife Lil imparted to him. It took place not long after Armstrong's arrival in Chicago. "You see, the way you really go by somebody seems to be by trying to please them," Murray said. "That's the way Louis Armstrong went beyond King Oliver. They were out there in this recording studio and Louis really wanted King Oliver to think he was good. But he'd developed so much that he was unbalancing the record. After all, King Oliver was running the group, he was the daddy, he's Poppa Joe! So the recording engineers said, 'We didn't get that quite right, let's do another take'—and they moved Louis back a little bit. Now Louis played even harder, so they wouldn't have to hide him! Next time they moved him all the way back against the wall, way away from the mike, for still another take. Louis still dominated the record! And the reason is, he's trying to be sure he don't mess up for King Oliver!"

The story was reminiscent of Marsalis coaxing his horn before taking the stage to try the Brandenburg Concerto. Indeed, Wynton's own sound—the fat, breathy tones; the singing, shouting, growling, whispering rise-and-fall—is in some ways strikingly reminiscent of Armstrong's. Marsalis marveled at Armstrong's creation of the first coherent, organized solos, the way he figured out how to connect themes while improvising.

"The question in jazz," says Marsalis, "is how do you make conflicting things harmonious. And achieving that balance is what Pops is basically all about. He could play with tremendous power and grace. In equal measure. He stayed calm within himself and had this great sense of tranquillity in his personality. But there was also this barely contained frenzy in his playing, like rice ready to boil over."

By the late 1920s, Armstrong's trumpet playing with two small recording units he organized—the Hot Five and the Hot Seven—had earned him a national reputation. During the Depression years, he became the first black performer sponsored on network radio and one of the first featured in major Hollywood film productions. In Europe, he was lionized; 10,000 people met his railway carriage when it arrived in Denmark.

Marsalis spent long evenings discussing "Pops" with Albert Murray, studying the transformation Armstrong wrought as he became America's "Ambassador of Sound." "Armstrong's music," Murray wrote in his most recent book of essays, *The Blue Devils of Nada*, "made him a globetrotting goodwill ambassador for the irrepressible idealism of his native land because it was such an irresistible expression of what so many people elsewhere think of as being the American outlook on human possibility."

As time passed, Marsalis came to his particular insights about Arms-

trong, insights which enlightened his own teachers. Sitting in a Greenwich Village café, Stanley Crouch recounted: "See, Marsalis pointed
out to me something about Armstrong that's very important. That
there was never a point in history when somebody had equal impact
as an instrumentalist and a vocalist. When you really listen to the way
American music sounded before Armstrong, and then the way people
started to play and sing after him, it's so monumental that it's hard to
believe sometimes. In fact, Armstrong is an unparalleled innovator in
all of Western music."

Not only did the leading trumpeters of the big-band period—Roy Eld-
ridge, Bunny Berigan, Harry James, Cootie Williams, and more—model
their styles on Armstrong's. Jimmy Rodgers, the father of country music,
recorded with him. So did Hoagy Carmichael and Bing Crosby. "Yes,
I'm proud to acknowledge my debt to the Reverend Satchelmouth,"
Crosby once said. "He is the beginning and the end of music in America." As Crosby's fellow crooner Rudy Vallee said in 1936: "Compare a
record by Crosby, in which he departs from the 'straight' form of the
melody and lyric and then listen to an Armstrong record and discover
whence must have come some of his ideas of 'swinging.' " Just listen to
Tony Bennett's phrasing, says Murray. Or Billie Holiday's, as Bennett
himself has said. It was, wrote Armstrong biographer James Lincoln
Collier, "as if he were a funnel through which twentieth-century music
had to pass before it could find its way."

For his part, Armstrong called Crosby "Papa Bing" and described
Guy Lombardo's band in a letter as "the sweetest music this side of
heaven. . . . Guy Lombardo inspired us so much with their sense of
timing—their beautiful tones (the most essential thing in music), their
beautiful way of phrasing—we stepped right into their footsteps with
our big band at the Savoy."

For all the joy he exuded, all the friends he had that knew no color
lines, Armstrong was not silent about racism in America. During the
1950s, his was a ubiquitous presence on the world's stages, radio and
TV, and in eleven movies. In 1956, during his first tour of West Africa
where more than 100,000 came to the concert, Armstrong made a
point of performing Fats Waller's *Black and Blue*. He had first established it as a kind of "protest song" in 1929: "They laugh at you—
what can I do? How would it end? Ain't got a friend. . . . What did I
do, to be so black and blue?"

During mid-September of 1957, Armstrong exploded when he
learned about events in Little Rock, Arkansas. Despite the Supreme
Court's decision mandating the integration of public schools, black
schoolchildren had been refused admission. The federal government

was doing nothing about it. "Louis made a statement in an interview," jazz pianist Dave Brubeck recalled. "He said President Eisenhower should go down there and take those little children by the hand and lead them into that school."

The remark caused a firestorm. One New York newspaper columnist demanded a boycott of Armstrong's appearances. Concerts were cancelled in the South. After Eisenhower took a stand and dispatched federal troops to Little Rock, Armstrong sent the White House a telegram: "If you decide to walk in the school with the little colored kids, take me along daddy. God bless you."

As Marsalis says of Armstrong, "He always stayed true to himself, his way of doing things, no matter what anyone, white or black, said. He just did his thing—and changed the world."

Briefly fingering the horn beside him on the couch, Marsalis continues: "Pops came under a lot of false criticism for the way he played in his later years. People wanted him to perform with the same velocity. A lotta times, we confuse velocity with technique. Velocity's just the ability to play fast, jump octaves or something. The highest level of technique is nuance. The solos Louis Armstrong was playing in his later period are virtually impossible to learn. The color of the tone is so refined, the rhythmic sophistication is so much more advanced than in the earlier recordings. It's just been worked on for so many years."

Forty years after he first revolutionized American music, Armstrong's recording of *Hello Dolly* displaced the Beatles as the number one record in America early in 1964. He continued to barnstorm the world, despite frequent hospitalizations for illnesses. He had spent two months recovering from a heart attack when he asked his doctor to bring his All Stars together for a rehearsal. Armstrong died the next morning, on July 6, 1971.

When it came out a few years ago that Armstrong's claimed birthdate of July 4, 1900, was a personal selection (baptismal records show the actual date as August 4, 1901), Albert Murray wrote: "The symbolism of the choice may well suggest that Armstrong was not unaware of the fact that he was in effect a culture hero (not unlike, say, Prometheus), the bringer of indispensable existential equipment for the survival of humanity."

Or, as Wynton Marsalis puts it, "The sound of that horn was a pure spiritual essence, the song of America and the freedom it had been supposed to offer."

"They all know I'm there in the cause of happiness. . . . Through all of the misfortunes, etc., I did not plan anything. Life was there for me

and I accepted it. And life, whatever came out, has been beautiful to me, and I love everybody."

                                                    —LOUIS ARMSTRONG

FOR FURTHER READING:
Louis Armstrong, *Satchmo: My Life in New Orleans* (New York: New American Library, 1954, repr. New York, 1961).
————, *Swing That Music* (New York/London/Toronto: Longmans, Green & Co., 1936).
Laurence Bergreen, *Louis Armstrong: An Extravagant Life* (New York: Broadway Books, 1997).
James Lincoln Collier, *Louis Armstrong, An American Genius* (New York: Oxford University Press, 1983).
Max Jones and John Chilton, *Louis: The Louis Armstrong Story, 1900-1971* (Boston: Little Brown, 1971).

BOOKS BY ALBERT MURRAY:
The Omni-Americans: New Perspectives on Black Experience and American Culture (New York: Outerbridge & Dienstfrey, 1970).
South to a Very Old Place (New York: McGraw-Hill, 1971).
The Hero and the Blues (Colombia, Mo.: University of Missouri Press, 1973).
Train Whistle Guitar (New York: McGraw-Hill, 1974).
Stomping the Blues (New York: McGraw-Hill, 1976; London: Quarter, 1978).
Good Morning Blues: The Autobiography of Count Basie as Told to Albert Murray (New York: Da Capo, 1986).
The Spyglass Tree (New York: Vintage, 1991).
The Seven League Boots (New York: Pantheon, 1996).
The Blue Devils of Nada: A Contemporary American Approach to Aesthetic Statement (New York: Pantheon, 1996).

BOOKS BY STANLEY CROUCH:
The All-American Skin Game, or, The Decoy of Race (New York: Pantheon, 1995).
Notes of a Hanging Judge (New York: Oxford University Press, 1990).

The Craft of Ralph Ellison

For Albert Murray—my friend who was schooled in the same briar patch, to confound the squares, bears and fools thereabouts. Passion is his, and with it consciousness, but best of all self-acceptance and self-respect. In his ear, my voice becomes richer for his love and knowledge of the experience we both love and share.
   "Sincerely, Ralph Ellison. Tuskegee, 1954—2 years late, but deeply felt."
      —The inscription on Albert Murray's first edition of *Invisible Man.*

   In the prologue to *Invisible Man*, Ralph Waldo Ellison's masterpiece published in 1952, there was this passage from the nameless protagonist who has taken up residence in an underground passageway beneath a manhole cover:
   ". . . when I have music I want to *feel* its vibration, not only with my ear but with my whole body. I'd like to hear five recordings of Louis Armstrong playing and singing 'What Did I Do to Be so Black and Blue'—all at the same time. Sometimes now I listen to Louis while I have my favorite dessert of vanilla ice cream and sloe gin. I pour the red liquid over the white mound, watching it glisten and the vapor rising as Louis bends that military instrument into a beam of lyrical sound. Perhaps I like Louis Armstrong because he's made poetry out of being invisible. . . ."
   Ralph Ellison, Stanley Crouch has written, "was from the same spiritual corner as Louis Armstrong, who knew of cutting and shooting but had danced in the gutter while doggedly staring at the stars."
   Ellison was living in a modest apartment above the Hudson River, where northern Harlem meets Washington Heights, the night that Crouch took Wynton Marsalis over to meet him in the mid-1980s. Crouch's initial relationship with Ellison had begun at a big party at Albert Murray's. That was more than forty years after Murray first encountered Ellison at Alabama's Tuskegee Institute. It turned out that Ellison had not started out to be a writer, but a musician—in fact, a trumpeter. So Wynton brought along his horn. They ended up playing a duet together.
   Asked what they talked about, Marsalis recalls saying very little,

simply listening and absorbing "like when I'm around Mr. Murray." He listened as Crouch, who had taught a college course centering on *Invisible Man*, discussed the novel's intricacies with its author. He listened as Ellison read aloud passages from a work-in-progress. He remembers being struck by Ellison's humor and the cadence of his speech, the way it "rolled down a certain way." He admired the absence of pontification, the down-home style.

Marsalis pauses and, somewhat at a loss for words, continues: "Except there was something *else* in it all, this quality of thought. I don't know how to describe it, just—this was *Ralph Ellison*."

Ellison was born in Oklahoma City on March 1, 1914. His father died when he was three, and he was raised by a politically active mother who worked as a domestic. According to Harvard professor Cornel West, "Ralph's mother was unbelievable. She was a Socialist, and part of a drive at one time to make Oklahoma a black state! In many ways, Ralph's creativity comes from her energy, talent, and determination."

Ellison began playing the trumpet in his early years. When he was a teenager, three jazz luminaries—Hot Lips Page, Jimmy Rushing, and Lester Young—all settled in his hometown. He arrived at Tuskegee to study classical composition. Murray, two years his junior, says he would often see him sitting at a library table surrounded by sheets of music, "or in the art department sculpting a model of someone's head." Every book that Murray went to check out of the library, Ellison's name was there first.

Murray shakes his head and laughs, reminiscing about the day Ellison ran into him on campus. Murray was reading a Modern Library hardcover of Sinclair Lewis's *Arrowsmith*. As his teacher often did, he had folded the book and stuck it in his pocket. "Ralph looked at me and said: 'What do you think this is? A *pocket* edition?' " Murray laughs again. "The tweed jacket, the contrasted slacks, the sporty shoes. Ralph was so fancy he'd even wear a bow-tie! He was sort of like a student concert master of the band. The guy who'd go"—and here Murray offers a loud, drawn-out imitation—"Touch-down Tigers, Touch-down Ti-gers! He had a nickname at Tuskegee: Sousa."

In the summer of 1936, Ellison traveled to New York to study sculpture and earn some money to finish his final year. He never came back. The very morning after Ellison arrived and checked into the Harlem YMCA, he recognized Dr. Alain Locke standing with someone in the entranceway. Locke had been a pivotal figure in promoting black artistic talent during the Harlem Renaissance of the 1920s, and had just met Ellison briefly on a visit to Tuskegee. Locke introduced the man beside him to Ellison. It was the poet Langston Hughes, who was carrying copies of André Malraux's *Man's Fate* and *The Days of Wrath*. After talking for a bit, Hughes told the young man, "Since you like to read so much, maybe you'd like to read these novels and return them to their owner." Hughes soon arranged for Ellison to meet Richard Wright, the author of *Native Son*, who encouraged him to pursue writing. The fates seemed to have ordained Ellison to a life's work other than music or sculpture.

Albert Murray stayed on to graduate from Tuskegee, which then hired him to teach composition and literature. He began to see book reviews by Ellison appearing in various journals. At Tuskegee, Murray fell in love with Mozelle Menefee, to whom he has been married since 1941. The next year Murray paid his first visit to New York, where a friend who knew Ellison arranged a reunion. By this time, Murray, too, was thinking of becoming a writer.

"Ralph was living over on Compton Avenue in an apartment with his first wife," Murray remembers. "When we walked in, first thing I saw was Malraux! That was impressive, because I'd read most of his books in college."

A lifelong friendship soon commenced. When Murray entered the Army Air Force during World War II, flying up to New York on weekends to buy bagfuls of books, he would see Ellison. After the war ended, Murray moved to the city to pursue a Master's degree in literature at New York University. Ellison was working not far away from Murray's main hangout—the 42nd Street Library—and often dropped by for a mutual walk over to the Gotham Book Mart.

Now, as dusk settles over the Harlem the two of them first explored together, Murray brings out his big stack of photo albums. "Ralph had all kinds of cameras—a Leica, a Roloflex, a Technica, a Hasselblad, Nikon, everything. You know what a Technica is? That's a wide-angle, sort of 3-D, that they take architectural pictures with. Ralph took these pictures. There's Ralph and me after the war. He was working on *Invisible Man* at this time. Ralph and Fanny [his second wife] came up at Christmas and stayed, then we were over there for a down-home New Year's in '48."

During the seven long years that Ellison spent writing *Invisible Man*, he would read passages aloud to Murray. Asked about the novel, Murray says: "The invisible man is a tragic hero with the possibility of redemption. Not really redemption, but rejuvenation, metamorphosis. Basically everything that happens to him is closer to a sense of tragedy. We're talking about the nobility of tragedy. Every American would be more knowledgeable of his own identity by being familiar with that aspect of American life."

How would Murray characterize Ellison's style? "Hallucinatory. It was like a nightmare, Kafkaesque." A brief pause, a nostalgia in his voice. "We were very close. We agreed on a lot of things. But we didn't have the same type of sensibility. So my books are not anything like his at all, except they represent the same basic values. With Ralph, the political implications are more obvious. I'm interested in epics. It's another literary strategy altogether. I write about heroic possibility."

Despite the stylistic differences, one often comes across the same reference points in the two writers' essays. For example, both use the phrase "antagonistic cooperation." Murray explains: "I got that from Joseph Campbell [author of *The Hero with a Thousand Faces* and many other studies of myth and ritual]. We were very good friends. And Ralph got the phrase from me. It has to do with looking at all opposition as potentially cooperative—since you need evil in order to have a saint, a war to have a general, a contender to have a champion."

Both Ellison and Murray also describe their philosophical debt to such thinkers as Lord Raglan, author of *The Hero*, and literary theorist Kenneth Burke. "I didn't get into either of those guys, except under Ralph's influence," Murray continues. "In literature you have two types of statements that Kenneth Burke likes to talk about—they're terribly important to me and I used to teach them to my students: you can set up a frame of acceptance or a frame of rejection. Now what you accept is the necessity of struggle. And it's out of that literary strategy that you get the epic."

The parallels of mutual influence continue. Ellison and Murray were enamored of the same literary figures: Hemingway, Malraux, Faulkner. Both pay homage to the little-known essayists Constance Rourke and John Kouwenhoven for their insights into American culture. Both were deeply affected by the blues tradition. Both knew well, and wrote about, musician Duke Ellington and artist Romare Bearden. Both were practitioners of sartorial elegance.

Was one the real wellspring for the other's work? We may know more when the extensive Ellison-Murray correspondence becomes available. Murray has all of Ellison's letters to him, but says, "I wouldn't presume to publish them unless his estate asked me to." (Ellison died in 1994.) What is evident is that the two men inspired one another's imagination through mutual discoveries. Murray's personality was more ebullient, Ellison's more saturnalian. One glimpses their similar vision, and their elegant means of expressing it, in these passages about the blues:

ELLISON: The blues is an art of ambiguity, an assertion of the irrepressibly human over all circumstance, whether created by others or by one's own human failings. They are the only consistent art in the United States which constantly remind us of our limitations while encouraging us to see how far we can actually go. When understood in their more profound implication, they are a corrective, an attempt to draw a line upon man's own limitless assertion.

MURRAY: *The blues affirm life in America in all of its infinite confusions, they affirm life and humanity itself in the very process of confronting failures and existentialistic absurdities. . . . [In the blues] there is, for instance, the seemingly inherent emphasis on rugged individual endurance. There is also the candid acknowledgment and sober acceptance of adversity as an inescapable condition of human existence— and perhaps in consequence an affirmative disposition toward all obstacles, whether urban or rural, whether political or metaphysical.*

Ralph Ellison once told the story of how, shortly after World War II where he had served as a cook in the merchant marine, he went to visit a friend in Vermont. He sat down at a typewriter one afternoon in an old barn looking out at a mountain and wrote: "I am an invisible man." At the time, he had no idea what the cryptic phrase meant, or what had inspired it. It seemed to Ellison a "wild notion," but the moment he started to abandon the idea, he thought: "Well, maybe I should try to discover exactly what it was that lay behind the statement. What type of man . . . would conceive of himself in such terms? What lay behind him?"

It is stunning to realize how much *Invisible Man* presaged. The civil rights movement and the urban riots of the '60s. . . . The rise of black nationalism and Afrocentrism. . . . The multicultural metaphor of the paint factory, where black mixes inextricably with white. Above all, the haunting question: How do people release themselves from that which makes races and individuals blind to one another's existence? "What on earth," as the Everyman narrator asks, "was hiding behind the face of things?"

The Invisible Man must learn how to break the codes—social, political, racial. His rite of passage begins at a Tuskegeelike school, then mirrors the rural-South-to-urban-North migration of so many African-Americans. Along each step of his journey, the hero encounters chaos and betrayal, mystery and revelation, and an assemblage of mythic characters who embody the paradoxes of the nation. Blending echoes of Dostoevsky's stark realism and Kafka's surrealism with reverberations of folklore and slave narrative and Twain and Faulkner, Ellison emerges with what Murray once described as "the literary extension of the blues. It was as if Ellison had taken an everyday twelve bar blues tune (by a man from down South sitting in a manhole up North in New York singing and signifying about how he got there) and scored it for full orchestra."

"Who knows but that, on the lower frequencies, I speak for you?"
—the last line of *Invisible Man*.

On a chilly February afternoon in Amherst, Massachusetts, John Edgar Wideman has just come off the road promoting his new novel, *The Cattle Killing*. He is a tall, good-looking man in his mid-fifties, dressed casually in a black sweatsuit. On one wall of his living room is a poster of a Romare Bearden painting. On a music stand next to a small piano, a book titled *Nothing But the Blues*.

When he first read *Invisible Man*, Wideman remembers, "I was a young African-American male with aspirations to writing. It struck me to be as good as the very best books I was reading, and that judgment had nothing to do with race but everything to do with race. The novel both transcended race in terms of its quality, but couldn't have been more personal and more culturally evocative. It took me down to the foundations of me. Suddenly, I had a hero and a champion."

In the years since, Wideman estimated he had taught *Invisible Man* a dozen times to his students at the University of Massachusetts. "And I've found the book a kind of inexhaustible source of enlightenment, and fun, and mystery. There is always a freshness to reading it. And layers that I hadn't uncovered, or reassessments I have to make—pretty radical ones sometimes—something I have discarded or am quite prepared to discard, I have to bring it back in and get rid of something else. So it's like your very best friendships, it has a life apart as well as a life that you share and that reinvigorates itself all along."

Besides being a storehouse of language—all the ways to represent distinct varieties of speech—and of an omnibus of novelistic techniques, there were Ellison's pivotal ideas about revolution and black separatism. Perhaps, above all, Wideman went on, "another aspect of Ellison is sharing him. It's a point of contact with other African-American writers, having read him and talking about him, knowing other people who have grown from the same roots and sources. Identifying a kind of kinship, a shared mentor if you will.

"I think that's very important because the kinds of chances that Ellison takes and the fact that he stands for a certain level of quality, where he's competing with the very best—those are things that are not easy to keep alive in a tradition. Particularly a tradition that gets periodically trashed, or rifled. Or abused. People come along and say 'All black writers this,' or 'All black writers that.' Or another time, praise something to high heaven simply beause it's the flavor of the month. So it's good to have some lodestones to refer to and keep in mind, on the level of continuity and tradition.''

Ellison's own explorations of continuity and tradition appear in the only other two books he ever published, the essay collections titled *Shadow and Act* (1964) and *Going to the Territory* (1986). ''Ralph's essays tell you as much as Emerson's,'' Albert Murray believes. ''Other [black] writers end up asking for acceptance, inclusion. Whereas Ralph was interested in changing perceptions, saying: 'This is American, too, basic American.' ''

Three years after *Invisible Man* won the National Book Award and catapulted Ellison to international fame, in 1955 he began work on a second novel. It is said to have centered around the relationship between a black preacher and his white friend, who becomes a U.S. senator and notorious racist. A very meticulous craftsman, Ellison often showed excerpts or read aloud from the book to Albert Murray. Twelve years after he began the work, Ellison's revisions were in the final stages. Suddenly, his personal continuity was irrevocably shattered.

It was November 1967 in the Berkshires. Ellison and his wife had extended their country respite from New York at their old wooden summer house in Plainfield, Massachusetts. ''Ralph was working so well there that he stayed longer than he normally would,'' Murray remembers. ''My wife and I had stopped by that summer on our way back to New York from the Cape. He figured he'd have the manuscript ready for his editors by the first of the year. Finally he and Fanny were getting ready to leave. He packed up everything and put it in the hallway, his cameras and his Scottish shooting piece. Then they went out to dinner at Dick Wilbur's, the poet.

''On the way home, they saw this fire reflection on the skyline, and the nearer they got, the more it seemed like it was their place. And as they turned in, they saw their house going up in flames.''

There had been an electrical failure. The home was in an isolated area, where it was difficult to get water. The local volunteer fire department was off fighting another blaze. Michael Harper, an African-American poet and friend of Ellison, was told what happened next by his wife Fanny: ''The fire department had arrived by this time. The manuscript, more than 350 pages, was inside on a table. Fanny could see it. She told me it was the great regret of her life that she didn't just go through the window and grab it. But Ralph had a dog, and they were intent on saving the dog.''

Author Saul Bellow, who had read considerable portions of the manuscript, described it as equal in scope to *Invisible Man*. Now the heart of his painstaking revisions was gone. Ellison tried to reconstruct what he could from earlier drafts he had left in New York. He would call Murray and read him passages, seeking to jog his friend's memory in order to rekindle his own. It proved too painful.

"Ralph was just devastated," Murray has said. "He couldn't forgive himself for not packing the trunk of his car that night. He just closed in on himself for a long time. He didn't see anyone or go anywhere. At a certain point, you knew not to say much about it. A wall, Ralph's reserve, went up all around him."

Two and a half years after the flames of Plainfield, an Ellison essay titled "What America Would Be Like without Blacks" appeared in *Time* magazine. It concluded on this note:

"There is no point in complaining over the past or apologizing for one's fate. But for blacks there are no hiding places down here, not in suburbia nor in penthouse, neither in country nor in city. They are an American people who are geared to what *is*, and who yet are driven by a sense of what it is possible for human life to be in this society. The nation could not survive being deprived of their presence because, by the irony implicit in the dynamics of American democracy, they symbolize both its most stringent testing and the possibility of its greatest human freedom."

> I reach from pain
> to music great enough
> to bring me back. . . .

Those lines are from Michael Harper's first book of poems, *Dear John, Dear Coltrane*, which was reviewed in the same issue of *Time* as Ellison's essay. In the years since, Harper has risen to be regarded as one of America's finest contemporary poets. His traditions run deep: his great-grandfather, an A.M.E. bishop, had been one of the presiding church elders at the funeral of Frederick Douglass. Harper's underlying philosophy, like Ellison's and Murray's, seeks to bridge the schism between black and white America. As Harper has written, "being a Black poet and an American poet are two aspects of the same story, two ways of telling the same story. I'm both/and, not either/or."

We met at Brown University, where Harper teaches literature and reigns as the Poet Laureate of Rhode Island. A burly, no-nonsense man in his late fifties, he wore a black beret and a Miles Davis T-shirt under his black sweatshirt. In 1979, he had arranged an Ellison festival at the school and had remained a close friend of the novelist until his death fifteen years later. Harper expressed distress that a rediscovered set of Ellison's early short stories was now being published. "He wouldn't have done this if he was alive, because he didn't think they were up to his standards."

What does it matter that Ellison only wrote one major work, Harper continued, when that book was *Invisible Man*? "It's very difficult to live in this country and maintain the kind of standards that Ralph Ellison had. That respect for what I will call the magical dimension is something which he never gave up, where suddenly you are transported into some other domain. And we are now seeing many of the parameters that he scoped out intuitively.

"What I love most about Ellison is his democratic persona. You see, you have to have a lot of experience, and you have to be magnanimous, in order to grant your enemies the kind of complexity you would give to your friends or to yourself. More people have read *Invisible Man* and struggled over that condition than we can possibly know. And his essays were not only formidable, they were informed in a way that raised the standard of discourse."

Talking with Harper, the complexities of the man who played one of literature's great fugues came into stronger focus. Harper described a meeting between Ellison and the son of German novelist Thomas Mann, which took place in the early 1940s. Mann's son was trying to develop a correlation between the Nazi Holocaust and American slavery. "Ralph tried to disabuse him of this easy analogy and basically said, even Germany will rebuild out of this and it will become part of the consciousness of modern man and I don't think it's the end of civilization. So the attention to order and the feeling of these huge glitches were very much what Ellison was always about. He wasn't going to diminish the effects of slavery, but he wasn't going to over-inflate them either.

"His wanting to serve as a citizen always kept Ralph in the public domain," Harper continued. "His papers are in the Library of Congress for that reason. They could have been at Brown or Yale or Harvard, but he made sure they were where people could have access to them."

At the same time, Harper described Ellison as a man of "incredible anger. Now it was not anger that would be easily expressed, but he's not somebody you wanted to cross. I'll give you a metaphor, it's a good one."

One night, Harper recalled, he had dinner at Ellison's home in New York. Ellison was doing some house-cleaning, throwing out all kinds of magazines, and was pleased at Harper's offer to take the issues of

Partisan Review back to his students. It was one o'clock in the morning when Ellison and Harper carted the magazines into the elevator, heading for the poet's car a few blocks away.

"He lived at 150th and Riverside Drive. This was a transition neighborhood. So I was saying to him, 'What if we run into some crazy stuff out here this late?' Ralph smiled. He reached into his pocket and pulled out what we used to call a shank. He just held it up and said, 'Don't worry about me.' He didn't make any bombast about it, but was letting me know that here's a guy who knew something about weapons. And I thought to myself, if I had to have somebody at my back, I couldn't choose a better person."

The ever-present possibility of chaos was, in the view of Stanley Crouch, crucial to Ellison's sensibility. Yet it was a chaos that in itself contained almost magical possibilities, dating back to Ellison's boyhood years in Oklahoma City. Crouch remembers: "He gave a lecture once about when they were getting ready to build a library in the Negro section, and for a while they put all the books in the pool hall. So Ralph could pull out Freud's *Interpretation of Dreams* in one hand and *David Copperfield* in another. You could see this carried over into *Invisible Man*, where something chaotic periodically breaks out. I think this was Ralph's central vision of life in this country—that strange balance between clarity and chaos, or reason and irrationality, order and disorder. Because the American story is some kind of combination of a tale of precision engineering and disorganization."

Crouch, a big, bald man with a deep bass voice, was sitting behind a desk in his Greenwich Village apartment, which overflowed with books and records much as Albert Murray's does. When he first met Ellison at Murray's place, they had spent a long time discussing film. Ellison was curious about how Orson Welles had used the deep-focus technique, and how the nature of a camera shot paralleled the creation of mood and the intensification of narrative in fiction. "Ellison was fascinated by the way time functions in aesthetic structures," Crouch said, "and also in the velocity of change that takes place in the United States: the traditions that are built up and decay or are dismissed so very, very quickly."

They communicated regularly over the years. Ellison would call with comments about one of Crouch's essays. Their discussions ranged from jazz to Oklahoma, contemporary politics to Melville. Ellison was a prodigious student of American history and its ambiguities. While most writers focused on a particular class of people, Ellison analyzed all the different ways that white and black Americans speak—"this incredible orchestration of American sound," as Crouch put it.

"Ellison studied the tensions and remakings of an individual on the basis of geography, in a country where you could invent your identity as you went along. And the various ways corruption functions, both for better and for worse." For example, Crouch cites the railroad barons having inadvertently created a group of traveling workers "who became some of the most sophisticated black Americans in the United States—the porters and waiters on trains!"

Thus was the Invisible Man endowed with an extraordinarily complex consciousness. Thus did he encounter the nation's dualities, emerging with what Crouch calls a "cynicism of engagement." Ellison recognized what Crouch describes as "the ignoble traditions—slavery, slaughter of the Indians, despoiling of the land, sexism, the exploitation of child labor and labor period, governmental hanky-panky, various versions of organized crime, underhanded deals between the industrial and military and political sectors. Then on the other hand you have the abolitionists, Red Cross, the women's suffrage movement, conservation, Pure Food and Drug Act, child labor laws, the union movement, city sanitation, boards of health, public education. What made Ellison's material so important was his capability to maintain optimism without sinking down into third-rate cub-scout morality.

"The necessity for empathetic and unsentimental morality that does not have to turn its back on the horrors of American life and the world, that's what he was after. What is so remarkable is, Ellison understands all the ramifications of the racial limitations that were imposed by discrimination. But he also saw this grand American epic that one would ignore at the cost of truly understanding how the country works, and has worked."

On March 1, 1994, sixteen people gathered at a French restaurant on New York's East Side to celebrate Ralph Ellison's eightieth birthday. Albert Murray raised the first toast. He recalled his youthful admiration for Ellison, as not only the most intelligent but best-dressed man at Tuskegee, the one who always checked the best books out of the library. "I even remember the poetry Ralph wrote," Murray said, and quoted: "Death is nothing,/Life is nothing,/How beautiful these two nothings!"

At the table, Murray's heavy-set, muscular friend with the neatly trimmed mustache savored his wine and said quietly: "Thanks for remembering so much." All evening long, Ellison talked about his friends in the jazz world, and the night he played his trumpet in Wynton Marsalis's presence—and wished he hadn't. Toward the end, as recounted by *New Yorker* writer David Remnick, Ellison turned to Murray and said the following:

"Isn't it interesting and worth a bit of thought that from Booker T. Washington's school, which was supposed to instruct youngsters in a vocation, two reasonably literate writers emerged? Isn't that just part of the unexpectedness of the American experience? It behooves us to keep a close eye on this process of Americanness. My grandparents were slaves. See how short a time it's been? I grew up reading Twain and then, after all those Aunt Jemima roles, those Stepin Fetchit roles, roles with their own subtleties, here comes this voice from Mississippi, William Faulkner. It just goes to show that you can't be Southern without being black, and you can't be a black Southerner without being white. Think of L.B.J. Think of Hugo Black. There are a lot of subtleties based on race that we *will* ourselves to perceive, but at our peril. The truth is that the quality of Americanness, that thing the kids invariably give voice to, will always come out."

Everyone raised their glasses.

A month and a half later Ralph Ellison was dead, from a pancreatic cancer that came on suddenly. Late that May, Wynton Marsalis interrupted rehearsals with his band in New Orleans, in order to return to New York and play at his memorial service. It took place at the Beaux-Arts Auditorium of the American Academy of Arts and Letters, an elite institution to which Ellison had long ago been elected.

Marsalis came on stage in an immaculately tailored, double-breasted suit. He opened with a trumpet solo of Ellison's favorite song, Hoagy Carmichael's *Stardust*. Then Marsalis told the gathering that Ellison had loved the music of Duke Ellington. In fact, he had once an opportunity to audition for a trumpet chair in the Ellington band—"but Ralph missed the gig."

Backed up by a piano and drums, Marsalis then performed Ellington's 1927 classic *Black and Tan Fantasy*. The trumpet section ended with an inclusion from Chopin's *Funeral March*. As Marsalis's note of farewell soared across the auditorium, the audience rose to a standing ovation.

"Wynton was simply magnificent," says Michael Harper. "I have never heard him play that well."

"And when the 'Black and Tan Fantasy' was played we were reminded not only of how fleeting all human life must be, but in its blues-based tension between content and manner, it warned us not only to look at the darker side of life, but also to remember the enduring necessity for humor, technical mastery and creative excellence."
—RALPH ELLISON, "Homage to Duke Ellington on His Birthday," 1969.

FOR FURTHER READING:

The Carleton Miscellany (A Ralph Ellison Festival), vol. 18, no. 3 (Winter 1980).

Ralph Ellison, *The Collected Essays of Ralph Ellison* (1995).

————, *Invisible Man* (2nd ed., New York: Vintage International, 1995).

Jerry Gafio Watts, *Heroism & The Black Intellectual: Ralph Ellison, Politics, and Afro-American Intellectual Life* (Chapel Hill: University of North Carolina Press, 1994).

4

From Duke Ellington to Wynton Marsalis

"In 1965, I was invited . . . to present a concert of sacred music in Grace Cathedral, San Francisco. . . . I recognized this as an exceptional opportunity. 'Now I can say openly,' I said, 'what I have been saying to myself on my knees.' . . . If a man is troubled, he moans and cries when he worships. When a man feels that that which he enjoys in his life is only because of the grace of God, he rejoices, he sings, and sometimes dances."
—DUKE ELLINGTON, *Music Is My Mistress*, 1973.

"I wanted to express the full range of humanity that arises in a church service, from deep introspection to rapture to extroverted celebration. . . . The momentum of the piece is based on Albert Murray's description of swing as 'the velocity of celebration.' That means that the sound of praise is in the rhythm, too."
—WYNTON MARSALIS, Liner Notes for *In This House, on This Morning*, 1994.

Ralph Ellison was a high school student in Oklahoma City when he began listening to the music of Duke Ellington. Discovering Ellington was his first "hint that jazz possessed possibilities of a range of expressiveness comparable to that of classical European music." He never forgot the day in 1934 when Ellington brought his orchestra to Slaughter's Hall, with "their golden horns, their flights of controlled and disciplined fantasy." Ellison's mother, a devout churchgoer, surprised him when she once expressed the hope that someday her son would have a band like Ellington's. "I suspect that she recognized a certain religious element in Ellington's music," he later wrote. "Either that, or she accepted the sound of dedication wherever she heard it, and thus was willing to see Duke as an example of the mysterious way in which God showed His face in music."

A few years later, Ellison paid a visit to Tuskegee Institute, where Ellison talked briefly with him about his studies and dreams. And when Ellison went on to New York, "a stranger in Harlem, I lived at the YMCA and spent many a homesick afternoon playing Duke's record on the jukebox in Small's Paradise Bar, asking myself why I was in New York and finding reassurance in the music." Shortly thereafter, Langston Hughes took Ellison up to visit the Duke in his apartment on Sugar Hill. To the young man's delight, Ellington remembered him. This was still twelve long years before the publication of *Invisible Man*, but marked the beginning of what would become a lifelong friendship.

Edward Kennedy Ellington was born on April 29, 1899, in Washington, D.C. His father had been a policeman and occasionally served as a butler at White House events. His mother, whom Ellington adored, often told him: "Edward, you are blessed." In the segregated schools he attended, his first principal taught him about proper speech and good manners "to command respect for our people." His friends started calling him Duke because his dress code was always so impeccable. He was, Albert Murray would write, "born and raised among people to whom quality mattered and who required your personal best no less as a general principle than as a natural reaction to the folklore of white supremacy. In neither case would they accept excuses for failure. You either had what it took or you didn't."

As with Ellison and Murray, there was another education to be found on the streets. Sneaking into Frank Holliday's pool hall, Ellington mingled with people from all walks of life. The railroad porters regaled him with tales of their journeys. Was it surprising then that train pistons, bells and whistles appeared in some of his future compositions like *Daybreak Express*—resonating, too, Murray has pointed out, "of the metaphorical underground railroad and the metaphysical gospel train."

Both his parents played the piano and Duke was drawn to ragtime. When he was fourteen, he penned his first composition, *Soda Fountain Rag*, while working part-time in a café. Ellington was a talented artist who received a scholarship to Pratt Institute after winning an NAACP poster contest. He decided to stick with music after a local bandleader taught him how to read notes. Dropping out of Armstrong High School three months shy of graduation, he soon formed his first band, Duke's Serenaders.

"Music is everything," he would write in his memoirs. "The oldest entity. . . . Without music I may feel blind, atrophied, incomplete, *inexistent*."

Ellington was twenty-one when James P. Johnson, known as "the father of stride piano," came to town from New York. Every day for weeks, Ellington had listened to a popular Johnson ragtime piece and worked to master it. After Johnson performed *Carolina Shout*, Ellington's friends shoved him up onto the bandstand at the Washington

Convention Center. Johnson let him play and applauded the young Ellington. Later that night the pair went out on the town and became "fast friends."

Yes, Daisy Ellington was right: her son seemed blessed. Leaving home, he took his band to New York in 1923, arriving at the nascency of the Harlem Renaissance. Tough-talking, cigar-chewing Willie (The Lion) Smith—one of Harlem's top pianists—took a liking to him. They spent long nights together in the speakeasies and cabarets. Ellington's jazz reputation, formed around a group now called The Washingtonians, began to blossom. Bandleaders like Paul Whiteman came around to hear them. By 1927, when a vacancy opened up at Harlem's Cotton Club, the Ellington band was on its way to stardom.

The first major hit of Ellington's more than 2,000 compositions was *East St. Louis Toodle-oo*. It was inspired, he said, out of this tradition: "Those old Negroes who work in the fields for year upon year, and are tired at the end of their day's labour, may be seen walking home at night with a broken, limping step locally known as the 'Toddle-O,' with the accent on the last syllable. I was able to get a new rhythm from this, and what better title could I find than the original? . . . The memory of things is important to a jazz musician. Things like old folks singing in the moonlight in the back yard on a hot night or something someone said long ago."

Ellington eventually owned some 800 books on black history, in which he underlined passages about two men who had orchestrated slave revolts, Denmark Vesey and Nat Turner. Ellington himself loved to "break the rules and even make new rules." His rebellion took form in early innovations such as *Creole Love Call*, where Adelaide Hall's growling, wordless solo made the human voice sound like an instrument. He used risky harmonies and long phrase lengths that broke the mold. "The common root, of course, comes out of Africa," he would say. "That's the pulse. The African pulse. It's all the way back from what they first recognized as the old slave chants. . . ."

Ellington once called his band a gathering of "tonal personalities." When he composed a certain note, he always knew ahead of time whose it was going to be. "You've got to write with certain men in mind. You write just for their abilities and natural tendencies and give them places where they do their best." So he planned spaces where a soloist could improvise, and wrote solos that *sounded* improvised.

Many of the arrangements with Ellington's sidemen were worked out collectively. The Duke would bring his ideas to a meeting, others would make their suggestions, Ellington would encourage them to devise counterlines, improvisations would be tried in the moment. After several performances, these might metamorphose into an entirely new piece. Perhaps the most evocative illustration of these sessions—of Marsalis's comment that "jazz is a music of conversation"—came when Ellington was composing his all-black musical, *Jump for Joy*.

The Duke sat in his bathtub alongside a container of chocolate ice cream and a glass of scotch-and-milk, scribbling notations and calling them out to his partner Billy Strayhorn, who in turn would hit the notes on a rented piano in Ellington's hotel room. Ellington would listen and write some more. Before long the other band members staying on the same floor were joining in with their lines.

On stage, Ellington choreographed everything from his piano. Albert Murray writes: "He not only set tempos, moods, and voicing as if the various sections of the orchestra were physical extensions of the keyboard, but he also inserted riffs and dictated phrasings, shadings, and even revisions. He actually played the orchestra from the piano."

And what a band it was! His players comprised a potpourri of origins; they came not only from Washington, New York, and Boston, but New Orleans, Alabama, California, even the West Indies, and each brought something special. During the Cotton Club years between 1927 and 1932, when Ellington's fifteen-man team made 200 recordings and became nationally prominent over CBS Radio, it came to include lilting baritone saxist Harry Carney, Cootie Williams with his plunger-muted trumpet, Lawrence Brown on his sensuous trombone, and an alto sax wizard named Johnny Hodges. Those four would still be with Ellington in 1967.

"An unbelievable esprit de corps held the Ellington band together for these many years," said cornetist Rex Stewart. "In a way, this was phenomenal, especially when one considers that we came from such divergent backgrounds with disparate degrees of musical training, heritage, and cultural environment. But we all learned to cleave together, think alike and play together as Duke's band."

"I am a minstrel, a pedestrian minstrel, a primitive pedestrian minstrel. Sometimes I imagine I paint, with water colors or oils, a crystal-clear lake in the sky reflecting the shadows of invisible trees upside-down beneath sun-kissed, cotton-candy snow. On the fringe, clouds so foamy white—tranquil on top, a raging storm inside . . . 'I'll write it,' I think, before returning to that half sleep as the plane roars on to Atlanta . . . or is it Atlantis?"

—DUKE ELLINGTON

He wrote *Mood Indigo* in fifteen minutes the night before a recording session in 1930, while waiting for his mother to finish cooking dinner. It was recorded the next day; before the year was out, there were five more recordings for various labels. *Mood Indigo* offered a rare combination of subtle voicings among the horns—the muted trumpet on top playing the melody, a muted trombone beneath that, and on the bottom a clarinet playing in the lower register. Of clarinetist Barney Bigard, Ellington said: "He had that woody tone which I love on the instrument and he was invaluable for putting the filigree work into an arrangement. Sometimes it could remind you of all that delicate wrought iron you see in his hometown, New Orleans."

The next year, Ellington arranged a new song called *It Don't Mean a Thing If It Ain't Got That Swing*. His and a few other orchestras, he said in 1933, "have exploited a [jazz] style characterized by 'swing,' which is Harlem for rhythm." He had preordained and named an entire era, the Big Band swing of Fletcher Henderson, Jimmie Lunceford, Benny Goodman, and the Dorsey brothers. By the end of the decade would come one of the legendary battles of bands that became popular in the '30s; a record crowd of 3,100 turned out in 1937 to watch Ellington compete against Chick Webb and then Lunceford at the Savoy Ballroom.

Ellington taps "the inner world of feeling and experience," wrote music critic R. D. Darnell in the early '30s. "Over the straining, strongly pulling bass and the fundamental beat, the true melody, or more often two or more melodies dip, curvet, swoop, and spiral in the untrammelled, ecstatic freedom of soaring gulls."

How the maestro must have captivated his audience! Entering the stage proffering that sly smile, standing a handsome six-foot-one with his glistening dark hair slicked back, sitting down before the keyboard in a double-breasted blue suit—Ellington is said to have owned over 150 suits and a thousand ties—introducing his beautiful vocalist Ivie Anderson and an orchestra that flew, as he put it, "beyond category."

After a performance, the Ellingtonians would often rehearse until sunrise. The Duke was forever jotting down ideas—on hotel stationery, the backs of envelopes. Then, arriving home at dawn, he might write an entire score before finally retiring to sleep. "You know how it is. You go home expecting to go right to bed. But then on the way, you pass the piano and there's a flirtation. It flirts with you. So, you sit down and try a couple of chords and when you look up, it's seven A.M."

Utterly devoted to his music, Ellington was an intensely private man. Although married for nearly five decades, he and his wife Edna lived together for only a few of those years. In the midst of the Great Depression, his mother's death in 1935 devastated him: "The bottom dropped out. . . . My sparkling parade was probably at an end." Albert Murray says: "Duke would never put on a brown suit again, because that's what he was wearing when his mother died." Yet out of his grief, in memoriam Ellington wrote his longest and most complex work of the period. It was a 13-minute composition called *Reminiscing in Tempo*, a manuscript he said was stained with his tears.

Nor was Ellington immune to the social currents of the time. He performed a benefit concert in Washington for the Scottsboro boys, nine young black men falsely accused of rape and sentenced to death by an all-white jury. He made a statement traveling through the Deep South by train, in two Pullman cars and a seventy-foot baggage car. "We commanded respect," he recalled. "We parked those cars in each railroad station and we lived in them." On some of those journeys, as Richard O. Boyer recounted in a *New Yorker* profile of the 1940s, the plague of racism followed.

The band arrived in St. Louis to play at the Fox Theatre. As the train pulled into Union Station, Ellington's two white employees—Tizol and Boyd—immediately got a taxi and went to one of the town's good hotels. Duke and the band members got taxis only after an hour and considerable begging, since most of the drivers didn't want Negroes as passengers, and then they were taken to a rickety hotel in the Negro section. The next day, when the colored members of the band went out for lunch after the first performance, they couldn't find a restaurant in the neighborhood that would serve them. They didn't have time to get over to the segregated district before they were due onstage again. They returned to the theatre and arranged for a white man to go out to buy sandwiches at a drugstore. When the proprietor of the store, making inquiry, found that the sandwiches were for a Negro band, he refused to fill the order. A few minutes later the men went back to work, hungry, the curtain rose, and from the white audience out front there came a burst of applause. The crowd cheered, whistled, and stamped its feet. As the curtain was going up, the dejection on the faces of the players vanished, and, as swiftly as an electric light is switched on, it was replaced by a look of joy. The music blared, Duke smiled, threw back his head, and shouted "Ah-h-h!," Rex Stewart took off on a solo that was greeted with fervor, and as he bowed, the musician next to him muttered out of the side of his mouth, "Bend, you hungry fathead! Bend!" Everything was flash and brightness until the curtain came down. Then the joy was switched off and there was just a group of angry, hungry Negroes arguing their right to food.

"Can't we eat in our own country?" Rex Stewart said. . . .

An hour after the show, Duke was introduced to a policeman who said enthusiastically, "If you'd been a white man, Duke, you'd been a great musician." Duke's smile was wide and steady as he answered quietly, "*I guess things would have been different if I'd been a white man.*"

One evening, in the midst of the Second World War, Ellington was listening to one of his new recordings that merged Cuban rhythms with those of his ensemble. Suddenly he shouted: "That's the Negro's life! Hear that chord?" He set the needle back and replayed it. "That's us!" Then he added, "Dissonance is our way of life in America. We are something apart, yet an integral part."

Jump for Joy, his 1941 all-black musical, was the first to portray African-Americans beyond the stereotypical dialects and shuffling gaits of the popular theater and movie entertainment. It became such a source of pride that a black weekly in Los Angeles wrote: "In *Jump for Joy*, Uncle Tom is dead. God rest his bones." It was one of Ellington's strongest regrets that the musical didn't gain enough acceptance for a nationwide tour. Nor was his 1943 *Black, Brown, and Beige* successful when it debuted at Carnegie Hall. It was a forty-minute musical epic, the longest Ellington ever wrote, following an African into slavery and across the landscape of America's Revolutionary and Civil Wars into twentieth-century Harlem.

"It's not about this or that generation," the Duke once told his nephew. "The issue in art is *regeneration*."

"Ellington's music contains so many characteristics of the nation," writes Stanley Crouch. "The intricate dialogues between individuals and communities, the awesome and heartbreaking difficulties to 'make it' or just plain survive, the urban skylines and rural landscapes. We hear the stone, glass, and steel of industrial achievement summoned up by brass, reeds, and percussion. No other music has so piercingly captured the bittersweet energy of modern life."

Ellington's work always seemed to herald the future. *Cotton Tail*, for example, laid the foundation for be-bop. His personnel went through many changes in the 1940s, but continued to break new ground and were lauded at annual Carnegie Hall concerts. "My biggest kick in music—playing or writing—is when I have a problem," he said. "Without a problem to solve, how much interest do you take in anything?"

After several band members left to form their own combo in 1951, some observers predicted that Ellington was finally over the hill. What happened at the first Newport Jazz Festival in 1956 put a stop to all such talk. Johnny Hodges had just returned after a five-year absence. It was a hot evening in July, the beginnings of the rock-and-roll era. As the fifty-seven-year-old Duke suddenly began hollering and clapping his hands and dancing around the stage, the fever became infectious.

Time magazine reported: "One young woman broke loose from her escort, and rioted solo around the field, while a young man encouraged her by shouting, 'Go, go, go.' " Couples began jitterbugging in the aisles. Dozens more surged toward the stage. Fearing a real riot, promoter George Wein could be heard shouting: "Duke, that's enough. That's enough, Duke. That's enough!"

He wouldn't quit. Tenor saxman Paul Gonsalves went wild on another twenty-seven choruses. Ellington had to lead four more numbers, including the *Jeep's Blues* he had written for Hodges years before, before the crowd would finally let him go at one o'clock in the morning. Nothing like this had been seen since the pandemonium that greeted Benny Goodman at the Paramount in 1938. *Time* did a cover story. A new contract was signed with Columbia, entering the world of the LP record, and *Ellington at Newport* hit the top of the charts. "I was born in 1956 at the Newport festival," Ellington said in later years.

"The man is a revelation," his longtime writing partner Billy Strayhorn commented. "He's continually renewing himself through his music." There followed a *Shakespearian Suite*, Ellington's personal interpretation of the Bard, and a visit with Queen Elizabeth; Duke went home to make a single copy of a new piece he'd played for her at Buckingham Palace, which she alone received. There followed adaptations of Tchaikovsky and Grieg, and movie scores, and Sacred Music concerts that fused jazz and church music for the first time. There followed joint recording sessions with Louis Armstrong and Count Basie, as well as new luminaries like John Coltrane—as if Ellington's mission was to encapsulate both past and present.

"I don't want to be modern . . . futuristic . . . and neither do I want to be hung by the plaintiveness of something we might have done years ago, even with success. I don't want to feel obliged to play something with the same styling that we became identified with at some specific period. I have no ambition to reach some intellectual plateau and look down on people. And, by the same token, I don't want anyone to challenge my right to sound completely mad, to screech like a wild man, to create the mauve melody of a simpering idiot, or to write a song that praises God."

—DUKE ELLINGTON, 1959

The civil rights movement dawned. After a concert at Johns Hopkins University early in 1960, Ellington heard that black students had twice been refused service at a Baltimore café. He went himself to the Blue Jay Restaurant, was also refused service, and the event made headlines.

He canceled a scheduled appearance in Little Rock, Arkansas, in 1961, after the NAACP informed Ellington that the seating would be segregated. Immediately after that, he played the music halls of Dallas and Houston—after ensuring that, for the first time in history, the seating arrangements make no distinctions based upon skin color.

In 1963, the year of Martin Luther King's March on Washington, Ellington wrote a musical theater production called *My People.* Its finale was *King Fit the Battle of Alabam',* based upon King's confrontation with the police authorities of Birmingham, and another piece titled *What Color Is Virtue?—What Color Is Love?* During the rehearsals in Chicago, King showed up backstage. He and Ellington met for the first time, and embraced as if they had known each other all their lives.

Will the circle be unbroken, bye and bye Lord, bye and bye. . . . Dr. Arthur C. Logan was a physician who had befriended Ellington at the Cotton Club in 1937, helped heal the ache left by his parents' passing, and always responded to the Duke's call no matter where in the world he was touring. He was also the personal doctor for Martin Luther King.

In 1969, Edward Kennedy Ellington was honored at the White House where his father had once been a butler. He sat at the piano next to one of his early mentors, the now seventy-one-year-old Willie (the Lion) Smith, and they played a duet. And he was presented with America's highest civilian honor, the Medal of Freedom, by President Nixon.

One by one, the members of the Ellington team began to die—first Johnny Hodges, then Ben Webster and Arthur Logan. By the spring of 1974, Paul Gonsalves and Tyree Glenn were gone. Ellington had fallen terminally ill with cancer. Selections from the three Sacred Concerts which he considered his greatest achievement were being performed in New York. He kept an electric piano at his bedside so he could keep working on one last song. It was mid-May when the Duke sent out his last Christmas card in gold letters. It bore only this message:

L

G O D

V

E

A fifty-year musical career ended on May 24, 1974. For a time, Ellington and his two band members Gonsalves and Glenn were laid out alongside each other in the same mortuary. More than 10,000 people came to the Duke's funeral, and 2,500 more had to be contained outside. Ella Fitzgerald sang *Just a Closer Walk with Thee.*

"Roaming through the jungle, the jungle of 'oohs' and 'ahs,' searching for a more agreeable noise, I live a life of primitivity with the mind of a child and an unquenchable thirst for sharps and flats. The more consonant, the more appetizing and delectable they are. Cacophony is hard to swallow. Living in a cave, I am almost a hermit, but there is a difference, for I have a mistress. Lovers have come and gone, but only my mistress stays. She is beautiful and gentle. She waits on me hand and foot. She is a swinger. She has grace. To hear her speak, you can't believe your ears. She is ten thousand years old. She is modern as tomorrow, a brand-new woman every day, and as endless as time mathematics. Living with her is a labyrinth of ramifications. I look forward to her every gesture.

"Music is my mistress, and she plays second fiddle to no one."
—DUKE ELLINGTON

"I have no idea where we will all be a hundred years from now, but if there is a classical music in which the American experience has finally discovered the voice of its own complexity, it will owe much of its direction to the achievements of Edward Kennedy Ellington. For many years he has been telling us how marvelous, mad, violent, hopeful, nostalgic and (perhaps) decent we are. He is one of the musical fathers of our country, and throughout all these years he has, as he tells us so mockingly, loved us madly. We are privileged to have lived during his time and to have known so great a man, so great a musician.
—RALPH ELLISON

After Ellington's death, his son Mercer—who had served periodically for the band as an arranger/composer—took over the orchestra for a time. The more than twenty years since have seen the production of an unfinished opera, a Tony Award-winning musical based on his work (*Sophisticated Ladies*) and the release of many recordings from some 500 hours of music that Ellington taped privately during the last decade of his life.

"Duke Ellington is now starting to be reconsidered in terms of the sheer weight of what he brought off," Stanley Crouch was saying over breakfast in a Greenwich Village café. "See, if you listen to his music from the late '20s until he died, you see this extraordinary development that I don't think is paralleled by anybody else in the history of jazz. You can't believe the same guy could do *Creole Love Call* all the way to a fantasy recording called *The Ellington Suites.* Though people like

Miles Davis and Coltrane are the ones usually pointed out as always changing, Ellington goes far beyond that."

All because, Crouch added, Ellington considered himself "the world's greatest listener."

After Crouch started loaning Wynton Marsalis records from his Ellington collection, he wanted the young trumpeter to talk to Albert Murray about the Duke. Murray had first met Ellington backstage at Carnegie Hall in 1946. In subsequent years, he attended many of his recording sessions. "Albert Murray," Ellington once said, "is a man whose learning did not interfere with understanding." As I looked through Murray's photo albums with him, he recalled teaching literature at Colgate University in 1970 when Ellington would call him from the road. "He remembered everything," Murray said. "He'd say, 'Hell, you're through with your lectures at five o'clock on Thursdays, you're not gonna have anything to do until Tuesday. Why don't you let me set up a flight out here?'—to New Orleans or Hollywood or wherever."

Later, after Murray took Marsalis under his wing, Wynton adopted the same habit of calling from the road. "Like when he was working on that series about jazz for National Public Radio, he'd have an assistant call and ask me, 'What's an Ellington number that would do such-and-so? What would you suggest?' "

In 1991, Murray seized an opportunity presented by the inauguration of Jazz at Lincoln Center—to incorporate first Ellington, then Marsalis. When Murray was named a member of the Board of Directors, he says, "We invented the repertory orchestra to play Ellington. Dave Berger, an Ellington scholar, was directing it. Wynton loved just being in the trumpet section and listening. I like to think that I tricked Wynton into becoming the conductor. He was already thinking in those terms, adding voices to his own combo. I knew how precise he was about things, wanting to take his time. Finally he took over the conducting, and he's in better control of the band than anybody has been."

It was all part of a process. After Murray's collaboration on Count Basie's autobiography had appeared in 1986, a big party reuniting Basie's original band with his comeback group was held at New York's Village Gate. Murray invited Marsalis, who was "delighted to get a chance to sit in with all these guys full of all that experience, the real jazz voicings."

Marsalis was already quite well known by that point. He had led a band for six years and become the only trumpeter ever to win Grammy awards for both jazz and classical recordings. He also displayed distinct Ellingtonian overtones, right down to his style of dress. This was a far cry from when he signed with Columbia Records in 1982. "When I met Wynton," Columbia executive George Butler remembers, "he would go onstage in tennis shoes. Nothing matched." Now, as Marsalis told one interviewer: "When you see me on the bandstand, I'm always going to look sharp. How can you get respect from an audience when you come on looking like a bum?"

Marsalis had also grown less enthusiastic about the modern jazz that he'd enjoyed as a teenager. The influx of electronic fusion, he felt, had all but killed the music. He considered that Miles Davis, whose early work he admired greatly, had "sold out and started imitating rock musicians." So, in the midst of a Davis concert in 1986, urged on by Stanley Crouch, Marsalis suddenly appeared on the bandstand with trumpet in hand, like the biblical Gabriel ready for battle.

While Murray did not approve of such grandstanding, he saw in Marsalis the man to carry forward jazz as a fine art. "All any real orchestra does," Murray explains, "is keep something alive. Your creativity comes out of the dialogue with the tradition, with the ongoing. If you're looking just for innovation, you're flirting with hysteria."

The Jazz at Lincoln Center program has come a long way since 1991, when the Center's symphonically and operatically inclined leadership was merely looking for summer fare to fill in during the slow August season. The program that Marsalis pushed forward, with assistance from Murray and Crouch, now includes not only the repertory orchestra but music lectures and educational clinics for young people. At Lincoln Center, Murray knew, "You gotta cut them dots or not! There's no rank except efficiency."

In the Ellington vein, Marsalis began writing prodigiously. First for more voices—a quintet, a septet. Eventually moving on to composing for the ballet (Twyla Tharp and Alvin Ailey), and for a full orchestra. His extended works—*Blue Interlude*, *Citi Movement*, *In This House, on This Morning*, and *Blood on the Fields*—all bear the unmistakeable Ellington influence.

"Underneath all of it," says Murray with a gleam in his eye, "is that we don't want Americans ever to forget how to sw——iiii——nnng. We don't ever want them to stop being re-sil-i-ent. We don't ever want them to stop improvising. At the same time, having the precision not to violate the beat."

When I sat down with Marsalis for two wide-ranging discussions over a period of several months in 1996, he was on an amazing roll. Over the first fifteen years of his career, he had released over thirty albums and won eight Grammys. Now, with Marsalis named as artistic director, Jazz at Lincoln Center officially joined the New York Philharmonic, Metropolitan Opera, and eight other organizations as a full-fledged equal entity, the first to be added since the Film Society in 1969. Wynton had performed, a la Ellington, for Queen Elizabeth and been made a member of London's Royal Academy of Music. His four-part Public TV series, *Marsalis on Music*, where he teamed with conductor Seiji Ozawa and cellist Yo Yo Ma, was considered today's successor to Leonard Bernstein's classical *Young People's Concerts*. (Since his first of four children, Wynton, Jr., was born in 1989, Marsalis estimates he has probably visited more than 1,000 public schools.)

His twenty-six-part National Public Radio series, *Making the Music*, was a history of jazz that included interviews and a wide display of styles. His eleventh classical album, *In Gabriel's Garden*, made number one on *Billboard*'s charts. The opening ceremonies of the Olympic Games in Atlanta began with his six-minute composition based on the music of the South. At the Olympic Jazz Summit, Marsalis conducted a seventeen-piece orchestra incorporating Latin jazz and Afro-Cuban music along with dance elements. He had become a truly protean figure.

Framed in the picture window of his L-shaped apartment, Marsalis was wearing a light-green, pin-striped shirt with a paisley tie and suspenders, olive-colored suit pants, and velvet-brown shoes. He sat facing the framed print of Ellington that rested above his traveling trumpet case in the hallway. In 1994, Marsalis's composition *In This House, on This Morning* was the first major jazz work to pick up where Ellington's *Sacred Concerts* of the 1960s left off. It was a representation of a black Baptist church ceremony, from the first call to prayer to local announcements, the sermon, and the pot-luck dinner.

When Stanley Crouch had first brought over to him the Smithsonian's Ellington collection—which Albert Murray, among others, had assisted in assembling—Marsalis remembered being intimidated. "I told Crouch, 'This stuff Duke writes is so *complex* I could *never* figure it out,' and Crouch said, 'Hey, man, you never know what you can do in ten years.'"

Marsalis had said to one interviewer that Jelly Roll Morton, jazz's "first intellectual," gave him a way to understand its greatest intellectual. "Ellington codified the music," Marsalis was quoted. "He put it down, like Bach did for European music. All the characteristics that we've gone through are in Ellington."

What did Marsalis mean when he said that Ellington embodied the mythology of America? Wynton nodded his head and replied: "First of all his tunes, and the range of his music. He could relate to anybody, man. Stuff with the church, stuff with that late-night whorehouse feeling, clubs, hotel scores, ballets, commercials. Goes from hamburger to caviar!"

He laughed and then, as Murray had, Marsalis amplified the definition of jazz. "All the devices are conversational. The vamp, which is something you repeat, come to. Polyphonic improvisation, that's when you're just stepping all on top of each other but still trying to communicate. Riff, same thing repeated over and over again. It's different from a vamp, in that a vamp is a point of rest. It can be introduction, it can be at the end. Whereas a riff is something that needs to be stated and restated, like a ground. Soloist is—you talk, I talk—we develop it."

I recalled what Murray had added about the break, or the temporary interruption of established cadence, in his book *The Blue Devils of Nada*: "Nor is the break just another mechanical structural device. It is of its very nature, as dancers never forget, what the basic message comes down to: *grace under pressure, creativity in an emergency, continuity in the face of disjuncture. . . .* The break is the musical equivalent to the storybook hero's moment of truth."

So how had Marsalis integrated into his music the "storybooks" to which Murray had introduced him? "Well, you're dealing with the same elements of form, dialogue. The nature of the insight into the human condition. The intensity of relationships in any work of art. In painting, it's the question of balance and form—where the subject is placed, what's in the background and foreground. Plus music is tied to memory. The greatest musicians can resurrect something, like it's still echoing. They can feel it, intuit it. You listen to Bach's music, you can hear Gregorian chant in it, all the church songs from long long ago. Beethoven in his late quartets was trying to bring Bach's sound back."

Thinking about the importance of the heroic in the work of his mentors, I wondered who Marsalis felt best exemplified this in American history. Without hesitation, he named Harriet Tubman, the runaway slave who led more than three hundred of her people to freedom along the clandestine Underground Railroad. Why Tubman?

"Because first, she never got caught. She sacrificed her freedom for others to be free. She's a real democratic figure. She's hard, too—but with soul. She had her networks together, very well-organized. She understood how to defeat the system and she did the best she could with what she had. And she kept goin' back. If she'd ever got caught, mannnnn! She was a woman, which was even harder. I think Robeson and Du Bois got tired. Harriet Tubman didn't get tired."

Outside, an afternoon fog over the Hudson River grew denser. Recalling a remark Marsalis once made—that the nature of the blues is to accept tragedy and move forward—I pursued the bridge between the blues and the authors he most admired. "Basically whenever you're dealing with the whole question of recognition, redemption, experience—there's some blues in there somewhere," Marsalis continued. "Somebody's gonna be confronted with something they don't want to deal with and have to. Harriet Tubman. Mark Twain. What his characters go through, the main thing that catches your attention is the unpleasantries. It's when they reach that crisis point, and you go—let's see now, what are they gonna do with *this*? And that's the blues. That's what's interesting. We all deal with it, some a little more than others. We can hide it, but we're not gonna escape it."

I thought of something else Marsalis had said before: "If you read Martin Luther King, most of what he's saying comes out of the Constitution. He didn't say 'I have to reinvent the United States of America'; he just tried to make it more of itself, of its best self."

Now Marsalis rose and walked over to the piano and started to play. It was a touch of Duke Ellington's *Black and Tan Fantasy*.

Over lunch, Stanley Crouch was effusive in his praise of Marsalis's growth and mastery. "I don't think anybody's ever appeared in jazz who can play as many different ways as he plays. With the authority that he plays. And sound like himself. I mean, he performs on his instrument the way Laurence Olivier was at his best, I would say. Olivier could do not only Shakespeare but Greek drama, Eugene O'Neill, be superb in Chekhov, whatever he wanted. And not just with a bag of tricks and mannerisms. Also as a composer, Wynton has something seldom seen in terms of the breadth and depth of what he does."

Since the advent of Marsalis, major record companies have established active jazz divisions, with hundreds of classics being reissued from their vaults. A whole generation of new jazz musicians seems to be studying earlier styles and returning to their roots. As Dan Morgenstern, director of the Institute of Jazz Studies at Rutgers University, explains: "Young men can now make a living playing straight-ahead jazz, and Wynton is responsible for that being possible."

Marsalis's master composition to date, *Blood on the Fields*, is a more than three-hour-long, twenty-one-movement stage piece which features three singers and the seventeen-member Lincoln Center Jazz Orchestra. Its receipt of the Pulitzer Prize for Music in April 1997 marked the first time the award has gone to anything but a classical composition. Indeed, in 1965, the Pulitzer's full committee had specifically rejected Ellington's nomination for a special award. "Fate is being very kind to me; fate doesn't want me to be too famous too young," the sixty-six-year-old Ellington had wryly commented at the time. After Marsalis won the Pulitzer, a visiting journalist observed a copy of Ellington's autobiography, opened on Wynton's living-room table to the page containing that statement.

In some ways, *Blood on the Fields* is an elaboration on the themes of over fifty years ago in Ellington's *Black, Brown, and Beige*. Ellington's historical narrative was, as his biographer John Edward Haase put it, one where an oppressed people "hold onto their faith and find life's joys along with self-esteem."

Marsalis traces the journey of an African prince who himself had owned slaves, and a common woman who falls in love with him in their Southern bondage. He rejects her and runs away; captured again, Jesse slowly learns through Leona's patient love and the wisdom of an elder named Juba to put the past behind him. In so doing, he discovers his own humanity and that real freedom can be found only through taking part in the struggles of others. It is a meditation on learning, religion, responsibility, and ultimately, love; "a piece finally about the power of care," says one reviewer, "to redeem even the most malevolent and persistent crimes."

Marsalis has said of it: "*Blood on the Fields* is about today. When I go to Civil War battlefields, I think about what is in the soil. It's in our nation, it's in us. I try to avoid referring to people by color. The colors in the piece are the social breakdown of America in the 19th century—white above, brown soil, and red down below."

Like Ellison and Murray, Marsalis seeks both to acknowledge and transcend race. Like Ellington, he works with the jazz tradition but is compelled to move it forward creatively. In *Blood on the Fields*, the orchestra itself recites transitional narrative passages; Marsalis has them play syllables of "speech" before the vocalists sing them—something he picked up from Ellington as well as his reading of Greek tragedies where the chorus comments. His singers often duel with the orchestra. "I wanted to hear the voices struggle, so I put things at extremes," Marsalis told one interviewer. "I had to write with these specific singers in mind, so the main thing was to find the meat of their range." Everything he knew, he says, went into *Blood on the Fields*: from stories he'd heard, to Stephen Vincent Benet's *Freedom Is a Hard Bought Thing*, to John Coltrane's recitation of a prayer inside his mellifluous saxophone on *A Love Supreme*.

We were talking about Coltrane now, in the kitchen of a temporary apartment along Central Park West where Marsalis was living while his Lincoln Center penthouse got fixed up. "That prayer," Marsalis was saying, "when he wrote the music out to go on top, what's in that music is so—like the Gregorian chant, man, so pure. I transcribed it for *Blood on the Fields*." He sang a few bars and went on: "Trane went all the way back to the spirituals, trying to get to a certain type of expression. His music had both the sound of field hollers and the psychological complexity that Bird [Charlie Parker] brought to the music."

Marsalis is not a fan of Coltrane's later avant-garde music. What happened to Coltrane in the mid-1960s? I asked. "I don't know," Marsalis said wistfully. "It's a combination—cats get tired, he knew he was dying. The whole of the twentieth century, there's been this big misconception in art, even the greatest artists suffer from it. First trying to be known. Second, trying to constantly come up with something new. Leonard Feather in an interview once asked [Thelonius] Monk, 'What about something new?' Monk said, 'Let somebody else invent something new. What about something *good*?' I mean, the tradition of the new is suicidal, man. I think with Trane, too, it was the times. Lot of people struggling, lot of pain."

Marsalis thought a moment, then continued: "Jazz is not dark music. It's light, you know. Then it started becoming dark because all the criticism was pushing it in that direction. Musicians started following the critics, which is a major mistake, worrying about how they were being reviewed and what the people will think about what they said."

Marsalis has taken his fair share from the jazz critics. Many complain that the Lincoln Center program refuses to include the avant-garde, or even traditional jazz that doesn't fit the particular standards of Marsalis, Crouch and Murray. Some have falsely accused him of excluding the work of such white luminaries as Bix Beiderbecke, Benny Goodman and Dave Brubeck, and charged that there are too few white players in his orchestra.

"That's just a tactic to draw the attention away from the real issues," Marsalis continued. "I mean, the fact of Benny Goodman's being the first integrated band is always elevated above the music. Benny was simply in possession of a great band and he worked them hard. But in the minds of many of those raised in the whole jazz world, a lot of it *is* racial. My position has matured as I've grown older. Now I say, thank the good lord for these white critics who are gonna attack you just because you're black, because what if they didn't comment at all? You think black critics would talk about this? There wouldn't be dialogue. Today you have more fights because people are coming more together. My kids don't see everything in terms of black and white. Not like we saw it.

"I've been very lucky, just to have this opportunity—and to understand it. That's two different things. Without the understanding, the real *joy* of representing something is not clear to you, only the tragedy of it. Because to represent something, that means you have to fight against the stuff that *it* fought against."

Which led us, once again, to the roots of his understanding, the respect Marsalis has for his elders, and his relationship with Albert Murray. "Well, I was raised like that. I was always around older people, my great-uncle and great-aunt. They were just soulful. I didn't realize that until I left home and got around other people and then I said, Okay. So with Mr. Murray, it was a natural progression. I've been to his house hundreds of times. Now I take my kids up to see him. It's like we're family. It's just—a certain feeling."

I remembered Albert Murray talking about the day Marsalis's musician father Ellis came to visit him. "He says to me, 'Well, people are saying Wynton is your grandson. So I guess I must be your son!' "

"The musicians who are the most successful are the ones who cause the most eras to resonate. . . . In democracy, as in jazz, you have freedom with restraint. It's not absolute freedom, it's freedom within a structure. . . . Played properly, jazz shows you how the individual can negotiate the greatest amount of personal freedom and put it humbly at the service of a group conception. . . . There are always going to be dragons to slay."

—WYNTON MARSALIS

Henry Louis Gates, Jr., the prominent Harvard administrator and author, concluded a recent profile for the *New Yorker*: "This is Albert Murray's century; we just live in it." The Pulitzer Prize-winning author James Alan McPherson calls Murray "the last of the giants. . . . Al was there when a lot of us needed instruction, and he gave us what he had."

Duke Ellington's *Echoes of Harlem* seems to hover in the air outside Murray's Lenox Terrace apartment, across from the old A.M.E. church. He has been reading aloud excerpts from his third novel, *The Seven League Boots*. It follows a semi-autobiographical protagonist named Scooter into the latest phase of his life, traveling with a band modeled on Ellington's and absorbing knowledge from his elders. Murray himself once played rhythm instruments and bass fiddle with pickup groups formed by members of the U.S. Veteran's Hospital staff and the faculty at Tuskegee.

Now he picks up his own autobiography, *South to a Very Old Place*, and continues to read, often laughing with delight. "Sumbitch is swingin', boy!" he cries out. Before he embarks on his next project, Murray adds, he is first rereading the complete works of Dostoevsky and Tolstoy. He quotes from Joseph Conrad, noting that a writer's style should "carry its conviction in every line."

We are leafing through more photo albums. There is Murray's daughter Michele on Broadway, when she was a dancer with the Alvin Ailey company. There is the English teacher, Mr. Sprague, who taught both Murray and Ellison at Tuskegee. There is Murray in World War II, "taking a course in camouflage, getting ready to go to the Pacific just before the atomic bomb." There is the fighter Sugar Ray Robinson, visiting Murray when he was a member of the ROTC staff at Tuskegee during the '50s. Murray turns to a skinny figure in a bathing suit standing on a beach. "Here's James Baldwin in Antibes. I tried to teach him how to swim, but he wasn't too good at that."

On another page are a group of jazz drummers. "Art Blakey, that's Wynton's first boss," Murray says and smiles. "You know, Wynton is very much impressed with the fact there's more dance accompaniment with the Latin music than the American." Music that loses touch with dance becomes too cerebral, Murray believes; stop dancing to jazz and you're way off in the wrong direction. Then he gets talking about Ellington again, his "fully orchestrated blues statement."

Murray glances over at a painting by Romare Bearden that hangs in the living room. "I plan to give that to Wynton when he moves into his new place," he says. He points to an expensive Macintosh CD player in another corner, near the pictures of Armstrong and Ellington. "Wynton got that for me. He always brings things back from various places. This watch"—he wiggles his wrist—"for my birthday."

Then Murray stands up, leading me over toward a cabinet beside his writing desk. "Wynton calls from Vienna, has me hold the phone, then the band plays *Happy Birthday*. Now that's a good place to get a musical valentine from!" He pulls open a drawer, and reaches for a small handsome case. Inside is a beautiful gold pocket watch.

The inscription reads: "To Albert Murray, Love and Admiration, Christmas 88, Wynton Marsalis."

"As he turns page after page, following the fortunes of the storybook hero, the reader is as deeply engaged in the educative process as if he were an apprentice in a workshop. Indeed, he is an apprentice, and his workshop includes the whole range of human possibility and endeavor. His task is to learn from the example of journeymen and master craftsmen such skills as not only will enable him to avoid confusion and destruction, but also will enhance his own existence as well as that of human beings everywhere."

—ALBERT MURRAY, *The Hero and the Blues*

FOR FURTHER READING:

James Lincoln Collier, *Duke Ellington* (New York: Oxford University Press, 1987).

Duke Ellington, *Music Is My Mistress* (New York: Da Capo, 1976).

————, *The Duke Ellington Reader* (New York: Oxford University Press, 1993).

John Edward Haase, *Beyond Category: The Life and Genius of Duke Ellington* (New York: Simon & Schuster, 1993).

Wynton Marsalis, *Sweet Swing Blues on the Road* (New York: W. W. Norton, 1994).

————, *Marsalis on Music* (with accompanying CD) (New York: W. W. Norton, 1995).

Eileen Southern, *The Music of Black Americans: A History* (New York: W. W. Norton, 1971/1983).

Variations on a Theme:
Romare Bearden, Artist

"Romare Bearden played around with artist's raw materials in much the same way as, say, Duke Ellington in search of a tune or in the process of working up an arrangement or composing a fully orchestrated blues sonata. . . . More often than not, [Bearden's compositions] began simply as neutral shapes with contours that were simply what they happened to be. What each original shape eventually became was always determined only as each collage evolved."

—ALBERT MURRAY

"I think the artist has to be something like a whale, swimming with his mouth wide open, absorbing everything until he has what he really needs."

—ROMARE BEARDEN

Not long after he began spending long evenings at Albert Murray's apartment, Wynton Marsalis became curious about the artist whose original works hung on walls in the foyer, the study, the living room, even the bathroom. Many of the compositions took the form of collage, where bits of photographs and colored paper were blended into striking color tones. The predominant human figures, set against backgrounds of trains and cabins and factories, cut razor-edged profiles. The sudden breaks and repetitions in the pieces reminded Marsalis of nothing so much as the music he loved.

Murray described to Marsalis the use Romare Bearden "makes of Byzantine painting and African art, his deliberate violations of scale, and his arbitrary use of color." One of the collages was titled *Duke Ellington on Stage*. Murray pointed out the variation: the different-colored rectangles, the half-moon glistening atop the piano, how the drumheads and the shine on Ellington's knee reflected light.

When Wynton wondered if Bearden might do an album cover for him, Murray took Marsalis to see Romie, as his close friends called him, at his studio in Lower Manhattan. Bearden knew who Marsalis was, and that he was a friend of Murray's. He agreed to do the record jacket.

More than a decade later, in his penthouse apartment, a sheepish look crossed Marsalis's face as he remembered: "Every day I would go down to his studio. I tried to tell him what I wanted him to do. Then when he finished it, I didn't like it. Of course I didn't *tell* him, but he knew. Because he told Mr. Murray, 'Yeah, I gave it to Wynton, he didn't like it.' But I mean, he understood—I was just young and dumb. I wasn't sophisticated enough to really understand who Romare Bearden was."

The Bearden collage appeared on the Marsalis album *Jay Moods*. Later Marsalis purchased the rights to additional Bearden works for several more of his record covers. He has continued to feature them since the artist's death, at age seventy-five, in 1988.

At the time of his passing, Romare Howard Bearden was described by the *New York Times* as one of America's preeminent artists and the nation's foremost collagist. Bearden had, as Lowery Sims of New York's Metropolitan Museum put it, "raised the medium of collage to a mode of expression so intensely personal that it is difficult to think of another artist so closely associated with it." Bearden was awarded the National Medal of Arts in 1987. Today, his works remain on display at every major New York art museum and over a dozen more across the United States.

He was a friendly bear of a man whose physical trademark was his shaved head. When Albert Murray first saw him in Paris in 1950, "I thought he looked like a Russian or a Frenchman, either Khrushchev or [the playwright] Jean Genet."

Bearden was born on September 2, 1912 and, Murray has written, "spent his early years in the bosom of the church, as the old folks in the pews used to say, down home in Mecklenburg County, on the outskirts of Charlotte, North Carolina; and in a transplanted down-home neighborhood in Pittsburgh, Pennsylvania."

His family moved to Harlem when he was eight, but Bearden continued to divide his time with grandparents in the rural South. There he awakened to red roosters crowing against a Matisse-blue sky, and rushed to the train tracks to watch the New Orleans Limited whistle by. He would go on to imitate and choreograph, Murray continues, "work chants, railroad rhymes, and field hollers that, along with the music of the kitchen, the washplace, the fire circle, the street corner, the honky-tonks and the dance halls, were the secular complements to church music."

Bearden's mother, Bessye, was a political leader during the Harlem Renaissance and the Great Depression years. She served as New York editor of the well-known black newspaper, *The Chicago Defender*, and as chairman of the local school board—indeed, the first woman ever appointed to such a post in New York City. "Bessye Bearden was a real fighter," the painter Jacob Lawrence remembers. "The movie people used to segregate the audiences at the Loews Theatre on 125th Street. All the Harlem restaurants were very, very discriminatory. But she broke down the segregation in the Harlem community during the '20s. By the time I came along [in the 1930s], that no longer existed."

Among Bessye Bearden's friends were such luminaries as Eleanor Roosevelt (who helped get her a senior appointment in 1935 with the Internal Revenue Service), educator Mary McLeod Bethune, jazz pianist Fats Waller—and Duke Ellington. In fact, Murray says, "I think Bearden and Ellington were distant relatives, somewhere back on their mother's sides of the family."

Jazz was one of Bearden's earliest influences. The Lafayette Theatre was right across the street from the family's apartment on 131st Street; the Savoy Ballroom opened about ten blocks away when he was eleven. "Regardless of how good you might be at whatever else you did, you also had to get with the music," Bearden would recall. "The clothes you wore, the way you talked (and I don't mean just jive talk), the way you stood (we used to say stashed) when you were just hanging out, the way you drove an automobile or even just sat in it, everything you did was, you might say, geared to groove. The fabulous old Harlem Renaissance basketball team, like the Globetrotters that succeeded them, came right out of all that music at the Renaissance Casino."

Bearden majored in mathematics at New York University, planning to go on to medical school as his mother desired. He was also an excellent baseball player, pitching for the Boston Tigers in the summer Negro Leagues. "Romie could've been in the major leagues if he'd wanted," Murray says, "because he was very light-skinned. But he didn't want to 'pass' [as white]."

Bearden's sidelight passion was cartooning. He found a publisher in a black weekly newspaper, the *Afro-American*. Several months after graduation from college, he took up study at the Art Students League under the German artist George Grosz. It was Grosz, whose paintings focused on the human pathos in the defeated and impoverished Germany after the First World War, who Bearden said "made me realize the artistic possibilities of American Negro subject matter."

During the Depression years, Bearden supported himself as a social worker with the New York Department of Welfare. After helping found the Harlem Artists Guild in 1935, he started working in a studio on 125th Street that his painter friend Jacob Lawrence "found for us at $8 a month and free electricity." Bearden, however, seemed to be getting nowhere fast. In a conversation that was filmed in 1978 between Bearden, Murray, James Baldwin and Alvin Ailey, Bearden recalled the turning point of his early artist years.

"I was living at home but I came to the studio all the time, but I couldn't really work. I remember a fellow had left a turtle there. He had two turtles, one named Abercrombie and one named Fitch. He left Abercrombie with me. Abercrombie used to come out every night, and I thought the turtle—you know how egocentric artists are—I thought it was because he liked my painting. I did a few turtle paintings, but that was about all in those days, in tempera."

Then, while walking down the street one day with Jacob Lawrence, "There was the homeliest looking woman I had ever seen in my life. . . . Standing on the street, shaking these keys, which told you what profession [she] was in. And we looked at her. 'Jesus Christ!' we said, 'this woman.' She said, 'Gentlemen, two dollars'; then she said, 'A dollar, fifty cents, a quarter, but for God's sake, please take me.'

"So I went to my mother and I said, 'You know, mother, I know the lady is a nice lady, but she's in the wrong profession, could you find a job for her?' And my mother found a job for this lady. [After that] she felt she owed me something. She came and cleaned my studio every Saturday."

One Saturday morning, the woman inquired about the huge brown sheet of paper that Bearden was using to paint on, because it was cheaper than canvas. "Romie," he recalled her asking, "is this the same brown paper I saw last week and all those weeks before?" Bearden replied, "Yes, I'm trying to get my mind together." The woman continued: "You know, you told me that I was in the wrong profession. . . . Why don't you paint me?"

Bearden remembered: "She could see from my look how I felt [about that]. She said to me, 'When you can look into me and find what is beautiful, you'll be able to paint something.' This was the greatest lesson in painting I've ever had in my life. . . . This woman got me to work."

In those early artist years, Bearden went from tempera to watercolor to oil. He began as a strict Cubist in the Picasso mode, then moved to the "Social Realism" of such Mexican masters as José Orozco. He visited the studio of Stuart Davis, a post-Cubist who had studied in Paris. Davis possessed a large collection of jazz records and, says Murray, "kept trying to make him [Bearden] see visual devices in terms of the way Earl Hines did things on the piano."

This marked another transition for Bearden. "The more I just played

around with visual notions as if I were improvising like a jazz musician," he later said, "the more I realized what I wanted to do as a
painter, and how I wanted to do it."

*"Once you get going, all sorts of things begin to open up. Sometimes
something just seems to fall into place, like the piano keys that every
now and then just seem to be right where your fingers happen to come
down. But there are also those times you have to keep trying something
over and over and then when you finally get it right you wonder what
took so long. And of course there are also times when you have to
give it up and try something else. But sometimes it turns out just great
as the beginning of another, totally different picture. By the way, this
sort of thing is much more likely to have to do with how something
fits into the design or ornamental structure of the painting than with
its suitability as subject matter."*

—ROMARE BEARDEN

Those were exciting years in Harlem. "You could walk down Seventh Avenue," Bearden remembered, "and see James Weldon Johnson,
Langston Hughes or Countée Cullen. They were very accessible. We
had a community." In 1936, Ralph Ellison arrived in the city and
hooked up with the Federal Writer's Project. Having taken a sculpture
class at Tuskegee, he was interested in art and soon ran into Bearden
through mutual acquaintances.

They quickly found common ground. Both shared interests in the
poems and plays of Spain's Federico García Lorca, the poetry of T. S.
Eliot, and the fiction of Ernest Hemingway. "Indeed," Ellison would
say years later, "I soon discovered that Romie knew about many matters that I in my naiveté hadn't expected a painter to know, and when
I accepted this fact my life was unexpectedly enriched."

Ellison would visit Bearden at his studio, where he had begun working on scenes of the Great Depression, depicting the unemployed of
Harlem in the style of the Mexican muralists. Ellison watched as he
"stood at his easel sketching and explaining the perspectives of the
Dutch and Italian masters. At other times he played with the rhythms
of Mondrian and related them to the structure of jazz, and on still
other occasions he explained some of the magic by which color became
space, space became perspective, and color became form. He also had
much to say about the nature of African sculpture."

Among all of Ellison's new friends, "Romie's approach to art and
his line of development seemed closer to my own" than the writers he
knew. "Thus when it seemed impossible that I would ever get any-

where with my writing, I could talk with him, take heart from his progress, and feel encouraged. Better, I could observe and discuss his search for more effective techniques with which to give artistic form to his conceptions of our general experience. Each of us was concerned with the relationship between artistic technique and individual vision, and we were especially concerned with the relationship between our racial identity, our identity as Americans, and our mission as writer and artist."

Bearden loved regaling his friends with tales. As Jacob Lawrence remembers: "He was a tremendous storyteller. He could tell these stories that were comical but at the same time full of pathos, about people on relief and what you had to do as a relief investigator, and the response and reaction to people who applied for it. He was a very scholarly person." Bearden was also fascinated by folktales; Ellison called it a shared ancestral lore which "made for a level of unspoken communication which connected the past to the present."

They went together to see the new stars at the Apollo Theater, danced the Lindy at the Savoy, cheered the ring exploits of Joe Louis. At the same time, the question for both Ellison and Bearden became how art fit into the picture in the throes of the Depression. "Art itself was a form of freedom," Ellison recalled, "and there was a world of art complete with all the styles and complex techniques through which artists had confronted experience and given it artistic form. That world was ours to draw upon. Yes, and there were the rituals—religious, fraternal, social—through which our people had imposed order upon the chaos of their lives. There were the interrelations between such rituals that were shared by Americans of various backgrounds to be drawn upon." Together they decided they had to draw on their own experiences to show the "variety and diversity, discord and unity."

By 1940, Bearden was getting his first exhibitions. After serving in the military during World War II, he went to study art in Paris on the GI bill. He lived across the street from where Victor Hugo wrote *Les Misérables*. One evening at twilight, Bearden was sitting in a café when:

"Someone hollered, 'Le maître passe,' the master is passing by. I looked and here came [Henri] Matisse, a young man supporting him and two young girls following. He may have been drawing them as models and they were taking him to a waiting car. All the waiters, about ten or twelve, ran to the curb and they began to applaud. Matisse was oblivious to this until the man pointed and said, 'Master, this is for you.' He was so delighted that he walked over and shook hands with all of the waiters. I was sitting back there as a young artist, and I was saying, 'My God . . . you have a chance in Paris.' It meant so much to me. Just that one incident."

Back in the United States, abstract art was more and more in vogue; descriptive narrative was considered passe. Bearden was still experimenting—with a more limited use of color, an increasingly shallow space, a more developed planar surface. When they met in Paris, Pablo Picasso told him, "You've got to tell a lie to get to a stronger truth." The implication was, art was a tale told by a magician.

So it was that Bearden commenced a lengthy series of drawings and paintings steeped in myth and ritual. They were inspired by Federico García Lorca's poem "Lament for Ignacio Sánchez Meijías." He had met Lorca when the Spanish poet was studying at Columbia University, and Langston Hughes was squiring Lorca around Harlem. This was the series Bearden was working on when Albert Murray met him in 1950 at a party at Peggy Guggenheim's daughter's Paris apartment, "right across from the famous restaurant where Hemingway used to write," Murray remembers. "I knew of him through Ellison because they'd been friends since 1937. Bearden and I became friends in Paris."

Bearden soon returned to Harlem. "Then when I came back to the States," Murray says, "I used my import quota to bring some extra perfume that he had left with me. I stopped by to see him on my way back to Tuskegee—and he gave me the first of a number of paintings he was to give me over the years, a watercolor from his Lorca series. He also gave Ralph a couple paintings from the Lorca, and Ralph let me have one when he picked up a larger Bearden. So now I had two!"

In 1951, Bearden had a breakdown; his art seemed to have dried up, and he ended up in the Bellevue sanitarium. He decided he had to go back and study the masters, and had photographs of their work enlarged. He recalled: "I did that with Giotto, Duccio, Veronese, Rembrandt—right up to Monet. I spent three years copying." Only after his marriage to Nanette Rohan in 1954 did Bearden resume his own work. He tried a dozen different styles before he found himself at home in collage. Just as with Murray, Bearden was in his fifties when it all started to come together. By the early 1960s, the works of two black artists—Bearden and Jacob Lawrence—were regularly appearing in New York's finest art galleries.

It was 1963 when Bearden helped found the Spiral Group, whose symbolic meaning was upward-and-outward for black artists. Originally they planned to limit their palettes to black-and-white, emblematic of America's racial conflicts. Bearden thought collage was something in which everyone in the group might take a creative hand. But when he cut pictures out of magazines and brought them to a meeting, nobody was particularly interested. Undaunted, he continued experimenting with collage on his own.

"I wasn't an abstract expressionist or a pop artist. I believe that it was because I had something unique to say about the life that I knew best. I took an art form that was different. What I had to say took a little different form than most of the paintings around; I used the collage. Especially in some of the earlier collages that I did, I chose some of the photographic materials for a certain reason. I wanted to give an immediacy, like a documentary movie. . . .

"I felt that the Negro was becoming too much of an abstraction, rather than the reality that art can give to a subject. What I've attempted to do is establish a world through art in which the validity of my Negro experience could live and make its own logic."

—ROMARE BEARDEN

In a 1967 collage, *Tidings*—part of a larger collage series called *The Prevalence of Ritual*—the ambiguity of Bearden's time sequence is reminiscent of portions of Ellison's *Invisible Man*. The face of an angel resembles an African mask; the Virgin holds not a lily, but a rose; human figures break along cubelike planes. Amid the juxtaposition of drawings, paintings and photographs, the background includes a sharecropper's shack and a remnant of an old Victorian mansion. Another sequence, *Baptism*, also bears the African mask and larger-than-life people in the foreground, against a small church bordering the railroad tracks somewhere in the rural South.

Another work, *Three Folk Musicians*, is clearly a takeoff on Picasso's *Three Musicians*, while *Artist with Painting and Model* is Bearden's homage to Matisse. "I really think the art of painting is the art of putting something over something else," Bearden said. "I would work with rectangular shapes that were in proportion to the overall rectangle of the whole painting." His crowded, lyrical human effigies shouted, worked, grinned, suffered, and made music. His most ambitious piece was eighteen feet long and called *The Block*.

Ellison wrote of Bearden's mask-faced Harlemites and other portrayals: "He knows that the true complexity of the slum dweller and the tenant farmer requires a release from the prison of our media-dulled perception and a reassembling in forms which would convey something of the depth and wonder of the Negro American's stubborn humanity." It was, Ellison saw, often a saga of birth and resurrection, a harsh beauty arising out of fragmentation as Bearden's explosive details encompassed tribal Africa, Northern bound-for-glory trains, and the teeming Harlem streets. "His combination of technique is in itself eloquent of the sharp breaks, leaps in consciousness, distortions, paradoxes, reversals, telescoping of time and surreal blending of styles, values, hopes and dreams which characterize much of Negro American history."

Following a hugely successful one-man show at the Museum of Modern Art in 1971, during that single decade Bearden created 342 collages, 128 oils on paper, 24 drawings, 25 prints, 5 tapestries, 4 murals and mosaics, as well as illustrations for the theater and movies, magazine covers, book jackets, banners and quilts.

"His impact as an artist was enormous," says Professor Richard Long of Atlanta's Emory University. "At the precise moment he began to use the collage technique, it opened up a lot of people's eyes in different areas. Collaging in music and in literature was a response to the great attention Bearden began to receive. His wife had a dance company, and there was also interaction between Bearden and Alvin Ailey. He did the sets for several of Ailey's ballets."

Bearden also became a mentor to numerous young artists. He was a founder of the Cinque Gallery, which has since given hundreds their first exhibitions. Lou Jones, today a prominent Boston-based photographer, recalls how Bearden inspired him to leave behind his college training as a physicist.

"My older sister was buying largely black art at a very early age, and she struck upon Romare Bearden," Jones says. "I had no idea who he was. When she told me she was going to New York to visit with him, I asked if I could tag along. Late one cold winter night, he showed us his studio and talked incessantly to my sister about everything. The more he talked, the more I knew that I wanted to be an artist. But I knew that I had no chance. So, toward the end of the evening, I asked him: 'Mr. Bearden, you've done commissioned works for museums and earned your living making art—what's your secret?' Of course, you couldn't ask a dumber question. But he just turned to me and answered with one of the most profound statements: 'I *outlived* everybody.' I didn't know what he was talking about at the time, but since then I've realized exactly what he meant. He outlived all of his competition. And eventually, people come to your work."

Even as Bearden's acclaim grew, he continued to live modestly in a fifth-floor walk-up apartment on Canal Street, maintaining a second abode on the Caribbean island of St. Martin, where his wife was born. Murray has described Bearden's on-the-spot improvisations as being very much like a jazz musician's. In fact, Bearden was also a songwriter. Twenty of his compositions were recorded, including a hit called *Seabreeze* that was done by Billy Eckstein and Dizzy Gillespie. Bearden's collage *Carolina Shout* is taken from the "stride piano" piece

James P. Johnson wrote, the same one that the young Duke Ellington memorized and was pushed onstage to play for Johnson. The trains in Bearden's pictures evoke not only the old guitar and harmonica folk blues, but Ellington's *Daybreak Express* and the locomotive themes in Murray's novels.

"Except for the American Indian, everybody who came here or was brought here becomes, starting with the second generation, four things: Part Anglo-Saxon, part Indian, part frontiersman and part black. These are the roots that form American music. I knew a lot of painters, abstract expressionists, who used to paint to jazz music. They even called it action painting. It wasn't done in Europe. Everything is American that comes out of America."

—ROMARE BEARDEN

If that comment sounds ever so Ellisonian/Murrayesque, it is not surprising. Ellison wrote the introduction to a catalogue of Bearden's works in 1968. Murray ghost-wrote several erudite lectures given by Bearden at a Yale University seminar on African-American art. He also came up with the names for many of Bearden's works. This story was told to the *New Yorker* by Columbia University scholar Robert O'Meally, who encountered the pair of them one afternoon in a bookstore as they were trying to decide on the title for the latest collage.

"It might be that Al Murray's eye was caught by the figure of a woman in one corner of the image. And he'd say, 'Who's that?' And Bearden would be looking embarrassed, because the woman in question had been an old girlfriend of his. Maybe Bearden would say, 'Oh, she's just a woman I once knew from North Carolina.' And then Murray would say, 'I've got it. Let's call it *Red-Headed Woman from North Carolina.*' Or, 'I know, call it *Red-Headed Woman from North Carolina with Rooster.*' And Bearden would go and write that on the back of his painting."

Murray says: "Romie would call my wife and say, 'Well, I've been pretty busy. Tell Al I got to see him. I've got all these orphans over here that need names.' I would think in terms of design, but in poetic and metaphorical terms. So he'd say, 'What can I do?' And I'd say, 'What about *Storyville Odalisque*?' You know, Matisse. Bing! He's off."

Looking around his apartment at the many works of his friend, Murray wrote: "And what finally is a Bearden if not design or ornament or decoration for a wall, where it hangs not primarily as a record but as an emblem or badge or shield or flag or banner or pennant, or even as a battle standard and existential guidon. And of what is it emblematic if not that in terms of which the fundamental rituals of the blues idiom condition one to survive (with one's humanity, including one's sense of humor, intact, to be sure). What indeed if not flexibility become elegant improvisation not only under the pressure of all tempos and not only in the response of all disjunctures, but also in the face of ever-impending nothingness. Yes, it is precisely in doing this that a Bearden wall ornament functions as a totemistic device and talisman for keeping the blues at bay, if only intermittently."

At a memorial service for Romare Bearden on April 6, 1988, Ralph Ellison looked around the Cathedral of St. John the Divine—where some of his friend's collages graced the walls—and concluded his eulogy:

"Now perhaps we should remind ourselves that we are a *collage of a nation*, and a nation that is ever shifting about and grousing as we seek to achieve the promised design of democracy. Therefore one of the reasons that *we* revere Romie is for his discovery that one of the ways for getting at many of the complex matters which we experience, but seldom find recorded in official history, is through art. Art is the mystery which gets left out of history."

FOR FURTHER READING:

Myron Schwartzman, *Romare Bearden: His Life and Art* (New York: Harry N. Abrams, 1990).

Essays on Bearden: Albert Murray, *The Blue Devils of Nada: A Contemporary American Approach to Aesthetic Statement* (New York: Pantheon, 1996) and *The Collected Essays of Ralph Ellison*, ed. John F. Callahan, intr. Saul Bellow (New York: Modern Library, 1995).

Part 2

CREATION UNDER FIRE

"My friends, the destiny of the colored American, however this mighty war shall terminate, is the destiny of America. We shall never leave you. The allotments of Providence seem to make the black man of America the open book out of which the American people are to learn lessons of wisdom, power, and goodness—more sublime and glorious than any yet attained by the nations of the old or the new world. Over the bleeding back of the American bondsman we shall learn mercy. In the very extreme difference of color and features of the Negro and the Anglo-Saxon, shall be learned the highest ideas of the sacredness of man and the fullness and perfection of human brotherhood."

—FREDERICK DOUGLASS, from a speech given
in 1862 at the height of the Civil War.

"The only progress is the progress of the human heart."

—ABRAHAM LINCOLN

Ancestors—Meta Warrick Fuller, Sculptor

"But what the Negro artist of to-day has most to gain from the arts of the forefathers is perhaps not cultural inspiration or technical innovations, but the lesson of a classic background, the lesson of discipline, of style, of technical control pushed to the limits of technical mastery. A more highly stylized art does not exist than the African. If after absorbing the new content of American life and experience, and after assimilating new patterns of art, the original artistic endowment can be sufficiently augmented to express itself with equal power in more complex patterns and substance, then the Negro may well become what some have predicted, the artist of American life."

—ALAIN LOCKE

The young female student at Paris's Colarossi Academy, just turned twenty-four, stood for a long time staring at the house behind the tall trees. It was the summer of 1901. Meta Warrick, raised in Philadelphia, was the daughter of a barber and a hairdresser whose promise as a sculptor had been recognized at the Pennsylvania School of Industrial Art. She was diminutive and strikingly beautiful. She had been in Europe for a year and a half, working diligently but often living a life of isolated desperation.

"Why didn't you tell me you were not a white girl?" the director of the American Girls Club had greeted her upon arrival. Meta had been turned away. The expatriate African-American artist Henry Ossawa Tanner, a friend of Meta's uncle, had found her a room in a small hotel and continued to serve as her guardian.

Now she was carrying a letter of introduction for a meeting with Auguste Rodin, France's grand master. "It was possibly the most exciting moment of my life when I found myself standing on the street outside the sculptor's home," Meta would remember.

The house in Meudon was set back behind a high black grille fence. Finally she gathered her courage to traverse the seemingly endless path to the front door. Rodin, an old man with a kindly smile, greeted her. Inside the house, she brought out to show Rodin a little figure—no more than eight inches high—cast from a clay mold. She called it *Man Eating His Heart*, or *Secret Sorrow*.

The idea had come to Meta while she lay awake one night, remembering a poem by Stephen Crane called "The Heart." "I used to clip poetry when I was still in my teens," she would say in later years, "and I remember clipping this poem from some newspaper or other. I don't know whatever became of it. I thought of this idea of a man eating his heart, and I got out of bed to start it."

Rodin carefully examined the oddly impressive work. "Mademoiselle," she recalled him saying, "you are a sculptor. You have the sense of form in your fingers. . . . Come with me, and I'll show you some things that will be of help to you." Rodin led her to a case with "myriads of little hands, feet, legs and arms" in clay and terra-cotta that he had used to study the human figure—"tiny writhing figures without faces, and often with missing limbs, whose whole simplified shape suggested the most incredible passion or agony. He didn't say a great deal while we looked at his studies and, afterwards, he took me around the studio where there were dried heads on wooden stands, a few tools and his own Oriental collection of things."

She remembered Rodin advising her to pick as models people "who did not know how to pose," so that her work would be spontaneous. At the close of their visit, Rodin offered to be her teacher. It was, Meta said, "a great honor." But she told him that, if she accepted, she feared her talent and individuality would merely become an imitation of his. Rodin understood and "offered to criticize my work any time I wanted him to. 'If the work is too large and cumbersome to bring to me, I will come to Paris to see you.' He did just that."

With Rodin's blessing, Meta Warrick soon established a studio in the French capital and was invited to exhibit in the great salons. The press called her "the delicate sculptor of horrors." For her subject matter was a bold departure from the customary beauty-extolling sculpture of the time. She sought to capture the theme of duty in *Man Carrying a Dead Comrade*. Exhibited in 1903 at the Art Nouveau Gallery was a new piece she called *The Wretched*—seven figures representing different forms of human anguish.

As Meta described it: "There was a woman suffering from loss— say, the loss of her child; a man suffering from shame; an old man, from poverty in his old age; a woman, from distress of mind; a child, from some hereditary malady; a man who realizes that he can never fulfill the task before him; and, topping them all, the philosopher who suffers from sympathy and understanding."

J. Velma Hoover, a close friend in Meta's later years, has written: "At the turn of the century in the United States, most black persons were afraid to publicly verbalize the pain, sorrow and despair of the black experience, and a woman was seldom expected to voice any opinion at all. Meta found creative expression of these feelings through her sculpture." Her early pieces, according to art historian James A. Porter, are "a hymn to tradition expressed in forms which reflect the intense struggle of a soul with its own nature."

Meta did not find a ready audience upon her return to America, where she was spurned by art dealers. Still, Hoover tells us that "as an artist she needed to live and work in the United States, where she could be near her cultural roots." In 1907, she was commissioned— for the then-remarkable sum of $1,500—to commemorate the 300th anniversary of the colonial Jamestown settlement by creating fifteen tableaux highlighting the progress of African-Americans. In a far more realistic style than before, Meta set about doing dioramas of 150 figures.

When she came to receive a gold medal for the *Warrick Tableau* that established her reputation on American soil: "I didn't know it at the time, but I couldn't eat at any of the restaurants. I became so hungry that, when I visited the exhibit of the Shredded Wheat Company and discovered they were handing out samples, I took some of them. That was all I had to eat during that day of my visit to the Jamestown exposition."

Two years later, she met Dr. Solomon Carter Fuller, a Liberian immigrant and already prominent neurologist who directed a pathology laboratory in Massachusetts. Married in 1909, the couple moved to Framingham outside Boston, into the house where Meta would remain until her death almost sixty years later. Initially, a petition was circulated among neighbors seeking to keep them out of the community— "inasmuch as Negroes, it was thought, would decrease the value of property," she would remember. "No sooner did we move in here than I used to go up and down the street, never looking right nor left. But little by little, the people on the block began to come over to ask favors, to borrow something—you know, sugar, or eggs or potatoes."

Fuller had stored her most valuable pieces with an aunt in Philadelphia, who had placed them in storage. The cause of a fire that destroyed the warehouse in 1910 was never explained. Nearly all of her sixteen years' work—including *Man Eating His Heart* that so impressed Rodin—was destroyed. Among the few surviving pieces was her seven pillars of suffering, *The Wretched*.

For the next several years, Meta Warrick Fuller abandoned her sculpture and settled down to begin raising three children. Then W. E. B. Du Bois paid her a visit. The first African-American to receive a doctorate degree from Harvard University, Du Bois was already regarded as the foremost black activist/scholar of his time: author of *The Souls of Black Folk*, publisher of the monthly *Crisis* magazine, organizer of the early NAACP. Du Bois had long been interested in Fuller's work, dating back to the Paris exposition of 1900. When she had been invited to attend the U.S. Pavilion's banquet there, she recalled:

"I said I would be delighted, and asked what the fee would be. Dr. Du Bois spoke up then and said, 'There will be no fee. You will come as *my* guest.' I decided to put on my best bib and tucker, which happened to be my white silk graduation dress, and I got it out and pressed it. Dr. Du Bois called for me, and I felt very proud to have such an escort! He was master of ceremonies, and I sat at his right. From then on, Dr. Du Bois and I enjoyed meeting from time to time with other friends visiting Paris."

Now Du Bois came again in 1913, asking Fuller if she could reproduce *Man Eating His Heart* for the fiftieth anniversary of the Emancipation Proclamation. No, she said of the work consumed in the fire, it would be too painful. She did agree, however, to produce *Spirit of Emancipation*. Standing eight feet high, the plaster grouping was unlike anything ever seen before; there were no discarded whips or chains, no grateful slaves kneeling before Abraham Lincoln. The sculpture depicted a boy and a girl standing beneath an overshadowing figure.

"They have just been set free," wrote her friend Velma Hoover, who studied the sculpture years later in Fuller's garage. "And behind them, Humanity personified is urging them on while race hatred holds them back. Bewildered, they stand looking to the future with nothing in their hands to help them, and with only the scantest clothing covering them. Humanity, while urging them forward, weeps for their discouraging state."

Spirit of Emancipation marked a new lease on life for Fuller. After the onset of the First World War, she created *Peace Halting the Ruthlessness of War*—a blind soldier riding a blind horse plunging through crowds of people, a human head impaled on his spear, forced to a halt by a figure of Peace with an upraised hand. More and more, Fuller turned to activism: becoming involved with the Women's Peace Party and the equal suffrage movement, crafting two powerful antilynching pieces, creating a relief for a black YMCA in Georgia that showed a youth rising from his knees to meet the morning sun.

Then came *Awakening Ethiopia*, a life-sized statue done in bronzed plaster which stands today at the Schomburg Center for Research in Black Culture in Harlem. Inspired by the philosophy of Du Bois, its Egyptian motif has a black woman emerging from a mummy's wrappings through enveloping hands. Unraveling the bandages of the past, the woman looks out upon life with anticipation and without fear. Fuller memorialized, as one critic put it, "the awakening defiance of her people." The piece was unveiled in 1922 at the Making of America exposition in New York.

There followed *The Talking Skull*, drawn from an African folktale, and other works relating to mythology, poetry, and song. "I love to interpret music in my sculpture," Fuller said. "I made two interpretations of the song 'Water Boy.' " The studio she had built near her home in 1929 "had two beautiful fireplaces and an ideal atmosphere. There I did much work. I held classes and the like. Friends and neighbors loved to congregate there, and came from near and far to sit by the open fire, chat and sip tea when I had open house."

Through an association with the Harmon Foundation in New York, Fuller served as a juror and exhibitor in showcasing the work of young black artists. She made reliefs, busts and statuettes of black and white friends, including composer Samuel Coleridge-Taylor and actor Richard B. Harrison.

In the mid-1930s, Fuller sculpted a clay group of Southern blacks about to begin their Northern migration. She called it *Exodus*. But when she began moving it from her studio, it suddenly crumbled into pieces.

There were long, difficult years ahead: first she had to care for her husband when he lost his eyesight. After his death in 1953, Fuller entered a sanatorium for two years with tuberculosis. She doubted she would ever sculpt again. But toward the end of her hospitalization, "A friend brought me some plasticene which I added to, and I made *The Good Shepherd* and *The Voice of the Cello*." Yet another comeback began in the mid-1950s. Fuller was already approaching eighty.

She would keep working until the end. During the early 1960s, Fuller donated the proceeds of her art sales to aid the voter registration drives in the South. One of her last pieces came in reaction to the tragic deaths of four little girls, in the September 1963 bombing of a Birmingham, Alabama church. It was a raised head of Christ. Fuller called it *The Crucifixion*.

She had come full circle. Long, long ago, her Pennsylvania college had awarded a metalwork prize for one of her very first pieces in 1898. That one was called *Crucifixion of Christ in Agony*. When some observers objected at seeing so tormented a portrayal, the young woman had replied: "If the Savior did not suffer, wherein lay the sacrifice?"

The first artist to probe the painful depths of the black experience died at the age of ninety in March of 1968, two weeks before Martin Luther King's assassination. "Unfortunately, she was not fully appreciated in her time," writes Samella Lewis in *African American Art and Artists*, "for the subject matter and emotional intensity of this dynamic artist intimidated many of her contemporaries. A transitional figure in the history of African American art, Warrick expressed ideals that are more in accord with the generation that followed hers than with the prevailing artistic views of her own period."

FOR FURTHER READING:

Samella Lewis, *African American Art and Artists* (Berkeley & Los Angeles: University of California Press, 1990).

The Painters:
Loïs Mailou Jones and Jacob Lawrence

"Art must be the quintessence of meaning. . . . Inspirations can come from most anything. Tell the world how you feel . . . take the chance . . . try, try!"
—META WARRICK FULLER

Loïs Mailou Jones was a teenager when she first encountered the woman she calls "my inspiration"—Meta Warrick Fuller—on Martha's Vineyard off the Massachusetts coast. "I used to get as close to Meta as possible on the beach to talk," Jones remembers. "When she told me she had met Rodin and worked in his studio, I was inspired to no end. I made up my mind very definitely—that's what I'm going to do someday, go to France to study."

Jones does not remember the exact year when the fateful meeting took place, only that it was sometime between 1919 and 1923. This was still the era of horse-drawn carriages, more than fifty years before Martha's Vineyard became the fashionable summer resort it is today.

Early in 1997, Loïs Jones had just turned ninety-one—a year older than Meta Fuller had been when she died in 1968 and had her ashes scattered over Vineyard Sound. I am sitting with Jones at the dining room table of her lovely three-story stone house in northwest Washington, D.C. After years of relative obscurity, today she is widely regarded as the finest female African-American painter of the twentieth century. Only recently has the mixture of American, European, Caribbean, and African cultural themes in her paintings come to be seen as "enlivening the whole vocabulary of art," as the Corcoran Gallery's chief curator Jack Cowart puts it. Her work is featured in New York's Metropolitan Museum of Art; Boston's Museum of Fine Arts; Washington's National Portrait Gallery and the Smithsonian National Museum of American Art, as well as nearly thirty other public collections.

Jones's home itself is a veritable museum. Dozens of her works adorn the walls and staircases leading up to the studio overlooking the backyard. Every available space explodes with color—oils, acrylics and watercolors covering such a diversity of places, subjects and styles that it seems impossible for the paintings to have been done by the same artist.

Surrounded by stacks of photographs and other mementoes, Loïs Jones is wearing an elegant, boldly-patterned dress. Combined with her bronzed hair, warm smile, and vivid memory, she appears considerably younger than her years. Only the cane she has begun using is a testament to her age. "My legs have started to give way," she shrugs, then points to some paintings leaning against a wall and adds: "These are things that are building up for another show, I have a big one going on now."

Back in 1932, it was Meta Fuller's sculpture *The Awakening of Ethiopia* that had inspired Jones's first oil painting. She called it *The Ascent of Ethiopia*, and it hangs today in the Milwaukee Art Museum. The profile of a beautiful black woman in Nubian garb looks on as five of her people ascend a long staircase past two pyramids beneath a blazing sun. They are moving toward circles within circles of art, drama, and music. A decade before she finished it, the world had thrilled to the discovery in Egypt of King Tut's tomb, just as the Harlem Renaissance was beginning. Jones's stunning painting pays homage to both realms.

Jones remembers: "When I was a child, Meta Fuller lived most of the year in Framingham, near some of my family who had a riding school out there. She was very dramatic and loved to give pageants and plays. She'd call on me to be the artist and make costumes with her. Sometimes I would even take a minor part, as I was a little actress."

Jones's parents had moved from New Jersey into the Boston area in 1896, looking for new opportunities. Jones was born there on November 3, 1905. Her mother was a beautician for upper-crust Brahmins, and "loved to make hats with the wire framing and flowers and veils and all." Her father started out as superintendent of a downtown office building, where the Jones family resided for thirty years on the top floor.

"He used to go across the street to City Hall to see his friend Curley [Mayor James, usually known as "Boss" Curley]. Daddy told Curley he really wanted to be something, maybe a lawyer. And Curley said, 'Why don't you go to Suffolk Law School?' So he did, at nights, because by day he was busy keeping that building clean. I guess he went for six or seven years. He got the degree in 1915 when he was forty, I have it upstairs. Much of my drive surely comes from my father."

As long as she could remember, Loïs Jones loved to draw her surroundings. From her parents she received her first set of watercolors at seven. When school let out, the family would take a train to meet the ferry bound for Martha's Vineyard. Jones's grandmother had been among the island's early settlers, "a housekeeper for a wealthy white family that had an express business." She saved enough to buy some property in Oak Bluffs. Eventually, this Vineyard town would be where numerous African-Americans—including Henry Louis Gates, Jr. and filmmaker Spike Lee—came to spend vacations.

Here nature captivated the young Jones: "The fields of daisies and buttercups and the beauty of the landscape and the ocean were overwhelming. When I was fifteen, my mother would put my watercolors on our clothesline and invite friends over to have a chance to be my patron! Mother's garden was my gallery."

Jones laughs, and begins talking about her then-next-door neighbor, Dorothy West. Later to become a prominent African-American novelist, West continues to reside in Oak Bluffs. "We grew up together on the island," Jones says. "Dorothy's mother loved children and gave us the courtyard in front of these little cottages as our playground. The husband, who worked in the marketplace in [Boston's] Faneuil Hall, would send down crates of fruit and she would pack them in the under-porches. That was our private meeting spot."

Jones's tone becomes more serious as she continues: "One afternoon the Wests were having a big card party on their veranda. Somebody must have thrown a match down the crack and about three o'clock— boom! Up went the wooden houses. It was a terrible fire. I remember my mother calling my father—'Where's Wesley? Where's Wesley?'— my one brother. He was asleep. Daddy went in and wrapped him in blankets and got him out. But our house burned to the ground." The Joneses, and the Wests, rebuilt.

Now Loïs Jones, who stands about five-feet-two, gathers her cane and we walk together into a sitting room. She points out a photograph on the wall. "There you see my first boyfriend, Adam Clayton Powell. He was such a devil, and so good-looking—I knew I couldn't hold him. His father was a preacher in Harlem and they came to Martha's Vineyard for vacation, and they heard about Loïs Jones, who went horseback riding every day. And they called me and wondered if I would take Adam with me. Of course I was delighted. I took him to meet the stable people and we'd go riding every morning. He was quite a character. Even later when he became a congressman, he'd go to the post office in his bare feet!"

In many ways it was an idyllic world, the Vineyard of the early 1920s, "so beautiful and elegant and dignified." But the color barrier existed even there. "The blacks had their own hotel in Oak Bluffs, because they couldn't stay anywhere else. That's where Meta came, and Harry T. Burleigh, who arranged so many of the spirituals. Oh, the cooking was wonderful! Even the white people would go up there and buy hot rolls and everything. And this was our place. We made part of it into a theater. Dorothy West would direct the plays."

The island became part of the blood of Loïs Jones. She still returns every summer, maintaining a studio in Edgartown, where her grandmother had bought additional land. Her paintings of the boats moored in Menemsha harbor and the clay cliffs of Gay Head are among her finest landscapes. When President Clinton arrived for his vacation on the Vineyard in 1993, he came to one of her exhibits. She gave Clinton a painting (*Breezy Day at Gay Head*), which is the first by a black artist to hang in the White House.

"I thought he was going to take something of Haiti because he said, 'Isn't this Haiti?' and I said yes. He said, 'Now that's something I'm going to do for Haiti.' He went on that he was going to give them a lot of money, Aristide would be promoted and he would help him. Then he continued to walk around and said he hadn't been up to Gay Head, and the Gay Headers were not pleased. He said, 'So I'm gonna take this painting of Gay Head!' Which was nothing more than a fence with grass blowing and the water!"

She laughs again. "But that's politics, I guess."

Loïs Jones's talent blossomed early. She won four consecutive scholarships to vocational drawing classes at Boston's Museum of Fine Arts, attending daily after high school to work on drawings based upon nineteenth-century sculptures. Apprenticed to Ripley Studios in Providence, Rhode Island, she was "introduced to Africa there through creating masks." Her free-lance fabrics and textiles won numerous prizes and appeared in the showroom windows of many department stores.

It was the summer of 1928 when Jones met Charlotte Hawkins Brown, the renowned founder of a black women's junior college in Sedalia, North Carolina. When Brown "mentioned the need for young educators to come to the South and teach," Jones convinced her to create an art department modeled along the lines of Boston's Museum School. At Palmer Memorial Institute, she began her long career as an art instructor. She also coached the basketball team, taught folk dancing, and played the piano at Sunday chapel.

In the spring of 1930, Jones was recruited to teach design at Howard University in Washington, one of the few black colleges that offered courses in art. She would remain there for forty-seven years, with many of her protegés going on to remarkable careers. They include sculptor-printmaker Elizabeth Catlett and painter Gwendolyn Knight, the wife of Jacob Lawrence.

"As students of Loïs Jones, we were taught that art must be the central focus of our lives," painter and art professor David Driskell has written. "She often spoke of the importance of being 'married' to one's art, and the devotion and discipline she brought to bear in her own career left a lasting impression on us. . . . She reminded us repeatedly, through precept and example, that the finer aspirations of the human spirit can tower over many of the obstacles that come one's way."

In her own work, Jones focused on portraiture through the mid-1930s. Then came a memorable summer afternoon next to Meta Warrick Fuller on the Highland Beach at Oak Bluffs. "I remember Meta turning to me and saying, 'You're not going to make it in this country, because they're not ready for you. You're going to have to go abroad.'" Shortly thereafter, the opportunity arrived: a fellowship to study at the Académie Julian in Paris for the 1937-38 academic year.

"Before I caught the boat, the director of the Harvard Foundation, Mary Beatty Brady, came over to me and said: 'Loïs, we expect an awful lot of you when you come back. I want you to sketch every day, don't ever be without your sketchbook.' When I arrived in Paris, African art was just the thing. All the galleries and museums were featuring African sculptures, African designs, and I sketched, sketched everything."

Jones's dream was to catch up with Henry Ossawa Tanner. He was the first prominent African-American artist, the man who had shepherded Meta Fuller through her own first year in Paris. Tanner, too, had studied at the Académie Julian and was preparing to return to France from America at the same time as Jones's trip. "I was thinking, oh, to be there and see him and maybe get advice from him. But he died three weeks before I arrived. So I never had the glory to meet him, only the inspiration of what the man had done."

Instead, a surprisingly different mentor awaited her. Jones remembers: "Being in France was so mystical, it really was the making of me. The first study I did was on the Seine. Everything looked so silvery gray, very beautiful, the quiet of the river. I was there with my easel looking down, doing a painting I called *Under the Bridge*. And there was an old man with long white hair, standing there watching me for a long time. Finally he said something in French. I had taken a course, but I couldn't understand him. There was a young woman who worked with me, Céline Tabari—and I called her over to translate. What he said was, 'It is good to see a young artist not wasting canvas and paint. She's going to make it.'"

The old man was Emile Bernard. He had been a colleague of the French Impressionist masters Van Gogh, Gauguin and Cézanne, and a co-founder of what became known as the French Symbolist school of painting. Jones loved the long Parisian daylight that allowed her to keep working until nine o'clock, but it was starting to get dark along the Seine. "And Emile Bernard said to Céline and me, 'Why don't you bring those big easels over to my studio and leave them overnight?' We were so grateful not to have to take the Métro with those wet canvasses.

"He invited us into his studio for tea and cookies. It was a magnificent place near Pont Sainte-Marie, with paintings on the walls, a huge fireplace, and antique furniture. He showed us his hundreds of Japanese prints and told us this had been Whistler's studio, and talked about all that Whistler had done.

"Then he brought out three paintings and asked, 'Who do you think did those?' Céline and I shouted out: 'Gauguin!' And he was furious. He said, 'They're mine! Gauguin took my style, went to Tahiti and got famous!'

"After that, Emile sort of adopted me. He always let Céline and me keep our easels and canvasses there, because we would return at the same time each day in order to have the same light and environmental conditions. When Emile would have his soirees at night—those elegant affairs with artists, writers and musicians—he would always invite me and any friend I was with. We kept in touch after I came back to the United States. I will never forget his kindness and generosity. He never really 'made it' until after his death."

Loïs Jones found a penthouse studio on a quiet Montparnasse street, with a balcony facing the Eiffel Tower. "That was the luxury of my life, that studio—to have a skylight, even a roof garden, for fifty dollars a month!" She painted "furiously, from morning to night": Impressionistic still lifes and street scenes, more than forty paintings during her nine months in Paris. When her professors criticized a change of style to a more angular geometry, "I had to remind them of Modigliani and Picasso and all the French artists using the inspiration of Africa, and that if anybody had the right to use it, I did. It was my heritage, so they had to give in." Her time in Paris allowed her "to be shackle free, to create and be myself." Twice during the 1960s, she would take groups of her students to visit the country that had so inspired her early work.

By the time Jones returned home from her first European journey, she had begun to develop her own style. As described in a *Christian Science Monitor* review of her first solo exhibition in 1939: "While in Paris, she was imbued with the qualities the Impressionists sought to achieve through painting with broad brush work, in summary patches of color which catch the effect of sunlight upon surfaces. Miss Jones is an Impressionist without the strict methods of divided color." Or, as French art historian Catherine Bernard said of Jones, "she proved to be a postmodern artist long before the term entered our vocabulary."

Her consciousness was changing, strongly influenced by encouragement from the African-American scholars Carter G. Woodson and Alain Locke. Even before she went to Paris, Jones had begun doing free-lance work for the Associated Publishers. The group had been organized by Woodson in 1921, putting out books by blacks that were not accepted by commercial publishers. Woodson had also initiated *The Journal of Negro History* in 1916, and the *Negro History Bulletin* in 1937. Jones would serve all of these as an illustrator between 1936 and 1965, including a thirty-work collection for Woodson's *African Heroes and Heroines*.

Alain Locke was that era's "Professor of Connection," the same man who introduced the young Ralph Ellison to Langston Hughes. He saw Loïs Jones off at the docks on her maiden voyage to Paris. "We expect from the Negro artist a vigorous and intimate documentation of Negro life itself," he wrote in 1939, while chairman of Howard University's philosophy department. Jones recalls a pivotal encounter with Locke one day on the Howard campus. "He said, 'I like what you did in France, but one thing, young lady: You have a heritage, you must do your heritage.' "

All through the 1940s, in what Jones calls her "Locke period," she did. The decade began with her decision to submit one of her paintings to an annual contest sponsored by Washington's Corcoran Gallery of Art. It was an oil called *Indian Shops, Gay Head, Massachusetts*. Jones remembers of its creation in 1940: "In those early days, they had two or three Wampanoag Indian teepees at the tip of Gay Head. In them they sold clay vases and ornaments, Indian beads, all things related to the area. As I drove up and stood looking at the landscape, there were these teepees with the background of the ocean behind. It was so beautiful, I said, 'This is my spot,' and set up my easel.

"I wasn't invited to the Corcoran show. It was a matter of delivering your painting with the hope that you might get in—but they forbid participation by blacks. If they saw me coming, it would go in the rejects real quick. Even the guards would have said, 'Put that thing over there, this Negro woman is not an artist.' But my friend from France, Céline Tabari, was visiting me at the time. She brought my entry over to the Corcoran."

Jones's painting was chosen to receive the prestigious Robert Woods Bliss Prize for Landscape. "They wrote and told me I had won it. But I felt I could not go and receive it personally. I was afraid they would take it away. So I had them send the certificate through the mail."

For years, the Corcoran had no idea that Jones's work had broken its longstanding color barrier. Recently she brought the painting out of storage and took it to be featured at a festive dinner at the Corcoran, where she related its history.

From her award-winning depiction of Native Americans, Jones's focus had shifted to the black experience. Her wartime character studies of blacks have since been compared to those of John Singleton Copley, among others. In works like *Jennie*, *The Pink Table Cloth*, and *The Banjo Player*, her figures capture the many facets of the African-American personality.

For what became her powerful *Mob Victim (Meditation)*, Jones found her model on the streets of New York. He was a tall, shabbily-dressed man, carrying a guitar over each shoulder. When he accepted Jones's invitation to have his picture painted, she told him he was to pose as a man about to be hung. His brother, the man revealed, had died this way down South—in his presence.

The 1944 painting shows a man with hands tied standing beneath a tree, his eyes focused on a far distant realm. At the last moment, Jones removed the rope she had originally fashioned around his neck—and allowed the portrait to be one of simple dignity in the face of imminent death.

She returned to live in France for a while after the Second World War—traveling around the Mediterranean, creating richly hued panoramas, the orange roofs of the North contrasting with the verdant green valleys she found in the South. "I stayed there at the country home of Céline's family. We'd be ready to go up to our rooms at night and Madame Tabari would say, 'Bon soir, Louise,' and kiss me here and here. And the sister would kiss me, and the father—I was kissed to death! And they'd bring the coffee up to my bed in the mornings. Ah, I wish I could die in France. I mean, I was treated like a human being."

In 1953, a new phase in Jones's life and career began. Louis Vergniaud Pierre-Noël, a Haitian citizen and outstanding graphic designer, had come to Washington on a commissioned assignment. He was a tall, handsome, cultured gentleman whom Jones had first met nearly two decades before, when both were doing graduate work at a summer session at Columbia University. They had become friends then, and corresponded afterwards, but lost contact when Jones went to Paris in 1937. Now here came Pierre again, paying a call at her home.

"I had always been very attractive," Jones says with a shrug of her shoulders. "Somebody was forever trying to be my boyfriend. One was

Justin Sandridge, the pianist. I was really in love with him, but his mother wouldn't let him loose. She wouldn't even let him carry my books across the campus, said it wasn't professional. Oh, she was tight!"

She laughs and continues: "My mother would warn me about staying single. 'Someday you're going to wake up and find yourself surrounded by paintings,' she would say. I just figured I was born to paint and teach. Now here I was, forty-eight years old, and suddenly Pierre walked back into my life."

The courtship was brief; the couple were married in the French hometown of Jones's friend Céline Tabari on August 8, 1953. It was her husband's native land, the French-speaking Caribbean island of Haiti, that would come to enthrall her. Her first visit combined a honeymoon with a commission from Haitian president Paul Magliore. "He invited me to do a series of studies portraying his nation—the gardens, the fields, all the life of Haiti for a major exhibit at the Pan American Union during his official visit as the guest of Eisenhower in 1954."

One of her subjects was Monsieur Cadet Jeremie, her husband's stepfather and then chief justice of the Haitian Supreme Court. Jones's oil portrait hangs on her living-room wall. It shows a wise-looking old man with a gray beard and beautiful long fingers, dressed in a dark suit with a white vest, reading and surrounded by books.

"He wrote three books. That's the balcony of his house, with the beautiful countryside behind. Every morning Pére Jeremy would come out full dress and walk forty-some steps or more to the church. Then he would return and sit on the terrace. There would be piles of money in front of him—he was quite wealthy—and a line of people coming to the house, I can't tell you how long a line, and he would give each one what they needed for the day. They loved him, he was like a priest. He was a perfect gentleman, always wore that clean white shirt and the suitcoat with cufflinks. The streets are named for him downtown, and a park. I can still see him today."

It was a whole new world to explore, which Jones did every summer through 1969 and periodically since. There were the lush countryside, the colorful garments, the voodoo dancers. "To see those black women selling chickens in the marketplace! And the cleverness of them, I mean they're smart!" Pointing to a painting of a mountainside home overlooking the Caribbean and the capital of Port-au-Prince, she adds reverently: "There's the view from my studio."

As Jones fell "increasingly in love with Haiti and its people," her artistic style took on a fluid energy compatible with the vitality of the life around her. Her biographer, Tritobia Hayes Benjamin, notes that—

as Jones had discarded modernism for Impressionism—her Haitian period went "in favor of an expressive, colorful, hard-edge style that
fused abstraction, decorative patterns and naturalism."

"Haiti never cut its ties with Mother Africa," Jones has said. "Many
of my works with an African theme and African motifs were actually
created in Haiti. Some of my most creative compositions, for which I
researched African icons, patterns, masks and sculptures were actually
done in my Haitian studio."

In the spring of 1970, Jones received a grant from Howard University to tour eleven African countries. Asked by the U.S. Information
Agency to lecture about African-American art, she became a kind of
cultural ambassador. "My husband met me halfway on the trip, we
called it our second honeymoon. I was able to see our ancestral arts
in their original settings as well as in museums and galleries. I met the
artists, and got quite a few young ones to come over to Howard, where
they got degrees. And I painted as I went."

The wonderful thing about being an artist, Loïs Jones has said, is
that there is no end to creative expression. The pieces from her 1970s
"African period" made a full circle—back to her studies of sculpture,
her earliest artistic endeavors in fabrics, and her first oil painting, *The
Ascent of Ethiopia*, done precisely forty years before. *Magic of Nigeria*
uses textile designs as a backdrop for a ram's head and two Ibo masks.
Moon Masque combines motifs from several African regions—the
Congo's Kwele mask at its centerpiece, overlaid against a pattern from
Ethiopian fabric. Western portraiture and the geometric contours of
African textiles mesh in *Ubi Girl from Tai Region*. In each painting,
the color schemes are the most stunning of Jones's career. They were
exhibited at the Second World Black and African Festival of Arts and
Culture in Lagos, Nigeria, in 1972, and again as part of a showing of
Jones's work at the Boston Museum of Fine Arts a year later (its first
solo retrospective for a black artist).

Her husband lived long enough to see Jones be one of ten artists
honored by President Carter at a 1980 national conference of artists.
After Pierre's death in 1982, Jones had his body returned to Haiti for
burial near his family's estate. Her regular visits continued for four
more years, until a coup ousted Jean Claude ("Baby Doc") Duvalier.
Then, with the 1987 mass exodus of the Haitian "boat people" seeking
sanctuary in America, Jones captured the tragedy in her *Haiti Demain?
(Haiti Tomorrow?)*. The painting, all in jagged shapes and bold, sharp
colors, shows a woman gazing starkly at a child in her arms as more
emaciated children stand peering up at them. Behind them falls a rain
of Haitian currency. "The rich Haitians," Jones says sadly, "care nothing about the poor people."

Shortly before he died, Pierre had advised his wife to consider returning to the Impressionist style. In 1989, when she returned to France for a reunion with Céline Tabari, she did so. Infusing Haiti and Africa, writes biographer Benjamin, "the tonalities of the same panoramic views are deeper, each color mass holds its own yet relates harmoniously to every other mass, and brush strokes, clearly visible in previous works, are economized, revealing few patches or strokes of color."

The rush of travel—Haiti in May, Paris in June, the Vineyard in July—proved too much. On her eighty-fourth birthday, Jones suffered a heart attack and underwent triple bypass surgery. Then she went right back to work. In January 1990, seventy-six of her works—her first major retrospective in almost twenty years—went on display at Washington's Meridian International Center. More than 700 friends, colleagues, and students from across America came to the unveiling. "The World of Loïs Mailou Jones" proved so popular that the exhibit toured America for four years; she was on hand for every opening.

"The Clintons seem to enjoy having me around," she is saying, looking at a photograph of herself talking with the President and the First Lady. "When the president of France was coming to a state luncheon at the White House, they invited me. It happened to fall on the same day that I was to take a plane to Florida to open the exhibit of one my protégés from Haiti, so the two things collided. But President Clinton reminded me, 'You wanted to give the president of France your original painting of *Jardin de Luxembourg*. So we will arrange for you to present it to him before the luncheon and then you can still get out to the airport.'

"We had it on a pedestal and draped, his wife stood near it. Then the procession started coming in the main doors, and I was standing with the painting of course. They all stopped before it, and I made my presentation. I have a picture of him leaning down kissing me—the president of France—so cute!"

Our afternoon together is drawing to a close, but Loïs Jones cannot resist one more walking tour. At the far corner of the first floor is her husband "Pierre's room. . . . That's a piece of his work in black-and-white; he did all the posters for the National Health Organization downtown. If you go back there to that statue, that's when Pierre was an illustrator for the field of natural history. Just look at the bugs! The detail! He was a genius."

The house seems to resound with the multifaceted hues of Paris, Martha's Vineyard, Haiti, Africa. I think of what Edmund Barry Gaither, curator of the Museum of the National Center of Afro-American Artists in Boston, said of Loïs Jones: "Every lover of the creative spirit in the visual arts should know her oeuvre, as well as the sweep of her triumphant life, stretching over virtually the whole of this century."

She stands beside a watercolor that not long ago carried a price of $1,500; today, she is asking between $40,000 and $50,000. "But I love them, I don't really like to sell them," Jones says. "I'm making my will now and going over titles—hundreds, hundreds, and good paintings! I mean, I'm amazed. What I would like is for many of them to go in museums or other places where people can see them, not in someone's dining room somewhere. Do you have any suggestions?"

We are seated again at the big table. There is a box of mail at her feet. "All these people saying, Where have you been? I'm getting hundreds of letters, I try to answer as many as I can. And the phone rings, people calling for interviews, or I'm running up to New York where I've had to speak several times. And when I start to talk, I talk—as you've learned."

A pause, and Loïs Jones's expression grows pensive. "It really was sort of a double handicap, to be not only a woman artist but a black woman. I had to fight that. They think you can cook well and wash dishes, and that's about it. But I loved my students. My life was really with them, for them. And all the places I went traveling, the people I met! It's been a very long life, a hard life, but I've loved every minute of it."

Then she offers her demure smile once more and adds: "At ninety, I arrived. And I will be painting until the last day."

"For me a painting should have three things: universality, clarity, and strength. Universality so that it may be understood by all men. Clarity and strength so that it may be aesthetically good. . . . It is more important that an artist study life than study the technique of painting exclusively. Technique will come with the desire to make oneself understood. It is more important for the artist to develop a philosophy and clarity of thought. My pictures express my life and experience. I paint the things I know about and the things I have experienced. The things I have experienced extend into my national, racial and class group. So I paint the American scene."

—JACOB LAWRENCE

Like Loïs Jones, Jacob Lawrence has been not only a painter but a teacher. Like Jones, he was drawn to Haiti—in the historical personage of the revolutionary Toussaint L'Ouverture. As with Jones, an extended trip to Africa in his later years found poignant expression in his work. Lawrence, too, was an iconoclast in all aesthetic trends of the time. Both received early encouragement from philosopher Alain Locke. Both created out of their own experiences, wherever the Fates took them. Both use color and shape brilliantly, and symbolically. And each in their own way believes in magic—as revealed through the power of the human spirit.

Unlike Jones, Lawrence had achieved success at an early age. In 1941, at only twenty-four, he became one of the first black artists ever to be represented by a New York gallery. By the time he was thirty, Lawrence was widely regarded as the country's leading African-American painter. The Whitney Museum held a major retrospective in 1974 that toured nationally and, in 1983, Lawrence was elected to the American Academy of Arts and Letters.

He was known as a "Social Realist," using narrative and serial imagery to depict the stories of Frederick Douglass, Harriet Tubman, the civil rights movement, and much more. His chosen subjects were, as one critic wrote in the mid-1950s, "a testament, an expression of his belief in man's continuing strength and will to achieve and preserve freedom." Or, as another critic put it, Lawrence emphasized a moral vision, "a man of the people, the world, [who] revels in the dynamics of human interaction."

It was August of 1996, shortly before Jacob Lawrence's seventy-ninth birthday, when I made the long drive from Boston into the pines and rolling hills of south-central Maine. He had been living in Seattle for twenty-five years, but was one of six resident artists teaching that summer at the Skowhegan School of Painting and Sculpture. Outside the old mill town, off Old Schoolhouse Road, a dirt road wound downhill toward a series of wooden cabins. On the back porch of Murch Cottage, Lawrence was sitting at a picnic table and watching the fish jump in Lake Wesserunsett.

A short, powerfully built man with close-cropped whitish hair and a thin mustache, he was wearing a blue knit-shirt and light-blue jeans. Accompanying his quiet, gracious demeanor, there was a courtly dignity about him. The eyes were of someone who had seen much. Using a cane required because of his arthritis, he moved slowly into the kitchen to get a pack of cigarettes. Jacob Lawrence lit a Lucky Strike and settled back onto the picnic bench.

"My mother's mother was born in slavery," he said, "I think she was about ten when the Civil War ended. So the people I later represented in my work, like Harriet Tubman and Frederick Douglass, were always close to us, almost a part of our daily life. These people became symbols, bravery against all odds. Harriet Tubman was a woman who, by academic standards, was illiterate. Yet she had the wisdom or the brilliance to free over 300 slaves just prior to the Civil War—moving through the woods, following the North Star. In fact, the black woman in general—the ones who are never written about—is a very powerful symbol which has held us together."

Lawrence's own mother exemplified what he was talking about. Jacob was born in New Jersey on September 7, 1917. When his parents separated, his mother was left struggling to support three children as a domestic. After spending his early years in a Pennsylvania coal town and a Philadelphia ghetto, Lawrence was placed in a foster home. His mother went alone to New York seeking better wages. In 1930, her children came to join her in Harlem. There, at thirteen, a new world opened up that would come to dominate Lawrence's early paintings.

"I've oftentimes been asked, where did my social awareness or conscience come from? Well, out of the Harlem community, because that's all I had to draw upon. The rhythm and geometry of the fire escapes, the grated windows. The tenements and roaches and people begging on the streets and some committing suicide." Lawrence swept a hand out across the Maine lake and continued: "Maybe if I had grown up in an atmosphere like this one, it would have been landscape."

After a pause, he went on: "You see, many of the shops in Harlem then did not hire blacks. The proprietors were people from outside the commmunity, yet they were making a living off the community. An ad would appear in the paper: 'Girls Wanted,' and the next morning that sidewalk would be crowded with girls from downtown somewhere. It was almost like blacks needn't apply. Resentment was easy, because people were going through the Great Depression and dissatisfied with their lives."

Still, amid the hard-knocks everyday life of people trying to make ends meet, there existed something else, something Lawrence calls "an essence. . . . Many of the people who inspired me, I never knew their names. Everywhere in Harlem, there were these streetcorner orators. They gave very passionate speeches—about slavery and how Toussaint L'Ouverture overthrew the French in Haiti, saying, Be ready to give up your life as John Brown did. Probably many of the things they said were romanticized or not true, but it was the passion and vitality and energy which they gave. Marcus Garvey [the black nationalist leader] had been deported, but many of his followers were still around. They would carry swords and give parades. Then the labor leaders, the Communists and the Socialists, saying *that* was the way of salvation. There was such an outpouring of everything then. A young person like myself, you just drank this in, the drama of it. You didn't bother about dates or about detail. These were symbols of spirit—for a minority living in a majority society."

There were other seminal influences, such as the Abyssinian Baptist

Church where Reverend Adam Clayton Powell, Sr., held forth. "I can remember some of his very dramatic sermons, one of his famous ones was called the 'Dry Bones Sermon.' " Then there was the way the Harlemites graced their living spaces. "They would use all sorts of colors to decorate their apartments, inexpensive throw rugs with bright patterns, like a Matisse painting. My mother used to weave and she liked color, more or less again to alleviate the drab existence. I got ideas from all of this."

Lawrence took to walking the sixty-some blocks from his home to the Metropolitan Museum of Art, where he would spend hours gazing at the Renaissance masters. At Utopia House, a day-care center where Lawrence's mother enrolled him after his day at Frederick Douglass Junior High School, the arts program was directed by Charles Alston. A well-known black artist, Alston took the young man under his wing. "It would [have been] a mistake to try to teach Jake," Alston would say years later. "He was teaching himself, finding his own way. All he needed was encouragement and technical information."

Lawrence dropped out of high school after two years, holding down odd jobs to help support his family. When Alston moved on to the Harlem Art Workshop, under the sponsorship of the Works Progress Administration (WPA), Lawrence came along with him. He used poster paint, a water medium, and egg tempera because he liked its translucency and ease of application. "Besides, I could buy a jar with a dime," he remembers. Initially, Lawrence set up shop alongside Romare Bearden. Later he worked in the studio of a sculptor, Henry Bannarn, where he paid two dollars a week in rent. The place was called "The 306 Group," after its 306 West 141st Street address, and it became a rendezvous for Harlem's arts community.

"So many different kinds of people! I met Ralph Ellison here when he first came up from the South, carrying his trumpet. Richard Wright stopped by on his way to France. People from the theater like Leigh Whipper, who was well known on Broadway in black roles. I'd hear them all talk about their craft, how closely the arts were related. I couldn't participate in the conversation because I didn't have the experience. But these were my early mentors. The writer Claude McKay in particular loved the work I was doing. He was much older, but we became good friends. When he was dying, it must have been in the late '40s or early '50s, he asked if I would be one of his pallbearers."

In one of his strongest formative experiences, Lawrence estimates he was about sixteen when he encountered "Professor" Seyfert. As Romare Bearden and Harry Henderson described the moment in their 1972 book, *Six Black Masters of American Art*: "One day, leaving the YMCA where he liked to shoot pool, Jake stopped at the door of a crowded meeting room. The speaker, a slender erect man, said Black people were never going to get anywhere until they knew their own history and took pride in it. Jake edged into the room. The speaker described the achievements of Black men in Africa, the golden city of Timbuktu, African use of iron when most of Europe was ignorant of it, the elegant bronze casting required to create the superb art treasures of Benin in Nigeria. . . . He believed that through their pictures, [Harlem artists] could show Black people their history and inspire them."

Lawrence smiled when I brought up Seyfert's name and elaborated: "He wasn't really a professor, but everybody called him that. I think he was a carpenter by trade, and must have been in his sixties. One of his projects was to call a few of the black artists together—I was one of the very young ones—attempting to inspire them to use these symbols. Seyfert was an exciting man, he helped to give us something that we needed at the time." When Seyfert arranged for the Harlem artists to view a show of West African sculpture at the Museum of Modern Art, "it made a great impression on me. I became fascinated by the African approach to form."

In the midst of the Great Depression, Lawrence joined the Civilian Conservation Corps and spent about six months "working on a dam in upstate New York. I learned the feel of a lot of things—of how it feels to shovel dirt up above your shoulders. Like any experience, it had things in it I could use for painting. FDR really saved the country through establishing these programs. He didn't have to include the arts, but he had the foresight to realize they were very important to the quality of life."

Indeed, without the WPA's Federal Arts Project, Lawrence doubts he would ever have continued as an artist. The times were simply too hard, money too scarce. But Augusta Savage, a well-known sculptor who maintained a basement studio in a Harlem tenement not far from Lawrence's home, insisted "that I should be on what we called the Project. That is, I was to be paid for my work. Augusta Savage plays a very important role in my life. She first took me downtown to the Project's hiring office in 1936, but they said I was too young. Then I completely forgot about it, but she did not. When I turned twenty-one in 1938, she brought me over to show them my work again. I was signed up and got paid $23.86 a week. That was a tremendous salary in those days, when you think that taking a bus cost a nickel and a pair of shoes was $3-something and a man's suit $22.50."

So, under the WPA's auspices, began Lawrence's first epic works. He drew upon the many sources that had crossed his path—the heroic African-American narratives, the Renaissance masters, the African sculptures, the Mexican muralists Rivera and Orozco. "I was influenced by the funnies, too—the old Katzenjammer Kids and Maggie and Jigs cartoon strips—and also by films like *The Blue Angel*. So the way I thought to tell the story of a person's life was through a series of panels, a kind of documentary, and a bit like the comics and the cinema."

His first subject was *Toussaint L'Ouverture*, a series of forty-one paintings each describing an episode in the fight by the Haitian slave to overthrow the French colonialists, which resulted in the founding of the first black Western republic in 1804. Lawrence spent hours studying Toussaint's life at Harlem's Schomburg Center for Research in Black Culture. In describing his admiration for Toussaint, Lawrence said at the time: "It's the same thing [Frederick] Douglass meant when he said, 'Judge me not by the heights to which I have risen but by the depths from which I have come.' " When the *Toussaint* series was exhibited in a special room at the Baltimore Museum in 1939, a *Baltimore Sun* review described it as "charged with feeling and movement . . . full of swift, racing vigor." Jacob Lawrence was on his way.

"If at times my productions do not express the conventionally beautiful, there is always an effort to express the universal beauty of man's continuous struggle to lift his social position and to add dimension to his spiritual being."

—JACOB LAWRENCE

In the years between 1938 and 1942, Lawrence completed four more historical series: *Frederick Douglass, Harriet Tubman, The Migration of the Negro,* and *John Brown.* "We have a tremendous history," he told me, "and I'm not just talking about the black, but the American people. This is part of that history. It's all one story. Exploring the American experience is a beautiful thing."

At the time, Lawrence had said of his style: "When the subjects are strong, I believe simplicity is the best way of treating them." The many narrative panels with their dramatic color schemes conveyed powerful emotion. Each panel is captioned as the story unfolds, with the necessity of the tale determining the number of tableaux (thirty-three with Douglass, thirty-one with Tubman, sixty in the migration series). They utilized a new water-based medium, casein tempera, about which Lawrence had learned through research and experimentation. "I was getting very inexpensive poster paint and working on brown wrapping paper before," Lawrence remembered.

Midway through his historical works, a friend arranged a meeting with the famed Mexican muralist, José Clemente Orozco. As for his friend Bearden, the dramatic social content and abstract forms of

Orozco had been a primary inspiration for Lawrence's early work. The visit took place at the Museum of Modern Art, where Orozco was painting a large fresco called *Dive Bomber and Tank.*

Lawrence has said: "It was around lunchtime and nobody was there. Orozco was working inside an enclosure, a very quiet man. He only had one arm. I'd been taught that you do a small version of what the work is going to look like—you know, a study. But Orozco took out a piece of cardboard, the kind you get with men's shirts from the laundry. And it had just a few vague chicken scratches on it. That was his study for the work. He told me, 'That's all I need.' It was a lesson he taught me. The point is that he was very spontaneous, very direct. Which is even more incredible because, with fresco, if you make a mistake, you have to dig out the plaster and start all over again. When I was leaving, I asked if I could do anything for him, I admired him so much. He said, yeah, he'd like to have a bag with cherries. So I went out to the street and brought a bag back to him. It was my little gift."

In the *Migration* series, which Lawrence completed after receiving in 1940 the first of three consecutive Rosenwald Foundation Fellowships, the intentionally distorted figures are more purposeful and the angles more intense. Here he captured the great wave of African-Americans who began leaving the South not long after the turn of the century, as his own parents had. "I had never been south until after I did the series," Lawrence explained, "but growing up, all my friends were from the same background. Before I knew the word migration, I knew another family had arrived because my mother would talk about it. People would give old clothing to help get the new migrants settled, or coal for heat. The migration was all around me."

Professor Alain Locke had been following Lawrence's career closely. They had first met at the 306 Studio. Locke reproduced a number of panels from the *Toussaint L'Ouverture* series in his book *The Negro in Art.* Now Locke brought the *Migration* series to the attention of New York's Downtown Gallery.

"Locke helped many people like myself," Lawrence recalled. "By some, he was considered too soft, but artists my age thought very highly of him. He wrote about us, lectured about us. He brought us to the stage where we could be recognized by the establishment. He encouraged us to probe and to be proud of the African heritage. You must have dignity, he said, because this was the image you were projecting to the world."

When the Downtown Gallery went on to open the first large-scale exhibit of African-American artists—including Tanner, Alston, Bearden and Lawrence—the Museum of Modern Art and Washington's

Phillips Memorial Gallery competed to buy Lawrence's *Migration* series. (Eventually, they agreed to divide it.)

Twenty-six of the *Migration* panels were also reproduced in color in the November 1941 issue of *Fortune* magazine, accompanied by an article by Locke. The magazine wrote: "Jacob Lawrence [is] a young Negro artist whose work promises to earn for him the same high recognition accorded to Paul Robeson, Marian Anderson, W. C. Handy, and other talented members of his race. His use of harsh primary colors and his extreme simplicity of artistic statement have extraordinary force." As America entered the Second World War, young Lawrence was receiving national acclaim.

In July of 1941, Lawrence had married Gwendolyn Knight, a beautiful young artist from Barbados. They first met when he was in his early teens and Knight was a student at Augusta Savage's workshop down the street from his home. Later, she had studied at Howard University under Loïs Jones. "Gwen's a romantic," Lawrence says admiringly. "She has some of the feelings in her paintings, I think, like Renoir. It's very luminous when she's working in oil, very spontaneous."

Soon after their marriage, Lawrence embarked on his twenty-two-panel *John Brown* series. His portrayal of the abolitionist leader, who believed it was his divine mission to rid America of slavery, contained some of the most powerful and graphic imagery of Lawrence's career. While John Brown had been a subject for many painters, this marked the first time a black artist depicted him. The first panel showed blood flowing from a crucified Christ. The last panel showed a wan, black-clad figure with a long white beard hanging from a rope against a stark background. It is captioned: "John Brown was found 'Guilty of treason and murder in the 1st degree' and was hanged in Charles Town, Virginia, on December 2, 1859."

Lawrence's biographer, Ellen Harkins Wheat, writes: "The *John Brown* series represents the apogee of Lawrence's dramatic abilities. Through economy of means—large flat forms, pure colors, and extreme reduction of details—expression is heightened. Lawrence's concern here is the universality of the theme in which a man lays down his life in a struggle for freedom and justice."

"All over the North men were singing the John Brown song. His body was in the dust, but his soul was marching on. His defeat was already assuming the form and pressure of victory, and his death was giving new life and power to the principles of justice and liberty. . . . What he had lost by the sword he had more than gained by the truth."
—FREDERICK DOUGLASS

*"And then we saw the lightning, and that was the guns; and then
we heard the thunder, and that was the big guns; and then we heard
the rain falling, and that was the drops of blood falling; and when we
came to get in the crops, it was dead men that we reaped."*
                    —HARRIET TUBMAN, describing the Civil War's
                                        Battle of Fort Wagner.

On my second day with Jacob Lawrence, we began by talking about
his experiences in World War II. He had been drafted into the U.S.
Coast Guard, which was then part of the Navy, in the autumn of 1943.
The Atlantic weather patrol vessel to which he was assigned turned
out to be the first integrated American ship. The captain of the USS
Sea Cloud, Lieutenant Commander Carlton Skinner, had received permission to conduct what one newspaper called an "experiment to combat racial discrimination at sea."

"I went in as a steward mate," Lawrence said, "to which many of
the minorities were relegated. But Captain Skinner helped me get a
public relations rating, so I could do documentary pieces of Coast
Guard life. I painted for all but six of the twenty-five months I was in
the service. We all got along; it was really the best democracy I'd ever
known. I still maintain contact with Captain Skinner."

Most of Lawrence's Coast Guard paintings disappeared after being
put into the service's archives, although a few went on display in October 1944 at the Museum of Modern Art. Of them, Lawrence had
commented at the time:

"It's the little things that are big. A man may never see combat, but
he can be a very important person. The man at the guns, there's glam-
our there. Men dying, being shot, they're the heroes. But the man
bringing up supplies is important too. Take the cook. He just cooks,
day in and day out. He never hears a gun fired except in practice. He's
way down below, cooking. Now the coxswain, or the gunner's mate,
the man at the wheel, people admire what they do. But the cook—the
cooks may not like my style of painting. But they appreciate the fact
I'm painting a *cook*."

After some eight months aboard Skinner's ship, Lawrence got reas-
signed to a troop transport carrier where Captain J. S. Rosenthal—his
commanding officer back in boot camp—had asked for him as his
combat artist. Aboard the USS *General Wilds P. Richardson*, Lawrence
first saw the world—making the rounds to England, Italy, Egypt and
India as the war wound to a close in 1945.

"I had been sheltered, relatively speaking. And the troop transport
was a pretty harrowing experience, though not physically. We went
over with 5,000 troops and we came back a hospital ship—all kinds

of cases, mental and physical disabilities. I tried to capture some of this in my *War* series later. In approaching the whole subject, I sought the essence of war through the feeling and emotions felt by the individual, whether fighter or civilian. A wife or mother getting a letter from overseas. The next of kin receiving notice of a casualty. The futility men feel when they're at sea or down inside a foxhole just waiting, not knowing what part they're playing in a much broader and gigantic plan."

The fourteen-paneled *War* series, unveiled at New York's Downtown Gallery in December 1947, was called "by far his best work yet" by *Time* magazine. Lawrence then headed into the Deep South for *Fortune*, which had commissioned ten paintings of postwar social conditions. When Jackie Robinson broke the color barrier in major league baseball that same year, Lawrence observed the historic moment with a work called *Strike*. The six illustrations he did for Langston Hughes's latest work of poetry, *One-Way Ticket*, marked his entry into the book world.

Then suddenly, in October 1949, Lawrence suffered a breakdown and checked himself into Hillside, a psychiatric hospital in Queens. "Like many of the men who'd been in the service, I guess the entire experience was a shock—and I think we didn't realize it. I was suffering from depression more than anything else. I was in Hillside getting treatment for almost a year. It wasn't a place where you found a lot of mad people running around; there were no guards or anything like that, and many of the patients were very knowledgeable and intelligent. It was a very deep experience, I think one of the most important periods of my life."

Indeed, as he always did, Lawrence used his time on the psychiatric ward to create. His *Hospital* series, first shown soon after his discharge in the summer of 1950, offers an introspective and emotional power in the patients of *Depression* and the frenzied activity of *In the Garden*. As Lawrence said later in considering these in the broader context of his work, "It still says struggle, doesn't it?"

Upon his recovery, Lawrence went back to the Harlem of his youth in disquietingly poignant paintings like *Slums* and *Photographer's Shop*. Next came a *Theater* series, harkening back to the nights when someone from the 306 Studio would take the teenaged Lawrence over to the Apollo Theater. "That was a wonderful experience: the big bands, the chorus girls. Especially the comedians and the stories they would tell. All very comical, but below that was a great deal of pathos, talking about the neighborhood and the people. What made the Apollo such a popular place was, it was a real community. It reflected everything we were going through and had gone through."

There followed another epic series in the mid-1950s—*Struggle: From the History of the American People*. Its thirty panels covered the period from the Revolutionary War through the first covered wagons headed west. "Years ago," Lawrence said then, "I was just interested in expressing the Negro in American life, but a larger concern, an expression of humanity and of America, developed. . . . The struggle that we go through as human beings enables us . . . to take on further dimension."

His continuing figural emphasis bucked the vogue of Abstract Expressionism. A no-holds-barred speech that Lawrence gave at the time to a group of artists and students provided this unequivocal explanation: "Maybe . . . humanity to you has been reduced to the sterility of the line, the cube, the circle, and the square; devoid of all feeling, cold and highly esoteric. If this is so, I can well understand why you cannot portray the true America. It is because you have lost all feeling for man. And the art of those that are devoid of feeling themselves cannot reflect the vital, strong, and pulsating beat that has always been humanity. And your work shall remain without depth for as long as you can only see and respect the beauty of the cube, and not see and respect the beauty of man—every man."

In 1955, Lawrence began teaching design and figure drawing at Pratt Institute, where he was eventually appointed a full professor. Before he accepted a permanent position at the University of Washington in Seattle in 1971, he also instructed at Brandeis University and the New School for Social Research. Lawrence retired as a full-time teacher in 1984. "I miss the students," he says. "My teaching has contributed so much to my own growth and development."

During the early 1960s, Lawrence was invited to Africa to show and discuss his work. "I became so excited then by all the new visual forms I found in Nigeria—unusual color combinations—textures, shapes, and the dramatic effect of light—that I felt an overwhelming desire to come back as soon as possible. . . ." He and his wife returned to West Africa in April 1964 and spent eight months there, Lawrence's eight paintings and several drawings echoing the teeming streets and marketplaces.

All through that decade, Lawrence's main concentration was the civil rights movement. He held back nothing. There were studies of battles between rioters and police. There was *Invisible Man among the Scholars*, raising the question of whether a black person could find a real education in America. In *The Ordeal of Alice*, the dress and stockings of a little black girl seeking to enter a Southern school are covered with seven piercing arrows. Grotesque and gleeful figures in various shades dance around her agony. Flowers are at her feet.

"People asked me, why do you want to paint *The Ordeal of Alice*?

Well, I think it's beautiful that people are able to go through this. People will ask, why do you want to do riots? I don't do them for sensationalism, I do them for our capacity to survive. Some terrible things went on during the civil rights period. But it was also a heroic time, part of the American struggle which I think paradoxically has made us a great country, too. I don't mean great only in a power sense, but that we continue to try to elevate our conscience, that we have this capacity to survive as a people.

"I've been asked to consider doing a series of paintings on Malcolm X," he continued. "But I couldn't do it. He was a monument, he built a monument and I don't consider myself that kind of a painter. I'd feel false, like I was capitalizing on something."

After moving to the Pacific Northwest, Lawrence began working on a series that still preoccupies him, called the *Builders*. Its focus is on manual labor, and he keeps a set of hand tools as props in his Seattle studio. "I can hardly drive a nail myself," Lawrence says with a laugh, "but I grew up in Harlem around three brothers about my age who were cabinet makers. After the 306 Studio closed down, they established their workshop there. They worked with tools that were aesthetically beautiful, like sculpture. I never realized at the time that this would become a major theme of my work. But I always say that I think the tool is an extension. The hand is a beautiful tool—its dexterity and what we do with it, the positions it takes."

In 1974, his *Builders-Family*—a black couple and their two children passing by several carpenters framing a house—became the poster for a one-man show presenting more than 160 of Lawrence's paintings. It began at the Whitney and moved on to five other cities. Spencer Moseley, a Seattle artist who came to the opening there, said afterwards: "It was the only exhibition I've ever attended where the works brought tears to the eyes of those who viewed the paintings."

Jacob Lawrence has never stopped. In recent years, he completed six murals, including *Games* for Seattle's Kingdome Stadium and *Exploration* for Howard University; an eight-tableaux series, *Hiroshima*; and many more *Builders* works. Now he is completing a New York theme as part of the renovation of Times Square. He is an artist whose work has kept evolving and is beyond labeling—a man with no formal training who has continued to paint at a small easel in basic water-soluble media and vibrant colors, as the old masters had since time immemorial.

Now, as the mid-day sun cut a swath through the pines along the lake, his wife Gwen joined us. The night before, she had given a talk to the sixty-five summer students at the Skowhegan School about the WPA programs during the Depression. "We talked about the freedom, and the worth of it in terms of making artists more secure," she said. "Right now the students here are doing what they call installations. One young man dug a big hole in the ground and stood there for six hours in the sun with a bowl of ice cream just out of reach. That was his performance piece."

Her husband laughed and shook his head. "Well, maybe they're reflecting the world we live in. There is so much today that gets away from the spirit of life. You see it in many of the young people. They're trying to make discoveries, but I guess they would say the space and form of this chair I'm sitting in is a discovery. Well, it's already there. They generally don't notice the lake or its relationship to the sky or the shore. Maybe people like me are considered old hat, but I think this is important. But where are the young people going to go? There's this tremendous frustration—because they have so little to relate to anymore that's healthy."

Lawrence lit a cigarette and thought for a moment. Finally he said: "Life is a mystery. Sometimes I think about this Blind Tom [Bethune], who was born a slave. He couldn't see, he couldn't read music, but he'd hear a piece once and he could play it. I believe in phenomena, things you can't explain. Sometimes, for no reason I can think of, these people who turn out to look like somebody I've known will appear in my paintings. I didn't start out to do them. I don't believe that people ever die, they live through others."

What would Jacob Lawrence like his own legacy to be? He contemplated the question for a time, and said: "Well, having contributed something, in the sense that this is the way one person saw things. So that it stimulates and provokes someone who comes in contact with my work, it creates an interest and adds some quality to their lives. I think that's it. That's the way I'd like to be remembered."

The forerunner of them all was Henry Ossawa Tanner. He was the painter who helped Meta Fuller through her first difficult days in Paris; whom Loïs Jones "never had the glory to meet . . . only the inspiration"; of whom Romare Bearden said, "I wouldn't be where I am today if Tanner had not paved the way."

Dr. Rae Alexander-Minter, the woman to whom Bearden made that comment, is the grand-niece of Henry Tanner. In New Brunswick, New Jersey, where she directs the Paul Robeson Cultural Center on the Rutgers University campus, she is discussing Tanner's renowned early works such as *The Banjo Lesson* and *The Thankful Poor*. Music plays in the background. It is the voice of Paul Robeson singing the spirituals.

Tanner, the son of a Baptist minister, had focused on religious subjects for most of his career. He spent most of his adult life in Paris, an expatriate who believed race a "ghetto of isolation and neglect" and largely removed himself from championing any cause but art. Yet, as his son Jesse said, "A Tanner can do more than give you enjoyment, it can come to your rescue, it can reaffirm your confidence in man and his destiny, it can help you surmount your difficulties or console you in distress."

In becoming the first internationally known black artist, Tanner was the pathbreaker. His own descendants, as Rae Alexander-Minter says, took the torch he lit and carried it far into the future. "Mine is an extraordinary family," she says reverentially. "Tanner's sister Hallie became the first woman, regardless of race, to pass the medical boards to become a doctor in 1891. Booker T. Washington walked her to take the boards in Montgomery, Alabama, and gave Hallie her first job as a physician for his Tuskegee Institute. Another sister, my grandmother Mary Louise, married the first black person to graduate from the University of Pennsylvania Law School. And one of Mary's daughters, my mother Sadie, became the second black woman in America to receive a Ph.D., and the first in economics. She then went on to be the first black woman to pass the bar and become an attorney in Pennsylvania; my father, Raymond Alexander, was the first black to become a judge of the highest court in Pennsylvania."

Alexander-Minter's parents had been champions of civil rights in Philadelphia. As a child, she remembers crowds of strangers gathered at night on the family's staircase and the parlor chairs, waiting to receive legal counsel. "These were primarily domestics who couldn't get off work until then, and if someone didn't have the money, my parents didn't charge them. They would work until two or three in the morning, and be in the office by eight."

She listens to the voice in the background singing: "And ol'man river, he just keeps rollin'along!" Alexander-Minter continues: "Paul Robeson was my grandfather's nephew by marriage. As a young man, he wanted to date my mother but when my father came along, that was that. But they all grew up around one another. I saw him once or twice at our home when I was a little girl."

Today, Alexander-Minter is planning an exhibition at Rutgers that will open the centennial celebration of Robeson's life in 1998. It is scheduled to move across the country, then on to Europe and South Africa. "It amazes me how many people still do not know who Robeson was," she is saying. "He is one of the towering figures of the century, but he hasn't been fully understood or appreciated. He was silenced for such a long time, we couldn't hear him, couldn't hear what he was trying to say. But he was prophetic. He was talking about a world that we are only now starting to realize we must become."

FOR FURTHER READING:

Tritobia Hayes Benjamin, *The Life and Art of Loïs Mailou Jones* (San Francisco: Pomegranate Artbooks, 1994).

Ellen Harkins Wheat, *Jacob Lawrence: American Painter* (Seattle: University of Washington Press, 1986).

All the World's Their Stage:
Paul Robeson and Ira Aldridge

"Had I been born in Africa, I would have belonged, I hope, to that family which sings and chants the glories and legends of the tribe. I would have liked in my mature years to have been a wise elder, for I worship wisdom and knowledge of the ways of men."

—PAUL ROBESON

"A child of the sun, black my countenance, yet I stand before you in the light of my soul."

—IRA ALDRIDGE

In the late 1920s, when Paul Robeson was living in London and preparing for his first portrayal of Shakespeare's Othello, he received a letter from a woman who resided in the city's West End. Amanda Ira Aldridge was writing to congratulate the young actor for a "magnificent performance" in the new musical *Show Boat*. Perhaps, she suggested, they might arrange to meet. She had a gift for Robeson— the earrings that her father had worn on stage when he made his own debut as Othello a century before.

Her father was Ira Aldridge, the first African-American actor to play roles reserved for whites, including Shakespeare's Macbeth, Shylock, and King Lear. For more than forty years, across the British Isles and Continental Europe and into the distant provinces of Russia, Aldridge brought these and many more memorable characters to an adoring public. He had received honors bestowed upon no other actor of his time.

Amanda Aldridge never knew her father, who died in 1867 when she was a year and a half old. But she had achieved considerable success herself, first as a concert contralto and, after severe laryngitis ended her singing career, as a composer and voice teacher. Now she would pass the Aldridge torch to Paul Robeson. Soon after the two met, she began teaching Robeson elocution as he set out to master the intricacies of Shakespeare.

The lives of Paul Robeson and Ira Aldridge, born ninety-one years apart, conjure a mysterious mirror image. Both were tall and handsome men. Both were the sons of East Coast ministers and lost their mothers at an early age. Both went on to become singers and activists as well as actors. Both studied Russian folklore and felt a deep affinity for the Russian people, for whom their performances engendered an unprecedented response. Both received worldwide acclaim, and possessed an uncompromising commitment to their art and to humanity. And both suffered deeply because of attitudes toward their race and, in Robeson's case, his politics.

A photograph of Robeson, discovered among Amanda Aldridge's effects after her death in 1956, is inscribed: "To Miss Aldridge—with many thanks for the fresh inspiration received from all the reports of [your] father's greatness. I realize that I can only carry on in the 'tradition of Aldridge.' Paul Robeson."

Paul Robeson, Jr., now in his late sixties, is seated at a corner table of a coffeeshop in midtown Manhattan. Though he is considerably thinner than his father was and walks with a slight limp, the resemblance remains striking. He has close-cropped hair and a warm smile. He is currently working on a biography of his father, tentatively titled *The Undiscovered Paul Robeson*. For several hours, we have been talking of fathers and sons, music and cultures, and much more.

Did your father, I ask, ever talk to you about Ira Aldridge? Robeson nodded affirmatively. "What dad discussed with Aldridge's daughter is how the experience of acting in Europe expanded the cultural vision. That is, the universal aspects of all cultures. In his time with Amanda Aldridge, it wasn't so much dad wondering what notes did he write on the script? That was sort of irrelevant. But what was in Aldridge's head? Not so that dad could imitate Ira Aldridge, but rather follow the same path in his own way, to seek those universal connections."

St. Petersburg, Russia, on the eve of the American Civil War: A hush descends over the audience as Ira Aldridge takes the stage as Othello. He stands over six feet tall, with broad shoulders and a muscular physique. Even before he speaks, an air of calm dignity seems to envelop him. Unlike many American actors of the nineteenth century, he does not stride onstage majestically—no picturesque poses or gestures, no artificially tragic gait. Every movement is deliberate, natural; the hands are as eloquent as the words. His voice is rich and sonorous, every syllable uttered with meaning, but his silences speak equally of the passion within him. It is the inner meaning that rivets the attention.

Aldridge delivers the lines of Othello in English, a foreign language that no one in the Russian audience understands. Yet through his char-

acterization, they grasp the universality of Shakespeare. By the final
scene, when Othello seeks revenge upon his wife Desdemona for her
betrayal of him, Aldridge's face contains every emotion—the strongest
doubts, the despairing sorrow, the hatred and anger, the most tender
love. As Desdemona succumbs to the Moor's dagger and offers a dying
whisper, and he throws himself at the foot of her bed and cries her
name, one critic described Aldridge's voice as sounding exactly like a
cello.

"Such is the power of his spirit," wrote the Russian historian M. P.
Pogodin, "that you surrender to him from the very first minute, you
understand what he says, you apprehend all that he feels, you listen,
it seems, to every beat of his heart . . . and deep in the heart of every
ecstatic spectator, sacred conscience is heard. . . . In my imagination I
saw the history of a whole people."

In Paul Robeson's notes, his son remembered, he referred to two European cultures which possess an affinity with African culture. One
was Spain, land of the Moors, ancestral home of Othello. The other
was Russia. The music of Mussorgsky which Robeson studied drew
from the Eurasian speech patterns and songs of the Russian peasantry;
Tartars, Mongols, and Africans all once passed along the southern silk
route through Uzbekistan and Turkestan. Then there was the poetry
of Alexander Pushkin. Pushkin's great-grandfather had been a captured
African who became part of the court of Peter the Great. In Pushkin's
rhythms, both Robeson and Aldridge found inspiration.

To prepare for his Othello, Robeson sought Shakespeare's nuances
by translating and comparing the English version to those of other
languages. Robeson was a gifted linguist, "fairly fluent in a dozen languages and functional in another dozen," according to his son. So
Robeson excavated some of Shakespeare's secrets from the Russian,
others from the French.

Paul Robeson, Jr.'s excitement intensified as he recalled his father's
painstaking effort. "Here you have this huge warrior who cut off people's heads. Yet with the French overtones, it's almost a caress when
Othello speaks of Desdemona. When he's describing the attack on Cy-
prus, there's German for that. If you want a touch of ironic humor,
try it in Yiddish. But Shakespeare wrote the play in the Elizabethan,
so let's take it back to the original. Then even further back, because
Shakespeare drew on Chaucer. As he went along, dad retranslated all
of this, matching lines, putting it all back together, finding the various
ways the poetry flowed."

The son paused momentarily, then continued: "When dad first
played the part in England in 1930, he got great reviews. But one very

perceptive reviewer said that Robeson's Othello was too tentative—as if he reflected the feeling of inferiority imposed upon Negroes in America. Othello is a king, working as a mercenary perhaps but certainly the opposite of inferior. Dad not only accepted that criticism but, to make this come alive in 1943 and '44, he carried it one step further in saying: Othello comes from an African culture that is the equal of Venetian culture. His crime, in killing Desdemona, is not simply one of passion. It's about the betrayal of his human dignity."

An All-American football player at Rutgers College in 1917, nearly thirty years later Robeson began rigorous workouts under the watchful eye of the physical trainer for Joe Louis and Louis Armstrong. Traditionally, actors had Othello give a sweeping bow from the waist when he first entered the court of Venice. Not Robeson.

"I'll never forget this," his son said. "He just glided across the stage at a rate fast enough so that the cape went out a little bit. It was almost like this human vehicle, not quite walking on water, but an extraordinary entrance. Then he came to an abrupt halt, inclined his head about fifteen degrees, and gave the line to the Duke: 'Most potent grave and reverend senior.' It's king to king."

At the finale, when in his realization that he must take his wife's life Othello appeals to the stars, Robeson's son recalled in a whisper: "He's talking to God, talking to his own soul."

The Ira Aldridge legacy bequeathed to Paul Robeson had its origins in West Africa. Aldridge, so the legend goes, was the grandson of a humanitarian Senegalese chief. When the chief ruled that prisoners of war from other tribes should be subject to exchange, rather than be offered for sale into slavery, his own tribesmen deposed and killed him. Only one son survived, rescued by an American missionary who brought him to the United States sometime during the late 1700s. The intent was that, after completing his education, he might return to his people as a Christian ruler. But Daniel Aldridge, as he came to be known, remained in America—a free black man who eventually became a Calvinist minister and presided over an all-black congregation at New York's Green Street Chapel.

His son Ira, born on July 24, 1807, was placed with his older brother in New York's African Free School, then an educational haven established by the city's Manumission [free slave] Society. Daniel Aldridge hoped that Ira would follow him into the ministry, but the boy began frequenting plays at a park where many leading British actors of the time performed. While still a teenager he joined the first black American drama group, founded in 1820 as the African Company and located in a ramshackle structure in what is now Greenwich Village. Its star attraction—and Aldridge's inspiration—was James Hewlett. He was a young waiter whose roots lay in the West Indies. The robes he wore as Shakespeare's Richard III were fashioned from discarded curtains. His performances quickly became so popular that a portion of the African Grove Theater was set aside for white audiences.

It was not long before the owners of New York's premier Park Theatre feared too much potential competition. The police ordered the African Company to close its doors. When the actors defied the edict, the authorities moved in. In a remarkable real-life drama, James Hewlett as Richard III concluded his last Shakespearean performance in America. A policeman interrupted one of his soliloquies to demand that Hewlett accompany him. "Fellow begone—I'm not at leisure," the actor replied. Several more officers ascended the stage to arrest him. "Where am I going?" Hewlett asked. "To the tower?"

As the entire cast was escorted into the nearby police station, King Richard suddenly became Macbeth, shouting:

> *"How now you black and secret*
> *Midnight hags—what are you about?"*

The actors, thrown together in a single cell, continued to plead their case in blank verse. Only as the long night ended did they accede never to play Shakespeare again. The African Company revived briefly but, according to Langston Hughes, "white hoodlums who came to laugh and jeer eventually forced the closing of the Negro playhouse." Its last performance was a drama about a black insurrection on a Bahamian island.

At this same time, a white actor named Edwin Forrest presented the first blackface portrayal of the Southern plantation Negro, mimicking the dress, dialect and gait that so came to amuse nineteenth-century American audiences. The genuine black performers were forced out to make way for the minstrel shows. James Hewlett left to try acting in London, where he soon disappeared without leaving a trace.

Ira Aldridge's talent had been recognized by Henry and James Wallack, British brothers who were among New York's most well-known Shakespearean actors and whom Ira assisted in carrying their wardrobe. At the age of seventeen, with scarcely any money, Aldridge secured passage as a steward on a ship carrying James Wallack to an engagement in Liverpool. There was, as Paul Robeson later wrote, "no place on our stages for one of the greatest actors in theatrical history."

By the fall of 1825, the young Aldridge obtained the lead in a London melodrama, *Revolt of Surinam or A Slave's Revenge*. Although England still persisted in exporting African slaves to its West Indian colonies, Aldridge's appearance coincided with a growing public outcry against the practice. The playbill called the melodrama "a most faithful portrait of the horrors that arise out of that dreadful traffic." In a tale not far removed from the legend surrounding his own heritage, Aldridge portrayed a noble, tragic African prince kidnapped and brought to the West Indies. As one newspaper put it, seeing the character of Oroonoko played by someone of African descent served to "awaken a trend of deep reflections."

Aldridge soon became known as "the African Roscius," after a renowned slave actor in ancient Rome, Quintus Roscius Gallus. He seemed preordained to stand as a symbol, and to break barriers. Still only eighteen, he married a white woman ten years his senior. Margaret Gill was described in one memoir as "an English lady of respectability and superior accomplishments" whom Aldridge met when he was invited to a private box after starring in a play called *The Slave*. The couple remained together until her death thirty-four years later.

Hostility toward Aldridge in the London press soon followed his wedding and forced his departure for the English provinces. Yet even in Liverpool, then the largest slave-trading center in the British Isles, in his debut as Othello in 1827 he was acclaimed alongside a white woman as his Desdemona. That same year, Haiti, which had become the first black Republic following Toussaint L'Ouverture's successful slave revolt against Napoleon, honored Aldridge with a commission in its Army.

There was a quality to Aldridge's art which transcended racial boundaries. He touched a chord in Irish peasants—considered the "inferior stock" of the British Isles and still beset by a famine that had cut their population in half only a decade before—who identified with his slave characters. Aldridge also began testing out his first white Shakespearean roles, notably as Richard III. And when he came to the Irish stage as Othello, the *Dublin Comet* said: "Away flew all our preconceived notions and prejudices. His performance through the whole play was so chaste, so judicious and so completely Shakespearean that we doubt we shall ever look upon the personation of Othello so entirely fulfilling all that we could imagine of the perfection of acting."

Still, the great halls of London's West End eluded Aldridge. The city's proslavery lobby was in the throes of its last battle to keep the practice from being abolished in the British colonies when he was finally permitted to appear as Othello at Covent Garden in 1833. His acting company had formerly been Edmund Kean's, who was considered the greatest Shakespearean actor of his time. Only sixteen days earlier, Kean had suddenly collapsed while portraying Othello on the same stage. It was his last performance; he died shortly thereafter.

So Aldridge's assuming of Kean's mantle was, in the eyes of many Londoners, doubly offensive. The city streets erupted in protest. Although Aldridge supporters distributed a handbill urging that talent hold sway over prejudice, a relatively empty house greeted him on opening night. Some of the unfavorable press reviews were blatantly racist; it was "impossible that Mr. Aldridge should fully comprehend the meaning and force or even the words he utters," said one journal. Ellen Tree, a well-known white actress playing his Desdemona, was urged not to allow herself to be further "pawed about by Mr. Henry Wallack's black servant."

The theater abruptly cancelled Aldridge's third performance. Nor did he appear in two other scheduled roles at Covent Garden. Indeed, he would never play there again; nor does his name appear in the elaborate two-volume history, *The Annals of Covent Garden Theatre*. For a time, he moved over to one of London's more important minor theaters with the help of the British actor who remained his benefactor, Henry Wallack. But the attacks against Aldridge continued. A large contingent of police marched into the neighborhood to keep order outside the theater.

Soon after Aldridge decided to depart London again, the British Parliament voted to end their slave trade forever. For the next nineteen years, accompanied by his wife, he continued to wander and work across the British Isles. He grew in acting stature and gathered such patrons as Sir Walter Scott and the Duke of Wellington. He also stirred controversy by raising the specter of slavery. Old playbills find him including among his Classic Entertainment such topics as *England, or the Negro Emancipation: The Slave's Gratitude*, and *Liberty and Equality, or the American Slave Market*. Often he performed the song *Jim Crow* on Spanish guitar.

Nor did Aldridge confine himself to the issue of his own people's plight. Shakeapeare's creation of the Jewish merchant Shylock in *The Merchant of Venice* had been written amid racial animosity that followed the trial and execution of a Jewish physician to Queen Elizabeth I. Ever since, customarily Shylock had been portrayed as a greedy and soulless individual. Aldridge presented a far more sympathetic character, proud and firm in his convictions. "In Shylock," one reviewer wrote, "he does not see particularly a Jew, but a human being in general, oppressed by the age-old hatred shown towards people like him, and expressing this feeling with wonderful power and truth." His appearance as Shylock coincided with English Jews' petitioning Parliament for expanded civil rights and an end to their own segregation. As he sought to raise consciousness, Aldridge came under fire from Shakespearean professors who charged him with being "in league with the Jews."

Frederick Douglass and other American abolitionists are known to have visited England during the long period of Aldridge's exile in the provinces. There is no record of any meetings between them, but Aldridge is known to have sent thousands of dollars back to America. His contributions were funneled into the Negro State Conventions that operated between 1830 and the Civil War's outbreak in 1861.

The long journey of Paul Robeson, which took him to many of the same locations as Aldridge and culminated with his own forced exile in America, began in Princeton, New Jersey, on April 9, 1898. His father had been born into slavery on a North Carolina plantation. At age fifteen, William Robeson escaped and made his way north on the Underground Railroad, serving as a Union laborer during the Civil War. After the war, he obtained an elementary school education. Earning his way through farm labor, he studied for the ministry at an all-black university outside Philadelphia. "Loyalty to one's convictions," Paul Robeson later wrote, "was the text of my father's life."

Reverend Robeson cultivated his son's deep and passionate speaking voice, coaching Paul in oratorical skills from an early age. It was within his father's A.M.E. Zion Church that Robeson first learned of two earlier legendary members, Harriet Tubman and Sojourner Truth, and about how Frederick Douglass printed his newspaper in the cellar of another of the denomination's churches. Here, too, Robeson first sang the spirituals in his father's choir. "The great, soaring gospels we love are merely sermons that are sung," he wrote in his autobiography, *Here I Stand*. Robeson traced his roots to the Ibo people of Nigeria. Years later, when he began studying the languages of West Africa, he "immediately found a kinship of rhythm and intonation with the negro-English dialect which I had heard spoken around me as a child." It was not an intellectual attraction, but a visceral recognition—one that came to permeate Robeson's singing and acting.

Robeson received an academic scholarship to Rutgers College, becoming the third African-American ever to attend. While barred from most social events, he excelled both scholastically (winning a Phi Beta Kappa key) and in four sports. Twice he was named an All-American end in the early days of college football. Honored as valedictorian of the Rutgers Class of 1919, in a speech titled "The New Idealism" Robeson expressed his vision of the post-World War I future. "We of the younger generation especially must feel a sacred call to that which lies before us. It is . . . the task of this new spirit to make national unity a reality, at whatever sacrifice, and to provide full opportunities for the development of everyone.''

In 1921, Robeson met and married a beautiful analytical chemist named Eslanda Goode. Robeson first entered the legal profession, becoming the third black graduate of Columbia Law School in 1923 and the first African-American to join one of New York's most prestigious law firms. Other horizons, however, were already beckoning. His son remembers it had much to do with the Harlem Renaissance, the unprecedented flowering of black artistic culture that took place during the 1920s.

"While dad was still in law school, he began going to the Harlem gatherings at the homes of James Weldon Johnson, J. Rosamond Johnson, and W. E. B. Du Bois. In the beginning he would sit and listen, asking questions, absorbing everything. These were the giants, men in their thirties all the way to their seventies, some of whom went back to Frederick Douglass's time. Dad loved to sing for people and they loved to hear him sing. And every once in a while he would speak up about something, and *they* would listen.''

Du Bois, who had been instrumental in the ascendancy of Meta Warrick Fuller, possessed an even stronger influence on Robeson. He had first learned of Du Bois during his student days—joining the NAACP that Du Bois helped organize and build, reading *The Crisis* magazine Du Bois edited, following Du Bois down Fifth Avenue in a civil rights protest.

Paul, Jr., recalled: "Dad always called him 'The Doctor.' It was like a student and a professor, even in private. I had the extraordinary experience of being with dad coming into a room where Du Bois was sitting. It was 1958, Du Bois was by then in his eighties. He was a very small man and I still see this image of dad, with his huge size, literally settling down on a cushion at Du Bois's feet. It was natural for Du Bois to accept this, and for dad to do it. He simply had infinite respect for him.''

Robeson had been drawn to the amateur stage while still in law school. He first sang in a professional summer production on a trip to London. Facing racial insults at his first job—in a time when black lawyers were yet a rarity—he resigned. Bearing a letter of introduction to Eugene O'Neill, who had seen one of his amateur performances, Robeson found himself cast as the lead in the playwright's new production, *All God's Chillun Got Wings*. The character, a black lawyer, is married to a white woman.

As happened to Aldridge a century earlier, Robeson's stage career stirred widespread controversy from the beginning. Even before the play opened, death threats came from the Ku Klux Klan. The Hearst newspapers assailed the play, and New York's mayor openly announced his opposition. So O'Neill cast Robeson simultaneously in *The Emperor Jones*, which opened right after the other production and received critical acclaim—with Robeson having learned both roles at once.

His rise, like that of Aldridge, was meteoric. When Robeson sang for O'Neill's theater group, the playwright and others were so transfixed that a concert was quickly arranged. By the spring of 1925, all of high-society New York came to the Greenwich Village Theatre to hear Robeson perform the spirituals he had learned in his father's church. It was the first all-spirituals concert in history. His bass-baritone voice, as one music critic described it, was one "in which deep bells ring." The following year, Robeson repeated the concert in New York's Town Hall, with similarly successful results.

What was it about the spirituals? "These songs are to Negro culture what the works of the great poets are to English culture: they are the soul of the race made manifest," Robeson wrote. He spent long hours analyzing their origins. The Bible was the only form of literature to which the slaves had had access. They identified with the captive Hebrews of the Old Testament, the liberation themes in the tales of Daniel, Joshua, Moses: "Let my people go!" New meanings, based upon their own experience, were infused into the ancient epics.

Robeson did the same with *Ol' Man River*, which was written with him in mind by Oscar Hammerstein II and Jerome Kern. Robeson altered its lyrics from despair to resistance. It became no longer a man "tired of living and scared of dying," but a man who "must keep fighting until I'm dying." He described the power of spirit in his people as intangible, but "of steadfast determination, exaltation in the face of trials . . . a great force that must be unleashed in the struggles of today." That spirit, he wrote, lived on "in the sublime grandeur of 'Deep River,' in the driving power of 'Jacob's Ladder,' in the militancy of 'Joshua Fit the Battle of Jericho,' and in the poignant beauty of all our spirituals." He probed the past in order to find his future.

Robeson performed *Ol' Man River* for the first time in the London production of *Show Boat* in 1928. Then, under the tutelage of Amanda Aldridge, he made his debut as Othello in England. He was the first black actor to play the part since Ira Aldridge's last performances. For twelve years, until the outbreak of the Second World War in 1939, Robeson and his family lived primarily in London. There, and during performances across Europe, he assiduously studied the varied cultures of the world, becoming expert in the languages and traditions of Africa, China, Germany, and the Soviet Union.

*   *   *

Ira Aldridge, still rejected by the London theaters in the 1850s, had set out on his first journey to continental Europe. No matter where he went, the expatriate American received the highest tributes. Presented to King Frederick William IV of Prussia, he was awarded the Golden Medal for Art and Sciences—an honor previously bestowed upon only three individuals. In Germany, hundreds of admirers carrying scrolls of greeting and garlands of flowers welcomed him at the railway stations. In Serbia, where Shakespeare was completely unknown, Aldridge taught the techniques to a young national theater movement. Today, inside the National Theatre in war-torn Belgrade, there remains a plaque of gratitude to "the African Roscius," erected by both the Serbs and the Croats.

A Polish newspaper of the period described an American slave family which had fled Baltimore and been captured in New York. The New York Society for the Manumission of Slaves had run out of funds. Put up for sale, the mother and father were to be transported to a Georgia plantation. Aldridge, performing in Austria, somehow learned of the situation—and dispatched the money to purchase the family's freedom.

Acclaimed by continental Europe, in 1858 Aldridge finally was allowed to bring Othello to London's West End after an absence of a quarter-century. This time, the audience called him out to receive their applause at the close of the third and fifth acts. The *Illustrated London News* wrote: "He is manifestly an intelligent man [who] has studied his art with earnestness. . . ." Advertisements of an impending appearance in America appeared in a New York newspaper. But Aldridge did not return from his self-imposed exile—apparently because, as he wrote in a letter, "my dear wife would not entertain the idea, her prejudice is so rooted against the Americans for their treatment of [my] oppressed race generally."

Instead, Aldridge set out with Margaret for the Russian capital of St. Petersburg. It was a trip that not only crowned his career, but changed his life. For in Aldridge, the Russian people—like the Irish and the English Jews before them—found a symbol. The great majority in Russia still lived as serfs. Some were virtually slaves of individual landowners who separated families, ordered and dissolved marriages, and sold them off at will. Harriet Beecher Stowe's *Uncle Tom's Cabin*, published in 1852, had become especially popular after its translation in Russia, where the American abolitionist movement was staunchly backed by progressive intellectuals. One wrote that the liberation of America's slaves "becomes something *internal* . . . for all of us. This is why for us, at this particular time, the role of Othello performed by this artist of genius, with all its subtleties of tribal and climatic character, has a universal mighty significance." In Aldridge's character's deep cry—"Oh misery, misery, misery!"—was contained "the groans of the whole of suffering mankind."

As Civil War loomed in America, a rage simultaneously erupted in Aldridge. It was so towering that European audiences who could not understand a single word came to fear for the lives of the actors portraying Desdemona and Iago. After the finale of one performance, a member of the troupe found him sobbing for several minutes behind the scenes. And, when he took the stage as King Lear in St. Petersburg, Aldridge played the Caucasian ruler with conspicuously unwhitened hands.

> *"Let me live heavenly Creator,*
> *Oh, let me live with feeling heart!*
> *That I may praise your wonder world,*
> *To my fellow-men my love impart!*
> *'Tis horrible slavery to face,*
> *To be free and sleep—is worse,*
> *To go through life and leave no trace—*
> *Life and death are then a curse!"*
> —TARAS SHEVCHENKO

One night, Count Theodor Tolstoy—uncle of the Russian author Leo Tolstoy—invited Aldridge to his home to meet a guest. Taras Shevchenko was a Jewish Ukrainian poet, artist, and revolutionary, seven years younger than Aldridge. A former serf whose freedom had been purchased by an artistic benefactor, Shevchenko's short poems and novels in verse all focused upon the plight of his people. In 1847, Shevchenko had been sentenced to lifelong imprisonment in a military fortress for having composed satirical poems about the Russian aristocracy. Now, following numerous pleas to the government by Count Tolstoy, he had been released after nine years of confinement.

The count's daughter, then only fifteen, served as interpreter at the first meeting between Shevchenko and Aldridge. Years later, in her memoirs, Mrs. E. F. Yunge described the actor sitting to have his portrait painted. Aldridge found it difficult to stay still. He began making faces. Shevchenko became angry and stopped painting. For a time, Aldridge sat quietly again. Suddenly he said, "May I sing?" An exasperated Shevchenko agreed. It was, the memoir recounts, "a touching, sad Negro melody, which gradually passed into a more lively tempo." It ended with a mad dance by Aldridge around the studio. Shevchenko then launched into a series of Ukrainian songs. When the long night ended, they were engrossed in conversation about folklore and the similarity of peoples.

These two men who could not speak each other's language quickly became close friends. They met regularly, sharing memories, comparing thoughts on slavery in America and among Russia's serfs. After witnessing Aldridge's King Lear, Shevchenko rushed into his dressing room and embraced him, tears streaming down his face. The poet of the Ukraine led the procession that saw Aldridge off at the St. Petersburg station. "In my person," the actor wrote Shevchenko while en route back to England, "you have shown your sympathy and love for my oppressed people."

They never saw one another again. Less than two years later, his health undermined by the long prison stay, Shevchenko died at the age of forty-six on February 26, 1861. He did not live to see Czar Alexander II's decision to liberate the Russian peasantry that same March, only one month before the attack on Fort Sumter that began the American Civil War.

In June of 1861, Aldridge embarked on a tour that took him to the Ukraine. On a hill above the Dnieper River, he stood alone, weeping over the grave of a kindred spirit.

The completed Shevchenko portrait of Ira Aldridge hangs today in Moscow's Tretiakov Gallery.

With London remaining his home base all through the turbulent 1930s, Paul Robeson made a few films but spent much of his time following Aldridge's path across Europe. "When I sang my American folk melodies in Budapest, Prague, Tiflis, Moscow, Oslo, the Hebrides, or on the Spanish front," he told an interviewer, "the people understood and wept or rejoiced with the spirit of the songs. I found that where forces have been the same, whether people weave, build, pick cotton, or dig in the mines, they understand each other in the common language of work, suffering and protest. Their songs were composed by men trying to make work easier, trying to find a way out."

Robeson began studying the Russian language, culture and music at the onset of America's Great Depression. He had first come in contact with Russians while in college and, hearing their folksongs, been struck by the similarities to Negro melodies and African music. The Russian composer Stravinsky, he learned, borrowed from the black traditions. While it took Robeson a prodigious effort to master French and German, he was able to speak Russian in six months with a perfect accent. It was likewise with Chinese, which possessed the same basic structure as African languages; Robeson found the Chinese intellect similar to the African way of thinking in symbols. "I found that I, who lacked feeling for the English language later than Shakespeare, met Pushkin, Dostoevsky, Tolstoy, Lao-tze, and Confucius on common ground," Robeson said. "I understood them. I found myself completely at home with their compatriots."

When Robeson paid his first visit to Moscow in the winter of 1934, at first it did not appear the feeling would be mutual. As he and his wife arrived by train at the Soviet border, customs officials informed the Robesons that their papers were not in order, and were about to turn them back. Then, searching their luggage, they came across some of Robeson's recordings. "Robeson! Robeson!" they exclaimed as Paul, laughing, burst out in song. Even in remote areas, the Russian people were familiar with Robeson through listening to filtered foreign radio broadcasts.

So the remarkable reception that he was to find in the Soviet Union was beyond ideology and beyond race. There existed a cultural identification, as the sons of serfs took the son of a slave into their hearts. The legacy of Aldridge and Shevchenko transmuted, timelessly, into a friendship between Robeson and the Russian filmmaker Sergei Eisenstein. "I hesitated to come," Robeson told Eisenstein. "I listened to what everybody had to say but I didn't think this would be any different than any other place. But—maybe you'll understand—I feel like a human being for the first time since I grew up. . . . Here, for the first time in my life, I walk in full human dignity."

Others were not so lucky. Josef Stalin's collectivization had led to a terrible famine. Robeson made friends among such reform-minded men as Eisenstein and the Soviet Foreign Minister, Maxim Litvinov. He also became acquainted with the Minister of Defense, Marshal Mikhail Tukhachevsky, who in 1937 would be among the thousands of Communist Party leaders murdered by Stalin in his infamous purges.

"Dad was a keen observer," his son says, "and, since his writings and personal letters reveal that he was devouring Marx in the original German as early as 1932, he knew very well that Stalinism had little to do with what Marx wrote. But dad concluded that it was in the interest of most of humanity, certainly the colored peoples, to support the Stalinists against the Nazis." (Indeed, Stalin's Soviet Union would become America's ally in World War II.)

When Robeson sang the words "Let my people go," it was a symbol for those seeking escape from the rise of fascism. By the close of the 1930s, his concerts often turned into massive anti-Nazi demonstrations. His message proved so powerful that eventually his recordings were outlawed for sale in Hitler's Germany and all the European countries it came to occupy.

In September 1939, with the coming of the Second World War, Robeson and his family set sail for a return to America. Here Robeson's popularity reached its peak during the war years. His portrayal of Othello on Broadway and across the land became, as Robeson wrote in the *American Scholar* in 1945, "painfully immediate in its unfolding of evil, innocence, passion, dignity and nobility and contemporary in its overtones of a clash of cultures ... the terrible agony of Othello, the irretrievability of his world, the complete destruction of all trusted and sacred values—all these suggest the shattering of a universe. ... Now, interestingly enough, we stand at the end of one period of human history and before the entrance of a new. All our tenets and tried beliefs are challenged."

Robeson was at the forefront of the challenge during the war years. He was the first leading concert artist to perform inside prisons, to refuse to appear before segregated audiences, and to steep himself in the labor movement on behalf of black and white workers. He led a delegation to the major-league baseball owners, applying pressure that eventually ensured Jackie Robinson's breaking of the color barrier in 1947.

"Dad sensed the Cold War coming soon after Franklin Roosevelt's death," says Paul, Jr. "For three years after the war ended, he was the most popular concert artist in the country. He felt he had a more important message to give through his art than attending political meetings."

Then, in 1948, Robeson took a group to the White House to discuss with President Truman the lynchings of blacks that were continuing in the South. A confrontation ensued. Truman said the political timing was not right to push an antilynching bill through Congress. Robeson responded that if the government would not defend the people, black veterans who had fought for their country might be forced to defend themselves.

His son remembers: "Truman jumped up red-faced, wagging his finger and saying, 'That sounds like a threat!' Dad stood up. Two Secret Servicemen on either side of the President stepped forward and opened their jackets. Someone else in the delegation said he'd certainly meant no threat. Dad said, 'Of course I meant no offense to the office of the presidency. I was merely expressing the way ten percent of the American people feel.' Both Truman and dad sat down. But headlines all across the country trumpeted Robeson talking about armed black self-defense. This became a metaphor for dad going against the stream."

As the Cold War swept America, the controversy around Robeson escalated. "In 1949," recounts Paul, Jr., "Hoover's FBI forced concert agents in different cities to cancel 100-some appearances. Dad wasn't looking for a fight, but they ambushed him. So he went to Europe. And then came Peekskill."

That September of 1949, rioting in protest of a Robeson appearance broke out in the little town of Peekskill, New York. Shortly before, Robeson had given a speech in Paris. He had said that American blacks would never go to war against the Soviet Union, a nation that had specifically outlawed racism in its constitution. Robeson was branded a Communist, although he never joined the Communist Party.

What happened in Peekskill remains a vivid memory to folksinger Pete Seeger, now in his late seventies. In his mountaintop cabin overlooking the Hudson River, Seeger spoke of having been slated to appear on the same concert program. When he ran into a monumental traffic jam en route, he pulled over to ask a state trooper whether the officer could somehow get him through. "There's not gonna be any concert," the policeman replied, and walked away. Seeger arrived to find it cancelled.

Robeson went back to address a huge rally in Harlem. This is America, he said, nobody could deny him the right to sing. When the Peekskill concert was rescheduled, Seeger recalled, this time 1,500 members of union Local 65 stood arm-in-arm around the perimeter.

"There was a crowd of maybe eighty people at the gate, hollering, 'Go back to Russia! Kikes! Nigger lovers!' When Paul sang, two men stood on each side of him, their eyes looking over the crowd to make sure nobody was raising a rifle sight."

Seeger and his wife were among the last to leave. On their way out, a policeman was forcing all cars to the right. Seeger glimpsed some glass in the road. Around a corner stood a group with stones as big as baseballs. For three-quarters of a mile, as the police watched idly, "it was like running the gauntlet." Seeger drove home with a shattered windshield, feeling lucky to escape with his life.

"Well now, here's the interesting thing, very interesting," Seeger continued. "The very next day, all through Peekskill were these signs: 'Wake up, America! Peekskill did.' They were in cars, in windows, in stores, in bars, in gas stations. They'd obviously been printed in advance. I told this story to someone who said, 'Those are the exact same signs that Hitler put up after Kristallnacht—Wake up, Germany!' But, about a month later, they *all* disappeared. How this happened, I don't know."

Talking to Seeger, it became clear that the coming together of Paul Robeson with the folk musicians of that era really marked the beginning of the civil rights movement. "Finding various ways that we could work together," Seeger said, "laid the foundation for a whole new period of American history."

There is a photograph of Robeson alongside Leadbelly, the twelve-string guitar player who wrote the now-classic *Good Night Irene*. During the early 1950s, Robeson did a recording session with harmonicist Sonny Terry and his partner Brownie McGhee. Worlds were merging, the American folk music revival of a decade later was being forged.

"We didn't call them folk festivals then," Seeger remembered. "Robeson simply sang for all sorts of peace and civil rights organizations, just everywhere. There was a tendency for speakers to boom out, but when Robeson's voice came over the PA system"—here Seeger's voice became a low whisper—" 'Good evening, friends,' in that deep bass voice. And the whole place melted. We're in safe hands, Paul is here."

Seeger's eyes were misting beneath his spectacles. "By and large, even many young black people don't know who Paul was anymore," he said finally. "But his work in history will be seen by a generation of people that he inspired, white and black, male and female: if Robeson is brave enough to do this, we've got to try, too. The plain raw courage of the man. He was just pure inspiration."

Late in 1860, Ira Aldridge accepted an invitation to return to Russia. As Civil War raged in America, he set off on several lengthy tours of the isolated Russian provinces. Along what Aldridge described in a letter as "such desperate roads," scarcely more than cart tracks, he made forays on stagecoach or by horse sleigh into villages that had never seen a foreign actor, let alone a Shakespearean drama. While he continued to perform in English to full houses, Aldridge added Russian serf folksongs in their own language.

He taught local companies acting skills, issuing instructions through a translator and cueing a prompter with his hands and feet during their performances. "If he did it once," one account said, "then you could be sure at the tenth time he would do exactly the same gestures or movements, and after that the prompter could safely give the cue to the next actor." Each time Aldridge departed, dozens of letters pursued him—from children, elderly women, entire families. He was referred to as "a strolling missionary of art," creating "a whole epoch in the cultural life of each town."

Back in Moscow, wild sell-out crowds greeted Aldridge at the Bolshoi Theater. Langston Hughes has written that Aldridge achieved such popularity "that the students unhitched the horses of his carriage and themselves pulled him from the theatre to his hotel."

Yet a backlash had set in against the reforms that abolished Russian serfdom. Amid tighter censorship and often police terror, a number of radical leaders were arrested and dispatched into exile, among them close friends of Aldridge. The reactionary press, which advocated a return to the old Orthodox Slavic culture, attacked an Aldridge performance for having "murdered and crushed the spirit." His interpretations of King Lear and Macbeth possessed such impact on the populace that, in 1862, he was banned from the stages in St. Petersburg and Moscow by the Czar's censor.

"I am very miserable and quite alone all the time," Aldridge wrote in a letter. "If I had known things were so bad in Russia I would have stayed at home." Still, there were moments of relief. E. F. Yunge, Count Tolstoy's daughter, recalled one of these, offering this poignant account of an Aldridge visit to St. Petersburg in the midst of the intensifying hostility against him.

"My eldest son was then about one year old," she wrote in her memoirs, "and, on taking him for the first time to see Aldridge, I was terribly worried that the child would be frightened by his appearance, and that my black friend, who so passionately loved children, would nevertheless be grieved. No doubt he also thought something similar— but the child soon dissipated our fears. He at once stretched out to Aldridge and settled into his arms. Aldridge's face lit up, he began to dance with the little fellow around the room and never let him go from his arms the whole day, even during dinner."

As had happened in London, Aldridge found himself forced by official animosity to leave the city for the Russian countryside. There, his biographers state, he brought "a modern, realistic style of production, acting and interpretation that was to leave an indelible mark on the theatre history of Russia."

Soon after Lincoln's Emancipation Proclamation, Aldridge returned to England. The American Civil War had just ended when he was again invited to play Othello in London's West End. A seventeen-year-old actress, later to become famous as Dame Madge Kendal, played his Desdemona. In her memoirs, she recalled the scene in which Othello asks for her hand. Slowly, slowly, Aldridge reached out for her, forcing the audience to absorb the moment of contrast—and of beauty—between black and white. The gesture never failed to receive a round of applause.

There is much that remains mysterious about the life of Ira Aldridge. His wife Margaret, whose health deteriorated over many years, was herself childless, but raised Aldridge's first-born son as her own. The boy was of mixed parentage, though his legitimate mother's identity is unknown. In 1860, Aldridge had a second child by a Swedish opera singer he met on one of his tours. Until Margaret's death four years later, he supported two families—one in London, another in Stockholm. Finally, in the summer of 1867, shortly after making out his will, Aldridge accepted an invitation to return at last to the New York stage. It never happened.

He decided first to honor a commitment in Poland, but arrived too ill to perform. "In two days a boil on the breast opened up," wrote the *Warsaw Courier*, "and though they called in seven of the most eminent doctors in the city, they could not save him." At the age of fifty-nine, Aldridge died on August 7, 1867, his body lying in state inside a hotel. He received a lavish funeral procession and was buried in Lodz's Evangelical Cemetery. A large cross was erected as a tombstone in 1890. It continues to stand after two catastrophic World Wars.

"Long afterwards in the provinces," the Russian author Davydov tells us, "one could see both in the albums and on the walls, faded with time, pictures of the talented artist whom the Russian public loved, and whom Fate brought to lie on Russian soil."

During the 1980s, Dr. Helen Armistead Johnson, a scholar of African-American theater history, made a pilgrimage to Aldridge's grave. She found it was still being cared for by the Society of Polish Artists of Film and Theatre. "They considered him a freedom fighter," Dr. Johnson said, "a kindred spirit."

> *His friends stood by, he slept,*
> *He was dying, they wept*
> *Like children. Softly he sighed.*
> *He sighed and sighed, he was gone!*
> *And the world has lost a prophet,*
> *And fame has lost a son!*
> —TARAS SHEVCHENKO

Paul Robeson always wanted to do a film about Ira Aldridge. The idea originated with Herbert Marshall, a British director friend of Robeson's, in the late 1930s. Marshall had studied filmmaking under Sergei Eisenstein in the Soviet Union, and it was the Russians who expressed interest in an Aldridge project. At the time, Robeson said he preferred to provide the narration, rather than portray Aldridge. The outbreak of World War II forced all plans onto the shelf.

In 1949, when Robeson was temporarily back in England, Marshall again brought up the Aldridge project. Work on a script commenced with a Robeson role in mind. It was then that Robeson told Marshall the story of having studied voice and diction with Aldridge's daughter while preparing for his first performance as Othello. But the film never materialized. Upon his return to the United States, Robeson was not permitted by the State Department to leave again. Marshall went on to co-author a 1958 biography, *Ira Aldridge: The Negro Tragedian*, for which Robeson wrote a preface to one edition.

The crowning parallel irony in the life experiences of Aldridge and Robeson focuses on Russia. Like Aldridge, Robeson was overwhelmingly popular there. Like Aldridge's kinship with the Jewish poet Shevchenko, Robeson became close friends with a Jewish poet named Itzik Feffer. Not long before the events in Peekskill, during one of his last journeys onto Russian soil, Robeson, too, was swept up in internal political turmoil.

Inside the Soviet Union, Stalin had embarked on an anti-Semitic campaign. When Robeson asked to see Itzik Feffer, he was told that his friend was on vacation. At the end of his tour, Robeson told Soviet officials that he would not leave Moscow until Feffer arrived. Robeson was informed that Feffer would be located by the next day. In fact, Feffer had been falsely accused of being a spy and jailed. Now Stalin's NKVD security forces descended on his cell within the infamous Lubyanka prison. They drove him home. Feffer's wife did not even know he was still alive. They allowed him a home-cooked meal. They had him put on a suit. On the way to the hotel where Robeson was staying, Feffer was instructed to assure his famous American friend that all was well, lest Feffer's family disappear. The NKVD dropped him off, saying they would return in ninety minutes.

Within weeks of this event, upon his return to America, Robeson privately told his son of his rendezvous with Feffer. Paul, Jr., remembers:

"Dad is in his suite when Feffer knocks on the door. They embrace and Feffer indicates in sign language to be careful, the place is bugged. Right on cue, dad continues the conversation in Russian. It's all on two levels. 'How are you doing?' dad asks. Feffer says, 'I am recovering from a bout with pneumonia, that's why I am pale.' He talks about his memoirs and dad talks about the U.S. Meanwhile they are doing sign language and passing occasional brief notes. Dad writes, 'Mikhoels?', referring to a prominent mutual Jewish friend. Feffer writes, 'Murdered on Stalin's order.'

"Toward the end, while discussing his music, dad points at Feffer and makes a questioning sign that indicates, 'What's to happen to you and your friends?' Feffer answers how much he loves the song *Deep River*. While saying this, he draws a finger across his throat. They embrace again, tearfully. Feffer is driven back to Lubyanka, and dad is left wondering what he can possibly do."

Robeson knew that any overt action he took would simply result in a denial by Soviet authorities—and would also seal Feffer's fate. But his farewell concert was scheduled for the next day in Moscow, to be broadcast by radio into every time zone of the vast USSR. After he concluded the concert with *Ol' Man River*, Robeson quelled the applause and announced he needed to preface one encore with a few remarks.

His son continues the story: "Dad says, 'I was greatly saddened to hear of my dear friend Mikhoels's death.' He uses a word in Russian which literally means 'happened too soon.' This could mean he fell or died in his sleep or was deep-sixed. The audience gasps, because even though Mikhoels was given a state funeral, his name is anathema. 'But I had a wonderful visit with my friend Feffer,' dad continues, 'who is in good health and working on his war memoirs.' Another gasp. The audience knows that Feffer has disappeared without a trace. They are mostly high party officials, the Moscow elite, and leading Jewish cultural people who are still at liberty. And they are all nervous about where Stalin's axe will fall next.

"Then dad goes on to say, 'I remind you of the deep ties between the Jewish culture in the Soviet Union and in the United States. My encore will be a song that must be done in Yiddish, because I learned it in the rubble of the Warsaw ghetto, from a survivor of the rebellion where Jewish partisans fought to the death against the Nazi Army.' By now the audience does not know quite what to do. He recites the last verse in Russian:

> 'Never say that you have reached the very end,
> When leaden skies a bitter future may portend,
> For sure the hour for which we yearn will yet arrive,
> And our marching steps will thunder: we survive!'

"Timid applause from the audience. Then dad begins to sing, straight from the heart, with this immense power: 'They sang this song drowning in their own blood, this people sang with guns in hand.'

"At the end, there was total silence. And then, dad told me, there followed the most extraordinary ovation any audience ever gave him. Russian and Jew sitting side by side fell into each other's arms weeping. Some rushed toward the stage, calling out his name: 'Pavel Vasilyevich!' It went on for ten minutes."

Not a word of this appeared in any Soviet newspaper, although the Warsaw press did report it. But Robeson had delivered his message like the chess master he was—to the Soviet people via radio, and to Stalin himself. It became politically impossible for Stalin to label Itzik

Feffer an enemy of the people and shoot him; he had, after all, just visited with Paul Robeson, the peoples' hero from America. "Dad played it straight—and hoisted Stalin on his own petard," his son says.

Feffer survived until 1952, when Stalin finally ordered him executed shortly before his own death. In 1994, the Russian archives released a recording of Robeson's concert. His remarks had been excised, but *Zog Nit Keynmal—Song of the Warsaw Ghetto Rebellion*—concludes the performance from Tchaikovsky Hall, along with the ovation.

Soon after the Korean War broke out in 1950, in an unprecedented action the U.S. State Department cancelled the passports of Robeson, his wife and son. His outspokenness against colonialism in Africa and on behalf of civil rights in America became anathema in the Cold War's McCarthy period. As his granddaughter Susan Robeson writes in her pictorial biography, *The Whole World in His Hands*: ". . . not a single concert hall or recording studio in the country was accessible to Paul. If an owner of a studio or hall did entertain the thought, the FBI immediately paid a visit and ended that. Denied any outlet to work, unable to travel, trapped in his own country rather than exiled from it, Paul's income dwindled from a hundred thousand dollars to five thousand in less than one year. Honors were withdrawn, and friends disappeared. Paul, once a national hero, was now an outcast."

According to documents acquired by Paul Robeson, Jr., under the Freedom of Information Act, the American Consul in the Gold Coast [now Ghana] recommended to the State Department in January 1951 that a "specially written" article about Robeson be authored by a credible black source—because the Communists were winning propaganda victories all over Africa "on the Robeson case" [his being denied a passport]. That November, "Paul Robeson—The Lost Shepherd" appeared in *The Crisis*, the African-American journal that W. E. B. Du Bois had founded. The article was written under a pseudonym, by a prominent black journalist and later politician whose name has never been publicly revealed. It described Robeson as a great artist and a well-meaning but duped man, so angered by discrimination against blacks that he had become a shill for the Stalinists. By order of Secretary of State John Foster Dulles, eventually thousands of copies were disseminated throughout the African continent.

"This image of dad has been recycled over and over," his son says, "that he was either naive or a knave. The mystery is, why did he defend Stalinism in the Soviet Union? Why didn't he say what he knew? The answer is really quite simple. You find it in his writings and his actions. With all of its vicious crimes, he believed that Stalin's Soviet Union was the main hope for the Third World to get out from under Western colonialism. Once you got rid of Hitler, the main enemy of colored peoples and the oppressed was the right wing of the West, and specifically the United States. As he passed through Germany in 1934, dad equated Southern right-wing racists as cousins, if not brothers, of the Nazis. He was very pro-Roosevelt, proliberal, all his life. So he could distinguish between which Americans—and which Russians—you were talking about."

Robeson's uncompromising stand cost him dearly. Gordon Parks, who at the time had recently become *Life* magazine's first black staff photographer, recalls one painful incident: "I saw a disaster with Paul. It was in a restaurant in Harlem called the Red Rooster. He used to hang out there. There was a famous black ballplayer at the bar. Paul walked over to him and said, 'I admire the way you're playing, you're a hero of mine.' The guy looked at him and said, 'Get the hell away from me, you're a Communist!' I felt so bad for Paul I didn't know what to do. All of us wanted to kick that guy in the mouth. But Paul reacted in his way. He just stood there, didn't say one word."

This story was elaborated upon by another observer, well-known black journalist James Hicks, in a documentary about Robeson. When Don Newcombe, a star pitcher for the Brooklyn Dodgers, stood up and began shouting his denunciations at the silent Robeson, suddenly Newcombe found himself surrounded by a dozen people. One flicked open a large switchblade and announced: "Well, you're a great pitcher, but ain't nothing gonna happen to Paul Robeson—not in the Red Rooster." Newcombe was led out of the bar.

Excerpt from testimony in 1956, before the House Un-American Activities Committee in Washington:

ROBESON: I stand here struggling for the rights of my people to be full citizens in this country and they are not. They are not in Mississippi and they are not . . . in Washington. . . . You want to shut up every Negro who has the courage to stand up and fight for the rights of his people. . . . That is why I am here today. . . .

CONGRESSMAN SCHERER: Why do you not stay in Russia?

ROBESON: Because my father was a slave, and my people died to build this country and I am going to stay here and have a part of it just like you. And no fascist-minded people will drive me from it. Is that clear?

Paul, Jr., was in his early twenties when the government net closed upon his father. Some of Robeson's chroniclers have suggested that father and son were never particularly close. Nothing could be farther from the truth, especially during the period of Robeson's forced exile.

The forging of their relationship had begun when Paul, Jr., was six-teen, and accompanied his father "into café society in New York. He introduced me to his friends, his lovers, I became really part of his life and of his political work."

Then, in the climate of fear surrounding Robeson during the early 1950s, the father sought to protect his son. "I had to fight my way into his circle of close associates," Paul, Jr., remembers, his voice rising as he tells the story. "Dad was very reluctant because he really thought he was going to get shot. And, of course, so could I. I was newly married, he didn't want to put me at risk. So he would say, 'The initiation fee is high.' He did everything but give me twenty lashes to discourage me from working with him. He was capricious, unreasonable, even insulted me a couple of times in public. I took it all. Then, one day, I cussed him out: 'Goddamn it, you know you're wrong, how dare you! You mess with me again, I might hit you! Even though you outweigh me, I'm in good shape.' When I did this, dad said: 'Finally. I wondered if you could do that—you've got the job, because the one thing I can't deal with is an-other yes-man.' He said that was the last test."

So an abiding relationship developed between father and son. Paul, Jr., became one of his chief advisers, both ombudsman and musical critic. He himself had perfect pitch, and recalls a recording session where he detected two flaws in an otherwise magnificent rendition of a *Boris Godunov* aria.

"Dad is saying, 'Boy, I knocked the hell out of that one. And I'm saying, 'Well, dad, maybe you'd better do it over.' He said, 'Do it over? What the hell for?' I explained, 'Well, the accompanist went a little off on the—' He got furious now. 'Accompanist? I've got ears, what the hell are you talking about?' So I said, 'Well, to tell you the truth, you went off key here and here.' He said, 'Let me hear it back.' He sat down and listened to the whole thing. Then, without looking at me, he got up and told the accompanist, 'Start from the beginning.' He did it four times until I said it was okay. From then on, he never questioned a decision I made. He said, 'Look, you pick the takes, edit them, and at the very end if you've got any problems you really want to come to me with, do it!' "

The two also worked together politically. Unlike his father, in the 1950s Paul, Jr., did become a member of the Communist Party-USA. Soon he was serving as its unpaid chairman for the Harlem region. In this capacity, the son often took strong positions that his father could not. He also cultivated private relationships with other black leaders who would have become targets of the FBI, had they been seen meeting with Robeson himself. Indeed, Paul Jr., says that his father made a conscious decision to "stay miles out of Martin Luther King's way. It was just a political reality, King had problems enough with black mainstream leadership." So, for the 1963 March on Washington where King gave his unforgettable "I have a dream" speech, Paul, Jr., quietly raised support money from among his own contacts.

According to Paul, Jr., his father had a trio of strange-bedfellow political heroes: Franklin D. Roosevelt, India's Premier Jawaharlal Nehru (a close friend of Robeson's), and Soviet Premier Nikita Khrushchev. After the McCarthy era ended and Robeson's passport was finally returned to him in 1958, he traveled first to London and then on to Moscow for concerts. Khrushchev issued an invitation to join him on vacation at a seaside resort, and the two struck up a friendship. In Robeson's view, Khrushchev's reforms represented an effort to restore a pure form of Communism that had been lost during the tyrannical reign of Stalin. He sensed that Khrushchev's rise to power might open up a thaw in the Cold War.

Robeson also had great admiration for President John F. Kennedy, and was excited about the growing accommodation between Kennedy and Khrushchev that followed the near-apocalyptic Cuban Missile Crisis of 1962. But shortly thereafter, Kennedy was assassinated and Khrushchev was ousted. In the arena of civil rights, the two great black leaders—Malcolm X and then Dr. King—would soon be shot down as well. Malcolm X's assassination occurred only days before he had a scheduled appointment to meet with Paul Robeson for the first time.

Then in his sixties and plagued with bouts of ill health, Robeson left the stage for good. His last public appearance came in 1965. He spent his last years in relative seclusion at the home of an older sister in Philadelphia. In 1972, his son accepted an honor on his behalf. It was the Ira Aldridge Award from New York's chapter of the Association for the Study of Negro Life and History. After suffering a stroke, Robeson died on January 23, 1976, at the age of seventy-seven.

As I sat alone with the son who has devoted himself to keeping his father's memory alive, I remarked how tragic it seemed that Robeson's radical views kept the civil rights movement from embracing him. Paul, Jr., shook his head and replied: "Dad didn't care about that, he really didn't. He'd say, 'I dreamed about this thirty or forty years ago, I didn't think I'd ever live to see something like this. This younger generation, it's great.' He just reveled in it—'Look what sprouted from the ground I plowed.' What difference does it make whether the *New York Times* says this crop was planted by him?"

Paul, Jr., was silent for a moment and then continued: "Both King and Malcolm, from their own direction, came to the place at about the same age where Paul Robeson left off in the prime of his life. There is an extraordinary symbolism there."

Equal rights, Robeson knew, was only the beginning; the struggle for equal opportunity would take far longer. As Amanda Ira Aldridge said of Robeson's struggle before her death in 1956: "It will take a little while yet before things get as they should be in your country."

What Robeson envisioned was that appreciating the differences of culture, not focusing on ethnicity, was all that could ever bring the world together. How would his son summarize his father's single greatest achievement? "It sounds a little pedantic," Paul, Jr., said, "but I would say being the first African-American in history to bring the universality of African culture into a *dominant* position in the main-stream—in theater, on the concert stage, and as a public figure. I think what made this possible was the American experience added to his experiences in Europe. Similar to Frederick Douglass in a way, who also lived in England for a time. And, again, similar to Ira Aldridge."

The son added: "Dad believed somebody up there was looking after him, until the day he died. Then he said, 'I'm going home—across the river Jordan.' "

As I said goodbye to Paul Robeson, Jr., and walked out into teeming Manhattan streets that felt suddenly very still, I recalled what Harvard Professor Cornel West had said when I asked him about Robeson. "I don't think we've ever had a black genius as thoroughly multitalented as Paul Robeson. So much so that he was almost forced to wrestle with an embarrassment of riches. Yet he was able not only to make such a grand contribution artistically, but was willing to pay a tremendous and painful price for his talent. He becomes a figure as much of courage as of artistic genius. And that is very rare."

FOR FURTHER READING:

Martin Bauml Duberman, *Paul Robeson: A Biography* (New York: Ballantine Books, 1989).

Philip S. Foner, ed., *Paul Robeson Speaks* (New York: Citadel Press Book Carol Publishing Group, 1978).

Herbert Marshall and Mildred Stock, *Ira Aldridge: The Negro Tragedian* (Carbondale, Ill: Southern Illinois University Press).

Paul Robeson, *Here I Stand* (Boston: Beacon Press, 1988).

Paul Robeson, Jr., *Paul Robeson, Jr., Speaks to America: The Politics of Multiculturalism* (New Brunswick, N.J.: Rutgers University Press, 1993).

Susan Robeson, *The Whole World in His Hands: A Pictorial Biography of Paul Robeson* (New York: A Citadel Press Book/Carol Publishing Group, 1990).

Gordon Parks:
A Lens on Humanity

"I've been born again and again, always finding something or someone to love, to win or lose, to mourn or celebrate. Now, with life quieting down around me, I look back through an autumn mind, searching the clear air for the roots of things I watched growing or expiring along the way. Wherever my feet have taken me I have found both goodness and pain; and that's all I have to give. I could depart with washed hands, keeping the silence and telling nothing. But I have no secret doors to hide the memories."
—GORDON PARKS, *To Smile in Autumn*

It is sundown on the Fourth of July, 1997. Eight floors below the spacious apartment in the United Nations Plaza building, crowds of New Yorkers are beginning to arrive for the annual fireworks display. From his living-room table, Gordon Parks gazes out the picture window toward the East River, his memory alighting on another summer afternoon some fifty-five years ago. He was in Washington, D.C., on one of his first photo assignments. It was for a book of profiles about black Americans called *13 against the Odds*. That day's subject was Paul Robeson.

"Paul was a man I had great respect for in those early days," Parks is saying. "When we first met, he gave me about an hour to photograph him. Afterwards he asked, 'You're going to be at the concert tomorrow?' I said, 'Yes, I'll be there.' He said, 'Well, our car will pick you up and I will accompany you.' *He* would accompany *me*!"

Parks smiles, shakes his head, and continues: "The concert was in a big open arena. As we walked through the crowd together, he put his massive hand on my shoulder—as if he was bringing me to the concert to introduce him. I never forgot that moment. He was very fatherly, very instructive. He told me to consider myself to have greatness within me, and to push toward it. Greatness? I couldn't quite grasp that. I'm just a little guy with a new camera. But I listened to him. And I clung to his words as much as possible."

What Paul Robeson once sensed in Gordon Parks has taken so many different forms that it is difficult to know where to begin describing them. This son of the Kansas prairies, who never completed high school, is today considered one of the premier photographers of the twentieth century. Altogether he has authored nineteen books. They include numerous works of photography, both essay and instructional; four autobiographies; four volumes of poetry; three novels; and two recent books that combine Parks's poetry and photographs with his paintings. He has directed six feature films, as well as written the screenplay and the musical score for his first one, *The Learning Tree*, which was based on his best-selling autobiographical novel. He has composed concertos, sonatas, symphonies, a ballet, and popular songs. In short, there is no field of artistic endeavor that Gordon Parks has not attempted successfully.

The apartment where Parks has lived since the 1970s resonates creativity. Nearly every inch of wall space is filled with pictures: family members (including two great-grandchildren), illustrations for Parks's poetry, and images from his twenty-four years as *Life* magazine's first black staff photographer. From one wall, Muhammad Ali faces off against two paintings by Chagall. In the far corner of the living room, surrounded by a curtain of Chinese tapestry, is a Bechstein grand piano. On a coffee table are proofs for a 350-page retrospective book. It was to be published simultaneously with a Parks photo exhibition, scheduled to open at Washington's Corcoran Gallery in September 1997 before touring the nation and eventually Europe.

Now in his mid-eighties, Parks is recovering on this Independence Day from surgery on the Achilles tendons of both legs. Temporarily forced into a wheelchair, he chafes at the inactivity. "I'm supposed to perform the piano sonata in November that I've written for my four children," he says. "But the doctors don't want me putting my feet to the pedals right now. It's very difficult to work just on notes, because sustaining sounds sometimes leads you into another theme. And I can't do that at the moment. So I'm in trouble." Then he adds with a shrug of his shoulders: "But I guess I've got plenty of time."

Over a yellow knit-shirt, Parks is wearing a short-sleeved green sweater with "Ireland" emblazoned on it. A blanket covers his legs, leading down to a pair of black sandals. A backwards-turned baseball cap does not quite cover a long mane of white hair jutting behind his ears. The thick, snow-white mustache which he has worn for years fills out a furrowed but still elegantly handsome face. ("My father looked like the black Clark Gable—and better," as his daughter Toni says.) One immediately notices, too, the long, thin, delicate-looking hands that have cradled many kinds of cameras and continue to linger long hours at console and computer keyboards.

Parks speaks huskily and very softly, in the voice of someone long accustomed to a necessary conservation of energy. For years, he is saying, he has preferred working in the wee hours of the night. "The telephone stops ringing, I put on my favorite composers and listen to them. This house is never without music. With this new novel I've been working on, it might be Rachmaninoff or Prokofiev. Maybe Ravel. Depending on what section I was writing. Certain chapters in the book demanded a certain kind of music. And the music immediately carries me back to where I left off."

After eight years of writing and revising, Parks had recently finished a long biographical novel. The subject is William Turner, the nineteenth-century British landscape artist. For Parks, "saturated" in Turner's life and times, the experience sometimes verged on a haunting. "He used to come knock on my bedroom door at three o'clock in the morning and say, 'Get up! Work on me!' " Parks says with a smile. "So I finally named this novel *The Sun-Stalker*. Turner always stalked the sun, he was absolutely mesmerized by it."

He continues: "Turner sort of changed my whole attitude toward my work. In terms of taking chances, not being afraid to attempt something new. You let your mind go where it's free to roam, and try to live up to it."

The result for Parks was an art form that one friend has called "poetography." Parks's two most recent books, *Arias in Silence* and *Glimpses toward Infinity*, are comprised of color plates that blend together nature photographs and abstract art, with poems on the facing page.

"All these are horizons of my imagination," Parks describes. "I've told other photographers that it's not really necessary to travel around the world to get good pictures—and most of the materials for these came right out of this living room. Like dry leaves, petals, or maybe a stone from the sea. Then some of the poetry I wrote accommodates the pictures, and some doesn't. But studying Turner stretched my mind. There are a lot of beautiful things in life, and this took me away from poverty and racism and crime for a while."

The latter are subjects to which Parks has never been a stranger, both professionally and personally. As his longtime friend and *Life* magazine colleague Philip Kunhardt, Jr., wrote in an introduction to *Gordon Parks: A Poet and His Camera*, Parks had decided "to wage his own personal battle against the world and for it, by using photography and words and music in place of fists and guns and blood. It would have been easy for him to take that other course."

"Sometimes I look back," Parks says, "and I'm most amazed that I survived at all."

*   *   *

When Gordon Parks was born into rural poverty in the little south-western Kansas town of Fort Scott, on November 30, 1912, the family doctor pronounced him dead. He was being wrapped up for disposal, when the doctor's young assistant asked if he might try something. "I was swished about in a tub of cold water like a slab of beef," Parks recounts in his 1990 autobiography, *Voices in the Mirror*. "Suddenly I started yelling, and they say I kept up the yelling for an hour." He was named for the Dr. Gordon who saved his life.

He was the last of fifteen children raised by Andrew Jackson Parks and his wife Sarah. The father sustained a small family farm, the mother worked as a maid. She died when Gordon was fourteen. Four of Parks's closest boyhood friends, he has written, "died of senseless brutality before they were twenty-one." On the Kansas prairies, where Parks attended a segregated grade school, "Blacks and whites moved about in deceiving air, seeming to avoid any sort of relationship that might somehow damage their pride. And as they lived, so were they consumed, one race by despair, the other by intolerance. . . .

"Where could I begin to build pride? In church, God and the saints and angels were always white. In school the textbooks always showed my ancestors picking cotton, dancing jigs or strumming banjos. Africans were always depicted as savages. My history books never mentioned heroic blacks like Hiram Revels, Peter Salem, Benjamin Banneker or Harriet Tubman. Much later I read about Russia's great poet Alexander Pushkin and France's revered novelist Alexandre Dumas, but not until years later did anyone tell me that they were men with black blood."

Now, as Parks taps his pipe against the table and reaches for a refill from his tobacco pouch, I ask whether he's always smoked a pipe. "A good part of my life. I'm following my dad there." He points to a framed photograph on the wall beside him, depicting a mustached man wearing spectacles and a farmer's hat, with a long pipe in his mouth. "I used to have all of his pipes," Parks continues, his hand moving toward a second picture of a beautiful woman in a long white dress. "Somebody asks me who my heroes were, it's mom and pop. They're always there looking at me—very sternly. When I have to make a decision, I look at them and they say, 'Don't do it that way, do it this way.' Yes ma'am, yes sir. Telling me what is right and what is wrong. Helping me to remember my teachings."

Parks draws out the word "teachings," pauses briefly, then continues: "In my books I write mostly poetry about my father; with my mother, I'm inclined to write prose. I don't know why. I would think it would be just the opposite, but it's not. I had fourteen brothers and sisters. The first five were by another mother, and my mother brought ten to birth. But I didn't even know they were half-brothers and -sisters until I was older. I never saw any violent arguments, either between them or between my parents. Because my mother was boss! When she says something, everybody listens, including my father. He was a magnificent man.''

Parks stares out the window for a long moment. "My mother was the one who told my father to get me out of Kansas. There was an awful lotta prejudice in Kansas at that time. I remember Miss Mc-Clintock in high school, a teacher who advised us black kids: 'Don't bother to go to college and spend your mother's and father's money, because you're gonna be porters and maids.' So I dedicated the twenty-ninth of my thirty [honorary] doctorates to her!''

Parks laughs, then adds quietly: "Before the flowers on my mother's grave had wilted, my father had me on a train to my sister in Minnesota. I ran into some hell there.''

That was in 1927. Still a young teenager who would never return to school, Gordon Parks spent his next fourteen years struggling to make ends meet. His troubles began soon after his arrival in St. Paul, when for no good reason his sister's husband threw him out into the cold winter. Parks moved into a rat-infested flophouse, found work washing dishes and then playing self-taught blues piano in a brothel. He had never taken lessons, merely toyed at his family's old keyboard. "My father was not one to consider the piano something for a boy to do," he says. "Mine was a natural gift. I don't know still where that comes from.''

When the Great Depression cost him a busboy's job in a wealthy white club, Parks hopped a freight to Chicago. There he briefly wound up in jail after a fight with three white men who jumped him. Bad luck seemed to stalk him. Parks had written a song, *No Love*, which caught the ear of an orchestra leader. Invited to travel with the group, Parks wound up in Harlem, where the fellow skipped town. Parks was left stranded and penniless. In 1933, he signed up for FDR's Civilian Conservation Corps, where he saved enough money to return to Minneapolis and marry his first love, Sally Alvis. Gordon Parks, Jr., was born a year later.

Parks sustained his family playing piano at a roadhouse. His compositions proved popular with the prostitutes and hustlers. In the autumn of 1935, he found a better job as a waiter on the North Coast Limited, a luxury train that ran between Chicago, St. Paul and Seattle. Parks began reading the magazines that wealthy passengers left behind on the train. One was *Vogue*, already a popular fashion periodical. Another magazine contained a portfolio of photographs of migrant workers driven from their homes by the Dust Bowl. Parks was stunned by the power in the pictures. He took the magazine home and studied it for weeks. He memorized the names of the photographers—Carl Mydans, Walker Evans, Dorothea Lange, Ben Shahn. These, and more, all worked under the auspices of the Farm Security Administration (FSA) that the Roosevelt Administration had established. "I never dreamt that I would one day work with them," Parks says.

On one layover in Chicago, Parks found himself in a theater, watching a newsreel that showed a courageous cameraman, Norman Alley, remaining at his post while Japanese fighter planes bombed the U.S. gunboat *Panay*. When Alley was introduced afterwards on stage, Parks "was carried away by his bravery and dedication to his job. From that moment on I was determined to become a photographer. Three days later I bought my first camera at a pawnshop for $7.50."

Still, his life remained wracked with turmoil. Parks got fired from the railroad after a dining steward provoked him into a confrontation. His wife would come and go, because of her domineering father. He tried playing semi-pro basketball, then landed a porter's job on a fast train between Minneapolis and Chicago.

Looking back in 1990 over the hardships of his early years, Parks would write: "They seem to have divided up my quietudes with things that lambaste me. I have learned to accept them without too much surprise; to know that each hour can be as changeable as the last. The years have also taught me that understanding rhymes with forgiveness." Through it all, he felt a need "to explore every tool shop of my mind." He became "devoted to my restlessness; to chasing down poetry in the best of what I found; to opening doors that allowed me entrance into their universe, no matter how small. If I found nothing, I tried another door."

Early in 1938, Parks walked through the door of an upscale women's clothing store in St. Paul and asked if they might need any fashions photographed. The manager wasn't interested, but the fellow's wife convinced him to give Parks a chance. Parks borrowed a Speed Graphic camera on credit, and spent a day photographing models. But when he developed the film, he was devastated to find that he had double-exposed all but one shot. Sally Parks suggested he take a chance and blow up the one good picture. When the store manager saw it, he was thrilled. Where were the rest? Parks told the truth. He was allowed to reshoot. Soon his pictures filled the windows of Frank Murphy's store. That was the beginning. Parks's work caught the eye of Marva Louis, wife of then-heavyweight champion Joe Louis. She urged him to relocate to Chicago, where she could help him find more clients.

So, soon after the birth of a second child, Toni, in 1940, the Parks family moved. Still haunted by the power of the Farm Security Administration's Dust Bowl photographs, Parks took his old Voightlander Brilliant camera into Chicago's South Side ghetto, feeling compelled to make "a serious comment on the human condition." Two months before Pearl Harbor, his scenes of poverty were first exhibited at the South Side Community Art Center. The Julius Rosenwald Fund, a cultural foundation that had been established to help promising blacks and Southern whites, offered him a fellowship. Parks was being invited to come to Washington, for a year's apprenticeship at none other than the Farm Security Administration. There, under the tutelage of Roy Emerson Stryker, photographers "used their cameras to speak for these people who couldn't speak for themselves."

By the time he arrived at the FSA, Parks is remembering, some of the photographers whose work had so stirred him in the Dust Bowl days were no longer there. "The FSA was in trouble by then with certain powers-that-be. But I learned so much there under Roy Stryker about the importance of using photographs as a weapon. Their files showed it all—the tragedy of the migrant workers, the eroding farmlands. I suddenly realized that if they could use the camera against poverty the way they were, why couldn't I use the camera against racism? And the very first picture I made there has become my most well-known."

It was a portrait of a lean black woman named Ella Watson, holding a mop and a broom, standing in front of the American flag. Parks called it *American Gothic*. Stryker told him it would get them all fired. Indeed, pressure from conservatives soon found the FSA absorbed into the new Office of War Information. Parks remembers thinking that his photograph had been destroyed—"because some Southern Congresspeople felt it was an indictment of the government itself." Some years later, after Parks had moved to New York and suddenly saw the picture appear on the front page of the *Washington Post*, he "immediately headed for Washington, saw the black guy then in charge of the FSA archives, and got my negatives out. Mine!" He points to a corner of the apartment. "They're over there in the closet."

During his year-long fellowship at the FSA, Parks had also first met the novelist Richard Wright. "In a literary sense, he was my first inspiration. My bible was his *Twelve Million Black Voices*. We used pictures from the FSA to illustrate that book. Then Wright was among the people, along with Paul Robeson, that I photographed for Edwin Embree's *13 against the Odds*. In retrospect, Wright seemed to be throwing his intellectual weight at me—but in a nice way, not in a way that I resented. It was, 'Hey, boy, learn *this*.'"

Back in New York after a brief photography stint with the Office of

War Information, a third child, David, was born in 1944. Now Parks decided to return to the realm of fashion photography. The editors at *Harper's Bazaar* loved his work, but informed Parks that the Hearst organization didn't hire Negroes. His FSA boss, Roy Stryker, suggested Parks pay a visit to the prominent photographer Edward Steichen, who in turn arranged an interview for him with *Vogue*. His first assignment resulted in an eight-page color spread of the winter's collection of evening gowns.

For a time, Parks rejoined Stryker, who had been hired by the Standard Oil Company to build a picture file on rural America. Parks went from shooting "thinnish, delicate women swathed in satin and silk" to a "farmer's wife carrying a stack of tobacco leaves under her arm." Stryker found the Parks family a "beautiful little bungalow" outside the city in White Plains. "During those early years when I was inclined to loathe all whites," Parks would write, "one [like Stryker] would invariably emerge to prove me wrong."

The Second World War drew to a close. "Young black men, having served overseas, were now returning to fight the kind of tyranny they had helped put an end to in Europe," Parks recounted in his memoirs. "The Civil War and two world wars had taught us that bigotry could not be legislated from a man's heart. It was up to black people to take things into their own hands, and they were on the move. And I was ready to move with them."

By now, Parks had become a close friend of Ralph Ellison. "Ralph was intense in a different way, a more friendly way, than Richard Wright," Parks remembers. "You learned from Ralph just from the experience of knowing him. He had a tremendous sense of humor. That's a part of Ellison a lot of people don't know, because Ralph was also very sophisticated. In those days, I was half-broke and Ralph wasn't making too much either. When my family went away to Maine one summer, he came to write at my house out in the country. He wrote part of *Invisible Man* up there. Ralph used to kid me that Ras, one of the characters in the book, he'd patterned after me!"

Parks and Ellison teamed up to do an article, "The Need of Psychiatric Treatment in Harlem," assigned by a magazine called *'48*. When the periodical folded, Parks decided to take the piece to *Life* magazine. Although *Life* didn't take the story, they did take on Gordon Parks. And, after the publication of *Invisible Man*, Parks would do a photo-essay for *Life* on his friend Ralph Ellison. The stars of both men were finally ascending.

As the first black staff photographer ever hired by *Life*, in 1948, one might imagine that Parks would have felt a certain isolation. Asked whether this was so, he shakes his head and responds: "I learned a lot about people, and life, at *Life* magazine. Of course I had worked at the FSA, which was practically all-white. Then I had gone to *Vogue*, which was lily-white, and Standard Oil, which was seeking a new image. So by the time I got to *Life*, I didn't feel any sense of isolation. Things happened so fast for me there. The first story I did was on the gangs in Harlem, there was nobody else who could get inside the black gangs. And there were no fashion photographers at *Life* then. When the fashion editor, Sally Kirkland, discovered I had worked for *Vogue*, before long she had me on the *Queen Mary* on the way to do fashions in Paris. Now she didn't have to go out and get an Avedon or a Penn to shoot at the collections. So they had reasons to treat me well, and the people I met there never showed disrespect for me in any way. In fact, they pushed me, they helped me.

"There was just a great sense of brotherhood amongst the people who worked at *Life*. If somebody in your family was sick, the magazine looked out after them. It's dangerous to say, but if I counted my friends, they'd be the vast majority. These were the people I saw every day of my life. So this helped me realize that the most important thing in the world was to judge someone by who they are, not by their color. One of the curators of my will is Phil Kunhardt, who used to be *Life*'s managing editor. Katy Strickler, who comes from Kansas, is another executor of my will. She's a white Southern woman. But I know I can depend upon these people. They know me, they know my kids, they care."

From the beginning it seemed a remarkable juggling act, moving between worlds at such opposite extremes, from Harlem gangs to Paris fashions. Did Parks see it that way?

"You know when it came to me what I was doing?" he responds. "I was shooting Red Jackson's gang. One of the kids had been killed by a rival group, I have a picture of him lying on the sidewalk. Three days later I'm photographing a gown by Jimmy Galanos, this famous American designer. And Sally Kirkland, my editor, is telling me, 'Gordon, try to capture the red in Jimmy's gown, it's so fragile, so beautiful.' I remembered the blood on this kid and compared it to the 'blood' on the gown. It was just about the same fragility in the light, you see. But that's how close I was to subjects, intertwining them."

In Harlem, Parks had won the trust of Red Jackson and his Midtowners gang. He had traveled with them for weeks. He had even protected them by showing his *Life* credentials when the police burst into their headquarters. And he did not let them down, in what became Parks's first test of integrity at *Life* magazine.

Parks remembers: "I had a picture of Red Jackson with a smoking gun in his hand, and they wanted to run it on the cover. I said, 'You can't do that, the kid'll be in jail next week.' They said, 'Oh come on Gordon, it's a gang shot.' I said, 'I don't care, I'm not gonna betray Red.' I wasn't sure what they'd do. So I took the negative and cut it up. I *knew* they weren't gonna run it then. And since I wasn't on the staff yet, I could do that."

Life acquiesced. After his cover story ran, Parks was given a full-time position. In a description of the Harlem gang story that seems as timely today as it was fifty years ago, Parks later wrote in his memoirs: "I found how indifferent death could be in this warring place, where honor meant spilling blood over the most trivial thing—an accidental bump on the shoulder; a dispute over a stolen bicycle; an invasion of the wrong territory; a girl's innocent wink; or a game of stickball. Teenagers, talking death, took blood oaths to die together. Mothers feared a knock at the door, afraid it was the police to say that a son was dead."

During his first eighteen months at *Life*, Parks was assigned fifty-two stories. Then, in the dream assignment of all photo-journalism, he was posted for two years to the Paris bureau. Almost overnight, the Parks family were living with a maid and butler in a four-story English Tudor home. There he rented a piano, began carrying a diary, and writing poetry. In between assignments covering everyone from General Dwight D. Eisenhower to fighter Sugar Ray Robinson, Parks went to work composing a concerto. "After several weeks," he has written, "I had devised an intricate mathematical system for using numbers that corresponded to notes—allowing me to establish themes and harmonic structures." In Paris, "for the first time in my life I was relaxing from tension and pressure. My thoughts, continually rampaging against racial conditions, were suddenly becoming as peaceful as snowflakes. Slowly a curtain was dropping between me and these soiled years."

In Paris, too, Parks was reunited with Richard Wright. The author had accepted an invitation from the French government to move his family there, after Wright's purchase of a home in a white New York neighborhood brought only broken windows and other indignities. Parks invited him to lunch. Just once, Wright said, he would love to dine at luxurious Maxim's. Parks agreed to meet him there. He wanted to give something back to the man who ten years before had "nudged me toward a more diligent use of my camera."

At the end of a long day together, Parks recalled Wright saying over a bottle of wine: "I didn't want to write ordinary books, but something akin to bombs." He wondered whether Parks had considered giving up on America? No, Parks replied, and quoted a line from Wright's

Will Marion Cook, composer/conductor and mentor to Duke Ellington. Photo: Portrait Collection, Photographs and Prints Division, Schomburg Center for Research in Black Culture, The New York Public Library, Astor, Lenox and Tilden Foundations.

Louis Armstrong, with famed vocalist Billie Holiday who, as Albert Murray writes, "used to say she didn't think of herself as singing but as blowing a horn." Photo: Photographs and Prints Division, Schomburg Center for Research in Black Culture, The New York Public Library, Astor, Lenox and Tilden Foundations.

Wynton Marsalis talks to his horn. Photo by Frank Stewart.

Author Stanley Crouch, who introduced Wynton Marsalis to his own mentor, Albert Murray. Photo by Martine Bisagni.

Wynton Marsalis (right), absorbing the wisdom of Albert Murray in the author's living room in Harlem. Photo by Michele Murray.

This picture of Albert Murray was taken by his friend Ralph Ellison in 1948, at the Ellison home on 749 St. Nicholas Avenue in New York, while Murray was on leave from Tuskegee Institute. Photo by Ralph Ellison, courtesy of Albert Murray.

This photo of Ralph Ellison was taken by Albert Murray, circa 1960, when both writers were visiting the author John Cheever at his farm in Ossining, New York. Photo by Albert Murray.

Gordon Parks took this picture of his friend Ralph Ellison in New York's Central Park during the early 1950s, around the time of publication of *Invisible Man*. Photo by Gordon Parks.

The *joie de vivre* of Duke Ellington in concert, captured by his friend Gordon Parks. Photo by Gordon Parks.

The artist Romare Bearden (right), hanging out on the rooftop of Albert Murray's appartment. Photo by Frank Stewart, courtesy of Albert Murray.

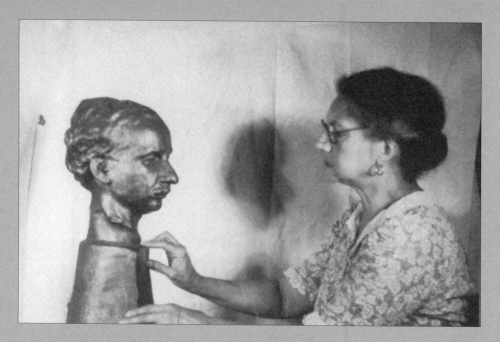

The sculptor Meta Warrick Fuller, at work on a bust of her husband, Dr. Solomon Carter Fuller. Photo: Photographs and Prints Division, Schomburg Center for Research in Black Culture, The New York Public Library, Astor, Lenox and Tilden Foundations.

Painter Loïs Mailou Jones, standing beside the painting she presented to President Leopold Senghor of Senegal in October of 1976. Photo courtesy of Loïs Mailou Jones and the Moorland-Spingarn Research Center.

Painter Jacob Lawrence in his Seattle Studio, 1994, at work on his Builders series. Photo by
Spike Mafford, courtesy of Jacob Lawrence.

The 19th-century actor Ira Aldridge, on stage as Othello. Photo:
Portrait Collection, Photographs and Prints Division, Schomburg Center for
Research in Black Culture, The New York Public Library, Astor, Lenox and Tilden
Foundations.

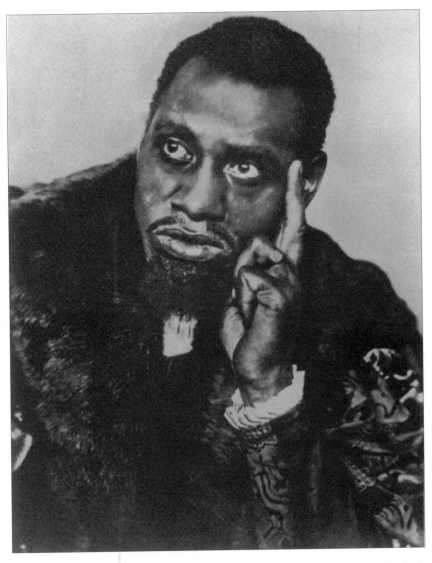

Paul Robeson, who learned elocution for his own Othello from Aldridge's daughter, in costume for the role. Photo: Portrait Collection, Photographs and Prints Division, Schomburg Center for Research in Black Culture, The New York Public Library, Astor, Lenox and Tilden Foundations.

The Robeson family on the front porch of their home in Enfield, Connecticut, 1941— Paul, Sr., his wife Essie, and their son, Paul, Jr. Photo: Portrait File, Photographs and Prints Division, Schomburg Center for Research in Black Culture, The New York Public Library, Astor, Lenox and Tilden Foundations.

Gordon Parks, as seen through the eyes of his daughter Toni. Photo by Toni Parks.

Mary McLeod Bethune applauding her friend Eleanor Roosevelt at a joint public appearance. Photo: Portrait Collection, Photographs and Prints Division, Schomburg Center for Research in Black Culture, The New York Public Library, Astor, Lenox and Tilden Foundations.

A snapshot of teacher Elma Lewis (right) with her friend Rosa Parks, one of the founders of the civil rights movement. Photo courtesy of Elma Lewis.

Harvard professor and author Cornel West. Photo American Program Bureau, Inc.

A 1943 portrait of Howard University scholar Alain Locke. Photo by James Latimer Allen: Portraits, Photographs and Prints Division, Schomburg Center for Research in Black Culture, The New York Public Library, Astor, Lenox and Tilden Foundations.

work that had so influenced him: "Black people are on the move back there, and I want to be moving with them." Wright smiled. As they parted company, Parks remembered the author of *Native Son* saying: "You know, Gordon, the substantial differences between black and white folk are not so much blood and color. I truly feel that it is what they both hope for that will bring a stronger kinship than any words or lawful legislation."

They would never meet again. Within a year, Wright was dead. Over the decades since, Parks remained "mindful of the description he penned in my daughter Toni's copy of his *Black Boy*. Bearing a lifetime of his experience, it says simply, 'Freedom belongs to the strong.' "

Parks had found himself able to journey across Europe "without judgments based on color." He had seen his first piano concerto performed in Venice. Now, at the end of 1952, he sailed back to New York. "I was black and I felt black," he has written, "but my aspirations had propelled me toward things most blacks were denied. . . . For me it seemed at times like I had won a rather pyrrhic victory. . . . Yet I was not unaware that America, with all its shortcomings, still had more to offer black people than any country in the world." From the skyscraper that housed the Henry Luce empire, Parks would soon embark on new journeys where his camera was indeed his "weapon" on behalf of the civil rights movement. The first of these took him to Birmingham, Alabama. The assignment was "Segregation in the South." It was shortly before Martin Luther King's crusade would begin in nearby Montgomery.

"I was only betrayed by one guy at *Life*," Parks is saying. "He was the Southern Bureau chief at the time. When I've written about what happened, I don't give his real name because I didn't want to embarrass his wife and children. He knew who he was. He was a scum-bum. He nearly got me killed down there."

The bureau chief was a secret member of a local White Citzen's Council. He alerted the group to the presence of Parks and a partner. They found themselves being followed constantly in Alabama, and briefly went into hiding. Then they headed for the little town of Anniston, to tell the story of a black sharecropper family. It took a week before the Citizen's Council discovered their presence at Willie Causey's farm. As Parks left by a back road, white townspeople closed in "with rope, tar and feathers." On a train leaving Birmingham, another group tried to seize Parks's film. Miraculously, the story made it into print.

By now, Parks's suspicions about the bureau chief had been confirmed. He remembers: "Irene Saint, who was head of the correspondents, called me into her office and asked me what was all this talk about our friend. I said, 'Well, I didn't tell you.' She said, '[Alfred] Eisenstadt told me.' See, I'd told Eisenstadt and he'd stormed into Irene's office to berate this guy for betraying another photographer. She said, 'I don't believe it.' I said, 'Well, you don't have to believe it, but I'm ready to go to Henry Luce since you brought it up. And I have proof.'

"Well, as so happened, next day down in Anniston, some of the bureau chief's associates took all of Willie Causey's belongings and put his family on the highway. The bureau chief was supposed to notify us in case anything happened to Causey when the story came out. You know what he did? He went off on a vacation. He *knew* about it. That's when *Life* pulled him back to New York, put him in a little inconsequential office outside of Irene Saint's, and that's the last I heard of him."

The magazine also sent two editors down to try to help the Causeys. They were met in the Anniston mayor's yard by several men armed with rifles and shotguns. *Life* relocated the Causey family and gave them $25,000. This was not the last time the magazine would be called into action by a Gordon Parks story.

Richard Stolley, who went on to become editorial director of Time Incorporated, recalls working with Parks in 1956 on a series about the desegregation of Southern schools. Racism, Stolley has said, "was almost an abstraction until this legendary photographer came into the South and there was no place we could have lunch. You suddenly realized, Jesus, here's this guy who's a brilliant photographer, writer, composer, soon-to-be filmmaker, a Renaissance man, for God's sake— we couldn't even have a meal with him in the South. The savagery of the system down there was never more apparent to us than when Gordon arrived."

Spring of 1961, Rio de Janeiro. Parks had been dispatched by *Life* to Brazil to do a photo-essay on poverty. He would later write: "Breathing hard, balancing a tin of water on his head, a small boy climbed toward us. He was miserably thin, naked but for filthy denim shorts. His legs resembled sticks covered with skin and screwed into his feet. Death was all over him, in his sunken eyes, cheeks and jaundiced coloring. He stopped for breath, coughing, his chest heaving as water slopped over his bony shoulders. Then jerking sideways like a mechanical toy, he smiled a smile I will never forget. Turning, he went on up the mountainside. . . . Catacumba was the name of the favela where I found Flavio da Silva."

For what would become his most famous piece, Parks moved into the favela with the family of twelve-year-old Flavio. "I left my clothes down at the hotel on the waterfront in Rio," he is recalling. "I knew it was dangerous coming up there. My interpreter told me, 'Don't leave at night, you'll get killed.' Even the police had to avoid the area. I slept on the floor of their shack, which was about as wide as from here to there." Parks points from where we are sitting to the wall about eight feet away. "All the family slept in one bed except for the baby Zacharias, who had a little cot."

Flavio, the eldest of eight children, kept the family going. Parks took the boy to a clinic, where a doctor diagnosed him with bronchial asthma, malnutrition and possibly tuberculosis. The prognosis was a year to live. Parks bought food for the family. When he said goodbye after more than two weeks, Flavio's words echoed behind his car: "Come back! Come back!"

Parks realized that *Life* was only intending for a single photograph to represent each country in a series on Latin America. Still, one editor had strongly encouraged him to pursue the Flavio story. When Parks saw the initial layout, he was appalled. In a letter to the magazine's managing editor, Parks wrote: "The layout shocks me. I gave so much to that story, perhaps too much. I can think of it now only as an exercise in frustration. To use one photograph of that dying boy juxtaposed against one of some socialite is, to my thinking, a journalistic travesty. You will, perhaps, think I am out of my senses. At this point I probably am. Nevertheless, I feel that I can no longer work here. With regret, I offer my resignation."

The editor who had supported Parks asked that he please wait out the weekend. "It seems reasonable that miracles happen on the Sabbath," Parks would recall. Dean Rusk, then secretary of state, suddenly gave a speech. Rusk warned that if the U.S. did not give substantial aid to the poor of Latin America, Communism would surely spread. *Life* reconsidered. It gave the Flavio story an eight-page spread. No one was prepared for what happened next. Thousands of letters poured into Time-Life headquarters. "We have never seen any reaction from readers as spontaneous as this one," said a publisher's office memorandum. "Queries are coming in from bureaus asking where people may direct money, food and clothing."

"In less than three weeks," says Parks, "thirty thousand dollars came in. Every night today, you look on TV and see thousands of kids starving in Africa or Asia. So I don't know whether Flavio would have the same effect today as it did then, I doubt it. Because people really rallied to this kid."

In Denver, the Children's Asthma Research Institute announced that, if Flavio was delivered to their door, they would do their best to save him without charge. *Life*'s Rio bureau cabled that Flavio's health was worse. If it was tuberculosis, as Parks recounted, "This could prevent his entering this country. I suggested that President Kennedy be asked to help. The President's message: 'Bring him on.' Two days later I was speeding toward Rio."

Parks continues: "The doctors in Rio are telling me, 'Why are you taking this kid to America? He's gonna die on your hands.' I said, 'Flavio wants to live, I've got the money.' I remember walking up the hill together, Flavio understood what was happening and he took me by the hand. He kept asking, 'What did the doctors say?' I said, 'You're gonna be alright, don't worry, I'm gonna take you to America.' Then, through my interpreter, Flavio said: 'I'm gonna tell you, Comrade Gor-don, I'm not afraid to die. But I'm worried about my brothers and sisters. The good people die young in a favela. You know that, right?' "

Parks's eyes mist over. His gaze is momentarily far away. "I never will forget that as long as I live. 'Good people die young in a favela.' It's so horrible. Over 26,000 kids died from malnutrition that same year up in that area. 26,000! *Life* had given me another $25,000 to move Flavio's family out of the favela. When I brought them down to the truck that morning, a woman grabbed me. She was screaming. 'What about us? Are we to stay here to die?' What could I say? I want to rescue the whole favela, I can't do it. I wished I could."

Parks stares down at the rug beneath his feet. "I asked his dad at the airport before we got on the plane, 'José, you know several people want to adopt Flavio, including me. What about it?' He said, 'Nah! I don't care how long you keep him, but bring him home.' His father wasn't about to let Flavio go. He's gotten his father a house and a truck. He's a meal ticket."

Besieged by newsmen's cameras upon arrival in America, Flavio had ducked under Gordon Parks's arm and burst into tears. For the next two years, the boy would remain at the Children's Asthma Research Institute in Denver. Fully cured, having learned English, he spent his last day on American soil in New York with Gordon Parks.

They had corresponded regularly for several years, then lost touch. In 1976, on another trip to Latin America, Parks sought out Flavio again. The favela was gone, bulldozed by Brazilian authorities not long after Parks's story appeared. Gone, too, by now was the weekly *Life* magazine. Flavio was married with two children. He was struggling, but surviving. He still dreamt of coming to America.

On the airplane home, Parks opened a package that Flavio had given him that afternoon. It was a handsome black billfold containing pictures of Flavio's family, including Flavio, Jr. "I opened the *Life* magazine and placed the two Flavios next to one another," Parks writes in *Voices in the Mirror*. "The resemblance was startling; their faces seemed to merge as one. Perhaps then, this was the point of Flavio da Silva's story—showing his son, his alert brown eyes and healthy body, a body not hampered by malnutrition and poverty. Such a father as Flavio would never allow that."

Now, almost thirty-five years after the story that aroused a nation's heart, Parks is saying: "Listen, Flavio and I talked less than a month ago. He's in some trouble again. He's not living with his wife and three kids. There's sixteen people living in that little bungalow I bought for them, with *Life*'s help. I just sent him a thousand dollars. There's no way for me to forget Flavio."

The turbulent 1960s were also so for Gordon Parks. His first marriage disintegrated after more than twenty years. He fell in love with a beautiful friend of his daughter Toni, thirty years younger than he was. They had a daughter, Leslie, in 1967. This marriage, too, did not survive the decade. Nor did the leading civil rights leaders whose lives he chronicled and whom, in the case of Malcolm X, he had closely befriended.

It was 1963 when *Life*'s editors called Parks in for a meeting. "*Life* had good reason to feel that my heart lay with the civil rights movement, which it did. They had been trying for a couple years to get a very capable white woman reporter inside for a story on the Black Muslims and Malcolm X. There was no way. Finally they asked me, 'Do you think you could do this with a white reporter?' I said no. 'Do you think you can do it with a black reporter?' I said, 'I don't know.' I told them I could try to do it myself, but I'd have to write my own text because my neck was gonna be on the line.

"That's when I first met Malcolm in Harlem. When Elijah Muhammad finally gave his consent to the story, he told me, 'Look, brother Malcolm's gonna be your guide into the Nation of Islam. If I like your story, I'll send you a box of cigars. If I don't like it, we'll be out to visit you!' "

Parks laughs. When he was assembling the story, he had convinced his editors to allow him to take issue with a guilty verdict, where fourteen black Muslims were convicted of assault in Los Angeles. That night, heading back to New York with Malcolm X on a red-eye flight, Parks recalls:

"Malcolm fell asleep and put his head on my shoulder. When he woke up, he looked at me and said 'Hey, brother'—before that, he'd always called me 'Mr. Parks'—'Hey, brother, I just read your book *A Choice of Weapons*. Quibilah [Malcolm's daughter] needs a godfather, and I elect you. How about it?' I said, Sure. The plane landed. Before

we got out of the taxi, I said, 'You called me brother for the first time.'
Malcolm laughed and said, 'You earned it. You traveled the fire with
me.' "

Parks remembers a time, not long thereafter, when *Life* invited Malcolm X to come talk to the editors over lunch. "Malcolm called me
and said, 'You want me to lighten up?' I said, 'No, say what you want.
Say what you'd say to somebody on the streetcorner.' So he did."

And what was the editor's reaction? "Well, they didn't need any hot
pepper for lunch!" Parks laughs again.

Then his tone becomes somber as he recalls a January afternoon,
early in 1965, when Malcolm X suddenly showed up at Parks's home
in Westchester County. Parks had long since sensed that something
was awry between Malcolm and the Muslim leadership. They had insisted he not appear in their group photograph. Now, having spent
most of the past year on a life-changing journey to Africa and Mecca,
Malcolm X had been expelled from the Nation of Islam.

"He stayed for about an hour at the house," Parks continues. "My
wife fixed us tea, in the bedroom. He told me he had been awakened
to the dangers of racism. 'It's not just a black and white problem,' he
said. 'The cords of bigotry have to be cut with the same blade.' He
said he'd done much as a Muslim that he regretted. He felt he'd allowed himself to fall under their spell, been pointed in a certain direction and told to march.

"That's when he told me they were trying to kill him. I asked him,
couldn't he get help from the police? He said, 'I taught the Muslims
their tactics. If they want to get you, they're gonna get you. They
already firebombed my house.' He invited me down to a meeting in
Harlem that Sunday, where he was speaking at the Audubon Ballroom.
We embraced. That's the last time I saw him alive. I intended to go to
the talk, but something happened and I couldn't.' "

After Malcolm X was murdered by several Muslim gunmen that
Sunday as he stood at the podium in the Audubon Ballroom, Parks
spent that evening with Malcolm's wife, Betty Shabazz, and their four
children. She showed Parks a blood-stained list that had been in Malcolm's pocket. It contained the names of probable hit men. Parks made
a copy for future reference. He had a story to write.

That March of 1965, after receiving three bomb threats, *Life* published Parks's "The Death of Malcolm X." The day after it came out,
Parks remembers, "*Life* was warned that I was next. They put my
whole family and me on a plane, boom!, out of the country. Well,
that's the way *Life* operated. They looked out after their people. When
I came back, they put bodyguards around me for two months. One

day I went up to this Muslim restaurant in Harlem and asked to see the head of *their* bodyguards, a man named Joseph X. We had some tea, talked about the weather. Ended with a handshake. I told *Life* to call off the bodyguards."

Now, a generation later, tragedy has struck again. Malcolm X's twelve-year-old grandson—the child of Parks's god-daughter, Quibilah—apparently set a fire that resulted in the death of his grandmother, Malcolm X's widow Betty Shabazz. "I've practically been Quibilah's father," Parks is saying. "I've helped her out with a number of problems." His voice is a near-whisper. "Her sister Malak called me last week and said she'd just been out to see the boy. He cries a lot. She was having a hard time accepting him as her nephew. I told her, 'He is *still* your nephew and you have to soften your attitude.' Because it's only going to get more difficult for him as time goes on. Malak called me back later and told me, 'Uncle Gordon, I've changed my mind about what I said.'

"They wanted me to come to Betty's funeral. But the only way right now, with my legs, was to put me in an ambulance and wheel me in. Furthermore, I couldn't put on any shoes or pants. So I just told the girls, 'Think of me as being there, in spirit.' They understood.

"I wrote a poem for Betty. Got a little carried away at that computer. I was just about to stand up and walk. Would have ruined the whole operation, because the doctors don't want any weight on my feet. It was five o'clock in the morning. Well, you know, the light through these windows is magnificent when the sunrise comes pouring in."

Such was the commitment, and the dynamism, of Gordon Parks that *Life* magazine gave his images and words the room to speak to the nation. During the Kennedy years, Parks watched a telecast of black protesters at a sit-in being doused with ketchup, salt and pepper. He recalled Attorney General Robert Kennedy having said of his attempt to build a bridge to Alabama governor George Wallace: "It's like a foreign country. There's no communication. What do we do?" Parks sat down at his typewriter and, the words "pouring from my insides like scalding water," he counseled:

"You keep trying, Mr. Kennedy. You keep going back for more, again and again, until you begin to realize what it is like for a black man to 'go slow,' to 'take it easy' while under the boot of a racist like 'Bull' Connor. Go down there sometime when the fire hoses are on full blast, when the dogs are snarling and tearing black flesh, when women, children and men are on their knees singing, crying and praying for deliverance from the agony of this beautiful land. Then go back and tell the President that if it's greatness he seeks, this is indeed his chance for it."

Life did not alter Parks's essay.

In April of 1968, the magazine sent him to Atlanta to cover the funeral of Martin Luther King, Jr. All across America after the assassination, the cities were on fire. Parks remembers: "My editor, Phil Kunhardt, said, 'Write what you feel.' Okay. I spent three days writing twenty pages on a yellow legal pad. Phil comes down to see me. He says, 'Goddamn, Gordon, I don't know whether the hell we can *say* this.' Loudon Wainwright was there to give me assistance. They're sitting there commiserating, getting drunk, and the magazine's wanting to know where my piece is. Finally Loudon says, 'Look, he was *there*. The man's written what he felt, like you told him to. Why are we going through all this bullshit?' Phil says: 'Put it on the wire to New York!' "

Life did not alter Parks's essay. It said, in part:

"Dr. King spent the last dozen years of his life preaching love to men of all colors. And, for all this, a man, white like you, blasted a bullet through his neck. And this has just about eliminated the last symbol of peace between us. We must struggle to distinguish between his act and your conscience. . . .

"We have grave doubts about your promises. We have grown to lack the patience to wait for God's deliverance. We want a new life. Our youths refuse to sit and wait to share in the affluence that you surround them with. They will cross your line—even if it means death. Dr. King's only armor was truth and love. Now that he lies dead from a lower law, we begin to wonder if love was enough."

When he saw his words in print, Parks "realized that my anguish had swept me dangerously close to hatred."

He could never separate himself from anguish, or from those who like himself had suffered it. Asked if he could name his three most memorable stories, Parks responds quickly: the Harlem gangs, Flavio, and the Fontenelle family. Yes, the Fontenelles. It was 1967. "Phil Kunhardt asked me, 'Why are black people rioting in the middle of America?' I said, 'Phil, I can live with one black family in Harlem for a week and show you.' He said, 'Go ahead.' Some people there didn't want to expose their life that way. Mrs. Fontenelle accepted me, because I told her she'd be doing her neighbors and her family a lot of good. What ultimately happened to the Fontenelles was a disaster. But if I had to do another Fontenelle family tomorrow, I would do the same thing. I would try to help them."

Parks asks his son David, who has come up from Texas to help care for his father during the recovery from surgery, if he would bring a book down from the shelf. Parks leafs to a page containing one of his most powerful images: a mother standing in a welfare office, surrounded by her four children. "Everybody in that photograph's dead but the little one," Parks says. "All of 'em."

Shortly before Parks's cover story on the Fontenelles appeared in March of 1968, he had gone to his editors and said he wanted the family moved to a bigger house. "They said, 'How we gonna do that? You get so attached to these families!' I said, 'How the hell am I gonna do a good story on these people if I *don't* get attached!' *Life* said, Okay, any time we get involved with one of your families, we've adopted them. I said, That's true, otherwise don't bother.

"You see," he explains, "somebody who's let down their curtains to allow you into their lives, and trusted you, they become part of your family. To the extent that you know you will be with them *forever* if they deserve it."

So had Gordon Parks forever remained with the Fontenelles. Through the dropped cigarette that lit the fire that killed the father and one son, in the home that *Life* had bought for them. . . . Through the deaths of two of the girls from AIDS, another from a drug overdose. . . . Through Mrs. Fontenelle's recent passing from cancer.

"The youngest boy, the one she had faith would someday amount to something, is the only one that's turned out. He wants to be a composer, I bought him some equipment. I keep telling him, 'Don't disappoint your momma.' He's a man now, living up to the standards that she set for him."

Parks is gazing out the window again at the East River, as he adds softly: "One of his kids is named Gordon."

Long, long ago, on the fateful train trip where he stared in awe at the magazine someone left behind with the pictures of the uprooted Dust Bowl migrants, one of the photographers who so impressed Parks was Carl Mydans. They had both ended up on the staff of *Life*. One day in 1963, they were talking about Parks's growing-up years in Kansas.

"Carl said, 'Man, you've got a novel in you.' I said, 'I've never written a novel.' He said, 'You ever try?' 'No.' 'Why don't you go home this weekend and try?' I said, 'I think I'll do that, Carl.' The very next week, I took some pages over to a guy Carl knew at Harper & Row. We all had lunch together. Evan Thomas offered me a contract for *The Learning Tree*. I couldn't believe it. Even ended up marrying my editor ten years later, Genevieve Young."

The book's title came from the words Parks's mother had spoken to him when he asked if they had to stay in Fort Scott forever. "I don't really know, son," she had said, "but you're to let this place be your learning tree." The book took Parks a year to write, in between photographic assignments. It became an overnight best-seller. Today, *The Learning Tree* is approaching its sixtieth printing, and has been translated into twelve languages.

"People ask me sometimes," Parks is saying, "did I plan to become a photographer or a writer or a motion picture maker? No. If anything, it was fright that drove me, that I would not live up to my mother and father's expectations. Since I had not even finished high school, I had this fear, you see. I was scrambling to do everything. People also ask me, how much was luck was involved? I say, a lotta luck. But like I tell kids, you'd better be ready when the luck comes. Otherwise it'll pass you by."

His son David brings his father a cup of tea. Parks takes a sip and continues: "I don't think until the day I die, I'll realize how I did it all. One thing is, I don't approach anything in a dilettantish manner. If I'm going to do something, do it and do it well. If you're going to compose music, listen to the great composers and absorb them. And all through my life, I listened to *people*, like that day with Carl Mydans. It wasn't easy. Lotta work. Lotta hard work. Like making a movie, the thrill is not when you walk down Broadway and look at the marquee and it says 'Gordon Parks's Learning Tree.' The thrill is when you're out there doing it. You do the best you can, and hope that posterity will give it its due."

Gordon Parks has done well by posterity. For the movie version of *The Learning Tree*, he not only directed but wrote the screenplay and the musical score. The 1969 Warner Brothers production marked the first time a black director was taken on by a major studio. Parks had opened the door that filmmakers like Mario Van Peebles and Spike Lee would walk through. Recently, *The Learning Tree* was listed by the Library of Congress as one of the twenty-five most important films ever made.

In filming *The Learning Tree* on location in Fort Scott, the native son had returned to Kansas for the first time in almost forty years. In his last autobiography, Parks wrote: "I was coming back to where I was born; where, as a poor black youth, I had been the victim of white racism and intolerance. Now I was returning with nearly an all-white crew and millions of dollars at my command. We passed a few miles south of the Evergreen Cemetery. There, in segregated graves, lay my mother, father, two sisters, a brother and several of my boyhood friends. . . .

"I climbed into the crane seat and it lifted me high into the air. Beyond, as far as I could see, were the rolling green plains of Kansas where I had spent the first fifteen years of my childhood. The cornfield beneath me had been the only means my father had for keeping his big family from starvation. . . . Our old clapboard house, standing against the storms and tornadoes, still leans into the oak tree shade where I used to sit and dream in the huge silence."

Parks put local townspeople in the film. He briefed Kyle Johnson, the young actor who portrayed him, about the night he spent lying beside his mother's coffin. The scene was shot in one remarkable take. *Life* commissioned Parks's son, Gordon, Jr., to photographically chronicle the filming. When the movie premiered in New York, two of Parks's sisters and a brother made airplane trips for the first time in their lives. They walked into the theater beside him.

Parks later had the crumbling headstones on his parents' graves replaced with matching rose-engraved granite tablets. "I have made my peace with Kansas to a certain extent," Parks is saying. "I've been out there since—they named me Kansan of the Year two times, I think they must've forgot they did that *twice*. But complete peace will be made when they move the segregated graveyards. They've sort of half-way beautified the plots and the land around them, and since my last trip they've stopped burning trash on the black side. But I've said I won't be laid to rest there until some more changes are made."

The Learning Tree had been followed by other films, starting with *Shaft* and a sequel in 1971-72. These were major box-office hits that marked the acting debut of Richard Roundtree, who had gone to high school with Parks's son David. They were action films starring Roundtree as a black private detective. The success of the *Shaft* pictures has been credited with saving the MGM studio, at a time of dire financial crisis. As filmmaker and critic William Greaves has said, they were also among the first movies "that dealt with black empowerment of a kind that is to say, here was a virile black man who had some measure of control over his destiny, which is something that American screens were very hostile to."

"We did as much as we could while we were writing the screenplay to make [John Shaft] a noble figure," Parks later told the *Washington Post*. "But I didn't think he'd become such a hero to black kids. Richard Roundtree was the first black hero to wear a mustache on screen—did you know that? I insisted on it."

Parks followed with *Supercops* in 1974, *Leadbelly* in 1976, and *The Odyssey of Solomon Northrup* in 1984. He had once spent time talking with Leadbelly, prior to the legendary folksinger's death in 1950. "I'd heard about him all my life," Parks remembers. "Frank Yablans at Paramount dropped the picture in my lap. Leadbelly was one of his heroes. Then Barry Diller took over the studio and tried to keep it out of distribution. He would've, too, if Charles Champlin hadn't come out in the *Los Angeles Times* and said it was one of the best films of the year. Diller didn't even know who Leadbelly was.''

Parks's firstborn son, Gordon, Jr., had followed him into film-making. The first of his several films was the popular *Superfly*. Then, on location in Nairobi, Kenya, in 1979, he was killed in a plane crash at the age of forty-four. Parks was finishing his third autobiography, *To Smile in Autumn*, when he received the terrible news. He wrote in an epilogue:

"Each road has its own winding; each night its own song—and there is no worse song to sing than one of grief. . . . I think back now and then, remembering the boy astride his favorite horse, galloping the wild fields; the strong boy beside me on his skis, sending snow flying as we plummeted down a mountainside. We had been close, very close, but now it seems we might have been even closer. There are so many things left unsaid, so many confidences and dreams left unshared. . . . Fortunately, he left good things for me to remember, to keep remembering, and to make conversation with.''

In *Voices in the Mirror*, Parks wrote: "Years later, Gordon III, the grandson Gordon left to me, landed on my chest as I awakened one morning. Lifting my mustache he said, 'Grandpa, I have never seen your lips before.' Then, in a brief puzzling way, he added, 'But then I've never seen my father either.' Any meaningful reply failed me. Perhaps he had said it all, but still I wondered what brought his young mind to place the two discoveries side by side. Perhaps I was seeing a future with the kind of poetry I probably wouldn't live to know.''

> *It's a wonder that in the midst*
> *of all the cold and darkness,*
> *flowered things go on flowering;*
> *that each dawn keeps drifting in*
> *with the lightness of a cloud.*
> *Despite the foul handiwork*
> *of those of us who resist*
> *understanding one another,*
> *faith blossoms—even in places*
> *of horror and terror. . . .*
> —GORDON PARKS,
> *Glimpses toward Infinity*

A few weeks before I met Gordon Parks, I had visited with his daughter Toni in his apartment. An attractive, vivacious woman now in her mid-fifties, she lives in England with her husband, British film editor Derek Parsons. But she had come to see her father through the operation on his legs. In recent years, they have begun a collaboration.

"When I was growing up, dad was directing me towards a musical career," Toni remembers. "I think he would have loved to go to Carnegie Hall and see his daughter playing concert grand piano. So I took composition lessons as a teenager, then went to the Boston Conservatory. In the '60s, I became a folksinger, which didn't last too long, and tried to act. Then I moved to California and raised my kid. I started quite late taking pictures."

On the living-room table is a calendar, containing twelve images of dancers which Toni Parks captured in 1990 during rehearsals of her father's ballet, *Martin*. It was his classical tribute to Martin Luther King, Jr., which debuted in Washington and aired that year on public television. And it marked Toni's debut as a professional photographer. Since then, a picture she took of her father has appeared on the cover of the *Washington Post Magazine*. An exhibition of her work is upcoming at England's Exeter University.

"I used to go in the darkroom with him in White Plains. He would talk about how you should treat people, that just because someone's the same color as you, it doesn't mean they're your friend. That you shouldn't judge people by the color of their skin or what they wear, but what comes out of their mouth. That's really the truth. I always call it 'lessons from my father.'

"Then when I finally got seriously into photography, what I got from him was like master classes. I'd bring my contact sheet, and he'd sit there with his loop and his red oil pencil. He'd mark the ones he thought were good, and I would ask him why. I'd say, 'Well, I sorta like that one,' and he'd tell me why it wasn't a good photograph. This went on for quite awhile. One day he said, 'You know, Gordon and David always questioned everything I said.' I said, 'But dad, I know for *sure* you know what you're talking about.' Also, they had been in their twenties, and by then I was pushing fifty."

The memories come rushing back: The voyage home from Paris on the *Queen Mary* in 1952, when Gordon Parks knew that Winston Churchill was somewhere on the boat but had been unable to find him. Suddenly, there came Toni, skipping along between Churchill and Britain's then-prime minister Anthony Eden. "This is my daddy," she introduced him. Calling her a "delightful child," Churchill invited Parks to his cabin for brandy and a good cigar, adding however that he himself was "getting too homely for photographs."

Toni continues: "I remember once Frank Sinatra came up to the house. Frankie was 'my guy,' you know. I was supposed to play the piano that night, but of course I just couldn't—my piano teacher filled in for me. And Frank and I stayed in the kitchen and ate ribs!"

There were also the painfully long absences when Parks was away on assignment. "When you get a little older, the missed birthdays and graduations all pile up and become confusing and frustrating. I'm very lucky that he's still alive, and that I could mature and see better what was happening. You have to learn how to share your father with the world. But life was very interesting with daddy, I must say. Basically my brothers and I had a ball. The only thing we were really spoiled with was books and music. We put in patios and driveways, painted, gardened, cooked, kept the house going. Our friends were always welcome. Unlike some of them, we didn't have our own telephones or get an abundance of clothes. If I wanted anything extra, I had to babysit. I think it's very good training."

She pauses and, very much like her father, looks long out the window toward the East River. "Dad said one of the problems in the world is that people can't get along in their families. So therefore how can you get along with your neighbors? It just spreads and spreads. I mean, our whole family will have arguments that get quite loud, but nobody holds grudges. He still keeps in touch with his three ex-wives."

Not long ago, she suddenly found herself doing a song cycle based on one of her father's books of poetry, *In Love*. "I just looked at the book, sat down, and started writing music for string quartet. I did about eighteen of these, one for almost every poem in the book. It was the first time in my life that I could just feel this stream going in and out. I'd never been so focused."

David Parks brings his father another cup of tea. He is a documentary filmmaker in Austin, Texas, and the author of three books. These include a diary his father had urged him to keep during his Army days in Vietnam. It became the first book to be published by a soldier who had served in the war. We are talking about David's other sister, Leslie, now a master chef at one of New York's finest restaurants.

There is a knock at the door. It is Toni Parks's son Alain, whose many tennis trophies are aligned along the top of a cabinet in Parks's workspace. He has just come from watching the Wimbledon tournament on TV, to check in on his grandfather. Now the conversation turns to Gordon Parks's own favorite recreational pastime.

"I played tennis with a lot of good players, especially in the professional-amateur tournaments," he says. "Jimmy Connors and I played together. I had the pleasure of beating [Ilie] Nastase twice. Some airline magazine once asked me what were my most exciting moments, and my buddy Ham Richardson—who was the world's doubles champion—read what I'd said and called me a damn liar. He believed my number one moment was when Tom Gorman and I beat him and Arthur Ashe on the court. Ham didn't speak to me for a week after our victory."

"Pepe, tell about the time you went up against Nastase and Bill Cosby," Parks's grandson coaches.

"Yeah, well, it was this tournament out in Hollywood and I was playing with a guy named Butch. He'd been a star at Princeton, and had one of the biggest serves in tennis. He never really made it big in the pros, but my God, he was outserving everybody out there! So anyway, there was this car worth about $12,000 that the tournament was giving away to the winning pro; the amateurs didn't get anything.

"The match is real close, Butch and I are ahead in the last set. Cosby walks up to the net and says to me, 'Hey man, you want to make $3,000?' I said, 'What are you talking about?' He said, 'Nasty [Nastase] wants the car. Drop these next two points and you've got $3,000.' I said, 'I gotta ask Butch, he's serving.' So I go back to Butch and tell him about the proposition. He says, 'Shit, I want the car, too!' He hauled off and that ball tore up the turf, man! Nastase couldn't even put his racket on it.

"Cosby yelled over, 'Is that the answer?' I yelled back, 'That's the answer!' And Butch went off with the car!"

With all his many talents, Gordon Parks is a marvelous raconteur as well. As the laughter settles in the room, the talk turns again to family and friends. For many years, Parks's closest friends have been women—the actress Dina Merrill, the writer Oriana Fallaci, the socialite Gloria Vanderbilt. Parks's relationship with Vanderbilt dated back to the summer of 1954, when he attended an exhibition of her paintings. "It was she," Parks has written, "who introduced me to poetry through notes, letters, scribblings, and an uninterrupted closeness. Perhaps if things had been different in this threatening society of ours, we might have married long ago. But I, much more than she, remained aware of the terrible distance between a black Kansas farm boy and a white heiress born to one of America's great families."

Parks says: "Women have been a great part of my life." He tells of how, when he was in the hospital recovering from his recent operation, he received seven simultaneous female visitors one afternoon. That was when his third ex-wife, Genevieve Young, happened to show up. "She said, 'You don't need *me* to come and visit you!' I said, 'I'm on drugs, Gene, I don't know where I'm at!' "

Parks asks if I would like to see the adjacent room where he works. He leads the way in his wheelchair. Here, too, the walls are lined with photographs and citations. At a writing desk facing the East River are

Parks's desktop computer and printer. The first thing a visitor notices, though, is the sprawling electronic console arrangement for recording music. "As in his photography and in his filmmaking, he has a great sense of continuity, of line, a tremendous linear aspect of his music," cellist Kermit Moore, who conducted a Brooklyn Philharmonic Chamber Orchestra's performance of Parks's music, has said. "He has a great choral understanding, too, a strong sense of subtlety and chords."

Within his inner sanctum, Parks is remembering another of his mentors—Duke Ellington. He was seventeen when he first met Ellington, asking him for an autograph behind the Orpheum Theater in Minneapolis. Parks's hero asked the youth his name. Then the Duke inscribed his signature to "Sir Gordon." Many years passed before they became close friends.

"So many stories about Duke," Parks says, a wide smile crossing his face. "His pals called him 'Monster,' 'Big Red,' all kinds of nicknames. Duke didn't like to ride the plane. He'd send everybody else on ahead. Harry Carney, his bass saxophone player, would drive him. So we were in the car together heading from Los Angeles to San Francisco, and Duke was sleeping in the back seat. As we were approaching the Bay Bridge, it seemed to be floating in the clouds. Just nothing underneath it, marvelous. Harry Carney said, 'Goddamn, look at that, isn't that beautiful.' Then he turned his head around. 'Hey, Monster! Wake up, goddamnit! Looks like there's something out here you might write music about.' So Duke stirred awake and sat up and said: 'Goddamn, these white guys are sure gettin' smart, they're floating bridges in the sky now!'"

When our mutual laughter subsides, Parks adds: "Duke taught me a lotta things. He's the one who told me, 'Listen to Ravel, listen to Debussy. Listen to all these guys, they've got something!' That's why he was so melodious, why he had such good construction."

Now Parks begins pointing out the various components of his console system. "This is the board here, where I can get the instruments—oboes, cellos, violins. And the master keyboard there. Over here is where it finally comes out on the machine—and it's ready to go to the movies!" He hands over a cassette to insert into the tape player.

"These are some excerpts from my ballet, *Martin*. Through the various movements, there were certain poignant moments in Martin Luther King's life where I try to show what he was all about. When he wrote the letter from Birmingham jail. The things that accentuated his becoming a civil rights leader. In the end, his death. And the mourning. Pretty sad piece, you know."

For the next fifteen minutes, the music fills the room. A cello speaks of the letter from the Birmingham jail. Violins cut the air, then dramatic percussion against a plaintive background of voices, bringing to mind the *Life* magazine essay that Parks addressed to the Kennedys. Finally comes the hauntingly beautiful, lonely sound of horns. One envisions Parks standing among the thousands gathered that day at Atlanta's Ebenezer Baptist Church for Martin Luther King's funeral.

"That's the end of the ballet," Parks says quietly.

Slowly, carefully, he angles the wheelchair around a tight corner leading back toward the living room. "When I first set out to make this turn, I thought I'd never do it," he says.

Dusk is settling over the city. The Independence Day fireworks will begin soon. How would he most like to be remembered? I ask. Gordon Parks thinks for a moment.

"Well, I can't honestly remember ever doing anything intentional to harm anybody. I've often thought of that, did I ever do such a thing? I might've had to hurt somebody along the way by doing something I had to do that I felt was right. But I was brought up the right way. See, even when I was hungry, I could've saved myself a lot of distress if I'd gone to the Salvation Army or somebody to help me. But Sarah Parks wouldn't have liked that. Nor would Jackson Parks."

From the wall beside him, the photographs of his parents loom large in the gathering darkness. "I wouldn't want anybody else's children to suffer what I suffered in the early days," Parks continues. "Yet I wouldn't take anything for what I went through. It's strange. Because what I've become has come from that. I don't say every kid has to suffer to learn something. But it doesn't hurt sometimes.

"I guess I have my own kind of religion. I believe more or less in the Ten Commandments. If you just respect everyone else in the world as you want to be respected, you've pretty much got it made. That's simple enough. That should take care of just about everything."

"As for all of us ordinary humans—for a long time I have entertained the impossibility of putting each one of us into a tiny room; of letting us remain silent for a moment, and then, separately, speak the absolute truth of ourselves, knowing the smallest lie could hurl us into fiery space. There we might realize how common our needs are; that hunger, hatred, and love are the same wherever we find them; that the earth, in relation to our time upon it, is hardly the size of a grain of sand. Perhaps then, in the justice of understanding, we could escape the past that imprisons us."
—GORDON PARKS, *To Smile in Autumn*

FOR FURTHER READING:

Books by Gordon Parks:

Flash Photography (Grossett and Dunlap, 1947).

Camera Portraits: The Techniques and Principles of Documentary Portraiture (F. Watts, 1948).

The Learning Tree (New York: Harper & Row, 1963).

A Choice of Weapons (New York: Harper & Row, 1966).

Gordon Parks: A Poet and His Camera (Deutsch, 1969).

Born Black (Lippincott, 1971).

Gordon Parks: Whispers of Intimate Things (Viking Press, 1971).

In Love (Lippincott, 1971).

Moments without Proper Names (New York: Viking Press, 1975).

Flavio (New York: W. W. Norton, 1978).

To Smile in Autumn (New York: W. W. Norton, 1979).

Shannon (Boston, New York: Little, Brown & Co., 1981).

Voices in the Mirror (New York: Doubleday, 1990).

Arias in Silence (Boston, New York: Little, Brown & Co., 1994).

Glimpses toward Infinity (Boston, New York: Little, Brown & Co., 1996).

Ancestors—Mary McLeod Bethune, Educator

"As the years have gone on the Negro woman has touched the most vital fields in the civilization of today. Wherever she has contributed she has left the mark of a strong character. The educational institutions she has established and directed have met the needs of her young people; her cultural development has concentrated itself into artistic presentation accepted and acclaimed by meritorious critics; she is successful as a poet and a novelist; she is shrewd in business and capable in politics; she recognizes the importance of uplifting her people through social, civic and religious activities; starting at the time when as a 'mammy' she nursed the infants of the other race and taught [them] her meagre store of truth, she has been a contributing factor of note to interracial relations. Finally, through the past century she has made and kept her home intact—humble though it may have been in many instances. She has made and is making history."

—MARY MCLEOD BETHUNE, 1933

For Gordon Parks, just beginning his sixty-year-long career as a photographer, the opportunity to meet Mary McLeod Bethune in the early 1940s had been a landmark in his life. "I had heard an awful lot about her," he says, "and her stature in the community was an example that I aspired to myself. She invited me down to Bethune-Cookman College for a week, and made sure that I met the whole student body. She asked me to pass parts of my life along to them as best I could. And we had several wonderful conversations about what I wanted to do. Mary McLeod Bethune told me not to ever give up along the way, that it would be tough for me because I was black, but that I could excel in spite of everything. I told her I intended to."

The story goes that when Mary McLeod Bethune came into the world on July 10, 1875, she was born with her eyes wide open. As the midwife who delivered Mary told her mother, she would possess an ability to see things before they happened. Both Mary's parents and all of her older siblings had been slaves in the little country town of Maysville, South Carolina. "I was the last of seventeen children, ten girls and seven boys," Bethune would remember. "When I was born, the first free child in their own home, my mother exulted, 'Thank God, Mary came under our own vine and fig tree.' "

The mother, said to be descended from African royalty in a tribe ruled by matriarchs, had "throughout all her bitter years of slavery . . . managed to preserve a queenlike dignity." She went on to supervise operation of the family's thirty-five-acre rice and cotton farm. Growing up in a two-room log cabin, Mary recalled working alongside her father: "When I was only nine, I could pick 250 pounds of cotton a day."

In the South during the Reconstruction period, it remained almost impossible for black children to receive an education. They were not permitted in public schools with whites, and there were entire Southern states without a single black school. But through the auspices of two older women who sensed something unusual about her desire to learn, Mary McLeod made a ten-mile daily walk to a nearby school. Eventually she received scholarships to North Carolina's Scotia Seminary and then Chicago's Moody Bible School.

After twice trying unsuccessfully to get a missionary appointment to Africa, she then ended up at the Haines Institute in Augusta, Georgia, "presided over by dynamic Lucy C. Laney, a pioneer Negro educator. From her I got a new vision: my life work lay not in Africa but in my own country." For the next seven years, Mary taught in various black rural schools of the Deep South. She married another teacher, Albertus Bethune, spending a year at home after the birth of a son.

Then, in 1904, she learned that hundreds of black construction workers had gathered in eastern Florida to build a railroad. And, with a dollar and a half as her capital, Bethune left her husband (they separated permanently in 1907) and journeyed to the growing resort town of Daytona Beach. Talking the owner into trusting her for the eleven-dollar-a-month rental of a shabby four-room cottage, she began fundraising at local churches. That fall, at the age of twenty-nine, "I opened the doors of my school, with an enrollment of my son and five little girls, aged from eight to twelve, whose parents paid me fifty cents' weekly tuition.

"We burned logs and used the charred splinters as pencils, and mashed elderberries for ink. I begged strangers for a broom, a lamp, a bit of cretonne to put around the packing case which served as my desk. I haunted the city dump and the trash piles behind hotels, retrieving discarded linen and kitchenware, cracked dishes, broken chairs, pieces of old lumber. Everything was scoured and mended." When parents began asking to leave their children overnight, "I took corn sacks for mattresses. Then I picked Spanish moss from trees, dried and cured it, and used it as a substitute for mattress hair."

The school expanded rapidly. In less than two years, with the addition of a large hall alongside the original cottage as a combined dormitory and classroom, Bethune had 250 pupils. Besides a number of volunteer workers, a few regular teachers were paid between fifteen and twenty-five dollars a month plus board. All worked in nearby fields in their blue uniforms and white aprons, to bring home sugarcane syrup, melons, pumpkins, tomatoes, peas and more.

Bethune recalled: "At last I saw that our only solution was to stop renting space, and to buy and build our own college. Nearby was a field, popularly called Hell's Hole, which was used as a dumping ground." The owner wanted $250, but eventually agreed to take $5 down, the rest within two years. "He never knew it, but I didn't have five dollars. I raised this sum selling ice cream and sweet-potato pies to the workmen on construction jobs, and I took the owner his money in small change wrapped in my handkerchief. That's how the Bethune-Cookman college campus started."

Slowly, the first building rose on Hell's Hole, along with an artesian well. Bethune implored contractors for sand and second-hand bricks, got local artisans to contribute a few hours of work in the evening in exchange for sandwiches and free tuition. She rang doorbells around Daytona Beach, "wrote articles for whoever would print them, distributed leaflets, rode interminable miles of dusty roads on my old bicycle; invaded churches, clubs, lodges, chambers of commerce." The entryway to Daytona Institute read simply: Faith Hall.

The warm climate and white sand beaches of Daytona had begun to attract a number of wealthy visitors, and Mary McLeod Bethune was not afraid to plead her case. John D. Rockefeller, who built a summer home on the peninsula, loved the Negro spirituals and invited Bethune's students over to sing for him. He became a patron, donating an organ to the school and giving Bethune a copy of *The Optimist's Good Morning*—a book to which she made reference for the rest of her life. James Gamble, of Procter & Gamble, became a trustee and, wrote Bethune, "for many years he was one of our most generous friends." So was sewing machine magnate Thomas White, who left a trust of $67,000 to the school upon his death.

Outraged that there were no hospitals in Florida where blacks could go, Bethune built one of her own. Staffed by white and black physicians, as it expanded it became "a refuge for the needy throughout the state" and was eventually taken over by the city to ease the financial strain on Bethune.

In 1909, Bethune's eloquent speech to the National Association of Colored Women brought further support. Around the same time, Booker T. Washington's visit to the school engendered considerable national publicity. By 1916, when its new White Hall was dedicated, U.S. Vice-President Thomas R. Marshall and Florida governor Sydney J. Catts were on hand to give speeches. From its foundations on a dump-heap, the Daytona School was flourishing. In 1922, it merged with Florida's first men's school for black higher education to become Bethune-Cookman College.

By now, Bethune had begun moving steadily into the political arena. After the Nineteenth Amendment granting women's suffrage was passed in 1920, she embarked on a voter registration drive. On election eve, members of the Ku Klux Klan descended on White Hall. "Turn on every light in the school! Let them know we're home!" Bethune instructed her students. As seventy-five hooded Klansmen passed by the windows with flaming torches, she gathered her frightened charges around her and sang: "Be not dismayed whate'er betide, God will take care of us!" The intruders disappeared into the night. "The next morning I was standing at the polling place at eight o'clock to vote with a line of Negroes behind me," Bethune would remember. "They kept us waiting all day, but WE VOTED!"

Elected to the board of the National Urban League and closely allied with the new NAACP, in 1924 Bethune was elected president of the National Association of Colored Women (NACW). Black women, she announced, were to carry "the steadying, uplifting and cleansing influence" to the struggle for racial equality. She led a successful fundraising effort that established the NACW's national headquarters in Washington.

Three years into her term, Bethune received an invitation to a luncheon meeting of the National Council of Women. It was at the home of Franklin D. Roosevelt, then governor of New York, hosted by his wife Eleanor at their Hyde Park estate. But when it came time to be seated, a palpable tension seemed to reverberate in the room. Who would sit next to the only black woman present? Sara Delano Roosevelt, FDR's mother, quickly took control of the situation.

"That grand old lady," Bethune later wrote, "took my arm and seated me at the right of Eleanor Roosevelt, in the seat of honor! I can remember, too, how the faces of the Negro servants lit up with pride when they saw me seated at the center of that imposing gathering of women leaders from all over the United States. From that moment my heart went out to Mrs. James Roosevelt. I visited her at her home many times . . . and our friendship became one of the most treasured relationships of my life. As a result of my affection for her mother-in-law, my friendship with Eleanor Roosevelt soon ripened into a close and understanding mutual feeling."

Eleanor Roosevelt had grown up listening to her Southern relatives reminisce about the slaves they had owned on their Georgia plantation. Her biographer, Joseph Lash, later recounted how "Eleanor worked with [Bethune] closely, but her reluctance to peck her on the cheek, as she did other friends, showed her the residue of racial feeling in herself, what the Negro resented and the White had to overcome. Not until she kissed Mrs. Bethune without thinking of it, she told her daughter Anna, did she feel she had at last overcome the racial prejudice within herself."

Influenced by Bethune, Eleanor began taking an active stand on civil rights issues soon after her husband's election as President. A Bethune speech about the needs of black youth led to her meeting FDR in 1934. Eleanor would recall Bethune listening quietly as the President outlined his plans for emergency education in the midst of the Depression. Then, when he suggested a division of funds between whites and blacks, Bethune stood up, walked over to the President and shook a finger in his face saying: "Mr. President, you've got to do better than that for me!" Initially taken aback, Roosevelt broke into laughter.

Bethune was named director of Roosevelt's Division of Negro Affairs within the National Youth Administration he had created—charged with supervising the training for 600,000 black youth. During her first year, Bethune traveled 40,000 miles across twenty-one states to assess the situation, gradually ensuring that blacks were directly involved in disbursing funds to their own communities. "The white man has been thinking for us too long," she said. "We want him to think *with* us."

Thousands were put to work clearing playgrounds and parks, building dormitories and schools, repairing roads, and assisting in the conservation of forests. Practical skills were implemented in new rural educational facilities. "Mrs. Bethune is a great woman," the President told his National Youth Administration director, Aubrey Williams. "I believe in her because she has her feet on the ground; not only on the ground, but deep down in the plowed soil."

In 1935, Bethune organized the National Council of Negro Women. It drew upon the more than 800,000 members of black women's clubs across the country, aimed at improving race relations. At sixty-one, she wore three hats—occupant of the first federal position created for a black woman, head of the National Council, president of Bethune-Cookman College. After more than three quarters of the black population voted for Roosevelt in the 1936 election, he made an unprecedented number of appointments of blacks to his administration; Bethune was known as the leader of the "Black Braintrusters."

Under her auspices, a special fund for black college students was implemented. The National Youth Administration's Civilian Pilot

Training Program at six schools became the spawning ground of the Tuskegee Airmen, whose instructors would include Albert Murray. Bethune opened other doors as well—recommending William Hastie to FDR as the first black named to a federal judgeship, demanding credentials for the *Atlanta World* to be the first accredited black newspaper at presidential press conferences. When Bethune needed treatment for her chronic asthma and was admitted to Johns Hopkins Hospital, her insistence upon the participation of two distinguished black physicians cracked the color barrier there. Twice a week during her recovery, Eleanor Roosevelt sent flowers from the White House greenhouse.

Eleanor and Mary often appeared on the same speaker's platform. Once, when Bethune began to cough in the middle of a speech, Mrs. Roosevelt left her seat, poured a glass of water, brought it over and stood beside her while she drank it—a gesture that was not lost on the audience. In 1938, Bethune refused to go along with the segregated seating policy of the Southern Conference for Human Welfare in Birmingham, Alabama. She called the White House. Eleanor flew out to join her in what became a successful protest.

In 1940, a Cookman College graduate named A. Philip Randolph began organizing a civil rights march on Washington. Before it could happen, a Roosevelt Executive Order abolished discrimination because of "race, creed, color, or national origin" in industry and the federal government.

At a rally before 20,000 people in Madison Square Garden, Bethune said in her heavy, melodious voice: "Your being here tonight is a new experience to America. Throughout the history of your life in this country—three hundred years—you have been regarded as a patient, submissive minority. . . . You had no rights. The Supreme Court held that you were chattels, like any horse, or plow. . . . Then came your emancipation. Still you were patient, experiencing discrimination, injustice, segregation, and denials of equal opportunities. Here and there a clarion voice rose above the rumblings of injustice. . . . But the pall of a slave experience still hung over the masses of our people. They had a right to speak out, but dared not speak. Today a new Negro has arisen in America. He is here tonight in Madison Square Garden. He is you!"

When America entered the Second World War, Bethune was named Special Assistant to the Secretary of War to help select the first black Women's Army Corps (WAC) officer candidates. Soon the Navy announced it would accept the enlistment of blacks as other than mess hall attendants. After two years of Bethune's persistence, black women were admitted to the WAVES and SPARS.

In 1942, Bethune resigned as president of the school she had founded on a dollar and fifty cents. "Today Bethune-Cookman College has fourteen modern buildings, a campus of thirty-two acres, and 600 students learning how to lead useful, happy lives," she said on one of her regular *We, the People* radio broacasts. "But there is still much to be done. I'm sixty-five years old now, and my doctor wants me to rest. But I'll never rest. Never as long as there is a single Negro boy or girl without the chance that every human being deserves—the chance to prove his worth."

On one occasion, when Bethune was at the White House discussing the problem of redistribution centers for black soldiers, she recalled FDR lighting a cigarette and handing her the pack. "Well, now, when are you going to learn how to smoke?" he asked. "I will smoke with you in celebration of your re-election this coming fall," Bethune replied. The President smiled and indicated he would eagerly await that moment.

They never saw one another again. Franklin Roosevelt died a few months after ascending to his fourth term. In April 1945, Bethune was among the guests invited to the funeral service in the East Room of the White House. "I looked at the flag-draped bier and my mind went back to the time when we first met and I had moved him to tears by my impassioned plea for my people's rights. I recalled holding his hands and looking into his fine, strong face, and telling him how much the common people depended on him. I remembered all this and many other wonderful little things that he had done for me and for my people."

At war's end, Bethune journeyed to San Francisco as a delegate to the founding conference of the United Nations in the summer of 1945. Forced to return to Washington when she became ill, she found a package waiting for her. Bethune had always carried a walking stick, although she didn't need it—"I carry it for swank," she said. Now, inside the package was a heavy oak walking stick, its polished shaft delicately carved to appear like gnarled wood. At the top was a silver plate bearing the name of Franklin D. Roosevelt. There was a note from Eleanor, in remembrance of their association through the Depression and war years.

Mary McLeod Bethune carried the walking stick with her daily, until her death from a heart attack where it all began, in Daytona Beach, on May 18, 1955.

"Nothing comes without faith and prayer. And nothing in my life has ever come without sweat too. . . .

"To Frederick Douglass is credited the plea that 'the Negro be not

judged by the heights to which he is risen, but by the depths from which he has climbed.' Judged on that basis, the Negro woman embodies one of the modern miracles of the New World."

—MARY McLEOD BETHUNE

FOR FURTHER READING:

Edwin R. Embree, *13 Against the Odds* (New York: Viking Press, 1946).

Rackman Holt, *Mary McLeod Bethune* (New York: Doubleday, 1964).

Gerda Lerner, ed., *Black Women in White America: A Documentary History* (New York: Vintage Books, 1972).

Catherine Owens Peare, *Mary McLeod Bethune* (New York: Vanguard Press, 1951).

Emma Gelders Sterne, *Mary McLeod Bethune* (New York: Alfred A. Knopf, 1959).

A Teacher's Mission:
Elma Lewis

"Mary McLeod Bethune and Elma Lewis both invested a life in not only the structural work, but also in the political and intellectual work, of trying to define a mission and finding a way to engage a large number of others in sharing that vision. Both shared commitment to a sense of peoplehood and of service to that peoplehood, of supporting the realization of human possibility by giving people the full, autonomous creative power of themselves."
—EDMUND BARRY GAITHER,
Director of the National Center of Afro-American Artists

"My work is a widening of the spirit. Each person's own creativity frees him if he is permitted to use it. Our society doesn't encourage that. It certainly was not encouraged among blacks. I encouraged my students to go way inside and find that deep wellspring and follow it where it leads, no matter what anyone says."

—ELMA LEWIS

Inside Boston's Museum of Science, a hush falls over the lavishly dressed crowd of nearly a thousand people. Kenneth (Kamal) Scott, star of the Broadway musical *The Wiz*, has been reminiscing about where his personal odyssey began, when he was not yet a teenager. "It was 1950, in a six-room apartment on Waumbeck Street in the heart of Roxbury. There was no furniture to speak of, no mirrors. We students would hold onto a few wooden folding chairs, twelve to be exact. If you were late, you had to hold onto the wall. And here was this lone woman, sitting on a stool for hours, teaching us ballet, tap, jazz—and about how to live."

Now, accompanied by a piano, Scott begins to sing—"If you believe in yourself. . . . If you believe in yourself. . . ."—his voice rising to a crescendo as a diminutive woman wearing an elegant red dress is brought onto the stage in a wheelchair. Her white-chocolate hair is folded in a bun and, although she wears glasses, she is legally blind. As one body, the audience rises to its feet.

"My cup runneth over," Elma Lewis tells them. "To see all of you in one place! All the little children who, *without permission*, grew up and came together yesterday and said, 'Here I am.' "

They had come from all across the United States, these many alumni of the Elma Lewis School of Fine Arts, come to pay a weekend-long seventy-fifth birthday tribute to a teacher of whom Boston University Chancellor John Silber has said: "Mother Teresa doesn't have anything on Elma Lewis, not one thing. She has devoted herself to the redemption of her community and the empowerment of children, without anything for herself."

She, too, is reminiscing now, about when Kenneth Scott graduated from high school in 1957 and "set off for New York to seek the Broadway theater. A few months after he arrived, he got his first job in *Jazz Train*, and was quite excited. He called me to say that his friend Ronald Frazier had an opportunity to join a German dance company, but didn't have the fare. I didn't know Ronny, but I'd recently heard about a club of young men who gave events to support other people's needs. Donald Sneed was one of them, but I had never met him either. I called his house and his wife answered. She said he would call me back, and he did. I told him that I wanted a loan, in cash and right away, and that I did not know when I could pay it back. I told him the story of Ronald Frazier and he said, 'The money will be under your door at five o'clock in the morning.' And it was. Everybody was going on faith here. But this was not as unusual as it might seem in the black community. Ron Frazier went to Germany and had quite a career."

A little later, Scott would elaborate: "When you take a chance because your heart says it's the right thing to do—that young man, Ronny Frazier, became the first black American to dance in the ballet in Germany. He is also the only black American buried in the cemetery there, with Beethoven, Brahms and Bach."

Elma Lewis goes on to recall how, after her school eventually moved into a spacious headquarters on Roxbury's Elm Hill Avenue, "we didn't have any heat in the building in winter. I was so mad at the property owner, I ran down the street in my ballet tights and shoes. People know I'm crazy. They may not understand the manner of madness but it seems to work. I ran into my friend, Senator [Edward] Brooke, and said: 'Brooke! Before they arrest me. . . . ' "

Whatever Massachusetts's first black U.S. senator replied is drowned out by the audience's laughter, but Elma Lewis makes it perfectly clear that her school ended up with its heat. Now she continues, her voice growing eloquently quiet: "You must respect what you come from. You must pay homage to it, you must analyze it, you must respect it, and teach it to your young. If the roots of the tree wither, the branches must die. . . . The thing which allowed the Jewish people to recover from the Holocaust was that they had a culture to feed back into. Think about it. Think about it. . . . Love yourself and then extend that love to the world."

Elma Lewis is a living legend. As Boston civil rights attorney and now Judge Margaret Burnham, puts it: "Boston's black community was never as distinguished nationally as, say, Harlem's or Atlanta's. Elma Lewis represented the complete antithesis of that. One cannot conceive of this city without her contributions to it. She put Boston on the map as far as black culture is concerned."

My own awareness of Elma Lewis began in 1993 when my son, who was then in junior high, became one of the 100-some young performers in her *Black Nativity* production. Written by Langston Hughes in 1961, this particular Christmas story is a stirring gospel tribute that has become a must-see for thousands of people annually at Boston's Tremont Temple. With a cast ranging in age from five to seventy-five, the Voices of (and Children of) Black Persuasion assemble as a white-robed chorus for a joyous celebration of life.

Evening rehearsals begin in early October at Roxbury's Eliot Congregational Church. It was there that I first witnessed the tough love of the woman the children reverentially call Miss Lewis. "You will become accustomed to the feeling of it," she was saying, standing before them in a neat gray skirt and a "Black Nativity" sweatshirt. "Stand still, stand still! You will become attuned. Stop it! You will feel the people move. You make so much movement, you can't tell one from the other! Calm down. You're making confusion. Be *intelligent*! Do that one more time. Do not walk on the other foot. Get on the *same* foot! Say I don't know what you mean."

"I *do* know what you mean," the young people's answer came back, as one voice.

"Then *do* it! Go back and try your entrance again. . . . When you do things like *Rise Up Shepherd and Fall*, you're not the show. The soloist is. You're just supposed to be keeping the rhythm! Don't get carried away."

It was not as a mere disciplinarian that Elma Lewis came across, but rather someone seeking to teach the children how to take charge of themselves. As their debut drew near, the rehearsals moved over to the big stage at the downtown Tremont Temple. Holding a microphone, Miss Lewis was at full throttle. "If you keep talking, I'll come over and hit you on the head with this microphone! I do understand how these acts of violence are committed, because people drive you to it."

The cast practiced its entrance first in the light, then twice more in the dark, carrying electric candles and singing *Go Tell It on the Moun-tain* as they made a stunning ensemble appearance both from above and behind the stage. Listening and nodding, Elma Lewis whispered: "This is not about religion, it's about spirit—which is *my* religion."

She smiled, then elaborated: "When I'm teaching, I parallel the oc-casion of Christ's birth to similar happenings today. Why were Joseph and Mary shut out? Because the Gentiles didn't want them in these inns, didn't want the Jews to have the good jobs. It's lovely music, but you have to make them understand the whole legend or you haven't done anything. Some of these children are six years old, they've never even seen a play. So they have to internalize it."

Afterwards, in an alcove of the auditorium, I stood talking with John Andrew Ross. A tall, thin, bearded man, he had just begun serving as music director for the Elma Lewis School of Fine Arts when he ar-ranged Boston's first *Black Nativity* in 1970. Before the cast ever gets down to singing, Ross explores with them the meaning of the Christ-mas story. They talk about good and evil, about Christ and Moham-med and Martin Luther King. And they talk about the legacy of Elma Lewis.

"There are different teaching styles," Ross was saying. "One was vividly demonstrated in a famous essay about Harvard's George Ly-man Kittredge, who believed in active mediation in a student's life. Another equally legitimate and effective style is to stand back and guide a student by asking probing questions that finally lead to an answer. Elma Lewis has learned to do both, although her involvement has often gone beyond the classroom. Parents of some kids she taught had such confidence in her that, particularly in the case of those who were not terribly good at parenting, they would just leave them in her care in an informal way.

"Her goal was that they go on to personal success," Ross continued, "not in a material sense, which if anything is perhaps a measure of the world's gratitude for what you've done. She steers children and adults to avoid acquisition for its own sake. Her special concern is unleashing potential, and she simply has this visceral feeling about young lives."

Ross went on: "So why would a black woman who possessed such an identification with empowerment and also with Africa find teaching classical ballet to be productive and relevant? The answer was, the form itself had been proven over time to have a salutary effect on the body—with the exception of dancing on point, which is not natural. But she noted that the discipline flowing from ballet had so many good effects and symbolically provided such a design for a person's life, she could use that as a pathway along which she could travel as a teacher in edifying students. She wanted them to have a sense that they could govern their whole expression, be the architects of their own success. To stand in a mirror all through class, get a sense of the line they want to create, then go on stage—and the mirror is reflected in their heads. You can do a whole life like that if you know yourself that actively, a desire to create a form and space that is gratifying to the human spirit."

The duplex on Homestead Street is in a quiet, tree-lined Roxbury neighborhood, not far from where both Malcolm X and Louis Farrakhan spent their formative years. Elma Lewis first moved here with her parents more than fifty years ago. The nine-room home looks much the same as it did in the 1940s. It contains pieces of antique furniture which Lewis's mother brought when she came to America from Barbados. The baby grand piano that dominates the living room was a gift from her mother to Elma's older brother Darnley when he was nine years old; now eighty-three, a retired professional organist and music teacher, Darnley still lives downstairs. Atop the piano are family photographs and various awards, including a medallion and citation that Lewis received from the Presidential Committee on the Arts and Humanities at the Reagan White House in 1983. On the wall is a picture of Elma's late brother George, a Harvard graduate and the first black doctor admitted to practice at Boston's Beth Israel Hospital before his untimely death from leukemia just shy of his thirty-fifth birthday.

In the parlor where Elma Lewis receives visitors, I am sitting on a purple sofa watching an old mantel clock quietly chiming the hour. She enters the room slowly, holding onto a cane for support. While her once-prodigious frame has slimmed considerably, she remains a powerful, no-nonsense presence. As she sits down, one of the first things she says is: "The genius of life is to believe you can, you are."

How did that feeling come to be inside you? I ask. What happened in your early years?

"I was thinking about that this morning," Elma Lewis replies. "I think about it every day. I had a blessed beginning. David Rockefeller was born with more money and this other one was born with more beauty—but I was born with it all. My father was a black nationalist and I never, ever saw anything better than me until I was eleven. When I realized then that white people thought they were better than me, I thought they were mixed up! It didn't bother me—that's how firmly my father taught us."

Her parents had met after both emigrated from the West Indian island of Barbados. Her mother Edwardine was already a widow with two small boys. Her father, Clairmont Lewis, was working as a janitor when Elma was born in Roxbury on September 15, 1921. Both parents

were among the thousands of followers of Marcus Garvey, the charismatic Jamaican whose Universal Negro Improvement Association
(UNIA) espoused black empowerment in a way that would not become
"mainstream" for decades. When Elma was three, her earliest memory
is of meeting Garvey and reciting a poem on the stage of one of his
Sunday gatherings.

"It was a poem my father had taught me about the beauty of 'colored women,' as they were called then. It seems to me that ever since
then, the arts were the love of my life. I was always taught the beauty
of my race. I knew there had been civilizations flourishing in Africa
before Europe was awakened. Our motto at the UNIA was 'Africa for
the Africans, at Home and Abroad.' My brothers were newsboys for
the Garvey newspaper, the *Negro World*, and I was a member of the
Girl Guides. And I still use Garvey's words when I work with the
children: 'Up, you mighty people, you can what you will!'

"So my father always wanted us to see each other as one people.
We were to know no distinctions of class, hue of skin, texture of hair,
or any of that. There was a great emphasis in my family on contribution. We were encouraged to become educated and to give our gifts
back to our people. My parents never said, Grow up and get rich.
Always, grow up and be important. My mother cleaned houses and
kept our house elegant, the greatest example of my life. And my father
was in every way I can think of the smartest person I ever met."

While her father loved the arts—regularly attending the Boston Symphony and encouraging Elma to visit local museums—her mother emphasized academics. Lewis recalls being one of the first children to
enter what were then experimental, predominantly white, nursery
schools. She began taking piano lessons at five and later elocution instruction. By the time she was eleven, Elma was making twenty to
twenty-five dollars a week doing poetry readings and dramatic
performances. That was twice as much money as her father brought
home unloading sugar on the Boston docks.

When she was thirteen, Lewis entered the Doris Jones School of
Dance and would study there through graduation from high school
and her sophomore year at Boston's Emerson College. She financed
her own education by working as a speech therapist and doing what
were called "platform readings" in local clubs and churches.

"When I was an eighteen-year-old freshman at Emerson," she says,
"Paul Robeson came to play Othello at the Colonial Theater. I used
to walk across the [Boston] Common and go in the back door and see
if there was an empty seat. And after one performance, he let me come
into his dressing room and read Desdemona against his Othello. I
thought I understood what kind of a privilege that was, but I had no

idea really. What an awesome thing I had asked of Paul Robeson—and he let me do it!"

After graduating in 1943 with a degree in Literature Interpretation (the college yearbook described her as "an analytical iconoclast with a zest for living"), Lewis received her master's degree in the education of exceptional children the next year from Boston University. In 1945, she played the role of Julie in Ferenc Molnar's play *Liliom* at the Copley Theater. "In my mind, I wanted to take the first opportunity and go to Broadway. But the first opportunity never came. I had a vision of being a great star, but in those days there weren't many black stars up there. In fact, I'd been the only black *student* at Emerson and B.U.!"

Doubling as an elementary school teacher and social worker/speech therapist, Lewis worked at ten schools and other organizations during the late 1940s. She was at the Harriet Tubman House when she began to reevaluate her life. "I taught girls above the age of six through college, about the direction they should take as young black women in this society. But I was always being thwarted by someone else's concept of adjusting to white America. Every day when I came home I would complain until my mother said, 'Well, why don't you start your own school?' My brother Darnley's advice was, 'Give it your own name and then everybody will know your name!' That's the best advice I ever got."

Elma Lewis laughs, recalling how her father scraped up $300 for her to put down a deposit on an empty apartment at No. 7 Waumbeck Street. She had just turned twenty-eight, one year younger than Mary McLeod Bethune had been when she founded her own school nearly fifty years earlier. "My father bought a second-hand piano, twelve second-hand folding chairs, and two second-hand folding tables—and I was off and running! I put the piano in the ballet studio, which was the living room and dining room opened together. One of the bedrooms served as an art studio and the kitchen was the dressing room. The doors opened on a Sunday, January 30, 1950. I started with four part-time teachers, twenty-five students, and me. I walked back and forth every day from my parents' house."

Lewis instructed the after-school drama and dance classes, as well as evening classes for adults. "I taught ballet as a means of understanding the possibilities of one's body. Standing at the barre working out, you understand that this is the leg you've got. This is what's good about your foot. This is what you can change to improve it. This is what you cannot change, but must adapt to and work around. You learn all about your body and how to make it the best possible instrument. Then we move from the body to the mind."

*　　*　　*

At a symposium—"A Spiritual Awakening: Elma Lewis's Legacy in the Arts"—held in September 1996 at the Boston Public Library, John Ross was remembering a conversation he'd had with his now-well-known actor friend Jackie Washington. "We were both teenagers and I remember Jack saying to me: 'Ah yes, Miss Lewis. I love the way she speaks to children. She elevates them by her respect for all their capabilities.' He said he was sitting there when a boy came to her asking something like, 'What time is rehearsal tomorrow?'—*after* it had already been drilled into his head. And Miss Lewis said, 'And you too, Brutus?' Now when Jack told me this story, I thought, wow! To assume that a child will grasp the full import of that eventually, if not then, is marvelous teaching—to the child.

"Miss Lewis was by all counts an outrageous person," Ross continued, "a person driven by the power of ideas. Here was a little girl or boy using not a barre for support, but the back of a chair in a rented house, where many professional dancers were made in the absence of anything like means. When Kamal Scott would take a leap it would be from one room, into the dining room and Miss Lewis would say, 'Duck your head as you go under the doorway.'

"She would tell her students, 'On the marquee tonight, your name is in lights. There you are on the stage, the band is tuning up, you hear the asbestos [curtain] start to go up. Now the light hits you in the face—*what color is your tutu?*'

"These young people were rigorously prepared, trained to take a bow before they began as a matter of respect, and after the performance they would evaluate one another. It was all about releasing what's inside, so that they might flower from within."

The school's first eighteen-and-one-half years were supported entirely by Roxbury's black community. Parents organized spaghetti dinners, raffles and cabarets to defray the costs. Lewis's students, who came every day after school and on Saturday mornings, paid fifteen dollars a month if they could afford it and were shown how to do all the administrative work. Friends pitched in to move scenery and make chiffon costumes. Lewis insisted that her students choose their friends from among the school community. "And if they had friends from outside, some would come to observe the class," Ross recalled. "Everybody who was around got taught, whether they took formal class or not."

Lewis would introduce them all to music they would otherwise never have heard—the *Pathétique* of Tchaikovsky, the *Scheherazade* of Rimsky-Korsakov. "And there were always the times when Elma Lewis sat the children down on the floor, and talked to them about life," Ross continued. "Sometimes the subject was, you know we have a community of ourselves. And when one succeeds among you, we will all celebrate the success because it reflects on all of us."

Many, such as Kenneth (Kamal) Scott, did indeed go on to achieve success. Eventually, Scott's broadway credits would include *Hello, Dolly*; *Golden Boy* and *Hallelujah, Baby!*, in addition to his lead role in *The Wiz*.

We were standing inside a big tent set up outside the National Center of Afro-American Artists that Lewis had also founded, as Scott reminisced: "I started at age twelve and stayed with her for six years. She used records. We would learn full-fledged ballets like *Cinderella* and *Swan Lake*, in addition to musicals such as *Guys and Dolls*. If you came to class at fourteen or fifteen years of age saying, 'I'm so tired' or 'My life is so hard,' her advice was simply: 'If you're dead, lay down. And if you're not, you're dancing!' Another favorite was: 'What do you think I have, a magic wand? If I had a magic wand I'd wave it over myself and I wouldn't be sittin' here!' And my personal favorite—she used to stare at us and say, 'Look at me, just look at my pretty blue eyes, *right now*!'

"I was the one who laughed at her all the time, she was funny to me. But it wasn't funny after I got a little grown, and realized what I had gotten from her. She was like a second mother. She wanted to know about our schoolwork, our report cards and our social life. You're talking about a giant, not just a mental giant, but somebody whose love for excellence and beauty was so far-reaching that every child everywhere should have one adult that cares like that. Whatever we became as human beings, we got from Elma Lewis. Trust me. She made us better people. When I look at how I teach and what I'm doing now with young people and adults, it's all foundation from her. All of it, everything."

Within a few years after the inauspicious beginnings of the Elma Lewis School of Fine Arts, there was such demand for her instruction that the school moved over to a building in Roxbury's Grove Hall area—and its first ballet barres and mirrors. "It was around 1956 that Miss Lewis realized she had students who were on a professional level," Kamal Scott had told the gala at the Museum of Science. "I was the first to go to New York to seek a career as a professional dancer. Shortly after that, Angela Bowen followed and we auditioned and were accepted in the revue *Jazz Train*."

By the late 1950s, more and more of Lewis's charges had their eyes fixed on the New York stage. However, as John Ross remembers: "She had made dancers, but the world was not really ready for black dancers. They would go off to New York for ballet theater school, but Broadway was not hiring." Elma Lewis notes that "the beginnings of

Talley Beatty's and Alvin Ailey's companies had been in high school and college auditoriums." Encouraged by the vision of a handful of women, including Lewis and her own teacher Doris Jones, things began to change. Lewis provided financial assistance to young Alvin Ailey, and later to Arthur Mitchell.

Elma Lewis recounts: "I've known Arthur since he was seventeen and going to the School of the American Ballet. Doris Jones asked me to come down and see him. She said, 'He's got it, he'll go to the top.' Arthur and I were very involved, and still are. I ran back and forth to New York and helped Alvin and Arthur put their companies together. Then we used to pinch our pennies at the school to bring the young people I had taught and was teaching down to New York and back. It just was never a part of my thinking that they wouldn't be accepted. If we'd have done what we were expected to do, we would all have been a nation of Pullman porters!"

When three of Lewis's female protégées—Leslie Hansell, Beverly Morgan, and Renee Rose—decided to strike out for Manhattan in 1961, Kenneth Scott recalls that "what Miss Lewis did was incredible. She went and found an apartment for these three young ladies and called upon the people of her small Roxbury community to donate furniture. They did, and she drove it down in a U-Haul van." With assistance from a parents' organization that called itself "Les Grandes Jetes," taken from the language of the ballet, four fully furnished apartments resulted in New York. "That was the era of green stamps, and they collected thousands of books of them to buy furniture," says Elma Lewis. "Housewives would buy clothes and prepare food to send down."

John Ross adds that "when opportunities finally did arise for black dancers, and they would audition these young adults who had learned Talley Beatty's *Toccata* and *The Road of the Phoebe Snow* and all these ballets from Elma as kids—that amazed the whole dance establishment in New York."

During the early 1960s, Kenneth Scott became a member of the Talley Beatty Dance Company. It was he who introduced Beatty to Elma Lewis, "having no idea theirs would become a friendship that would last forever." Beatty, who had first received rave reviews as an ebullient dancer in Katharine Dunham's troupe and then with his own touring show called *Tropicana*, was considered the preeminent black ballet performer and choreographer/composer of his era. His modern jazz composition *The Road of the Phoebe Snow* later became a permanent part of the Boston Ballet Company's repertoire.

"When Alvin Ailey started," says Ross, "the only repertoire he could build on was the existing black repertoire—and that was Talley

Beatty's. Talley's choreography was exceedingly difficult. He made tremendous demands and was impossible to work with. He'd get mad in the middle of something—you'd never know why—and just disappear. Nobody would have dreamed of asking somebody of his stature to work with teenagers. But when he and Elma became friends, Talley began making regular trips to the school. And she would say to the students: 'You are to be visited by one of the greatest creative intelligences on the face of the earth. That in itself is a commendation of you. But I will forewarn you—he is so singularly driven by whatever his muse is, he is given to excess. He's going to use bad language, confound your expectations of what is acceptable human behavior, and may even throw a chair at you.' And that is exactly what he would do. But she had prepared them, saying that the cost of being this close to genius is frequently expensive in terms of your emotions and humanity; nevertheless, you can't get this anywhere else, so endure it and show him proper respect."

When I discussed Talley Beatty with Elma Lewis, not long after his death in 1995, she elaborated: "We were sitting on the front porch one day and Talley was watching a taxicab going up the street. And he said, 'Elma, did you ever see how beautiful it was when those colors went by and how it organized itself on the way through?' He had the ability to see another dimension. Yes, he was mercurial. A very difficult man. But—I'm mercurial! Talley Beatty used to say, 'Show me the body of your work, that's all.' Well, when I leave here, the body of my work will be all these wonderful people out there in the world, doing great things."

Among the many dance stars produced by Elma Lewis are Fred Benjamin, who started out with Beatty and now has his own company in New York, Renee Rose and the late Consuelo Houston. Musician Leon Mobley also got his start at the Elma Lewis School. So did Lauren Jones, who has appeared in numerous Broadway and TV roles as well as starring in the film, *The Liberation of L. B. Jones*. Her success, Jones has said, was due to "a fantastic woman in Boston named Elma Lewis."

By the mid-1960s, the building in Grove Hall was deteriorating and Elma Lewis was forced to shop around for another location. The school moved three times in the next several years, being ousted from a VFW hall that had been purchased by a Pentecostal church which Lewis says "saw dance as sinful." Then the Boston School Department kicked her out of a junior high. "Everything went into storage. We had nowhere to go. For many years, we had survived on the resources of black people. Don't let anyone tell you our people won't support each other. However, I finally realized that we would need a larger, permanent home, an endowment and other funds. That's when I decided to branch out."

Lewis's first move for a greater awareness was to inaugurate a series of free summer concerts in Roxbury's Franklin Park. Since she envisioned an open-air theater like the one Joseph Papp had set up to bring Shakespeare to Central Park, she flew to New York to find Papp and ask how he'd done it. Lewis remembers him saying: "Don't ask anyone, just go on into the park. I asked New York and it took me seven years to get in. So just do it and, by the time they decide to throw you out, you'll have been a huge success. The people will love it, and they won't be able to do anything to you."

Papp advised Lewis to build a temporary stage with Safeway scaffolding, use a generator for lighting, and advertise the productions driving around town on a flatbed truck. In 1966, she persuaded Boston city officials to allow her to use what remained of a burned-out fire station. The building had been demolished and its excavation was basically a dump site where large rats rambled across Seaver Street. Lewis got black contractors to volunteer to clean up the garbage-strewn area and build a makeshift theater.

The first summer's productions—used her students and other local youth, in front of footlights powered by "an old generator that used to run out of gas in the middle of a performance." But within two years, Lewis's Playhouse in the Park was bringing capacity crowds of both blacks and whites into what had been an off-limits neighborhood. Here came local entertainers and national stars including Duke Ellington and his orchestra, Arthur Fiedler's Boston Pops, the Billy Taylor Trio, Odetta, Oscar Brown, Jr., and Olatunji and his Drums of Africa. The president of Eastern Gas and Fuel Associates, Eli Goldston, enlisted Boston businesses to contribute the entire funding for the second season. Between 1966 and 1975, nearly 700,000 people attended the concerts.

"Duke Ellington came every year," Elma Lewis recalls fondly. "He often came to our school as well, and we were very good friends. At the park concerts, we had him twice a summer. My children would say, 'Why does he come twice?' And I'd say, 'Once is for the public—and once is for me!' He was a professional in the complete sense of the word. One year the bus broke down, and he got off and came along ahead of the orchestra. He showed up wearing a dashiki and an old mashed-down hat—because his clothes were in the bus. If you know how splendid Duke always liked to be, you understand what kind of a sacrifice it was for him to get up there and play solo piano until the rest of the band arrived. But he did. He said, 'Those people have been waiting for me, I couldn't let them wait another minute!' His point was, you owe the audience homage."

Like Mary McLeod Bethune, whom Lewis says she never met but who "was a woman I much admired," she set out to enlist support wherever she could. After two years of negotiations, the Elma Lewis School moved into two magnificent old buildings that had long housed a Hebrew Academy and synagogue on Elm Hill Avenue. A friendship between Lewis and Eli Goldston had resulted in his arranging for ten businessmen to contribute $25,000 apiece to the Combined Jewish Philanthropies of Greater Boston. These funds enabled the Academy and synagogue to move to another location in suburban Brookline, where the majority of their students now lived. The old property, valued at $1.4 million, was donated to the Elma Lewis School.

Goldston said at the dedication ceremony: "These buildings have long stood as a majestic expression of our religious heritage. We sincerely hope that they will continue to serve as a symbol of the common bond that unites. . . ." And Elma Lewis responded: "I hope we have started something here that will give an idea of how the entire country should proceed. We're finally beginning to understand what black and white have to do for each other. . . . It seems singularly appropriate that buildings which have symbolized the heritage of Boston's Jewish community should now announce to the world the proud heritage of Boston's black community."

Near a Star of David that remained chiseled into the facade, the upper wall of the school had large letters engraved in the cement from the Book of Zechariah: "Not by might, nor by power, but by My Spirit, saith the Lord."

The school's first classes here—with an enrollment of 250 students— began on November 1, 1968, as Lewis set about raising almost two million dollars to refurbish the buildings. More than half of what was needed came through a "soul food" fund-raiser where many of Lewis's former students—Kenneth Scott, Renee Rose, Beverly Morgan and Fred Benjamin—all came from New York for the occasion. Soon jackhammers and blowtorches were mingling with piano lessons, while Skil-saws resounded not far from ballet rehearsals. "We have to suffer some things," Lewis told *Ebony* magazine. "Sometimes we don't turn the heat on on winter days and it's cold and that's alright too. Because if you're black and you can't stand much, you're finished already."

John Ross remembers: "We used to have a big, big music department—twenty-six teachers—when funding was available to the arts." Although the Ford and Rockefeller Foundations contributed $700,000 to funding various departments in the school during the 1970s, Lewis says today that "I haven't conquered that many people for money. My philosophy was that the energy of black performers—those who make records and do shows—should plow the money back into noncommercial things and build a community. Most of the things we did were unfunded and we funded them ourselves. Like *Black Nativity*—it pays for itself and makes a profit to put back into the work."

By 1973, the American Revolution Bicentennial Administration had selected the Elma Lewis School as a national representation of the "symbol of the arts made meaningful in current history." The school's annual budget rose to nearly $750,000. There were more than 500 pupils roaming the halls in leotards and flared jeans, with 350 more on the waiting list. Preschoolers were being sent over once a week by the Community Schools of Roxbury. Some 200 adults were taking evening classes. The staff numbered more than 100.

The full after-school curriculum included music, dance, art, drama, African heritage, drumming for boys and sewing/costuming for both boys and girls. Lewis did not believe in limits. "We do *Swan Lake* and *Les Sylphides*," she said at the time. "I'm getting ready a concert of African dance, too, but I don't know any little girl who doesn't love point shoes. There's no way for me to say that Brahms isn't a great musician or Shakespeare a great playwright. That's folly. Why should I tell lies?"

Her teaching year was divided into seven sections, each exploring a different level of identity—the strengths, role and value of the black family; relationships to one another; the function of institutions in a society; who black heroes were and why they should be honored; the people of Africa; and the black artist. "It was not a black school or a community school," says Lewis, "it just celebrated the black condition and tradition. We circled around one theme, in depth. It could be the ancestors. It could be the founding of the first college on the African continent, somewhere around 1840, in Sierra Leone. It could be about family. Honor."

First-graders might find Harry Belafonte giving them lessons one day, and Ossie Davis the next. One of the most popular classes was offered by a world-class Nigerian drummer named Michael Babatunde Olatunji. "I think we first met when he came to give one of our summer concerts in the Park. He came twice a week to teach for years, flying in from New York. He's my family. And he taught in my school many of the drummers who play percussion today."

Olatunji would describe how African drums speak a language, with their own alphabet. He would tell how African music based upon sounds like the "gun" (pronounced goon) originated in Nigeria, but could be heard today in Brazil, Haiti and Trinidad. He would instruct how the spirituals and the blues, calypso and bossa nova and rock music, all drew upon a legacy of African sound patterns.

As Emerson College History Professor Claire Andrade Watkins described to the 1996 symposium audience, Lewis "is a catalyst of collective memory. That is, the informal record about our traditions, forged by human links that pass from generation to generation over the centuries. An intangible spirit, an intangible feeling—of which Elma Lewis is the epitome. She has personified the ancestor, the teacher who will transcend the boundaries of W. E. B. Du Bois's statement that 'the problem of the twentieth century is the problem of the color line.' "

With the school's acquisition of substantial space, in 1969 Lewis also became founder/director of the National Center of Afro-American Artists. The school was intended as its teaching arm. Lewis had first conceived of such an idea at the 92nd Street YMCA in New York, where Talley Beatty and Alvin Ailey presented their first concerts. "Originally," she says, "it was a place where Jewish immigrants were serviced as they entered America, with intellectual forums, poetry readings, everything you can imagine."

Her new National Center took on the fourteen-member Talley Beatty Dance Company as its first professional component. It also created an African dance company, a chorus, theater and mime troupes, with Lewis often serving as both producer and choreographer of the productions. "I think in terms of my black community just as whites have always built museums and symphony halls and theaters and opera houses for their white community," Lewis said at the Center's opening. Today, looking back on the Center's mission, Lewis adds: "People at the center of their being differ. And they need an opportunity to tell their differences in praise song to their coming generations. It's not to be entertained. If you're just playing music to enjoy yourself, you're not speaking very deeply. It's an inner ear, parts of which you alone hear."

The *New York Times* noted that Lewis "could be black America's version of Sol Hurok, Tyrone Guthrie and P. T. Barnum—all fused into one generous package." Muhammad Ali came to town for a fundraiser, and the National Center's board was formidable. It came to include actor Robert Hooks, painter Charles White, author John Howard Killens, TV commentator Tony Brown, and U.S. Senator Edward Brooke. Reverend George Thomas, a successor pastor to Andrew Young at the First Congregational Church in Atlanta, served for years as the board's chairman and recalls that "most of the members liked to preach sermons while I tried to control *them*! Elma would get so excited and was so articulate, she'd just go to town, you know? I used to have a habit of putting my hand on her shoulder when Elma started to talk, and she'd shut up. Until one night she turned to me and said: 'Don't put that hand on my shoulder! I've got as much right to talk as anybody else!' "

Edmund Barry Gaither was a twenty-four-year-old art historian when Lewis recruited him in 1969 for a joint venture between Boston's Museum of Fine Arts and the National Center. As Director of the Center's museum, Gaither's first show featured under one roof—for the first time—the works of Romare Bearden, Jacob Lawrence, Charles White, Hale Woodruff and Horace Pippin. In 1978, the museum would move into a vacant stone mansion overlooking Roxbury's Walnut Avenue, with a $300,000 yearly budget, and Gaither eventually oversaw a permanent collection of 3,500 works by black artists.

One of these, a sculptured bronze head of a youth gazing steadfastly into the future and called *The Eternal Presence*, was crafted especially for the museum grounds by John Wilson. "I had been working on this head for years," Wilson has said, "and wanted a kind of natural setting for it. When I saw this lawn in front of the museum, I thought—the head has to go there."

Lewis recalls watching the large sculpture being set in place when a young boy walked up and jauntily asked, "What are you all putting up there?" Lewis says: "I told him, 'A boy just like you.' He asked, 'What's he going to be doing?' And I said 'Nothing—he's gonna sit on the side of the hill forever, just like you. Because did you know that we were the first people on earth?' He said, 'It seems like it.' I said, 'It is. Come Sunday after church and bring all your friends!' "

Looking back over the National Center's nearly thirty-year history, Gaither told the Elma Lewis symposium that her vision had "involved the presentation of art at its finest, but also a commitment to tying that to values which were genuinely humane." At meetings that took place every Wednesday at noon, Lewis called together the chiefs of the various departments and, as she did with her younger folk, "pulled forward lessons which she believed we ought to learn. Everyone who knows Miss Lewis well will realize that she is never at a loss for stories from which such lessons can be taken. And you are very lucky if you're not the subject of the story, because the story can sometimes be caustic and you always really get the lesson!"

Gaither recalled that the museum based its standards upon cultural traditions, but set them high—"we're not interested in some formula of what it is to be black." Programs have been presented over the years of Afro-Canadian, Brazilian, English Caribbean, Spanish Caribbean,

French Creole Caribbean, and Cape Verdean art, "trying to show a spectrum of who black people are.

"There are some things we have sought *not* to do," Gaither continued, "such as getting sucked into seeing ourselves through a pathological lens. For example, a couple of years ago, *The Black Male* was shown in New York. An exhibition by a black curator in a predominantly white institution, which found every kind of social collapse that could possibly associate itself with maleness, and found no redeeming spark anywhere. If our lives were so unrelentingly horrible, then we should have done as some did in the Middle Passage—and jumped off the boat. If we didn't do that, it represents some sense of faith, some notion that there is something better and more important, that there is some possibility in tomorrow.

"We have tried to see art and values as inseparable, that we must constantly remake ourselves from the knowledge of who we were and are at this moment. . . . And the applications of these values are very much based on the principles of human substance, the embrace of human imagination, and the acceptance of human responsibility. Which Miss Lewis strove nobly to try and get us to see, in those Wednesday meetings over that long period of time."

In the summer of 1969, Elma Lewis received a letter from an inmate at Massachusetts's Norfolk state prison. "Today we present an image of the prisoner as an illiterate bum, which is true to some degree," she says. "But this letter was flawless, unbelievably elegant, and he was asking us to bring our program in. So we went up to visit. When men are in prison, they prepare them for a nine-to-five job. Well, if they could work nine-to-five, they wouldn't be in prison, so it's foolish to do that. After thinking about it, we took a program in that taught backstage skills of the theater. Script-writing also. And the men turned out jewels."

After an experimental year, the Massachusetts Department of Corrections agreed to include the Elma Lewis School on its regular agenda. Four times a week her instructors made the drive out to Norfolk, where the men on the inside wrote and performed four stage productions. Little by little, prison rules were changed. For the first time, inmates could communicate with the press, and their friends and relatives could attend evening performances.

"Now when the inmates realized they could write newspaper articles and get paid for them, they decided to present all kinds of things for sale. Prior to our program, a prisoner was not paid for his work. But now they started selling their writing and they put together a book called *Who Took the Weight,* which was from a song by Kool and the Gang. They would not allow anybody to edit them—and they were *very* salty."

In 1973, Little, Brown published *Who Took the Weight*—the first time a major publisher had ever signed a contract with more than a single author or co-author. It consisted of poems, short stories, essays and plays by eleven Norfolk prisoners, who received a nine percent-plus royalty arrangement. Elma Lewis, who had made it happen, wrote the foreword.

In the mid-1970s, all hell broke loose in Boston over a court decision to further integrate the public schools by busing black and white students outside their own districts. The Elma Lewis School set up workshops on what Lewis calls "building emotional strength as a fine art." When violence flared one morning in a white enclave of Hyde Park, forcing the closing of the high school there, Lewis selected seventeen of her students to go with their parents and join with white counterparts to form a negotiating team. The biracial committee soon had Hyde Park High reopened.

"She was always active in the political life of the community," former Massachusetts Senator Edward Brooke was saying at the 1996 symposium. Brooke had flown in from Washington to join in the birthday tribute for Lewis. He recalled having met her when he first came to Boston, while serving in an infantry regiment at Fort Devens. Then he had gone on to law school "and for some unknown reason, decided to enter politics. Elma was one of my first supporters when I ran for state representative in Ward 12, Roxbury. I'd never even voted before!

"She would stand up on all issues she felt passionately about—and she felt passionate about almost everything! She'd tackle anyone. She'd go to the mayor, the governor, anywhere she had to. When I served as chairman of the Boston Finance Commission, which was rooting out corruption in Boston government—and you know that's a lifetime job—she worked with me. Then again, when I was attorney general for several terms in Massachusetts before I got to the United States Senate; she'd come to Washington to visit with me on legislative matters she was interested in. They weren't really her own causes, but causes that affected the lives of millions of people. We struggled and suffered through the housing problems, the busing problems. Elma has always been there."

The Elma Lewis School became a focal point for the Boston area. Its staff members drove needy people to the hospital or the store, searched for runaway kids, offered voting advice and provided transportation to the polls. After Lewis was named a consultant to the Office of Program Development for the Boston public schools, workshops based on her work sprang up in the city and suburbs. A number of colleges, including Harvard, Boston University, and Wellesley, implemented teaching programs drawing upon her model.

It was early in 1976, Lewis remembers, when "the head of the two zoos here in Massachusetts asked me to meet a guy who used to be governor of Georgia. I said I didn't know if I wanted to do that, since Georgia at that point was not one of my favorite states. Finally I agreed and the man came and said: 'I'm going to be President of the United States.' As I looked at Jimmy Carter, I knew that he would. You could just see that that was true. Well, as he went across the country through the primaries, the vote was not going quite as he expected. So he came back to my office again with Andy Young, who vouched for him. I'd known Andy for years. Earlier, actually before there was so much desegregation, blacks knew each other nationally better than they do today. I trusted in Andy Young and said I would help with Jimmy Carter's campaign. We worked at this very hard, in various communities, not only in Massachusetts."

Lewis hosted two lavish receptions for Carter along the campaign trail. The black vote became the key to his victory. After the November election, he said: "That's the lady who made me President." In 1983, Elma Lewis would have occasion to visit with another President, when she was called to the Reagan White House to receive the citation which honored her "leadership in providing long-standing and continuing artistic excellence."

When I visited Elma Lewis at her home, she had mentioned a recent phone call from Senator Brooke. "He said, 'Weren't those wonderful years when we started out.' They were. They were wonderful years."

What made them that way? I asked.

"Because everybody was well-intentioned and hopeful and vigorous of work and purpose, and well-meaning each for the other. Not so self-centered. Now everybody's so—me, me. People becoming free to express their ugliness. Looking out for number one. It's going to be a bad time for your son's generation, but then it's going to get better. They're going to be called upon to be strong people. But they have to know a lot more than they know, and people who try to make them believe that the hardships don't exist are doing them a disservice.

"I don't know," she continued, "I just still feel like a mother. Perhaps that's why it was not given to me to have a family and children of my own. Because I could have a bigger family, a huge family. And one that I love very much."

Today the Elma Lewis family is spread out around the country, even the world. Former students have developed their own schools—Sally

Daniels in Houston, Renee Neblett in Ghana. "People say to me, how nice, an Afrocentric institution," Neblett says. "I tell them it's not that, it's about exposing West Africa, the old world, to the Americans—as part of all Americans's shared cultural heritage, the same way Europe is. I'm only doing this because I had a teacher like Elma Lewis in my life, who made me understand that education is not only about the acquisition of skill but the development of character—and that we had a right to know who we are."

The honors have poured in for Elma Lewis in recent years. In 1981, she was among the first ten individuals selected for a MacArthur Foundation "genius" award. All told, she has received more than 400 awards. These include being named a Fellow of the American Academy of Arts and Sciences, and twenty-eight honorary degrees, including Harvard, where she has served as a housemother. She has been a trustee at Boston's Museum of Fine Arts, the Massachusetts College of Art, and WGBH-TV. "I'm not a *community* leader," Lewis says. "It would be foolish to urge black people to take the community and give everybody else the world."

Yet in Boston, time has taken its toll. Not only upon Elma Lewis physically, but upon what she founded. Although the museum at the National Center and the annual *Black Nativity* event remain ongoing, the school was forced to suspend its activities a few years ago. The reason was a series of three unexplained fires over a fifteen-year period at the Elma Lewis School of Fine Arts on Elm Hill Avenue.

It is painful for Lewis to discuss what happened, but she says: "Firemen say, and we believe, that they were arson fires. We know why and who, but that's not something I can really talk about publicly, without causing great disruption. The last fire became harder to tolerate because some students were in production inside the school at the time. We then moved out to scattered sites, but it's very hard to run a moving school.

"I believed that people would understand that we were being persecuted," Lewis continues. "But the painful concept that our friends succumbed to was the rumor that we were in financial disaster. No, going broke came later. Much other hostility had been shown us by people entering our community, and I was disappointed because the people of *our* community finally did not stand up. All they'd do was lament."

Edmund Barry Gaither adds that, after the last fire in the early 1980s, the money could not be found "to spring back from that. At the time when we were operating at full speed, it was impossible to develop an endowment. And an endowment is really the difference between staying alive and dying. I don't know that we will ever see the original vision in the same formula that it had. But we are all committed to finding ways of preserving the thrust of that vision and embodying it in ongoing programs."

At the 1996 Elma Lewis Symposium, a former student in the audience spoke plaintively about the school's demise. "It's been devastating to our area," she said. "That is where I was every day after school, no matter what. There was constant exposure to people coming in from all over the world to talk to us, take us to a performance. That is missing in our community, desperately missing. The school needs to be reopened!"

The city of Boston took control of the school's Elm Hill property in 1996, but the National Center board estimates it would take less than $200,000 to take care of the outstanding bills and revive it. "I wonder whether the work will be carried on," Lewis says. "But it goes the way God wants it to go. I've worked at it as hard as I could. I've pushed every inch of the way, but now I have to stop pushing. I am not physically equal to the task."

She used to read a book a night—"I read everything, including the phone book"—but now her eyesight has failed because of diabetes. Yet her spirit, as Reverend George Thomas says, remains undaunted. "Recently she said to me, 'My mind is like I'm eighteen, but my body's more like ninety.' One night I was in Atlanta and had a feeling to call her. She had fallen down the steps a few days before. As she told me the story, she laughed about it. And I appreciated more than ever that, although her body is broken, she just feels that whatever happens, she'll deal with it."

Inside the home where Elma Lewis has lived for more than five decades, she is cared for by former students, younger relatives, and a devoted housekeeper. Her upstairs sewing and costume room is filled with boxes of memorabilia, on their way to an Elma Lewis Archive being established at Northeastern University. In the downstairs parlor, she is talking about how her teaching methods changed over the years, something Reverend Thomas had alluded to at a prayer breakfast during her birthday tribute, saying: "When Elma was young, there was a formula, a pattern, an order. Then as she got older, she told the students to sit on the floor, listen to the rhythm, feel the music and move to its flow—as the music flowed inside of them."

Reminded of this, Lewis nods her head and says: "Actually, people don't change. You soften your expressions, but your basic philosophy doesn't change. I was much, much more of a disciplinarian when I was a young woman. I really didn't understand the degree to which children knew things. All they lack are experience and wisdom. So I talk things over and make them understand consequences, and I don't give them an inch. But I really make them understand they're loved and secure. Find your focus, listen to your internal rhythm.

"I don't promise them that life is fair, because if there's one thing sure, life is *not* fair. I don't know how the gifts are given out. I know you're going to get some. Work as hard as you can and let's see what you're given. Let's see what you'll throw away and what you'll keep, because you'll be able to sift it over and pick out some that are usable to you, and you'll learn how to bear the others, and you'll get the best possible life. You'll make a difference in the world. Let's go and I'm with you! Whatever happens, I'm *with* you!"

She talks for a while about her four "very exhilarating" trips to Africa. . . . Being invited to the palace to participate in the celebration of Senegalese President Leopold Senghor's seventieth birthday. . . . Encountering several of her former students and employees during the course of her journey. Was there one experience that stood out from the rest? Oh yes, oh yes. . . . "The day I spent on the tiny island of Goré, right off Senegal. We saw the slavehouse from which we were launched. That's where so many blacks passed through that door, onto the ships. And they had a day for us on the island. The Creoles sang us into history, because we had gone away—and yet we had returned."

Always, the return. . . . When Nelson Mandela was released from prison after twenty-seven years and came to Boston, it was Elma Lewis who organized a chorus of 450 interracial students to serenade him with the South African National Anthem.

She looks out at the twilight etching across her window and remembers two other leaders who came of age in this same Roxbury neighborhood. One was Louis Farrakhan, then known as Eugene Walcott, who spent much of his youth in Lewis's parents' household. "He came to visit me not that long ago. One of my mother's favorite favorite boys, a wonderful choir member at our church. And he's still a marvelous musician, he plays the violin, he's never stopped."

She pauses a moment, then goes on: "I don't know what this other dimension [of him] is. He doesn't ever talk about that with us, it's not part of our life with him. To me, he's still a wonderful man. When he's here, he has to do what my brother wants. He wouldn't talk out of turn!"

Elma Lewis laughs and remembers a moment more than thirty years ago with Malcolm X, whom she had first known as Malcolm Little when he was a teenager just down the street. "I went to see him at a hotel room in New York. This was not too long before he was assassinated. And his presence was so overwhelming, some people couldn't bear to even stay in the room. The spirit was so strong, they had to open the windows. It was an internal energy, you see."

I thought of something John Ross had said, harkening back to Elma Lewis's upbringing. "Marcus Garvey really started the black consciousness movement. It was he who inspired people like Malcolm X and Farrakhan. It seemed as though Garvey had failed, because eventually he was deported back to Jamaica, feeling he had been defeated. But Miss Lewis had the capacity to absorb that same spirit. It was, you might say, a kind of madness—one that allows you to forge ahead without knowing what the end will be. And to endure suffering of being without means to any end at all. And to be supported by the faith in the power of what you are doing. The most striking aspect of Elma Lewis's life is that one proceeds, having faith yet not necessarily having seen."

Now she is talking again about the children, about the *Black Nativity* pageant she will soon present again. "I am not particularly dedicated to gospel," she explains. "I am particularly dedicated to the fact that a child can take a piece of black folklore, and examine it minutely, and see in this piece of blackness which has been discarded, a precious jewel, and say—that's a piece of me. And I say to them, 'You are to make everyone in that audience a committed Christian.' They may forget it by the time they get to Park Street subway, but when they're in that auditorium, they have to believe it!"

The sun is setting over Homestead Street in Roxbury. A young woman enters to let Elma Lewis know that supper is ready. She reaches for her cane and stands up. "When they write my eulogy," she says as she exits, "I hope they'll say: 'She has been happy, she has been unhappy, but she has *never* been bored!'"

FOR FURTHER READING:

Alvin Ailey with A. Peter Bailey, *Revelations: The Autobiography of Alvin Ailey* (Secaucus, N.J.: Carol Publishing Group, 1994).

Jennifer Dunning, *Alvin Ailey: A Life in Dance* (Reading, Mass.: Addison-Wesley, 1996).

The Philosophers:
Cornel West and the Du Bois/Locke Legacy

"W. E. Burghardt Du Bois is a human being full flowered—of the highest intellectual training in most diverse fields, and with it all so direct, so devoted to the finest simplicity. His is a rich life of complete dedication to the advancement of his own people and of all the oppressed and injured.

"First, let us not forget that he is one of the great masters of our language: the language of Shakespeare and Milton on the one hand; and, on the other, of the strange beauty of the folk speech—the people's speech—of the American Negro. He is a great poet, one of whom all America is proud.

"In these days of stress and struggle I often pick up one of his many volumes, most frequently The Souls of Black Folk. *How I love to give myself up to those rich cadences, to receive sustenance and strength from those lines so deeply imbedded in the folk style of our people; yet enriched and heightened by the artistic gift of this deep-feeling prophet.*

"For Dr. Du Bois gives us proof that the great art of the Negro has come from the inner life of the Afro-American people themselves (as is true of the art of any group)—and that the roots stretch back to the African land whence they came. . . ."

—PAUL ROBESON, 1951

It is a Saturday morning on the Harvard University campus. An auditorium is rapidly filling to capacity, awaiting the next lecturer at a conference on "The Future of Black Leadership." Shortly after ten A.M., approaching the microphone comes a tall, slender man in his early forties. He has an Afro hairstyle, a mustache and a Vandyke beard, and is wearing a dark-blue three-piece suit. Cornel West pushes his glasses back over the bridge of his nose, looks out across a room crowded with students, and says: "When I was an undergraduate, I wouldn't come out to hear myself. On a Saturday morning, I'd watch *Soul Train!*"

The students laugh, and Cornel West begins to speak. In the tradition of the great orators, he commands the stage—using no notes, stalking back and forth, his voice rising to crescendos and falling to whispers. A professor of philosophy of religion as well as Afro-American studies at Harvard, West is the author, co-author or editor of eleven books. Along with Henry Louis Gates, Jr., the man who brought him to Harvard, West is regarded as one of the foremost African-American scholars in the world.

Now he is talking about W. E. B. Du Bois, the forebear who, he has written, "is the brook of fire through which we all must pass in order to gain access to the intellectual and political weaponry needed to sustain the radical democratic tradition in our time."

"I'm sure many of you have read *The Souls of Black Folk*," West suggests to the students. "That's a book you ought to read and reread the same way you'd listen to Babyface, over and over." More laughter. "I'm serious," West continues. "Because Du Bois is not simply the greatest black scholar—it's not a question of viewing scholars like they're racehorses in some kind of derby, on one level who gives a damn?—but we read Du Bois because of insights of wisdom, because *he* had courage. Because he was willing to sacrifice and he has something to say.

"We turn to his text, he begins with art. Very important to begin with art, in talking about race—or evil in America. Because there is no way that one can engage in a discourse about race that is exclusively rational. This is an irrational subject. Which is to say, if you have a dialogue about race and you are not dealing with some rage and some anger and some bitterness and some fury, then you are having a chit-chat, not a conversation. And that's true for folks right across the board—white, brown, yellow, red brothers and sisters. A whole lot is at stake.

"But art has a way of opening us up and allows us to be vulnerable, to deal with our ambiguities and incongruities and contradictions—so that we can grow and mature and develop. And it's hard, to open people up. It's hard to have a black-on-black conversation and get beyond the superficial and the supercilious, to really get down to crucial issues that effect your *life*.

"So Du Bois begins with a poem called "The Crying of Water"—eight references in those thirteen lines to guttural cries that echo the Africans who jumped off or were tossed off those slaveships. He's saying in part, to talk about race is to come to terms with the wrenching moans and visceral groans—but that's at the deeper existential level. You can still hear those moans and groans at prayer meetings in some churches I know. You can hear the primal screams in the solos of John Coltrane on the saxophone. Or if you listen closely to Bessie Smith's *St. Louis Blues*. It has to do with a certain sadness and sorrow, as well as creativity and originality. It has to do with heartbreak and heart-ache, agony and anguish, as well as resiliency and resistance. Du Bois says, this is how we begin our dialogue, opening ourselves.

"Does anybody recall that spiritual he invokes in the first chapter? 'Nobody knows the trouble I've seen, nobody knows but Jesus. Nobody knows the trouble I've seen—glory, hallelujah!' Where does that last line come from? Doesn't logically follow, does it? Trouble, grief, yet the last line is about joy and ecstasy. Something going on in terms of the tradition of struggle that allows black folk to keep keeping on, even when they look at life's abyss. They look at a world closed in upon them, and yet they still respond. Hip-hop culture, rap music, is just one crucial moment within this much larger tradition. If only through language, you still fight and create some option, some alternative."

"Your country? How came it yours? . . . Around us the history of the land centered for thrice a hundred years; out of the nation's heart we have called all that was best to throttle and subdue all that was worst; fire and blood, prayer and sacrifice have billowed over this people and they have found peace only on the altars of the God of Right. Nor has our gift of the spirit been merely passive. Actively we have woven ourselves with the very warp and woof of this nation—we have fought their battles, shared their sorrow, mingled our blood with theirs, and generation after generation have pleaded with a headstrong, careless people to despise not Justice, Mercy and Truth, lest the nation be smitten with a curse. Our song, our toil, our cheer and warning have been given to this nation in blood brotherhood. Are not these gifts worth the giving? Is not this worth the striving? Would America have been America without her Negro People?"
—The Souls of Black Folk, 1903.

A few days before Cornel West's lecture, I was sitting with him in his office three floors above Harvard Square. Books lay stacked everywhere—horizontally, vertically, diagonally—on the floor and peering down from overloaded shelves. The hallway outside was lined with students waiting to see him. Given a schedule that finds him at some 150 speaking engagements a year, I had been told that West was about as difficult to meet with privately as the President. Yet there was nothing at all aloof or patrician in his demeanor. He seemed to contain the quality he so admired in Du Bois's writing—a personal openness and vulnerability. And, when I asked West whom he most admired in American history, his answer was not at all what I expected.

"After my parents?" he replied. Yes, I said. "Probably Coltrane," he said. I was momentarily stopped, having anticipated West would cite Du Bois or perhaps Martin Luther King, rather than the great jazz saxophonist whom I'd discussed with Wynton Marsalis. Why Coltrane? I asked.

"I think brother John was just an amazing guy. His music reminds me of what Melville said: he loved divers who would go far into the depths of the sea—and emerge with bloodshot eyes. And of a phrase from the great European lyric poet, Giacomo Leopardi, in the early part of the nineteenth century: he wants to emerge with tear-stained hope. Bring the blues to those, you've got Coltrane. It's a matter of courage, willingness to take risks.

"There's something else, too, that I think is overlooked. Coltrane, and Toni Morrison, recognize that the doings and sufferings of people of African descent in the United States constitute one of the epic stories, of a deep tragicomic nature. People who have very little chance of ever being thoroughly accepted by the mainstream, because the legacy of white supremacy cuts so deep. Therefore, you have to talk seriously about respect and love among each other. At the same time, being so tied to America that there's no way to separate yourself from it. Recognizing that the very glue that holds you together is also the source of your pain. That's the blues right there. No way out, but to sing about there's no way out. And in the end, that's part of the *human* condition.

"Coltrane had so much love in him, compassion in him. Struggled with indescribable pain, kept a lot to himself as a heroin addict for many years. But Coltrane broke loose, continued to gain his voice, and still was gentle—as well as subversive."

Subversive in what sense? I wondered.

"In terms of the musical bars in jazz, free jazz. In terms of his own attitude and stance against white supremacy, in his music as well as in his support of Dr. King. He was just such a spiritually-culturally rich human being. And I think probably the best of American culture is that kind of existential democratic mode of being in the world."

Thinking of Coltrane soon had West riffing about one of the saxman's leading precedessors, Johnny Hodges of the Ellington band. "He'll relax you, he's got such a gentle touch. Reminds you of Coltrane in that regard, too. But I mean, Johnny Hodges is about as deep as they come without being the genius that Coltrane was. Hodges has that way of being in the world that accents the worth of other people, soft-spoken to the degree it allows others to open up. But wanting to be himself such that he can act the fool when he wants and not be ashamed, and act the gentleman when he ought—knowing that it's gonna help somebody else out.

"You see, somebody like Hodges or Coltrane, they would be like me in the sense they're much more concerned with being good people than being great so-and-so. To me, that's basically what life is all about, the way Coltrane put it, trying to be a force for good—through being a good servant."

"The Younger Generation comes, bringing its gifts . . . Here we have Negro youth, with arresting visions and vibrant prophecies; forecasting in the mirror of art what we must see and recognize in the streets of reality tomorrow, foretelling in new notes and accents the maturing speech of full racial utterance. . . . All classes of a people under social pressure are permeated with a common experience; they are emotionally welded as others cannot be. With them, even ordinary living has epic depth and lyric intensity, and this, their material handicap, is their spiritual advantage."

—Alain Locke, *Negro Youth Speaks,* 1925.

Cornel West was born on June 2, 1953, one year before Alain Locke died and ten years before the passing of W. E. B. Du Bois. Like both of them, West attended Harvard as an undergraduate and later earned a doctoral degree in philosophy. Like both of them, West always appears publicly in a well-tailored suit. Like both of them, West is a prolific and best-selling author, national spokesman, and mentor to the next generation. And, like both of them, he is very much a part of his own generation—as much a product of the civil rights movement as Du Bois was of the Reconstruction era and Locke was of the Harlem Renaissance. If Du Bois may be described as the yang and Locke as the yin of the African-American humanistic philosophical tradition, West embodies qualities of each.

Du Bois and Locke, nearly eighteen years apart in age, walked a remarkably similar road in their formative years. Both lost their fathers at an early age. Du Bois's father abandoned the family when William was small, and he grew up in near-poverty in a rented room along the railroad tracks in the western Massachusetts town of Great Barrington. Locke's father, one of the early black graduates of Howard University Law School, died in Philadelphia when his son was six.

Each young man was gifted with a tremendous intellect; Du Bois entered Harvard in 1889, Locke in 1904. The university's golden age of philosophy was in bloom, and both studied under William James and Josiah Royce. As Cornel West would later achieve, Locke completed Harvard's four-year course in three years. While Du Bois became the first African-American to receive a doctorate from Harvard,

Locke followed suit and, in 1907, was the first African-American (and the only one during the course of his lifetime) to be selected as a Rhodes Scholar. Du Bois and Locke also both studied at the University of Berlin. Visits to the South, immediately following their education, proved pivotal experiences in shaping their consciousness.

While Du Bois rose to national prominence at the age of thirty-five with the publication of *The Souls of Black Folk* in 1903, Locke was forty when his book *The New Negro* captured America's attention in 1925. "In many respects," writes historian Arnold Rampersad, "*The New Negro* was the first literary attempt to review the collective portrait of black America painted by [Du Bois]." Indeed, Du Bois contributed a major essay titled "The Negro Mind Reaches Out" to Locke's later work. Locke, in turn, paid homage to "the great service of Dr. Du Bois in his unforgettable chapter on the Sorrow Songs in *The Souls of Black Folk.*"

In temperament and style, however, the two scholars were vastly different. Locke believed that art itself offered "an emancipating vision to America." Du Bois viewed the arts more as a vehicle to advance the cause of his people. He was the foremost black political activist of his time—a founder of the Niagara Movement and its successor, the NAACP. Locke remained largely within the confines of academia at Howard University. He was a quiet, introspective and lonely man who never married. By contrast, Du Bois was possessed of towering energy, appetites and ambition. Like his hero Frederick Douglass, he authored three autobiographies. Where Locke preferred to highlight the creativity of others, especially the young, Du Bois used his own poetic abilities and political talents to carve a far more potent image across twentieth-century America.

Looking back at their writings, it is striking to realize how much of what they saw about this country remains equally prescient today. As a point of departure, consider these words written by Du Bois in 1920, in his *Darkwater: Voices from within the Veil.*

"High in the tower, where I sit above the loud complaining of the human sea, I know many souls that toss and whirl and pass, but none there are that intrigue me more than the Souls of White Folk.

Of them I am singularly clairvoyant. I see in and through them. I view them from unusual points of vantage. Not as a foreigner do I come, for I am native, not foreign, bone of their thought and flesh of their language. . . . I see these souls undressed and from the back and side. I see the working of their entrails. I know their thoughts and they know that I know."

The following excerpts are from a Locke essay, *The American Temperament*, written in 1911:

"*It is a curious but inevitable irony that the American temperament, so notorious for its overweening confidence and self-esteem, should be of all temperaments least reflective, and for all its self-consciousness, shoud know itself so ill. . . . Individualism and a certain self-willed energy has possessed us . . . and the modern demand for material progress is the result. . . . Peculiarly characteristic . . . is the national will in any moral issue. Only at times of the greatest tension is the popular mind in sight of principles. . . .*

"*Its politics are a professional game played by professionals . . . for the amateurish amusement and approval of the public. Exactly to what this is due is a very great puzzle. Perhaps it is an American trust and belief in experts, a trait which . . . exacts from us more unquestioning reverence for authority and greater faith in delegated power. . . . The autocratic possibilities of our nominally democratic institutions are only lately beginning to reveal this essential and deeply lodged strain in the American character. A country that worships power, respects the autocrat, and may even come to tolerate the tyrant. . . .*

"*American democracy is not a political theory, but a social instinct. As patriotism, it is sheer rhetoric, bombastic and effusive; as a deep conviction, it is almost religious in its intensity and individual hold upon every citizen. It differs from other continental forms of patriotism in being so associated with the personal and individual well-being of each man, and in having slight reference either to a national past or future. . . . America is too engrossed with the present to have anything but empty and boastful claims upon the future. . . .*

"*As soon as one examines this trait on an intellectual plane, one sees what curious laws of association govern the American mind. Its superb eclecticism, its voraciousness, its collector's instinct for facts and details, and its joyous disregard for proportion and an artificial order are still in need of adequate exposition. . . . The temperament is, however, extensively catered for: the informational press is its creature. To instruct pleasantly and with the minimum of effort is the debased aim of present-day art; a wide-spread and ever-growing disease of taste. . . .*

"*There is a greater measure of content and less of a sense of environmental injustice in America than anywhere else in the world to-day. And the principles of conduct and social relationships . . . are like the rules of a game, there is an immediate appeal to public censure or approval. . . . Where every man is supposed to consider his own interests, no social blame is imputed. . . .*

"*If it is too early to make up our minds as to what we are, or, better, what we intend to be, surely it is time to rid ourselves of the illusion that we already know both. . . ."*

Here is Du Bois, in a speech given about Abraham Lincoln in 1907:

"America today stands for hurrying and rush and work. We call ourselves a hustling nation. We do or we try to do a great deal more in a day than the average person in other lands, in other ages have done. But when we look at the life of this first American we see something that gives us pause. Why was it that Lincoln thought so clearly? It was first of all, because he thought and because he gave himself leisure to think. Many are the stories that they tell of him stretched out doing nothing, loafing here and there, whittling a stick, looking leisurely at the world. He thought. And that is one thing that the average American today does not do. That is one thing we do not do in our schools. The poor, hurried, worried children get no time to think, get no time to get acquainted with themselves. We then, as Americans, must take pattern of Lincoln and remember that before all, we must get acquainted with ourselves. We must get acquainted with this country of ours and not take the image or hearsay for the reality. This is in many respects a wonderful country, but it is not wonderful in the sense that it will not have to go through the same birth pains and have the same troubles of growth, find the same great difficulties of living, the same evils, the same great shadow of Death that all nations have found; and the quicker it realizes this the more carefully will it pause and think and plan. Abraham Lincoln's life gives us little sense of hurry. And yet Lincoln, as the world has known him, has been one of the world's great workers. And the reason is clear; if the human soul gets time to think and expand how much better it can work."

Finally, from Cornel West's speech to the Harvard students in 1996:

"It is very difficult to have a sense of history in America, because America is a hotel civilization. I mean a civilization that's obsessed with comfort and convenience and contentment. That's precisely what a hotel is, a fusion of the home and the market. Makes you feel at home if you have the cash to pay. Leave the room, everything's dirty, you come back and everything's clean. Hardly even see who's engaged in the work. They're hidden, they're concealed, it's a manicured space. Everything's Disneylandlike, clean. And yet we know, the world is not like that. There's evil in the world, there's unjustified suffering in the world, there's unmerited pain in the world, there's undeserved harm in the world, there's tears in the world, there's lament, there's cries.

You don't hear that in a hotel. America is very much like that, spoiled,
privileged. And that's precisely why America doesn't like to talk about
evil, and that's precisely why America doesn't like to talk about the
legacy of white supremacy."

In his 1993 best-selling book, *Race Matters*, West wrote: "We need
leaders—neither saints nor sparkling television personalities—who can
situate themselves within a larger historical narrative of this country
and our world, who can grasp the complex dynamics of our peoplehood and imagine a future grounded in the best of our past, yet who
are attuned to the frightening obstacles that now perplex us. Our ideals
of freedom, democracy, and equality must be invoked to invigorate all
of us, especially the landless, propertyless, and luckless. Only a visionary leadership that can motivate 'the better angels of our nature,' as
Lincoln said, and activate possibilities for a freer, more efficient, and
stable America—only that leadership deserves cultivation and support."

When *Race Matters* appeared—West's first book aimed at a general
audience—the *Washington Post* called it "as profound as W. E. B. Du
Bois's *The Souls of Black Folk.*" Like Du Bois, West is very much a
political activist although, like Locke, he has thus far chosen to remain
within the realm of academia. As Du Bois issued a challenge early in
the century to the conservative black leadership of Booker T. Washington, West does similarly in taking on the Clarence Thomases and
Dinezh D'Sousas of our day—as well as the nationalist stance of Louis
Farrakhan.

Yet, as the most prominent professor within Harvard's Department
of Afro-American Studies, West is also heir to what Locke began at
Howard University in Washington. For it was Locke who first proposed such a program there in 1924 (although it was not fully implemented until shortly after his death thirty years later). Locke was the
first to call for a "base for re-establishing the broken contacts of the
American Negro, and for re-educating him to a knowledge of his past
and a realization of his duty and mission with respect to Africa."

At that time, Howard was an all-black school but run by a white
administration. In the summer of 1925, Locke was among several professors who were suddenly fired on the alleged grounds of university
reorganization, consolidation and efficiency. A student strike erupted
in protest. "If such a man of ripe scholarship as that of Dr. Locke
cannot teach at Howard University," a statement said, "the administration cannot be endeavoring to run Howard as an institution of
learning." There were also protests in the black press and mass meetings in a number of cities. After a three-year period of exile, Locke

returned to Howard under the leadership of its first black president, Mordecai Johnson.

Locke would remain there until his retirement in 1953, when Johnson said in awarding him an honorary degree of Doctor of Humane Letters: "Your intellectual interests have been as broad as life itself. You have been a valuable critic of dogmatic ideology, a creator of free-moving ideas, an appreciator of the great cultural diversity in American life and a gentle but persuasive apostle of that unity of America and the world which thrives upon the coexistence and cooperation of individual and cultural differences."

Mutual understanding, Locke believed, was the key. "The fiction is that the life of the races is separate," he wrote. "The fact is that they have touched too closely at the unfavorable and too lightly at the favorable levels. . . . The Negro question is too often put forward merely as the Negro question. It is just as much, and even more seriously, the question of democracy. . . .

"Cultural recognition . . . means the removal of wholesale social proscription and, therefore, the conscious scrapping of the mood and creed of 'White Supremacy.' It means an open society instead of a closed ethnic shop. For what? For making possible free and unbiased contacts between the races on the selective basis of common interests and mutual consent, in contrast with what prevails at present—dictated relations of inequality based on caste psychology and class exploitation."

Du Bois echoed Locke in looking back at "the dark and flying slave ship in the sixteenth century, the expanding plantations of the seventeenth, the swelling commerce of the eighteenth, the fight for freedom in the nineteenth" and concluding: "It was the black man that raised the vision of democracy in America." What was crucial was to lift "the veil"—but first it had to be remembered, analyzed, and understood.

For both Du Bois and Locke, it was their first trips to Africa—made independently in the same year, 1924—that heightened their awareness of where their missions lay in America. Du Bois had been an organizer of the first Pan-African Congress five years earlier, which brought together for the first time blacks from America, Europe and Africa with white leaders to discuss racial problems, and which would continue periodically through 1945. Visiting the land from whence his ancestors sprung, he wrote:

"The spell of Africa is upon me. The ancient witchery of her medicine is burning my drowsy, dreamy blood. This is not a country, it is a world—a universe of itself and for itself, a thing Different, Immense, Menacing, Alluring. . . . It is life so burning, so fire encircled that one bursts with terrible soul inflaming life. . . . Three things Africa has given the world, and they form the essence of African culture: Beginnings, the village unit, and art in sculpture and music."

Locke, who journeyed to Sudan and Egypt and was present at the reopening of King Tutankhamen's tomb at Luxor, wrote upon his return that the first great "cultural renaissance" was "focalized here in an African setting. . . ." Yet his assessment of the richness of African arts differed from Du Bois's. Du Bois waxed lyrical about "the primitive art of Africa [being] one of the greatest expressions of the human soul in all time" and of how "the African not only sang beautiful melodies but he invented part singing, and his instinct for rhythm developed syncopation." Locke, however, saw the "characteristic African art expression [as] sober, heavily conventionalized, restrained." In contrast, black Americans were "freely emotional, sentimental and exuberant, so that even the emotional temper of the American Negro represents a reversal of his African temperament." What needed to be learned from the ancestors, Locke felt, was respect for technique, craft, discipline, and form.

Such was the message Locke sought to impart to the young writers that he introduced to a national audience in *The New Negro*: Langston Hughes, Countée Cullen, Claude McKay, Zora Neale Hurston, Jean Toomer, and more. Locke helped support them, as well as artists like Aaron Douglas and Richmond Barthe, through the patronage of an eccentric, wealthy white widow named Charlotte Mason. She edited Hughes's *Not without Laughter* and directed Hurston in her collection of Southern folkore. She subsidized Locke's annual trips to Europe for thirteen years, as well as his development of one of the finest collections of African art in the world.

It all centered around Harlem, where Locke spent considerable time with his protégés and where he felt that "Negro life is not only founding new centers, but finding a new soul." In "a deliberate flight not only from countryside to city, but from mediaeval America to modern. . . . Each group has come with its own separate motives and for its own special ends, but their greatest experience has been the finding of one another."

Ralph Ellison—whose chance meeting with Locke upon arriving in Harlem in 1936 led to his introductions to Langston Hughes, Richard Wright and his decision to become a writer—said of him at a Harvard symposium in 1973: "What Locke did for me, as he did for Al Murray, was to act as a guide. He stood for a conscious approach to *American* culture." While Ellison said he did not always agree with Locke, he found the philosopher a role model, "in the direction of some sort of conscious assessment of the pluralistic condition of the United States."

When you went back in time, Ellison continued, you did not find a pure stream: "After all, Louis Armstrong, growing up in New Orleans, was taught to play a rather strict type of military music before he found his jazz and blues voice. Talk about cultural pluralism! It's the air we breathe; it's the ground we stand on." While for years Locke was "thought of as simply a spokesman for a minor aesthetic position mainly of interest to minority people," Ellison concluded, "Don't kid yourself: he was talking about all of us."

"That Dr. Locke saw the importance of trying to define us in that sophisticated moment, in that moment of great transition, in that moment wherein jazz was being felt (if not understood as being more than a primitive folk music), in that moment when we were far enough away from the traumas of Reconstruction to begin to think of leadership on a very broad scale, in that moment when we realized whatever the new leadership, there would not be another Frederick Douglass, or Williams and Walker, or Scott Joplin. There would be a metamorphosis of their ideas and styles. There would be an incarnation of young people still unknown who would have some sense of what lay back there, some sense of the unspoken meaning, and who would try to translate into articulate forms that feeling about life, that assertion of identity which always made our contributions to the arts in this country immediately recognized as what America has instead of a sacred past."
—RALPH ELLISON

Cornel West was standing before about 650 young, mostly black, teenagers at the William Barton Rogers Middle School auditorium in the Boston suburb of Hyde Park. His overarching theme was self-love, leading to self-respect and finally self-confidence, without which you could not make a difference in the world. In certain respects, West's mesmeric speaking style was similar to what I had seen at engagements with adults and college students—arms now outstretched, now folded against his chest; now leaning forward, now bending backward; drawing out some words for emphasis and pausing to allow other ideas to settle in. But he was at the same time more deeply personal here, reaching out across the generation gap to include himself in their world, and to bring them into his.

West was talking now about the need for roots, for mentors, recalling the encouragement he received from his family and the seventy-five-year-old retired white schoolteacher who came into his segregated neighborhood in Sacramento, California, driving a bookmobile. "How many of you actually enjoy reading?" he asked. Not that many hands went up. "Oh, we've got to have more than that! Somebody stand up and tell me why you like to read." A boy rose to his feet and said:

"Because you get to imagine what it's like to be somebody else." West smiled and added: "To expand my imagination. Now how many of you all like to listen to hip-hop?" Many hands went up this time, and he asked why? Another student responded that it was the lyrics.

"What do the lyrics do?" They rhyme, the boy said. "And what else?" They tell stories. "Ah-ha!" West exclaimed. "What kind of stories do they tell?" Some good, some bad, the boy said. "If you are reading a short story or a novel or history, or if you are listening to some *good* music," West imparted, "this expands you. It deepens you. So as you listen and as you read, you have a deeper sense of the world."

Later he returned to the same theme, describing the excitement he felt when he went into a record store or a bookstore. "I listen to music every day, all kinds of music, from Luther Vandross to Mozart. It's about movement, the rhythm of life. And that's the way reading must be; if you are serious, you will read and write in the same way that people listen to music. Anybody heard of Wynton Marsalis? One of the greatest jazz musicians alive. What does he play? . . . How many hours does he practice every day? . . . And what about John Coltrane?" West spelled the last name slowly and continued: "I would hope that some of you who are serious about life, instead of buying the next CD of hip-hop, will buy John Coltrane. The reason why I say that is because John Coltrane represents the height of a tradition—he's gonna take you so high you can't stand yourself!"

This was the third time I had heard West discuss the impact of Coltrane. Addressing the Harvard student symposium, he had said: "I want to see a Coltrane revival among young folk! Not only because his music is so complex, but when you listen to *A Love Supreme*, you know this brother from gut-bucket North Carolina through Philadelphia who played his horn eighteen hours a day, went to sleep with the horn in his mouth and woke up blowing, was disciplined! And you also know that he was who he was because Dizzy Gillespie, Thelonius Monk and Miles Davis invited him to become parts of their group, so he could actually discover his voice. So there's a connectedness and an interrelatedness, there's an attempt to *empower* one another. When they criticized one another, they criticized in order to empower. That's crucial."

But it was not an easy road, being open to criticism and having respect for others, West told the middle school students. "To do something together without a whole lot of jealousy or envy, we've got to keep our eyes on something bigger than us. So many of us like to wear that mask, you know? Not lying to yourself is difficult. Even as a forty-two-year-old brother, I still have to wrestle with that. It takes work.

At certain moments in your life, there will be crises where you have to re-evaluate. You say, what am I really doing, what kind of person am I really, what do I want to do in this life. Raising those kinds of questions is tough, very tough. There's only way out—and that is courage."

Then West looked back to when he was a boy. "See, when I was in third grade, I got kicked out of school. I was on the wrong track. A lot of my friends I grew up with, they assumed I would end up in jail. Because they remembered my rage. Now I'm still full of rage. But I'm translating it into trying to be a force for good."

Like Ralph Ellison, West was born in Oklahoma. His mother was a schoolteacher in Tulsa, and his father a civil servant working for the Air Force. "The most significant stage-setting for my own life pilgrimage," West later wrote, was "closely knit family and overlapping communities of church and friends."

His grandfather, the Reverend C. L. West, was the minister at Tulsa's Metropolitan Baptist Church. "He was self-taught," West was saying, at the corner table of a restaurant near Harvard Square. "Started a church with three people in his basement when he was thirty-three, and left that church with 3,000 people! He was a great preacher, if you define greatness as profound love for your people.

"We were very close. I remember he used to tell me a story. He said that when I was christened at Paradise Baptist Church, maybe six months old, all the folk came. Right when the preacher was praying, the holy ghost just hit the church! Everybody went off for about forty-five minutes, he couldn't get control. My godmother Miss Williams, who weighed about 400 pounds, started swaying. Then people started singing songs, 'This special child he's gonna do so-and-so, Lord gonna be watchin'.'

"Then when I was ten, grand-dad brought me up in front of the church again. He said, 'I want you to sing a song, "Jesus built a fence all around us every day."' Then he told the congregation, 'See this boy right here? He's gonna change so-and-so. You keep your eye on him! Jesus built a fence around him! People gonna come at him, bullets flyin'!' I'm thinking to myself, what's going on with grand-dad? Has he lost his mind?"

West shook his head and laughed, then went on: "My father got sick when he was thirty-one years old. All the doctors gave up on him, they basically pronounced him dead. My father was in the hospital for about nine months. Grand-dad left his church to stay with us. Much as he loved his people, he loved his family more. Then dad bounced back. It happened after a big prayer meeting. The doctors didn't know what was going on. My father lived to be sixty-five. When I preached his eulogy at the funeral, I talked about this. It's been that kind of pilgrimage."

West had told the middle school students: "I realized a long time ago that I could never be one-third the person that my father was. He didn't have the same opportunity I had for education. But never confuse knowledge with wisdom. By wisdom, I mean wrestling with how to live."

West's older brother Clifton taught Cornel to read before he started school, and they were so close that Cornel named his own son after him. "In my case," West says, "family is really the foundation, the consecration of it all. The rest is embellishment."

After a brief move to Topeka, Kansas, with his parents and three siblings, West ended up in Sacramento in 1958. He attended an all-black elementary school. "When I go back and look at my second-grade picture," he says, "only two of my male classmates are still alive." West himself was "kind of the bad boy in class when I was growing up. I'd get in fights five or six times a week. I was full of energy and anger. I don't know where it came from, because my family was very loving."

One day in third grade, West refused to salute the flag as a protest against segregation. "I had heard stories of relatives coming back from the [First World] War and being shot in their uniforms and black people being lynched with the flag wrapped around them," he remembers. It was not dissimilar from Du Bois's own radicalization, when he learned of the 1,700 lynchings of blacks that took place in America between 1885 and 1894—"each death a scar on my soul."

When his teacher lambasted the young West for being unpatriotic and slapped him, West punched her in the face. He was suspended from school. "My mother taught me for a while," he says. West was eight when he discovered a biography of Theodore Roosevelt on the neighborhood bookmobile. Like West, Roosevelt was an asthmatic youth who overcame his physical ailment. Although Cornel had no idea what or where Harvard was at the time, after finishing the book he made up his mind he would someday attend Roosevelt's alma mater.

"I transferred into an integrated school. I had never been in a place with white students. They lived in a very different world, that was clear: different music, different language, different shows. And I was curious about it."

West was also curious about "all the entrenched evil in this world," during discussions about the Old Testament's Job in Sunday school. As he entered his teenage years, he became a devout Christian. "I was trying to get myself together," he told the middle school students.

"And I decided that for the rest of my life, I was going to try to make the world a better place, to fight for justice. Also, to be able to read and write the way James Brown danced and the way Aretha Franklin sang!"

The Black Panther Party had an office near his family's church. In the late 1960s, West found himself drawn both to their militance and their charitable community programs. He worked with the Panthers occasionally, and first heard about Karl Marx through their streetcorner discussions. But as time passed, West realized he could not give up his religious faith for their "grassroots Marxism," and did not like their contempt for Christianity.

West became president of the student body at John F. Kennedy High School, and entered Harvard on a scholarship in 1970—"part of the first generation of young black people to attend prestigious lily-white institutions of higher learning in significant numbers." This shift came about, he says, in the immediate aftermath of Martin Luther King's assassination. "For the first time since the Civil War, the United States government had to bring out the National Guard to protect the White House. It shook the foundations of the American empire when brother Martin was so viciously murdered. Finally then, conservative elites in America said, 'I think we've got a problem, we've got to do something about the Negroes.' And what did they do? They opened up, finally, and let people like me in. They weren't going all the way to working-class Sacramento and snatching somebody like me off the street before. My class at Harvard had ninety-six [blacks], the year before, they had about fourteen."

As a sophomore, West and two black roommates were hauled off by the police, after the rape of a white co-ed who lived next door. "They took us down and threw us in the clinker across from the Cambridge city hall," he recalls. Mug shots were taken and the three were detained for an entire day, while the police "tried to convince this white sister that we were the ones who really did it. Ironically, if it wasn't for her sitting there shaking and saying, 'No way, these are not the ones'—when the police were saying, 'C'mon, you know these are the guys'—we'd have been just another statistic, another set of innocent brothers gone to Norfolk [State Prison] or somewhere."

Initially West majored in philosophy, then switched to Near Eastern languages—studying the original Hebrew and Aramaic—and literature. His junior year, he took a double load of sixteen courses while working two jobs simultaneously. He cleaned toilets, washed dishes, and worked as a mailman at three different Harvard dormitories.

"I was running out of money, and mom and dad were in a tough situation financially," he explains his motivation. One of his profes-

sors, Martin Kilson, later called West "the most intellectually aggressive and highly cerebral student I have taught in my thirty years here."
Still, he was seen by professors and peers as a regular guy, a notorious
dancer of the "funky chicken," a fellow who his brother says "always
liked to go to two or three parties every weekend, but only after reading two or three books."

West went on to Princeton for post-graduate work in philosophy,
and landed his first teaching assignment in 1977 at New York's Union
Theological Seminary. One night, he recalled driving between New
York and Massachusetts when a state trooper pulled him over. "I
wasn't speeding. The cop peered into the car and said, 'I see you going
back and fourth once a week; this is the fourth time I've seen you.'
That made him feel that I was dealing in cocaine. I said to him, 'You've
been seeing me that often because I teach at Williams College once a
week. I'm a professor of philosophy and religion.' 'Yeah,' he replied,
'and I'm the Flying Nun. Let's go, nigger.' It was a moment that reminded me how much race does indeed matter in our society." It took
phone calls to both Union Theological Seminary and Williams College
before West got out of jail.

His first book, *Prophecy Deliverance*, was published in 1982. As
West described its purpose: "The basic contribution of prophetic Christianity, despite the countless calamities perpetrated by Christian
churches, is that every individual, regardless of class, country, caste,
race, or sex, should have the opportunity to fulfill his or her potenti-
alities." He moved back and forth between Union and the Yale Divinity School during the '80s, until Princeton asked him in 1988 to join
its faculty as professor of religion and director of the Afro-American
Studies program. Toni Morrison, a humanities professor there and a
novelist who would soon receive the Nobel Prize for literature, was a
major factor in his decision to accept. "She told me in one of our talks
that she wanted me to become a part of her 'intellectual neighborhood' " In Princeton, another prominent novelist, Russell Banks, lived
across the street from West. Seeing West's light still on at two A.M.,
Banks would go visiting and the two would often hang out through
the night.

West went against the grain of those pushing for an Afrocentric
curriculum at Princeton. He sought a more cosmopolitan approach of
cultural and historical studies. As he would write in *Race Matters*:
"Afrocentrism, a contemporary species of black nationalism, is a gal-
lant yet misguided attempt to define an African identity in a white
society perceived to be hostile. . . . It is misguided because—out of fear
of cultural hybridization and through silence on the issue of class, ret-
rograde views on black women, gay men, and lesbians, and a reluc-

tance to link race to the common good—it reinforces the narrow discussions about race."

In 1989 came the publication of West's book *The American Evasion of Philosophy: A Genealogy of Pragmatism*. West is an advocate of what he calls "prophetic pragmatism," whose roots he traces to Emerson (one of West's favorite quotations is Emerson's "Conversation is our account of ourselves"), and onward through William James and John Dewey. "The distinctive appeal of American pragmatism in our postmodern moment," West has written, "is its unashamedly moral emphasis and its unequivocally ameliorative impulse."

Here West harkens back to Du Bois and, as noted earlier, both Du Bois and Locke had studied philosophy under William James. "It was James with his pragmatism and [history professor Albert Bushnell] Hart with his research method," Du Bois wrote, "that turned me back from the lovely but sterile land of philosophic speculation, to the social sciences as the field for gathering and interpreting that body of facts which would apply to my program for the Negro." Later, when James wrote his former student questioning the often-despairing tone of *The Souls of Black Folk*, Du Bois responded: "You must not think I am tuned to the most aggressive and unquenchable hopelessness. I wanted in this case simply to reveal the other side to the world."

West set out to reveal an "other side" in his next work, *The Ethical Dimensions of Marxist Thought*. His reappraisal examined Marxism's relevance in the post-Cold War period. Personally, he declared himself "a non-Marxist socialist" whose Christian tradition and "ungrounded leaps of faith" were basically alien to the Marxist economic paradigm. Then came *Race Matters*, where West urged that "we must delve into the depths where neither liberals nor conservatives dare to tread, into the murky waters of despair and dread that now flood the streets of black America."

But he did not spare black leadership, criticizing the majority as "too hungry for status to be angry, too eager for acceptance to be bold, too self-invested in advancement to be defiant." When blacks are cast as "a problem people, rather than people with problems," as he told the Harvard student symposium, "black middle classes often feel as if they have to prove themselves to the larger white society—rather than just take their own creativity and humanity for granted."

As West explained his mission to one interviewer: "To be a philosopher in a society that understands itself to be democratic puts a special kind of burden on [you], because . . . you want to hold that society to its own self-understanding, its own ideals. . . . Socrates said that the unexamined life is not worth living. But we could say the examined life is painful. America's always been in flight from pain." His goal was to be an "organic intellectual" like Emerson—"someone who tries to fuse the life of the mind with the public affairs of the nation, who tries to shape public opinion. I'm trying to revive a grand yet flawed tradition, to take the best from liberalism, Populism and the Gospel while keeping track of what happens to everyday people, the ones the Bible calls the least of these."

Or, as West put it in a 1990 discussion with Bill Moyers: "I understand the vocation of the intellectual as trying to turn easy answers into critical questions, and ask these critical questions to those with power. The quest for truth, the quest for the good, the quest for the beautiful, for me, presupposes allowing suffering to speak, allowing victims to be visible, and allowing social misery to be put on the agenda of those with power."

"You whose nation was founded on the loftiest ideals, and who many times forget those ideals with a strange forgetfulness, have more than a sentimental interest, more than a sentimental duty. You owe a debt to humanity for this Ethiopia of Out-stretched Arm. . . ."
—W. E. B. Du Bois, Commencement address at Harvard, 1890

"I sit with Shakespeare and he winces not. Across the color line I move arm and arm with Balzac and Dumas, where smiling men and welcoming women glide in gilded halls. From out of the caves of evening that swing between the strong-limbed earth and the tracery of stars, I summon Aristotle and Aurelius and what soul I will, and they come all graciously with no scorn nor condescencion. So, wed with Truth, I dwell above the veil. Is this the life you grudge us, O knightly America?"

—The Souls of Black Folk

In 1994, Cornel West was lured away from Princeton by Henry Louis Gates, Jr., who heads Harvard's Department of Afro-American Studies as well as its W. E. B. Du Bois Institute for Afro-American Research (the oldest in the field). Here West is part of a team of prominent black scholars, including British philosopher/novelist Kwame Anthony Appiah and sociologist William Julius Wilson. Gates was enamoured of West's ability to "speak two languages . . . both fluently"—those of the street and of the academy.

Gates and West teamed up to write *The Future of the Race*, essays by each published in 1996 that take up the Du Bois legacy. Here, while giving Du Bois full credit for "a level of genius unequaled among modern black intellectuals," West also levels a critique of his forbear's "mild elitism" and "inability to immerse himself fully in the rich cultural currents of black everyday life." Du Bois's understanding, West tells us, was filtered "through the medium of an *Enlightenment world-view* that promoted *Victorian strategies* in order to realize an *American optimism*." Therefore Du Bois "pits autonomy against authority, self-mastery against tradition," and espouses a black "Talented Tenth" that "must civilize and refine, uplift and elevate the benighted masses."

So, in the spirit of the son who must necessarily strive to transcend the spiritual father, West proffers a razor-edged contemporary assessment and, ultimately, a new vision:

"Public life deteriorates due to class polarization, racial balkanization, and especially a predatory market culture. With the vast erosion of civil networks that nurture and care for citizens . . . and with what might be called the gangsterization of everyday life, characterized by the escalating fear of violent attack, vicious assault, or cruel insult, we are witnessing a pervasive cultural decay in American civilization."

In his later years, Du Bois had turned increasingly toward Marxism as the only hope for global salvation. Eventually, he even joined the Communist Party. Yet he never could quite forsake his sense of being an American. Paul Robeson wrote of having Thanksgiving dinner at Du Bois's home shortly after World War II. The United Nations had just been formed, and "the Doctor" had invited several of its delegates from other countries. As they had no understanding of the American holiday, Robeson remembered Du Bois having explained it all—"from turkey and cranberry sauce to pumpkin pie and early American history. After the delicious dinner, over coffee and brandy before the log fire burning in the spacious living-room fireplace, he spoke of Frederick Douglass, whose portrait hung over the mantel, and of his place in American history."

The unbroken circle . . . At around the same time, Alain Locke wrote that Robeson's casting as Othello "presents at last with such illuminating force Shakespeare's original values undistorted and unblurred." As Du Bois and Robeson spent long hours together comparing African-American folk music to similar traditions around the world, Locke looked back and noted "how suddenly the Negro spirituals revealed themselves; suppressed for generations under the stereotypes of Wesleyan hymn harmony, secretive, half-ashamed, until the courage of being natural brought them out—and behold, there was folk-music."

Du Bois had been among the founders in 1897 of the first black institute of arts and letters, the American Negro Academy; its work was carried forward by Locke in his promotion of the black theater movement, exhibitions of African art, and such books as *The Negro and His Music, Negro Art: Past and Present* and *The Negro in Art*. In *The Crisis*, the country's first major black magazine which Du Bois edited between 1910 and 1933, many of the young black artists initially promoted by Locke came to be featured. Later, Locke wrote cultural accounts for Du Bois's *Phylon* magazine.

Professor Richard Long, of Atlanta's Emory University, was in touch with Locke on "a fairly regular basis" during the last decade of Locke's life. "As a very young person, my contact with him was very stimulating," Long remembers. "I admired him as an exemplar of the kinds of things I was interested in becoming. Locke's overall range was narrower than that of Du Bois, and he was not nearly as visible to the larger community. But he had much more impact on writers and visual artists, who were very affected by his ideas. An article Locke wrote about black drama in the late 1920s is strikingly close to some of the things talked about in the black arts movement of the 1960s. And Locke's annual reviews of the literature of the Negro, which began in 1929 and continued up to 1953, were extremely influential among the literati."

Locke was also a major reformer in American higher education, who in 1945 was elected the first black president of the American Association for Adult Education. He lived long enough to witness the landmark Supreme Court decision that compelled integrated schools in 1954. Three weeks after Brown v. Board of Education, Locke died at the age of sixty-eight. W. E. B. Du Bois said at his funeral:

"Alain Locke stood singular . . . as a rare soul who pursued for nearly half a century, steadily and unemotionally, the only end of man which justifies his living and differentiates him from the beasts and birds; and that is the inquiry as to what the universe is and why; and how it exists and how it can change. The paths pointed out by Socrates and Aristotle, Bacon and Descartes, Kant and Hegel, Marx and Darwin, were the ones Locke followed and which inevitably made him unknown and unknowable to a time steeped in the lore of Mickey Spillane.

"And yet in Locke's life lay a certain fine triumph. He knew life's greater things: pictures and poetry; music and drama. . . . His severe logic, his penetrating analysis, his wide reading, gave him a world within . . . finely furnished and unforgettable in breadth and depth. It built a man not fit for war but nobly courageous and simply consistent, who could bear pain and disappointment and yet live and work."

Cornel West looks upon Locke's legacy in these terms: "I remember reading his dissertation when I was a graduate student. What I love about Locke is that he was, in the broadest sense, a man of letters. In the highbrow Victorian sense, which I think is a positive thing. Interdisciplinary, broadly gauged, synoptic vision, synthetic analysis. We've lost much of that in the academy [of scholarship] today. Brother Locke is about as complex as they come. He was gay, and that made it rough on him, especially among the black bourgeoisie. He was often pushed to the margins. But what a pioneer he was!"

Du Bois ended up "pushed to the margins" as well. After he avowed Communism, he became a prisoner of the Cold War and abandoned by the "Talented Tenth" whose rise he had championed. He renounced his citizenship and, writes West, "left America in militant despair." Du Bois spent most of the last two years of his life in West Africa. One of the last old friends he saw was Paul Robeson in London. They talked for hours of the Encyclopedia Africana that Du Bois had embarked upon, and the burgeoning civil rights movement, and simultaneous African uprisings against European colonial rule.

In Ghana, in his *Autobiography*, Du Bois wrote: "Let then the Dreams of the Dead rebuke the Blind who think that what is will be forever and teach them that what was worth living for must live again and that which merited death must stay dead. Teach us, Forever Dead, there is no Dream but Deed, there is no Deed but Memory."

Du Bois died, at ninety-five, on the very morning of Martin Luther King's August 1963 March on Washington. King, on the 100th anniversary of Du Bois's birth and in one of his last addresses before he was assassinated, said in 1968 that Du Bois's "singular greatness" was the "unique zeal [which] rescued for all of us a heritage whose loss would have profoundly impoverished us."

"My initiation into Ethiopian life raises urgent issues of inheritance and rootlessness, tradition and homelessness. What is my relation to my African heritage and Ethiopian house? How do I understand my African American tradition and sense of black homelessness in America?"

—CORNEL WEST, *Keeping Faith*, 1993.

Married twice before, Cornel West first met Elleni Gabre Amlak— the beautiful daughter of a prominent Ethiopian family—when he was teaching at Yale. They were married in 1992 in Addis Ababa, where West received the honorary Ethiopian name of Fikre Selassie. Elleni's mother transferred ownership of the ancestral house to the newlyweds, and since then West and his wife have spent nearly every summer there.

What this may portend for West's future is difficult to say. He has said of Afrocentrism: "There is nothing wrong with affirming African humanity if we recognize that African civilizations, like European civilizations, have an ambiguous legacy—barbarism on the one hand and humanism on the other." And, having spoken out against what he views as Louis Farrakhan's homophobia, sexism and anti-Semitism, he has faced criticism from Farrakhan's Nation of Islam.

In the midst of a speech at MIT, where West and his friend Michael Lerner shared the podium to discuss their dialogue published in *Jews & Blacks*, one of Farrakhan's ministers harangued West for building bridges with the Jewish Lerner and white America. West remained gracious, even-tempered—and uncompromising. Later he joined Farrakhan's Million Man March in Washington, explaining why in an op-ed article for the *New York Times*: "Although Minister Farrakhan—with whom I have deep disagreements—initiated this demonstration, the demonstration is about matters much bigger than he is. . . . We agree on highlighting black suffering. . . . To stand on the sidelines and yield the terrain to Minister Farrakhan and other black nationalists would be to forsake not only my [Martin Luther] King legacy but, more importantly, my love for black people."

Sitting in his office, I asked West to elaborate on something he told another interviewer: "We might be in a situation in the next ten years, if these vicious conservative attacks continue, that the consolidating of forces in the black community, the need for a black united front, might require a shift in what I am doing and where I am."

Could he envision himself living outside academia, in an entirely different way? "Maybe," he replied. "You just don't know. You're open to a variety of different possibilities. One thing you try to keep in mind is that you want to create conditions under which your loved ones will experience the least amount of pain. So that as things got real bad, you'd have to come up with some ways to make sure they're safe or get them out of the country or whatever.

"But for me personally," he continued, "I just go down fighting. Every day is borrowed time. You want to be able to use life as well as death as a form of service to something bigger than you. That makes life meaningful, basically. I believe we've got to confront the decay and decline, to look at the night side of the civilization to get a sense of why it's setting in—alongside the tremendous breakthroughs of whites and blacks and browns and yellows and Americans in general. And acknowledging the tradition of black genius that's been at work, culturally and artistically as well as politically and morally. It's *all* got to be there."

We talked for a time then about his particular legacy, the period when he came of age in the 1960s. "Robert Kennedy is a very important figure in the white psyche, these last thirty-five years, regarding a sense of multiracial activism and possibilities. He was like Malcolm, in that he had the courage to grow, mature and develop. And like my wife was telling me—she's so wise—the most difficult thing to do is to confront that truth in yourself. Once you confront that truth, in fact it enables you, it frees you up as it were, to grow and develop. Robert Kennedy and Malcolm X, in their own ways, were like that."

When a student at the William Barton Rogers Middle School asked West "what book inspired you to be who you are today," he named three works. One was a short story called "The Student" by Anton Chekhov, "about a young person who's going through life having to deal with all these different forces coming at him, and at the same time keeping his eye on the prize." Another was Toni Morrison's first novel, *The Bluest Eye*—"a painful, powerful story about how black people wrestle with their ideals of beauty." But the first book he mentioned was one he read "when I was about sixteen years old—James Baldwin's *The Fire Next Time*."

Both Baldwin and Ellison, West said now, "are deeply rooted in the culturally hybrid character of American culture. The difference, of course, is that Baldwin was much more explicit about his rage and his anger. Baldwin is one of the greatest essayists of the twentieth century. His rhythm, his truth-telling, the witness-bearing, the self-criticism that people often overlook. The way he's honest about his rage, without it necessarily becoming so bitter that it closed him up. Ralph Ellison always struck me as a deeply angry man, but it was hidden and concealed. You knew that behind a certain persona, there was just this boiling. He was one of the most elegant men I ever met in my life. I went to hear him speak a number of times, and I went to his place once just to ring and say hello, but he was gone.

"Of course, what Ellison is saying is, How hypocritical and ironic that a people whose epidermis is most visible find their humanity *invisible*. But I'm actually much closer to Richard Wright. That sets me a little off-key with brother Stanley Crouch and brother Al Murray—I think Murray's work on jazz is peerless, the best we have—but they see Wright primarily as a protest writer. I think he's an existential writer with a strong protest element. Because like Baldwin, he was open about black rage, in a way that Ellison was not. The sense of the picturesque and the comic in Ellison holds it at arm's length. So while the Invisible Man stays underground, Wright is always above-ground—with all the bats and the hatred and the contempt and the bullets comin' at him, you know what I mean? Toni [Morrison] is always above-ground, too. It takes a certain courage to do that and actually come to terms with your body and your soul, not just your *consciousness*. Ellison's much more linked to Dostoevsky and that tradition, with the prisoners of consciousness. It's a great tradition but it's limited, at least for me."

West thought some more, about others he considered his personal inspirations. He smiled and said: "I must say, I resonate deeply with old Herman Melville. I think he's our greatest literary artist. He and Tennessee Williams would be two of my greatest soulmates. And then Toni, who is in some ways like Coltrane for me."

I remembered a striking and surprising statement that West had made, comparing Ralph Waldo Emerson to Louis Armstrong. "Well I mean, Emerson is all about experimentation—being open, fluid, flexible. With Armstrong, jazz was also all about experimentation, improvisation, openness, fluidity, flexibility. A protean identity that is open enough to be adjusting or adapting to new circumstances—but strong enough based on discipline to sustain various levels of spontaneity. Because the discipline, of course, is inseparable from the spontaneity. And so with both Emerson and Armstrong—and these insights, I know, are very Ellisonian—it's profoundly American.

"Emerson is the greatest American man of letters, there's no doubt about that. It's through Emerson that we get the various kinds of democracies. Whitman's cultural democracy, *Democratic Vistas* and *Leaves of Grass*. Gertrude Stein's grammatical democracy, one that democratizes a sentence and forces us to give as much attention to each word as opposed to the hierarchical structure. You get the ecological democracy in a Robert Frost, that allows us to pay attention to and even ascribe tremendous worth to natural objects. Similarly so in terms of the political and economic democracy of John Dewey— that's right out of Emerson. Then we go on to the musical democracy that you get in Louis Armstrong and jazz. It's very Emersonian. Very Emersonian."

West continued: "The greatness of the country is primarily seen in its music, and in its humor. Now the democracy that's been able to stay in place for so long has its great moments, the constitutional rule of law and so forth. But look at American politics compared to American music and humor. It just pales in the face of those two! Then think of how so much has been the creations of working people, everyday people. Bing Crosby's an everyday brother from Spokane who sounds regal. He *is* regal. Frank Sinatra's a working-class brother from Hoboken, same way. Nat King Cole, black working-class preacher's kid from funky Alabama—and he sounds like a king, which he was. Sarah Vaughn, divine Sarah, who comes out of working-class Mount Zion Baptist Church in Newark. I mean, all this is profoundly American. Which is to say, profoundly democratic. Which is to say, America at its best."

I decided to tell West a story I had heard from Pete Seeger. It was about Woody Guthrie, who wrote *This Land Is Your Land*. Seeger's story went like this:

"Woody had come from a racist background in Oklahoma. His father had even participated in a lynching. But when he came to New York, and became close to Leadbelly, he started to change. In spite of all the separation between the races, Woody knew some of the same songs that Leadbelly knew. Leadbelly knew some of the same songs that Woody knew. The blues and the gospel songs and so on. And there they both found themselves in New York, with a bunch of strange Yankees and people of Jewish background and Italian background.

"Around 1942, Sonny Terry and Brownie McGhee came up from North Carolina and moved into Harlem with Leadbelly. Now did you ever hear the story of when Woody, Sonny and Brownie were singing in Baltimore? It was part of a war bond drive, so they were doing songs like, *We're Gonna Tear Hitler Down*. Afterwards, the chairman comes up to Woody and says: 'Mr. Guthrie, we have a seat for you at the table here, and a table for your friends out in the kitchen.' Woody says, 'What do you mean? You heard us sing together, why can't we *sit* together?' Chairman says, 'Oh, Mr. Guthrie, this is Baltimore, you realize.'

"And Woody simply said: 'This fight against fascism has got to start right here!' He picked up the whole table full of dishes and everything, tipped it over onto the floor. Went to the next table, same thing! Finally some people grabbed him, and hustled him out of the place. Brownie McGhee told me the story. He remembered saying, 'Hey, Woody, you're gonna get us all in trouble. Because I'm lame. And Sonny's blind!' "

Cornel West burst out laughing. "That's incredible!" he exclaimed. "Whoooo, my God, that's a helluva story! Lord, lord, lord!"

I told him what Seeger had said, too, about how the folk-music world of the 1940s was in many ways the precursor of the civil rights movement. West thought a minute and then responded: "That's true, very very true. The spirit building up. And creating spaces for more honest truth-telling. That's building on the blues. My good friend Russell Banks, another great American novelist, says that the blues is probably the only true history of America—in terms of being willing to confront the kind of things that Melville and Twain and Faulkner were pushing us toward, in their own ways, on the so-called white side of the culture. And the blues laying it out on the black side of the culture. But both ultimately recognizing that our destinies are intertwined. I think that's the fundamental lesson that we all have to learn."

"I believe in God who made of one blood all nations that on earth do dwell. I believe that all men, black and brown and white, are brothers,

varying through time and opportunity, in form and gift and feature,
but differing in no essential particular, and alike in soul and the pos-
sibility of infinite development."
                    —The Credo of W. E. B. Du Bois, *Darkwater*, 1920.

FOR FURTHER READING:
The Oxford W. E. B. Du Bois Reader, edited by Eric J. Sundquist
(New York and Oxford: Oxford University Press, 1996).
W. E. B. Du Bois: Biography of a Race, 1868–1919, by David Lev-
ering Lewis (New York: Henry Holt, 1993).
The New Negro: Voices of the Harlem Renaissance, edited by Alain
Locke (New York: Atheneum, 1992).
Voices from the Harlem Renaissance, edited by Nathan Irvin Hug-
gins (New York: Oxford University Press, 1976).
Race Matters, by Cornel West (New York: Vintage Books, 1994).
The Future of the Race, by Henry Louis Gates, Jr., and Cornel West
(New York: Alfred A. Knopf, 1996).
Breaking Bread: Insurgent Black Intellectual Life, by bell hooks and
Cornel West (Boston: South End Press, 1991).
*Jews & Blacks: A Dialogue on Race, Religion, and Culture in Amer-
ica*, by Michael Lerner and Cornel West (New York: Plume/Penguin
Books, 1996).
Keeping Faith: Philosophy and Race in America, by Cornel West
(New York: Routledge, 1994).

Toni Morrison:
Nobel Prize for Literature

"I write . . . village literature, fiction that is really for the village, for the tribe. . . . If anything I do in the way of writing novels isn't about the village or the community, then it's not about anything. I am not interested in indulging myself in some private, closed exercise of my imagination that fulfills only my personal dreams."

—TONI MORRISON

Sitting in a bar just off Harvard Square, Cornel West is sipping a cognac and talking about the unforgettable night of December 7, 1993. He was then at Princeton. West and his wife Elleni had been invited by their close friend Toni Morrison to accompany her to Stockholm. There she was to receive the Nobel Prize for Literature—the first author ever to have been awarded both a Nobel and a Pulitzer.

"You talk about grace, dignity, class, elegance—when Toni walked down that aisle on the arm of King Gustav of Sweden!" West is saying, his eyes aglow. "But what I could really see was these millions and millions of black folk who had come and gone. I could see it in her walk, I could see it in her face. All kinds of humiliation and cruelty coming their way. And they just kept comin' on! Nigeria's Wole Soyinka was sitting with us. He had been the first [black] to get a Nobel, in 1986. Now here was Toni, for the world to see. Tears flowing from everybody's eyes. That was one great moment, man."

Toni Morrison's Nobel speech had taken the form of a fable. It was the tale of an old clairvoyant blind woman, the daughter of slaves, who lived alone in a little house outside a small American town. "Her reputation for wisdom is without peer and without question," Morrison began. "Among her people she is both the law and its transgression." A group of young visitors comes to her door, intent on exposing the old woman as a fraud. They ask but one question she seemingly could not answer: "Is the bird I am holding living or dead?" After a long silence, she tells them she does not know—"but what I do know is that it is in your hands."

Morrison went on to use the bird as a metaphor for language. She described the old woman as a practiced writer who "thinks of language partly as a system, partly as a living thing over which one has control, but mostly as agency—as an act with consequences." Language could die "out of carelessness, disuse, indifference." If the metaphorical bird is dead, its "custodians are responsible for the corpse. . . .

"She would not want to leave her young visitors with the impression that language should be forced to stay alive merely to be. The vitality of language lies in its ability to limn the actual, imagined and possible lives of its speakers, readers, writers. Although its poise is sometimes in displacing experience, it is not a substitute for it. It arcs toward the place where meaning may lie."

Then Toni Morrison summoned up the presence of Abraham Lincoln. "When a President of the United States thought about the graveyard his country had become, and said, 'The world will little note nor long remember what we say here. But it will never forget what they did here,' his simple words were exhilarating in their life-sustaining properties because they refused to encapsulate the reality of 600,000 dead men in a cataclymic race war. Refusing to monumentalize, disdaining the 'final word,' the precise 'summing up,' acknowledging their 'poor power to add or detract,' his words signal deference to the uncapturability of the life it mourns. It is the deference that moves her, that recognition that language can never live up to life once and for all. Nor should it. Language can never 'pin down' slavery, genocide, war. Nor should it yearn for the arrogance to be able to do so. Its force, its felicity, is in its reach toward the ineffable."

Late that same night, Cornel West remembers, Nelson Mandela arrived. "He'd just received the Nobel Peace Prize in Oslo, and he came with all of his people from South Africa over to our hotel. Ohhhh, brother! Stayed up till four o'clock, Mandela and all with Toni over there. Stockholm ain't never *seen* nothin' like that! And never will."

To West, Toni Morrison is "*the* great storyteller, the great literary artist, of black folk. She's our Tolstoy, our Joyce, our Walter Scott. It's quite extraordinary when you think about it, because she started late."

Morrison's first novel was published in 1970, when she was thirty-nine. Her seventh is scheduled to appear in the spring of 1998. Only since mid-life has she received both critical acclaim and commercial success. *Song of Solomon* received the National Book Critics Circle Award for fiction in 1977. *Beloved* was awarded the Pulitzer Prize in 1987. Six years later, the Nobel was given for the body of her work. All the while, as a single parent who raised two children, Morrison has maintained second careers as either an editor or a teacher.

Her variegated tales cover the range of African-American experience from the times of slavery into the present. They are peopled with extraordinary characters with names like Pecola, Sula, Milkman Dead, and Sethe. The style is at once refined and improvisational, weaving vast circles in and out of her characters' lives. In Morrison's narratives, devastatingly painful realities merge with the paranormal realm of ghosts and flying ancestors. And, as her Princeton University colleague and literary critic Claudia Brodsky Lacour puts it, "The originality of Morrison's stories owes to the drama she finds where few have looked before."

Maryemma Graham, scholar-in-residence at the Association for the Study of Afro-American Life and History in Washington, adds: "When we enter a Morrison novel, we are participating in a narrative of community, complete with the rituals and cultural baggage that compel the reader's complete engagement."

As Morrison herself has described her work and goals: "My books are frequently read as representative of what the black condition is. Actually, the books are about very specific circumstances, and in them are people who do very specific things. But more importantly, the plot and characters are part of my effort to create a language in which I can posit philosophical questions. I want the reader to ponder those questions not because I put them in an essay, but because they are part of a narrative. . . .

"I would like my work to do two things: be as demanding and sophisticated as I want it to be, and at the same time be accessible in a sort of emotional way to lots of people, just like jazz. That's a hard task. But that's what I want to do."

Toni Morrison has never been a stranger to hard tasks. Born Chloe Anthony Wofford on February 18, 1931, in the little Ohio town of Lorain, she was the second of four children and grew up in poverty. (Toni was a nickname she adopted in college, Morrison her married name.) Her father found whatever jobs he could to support the family. As a young teenager, Morrison began doing after-school housecleaning to help out.

It is impossible to understand the many manifestations of African-American "village life" in Morrison's novels without focusing upon her formative years. This is a subject she has addressed with several interviewers, before going into recent seclusion to complete her latest book.

"Where I was before I came here, that place is real. It's never going away. Even if the whole farm—every tree and grass blade of it dies. The picture is still there and what's more, if you go there—you who

never was there—if you go there and stand in the place where it was, it will happen again; it will be there for you, waiting for you."
        —Sethe speaking to her daughter Denver, in *Beloved*.

Both of Morrison's parents had spent their formative years in the South: her father George in Georgia, her mother Ramah in Alabama. Morrison's maternal grandparents, she recalls, "lost their land, like a lot of black people at the turn of the century. They were sharecroppers, which meant they were never able to get out of debt. My grandfather had left Greenville for Birmingham to earn money playing the violin. He sent money back, but my grandmother began to get nervous, all alone in Greenville, because her daughters were reaching puberty and that was a dangerous business in the South, in the country. . . . So my grandmother decided to leave. She sent her husband an oral message: 'We're heading north on the midnight train. If you ever want to see us again, you'll be on that train.'

"She didn't know if he got the message, but with eighteen dollars to her name she packed up six or seven children and got them all to the train in Birmingham. It was the first city my mother had ever seen— she still remembers, 'We had *white* bread!' My grandfather was nowhere in sight. As the train left the station the children began to cry— then, about an hour later, he showed up. He'd been there all along, hiding, for fear somebody would recognize him and stop them for owing money."

They had made a brief sojourn to Kentucky, where Morrison's grandfather worked in a coal mine. "My grandmother did washing, and my mother and her sister went to a little one-room school. One day the teacher, who was about sixteen and white, was doing long division and having trouble explaining it. Since my mother and her sister already knew long division, they explained it to the teacher and the class. They came home all excited and proud of themselves, crowing, 'Mama, guess what we did? We taught the teacher long division!' My grandmother just said to her husband, 'Come on, Johnny, we have to move.'"

The family of John and Ardelia Willis had continued north, finally stopping in Lorain, a steel mill town on the banks of Lake Erie. There, Morrison's mother and father met. Ship welder George Wofford's story, Morrison says, was "different but the same. As a child in Georgia, he received shocking impressions of adult white people, and for the rest of his life felt he was justified in despising all whites."

But, Morrison continues, as a little girl "I knew he was wrong. I went to school with white children—they were my friends. There was no awe, no fear. Only later, when things got . . . sexual . . . did I see how clear the lines really were. But when I was in first grade nobody thought I was inferior. I was the only black in the class and the only child who could read!"

From her earliest years, her parents had nurtured in Morrison a desire for reading. "The security I felt, the pleasure when new books arrived, was immense. My mother belonged to a book club, one of those early ones. And that was hard-earned money, you know. . . . My parents made all of us feel as though there were these rather extraordinary deserving people within us. I felt like an aristocrat—or what I think an aristocrat is. I always knew we were very poor. But that was never degrading. I remember a very important lesson that my father gave me when I was twelve or thirteen. He said, 'You know, today I welded a perfect seam and I signed my name to it.' And I said, 'But, Daddy, no one's going to see it!' And he said, 'Yeah, but I know it's there.' "

There was also Morrison's mother's constant singing, "a kind of meditation . . . of talking to oneself musically." She remembers: "I could even hear the different ways that my mother would sing a song, whether it was classical [music] or spirituals or whatever, depending upon what was on her mind. It wasn't just to make herself feel better. It was also a kind of probing into something and then working it out in addition to whatever release it provided. It had a great deal to do, actually, with my feeling that writing for me is an enormous act of discovery. I have all these problems that are perhaps a little weary and general and well-worked-over that I want to domesticate and conquer. Then I can sort of figure out what I think about all this or get a little further along."

Because Lorain was a steel town, it had attracted immigrants of many nationalities—Eastern European, Irish, Italian—and Morrison recalls becoming "sensitive to languages" very early both in school and on the street. Within her family, "when something terribly important was to be said, it was highly sermonic, highly formalized, biblical in a sense, and easily so. They could move easily into the language of the King James Bible and then back to standard English, and then segue into language that we would call street. It was seamless, and this was extremely attractive to me to hear. Just listening to my great-grandmother, whom I knew, and my grandparents and my uncles and my mother and father and all their friends, it was fascinating."

Equally fascinating were the tales of black folklore and myth. Her parents told exciting, frightening ghost stories. Her grandmother, who lived in the household, decoded the symbols she saw in her dreams and placed bets on these in local numbers games. "We were intimate with the supernatural," Morrison has said.

Years later, in *Tar Baby*, whose story derived from one of those folktales, blind slaves would gallop across the hills on their horses while the watching trees readied themselves for war. And, at the close of the progatonist's quest for his heritage in *Song of Solomon*, Milkman learns about his grandfather:

"... 'according to the story he wasn't running away [from slavery]. He was flying. He flew. You know, like a bird. Just stood up in the fields one day, ran up some hill, spun around a couple of times, and was lifted up in the air. Went right on back to wherever it was he came from. There's a big double-headed rock over the valley named for him.' ... If you surrendered to the air, you could *ride* it."

Morrison's first novel, *The Bluest Eye*, originated with an experience that had haunted her since elementary school. It had to do with a little black girl who dreamed of having blue eyes; then, only then, might she be beautiful. Morrison had listened to the girl's sorrowful voice, tried to picture this incarnation, and was "violently repelled by what I imagined she would look like if she had her wish." At the same time, Morrison wrote in 1993, she realized that beauty "was not simply something to behold; it was something one could *do*. . . .

"*The Bluest Eye* was my effort to say something about that; to say something about why she had not, or possibly ever would have, the experience of what she possessed and also why she prayed for so radical an alteration. Implicit in her desire was racial self-loathing. And twenty years later I was still wondering about how one learns that. . . . The novel pecks away at the gaze that condemned her."

Both the lessons gleaned from hard work, and material for her future, came with Morrison's first employment as a part-time maid, around the age of thirteen. "The normal teen-age jobs were not available. Housework always was. It wasn't uninteresting. You got to work these gadgets that I never had at home: vacuum cleaners. Some of the people were nice. Some were terrible. Years later, I used some of what I observed in my fiction.

"In *The Bluest Eye*, Pauline lived in this dump and hated everything in it. And then she worked for the Fishers, who had this beautiful house, and she loved it. She got a lot of respect as their maid that she didn't get anywhere else. If she went to the grocery store as a black woman from that little house and said, 'I don't want this meat,' she would not be heard. But if she went in as a representative of these white people and said, 'This is not good enough,' they'd pay attention."

As an adolescent, Morrison's reading became prodigious—Jane Austen, Flaubert, the great Russian novelists. "Those books were not written for a little black girl in Lorain, Ohio, but they were so magnificently done that I got them anyway—they spoke directly to me. . . . I wasn't thinking of writing then—I wanted to be a dancer like Maria Tallchief—but when I wrote my first novel . . . I wanted to capture . . . the nature and feeling of the culture *I* grew up in."

Morrison remembers skipping over the racial stereotypes in Hemingway, Faulkner, and Willa Cather—themes to which she would return in a 1990 book of essays, *Playing in the Dark: Whiteness and the Literary Imagination.* "Because I loved those books," she recalls. "I loved them. So when they said these things that were profoundly racist, I forgave them. As for Faulkner, I read him with enormous pleasure. He seemed to me the only writer who took black people seriously."

It would be William Faulkner, a Southern Nobel Prize winner, with whose multilayered prose style Morrison would eventually be most closely compared. According to Cornel West, Morrison's other early influences were D. H. Lawrence, Virginia Woolf, and James Baldwin.

Finally, there was the influence of ambience in Lorain itself. "The racial and ethnic mix was so tight and so unhostile, and there were no black neighborhoods. I mean there were wealthy neighborhoods but all of the poor people, which we were—the workers—lived next door to each other. Of course, they went to different churches, and so on, as adults. Even now I think of the names of the people who lived next door to my mother's house. We all shared the same space, one high school, three junior high schools, these totally dedicated teachers. . . .

"I remember, as a teenager, walking down the street in Lorain, and somebody came up to me and said, 'Are you a Willis?' which is my mother's maiden name. And I said, 'Yes.' And he said, 'I thought so. You walk like one.'

"Now when I moved to New York . . . people said, 'What do you do? What job do you have?' But the place where somebody has some notion of what a Willis female walks like is entirely different. That kind of comfort of being recognized for those things that are—you know, I didn't even know what a Willis walk was—but it's a kind of comfort that I wish everybody had.

"At the same time, I was very, very interested in getting out of there."

After graduating from high school with honors, Morrison had moved on in 1949 to then all-black Howard University in Washington. There she majored in English and minored in the classics. She began doing some experimental prose with a college writer's group, the first time she toyed with the story of the little girl who wanted blue eyes. As a member of the Howard Repertory Theater, she also received her first opportunity to visit the South from which her parents migrated.

One of Morrison's professors, Cornel West remembers, was Alain Locke. "Toni took his philosophy course. In fact, it's the only 'C' she got on her transcript, because that's the highest grade Locke ever gave. Toni's told me all the stories about him, how he was into parapsycholgy, even had ouija boards. And how he always wore gloves, never allowed his hands to touch the door when he turned the knob!"

Going on to Cornell University for her graduate work, Morrison received her Master's in English in 1955; her thesis covered the theme of suicide in the works of Faulkner and Virginia Woolf. She had taught English first at Texas Southern University, then at her alma mater, Howard. There she met Harold Morrison, an architecture student from Jamaica. They were married in 1959.

The early 1960s were quite a time to be at Howard. She got to know the playwright Amiri Baraka (then LeRoi Jones), who Morrison says "really turned that campus around." One of her English students was Kwame Toure, known at the time as Stokeley Carmichael. He was, Morrison recalls, "the kind of student you always want in a class—smart, perceptive, funny and a bit of a rogue. He *never* worked, and he stimulated all the others to think." When Carmichael graduated in 1964, he told Morrison that he had been accepted into the Union Theological Seminary in New York. First, though, he wanted to head for Mississippi to spend the summer helping the civil rights struggle. Carmichael went on to become one of the leading figures in the Student Non-Violent Coordinating Committee and "Black Power" movement.

Another of Morrison's students was Claude Brown. One day, he asked if she would read a manuscript that he had written. It was some 800 pages long. "I said, What? Eight hundred pages? Claude, *come on*! A nickel a word, I'll read it for you." The manuscript turned out to be one of the recent classics of African-American literature, *Manchild in the Promised Land*.

As Morrison's marriage started to fall apart in 1964, she sought solace in writing, like "someone with a dirty habit." When she and her husband separated, Morrison was pregnant with a second child. He returned to Jamaica. She resigned from Howard University. Taking her three-year-old son along, she went home to Ohio to have the baby, having no idea what the future might hold. She was thirty-three.

Morrison did not linger long in Lorain. After Slade was born, she moved with the baby and his brother Howard to Syracuse, New York, where she took a job editing textbooks for a subsidiary of Random House. Her reading came to focus on African novelists such as Chinua Achebe and Camara Laye. "They did not explain their black world," Morrison says. "Or clarify it. Or justify it. White writers had always taken white centrality for granted. They inhabited their world in a central position and everything non-white was 'other.' These African writers took their blackness as central and the whites were the 'other.' "

At night after putting her children to bed, Morrison dove into *The Bluest Eye*, set in a little Ohio town just prior to the outbreak of the Second World War. "It was 1967 and the slogan 'Black is beautiful' was in the air," Morrison says. "I loved it, but something was missing." Morrison wondered why the concept of black beauty needed "wide public articulation to exist?" She set out to describe "the people who in all literature were always peripheral—little black girls who were props, background; those people were never center stage, and those people were me."

As another character in her novel comments about Pecola Breedlove: "The end of the world lay in their eyes, and the beginning, and all the waste in between."

Morrison decided she "did not want to dehumanize the characters who trashed Pecola and contributed to her collapse." The father who eventually rapes his daughter thus becomes a tragic figure, ensnared by social forces beyond his control, his terrible act ultimately becoming his only means of expressing love. "The writing," Morrison has said, "was the disclosure of secrets, secrets 'we' shared and those withheld from us by ourselves and by the world outside the community."

Shortly before the book's publication, Morrison had transferred into Random House's New York City headquarters as a senior editor. When *The Bluest Eye* appeared in 1970, she recalls, "I was upset. They had the wrong name: Toni Morrison. . . . Well, I sort of knew it was going to happen. I was in a daze. I sent it in that way because the editor knew me as Toni Morrison. . . . I write all the time about being misnamed. How you got your name is very special. My mother, my sister, all my family call me Chloe. It was Chloe, by the way, who went to Stockholm . . . to get the Nobel Prize."

Painfully evocative as it is, *The Bluest Eye* did not initially receive much attention. It was, Morrison says, "like Pecola's life: dismissed, trivialized, misread." Undaunted, six months later she began working on her second novel, *Sula*. She wrote considerable portions in her head, riding the subway back and forth to her home in Queens. In *Sula*, Morrison took up another subject that had rarely surfaced in literature—the complex friendship between two black women. When Sula Peace and Nel Wright discover that they were "neither white nor male, and that all freedom and triumph was forbidden to them, they had set about something else to be." Morrison followed their lives between 1919 and 1965, again in a small Ohio town. The saga became one that intertwined two psyches in an archetypal relationship.

Published in 1973, *Sula* did not bring Morrison much visibility either. That would happen five years later, with *Song of Solomon*. Here Morrison wove her tale around the quest of a male figure, for the first and only time. "I learned a lot from my sons," she says, "seeing how excited they got by going near danger, for instance—they'd come away *charged*, lifted, as if somebody'd turned the volume up. And my father taught me, too. He died before I started *Song of Solomon*, but I had long conversations with him in my head anyway, to learn what he knew about men. So you see, I have my own version of the supernatural."

This same theme surfaces early in the novel, when Milkman's all-knowing aunt Pilate recalls seeing her father blown off a fence and killed on the old family homestead in Virginia, only to emerge in visitations. "I see him still," says Pilate. "He's helpful to me, real helpful. Tells me things I need to know."

Whenever things were difficult for Morrison during that first decade in New York, she would think about her grandmother fleeing from Alabama with her children in search of a better life. "There was an urgency—that's all I remember. Not having the leisure to whine. Not paying close attention to what others thought my life should be like. Not organizing my exterior and interior self for the approval of men— which I had done a lot of before. . . .

"I remember one day when I was confused about what I had to do next—write a review, pick up groceries, what? I took out a yellow pad and made a list of all the things I had to do. It included large things, like 'be a good daughter and a good mother,' and small things, like 'call the phone company.' I made another list of the things I wanted to do. There were only two things without which I couldn't live: mother my children and write books. Then I cut out everything that didn't have to do with those two things. . . . Writing is what centered me. In the act of writing, I felt most alive, most coherent, most stable and most vulnerable."

After *Song of Solomon* became a best-seller, Morrison was walking along a dock on the Hudson River north of Manhattan one day. She looked up and saw what had once been a boathouse, a four-story colonial wood-frame. She says she felt her father's voice of delight echoing around her. She bought it, and moved with her two sons into Grand View-on-Hudson.

Morrison's next novel, *Tar Baby* (1981), was set primarily in a fictional Caribbean village. Here, for the first time, white people walked the pages, as the well-educated middle-class heroine Jadine sought to assimilate into their world. Finally she becomes a tragic figure because "she has lost the original and ancient characteristics of her tribe." As in each of Morrison's works, the style evolved to fit the subject. In *Tar Baby*, there was less narrative, stronger dialogue. It, too, received excellent reviews and had strong sales.

Then came Morrison's most difficult, challenging self-imposed task: a six-year-long quest to immerse herself in the period of slavery. As Cornel West puts it, "Most of our novelists won't touch it. Toni had the courage to walk right *into* the Hades of the black experience. To put it in Faulknerian terms, it's the book where she takes the most risk and therefore has to deal with the possibility of highest failure. In doing this, she's able to accomplish so much. To capture the variety of different dimensions of black people's experiences on so many levels—the ritualistic, the psychic, the social, the political, the soul-making, the soul-tormenting, the interaction with the larger society. There's a courage, as well as a talent, at work in *Beloved* that we simply have never seen in the black novel."

In painstakingly probing the world of Sethe, an escaped slave who murders her daughter rather than see the child live in the same circumstance, Morrison says: "I had never been so frightened. I could imagine slavery in an intellectual way, but to feel it viscerally was terrifying. I had to go inside. Like an actor does. I had to feel what it might feel like for my own children to be enslaved. . . .

"With *Beloved*, I wanted to say, Let's get rid of these words like 'the slave woman' and 'the slave child,' and talk about people with names like you and like me, who were there. . . . I was trying to make it a personal experience. The book was not about the institution—Slavery with a capital S. It was about these anonymous people called slaves. What they do to keep on, how they make a life, what they're willing to risk, however long it lasts, in order to relate to one another—that was incredible to me."

By the time of *Beloved*, Morrison had left Random House after twenty years. Yet her legacy as an editor is, in some ways, as striking as her prose. There had been a few outstanding, if little-known, black female novelists before Morrison—Zora Neale Hurston, Dorothy West, Paule Marshall. Today, there are dozens. "Toni has done more to encourage and publish other black writers than anyone I know," says Andrew Young, former mayor of Atlanta, U.S. ambassador to the United Nations, and one of those whose book she edited. Due to Morrison's influence, there is now a popular black women's literature. In 1992, four works by black women apeared on the best-seller lists simultaneously—Terry McMillan's, Alice Walker's, and two by Morrison (her novel *Jazz* and an essay collection).

Among the African-American women authors whom Morrison

served as editor and brought to the fore are Angela Davis, Gayl Jones, and Toni Cade Bambara. According to Bambara, Morrison is "a superb editor, a real wizard. She floats little suggestions past my eyeballs and smiles her magical smile—I trust her judgment absolutely."

Erroll McDonald came to Random House "through Toni's auspices" as an editorial assistant in 1977. Today, McDonald is executive editor of Pantheon Books, the highest book publishing position ever achieved by an African-American. Since the early 1990s, he has also served as Morrison's editor. "On the wings of Bambara and Jones, whom Toni brought along," McDonald says, "America became aware of a literary phenomenon actually. These writers were reviewed together, celebrated together, even as their singular achievements were respected."

Thus did Morrison create her own literary village, midwifing into existence an African-American literary resurgence that she herself had initiated. Ever since her coming to New York, she says, "I needed people who felt responsible. So what I had to do, along with some other people, was make a community. Now that means not the people on my street necessarily or on my block, but the people nationally, if not globally, the people that you could count on. If a friend's child was in trouble, I could say, 'Send her to me.' Or if my children needed respite from me, somebody would say, 'Send them to me for a week,' or a summer, or what have you. Or they would just appear under times of stress and clean house and go to the market."

This sense of *communitas* continued after Morrison left New York for New Jersey's Princeton University in 1989, where she remains the Robert F. Goheen Professor of Humanities. Wahneena Lubiano, currently in the literature and African-American studies programs at Duke University, was a colleague and close friend of Morrison's at Princeton for six years and says: "My son was a high school student, and there were times when he was not comfortable with me but he would be in Toni's presence. When I was at my wit's end, she could say so very easily and calmly things that made me realize being a parent is a life-long enterprise."

Cornel West, who was also at Princeton between 1988 and 1994, remembers: "Toni called me up before I'd met her and said, 'Corn, we've got a chance to create an intellectual neighborhood here at Princeton, should we make a go for it?' I'd planned to stay in New York, but after we talked, I started thinking seriously about making the move to be there with her. Best thing I did, intellectually."

West believes that much of the power in both Morrison's writing and personal life emanates from a little-known fact about her. "Toni's been Catholic since she was seven years old. Her own choice. Her family's A.M.E. [Methodist]. When she was at Howard University, there were two Catholics in the whole school and they roomed to-gether: Toni, and [future New York mayor] David Dinkins's wife-to-be, Joyce.

"So I've thought about this a great deal in terms of Toni," West continues. "What is it about Catholicism? You see, with Ralph Ellison and Richard Wright, they're profoundly Protestant writers because their work is very much about *individuals*—against the world, wres-tling with conscience. You find very little about what mediates the individual in society. Whereas Toni *always* focuses on the communal character of our individuality. It may be fractured or broken, but there's a relationship to the consequences of one's actions for family and community. That's not Hawthorne or Emerson or Melville. It's profoundly Catholic."

Another aspect of Morrison's work is her shattering of taboos on sexuality. "I wanted to write books that ran the whole gamut of women's sexual experiences," she has said. "I didn't like the imposition that had been placed on black women's sexuality in literature. They were either mothers, mammies or whores. And they were not vulner-able people."

West points out that this, too, seems connected in part to Morrison's Catholicism. "In some ways, there is a certain Protestant, if not down-right puritanical, character to the taboo on sexuality in so much of black writing. Whereas in the James Joyces, Flannery O'Connors, and other great Catholic or lapsed Catholic writers, there is a certain rev-eling in sexuality where it becomes just part and parcel of our everyday lives."

Albert Raboteau, a prominent professor of religion at Princeton, views Morrison in similar terms. "I would use a liturgical term from the Greek, *anamnesis*, which means 'not forgetting.' One of the strong-est dimensions of Toni's work can be summed up in that. This includes the horrendous suffering, and its effects, upon the black community and individual black psyches. But also the ways in which that suffering has created people of wisdom and humanity."

A colleague of Raboteau, Davíd Carrasco, is a Chicano scholar at Princeton in the history of religions and is currently doing a study on these dimensions of Morrison's novels. "First, you have the overt scenes of religiosity," Carrasco notes. "In every novel, you find im-portant moments in a sermon or a church or a funeral. Like in *Beloved*, where the remarkable Baby Suggs sermon takes place in the clearing. Secondly, she mixes African religious meanings and practices with Christian traditions—the conjuring women like Pilate in *Song of Sol-omon*, or the folk healer who brings access to the ancestors in *Sula*. Finally, you have what she calls 'strange things,' where sacred moments take place that may or may not have to do with church, these ghosts and mysterious events in nature. Part of the strategy is to move the novel along, but always give the reader the sense of being on edge.

"Toni talked to me once about this," Carrasco adds. "She said she grew up hearing stories about ghosts, and knowing these were real to the people who told them to her. When she went to college, she was encouraged to put all that stuff aside. But when she started writing these novels, there was great freedom to be able to bring it back: that the spiritual world is a living tradition in the black community, accessible and alive and just outside your door or your rational discourse."

Not long ago, Carrasco had escorted Morrison on a week-long trip to Mexico City, where he "wanted to share with her some of the research I was doing in the valley of Mexico on sacred spaces. Also, frankly, I wanted to try to stimulate an enlargement of her discourse on race to reflect on the [mixed-race] *mestizos* of Mexico."

So they had set out for the land of the Aztecs, visiting the pyramids at Teotihuácan, meeting with excavators of the Great Aztec Temple. Observing Morrison standing before the early murals of the great Mexican artist Diego Rivera, Carrasco was struck by how involved she became, "open to the messages that come from these artworks. She possessed such focus and attention that people around her seemed to pick up a certain vibration; they would step back and let her look."

When Morrison gave a talk at the National University of Mexico on their third day, Carrasco remembers: "We had just let people know the day before, but the crowds came in droves. They had signs up everywhere in Spanish—'Toni Morrison Entre Nosotros'—Toni Morrison Among Us. It was fascinating that the Mexicans had not only read her in translation, but identified very much with her characters. Particularly with *Song of Solomon*, and its theme of the ancestors becoming present and the lifeline coming down through them. Toni was very comfortable among these people, it was like home."

As Morrison's editor Erroll McDonald says: "Her influence has to be seen not strictly in American terms, but global ones. Over the last twenty-five years or so, we've witnessed an increasing awareness of what can only be called a global literature—in that readers throughout the world are sensing a universality as practiced by a wide range of writers, ranging from Toni Morrison to Salman Rushdie to Gabriel García Marquez."

The only request Morrison had made of Davíd Carrasco in planning their trip was whether he could arrange for her to meet with Gabriel García Marquez. There were many similarities between Morrison and Colombia's literary giant, author of such novels as *One Hundred Years of Solitude* and *Love in the Time of Cholera*. Marquez had received the Nobel Prize for Literature in 1982. His work has been described as "magical realism." Like Morrison, he, too, created a character who ascended into the air. Like Morrison, he, too, once conceived butterflies as soulmates for his book's lovers.

At Carrasco's request, Mexico's prizewinning novelist/essayist Carlos Fuentes arranged a dinner at his home for Morrison with his friend "Gabo." Carrasco says: "When we were driving back to the airport in a taxi, Toni leaned forward, tapped me on the shoulder, and said: 'Coming to Mexico and meeting García Marquez was as important to me as going to Stockholm to receive the Nobel Prize.'

"It was one genius transmitting to another. Morrison and Marquez didn't talk about racial questions, but about the dynamics of writing novels. Through translators, they spoke of how Latin American writers—Marquez, Fuentes, Vargas Llosa—were all very much influenced by William Faulkner. García Marquez discussed some of the different ways of structuring a novel between Morrison and Faulkner. She has long recognized Marquez's genius, and was impressed with the profound commitment of his taking fourteen years to write *One Hundred Years of Solitude*. And he had obviously read all of her books. Marquez knew when each was published—what year, the sequence. He was particularly fascinated by the ways in which she constructs her novels. He said, 'The reader needs to angle himself in.' "

In Morrison's most recent published novel, *Jazz* (1992), the angles come from many divergent points of view. She wanted "to get rid of that notion of the omniscient narrative voice," seeking to leave behind the "kind of classical, spiritual gospel feel" of *Beloved*. The book takes off from a story Morrison heard about an eighteen-year-old girl who was shot by her ex-lover at a party in 1926; refusing to tell anyone who had committed the deed, she had bled to death. Set in Harlem during the early part of the twentieth century, Morrison sought to capture the "unanticipated things" that occur during a jazz performance.

When she listens to jazz, Morrison says, "you hear the melody and then it goes away or seems to, or they play against it or around it or take it off to another zone. Then sometimes it comes back and you can recognize it. I wanted that narrative line or melody to be established immediately in the first pages, and when the question becomes whether the narrator was right in his or her expectations of exactly what the story was, that is the 'melody' being taken to another zone."

Morrison's home, says Cornel West, is never without music. "You walk in and there's often one person on the CD—and that's Sarah Vaughan." Morrison is also known to relax with mystery novels, or watching Court TV and soap operas. On days when she is not teaching at Princeton, she gets up before dawn, writing in the morning and generally reading in the afternoon. "There is such an intellectual curiosity about Toni, an obsession with ideas," West adds. "I mean, she can sit there and talk to you about the *variety* of the different biographies of Faulkner—and each one is 800 pages. I say, 'Toni, how do you read all that stuff?' She says, 'That's my life.'"

Wahneena Lubiano adds: "She's one of the few writers I've known who is avidly interested in literary criticism. Aware of the different currents in thinking, Toni brings this not only to her own work but her encounters with students. I've sat in on a number of her classrooms, and she's also one of the funniest people I know. I've never known anybody whose radar is out for humor the way Toni's is."

When in 1993 Morrison became the first African-American and the eighth woman to receive the Nobel Prize for Literature, she was stunned. "Because I never thought I had that many supporters. . . . I felt a lot of 'we' excitement. It was as if the whole category of 'female writer' and 'black writer' had been redeemed. I felt I represented a whole world of women who either were silenced or who had never received the imprimatur of the established literary world."

Others were shocked, too, but for different reasons. Michael Thelwell, a Jamaican-born college professor and author whose first novel *The Harder They Come* was widely acclaimed, remembers "driving along half listening to the news when I heard 'Nobel Prize for Literature.' Since I'd long ago dismissed that as a European arrogance and conceit, I reached out to change the station. Then I heard 'African American writer' and my heart *really* sank.

"I was absolutely sure the committee would screw up again as it invariably seemed to do—by omission *and* commission—on those rare occasions when it got around to writers of the black world. Then they read the name. I damn near ran off the road. I found my fist pumping the air. I was jumping up and down in my seatbelt. A totally spontaneous excitement and pride.

"What could account for a mood swing so total in exuberance and intensity? I had to really think about that for a long time. Figured it out, too. Despite some superficial differences, deep down I really admired and respected Toni Morrison's clarity of vision and sense of mission. The unswerving integrity of the cultural intelligence which was at the source of her craft. Her sustained purposefulness, commitment, courage and independence in an age of expedience, confusion and sycophancy."

Morrison had immediately put the $817,771 Nobel award away for her retirement. Then, suddenly, on Christmas Day, only two weeks after the accolade in Stockholm, an ember leapt from the fireplace onto a sofa in her Hudson River home. Her twenty-two-year-old son Slade, alone in the house at the time, tried to put out the fire. It quickly raced out of his control. He fled, unhurt. One hundred firefighters fought the flames for five hours. Alerted in the city, Morrison rushed to the scene. She arrived to see the final stages of her treasured home burning to the ground.

"In the two years around the Nobel, I had a lot of bad luck, a lot of very serious devastations," Morrison says. "My mother died, other things. . . . When I think about the fire, I think I may not ever, ever get over it. And it isn't even about the *things*. It's about photographs, plants I nurtured for twenty years, about the view of the Hudson River, my children's report cards, my manuscripts."

Ever since the Nobel and the fire that followed, Morrison has been hard at work on her seventh novel. It is called *Paradise*, and centers around four young women who are brutally attacked in a convent near an all-black town in the 1970s. In *Paradise*, Morrison has said, she is trying to imagine the language to describe a place where "race exists but doesn't matter."

All of Morrison's books, in one way or another, have been about coming to terms with the past. "A certain kind of amnesia is just intolerable," she believes. "In personal life, you have to know what happened and why and figure it out, and then you can go to another level freer, stronger, tempered in some way. Constantly burying it, distorting it, and pretending, I think, is unhealthy."

In words that echo both Ralph Ellison and Albert Murray in their contention that blacks are really the consummate Americans, Morrison wrote in her assessment of American literature, *Playing in the Dark*: "The concept of freedom did not emerge in a vacuum. Nothing highlighted freedom—if it did not in fact create it—like slavery.

"Black slavery enriched the country's creative possibilities. For in that construction of blackness *and* enslavement could be found not only the not-free but also, with the dramatic polarity created by skin color, the projection of the not-me. The result was a playground for the imagination. What rose up out of collective needs to allay internal fears and to rationalize external exploitation was an American Africanism—a fabricated area of darkness, otherness, alarm and desire that is uniquely American. . . .

"I want to suggest that these concerns—autonomy, authority, newness and difference, absolute power—not only became the major themes and presumptions of American literature, but that each one is made possible by, shaped by, activated by a complex awareness and employment of a constituted Africanism. It was this Africanism, deployed as rawness and savagery, that provided the staging ground and arena for the elaboration of the quintessential American identity."

Stockholm, 1993. In the great hall where she has received the world's most esteemed literary prize, Toni Morrison stands at the podium in her elegant full-length black dress and her salt-and-pepper dreadlocks. She is continuing her fable about the clairvoyant old blind woman and the youths who have come to her door. At last, the young visitors offer their response. It takes the form of a plea. Clearly, desperately, they want the bird in their hands to be *alive*. They ask:

" 'Is there no context for our lives? No song, no literature, no poem full of vitamins, no history connected to experience that you can pass along to help us start strong? . . . Think of our lives and tell us your particularized world. Make up a story. Narrative is radical, creating us at the very moment it is being created. We will not blame you if your reach exceeds your grasp; if love so ignites your words that they go down in flames and nothing is left but their scald. Or if, with the reticence of a surgeon's hands, your words suture only the places where blood might flow.

" ' . . . tell us what the world has been to you in the dark places and in the light. . . . Tell us what it is to be a woman so that we may know what it is to be a man. What moves at the margin. What it is to have no home in this place. To be set adrift from the one you knew. What it is to live at the edge of towns that cannot bear your company. . . . Tell us about a wagonload of slaves, how they sang so softly their breath was indistinguishable from the falling snow. . . . ' "

Then Morrison says: "It's quiet again when the children finish speaking, until the woman breaks into the silence.

" 'Finally,' she says, 'I trust you now. I trust you with the bird that is not in your hands because you have truly caught it. Look. How lovely it is, this thing we have done—together.' "

For Toni Morrison, in the beginning, too, was James Baldwin. "He could say something in a phrase that clarified all sorts of conflicting feelings," she remembers. Above all, Baldwin admired in her writings "a sense of humor that is the key to a sense of life." They had come to know one another well, and Morrison remains very close friends with Baldwin's sister, Gloria.

At the eulogy Morrison gave at Baldwin's funeral in 1987, she said near the beginning: "I never heard a single command from you, yet the demands you made on me, the challenges you issued to me, were nevertheless unmistakable, even if unenforced: that I work and think at the top of my form, that I stand on moral ground but know that ground must be shored up by mercy, that 'the world is before [me] and [I] need not take it or leave it as it was when [I] came in.' "

Morrison went on that she had just read again through the 6,895 pages of Baldwin's published work. "No one possessed or inhabited language for me the way you did. You made American English honest—genuinely international. You exposed its secrets and reshaped it until it was truly modern dialogic, representative, humane. You stripped it of ease and false comfort and fake innocence and evasion and hypocrisy. And in place of deviousness was clarity. In place of soft plump lies was a lean, targeted power. . . .

"The second gift was your courage, which you let us share: the courage of one who could go as a stranger in the village and transform the distances between people into intimacy with the whole world; courage to understand that experience in ways that made it a personal revelation for each of us. . . .

"The third gift was hard to fathom and even harder to accept. It was your tenderness—a tenderness so delicate I thought it could not last, but last it did and envelop me it did. . . . Yours was a tenderness, of vulnerability, that asked everything, expected everything and, like the world's own Merlin, provided us with the ways and means to deliver. I suppose that is why I was always a bit better behaved around you, smarter, more capable, wanting to be worth the love you lavished, and wanting to be steady enough to witness the pain you had witnessed and were tough enough to bear while it broke your heart, wanting to be generous enough to join your smile with one of my own, and reckless enough to jump on in that laugh you laughed. Because our joy and our laughter were not only all right, they were necessary. . . .

" 'Our crown,' you said, 'has already been bought and paid for. All we have to do,' you said, 'is wear it.'

"And we do, Jimmy. You crowned us."

FOR FURTHER READING:
Books by Toni Morrison:
The Bluest Eye (New York: Rinehart & Winston, 1970; Plume paperback edition, 1994).
Sula (New York: Alfred A. Knopf, 1974; New American Library paperback, 1993).
Song of Solomon (New York: Alfred A. Knopf, 1977; Plume paperback edition, 1987).
Tar Baby (New York: Alfred A. Knopf, 1981; Plume paperback edition, 1987).
Beloved (New York: Alfred A, Knopf, 1987; Plume paperback edition, 1988).

Jazz (New York: Alfred A, Knopf, 1992; Plume paperback edition, 1993).

Playing in the Dark: Whiteness and the Literary Imagination (Cambridge, Mass.: Harvard University Press, 1992).

Timeless Voices, Parallel Realities:
James Baldwin and Frederick Douglass

"We are fighting for something incomparably better than the old Union. We are fighting for unity; unity of idea, unity of sentiment, unity of object, unity of institutions, in which there shall be no North, no South, no East, no West, no black, no white, but a solidarity of the nation."
                                        —FREDERICK DOUGLASS, 1863

"Until the moment comes when we, the Americans, are able to accept the fact that my ancestors are both black and white, that on that continent we are trying to forge a new identity, that we need each other, that I am not a ward of America, I am not an object of missionary charity, I am one of the people who built the country—until this moment comes there is scarcely any hope for the American dream."
                                        —JAMES BALDWIN, 1965

Inside a warmly rustic house on the edge of a woods in western Massachusetts, Michael Thelwell is making a pot of tea and talking about the mentor and friend who he says "completely and forever revolutionized the way the question of race was engaged in the discourse of the nation." Although Thelwell was twenty years younger than James Baldwin when both were teaching at the University of Massachusetts/Amherst in the mid-1980s, he was among Baldwin's closest spiritual companions during the last years of his life. They had first met in 1961, when Baldwin came to speak at Howard University, where Thelwell was a student. In the years since, the professor of Afro-American studies had written widely about Baldwin, who in turn had authored the introduction to Thelwell's 1987 book, *Duties, Pleasures, and Conflict: Essays in Struggle.*

Now Thelwell is recalling, painfully as someone who deeply misses an older brother, the all-night discussions in the closing chapter of James Baldwin's remarkable life. "Usually it would begin in a restaurant somewhere, with students hanging around him, ten or fifteen people sitting at a table eating and drinking. He was a very accessible guy, and he would always pick up the bill. We would sometimes have arguments about that: whether I should at least on occasion pay my share. Some people crowded around him because he was a celebrity. Others were friends, the instant friends that he had such a talent for forming. He would just spontaneously like the most unlikely people, he'd see something about them that would appeal to him. But he never really felt the need to hold court, or to dominate the discussion. So these were democratic gatherings, very lively, very inclusive.

"Then when the place closed, Jimmy often would ask me to come over to his house. We shared a common background of the [civil rights] movement. By the time he came here at sixty—I was then in my forties—the distinction created by my thinking of him as someone of the older generation had long disappeared. We understood each other's references for the most part. Particularly we shared the experience of the political struggle of the '60s. So I think it was a comfort for him, like having a homeboy come over. Also I think I was unusual in that I didn't really want anything from him, except his friendship and his conversation. I think we were both fairly lonely and isolated figures here. We spent a lot of time discussing politics and literature. And we both drank and loved language and spirited conversation, so sometimes we'd still be sitting at the table when the sun came up. Then I'd run home, sleep a couple hours, and rush back to his house to wake him up to go to class."

A tall, bearded, handsome man who grew up in Jamaica, Thelwell pours the tea and then goes back to the stove to arrange the fixings for his luncheon specialty, a West Indian soup. "I think what a lot of critics, even black critics, have against James Baldwin is his unshakeable integrity," he goes on. "Jimmy was never for sale. I mean, he would speak the fucking truth—and he saw that as a writer's sacred responsibility. When Jimmy wrote [the 1955 novel] *Giovanni's Room*, his publisher didn't want to bring it out. They said, 'This book will not do your career any good,' because it was about the, at the time, undiscussable subject of homosexuality. Which it is about only peripherally, it's really about love and honor. So he changed publishers. Here's Jimmy, who didn't have a pot to piss in nor a bed to put it under, a high school graduate, a young black man in racist America trying to make his way as a writer, with the courage and integrity to say: 'Well, fuck you. This is what I have to say at this time, I think it's important and I will pay the price.' And Jimmy always paid the price."

Thelwell contemplates as he lights a cigarette. "People might say, well Jimmy Baldwin always wrote out of his own experience and referred to his own life. And that appears to be true. But only superficially: the most obvious part of the equation, of the phenomenon. What is not so obvious is how skillfully and purposefully he did that—and always managing to illumine a larger truth. So that he could go from the individual and the particular to the universal, or at any rate the American, with consummate grace. And an illuminating intelligence such as we have not seen since."

There is another long pause, as a look appears in Thelwell's eyes that seems to be reaching across a vast expanse of time. "Jimmy is really the Frederick Douglass of our time," he says finally. "Not in the sense of sustained and purposeful political organizing. But in the sense of a totally uncommon, inspired vision and intelligence, and the eloquence to articulate in timeless ways certain enduring American realities. In the same way that people recourse to Douglass's text whenever they need a quotation—which like a great African proverb, will aptly summarize and crystallize a truth, say the state of the relationship between the races—I have often advised people making documentary films and needing a title or a quotation to read Jimmy Baldwin. You'll find exactly the insight and the language you're looking for. There is a quality to both men—in their language, in their vision, their thought—which is not independent of black culture. That is, it certainly comes out of a sensibility and from a set of perceptions of American reality—which no white person could come up with—something that is fundamentally and ineluctably African-American. Yeah, Jimmy is the Frederick Douglass of our time."

They were born almost a century apart: Baldwin in a Harlem tenement on August 2, 1924, and Douglass on a Maryland slave plantation on an unknown date in mid-February of 1818. As writers and orators of genius, as spokesmen for the great movements of their day, as men whose periods of exile only gave them a stronger sense of their native land, they became voices of conscience in the most momentous of times. Douglass, like Baldwin, also wrote novels. In their journalism, both often employed the form of the "open letter." In telling their own stories, their ongoing autobiographies made the utterly personal become universal.

Each was cast in the mold described by Douglass in his essay on self-made men: ". . . the men who owe little or nothing to birth, relationship, friendly surroundings; to wealth inherited or to early approved means of education; who are what they are, without the aid of any of the favoring conditions by which other men usually rise in the world and achieve great results."

Neither man knew who their father was. Douglass was a boy when he heard it "whispered . . . that my master was my father. . . . My father was a white man. He was admitted to be such by all I ever heard speak of my parentage." Baldwin, who long suspected that he was illegitimate, had this confirmed as a teenager when he overheard a conversation between his mother and the Baptist minister who was his stepfather. For both Douglass and Baldwin, the mysterious circumstances of their births came to symbolize the illegitimacy of their entire race, as seen by the America in which they sought so passionately to feel at home.

To each, the ancestors loomed large. Here is Baldwin, describing the grandmother who lived in his house: ". . . she had been born in slavery. She was so old that she never moved from her bed. I remember her as pale and gaunt and she must have worn a kerchief because I don't remember her hair. I remember that she loved me; she used to scold her son about the way he treated me; and he was a little afraid of her. When she died, she called me into the room to give me a present—one of those old, round, metal boxes, usually with a floral design, used for candy. She thought it was full of candy and *I* thought it was full of candy, but it wasn't. After she died, I opened it and it was full of needles and thread.

"This broke my heart, of course, but her going broke it more because I had loved her and depended on her. I knew—children *must* know—that she would always protect me with all her strength. . . ."

And here is Douglass, whose grandmother had "toted" him on her shoulders that day when, just shy of seven, he had been sold to a new owner to work the fields. "Advanced in years as she was, as was evident from the more than one gray hair which peeped from between the ample and graceful folds of her newly and smoothly-ironed bandana turban, grandmother was yet a woman of power and spirit. . . . Lo! she was indeed gone, and was now far away. . . . heartbroken at the discovery, I fell upon the ground and wept a boy's bitter tears, refusing to be comforted. . . . The hearth is desolate." At the same time Douglass said goodbye to his family and entered the dark world of the strangers who possessed him, Baldwin tells us in his own *Dark Days*: "I hit the streets when I was seven. It was the middle of the Depression and I learned how to sing out of hard experience. To be black was to confront, and to be forced to alter, a condition forged by history."

And so, as Baldwin went on to Frederick Douglass Junior High School—shining shoes for pocket change as Douglass had—they came to discover their paths through books. Both received early assistance from white teachers. Forbidden by law to learn to read and write, Douglass hid bits of old newspaper and used "fences and pavements for my copybooks." When he was thirteen, he came upon *The Columbian Orator*. It contained a dialogue between a master and a slave, which opened Douglass's eyes as nothing ever had. "The master was vanquished at every turn in the argument, and, appreciating the fact, he generously and meekly emancipates the slave, with his best wishes for his prosperity. . . . I could not help feeling that the day might yet come when the well-directed answers made by the slave to the master . . . would find a counterpart in my own experience."

The book was also filled with the speeches of the grand English orators. "I met there one of Sheridan's mighty speeches on the subject of Catholic emancipation, Lord Chatham's speech on the American War, and speeches by the great William Pitt, and by Fox. These were all choice documents to me, and I read them over and over again, with an interest ever increasing. . . . The reading of these speeches added much to my limited stock of language, and enabled me to give tongue to many interesting thoughts which had often flashed through my mind and died away for want of words in which to give them utterance. . . . I had now penetrated to the secret of all slavery and of all oppression, and had ascertained their true foundation to be in the pride, the power, and the avarice of man. With a book in my hand so redolent of the principles of liberty, and with a perception of my own human nature and of the facts of my past and present experience, I was equal to a contest with the religious advocates of slavery."

For Baldwin, "the first book I can remember having read" was the famed antislavery novel of which Douglass had said: "Nothing could have better suited the moral and humane requirements of the hour. Its effect was amazing, instantaneous, and universal." The book was Harriet Beecher Stowe's *Uncle Tom's Cabin*. Baldwin read it, along with Dickens's *A Tale of Two Cities*, "over and over again . . . obsessively; they had something to tell me. . . . [They] were keys relating to something essential to my feelings about black life in this country. As a black, these two choices were stark. The one was about accommodation and acceptance. The other was about revolution. If I saw myself and mine in *Uncle Tom's Cabin*, I would have to accept the status quo. . . . On the other hand, the *Tale of Two Cities* suggested the possibility of change through revolution. Or at least through action. But action was apparently taboo for blacks. With these two books in my head, I looked around me at Harlem, at my father and the world."

Thus did Baldwin and Douglass come of age, reaching back in order to carry the vision forward one day. Growing up in fear of his stepfather, a man who called him ugly, for a time Baldwin had found refuge in his stepfather's world of the pulpit. As a remarkable "boy preacher" in Harlem, he had learned about cadence and measured speech, been thrilled by the "power and glory" that he felt when he used "the Word" effectively. Then, at sixteen, he left the church and his stepfather's house—and met a man who changed his life. Beauford Delaney, then in his late thirties, had come north from Tennessee the year that Baldwin was born. Like Baldwin, Delaney was a minister's son, an artist who would become his lifelong friend: "The reality of his seeing caused me to begin to see."

Douglass had also left behind his past at sixteen. It was an epic confrontation, his battle with the cruel overseer Edward Covey in 1833. And it was Douglass's encounter with a wise elder in the woods that gave him the courage to fight. Douglass had been badly whipped and run off to hide when he "heard the step of a man in the woods." Douglass knew the "old adviser" who sheltered him that night as Sandy, a slave on a nearby plantation. "He was a genuine African, and had inherited some of the so-called magical powers said to be possessed by the eastern nations. He told me that he could help me, that in those very woods there was an herb which in the morning might be found, possessing all the powers required for my protection. . . . He told me, further, that if I would take that root and wear it on my right side, it would be impossible for Covey to strike me a blow, and that, with this root about my person, no white man could whip me." At first Douglass found the notion "very absurd and ridiculous"; but, when he returned to face Covey, he was carrying the herb in his back pocket.

James Baldwin, recalling to an interviewer his years on the Harlem streets around 1933: "Well, if you wanted to beat me up, okay. And, say, you were bigger than I was, you could do it, you could beat me, but you gonna have to do it every day . . . every single day. So then the question becomes which one of us would get tired first. And I knew it wouldn't be me. . . . So then the other person would have to begin to think, and to be bugged by this kid he had to beat up every day. And some days perhaps he just didn't feel like doing it. But he would have to, yeah, because he said he was going to do it. So then come beat me up."

Edward Covey sprang upon Frederick Douglass, and had him on the floor. "Whence came the daring spirit necessary to grapple with a man who, eight-and-forty hours before, could, with his slightest word, have made me tremble like a leaf in a storm, I do not know; at any rate, I was resolved to fight. . . . The fighting madness had come upon me. . . . Taken completely by surprise, Covey seemed to have lost his usual strength and coolness. . . . After resisting him, I felt as I had never felt before. . . . It rekindled the few expiring embers of freedom, and revived within me a sense of my own manhood. . . . The gratification afforded by the triumph was a full compensation for whatever else might follow, even death itself. . . .

"Mr. Covey enjoyed the most unbounded reputation for being a

first-rate overseer and Negro-breaker. It was of considerable importance to him. That reputation was at stake; and had he sent me—a
boy about sixteen years old—to the public whipping-post, his reputation would have been lost; so, to save his reputation, he suffered me
to go unpunished. . . . I was determined on doing him serious damage
if he ever again attempted to lay violent hands on me."

James Baldwin, remembering: "But of course something happened
to him, something has to happen to him—because someone beating
someone else up is not so easy either. Because I would be standing in
the schoolyard with a lead pipe as a deterrent. So, you know, eventually it was just too dangerous. People began to leave me alone. . . .
That was the beginning of it and then later on it was cops, you know.
. . . They wanted me to beg. And I couldn't beg, so I got my ass kicked.
But I learned a lot, a lot about them. I learned there were very few
who were humane; they just wanted you to say what they wanted you
to say. They wanted to be confirmed in something by you. By your
face, by your terror of them."

Frederick Douglass, remembering:

> *"Hereditary bondmen, know ye not*
> *Who would be free, themselves must strike the blow?"*

In September 1838, when Douglass was twenty, he escaped from
slavery in disguise carrying false papers that identified him as a seaman
and, with the assistance of white abolitionists, settled first in New Bedford, Massachusetts. It was now that he changed his surname, aban-
doning his mother's name of Bailey and recasting himself after the hero
of Sir Walter Scott's *Lady of the Lake*. Douglass also married a freed-
woman, Anna Murray, with whom he would remain until her death
forty-four years later. And, within three years after his escape,
Douglass found himself telling his story to white audiences of William
Lloyd Garrison's American Anti-Slavery Society. Almost overnight, his
speeches took on a magnitude comparable to the words of Patrick
Henry that had so stirred him in *The Columbian Orator*: "Give me
liberty, or give me death!" By 1845, when Garrison's Boston office
published his *Narrative of the Life of Frederick Douglass*, Douglass's
voice had already been heard by thousands. Fearing that his notoriety
might imperil Douglass's safety, his abolitionist friends helped him sail
to Europe and out of reach of American fugitive slave laws. For almost
two years, Douglass would reside in the British Isles, lecturing to huge
audiences. Late in 1846, his English admirers purchased his freedom
from his Maryland master.

"I can truly say I have spent some of the happiest days of my life since landing in this country," Douglass wrote in a letter from Ireland. "I seem to have undergone a transformation. . . . I breathe, and lo! the chattel becomes a man! I gaze around in vain for one who will question my equal humanity, claim me as a slave, or offer me an insult. . . . Thank Heaven for the respite I now enjoy!"

Baldwin, who settled in Paris slightly more than 100 years later to complete his first book, *Go Tell It on the Mountain,* would look back upon his own first time in Europe and say: ". . . we are speaking about a voyage which we all have to make seemingly far away to come full circle. To redeem a tradition which was not yet called a tradition because it was not yet written down except by Bessie Smith, Duke Ellington . . . and by preachers like my father. . . .

"In my case, I think my exile saved my life, for it inexorably confirmed something which Americans appear to have great difficulty accepting. Which is, simply, this: a man is not a man until he is able and willing to accept his own vision of the world, no matter how radically this vision departs from that of others. . . . What Europe still gives an American—or gave us—is the sanction, if one can accept it, to become oneself."

Both men felt themselves compelled to return to participate and give voice to the struggles of their homeland. Douglass would write: "America will not allow her children to love her. She seems bent on compelling those who would be her warmest friends to be her worst enemies." And Baldwin would write: "Love is a battle, love is a war; love is a growing up. No one in the world—in the entire world—knows more— knows Americans better or, odd as this may sound, loves them more than the American Negro. This is because he has had to watch you, outwit you, deal with you, and bear you, and sometimes even bleed and die with you, ever since we got here, that is, since both of us, black and white, got here—and this is a wedding."

Since they first met in Nantucket in 1841, William Lloyd Garrison had been Douglass's staunchest white supporter. " 'Tell your story, Frederick,' would whisper my revered friend, Mr. Garrison, as I stepped upon the platform." But when Douglass came back from Europe to settle in Rochester, New York, he was carrying funds from British friends to start his own newspaper. Garrison, who had his own publication (*The Liberator*), did not like the idea. He wanted Douglass to remain the black orator against the antislavery cause, not a potential rival entrepreneur in the movement. Douglass eventually insisted upon publishing his own *North Star.* "I still see before me a life of toil and trials," he said, "but justice must be done, the truth must be told. . . . I will not be silent."

So a rift developed between Douglass and the man who had championed his rise. It was not made easier when Garrison introduced him at the annual meeting of the American Anti-Slavery Society in 1847, and the largest crowd ever gathered interrupted Garrison with shouts of "Douglass! Douglass!" In 1855, Douglass would write of his decision to start the first black newspaper: "The most distressing part of it all was the offense which I saw I must give to my friends of the old antislavery organization, by what seemed to them a reckless disregard of their opinion and advice." For his part, Garrison said of Douglass: "His conduct . . . has been impulsive, inconsiderate, and highly inconsistent." The Garrisonians, as Douglass's biographer William McFeely has described, "despite their official secularism, regarded any deviation from their leadership as heresy; theirs was the only way; all others were wrong."

Douglass wanted something bigger; he wanted to unite the entire antislavery world. Garrison began staying away from Douglass's speeches. He assaulted Douglass's positions in his own paper. And he published false rumors about the alleged discontent that "a certain person"—implying a white female friend of Douglass—was causing in the man's household. Harriet Beecher Stowe took Garrison to task and sought to mend the relationship. It proved impossible. "What Douglass *is* really," wrote the author of *Uncle Tom's Cabin*, "time will show."

In the life of James Baldwin, the closest parallel to what happened between Douglass and Garrison was his relationship with Norman Mailer. Not that Mailer was a political activist on behalf of African-Americans. But he considered himself, perhaps not dissimilarly from Garrison, a kind of "radical humanist." And Mailer became a personification of Baldwin's estrangement from the white liberal establishment.

Mailer had risen to fame with his towering novel about World War II, *The Naked and the Dead*. Baldwin's *Go Tell It on the Mountain*, published not long thereafter, had also established him as a major literary figure. When they first met in Paris in 1956, theirs had begun as a warm and mutually admiring friendship. Baldwin introduced Mailer to the late-night jazz scene, and Mailer helped Baldwin by writing a very favorable pre-publication comment about his new novel *Giovanni's Room*.

In their work, Mailer and Baldwin were undoubtedly the most astute social commentators of their time, and there was a natural competitive rivalry between them, which was fueled by the media. "Both [of us] tend to suspect others of putting us down, and we strike before we're struck," as Baldwin wrote. But beyond this, Baldwin believed, Mailer could not admit his own limitations in examining black culture—something Mailer had attempted in his 1957 essay *The White Negro*. While Mailer remained "very dear to me," Baldwin wrote in 1961, "there is a difference, though, between Norman and myself in that I think he still imagines that he has something to save, whereas I have never had anything to lose."

As the years went by, the friendship grew more and more strained. Baldwin, Mailer wrote, was "too charming a writer to be major" and publicly panned his novel *Another Country*. After what Mailer referred to as "another brotherly quarrel" in a Greenwich Village bar, Baldwin responded: "He still sees us as goddamn romantic black symbols. We still haven't been granted ordinary human status." In 1962, when both were covering the heavyweight title fight between Sonny Liston and Floyd Patterson, at a party they exchanged strong words and Mailer is said to have reduced Baldwin to tears. In later years, Baldwin would say: "Talking about Norman is very painful, very difficult for me."

Late in 1995, eight years after Baldwin's death, I visited with Mailer in his Brooklyn apartment to try to discover what time's passage had wrought. Mailer was now in his early seventies, looking very leonine with his long curly hair and charming smile. Much of the pugnaciousness of his younger years appeared to have mellowed in him. We sat over a chicken-and-rice dish that he had chefed up for lunch, in the dining room directly below Mailer's work space—a ship's crow's nest-type area with a ladder leading up to a nylon-mesh overhang. Outside the adjacent living room picture window, beyond a seeming acre of bookshelves, a tugboat whistled along the East River.

"Painful for Jimmy? How?" Mailer asked, a quizzical expression on his face when I brought up the difficult later years of their relationship. "Well, I'd just lost my temper with him a time or two, and said some things to him. But that piece he wrote about me, called 'The Black Boy Looks at the White Boy,' I thought it was all wrong, he had me wrong. He had me muscling him at times, in terms of face-offs. And I resented that. I wrote something to *Esquire* [the magazine that published Baldwin's essay] about it, and referred to his writing how Mailer really didn't understand blacks at all. That had nettled me, so I wrote in return, 'Well, that is one black boy who doesn't understand this white boy at all.' And that irritated the hell out of *him*. So these things put a chill between us."

I brought up the striking line that Baldwin had written, about the difference between Mailer's imagining there was still something to save while Baldwin had never had anything to lose. Mailer thought for a long moment, then said: "Well, there he could have been absolutely right. I certainly did feel there was a world to save in those days, and his attitude may have been more profound than mine."

It felt as if Mailer was still wrestling with something as he continued: "The honor that I think Baldwin has in my mind is this: there's never been a black literary artist in America that whites have loved more than Jimmy Baldwin. But he did have the balls to turn on them, and he was also trying to warn all the whites in America—'Look, you think all we blacks are just as friendly as I am, and it's just not so. There's a rage going on among my people that you had better start to comprehend.' At first we thought, all right that's hyperbole, because look at Jimmy, he obviously loves whites. And he did, you know. But when black power came along, everybody was saying, 'Yeah, I see now what Jimmy was talking about.'

"There *is* so much white hatred of blacks," Mailer continued. "You know, is there any hatred greater than the hatred that comes from guilt? It's much easier to forgive somebody who's done you a harm, than to forgive somebody to whom *you've* done a harm."

Mailer had known Ralph Ellison as well, and I was curious how he would compare Ellison to Baldwin. "You could never get two guys who were more different," Mailer replied. "Not only in their work, because Baldwin was always in the fray. But Ellison rarely showed you anything of himself. Baldwin was *there*. What you got in his style—and his essays were incandescent—was what you got in his presence. His charm was enormous. You could feel his immense sensitivity to everything. He had a sort of unbelievable intimacy. When you were with him, you had the feeling that you and he were the two people most attuned to one another in the whole world."

The more he talked about Baldwin, the more animated Mailer became. He had said from the outset that he really hadn't wanted to discuss Baldwin in detail, as he was "saving this for my memoirs." Yet as the years passed through him, it was as though Mailer was reconciling a kind of war inside himself.

"Oh, Jimmy was magical," he was saying. "If you can imagine the amount of energy coming off him, a sort of pale Louis Armstrong. Slight, small, finely tuned, but he had that warmth that Armstrong had. He looked a little bit like Armstrong. He was not a handsome man. But he was beautiful. The pain was in his eyes. It was like all the sensitivity pushing forward to pick up everything because he couldn't afford to miss a thing. Where he grew up, if he missed one thing, he would be gone. There was great weight on the eyes, all the suffering he'd seen."

As he spoke, Mailer's own eyes exuded a quality that was beyond sentimentality, more like a lament for something he could see and feel only from the vantage point of many years. "We did love each other," he said quietly. "I loved him, and I think he loved me."

From Mailer's *The White Negro*, 1957: "...it is perhaps possible that the Negro holds more of the tail of the expanding elephant of truth than the radical, and if this is so, the radical humanist could do worse than to brood upon the phenomenon."

Frederick Douglass, 1861: "The human heart is a seat of constant war."

"The whole history of the progress of human liberty shows that all concessions yet made to her august claims, have been born of earnest struggle. The conflict has been exciting, agitating, all-absorbing, and for the time being, putting all other tumults to silence. It must do this or it does nothing. If there is no struggle, there is no progress. Those who profess to favor freedom, and yet deprecate agitation, are men who want crops without plowing up the ground. They want rain without thunder and lightning. They want ocean without the roar of its many waters. The struggle may be a moral one; or it may be a physical one; or it may be both moral and physical; but it must be a struggle. Power concedes nothing without a demand. It never did and it never will.... The limits of tyrants are prescribed by the endurance of those whom they oppress."

—FREDERICK DOUGLASS, 1857

"But for power truly to feel itself menaced, it must somehow sense itself in the presence of another power—or, more accurately, an energy—which it has not known how to define and therefore does not really know how to control.... When power translates itself into tyranny, it means that the principles on which that power depended, and which were its justifications, are bankrupt. When this happens, and it is happening now, power can only be defended by thugs and mediocrities—and seas of blood. The representatives of the status quo *are sickened and divided, and dread looking into the eyes of their young; while the excluded begin to realize, having endured everything, that they can endure everything. They do not know the precise shape of the future, but they know that the future belongs to them. They realize this—paradoxically—by the failure of the moral energy of their oppressors and begin, almost instinctively, to forge a new morality, to create the principles on which a new world will be built."*

—JAMES BALDWIN, 1972

In a café not far from Harvard Square, historian David Blight—the author of *Frederick Douglass' Civil War*—was talking about Douglass and Baldwin. "They were two people in very different times, very much marginalized by their circumstances and their world, who desperately wanted to be at the center. They each wrote for and aimed at a national consciousness. They wanted to reshape America, wanted all of America to be their audience."

One hundred years apart, Douglass and Baldwin found themselves at that center with an opportunity to reshape America. On August 10, 1863, Douglass—who in his newspaper had excoriated Abraham Lincoln for the President's equivocation on slavery in the midst of the Civil War—became the first black man ever to have a private audience with an American President. On May 23, 1963, Baldwin—who had just sent Robert Kennedy a telegram blasting the Administration for its indifference to events in Birmingham, Alabama, at the height of the civil rights movement—accepted a breakfast invitation with the President's brother. What eventually emanated from these meetings did indeed shape the national consciousness.

Douglass, who had campaigned for Lincoln's election in 1860 and viewed him as "a man of will and nerve," grew strongly critical after what he termed the new President's "double-tongued" inaugural speech. There, Lincoln stated he had no "lawful right . . . to interfere with the institution of slavery in the States where it exists." Born poor in Kentucky and raised in the Midwest, Lincoln was not without innate prejudice. "There must be the position of superior and inferior," he said, "and I as much as any other man am in favor of having the superior position assigned to the white race." While Lincoln had long believed that slavery was morally wrong, his primary concern was preserving the Union. His ultimate solution, which he first broached in the 1850s and would hold onto for ten years, was a colonization scheme where blacks would be dispatched from American soil to Africa or Central America.

Douglass, however, was ready for war, for "any upheaval that would bring about an end to the existing order of things." After the Civil War broke out, he assailed what he saw as Lincoln's ambivalence, describing him in 1862 as "a genuine representative of American prejudice and Negro hatred and far more concerned for the preservation of slavery, and the favor of the Border Slave States, than for any sentiment of magnanimity or principle of justice and humanity."

Lincoln is known to have read *Douglass's Monthly*, and could not have been unaware of his viewpoints. By September of 1862, as he prepared the Emancipation Proclamation that would become law the following January, Lincoln said: "The subject is on my mind, by day and night, more than any other. Whatever shall appear to be God's will I will do." When the Proclamation was issued, nothing was said about colonization. Douglass said he "saw in its spirit a life and power far beyond its letter. . . . If he [Lincoln] has taught us to confide in nothing else, he has taught us to confide in his word." Douglass set out on a 2,000-mile speaking tour pressing for the enlistment of black soldiers in the Union Army.

That summer of 1863, aware of blacks' inferior treatment from Union officers and brutal mistreatment when captured by the Confederates—including the bloody defeat of Massachusetts's 54th Regiment in which Douglass's own two sons fought—Douglass journeyed to Washington seeking a meeting with the President. It was now a quarter-century since he had fled to freedom. He expected to have to wait for half a day, but only moments after his arrival at the Executive Mansion, Douglass was summoned inside to see Lincoln.

"When I entered he was seated in a low chair, surrounded by a multitude of books and papers," Douglass wrote years later, "his feet and legs were extended in front of his chair. On my approach he slowly drew his feet in from the different parts of the room into which they had strayed, and he began to rise, and continued to rise until he looked down upon me, and extended his hand and gave me a welcome. I began, with some hesitation, to tell him who I was and what I had been doing, but he soon stopped me, saying in a sharp, cordial voice: 'You need not tell me who you are, Mr. Douglass, I know who you are.' . . . He then invited me to take a seat beside him."

Douglass got right to the point. He criticized Lincoln's "tardy, hesitating, vacillating policy" in conducting the war, and Lincoln shot back that this was unfair. "I think it cannot be shown that when I have once taken a position, I have ever retreated from it," he said. Douglass bluntly stated his demands. Black soldiers needed equal pay and protection, and promotions for distinguished battle service; retaliation was needed against Confederate killings of black POWs. Lincoln shook his head and responded painfully that such retaliation was impossible. But he would take steps to ensure that Douglass's other requests were met.

Douglass left the meeting feeling not only that he "was in the presence of a very great man . . . [but] in the presence of a big brother." A Lincoln associate recounted the President's telling him that "considering the conditions from which Douglass rose, and the position to which he had attained, he was, in his judgment, one of the most meritorious men in America."

A year later, on August 19, 1864, this time it was Lincoln who called Douglass back to Washington. A man named Joseph T. Mills also had a scheduled appointment with the President that day and, when he walked into the waiting room: "It was dark. I supposed that clouds & darkness necessarily surround the secrets of state. There in a corner I saw a man quietly reading who possessed a remarkable physiognomy.

I was rivetted to the spot. I stood & stared at him. He raised his flashing eyes & caught me in the act. I was compelled to speak. Said I, Are you the President? No replied the stranger, I am Frederick Douglass."

Mills had come from Wisconsin, as Lincoln scholar Michael Vorenberg tells the story, "to ask Lincoln basically to renege on his commitment to abolition. On the same day—we don't know if it's coincidence—Lincoln had set up this meeting with Douglass. And his reason to see Douglass is very interesting. He is afraid that he might lose the [1864] election and that his successor will accept terms in ending the war that don't involve the universal abolition of slavery. In which case, Lincoln realizes what he needs to do is get as many slaves into Union territory as he can. So he proposes this plan to Douglass, which is basically another underground railroad: find a way to establish black agents to infiltrate the rebel states and accompany the others back North. And Douglass agreed to do this."

At the same meeting, Lincoln asked Douglass's advice about a concessionary letter on slavery that he had written to Horace Greeley, a prominent New York editor. Don't send it, Douglass said emphatically, or this will be interpeted as "complete surrender of your antislavery policy." Lincoln held onto the letter. In this most momentous of visits, Douglass assumed the role of wise statesman while Lincoln proposed a radical scheme to ensure black freedom.

It was reminiscent, Douglass felt, of his earlier meetings with John Brown. "What he [Lincoln] said on this day showed a deeper moral conviction against slavery than I have ever seen before in anything spoken or written by him. . . . I think that, on Mr. Lincoln's part, it is evidence conclusive that the [Emancipation] proclamation, so far at least as he was concerned, was not effected merely as a 'necessity.' "

Lincoln's "underground railroad" proposal proved unnecessary, as the tide of the war soon turned in the Union's favor. Lincoln came to realize that the enlistment of 180,000 black troops "constitute the heaviest blow yet dealt to the rebellion." Behind the scenes, he began deliberately moving toward the Thirteenth Amendment granting full citizenship to blacks. On April 11, 1865, a few days before his assassination, in his last public address Lincoln would advocate limited suffrage and public education for Southern blacks.

Six weeks before, Douglass had come to Washington a third time to attend Lincoln's second inauguration. "I felt then that there was murder in the air," Douglass wrote in 1889, "and I kept close to his carriage on the way to the Capital, for I felt that I might see him fall that day. It was a vague presentiment. . . . I could feel it in the atmosphere here." Douglass moved right to the front in the East portico of the

Capitol building. When Lincoln emerged to give his address, Douglass saw the President point him out in the crowd to Vice-President Andrew Johnson, who "looked quite annoyed that his attention should be called in that direction. So I got a peep into his [Johnson's] soul. . . . I felt that, whatever else the man might be, he was no friend to my people."

Douglass listened raptly to Lincoln's stirring words: "Fondly do we hope, profoundly do we pray, that this mighty scourge of war shall soon pass away, yet if God wills it continue until all the wealth piled up by two hundred years of bondage shall have been wasted, and each drop of blood drawn by the lash shall have been paid for by one drawn by the sword, we must still say, as was said three thousand years ago, the judgments of the Lord are true and righteous altogether."

That night, when Douglass stood in line with other well-wishers waiting to see the President: "As I approached the door I was seized by two policemen and forbidden to enter." Douglass asked a passerby to please let Lincoln know he was here. A few minutes later, Douglass was ushered into the elegant East Room where "like a mountain pine high above all others, Mr. Lincoln stood, in his grand simplicity and homely beauty. Recognizing me, even before I reached him, he exclaimed, so that all around could hear him, 'Here comes my friend Douglass.' "

The President took Douglass's hand, who remembered him saying, "I am glad to see you. I saw you in the crowd today, listening to my inaugural address, how did you like it?" When Douglass, not wishing to detain Lincoln, shied from responding, Lincoln went on: "No, no. You must stop a little, Douglass; there is no man in the country whose opinion I value more than yours."

The speech, Douglass told Lincoln, was "a sacred effort."

"I am glad you liked it!" the President replied.

On Good Friday a little more than a month later, he was assassinated. Years afterwards, Douglass would describe a gesture from Mary Todd Lincoln: "when Mr. Lincoln died and she was about leaving the White House, she selected his favorite walking cane and said: 'I know of no one that would appreciate this more than Fred. Douglass.' She sent it to me at Rochester, and I have it in my house to-day, and expect to keep it there as long as I live."

Eighty years would pass before Eleanor Roosevelt proffered her similar gift upon Mary McLeod Bethune.

"In all my interviews with Mr. Lincoln," Douglass wrote six years before his own death in 1895, "I was impressed with his entire freedom from popular prejudice against the colored race. He was the first great man that I talked with in the United States freely, who in no single instance reminded me of the difference between himself and myself, of the difference of color, and I thought that all the more remarkable because he came from a State where there were black laws. I account partially for his kindness to me because of the similarity with which I had fought my way up, we both starting at the lowest round of the ladder."

When, in 1876, Douglass had delivered a speech at the unveiling of the Freedmen's Monument in Washington, his summary of Lincoln's evolution began with these words: "Abraham Lincoln was not, in the fullest sense of the word, either our man or our model. In his interests, in his associations, in his habits of thought, and in his prejudices, he was a white man." Yet, despite his people's faith in Lincoln often having been taxed and strained, in the end he had been "swift, zealous, radical, and determined. . . . You are the children of Abraham Lincoln. . . . He calmly and bravely heard the voice of doubt and fear all around him, but he had an oath in heaven, and there was not power enough on the earth to make this boatman, backwoodsman, and broad-handed splitter of rails evade or violate that sacred oath."

The "more perfect union" was forged of a common soul.

"Nothing seems more evident than that our destiny is sealed up with that of the white people of this country, and we believe that we must fall or flourish with them. . . . One ground of hope is found and that is the discussion concerning the Negro still goes on. . . . This discussion will go on until the American people shall make character and not color the criterion of respectability. This discussion will go on.
—FREDERICK DOUGLASS

"To act is to be committed, and to be committed is to be in danger. In this case, the danger, in the minds of most white Americans, is the loss of their identity. Try to imagine how you would feel if you woke up one morning to find the sun shining and all the stars aflame. You would be frightened because it is out of the order of nature. Any upheaval in the universe is terrifying because it so profoundly attacks one's sense of one's own reality. Well, the black man has functioned in the white man's world as a fixed star, as an immovable pillar: and as he moves out of his place, heaven and earth are shaken to their foundations. You, don't be afraid.
—JAMES BALDWIN, *The Fire Next Time*, 1963.

By the spring of 1963, Robert Kennedy was well aware of the impact of Baldwin's book-length essay, *The Fire Next Time*. The U.S. attorney general, President John Kennedy's brother, had grown up wealthy, and had almost no contact with or understanding of James Baldwin's world. Jack Newfield, a writer who was a longtime close friend of Robert Kennedy, recalls what the singer Harry Belafonte told him: "Bobby was very ignorant at the beginning. In 1959, he came to see Harry for the first time, very upset because, he said, 'we just found out that Jackie Robinson is going to support Nixon against my brother [in the 1960 presidential race], and you've got to talk him out of this.' Harry told Bobby, 'Forget about Jackie Robinson. There's a twenty-eight-year-old minister in Montgomery [Alabama] named Martin Luther King, Jr., who would be much more important to your brother's candidacy.' Harry was the first person to begin to educate Bobby Kennedy about the black community, the diversity of black leadership. A year later, on the eve of the election, Bobby made a phone call to get King out of jail—which shifted the black vote in some key states."

Kennedy and Baldwin first met in 1962, at a White House dinner for Nobel Prize laureates, and agreed that they wanted to talk further. In the aftermath of having to call out the National Guard to allow James Meredith's admission as the first black to enter the University of Mississippi, the attorney general was alarmed at an escalating level of violence in America that had not been seen since the Civil War. He believed that the cities would be the next great battleground for racial justice. And he knew that Baldwin had grown up in Harlem, and wanted to talk to him about this.

They met for breakfast at Robert Kennedy's home on Washington's Hickory Hill. "What do Negroes want?" Kennedy wondered. "Which Negroes will other Negroes listen to?" Baldwin responded that they simply wanted to be treated as Americans, and that the President should take a more militant stance on civil rights, treating this not politically but as a "moral issue." Watching Kennedy, detecting an inner strength that he had not seen on television, Baldwin came away "really quite impressed by him. He seemed honest and earnest and truthful."

But Baldwin's plane had been late and the visit lasted only half an hour, so Kennedy suggested they reconvene the next day, May 24, 1963, in New York. "I said I'd meet him for a drink," Kennedy later recalled. "If he had some friends, maybe we could meet, and we could talk some more. So he said, 'Fine.'" Arriving back in the city, Baldwin set about feverishly assembling quite a gathering.

The more than three-hour-long conversation began in a hotel and moved to the Kennedy family apartment along Central Park. Besides such experts on the inner city as sociologist Kenneth Clark, Baldwin brought along Belafonte, playwright Lorraine Hansberry, singer Lena Horne, and a young civil rights worker who had probably been beaten and jailed more than any other, named Jerome Smith. Kennedy had spent the morning urging the owners of Southern chain stores to de-segregate their lunch counters, and anticipated a congenial and edu-cational discussion. Educational for him it was; congenial it was not.

From the outset, Kennedy felt pushed into a corner by Jerome Smith's seeming militancy. Baldwin later remembered Smith "set the tone of the meeting because he stammers when he's upset and he stam-mered when he talked to Bobby and said that he was nauseated by the necessity of being in that room. I knew what he meant. It was not personal at all. Bobby took it personally, and turned away from him. That was a mistake because he turned toward us. We were the rea-sonable, responsible, mature representatives of the black community. Lorraine Hansberry said, 'You've got a great many very, very accom-plished people in this room, Mr. Attorney General. But the only man who should be listened to is that man over there.' "

Smith continued to speak passionately about all he had gone through in the South, saying he was not sure if he could stay nonviolent: "When I pull the trigger, kiss it goodbye." Would he fight for his country? Baldwin asked. And when Smith cried "Never!" three times, Kennedy's face reddened and, Kenneth Clark recalled, he "in a sense accused Jerome of treason." This led everyone else in the room to protect Smith who, said Lena Horne, "communicated the plain, basic suffering of being a Negro. The primeval memory of everyone in that room went to work after that." Later, Lena Horne castigated Kennedy: "Look, if *you* can't understand what this young man is saying, then we are with-out any hope at all because you and your brother are representatives of the best that a white America can offer; and if *you* are insensitive to this, then there's no alternative except our going in the streets . . . and chaos."

Kennedy tried to defend himself, saying that he and his brother were indeed sensitive to the black plight and aspirations. Other Americans had had to endure periods of oppression, he went on, pointing out that his grandfather had been an Irish immigrant. Baldwin countered: "You do not understand at all. . . . Generations before your family came as immigrants, my ancestors came to this country in chains, as slaves. We are still required to supplicate and beg you for justice and decency! . . . Why is your brother at the top while we are still so far away? That's the heart of the problem."

Kenneth Clark, who would call this "the most dramatic meeting I have ever attended," said that "at Baldwin's outburst Robert Ken-nedy's face turned purple but he remained silent." Finally Kennedy said he had come looking for ideas. Why then, Baldwin suggested—echoing Louis Armstrong's message to President Eisenhower about Little

Rock—didn't President Kennedy personally escort some black children into the newly integrated schools of Alabama? Kennedy fired back that this was unrealistic, it was transparent theatrics. When he sought to explain how closely he had worked with Martin Luther King, he was greeted with unanimous shouts of: "That's not true!" Kennedy, Clark remembered, grew "more silent and tense, and he sat immobile in his chair. He no longer continued to defend himself. He just sat, and you could see the tension and the pressure building in him."

Afterwards, Baldwin was deeply upset. He had committed himself in *The Fire Next Time* to an alliance of "the relatively conscious whites and the relatively conscious blacks"; Robert Kennedy was supposed to be one of these. "Bobby didn't understand what we were trying to tell him," Baldwin said, "didn't understand our urgency." Yet, at the same time, Baldwin thought as he departed for Paris, the meeting had been useful and might even lead to concrete action.

"Why Bobby Kennedy convened this meeting was a mystery to many of us," Harry Belafonte would later say. "[But] he had been into a whole kind of self-examination and was arriving at a new place in his morality and humanism. . . . I'd look at Bobby Kennedy at that stage now as being in search of his soul. But his moderate attitude brought all the passion to the fore. It was quite jarring to him, but I thought it very cathartic."

Two weeks after the confrontation, President Kennedy went before the nation to give a major address on civil rights. In his speech, for the first time he emphasized that segregation was morally wrong. Not long thereafter, Kennedy would send to Congress the most comprehensive civil rights bill ever drawn up by an American President. Baldwin's biographer, David Leeming, says: "I think that May meeting, to some extent, had the effect of forcing the Kennedys to speak publicly about racism—not simply as something politically bad, but about the moral dilemma that was the result of racism."

Jack Newfield, too, feels that "the fury and passion of that day eventually burned through Bobby's reserve and resentment and arrogance." Over the next several months, Kennedy tried to establish for himself why the meeting had been so angry and painful. As his biographer Arthur Schlesinger, Jr., has said: "It pierced him. . . . His tormentors made no sense; but in a way they all made sense. It was another stage in [his] education."

That summer of 1963, Mississippi civil rights leader Medgar Evers became the first victim in a series of assassinations that still haunt the American consciousness. It was then, in part as a eulogy for Evers, that Baldwin wrote in his essay *Nothing Personal*: "One must say Yes to life and embrace it wherever it is found—and it is found in terrible places. . . . For nothing is fixed, forever and forever, it is not fixed; the earth is always shifting, the light is always changing, the sea does not cease to grind down rock. . . . The moment we cease to hold each other, the moment we break faith with one another, the sea engulfs us and the light goes out."

Martin Luther King's March on Washington followed on August 28. Watching on TV from the White House, Robert Kennedy marveled: "Boy, he made a helluva speech." James Baldwin, who was among the vast crowd at the Lincoln Memorial, said: "The day was important in itself. And what we do with this day is even more important."

After President Kennedy was assassinated a few months later, Baldwin called it "a tremendous loss. . . . You could argue with him. He could hear. He began to see. There was no reason for him, a Boston millionaire's son, to know more about blacks than anybody else. But he could listen." Baldwin telephoned David Leeming, who had just gone to work for him as a personal secretary, and described the assassination as "only the beginning." Everyone was in trouble—"not just the Negroes, but every living soul."

When Martin Luther King heard the news, Baldwin had also been informed that day, King said to his wife Coretta: "I don't think I'm going to live to reach forty." Baldwin responded in anguish: "I can't deal with that. They wouldn't dare. No, anybody but Martin."

He had already written widely about Dr. King, meeting with him on several occasions. And he very much wanted to sit down with Malcolm X, particularly after Malcolm returned from his trip to Mecca far more open to the possibility of a unified struggle with progressive white Americans. Kenneth Clark arranged for Baldwin, King and Malcolm X to spend the afternoon together on February 23, 1965. Two days before this was to happen, Malcolm X was gunned down by his former compatriots among the Black Muslims.

The metamorphosis that began in Robert Kennedy at the meeting in 1963 did not abate. In the griefstricken months after his brother's death, he read widely and underlined in Emerson's *Essays*: "Abide by it, and do not weakly try to reconcile yourself with the world. . . . Adhere to your own act, and congratulate yourself if you have done something strange and extravagant, and broken the monotony of a decorous age."

Early in 1967, Kennedy made a tour of the Mississippi Delta, witnessing black poverty firsthand for the first time. A reporter remembered Kennedy's reaction to a small child, sitting on the floor rubbing grains of rice: "His tummy was sticking way out. . . . Bobby looked down at the child, and then he picked him up and sat down on that dirty bed. He was rubbing the child's stomach. He said, 'My God, I didn't know this kind of thing existed. How can a country like this allow it? Maybe they just don't know.' " The late Medgar Evers's brother, Charles Evers, said the child never looked up. "Tears were running down [Kennedy's] cheek, and he just sat there and held the little child. Roaches and rats were all over the floor. . . . Then he said, 'I'm going back to Washington to do something about this.' No other white man in America would have come into that house."

When Robert Kennedy declared for the presidency in 1968, Jack Newfield remembers a walking tour they made together through the Brooklyn ghetto of Bedford-Stuyvesant. "He felt cheated by his affluent, elitist life," Newfield says. They were on a plane together on April 4, going to Indianapolis for a prearranged rally in the black community, when word came of King's assassination. "Bobby had never had that much personal chemistry with King. But even from a distance, King was a significant catalyst in his growth and education about race. It is a helluva journey he made, going from allowing the FBI to wiretap King when he was attorney general, to being transformed by his assassination. The crowd was waiting for him in Indianapolis, and most of the people had no idea that King had been shot and killed. Bobby broke the news, and you could hear this wounded gasp from what must have been 5,000 to 7,000 people. Then he gave his incredible, improvised speech."

On that cold windy spring night, Robert Kennedy said: "Martin Luther King dedicated his life to love and to justice for his fellow human beings, and he died because of that effort. In this difficult day, in this difficult time for the United States, it is perhaps well to ask what kind of a nation we are and what direction we want to move in. . . ." And he concluded: "Let us dedicate ourselves to what the Greeks wrote so many years ago: to tame the savageness of man and to make gentle the life of this world."

Kennedy sent a private jet to Memphis, to bring Dr. King's body home to Atlanta. Inside the Ebenezer Baptist Church, he saw James Baldwin for the first time since the fateful meeting five years before. They looked in one another's eyes. But in that moment there was nothing to say. Baldwin described the feeling at the service "as though something, perhaps the heavens, perhaps the earth, might crack. . . . Everyone sat very still. I did not want to weep for Martin; tears seemed futile." As the silent mourners filed toward the casket, he broke down in a friend's arms.

Jack Newfield remembers: "The night of the funeral, Bobby stayed up all night talking to what was then the national black leadership. He knew he had to do something. He realized that he had to become the inheritor of King's orphaned constituency. By then, his own politics had evolved almost to the same place where King's politics were, in terms of King's Poor People's campaign. The eight weeks left of Bobby's life, he was much more consciously talking about poor people, rather than the Vietnam War. If Bobby had been elected in 1968, and if King had still been alive, I think this would be a totally different country."

Harry Belafonte said in 1997: "Robert Kennedy, by the end of his life, embraced our cause fully and passionately. . . . I believe . . . that the May, 1963 meeting was only one of many experiences that led to Mr. Kennedy's greater understanding of our cause, hence his support."

To James Baldwin, the assassination of Robert Kennedy on June 4, 1968, was "simply one more indication of the sickness in the country," David Leeming remembers him saying, "one final example of the mentality of violence that was to some extent created or brewed by the racist and classist lies of America."

When Baldwin died in 1987, the man who led the way into the cathedral and joined the Baldwin brothers carrying the casket, who seemed almost to stand guard over the grave as people filed past leaving flowers, was wearing the overalls of his days in the civil rights Freedom Rides. His name was Jerome Smith, who on that long-ago day in 1963 with Robert Kennedy had been the living embodiment of *The Fire Next Time.*

In his living room, John Edgar Wideman is talking about the impact of Baldwin on his own work. After Wideman came to teach at the University of Massachusetts/Amherst in 1986, he had known Baldwin only briefly but "felt his loss personally, both because of the scope and the intimacy of his work and the sense that we all owed so much to him. He made us part of his thoughts and feelings in such a direct way. Other writers have often served me to help work out some of the irresolveable issues that we face—and Baldwin did this in a very important way, because he stood for certain things so clearly. Quality of writing, originality of mind, and political engagement. Plus, he was someone who embodied the great rhetorical tradition of not only black writing but black oral culture, because of his use of the Bible. Not only Bible theology and metaphor, but the preacher's gift of persuasion that took me back to the churches where I grew up as a kid.

"The point of view that is articulated by Baldwin in such a memorable way," Wideman continues, "a way you can't avoid and that makes you feel something, is not all that complicated. It's that we as a nation, as a people, don't want to hear it. There's too much investment in things as they are, it's not that we're lacking for solutions. What's complicated is what Baldwin said, changing the human heart, changing your motivation. Who wants less when they think they have more? Who has the power and the force to seek through material advantage to spiritual disadvantage? The key is willingly changing the power relationship; otherwise, you go around in a circle because you're only accountable to yourself."

When one looks at Baldwin's fiction, Wideman believes, "you see the inner torment, the personal struggle to realize some of the moral and ethical goals that he talks about in a larger canvas of society, them and us, white Americans and black Americans, in the essays. For instance, in *Giovanni's Room*—one of the finest lyric novels in American literature—there are no racially defined characters. But in that book, you can probably learn more directly and simply what Baldwin's address to racial issues is. It's all there."

I ask Wideman what he thinks of drawing a comparison between Baldwin and Frederick Douglass. "I think the analogies and parallels are right there with Baldwin. On issues of race, he clarified the national thinking and said things that—whether or not people read Baldwin—seeped into consciousness, permeated the way we understood things. And then for the whole '60s, Baldwin is a seminal voice. His was again a very simple point in a way, an old-time fundamental Christian point: you do evil to somebody else, you're destroying yourself. That notion of the conjoining of the victim and the perpetrator, and that there was a moral and ethical edge to all of this, a transcendent set of values. Which, if you held our everyday behavior up to it, you're in a lot of trouble. Baldwin made those kinds of points clear.

"Like Baldwin, Douglass had the capacity to cut through the nonsense and get down to the nitty-gritty issues, and left a body of work that is definitive. His autobiography is very analagous to the work Baldwin did. Then, too, like Douglass, Baldwin was an itinerant at certain times in his life. He did a lot of traveling and speaking, with the advantage of TV and other media that Douglass didn't have. But Douglass was dealing in a smaller world. The only way you could do it in those days was to travel so much and repeat yourself, which is the way Douglass made such a tremendous impact."

The itinerants . . . Baldwin, at mid-life, and Douglass, late in life, each made their pilgrimage to the biblical Holy Land. Here was what they saw:

". . . Jerusalem—God knows is golden when the sun is shining on all that yellow stone. What a blue sky. What a beautiful city—you remember that song? Oh, what a beautiful city! Well, that's the way Jerusalem makes one feel. I stood today in the upper room, the room

where Christ and his disciples had the last supper, and I thought of Mahalia and Marian Anderson and Go Down, Moses *and of my father and of that other song my father used to sing,* I want to be ready To walk in Jerusalem, Just like John. *And here I am, far from ready, in one of the homelands which has given me my identity.* . . . *To ask oneself, 'What is a Jew?', is also, for me, to ask myself, 'What is a black man?' And what, in the name of heaven is an American Negro?* . . . *This trip has had the effect of opening something in me which I must pursue.* . . ."
> —JAMES BALDWIN, *Letters from a Journey*, 1961.

"Religious ideas have come to us from the wilderness, from mountain tops, from dens and caves, and from the vast spaces from which come the mirage and other shadowy illusions which create rivers, lakes, and forests where there are none. The song of the angels could be better heard by the shepherds on the plains of Bethlehem than by the jostling crowds in the busy streets of Jerusalem. John the Baptist could preach better in the wilderness than in the busy marts of men. Jesus said his best word to the world when on the Mount of Olives. Moses learned more of the laws of God when in the mountains than when down among the people. The Hebrew prophets frequented dens and caves and desert places. John saw his wonderful vision in the Isle of Patmos with naught in sight but the sea and sky. It was in a lonely place that Jacob wrestled with the angel. The Transfiguration was on a mountain. . . . The heart beats louder and the soul hears quicker in silence and solitude."
> —FREDERICK DOUGLASS, in Egypt, 1886.

Looking back in 1978 on his first days in Paris, Baldwin said: "I lived in a real silence. . . . But I was absolutely active because in that silence I began to hear another language; began to hear French. . . . Which allowed me to hear my father and behind my father, my grandmother and the church I came out of and the pulpit I had just left. . . . It always struck me that out of that church which we, after all, in a way were forced to accept—one thing that black people did with it was to recognize all the symbols we were given—birth, resurrection, death—and to take them completely out of the Christian context and . . . back to where they began."

When Douglass was studying *The Colombian Orator*, he paid particular attention to how the great speech-makers related to their audiences. The book's introduction contained a quotation from Cicero: "All the passions of the soul are expressed in the eyes, by so many different actions."

So it was with Baldwin. "The thing I remember most about him were his eyes," Mel Watkins was saying at a jazz nightclub in Greenwich Village. "He had incredible eyes. I mean, he referred to himself as bug-eyed and ugly. But in fact, his eyes were like magnets. People could not take their eyes off his, because of the way he used them. In talking he immediately took center stage because of his way of presenting things, the way he visualized the world and then acted it out through his own gestures."

Watkins was an editor at the *New York Times Book Review* when he first got to know Baldwin. When Watkins was preparing an essay about Baldwin for a collection, he studied a theological treatise "that articulated or elucidated all those various elements of the preacher's presentation. Practically every one of those verbal techniques, you can find in Baldwin's writing—including repetition in order to make a point. The rhythm of his prose was one of the most attractive and disarming things about it. People would be pulled in simply on the rhythm and be mesmerized by it."

"My desire to learn increased, and especially did I want a thorough acquaintance with the contents of the Bible. I have gathered scattered pages of the Bible from the filthy street-gutters, and washed and dried them, that in moments of leisure I might get a word or two of wisdom from them. While thus religiously seeking knowledge, I became acquainted with a good old colored man named Charles Lawson. . . . [who] told me that the Lord had great work for me to do, and I must prepare to do it; that he had been shown that I must preach the gospel."
—FREDERICK DOUGLASS, *Narrative*, 1845.

"We won our Christianity, our faith, at the point of a gun, not because of the example afforded by white Christians, but in spite of it. It was very difficult to become a Christian if you were a black man on a slave ship, and the slave ship was called 'The Good Ship Jesus.' . . . it becomes necessary for me . . . not to read your pronouncements but to go back to the source and check it for myself. . . . it may very well mean that the revolution which was begun two thousand years ago by a disreputable Hebrew criminal may now have to be begun again by people equally disreputable and equally improbable."
—JAMES BALDWIN, *White Racism or World Community?*, 1968.

Both Douglass and Baldwin were very protective of their personal lives. And both suffered over their departure from convention—Douglass in marrying his white secretary eighteen months after the death of his first wife, and Baldwin for his homosexuality. Having moved to Washington, Douglass arranged his wedding to Helen Pitts secretly to avoid public outcry in 1884, but had no idea how startled his old friends would be. His wife's Abolitionist father—once proud to know Douglass—refused the couple entry to his house and would visit Washington only when he was certain they were away from the city. The father's brother, a next-door neighbor of the Douglasses, broke off all relations with his niece and her famous husband. Even Douglass's own children from his first marriage had difficulty in accepting what had happened, and many black Americans felt betrayed by Douglass.

As he explained in a letter to his friend, the woman's suffrage leader Elizabeth Cady Stanton: "Circumstances have during the last forty years thrown me much more into white society than in that of colored people. While true to the rights of the colored race my nearest personal friends owing to association and common sympathy and aims have been white people and as men choose wives from friends and associates, it is not strange that I have so chosen my wife and that she has chosen me."

It was with Helen Pitts that Douglass visited North Africa for the first time. Following their long tour the summer after their marriage, he wrote in another letter: "What business has the world with the color of my wife. It wants to know how old she is,? how her parents and friends like her marriage,? how I courted her,? whether with love or with money,? whether we are happy or miserable now that we have been married seven months? You would laugh to see the letters I have received and the newspaper talk on these matters—I do not do much to satisfy the public on these points—but there is one upon which I wish you as an old and dear friend to be entirely satisfied and that is: that Helen and I are making life go very happily [and] that neither of us has yet repented of our marriage."

Mel Watkins says of Baldwin that "many people read him for reasons nothing to do with race, because he was also talking about another kind of victim of American prejudice." Yet, as John Wideman sees it, "There was the whole issue of at how much distance Baldwin was kept from the center because he was gay, because it wouldn't be 'good press,' and the deep level at which that hurt him."

Baldwin broke the taboos over homosexuality in the mid-1950s with publication of *Giovanni's Room*. When he turned in the novel, he later recalled, "I was told I shouldn't have written it. I was told to bear in mind that I was a young Negro writer with a certain audience, and I wasn't supposed to alienate that audience." But Baldwin was not an advocate of any coalition based upon sexual preference. Indeed, in a rare interview about the subject, he said that the word "gay" had always rubbed him the wrong way: "It seems to me that a coalition has to be based upon the grounds of human dignity. Anyway, what connects us, speaking about the private life is mainly unspoken. . . . Even when I began to realize things about myself, began to suspect who I was and what I was likely to become, it was still very personal, absolutely personal. It was really a matter between me and God. I would have to live the life he had made me to live."

Above all, Baldwin and Douglass were spokesmen for the *human* condition, drawing no false boundaries and addressing themselves continually to the nature of relationships. Particularly after the Civil War, Douglass espoused the cause of women; the last speech before his death was to a women's rights rally. "Woman knows and feels her wrongs as man cannot know and feel them," he told the Woman Suffrage Association in 1888, "and she also knows as well as he can know, what measures are needed to redress them. . . . Her right to be and to do is as full, complete and perfect as the right of any man on earth. . . . Man has been so long the king and woman the subject—man has been so long accustomed to command and woman to obey—that both parties to the relation have been hardened into their respective places, and thus has been piled up a mountain of iron."

Baldwin, writing in a 1954 essay called "The Male Prison," expanded on the theme: "It is one of the facts of life that there are two sexes, which fact has given the world most of its beauty, cost it not a little of its anguish, and contains the hope and glory of the world. And it is with this fact, which might better perhaps be called a mystery, that every human being born must find some way to live. For, no matter what demons drive them, men cannot live without women and women cannot live without men . . . living as we do in a time and country where communion between the sexes has become so sorely threatened that we depend more and more on the strident exploitation of externals. . . . It is worth observing, too, that when men can no longer love women they also cease to love or respect or trust each other, which makes their isolation complete. Nothing is more dangerous than this isolation, for men will commit any crimes whatever rather than endure it. . . ."

Douglass and Baldwin also sought to come to terms with the bitternesses of their past, as personified in Douglass's case by his former slavemaster and in Baldwin's by his stepfather. Each, in their writings, describe remarkable deathbed scenes of reconciliation.

It had been forty years since his escape when Douglass, then serving as U.S. marshal of Washington, D.C., received a message that Captain Thomas Auld wished him "to come to the side of his dying bed." All this time, Douglass had "denounced in all bitterness of spirit and fierceness of speech" Auld's world: "He had struck down my personality, had subjected me to his will, made property of my body and soul." It was Captain Auld who had stopped his wife from teaching Douglass literacy. Now, thinking back, Douglass realized: "In learning to read . . . I am not sure that I do not owe quite as much to the opposition of my master, as to the kindly assistance of my amiable mistress."

So, when he traveled back to Talbot County, Maryland, to see the more than eighty-year-old captain, "He was to me no longer a slave-holder either in fact or in spirit, and I regarded him as I did myself, a victim of the circumstances of birth, education, law and custom. Our courses had been determined for us, not by us. We had both been flung, by powers that did not ask our consent, upon a mighty current of life, which we could neither resist nor control. . . . Now our lives were verging towards a point where differences disappear, where even the constancy of hate breaks down and where the clouds of pride, passion, and selfishness vanish before the brightness of infinite light. At such a time, and in such a place, when a man is about closing his eyes in this world and ready to step into the eternal unknown, no word of reproach or bitterness should reach him or fall from his lips, and on this occasion there was to this rule no transgression on either side."

As Douglass held the old slavemaster's hand, Captain Auld began to weep. "Frederick," Douglass recalled him saying, "I always knew you were too smart to be a slave, and had I been in your place, I should have done as you did." And Douglass replied: "Capt. Auld, I am glad to hear you say this. I did not run away from *you*, but from *slavery*; it was not that I loved Caesar less, but Rome more."

Baldwin's minister stepfather was very ill the last time he went to visit him. "The moment I saw him I knew why I had put off this visit for so long. I had told my mother that I did not want to see him because I hated him. But this was not true. It was only that I *had* hated him and I wanted to hold onto this hatred. . . . I imagine that one of the reasons people cling to their hates so stubbornly is because they sense, once hate is gone, that they will be forced to deal with pain."

At the funeral, Baldwin realized: "It was better not to judge the man who had gone down under an impossible burden. It was better to remember: *Thou knowest this man's fall; but thou knowest not his wrassling.* . . . It began to seem that one would have to hold in the mind forever two ideas which seemed to be in opposition. The first idea was acceptance, the acceptance, totally without rancor, of life as it is, and men as they are: in the light of this idea, it goes without saying that injustice is a commonplace. But this did not mean that one could be complacent, for the second idea was of equal power: that one must never, in one's own life, accept these injustices as commonplace but must fight them with all one's strength. This fight begins, however, in the heart and it now had been laid to my charge to keep my own heart free of hatred and despair. This intimation made my heart heavy and, now that my father was irrecoverable, I wished that he had been beside me so that I could have searched his face for the answers which only the future would give me now."

One might have thought that Baldwin and Ralph Ellison, as the two leading African-American authors of their time, would have had a close relationship. But this was not the case. First, in both their personal and writing styles, the two men were vastly different. As Mel Watkins put it, "Ellison was much more inclined to a methodical examination of issues, while Baldwin would grasp one part of an argument and use that to prove his point in a way Ellison never would have done."

There was also Ellison's chosen distance from political activism. "Jimmy told me a story of the first time he went South to report on the civil rights movement," says Michael Thelwell. "He was driven to the airport, or the train station, by Ellison, who lectured him—belaboring the subject really—on the inappropriateness of what he was doing. Because, Ellison felt, he was an artist and therefore could not afford to be involved, except at great peril to his 'Art.' "

Involvement, for both Baldwin and Frederick Douglass, often meant that they had most interesting friendships with whites. Perhaps Douglass's closest associate, especially in the critical years leading up to the Civil War, was a wealthy white landowner named Gerrit Smith. More so than William Lloyd Garrison, Smith practiced what he preached. His estate in Peterboro, New York, was an underground railroad stop. He often attended black churches, rather than condone the segregated "Negro pews" found in most churches. He gave financial aid to black schools. He provided land grants to blacks from among his nearly a-quarter-million-acres spread across four states, seeking to help as many as possible meet property qualifications to get the right to vote. And Smith fought the Garrisonians in their efforts to undermine Douglass, helping him get his *North Star* newspaper on firm footing and later merging it with his own Liberty Party periodical with the new name of *Frederick Douglass' Paper.*

Interracial friendships remained extremely rare in the 1850s, but Douglass and his family were welcome guests at Smith's vast estate. In their correspondence, they made continuing inquiries about the well-being of one another's families. When Douglass reported that he had been accosted for accompanying a white woman on a New York City street, Smith wrote to him: "Think not, my dear Douglass, that it is you colored men alone who suffer from this insane and rampant prejudice. The wound it inflicts on you, it inflicts on us who sympathize with you, and who have identified ourselves and made ourselves colored men with you. In your sufferings, we suffer.—In your afflictions, we are afflicted. . . . How can I enjoy that in which my equal brother is permitted no participation? Even the attempt to enjoy it, I feel to be traitorous to him. . . ."

In the final volume of his autobiography, Douglass recalled: "Invited to accompany Hon. Gerrit Smith to dine with Mr. E[dward] C. Delavan at Albany many years ago, I expressed to Mr. Smith my awkwardness and embarrassment in the society I was likely to meet there. 'Ah!' said that good man, 'you must go Douglass; it is your mission to break down the walls of separation between the two races.' "

Both Douglass and Smith became secret supporters of John Brown. During Smith's brief tenure as a U.S. congressman, Douglass reprinted his speeches. Smith's speech opposing the Homestead Act that barred blacks from obtaining land was, Douglass wrote, "the mightiest and grandest production ever before delivered in the House or Senate or this nation." The two men went through brief periods of estrangement over strategical differences. But, as historian John R. McKivigan has written, "In Smith, Douglass had found an understanding friend who could overlook minor points of disagreement in their shared commitment to the cause of freedom."

In certain ways, Baldwin's friendship with the novelist William Styron mirrors the Douglass-Smith relationship. When Garrison began chastising Douglass in his newspaper, Smith stood staunchly beside his friend. And, if Norman Mailer's break with Baldwin might be loosely compared to Garrison's with Douglass—"at that time," Mailer told me, "Bill Styron and I were having our feud, and Baldwin became very friendly with Styron, so that didn't improve matters"—in the same vein, Styron and Baldwin stood by one another against assaults during the most difficult of times.

Beginning in the fall of 1960, Baldwin moved into Styron's guest house in Connecticut for almost a year. Styron was assembling notes for his next novel, taking on the saga of Nat Turner's slave rebellion; Baldwin was completing his novel *Another Country*, and gathering his thoughts for what became *The Fire Next Time*. They had first met at a Manhattan dinner party, then again at the home of their mutual novelist friend James Jones in Paris. For both of them, as Styron looks back upon it, the long evenings they spent together in Connecticut proved revelatory.

A hurricane was bearing down upon the island of Martha's Vineyard, the afternoon I sat down with William Styron at his summer home in Edgartown in the late summer of 1996. A contemporary of

Mailer in age, Styron had also risen to early fame with the publication of *Lie Down in Darkness* and *Set This House on Fire*. He was a stocky man with long curly white hair, and beneath a gruff veneer was a gentle demeanor.

"I was the grandson of a slave-owner," Styron began, "and Jimmy was the grandson of a slave. We talked about this quite a bit. Most of his relationships with white people had been either French or basically Northerners. I was one of the first Southern-born white men he had met. And this was the first time that I had ever really had any intimate contact with a black person."

Had Styron's getting to know Baldwin forced him to confront parts of himself that he had never faced before? It was a difficult question, and one that Styron pondered before answering: "Yes, it required some time for me to get over my self-consciousness about his blackness. But what was most revealing to me was examining my preconception that black people were not quite as intelligent as white people. I had been raised in a segregated society and been conditioned to believe that most black people I had met, at least on the surface, were not as witted or as bright or all those 'good things' I had been told you needed to have to be a decent citizen. Well, all you had to do was spend a few hours with Jimmy and be absolutely overwhelmed by the counter to that. This was as keen an intelligence as I had ever encountered.

"I began to learn many things from Jimmy," Styron continued. "For one, just how tough it was to be black. It was illuminating for me to learn that blacks were treated as despicably in the North as they were in the South. Just because he was brought up in Harlem, he had suffered really the same deprivations that he might have suffered had he been born in Alabama. And I think it was fascinating for Jimmy to discover that there were white Southerners who weren't the standard caricature of a racist."

They spent considerable hours together listening to records. "He was a great fan of Nina Simone, and Miles Davis was very much in the ascendancy then. Odetta was coming on the scene and Jimmy introduced me to her music, which was enormously impressive, I thought. Then there was Bessie Smith. And a lot of gospel records. Paul Robeson was a big figure to Jimmy. I came more from the classical side, but we intersected; Jimmy could listen to classical music with great responsiveness too."

It was the gatherings at his home, the encounters between Baldwin and Styron's friends, that were the most vivid and extraordinary moments. "This was a little western Connecticut town, and I had a lot of very well-meaning white friends who would come to dinner. You have to remember that the early '60s had been preceded by the smug, complacent Eisenhower years, where the civil rights movement had not really gone anywhere. The black power movement had not yet developed. And there was a great deal of naiveté on the part of whites about what black people were up to. Everyone associated black people's sense of their own progress with Martin Luther King at that moment. And they didn't realize the extent of black rage."

The storm outside was escalating in intensity, and Styron got up to let in his dogs and close the windows on his porch. Then he resumed: "So Jimmy would say to these liberal white people assembled at my house, 'You cannot any of you imagine the horror of what it is to be a Negro in this country. And we're gonna *burn* your houses down, burn them right to the ground.' And these people's eyes would pop out! He would say these things with such eloquence and force, it would just make people shiver. They were astounded at the extent of Jimmy's passion and rage. Some people would really go away shaking their heads.

"But Jimmy was not in any sense intimidating, he was merely telling it like it was. He was bringing The Word. This really was high-level prophecy, because no one had yet imagined as he had that this would actually happen, that whole cities would burn down during the '60's. I would get very moved by the mobility of his face when he got impassioned. It really was a kind of almost biblical passion, as he spun out this artful monologue, and his rhetoric was extraordinary.

"It didn't really scare me, because this was my preoccupation at the time, writing about a black revolutionary. I actually had not begun *The Confessions of Nat Turner*, but I was making notes and doing a lot of heavy reading, trying to immerse myself in the historiography of slavery. I was from that part of the world, Tidewater, Virginia, where Turner's rebellion took place. But I had not really developed a feeling for it. So on many of these nights, Jimmy and I would end up reading to each other. He would read *Another Country* to me, and I'd read some of my previous work or from the notes I was putting together, fascinating sorts of details about slavery. And he began making notes for *The Fire Next Time*, based in part on our discussions and the get-togethers with my liberal friends."

Styron believed he could not have written *The Confessions of Nat Turner*, which went on to win a Pulitzer Prize after its publication in 1967, without the insights he gained from James Baldwin. "Jimmy turned me on to Frederick Douglass," he remembered. "I had heard of him, but he said, 'Douglass is *essential* reading.' And he was. For instance, there is what Douglass points out: that if you humiliate a slave, keep him in a state of perpetual subservience, that person is a slave for life. But if you treat him with decency and encouragement, he'll want to slash your throat. The point being, obviously, that slavery was such a monstrous institution, one that paralyzed people. Give someone a little hope and that's the moment he's ready to kill you—because he doesn't want just that, he wants freedom. Douglass implied this over and over again. When I was writing *Nat Turner*, I used that as a kind of touchstone throughout the whole book. Using such insights as that from Frederick Douglass, I was able to build certain psychological truths into my work. It was very important, and Jimmy and I discussed this.

"We drank a lot in those days, and all night long we would have these incredible cross-fertilizations of cultural things. He'd tell me about Harlem and I'd tell him about what it was like to live in the South. As segregated as the North was, nonetheless it was different in that a black man could theoretically walk down Fifth Avenue without being molested. But not in the South, where if you were caught in the wrong place at the wrong time, you suffered for it. There were these differences, which I learned from Jimmy and he learned from me.

"And it was certainly of value for him to encourage me, to plunge into this story of mine from the point of view of a black person. Because by this time, we both agreed mutually that there should be no impediment to a writer of one race taking on a character of another race. And he did that, of course, in *Giovanni's Room* especially. This was a kind of cardinal rule of his belief about himself and his writing. We were both, I now realize, almost twins in being politically incorrect. Because we were both attacked, separately, for the same reason—that we had been arrogant and presumptuous in trying to take on these worlds where we didn't belong. Black people attacked him for this, and they attacked me."

After *The Confessions of Nat Turner* came out, Styron indeed faced severe assessments, particularly from black critics. "But Jimmy took my side immediately after the book was published. He defended me, and I was always grateful for that. Basically he was extremely loyal to our friendship, which we maintained right to the very end."

The winds were beginning to rattle the windows of Styron's wood-frame house, and we ended our conversation talking again about Baldwin and Douglass. "It's not that Jimmy has some exclusive claim to the mantle of Douglass," Styron said. "But in terms of his eloquence, his persuasiveness, the parallels are right there. Also, Douglass, with all of his pride and dignity, realized nonetheless how important it was to talk to white people. Jimmy did, too. Douglass saw the necessity of dealing with the white world if he was going to get anything done. And I think Jimmy felt the same way."

"Every fact in our circumstances here marks us as a permanent element of the American people. Mark the readiness with which we adapt ourselves to your civilization. You can take no step in any direction where the black man is not at your side."
—FREDERICK DOUGLASS

"I suggest that the role of the Negro in American life has something to do with our concept of what God is, and from my point of view, this concept is not big enough. It has got to be made much bigger than it is because God is, after all, not anybody's toy. To be with God is really to be involved with some enormous, overwhelming desire, and joy, and power which you cannot control, which controls you. I conceive of my own life as a journey toward something I do not understand, which in the going toward, makes me better. I conceive of God, in fact, as a means of liberation and not a means to control others. . . . these walls—these artificial walls—which have been up so long to protect us from something we fear, must come down. I think that what we really have to do is to create a country in which there are no minorities—for the first time in the history of the world."
—JAMES BALDWIN

Neither man lived to see the fruition of the seeds they had worked so diligently to plant in the turbulent decades of their respective '60s. The harvest still waits. As the poet Michael Harper says, "After the Civil War was over and Lincoln was gone, Reconstruction politics undid much of what Douglass would have done only had Lincoln lived." Undone, too, was much of Douglass's own past, when an arson fire in Rochester, New York, in 1872 destroyed most of his memorabilia.

In a speech given in 1880 to celebrate the emancipation of the West Indies, Douglass lamented: "The citizenship granted in the fourteenth amendment is practically a mockery, and the right to vote, provided for in the fifteenth amendment, is literally stamped out in face of government. The old master class is today triumphant, and the newly-enfranchised class in a condition but little above that in which they were found before the rebellion. . . . In the hurry and confusion of the hour, and the eager desire to have the Union restored, there was more care for the sublime superstructure of the republic than for the solid foundations upon which it could alone be upheld."

Yet Douglass did not despair that his vision of America would one day come to pass. Nor did Baldwin. As Michael Thelwell said of his friend: "He was in a state of deep distress about the country through the '70s and '80s. Anybody would be, who embodied in such a direct way the hopes of what one might call the better angels of our nature, and who was so passionately committed to what had seemed at one point a real possibility to transcend some of the burden of our history. But there wasn't bitterness in Jimmy. He was a much larger person than that. Jimmy was too wise for that."

I am sitting alone, watching a videotape that Thelwell loaned me, of the memorial service given James Baldwin in Amherst in 1987. I am watching the white university chancellor, Joseph Duffy, describe how Baldwin "illuminated a common search for humanity that we all share" and quote from his writings: "Human freedom is a complex, difficult, and private thing. If we liken life for a moment to a furnace, then freedom is the fire which burns away illusion. Any honest examination of the national life proves how far we are from the standard of human freedom with which we began. The recovery of this standard demands of everyone who loves this country a hard look at himself, for the greatest achievements must begin somewhere and they always begin with the person. And if we are not capable of this examination, we may yet become one of the most distinguished and monumental failures in the history of nations."

I am watching the white dean of the College of Humanities and Fine Arts, Murray Schwartz, discuss how Baldwin changed his life in 1963 when he read *The Fire Next Time*. He, too, reads aloud from the work: "We are controlled here by our confusion, far more than we know, and the American dream has therefore become something more closely resembling a nightmare on the private, domestic and international levels. . . . One is responsible to life. It is the small beacon in that terrifying darkness from which we come and to which we shall return. One must negotiate this passage as nobly as possible, for the sake of those who are coming after us." And now, Schwartz adds, twenty-four years later, Baldwin's words "burn with the fire of the burning bush, which illuminates and is not consumed."

I am watching Professor Esther Terry, of the Department of Afro-American Studies, recall her days in the civil rights movement. "While it was Dr. King who moved us to action, it was James Baldwin who sustained us. For he validated us and the righteousness of our cause, for us and for all time." Baldwin "went before us in every nook and cranny, every high and lofty place, disturbing every unjust peace he ever encountered."

The organ is playing *Amazing Grace*, and then dancers take the stage to send him on his way to the home of the ancestors with an African war dance, and all is still but the echoing of the drum, and across the ages Frederick Douglass is saying: "This they would sing, with other words of their own improvising. . . . In the most boisterous outbursts of rapturous sentiment, there was ever a tinge of deep melancholy. . . . They spoke to the heart and to the soul of the thoughtful." And James Baldwin is answering: "White Americans seem to feel that happy songs are *happy* and sad songs are *sad*. . . . Only people who have been down the line, as the song puts it, know what this music is about."

I am watching a white English professor, James Tate, speak of a man who "had the burden of such terrible knowledge and yet was radiant with love." He reads aloud a poem written long ago by François Villon: "I am hot as fire, I am shaking tooth on tooth. In my own country I am in a distant land. Beside the blaze I am shivering in flames. . . . I cheer up in sad hopelessness. . . . Warmly welcomed, always turned away."

I am watching John Edgar Wideman read a poem he has written: ". . . How do we speak to you, who is our voice and still now. . . . We wait for the earth to turn and tilt again, the shadow to lift. . . . Your words tell us the circle is strong, will not be broken. . . . Steal away, steal away."

I am watching and remembering the words of Frederick Douglass's friend James McCune Smith: ". . . when a man raises himself from the lowest condition in society to the highest, mankind pays him the tribute of their admiration; when he accomplishes this elevation by native energy, guided by prudence and wisdom, their admiration is increased; but when his course, onward and upward . . . furthermore proves a possible, what had hitherto been regarded as an impossible, reform, then he becomes a burning and a shining light, on which the aged may look with gladness, the young with hope, and the downtrodden, as a representative of what they may themselves become."

I am watching Chinua Achebe, the great Nigerian novelist, recall a time with Baldwin on a speaker's podium when a mystery voice came over the public address system and "began to hurl racial insults at him, and us. I will see that moment to the end of my life: the happiness brutally wiped off his face, the genial manner gone, the eyes flashing in defiant combativeness, the voice incredibly calm and controlled, and the words of the remorseless prophet began once again to flow."

I am watching Michael Thelwell speak of the first time he saw him in 1960, when James Baldwin stayed up all night talking with a small group of Howard University students. Thelwell is talking about all the elements so mixed in the man—the gentleness and the boldness, the painfully penetrating insights and the generosity of spirit.

"In the sanctified church from which his roots come," Thelwell is saying, "on such an occasion one should take a text. . . . Where to begin? Do we go to one of the many streams that flowed into his art, nourished his vision, and was transformed by his genius? A line maybe

from a hymn, the battle hymn: 'We have *seen* his righteous witness.'
That would do. Or from Shakespeare . . . 'Let us sit down on the
ground and tell sad stories of the death of kings.' Because there was a
regality to him. That might do. Or a line from the Bible: 'Let us now
praise famous men.' Or from the Blues, because he never wandered far
from his raising and that tradition: 'You was a rambling man, daddy,
but your spirit done stayed home.' Or to the streets, the streets of
Harlem, a line I overheard in a bar one night when he engaged the
then-attorney general of the country: 'Wooooo, baby, that little dude,
he be whoppin' ass! He sure don't take no shit, do he?' That would
serve, too.

"But I think . . . I will recourse to the proverbial wisdom of the Ibo elders. To the source. An African ancestor said, 'If you want to see a mask
dancing, you cannot stand in one place.' And so it was with Jimmy. He
was indeed one of the luminous presences, the great ancestral mask spirits of our time—covering so much space in his prophetic dance that one
had to keep moving just to see it truly. And these same ancestors also
said, 'Truth is like a goatskin bag; each man carries his own.'

"And that is the text. Because truth and Jimmy were great friends.
Indeed, truth was his constant companion; they were one and inseparable. And all of us in this room . . . carry our own version of his truth.
We all in our manner loved him. Because you could not but love him,
if you read him, and especially if you knew him. We all carry a version
of his truth—each different, each personal, each in its own way true."

"I hear the piercing sound of trumpets. . . .
There is about Truth an inherent vitality, a recuperative energy. . . .
Here may come all who have a new and unpopular truth to unfold
and enforce. . . .
We who have long been debarred the privileges of culture may as-
semble and have our souls . . . lifted to the skies on the wings of poetry
and song. . . .
Well the nation may forget, it may shut its eyes to the past, and
frown upon any who may do otherwise, but the colored people of this
country are bound to keep the past in lively memory till justice shall
be done them.
We shall speak . . . for our race. . . . But we speak not the less for
our country. . . .
We need the storm, the whirlwind, and the earthquake. The feeling
of the nation must be quickened; the conscience of the nation must be
roused. . . .
I bring you the living present."
                              —THE SPEECHES OF FREDERICK DOUGLASS

FOR FURTHER READING:

James Baldwin, *The Price of the Ticket: Collected Nonfiction 1948-1965* (New York: St. Martin's/Marek, 1985).

David W. Blight, *Frederick Douglass' Civil War: Keeping Faith in Jubilee* (Baton Rouge: Louisiana State University Press, 1989).

The Life and Times of Frederick Douglass: Written by Himself (1881; Bonanza Books, 1962).

David Leeming, *James Baldwin: A Biography* (New York: Alfred A. Knopf, 1994).

William S. McFeely, *Frederick Douglass* (New York: W. W. Norton, 1991).

Eric J. Sundquist, ed., *Frederick Douglass: New Literary and Historical Essays* (Cambridge, Mass.: Cambridge University Press, 1990).

Michael Thelwell, *Duties, Pleasures, and Conflicts: Essays in Struggle*, intr. by James Baldwin (Amherst: University of Massachusetts Press, 1987).

Quincy Troupe, ed., *James Baldwin: The Legacy* (New York: Touchstone/Simon & Schuster, 1989).

W. J. Weatherby, *James Baldwin: Artist on Fire* (New York: Dell Publishing, 1989).

Novels by Baldwin:

Go Tell It on the Mountain (New York: Alfred A. Knopf, 1953).

Giovanni's Room (New York: Dial Press, 1956).

Another Country (New York: Dial Press, 1962).

Going to Meet the Man (New York: Dial Press, 1965).

Tell Me How Long the Train's Been Gone (New York: Dial Press, 1968).

If Beale Street Could Talk (New York: Dial Press, 1974).

Just above My Head (New York: Dial Press, 1979).

Part 3

BUILDERS OF AMERICA:

Science, Invention, Mathematics and Architecture

"Out of many things that these beginnings emphasize we may select one: the discovery of the use of iron. . . . it seems likely that while Europe was still in its stone age and while neither Egypt nor Western Asia nor ancient China knew iron, the black Africans had invented the art of smelting. It was a moment big with promise for the uplift of the human race. . . .

"The African villagers from early days . . . worked in iron, copper, brass, bronze, gold, silver, bone, and ivory. They built in fibre, wood, and stone. They developed an original division of industry. . . . among the villages so that they were grouped according to their reciprocal activities and became complements one to another."

—W. E. B. DU BOIS, *What Is Civilization?*

Ancestors—Lewis Latimer and the Early Black Inventors

" 'Tho' the waves seem sweeping o'er you,
Do not yield you to dismay:
You are part and parcel of it.
Let the tide turn as it may,
You must still be in, and with it,
Let who will laugh and deride;
Hold your way, and make all others,
Go ahead or stand aside!"
—from a poem by Lewis Latimer

Frederick Douglass was only four years removed from slavery when he sent the first public letter of his life to his fellow abolitionist leader William Lloyd Garrison. "I have for a week past been laboring," Douglass wrote on November 8, 1842, ". . . in New Bedford, with special reference to the case of our outraged brother, George Latimer, and speaking almost day and night in public and in private. . . .

"Slavery, our enemy, has landed in our very midst. . . . Just look at it; here is George Latimer a man—a brother—a husband—a father . . . hunted down like a wild beast, and ferociously dragged through the streets of Boston, and incaracerated within the walls of Leverett-st. jail. . . . what crime had George Latimer committed? He had committed the crime of availing himself of his natural rights."

As in Douglass's case, George Latimer's father was a white slave-holder. Latimer had already made several failed tries to escape from a plantation in Norfolk, Virginia. After he married twenty-year-old Rebecca Smith, who was bonded to a storekeeper, they were allowed to see one another only in the evenings. When Rebecca became pregnant, the couple decided to make their break for freedom. Working odd jobs, Latimer had secreted away enough money to buy two railroad tickets. They concealed themselves first in the hold of a steamer and then boarded a train, the fair-skinned Latimer posing as a Southern planter. But when they arrived in Boston, a former employee on the plantation recognized Latimer and set out to claim a fifty-dollar reward by alerting his owner. When the slaveholder arrived seeking his return, Latimer was jailed on charges of "larceny" while Rebecca was helped into hiding by the abolitionists.

Overnight, the Latimer case became the biggest cause célèbre of the abolitionist era. The day after he was taken into custody, close to 300 black freedmen surrounded the jail, forging a human chain to prevent any effort to return Latimer to his owner. John Greenleaf Whittier penned an epic-length poem, *Massachusetts to Virginia*, in Latimer's honor. It said: "No slave-hunt in our borders, no pirate on our strand!/ No fetters in the Bay State, no slave upon our land!" A mass meeting ensued at Boston's Faneuil Hall, after which the cry of "Latimer shall go free!" echoed through the city's streets. Massachusetts abolitionists even founded a newspaper, *The Latimer Journal and North Star*, which began publication three times a week during Latimer's trial and was read by some 20,000 people.

When the chief justice of the Massachusetts Supreme Court ruled that Latimer legally remained his slavemaster's property, negotiations began. After a month, the Virginia owner agreed to accept $400 from a black minister, Reverend Samuel Campbell, to buy Latimer's freedom. The case went on to have even greater impact. A petition signed by 60,000 people headed by Latimer's name was presented early in 1843 to the Massachusetts House of Representatives. It resulted in the passage of a landmark law, which made it a criminal offense for state officials to assist in the arrest or delivery of anyone claimed as a fugitive slave.

Latimer was reunited with his wife, and their first child arrived shortly thereafter. On September 4, 1848, the family's fourth child was born in Chelsea, a small town right outside of Boston. He was named Lewis Howard Latimer. And he would go on to become a pioneering black inventor who worked alongside three of the giants of the nineteenth century—Alexander Graham Bell, Hiram Maxim, and Thomas Edison. The first book on the subject of *Incandescent Electric Lighting: A Practical Description of the Edison System* would be written by Lewis Latimer and published in 1890. It was Latimer himself who made electric lighting practical, by devising a longer-lasting filament for the bulb.

The University of Massachusetts at Amherst is home to a number of African-American scholars. One of its longest-tenured is Professor Emeritus Asa Davis, who now lives in retirement in a large white wood-frame house near the campus. His specialty as a comparative researcher is African-American science and invention.

In his book-filled living room, Asa Davis is remembering the first time he heard Lewis Latimer's name. "I had a teacher at [New York's] P.S. 157 in 1933, a Jewish teacher. She used to turn the lights off and then turn them on and say, 'Someday you ought to take a look at the colored man who worked with Edison.' "

Yet the story of Lewis Latimer, Davis points out, "springs out of a whole consortium of things." You must go back several centuries to discover: "An African from Ghana, named Kwakwe, actually wrote down in a little book of about 100 pages a classification of all the plants around him, for example what medicine men had come up with for snakebite. Somehow that manuscript made its way to Europe, where a Swedish scholar took it and showed it to Linnaeus. Now we can't say that Kwakwe invented biology—he didn't—but his method of classifying plants was imitated by Linnaeus in his own classification of human beings. So I argue that the father of biology was a plagiarist!"

Davis chuckles and continues: "Now in our century, Edward Everett Just knew all that when he began looking at the nucleus of the cell. The inspiration behind Just was his awareness of this pattern."

Just, a black biologist originally from South Carolina, became the first scientist to unlock the secrets of cell function during the 1920s and 1930s. He discovered the essential part that the outer surface played in the development of the egg and the entire cell, shattering then-accepted thinking that only the nucleus was important.

"At one time, there was a black astronomer in Russia named Bolotov," Davis continues. "He was peering through his telescopes and looking at two stars. And he noticed that when he looked at them at intervals of two weeks, the distance between the stars got shorter. Then, in another two weeks, the distance became broader. So Bolotov discovered that instead of distances decreasing and increasing between the stars, the *mass* was increasing and decreasing. He was among the first to point out that mass and time in space interlock, which ties into some things Einstein worked on for his theory of relativity. Today, what we know as Riemann geometry is really based on Bolotov's observation."

Moving on to discuss America in the early part of the nineteenth century, one aspect of the Latimer story that has long fascinated Davis concerns the abolitionist supporters of his father, George Latimer. "Men like Dr. Henry Bowditch, and others, had made their fortunes in cotton manufacturing. Eventually cotton cloth, which was shipped not only to the northern factories but also out to England, was developed into something called 'Osnoborg.' It's an old Viennese name, and the synonym for 'Osnoborg' is 'Negro cloth.' So Lewis Latimer's father lived at a time when he knew that the cloth from cotton was named after runaway slaves from the plantation like himself. And Lewis knew about this, too, because I've seen it in some of his papers."

So Latimer's contributions fall within a much larger cultural context—"the genius of technology, trade and commerce that made this country," as Davis puts it. It is a context where the contributions of inventive African-Americans "reveal that textile manufacturing, the sugar industry, the railroads, electrical power—even a certain type of machine for sewing the soles on shoes—are all hooked up together."

Davis cites a number of instances to illustrate his point. "The Germans and French long took credit for developing the process for refining sugar, but now they're beginning to recognize a man named Norbert Rillieux as the inventor." The free son of a slave mother and a wealthy white engineer in New Orleans, Rillieux changed the sugar industry forever. The original sugar-making process, known as the "Jamaica Train," found primarily slaves toiling above open and scalding kettles, ladling the sugarcane juices through containers to produce a thick and syrupy substance.

The granulated sugar that we know today had its beginnings in a method discovered by Rillieux in 1843—when he used vacuum pans in a sequence to take liquid sugar to the boiling point and let it evaporate before it became too hot. This procedure resulted in crystallized sugar. Rillieux's machine, first used on a Louisiana plantation, remains the basic notion behind not only sugar but the manufacturing of soap, condensed milk, gelatin, and glue. His evaporation idea continues to be utilized in freeze-drying food and with industrial products such as pigments.

Then there was a railroad worker named Elijah McCoy, born the same year that Rillieux came up with his revolutionary means of sugar processing. The son of slaves who had escaped to Michigan on the underground railroad, McCoy was among the men who greased the engines of steam locomotives which were forced to lay idle until they could be relubricated with hand-held oil cans. Setting up a little shop not far from the tracks, after his workday McCoy began experimenting with finding a way to carry oil through an engine's inner workings. In 1872, he patented the first automatic lubricator—and sent American industry into a new era, with no more downtime for mechanical motors. Millions of machines came to depend upon "the real McCoy." By his death in 1929, McCoy was credited with patents for more than fifty lubricating units and twenty-five mechanical devices. (The latter came to include the first folding ironing table, because his wife needed a place to iron clothes—and the lawn sprinkler, because McCoy wanted to make watering his garden more efficient.)

As with McCoy, Jan Matzeliger's invention enabling shoes to be made completely by machine came directly out of his work in the cobbling trade. Born in Dutch Guiana, Matzeliger was the progeny of a plantation slave mother and a Dutch engineer, who showed a remarkable early talent for mechanics. Shipping out as a sailor at age nineteen, he ended up by 1876 in Lynn, Massachusetts, which was already the biggest shoe manufacturing center in the United States. Barely speaking English and lacking any formal education, Matzeliger attended night school while working at several different shoe factories. Although dozens of shoemaking machines were in existence, it was then thought impossible to connect the upper portion to the sole except by hand.

Matzeliger set up shop in a little room and began experimenting with pieces of wood, old cigar and packing boxes, and improvised tools. He was obsessed by his idea and it took him twelve years to perfect a simplified shoe-lasting machine. As historian J. A. Rogers has written: "No other machine has been invented that is capable of manipulating and shaping a shoe on all styles of lasts, and it is practically impossible to make shoes to meet commercial requirements without using Matzeliger's machine."

Matzeliger received a patent in 1883. Within six years, the demand for his invention was worldwide. He died in 1889 at the age of thirty-seven from tuberculosis, not living to see his work result in formation of the multi-million-dollar United Shoe Machinery Corporation.

Realizing that he was dying, Matzeliger made out a will. He left a few shares of stock in the original company he had formed to Lynn's North Congregational Church, a white congregation which had allowed him to join. Some years later, when the church fell into financial trouble, its sale of the stock for nearly $11,000 allowed its survival.

"In Matzeliger's will," says Asa Davis, "it's evident that certain things were happening to the black inventor. One of them was the fact that an old federal law said if a slave invented something while working for a white man, the patent rights go to the owner. Later, the corporations took over this same basic idea. Matzeliger's legacy became America's first big international company. But no one looked at the internal processes."

There is no evidence that Jan Matzeliger and Lewis Latimer ever knew each other, although the proximity of their locations overlapped for a three-year period in the late 1870s. However, as another Latimer scholar, Dr. Bayla Singer, says: "Within the corpus of Latimer's miscellaneous drawings is one that looks much like a couple of boot-lasts. It is not labeled in any way. But was he doodling, thinking of possible improvements to Matzeliger's machine?"

From the time he was small, Lewis Latimer seems always to have been "thinking of possible improvements." Undoubtedly aware of his father's escape from slavery with aid from the abolitionists, young Lewis worked as a newsboy for William Lloyd Garrison's *Liberator* newspaper. When he wasn't attending grammar school, he spent much of his first ten years at George Latimer's side—cleaning out his father's barbershop and later "becoming quite expert" as an apprentice paper-hanger.

Despite the elder Latimer's notoriety in the landmark fugitive slave case, he did not prosper monetarily and moved his family regularly after the U.S. Congress's passage of the Fugitive Slave Act of 1850. Since his wife Rebecca remained in that category, the Latimers lived for two years in Boston right next door to a station of the Underground Railroad. Among Lewis's earliest recollections was residing for a time among recent Irish immigrants. As set down in an unpublished auto-biography that he began writing at the age of seventy-nine, Latimer described the supposition that "the greatest enemy the Negro had was the Irish boys, but if you lived right in among them you could have no better neighbors."

In 1857, the U.S. Supreme Court issued its Dred Scott decision, as-serting that a slave had no rights of citizenship and that all fugitives could rightfully be returned to their owners. Within a year after this ruling, George Latimer disappeared.

"He left the family, but he didn't go very far," Winifred Latimer Norman is saying, "only far enough away that they couldn't find him. Because things were getting serious in legislation then, and he didn't want the family to become involved."

Norman, the granddaughter of Lewis Latimer and now in her early eighties, is sitting on a couch in her apartment near New York's Penn Station. Mementoes of Latimer's life are everywhere. On a china cab-inet above the entryway sits a group portrait of Latimer among other of the "Edison Pioneers." Above Norman's piano is a portrait that Latimer drew of an Italian youth. Several more of his sketches and paintings grace the living room. "My grandfather," she says, "was a kind of Renaissance man."

Since her retirement as a prominent social worker in 1980, Winifred Latimer Norman has devoted herself to keeping Lewis Latimer's mem-ory alive. "He saved so many things," she says. "In fact, that was what got me started in relation to being sort of the historian for the family. After my grandfather died in 1928, my aunt stayed in his house in Flushing [Queens, New York]. Before she died in 1963, she showed us the papers and documents that he had left behind. Then before the house was sold, I knew there must be some more material in the attic, where my brother and I used to play. It was pretty dirty and cobwebby after thirty years. But I went to the front and found a lot of blueprints from the early days of the electric industry."

Among the rediscovered collection were Latimer's logbook and autobiographical journal, which filled in for his granddaughter the story behind one of her earliest memories: "I knew my grandfather, as an old man of course, through my fourteenth birthday. My father had chosen to buy a house a block away from his house in Flushing to be near him, and my parents decided that both my brother and myself would carry the middle name of 'Latimer.' And I have never forgotten the Decoration Day parade that my grandfather was always so proud to be in. Today we call it Memorial Day, but it was always a holiday for schoolkids. I remember Lewis Latimer standing short and erect, marching down the street with the veterans. This was sometime after the end of World War I. I would tell my friends, 'There is my grandfather. He fought in the Civil War!' "

When the Civil War broke out in 1861, Latimer was only twelve. His mother, struggling to raise four children alone, had been forced to send first Latimer's two older brothers and then Lewis to a Massachusetts "Farm School." It was not a happy experience and, like his father before him, Lewis recalls having "pined for freedom" and running away with his brother William and a white youth. Later describing his experience in a third-person journal, he writes: ". . . they started for Boston 84 miles away, and by walking and stealing rides on the railway, begging and otherwise procuring food they after several days arrived in Boston, much to the surprise of their mother and sister who were keeping house."

Latimer went to work there as an office boy. Then, after his brothers joined the Union forces in the fight against the Confederacy, he lied about his age in order to join them. In mid-September of 1864, at fifteen, Latimer "became a cabin boy on the man of war *Massasoit* and was soon away to the front. He was in a number of engagements on the James River, Virginia." Further research by Winifred Norman found that the USS *Massasoit* was part of the North Atlantic Blockading Squadron that protected Union ships and blocked the way to Confederate vessels. The ship took part in the Battle of Howelett's House and carried crucial messages down to Union general William Tecumseh Sherman in North Carolina. Latimer received his discharge in July 1865, shortly after the Civil War's end.

"People said that the fact he even fought in the Navy was quite unusual in those days," says Latimer's granddaughter. "But then, he did so many unusual things. Later he became the adjutant (secretary) at the Civil War veteran's post in Flushing, Queens. One of the ways that the post's members educated young people about what their role was and why they did it was to present an American flag to the local school, which he did."

With the number of Irish immigrants increasing in Boston after the Civil War, finding work again had proved difficult for Latimer. Eventually he landed a job as office boy with a law firm which specialized in patent applications called Crosby and Gould. His salary was three dollars a week. As Winifred Latimer Norman describes in a 1994 book about her grandfather, *Lewis Latimer: Scientist*: "Every day, Latimer saw the draughtsmen at Crosby and Gould turn the applicants' sketches of their inventions into scientific drawings that could be presented to the U.S. Patent Office in Washington, D.C. He was eager to learn this trade, and he said of himself in his journal, 'He watched to find out what tools were used, then he went to a secondhand book store and got a book on drawing.' "

Saving money from his meager salary to purchase a few drawing tools, Latimer began practicing at night. After some months, he felt confident enough to approach the firm's head draftsman and ask, "May I do some drawings for you?" At first the man laughed, but eventually gave him his chance. Latimer ended up at Crosby and Gould for eleven years, rising to become head draftsman himself at a then-decent salary of twenty dollars a week—and supervising "putting the final touches on working models of inventions" before their submission for patent approval. By 1874, a year after Latimer met and married Mary Wilson of Fall River, Massachusetts, he had received his own first patent—an invention for the "Improvement of Water Closets" on trains.

Latimer was still working his way up at Crosby and Gould when, in 1876, he encountered a fellow one year his senior named Alexander Graham Bell. They were working a block apart from each other and, for two years, Bell had been conducting certain unusual experiments. "The father of Mr. Bell," Latimer writes, "an English subject, had invented a system of 'visible speech' by means of which deaf mutes could talk to each other, and at the time of which I write Alexander Graham Bell was teaching this method in the College of Liberal Arts, located on Beacon Street. Here he had day and night classes and I was obliged to stay at the office until after 9 p.m. when he was free from his night classes, to get my instructions from him as to how I was to make the drawings for the application for a patent upon the telephone."

Bell, who had emigrated to Boston from Scotland, had long been fascinated with sound. His mother was almost deaf, able to hear only by placing a rubber tube against her ear. His father's devising of a picture-image system showed someone how to position his or her mouth to make certain sounds. Now Bell was seeking to create a machine that could convert the human voice into electrical waves, and transmit it just like Morse's telegraph did. The year before he met Latimer, Bell achieved a remarkable breakthrough—coming up with a device that went beyond an electrical pulse, and able to vary in pitch with rising and falling tones.

Beyond Latimer's brief written description, little was known about his relationship with Bell until his granddaughter interviewed a cousin named Frank Holbrook. "Both Frank and his brother James became engineers as a result of my grandfather's inspiration and encouragement," Winifred Norman says. "Frank was very close to my family, especially my aunt. She called him when my grandfather was dying. Frank took the trolley from Brooklyn and got to the house just in time to see him. Frank said that my grandfather told him that he and Bell were young men in Boston together, talking about what they were doing. Bell found out that he had learned all about patent drawings, and Bell didn't have the ability to do that. So my grandfather did all the very original ones. He said it was really a moonlighting job after he finished his work at Crosby and Gould. He would then meet Bell and they would go over what should go into these drawings. He may not only have drafted Bell's plans for the telephone, but helped with the wording of the patent application."

Three days after the Bell-Latimer collaborative application was filed with the U.S. Patent Office, came the immortal words of the first telephone conversation between Bell and his assistant Tom Watson, on February 17, 1876: "Mr. Watson, come here. I want you!"

As far as is known, Bell and Latimer did not remain colleagues after their initial association. But the seeds of Latimer's interest in electricity had been planted. In 1879, Latimer and his wife moved to Bridgeport, Connecticut—a place, he wrote in his journal, "perfectly alive with inventors. It would be next to impossible to throw a stone into any company of men gathered anywhere about in the street without hitting one."

Before long, Latimer found employment as a draftsman at the Follandsbee Machine Shop. One afternoon, a stranger walked in. "I never saw a colored man making drawings," Latimer remembered him saying. "Where did you learn?" The man turned out to be well aware of the reputation of the Boston company Crosby and Gould, where Latimer had risen to head draftsman. He was Sir Hiram Maxim, founder and chief electrician for the new U.S. Electric Lighting Company. And Maxim was looking—as Bell had been—for someone who could make some patent application drawings for him.

Maxim came from a family of renowned inventors, which had developed the first machine guns—known as the Maxim guns—in the U.S. and England. "Within a week from the time we first met," Latimer wrote, "I was installed in Mr. Maxim's office busily following my vocation of mechanical draughtsman, and acquainting myself with every brand of electric incandescent light construction and operation."

One year earlier, a Maxim rival named Thomas Edison had received his first patent for the electric light bulb, which it was hoped would soon supplant candles, gas lamps, and oil lamps in illuminating homes and businesses. It was made of glass, with a carbon wire filament inside fashioned out of paper, bamboo, or thread. An electric current sent through the wire made the filament hot enough to glow. But there was one major problem: the filament lasted no more than a few days, after which it had to be replaced. Edison, Maxim, and others were struggling for a solution. Otherwise, the remarkable new possibility would simply prove too frustrating and expensive for mass production.

In her book about her grandfather, Norman recounts what transpired: "In his typically organized manner, Latimer meticulously studied the problem and tried to make the puzzle pieces fit. He conducted hundreds of experiments with different methods and materials. It was important not only to make the electric light glow longer but also to use materials that would be cheap enough for the average consumer to afford.

"Finally, after days and nights of trial and error, Latimer succeeded in solving the mystery. His method combined previous manufacturing techniques with several new materials that allowed the carbon filaments to last longer and to be made much more inexpensively. Latimer's procedure involved stuffing blanks, or shapes, of such fibrous materials as wood or paper into small cardboard envelopes and then exposing them to extremely high temperatures in an airless environment. . . .

"It was the cardboard envelopes that made Latimer's invention different from existing filaments—and that made it work so well. The envelopes expanded and contracted at the same rate as the wood or paper from which the blanks were made. This prevented the carbons from becoming misshapen or broken, as they had in the method used before Latimer made his discovery.

"Even more important, Latimer's method allowed for the first time the easy—and cheap—production of carbon filaments. At last, average families and businesses could afford to illuminate their homes and workplaces with the brilliance of electricity—and to live by lights that would last."

But while Latimer's improvement paved the way to a new era in artificial lighting, Maxim and his company claimed the credit—and all the profits. Although Latimer discovered a new means of attaching the carbon filaments to a lamp's base, it was Maxim's initial "M" that was displayed in the glowing light. Latimer received a patent for a different type of lamp that needed no filaments at all, which became the base for electric arc lamps. And Latimer was dispatched by Maxim to help build the first electrical plants in the Eastern U.S.

As Latimer wrote in his autobiographical sketch of his first days with the New York factory: "I had qualified myself to take charge of producing the carbons for the lamps, when I was not drawing, and worked through the day helping to make lamps and at night locating them in stores and offices. Electrical measurement had not then been invented and all our work was by guess. Office bell wire was the only kind on the market, and our method of figuring was that it was a good guess that that size wire would carry a certain number of lamps without dangerous heating. A number of mysterious fires about this time were probably the fruit of our ignorance."

After getting the New York factory in working order, Latimer moved on to Philadelphia and Montreal on Maxim's behalf. He seemed tireless; sent by Maxim to oversee a factory that opened in London in 1882, the task was completed three months ahead of schedule. But when Latimer returned home, he found himself out of a job. Nor did Maxim ever mention his name when the entrepreneur penned his own "success story."

Latimer, however, says little in his writings about Maxim's treatment of him, only that upon arrival back in New York, "we found the ranks closed and every place filled." He moved on briefly to a Brooklyn lighting company as draftsman and superintendent. "While Latimer was employed there," his granddaughter writes, "he constructed the Latimer lamp—an example of which has been preserved in the [William] Hammer Historical Collection in New York City. Incredibly, more than 100 years after it was made, the Latimer lamp still works."

After this, Latimer tells us, "the Edison people sent for me and I became one of the faces at 65 Fifth Avenue." Latimer would remain with Thomas Edison's firm, which soon became known as General Electric, for the next thirty years. The Wizard of Menlo Park, as Edison was called, was responsible not only for the first commercially viable incandescent lighting and electrical distribution systems. His nearly 1,100 patents included the phonograph, microphone, motion pictures, and alkaline battery.

There exists little documentation concerning whatever relationship Edison had with Latimer. One indication that survives is a letter in New York's Schomburg Library collection, addressed to Latimer by

Edison's colleague John Randolph on July 29, 1889: "Dear Latimer—
Your letter came to hand a day or so ago and after reading the poem
I handed same to Mr. Edison and he read it over my shoulder and said
it was d--m good."

As historian Bayla Singer notes, "Latimer was not at West Orange
or Menlo Park [the New Jersey locations where Edison spent most of
his time]. He was associated with the Electric Light Company in New
York, both as a draftsman and later what was then called a patent
examiner. He would go investigate whether others were infringing on
Edison's patents. Latimer seems to have been well-respected by his coworkers. He was very competent, personable, and somehow made his
philosophy stick—which was that if the African-American simply
showed what he was worth, then he would fit into mainstream America. And he appears to have been accepted on that basis, as far as he
could have been in those times."

Winifred Norman believes that "there was a close professional relationship. They were actually quite similar in certain ways, if you look
at both of their lives. Edison didn't get much education either. His age
was not too different from my grandfather's, and he died a couple of
years later. Edison certainly had to have admired my grandfather and
to recognize the role that he could play in Edison's life. The fact that
Latimer had worked for Maxim, who was one of Edison's big competitors, made him again most valuable. When it came to deciding who
were the original owners of certain inventions, my grandfather was
one of the best persons to testify. My brother used to say he was one
of the first patent attorneys, because they didn't have them in those
days. He traveled around and got pictures, some of which I have. His
testifying in these cases really helped move Edison along. And, as far
as I can tell, in most of these patent fights, Edison won."

Ironically, among the few patent infringement cases that Edison lost
were two court decisions in favor of a black inventor named Granville
T. Woods. These concerned an electric motor regulator, where Woods
was the first to reduce the size of resistances using a dynamotor and
series of coils and thereby eliminate substantial waste of electricity.
When Edison tried to hire him after losing the suits, Woods turned
him down, although Woods did end up selling General Electric the
rights to several of his patents.

Like Latimer, Woods was a self-taught inventor who crossed over
between the nascent fields of telecommunications and electricity. Born
in Columbus, Ohio, in 1856, he was another overlooked pioneer of
America's Industrial Revolution. At the age of twenty-eight, he created
an electrical telephone transmitter able to send a voice with better
sound and quality over a greater distance. Shortly thereafter, Woods

patented another device that he called "telegraphony," a combined telegraph and telephone that provided the first opportunity to use Morse code and oral communications simultaneously. Woods assigned both innovations to the new American Bell Telephone Company.

Between 1884 and 1907, Woods would patent some thirty-five inventions that proved vital to the development of electrical and mechanical equipment. These were particularly useful in modernizing transportation, making obsolete the old steam-driven trains in favor of electrically-run engines. His railway telegraphy allowed messages to be passed between moving trains, then on to railroad stations and back via static electricity, and thus served to alert engineers to potential hazards ahead. His overhead conducting system for electric railways drew electricity from a power line along the train or trolley paths. His series of electrical conductors running along and parallel to the tracks became known as the "third rail" system, and is still employed in the subways of New York and elsewhere. Another set of inventions in the early 1900s resulted in the automatic air brake, for which Elijah McCoy later came up with his system of lubrication.

Whether Woods's path ever crossed Latimer's is unknown—except in death. Woods died impoverished in 1910, and his unmarked grave in a Queens, New York cemetery was discovered in the mid-1970s by Middleton (Spike) Harris, a retired state parole officer. It was Harris, founder of an organization called Negro History Associates, who also first located Latimer's papers in the possession of the inventor's grandchildren.

Latimer, who had never gone beyond grammar school in formal education, was eventually able to read the works of Alexandre Dumas in the original French. He also played both flute and violin, painted and sketched family members and others, made his own book plates, and wrote one play and prodigious poetry.

"My grandfather had a feeling of mission, I believe," Winifred Norman is saying, "which came originally from his father and also his philosophy of life. It had to do with the brotherhood of man."

She walks over to a dresser and brings forth a photocopy of a handwritten letter dated September 16, 1894. It is addressed to Lewis Latimer by Frederick Douglass, written a few months before Douglass's death. It is the only record that survives of any communication between the inventor and the abolitionist leader who had helped save his father's life. It reads:

"Dear Mr. Latimer:
I give thanks for your excellent letter. It made me proud of you. I was glad to hear of your mother and family. I saw your father for [a]

moment in Boston, last Spring. He seemed in good health then and I am surprised to learn of his condition now. It is fifty two years since I first saw your father and mother in Boston. You can hardly imagine the excitement the attempts to recapture them caused in Boston. It was a new experience for the Abolitionists and they improved it to the full extent of which it was capable. I sincerely thank Dear Mrs. Mathews for bringing me to your attention. I shall be very glad to see you if you should ever visit Washington. I am overwhelmed with correspondence, hence pardon this brief letter—kind regards to your Mother.

Very truly yours—
Frederick Douglass"

Winifred Norman carefully replaces the letter in a folder and says, "We don't know what my grandfather had written to Douglass. And we don't have any documented evidence whether he ever saw his father again before George Latimer died. But I suspect he did; he wasn't that far away." Then Norman brings out another letter, written by Lewis Latimer late in 1895 concerning a "Call for a National Conference of Colored Men." This, she adds, was an example of her grandfather's "quiet activism."

In the letter, Latimer writes that he is "heart and soul in the movement because (1) It is necessary that we should show the people of this country, that we—who have by our martyrdom under the lash; by our heroism on the battle field; by our christian forbearance beneath an overwhelming burden of injustice and by our submission to the laws of our native land, proven ourselves worthy citizens and conscientious patriots—are fully alive to everything which affects the interests of our common country.

"(2) Because, there is no separation in the interests of the Colored American from those of the White American, and it is our duty to show to our country, and to the world, that we are looking to the interest of the people at large, when we protest against the crime and injustice meted out to any class or condition of our citizens. . . ."

Then, in words strikingly reminiscent of Douglass and later James Baldwin, he describes how "our history conclusively proves that the attempt to degrade any portion, class or race of our common people, has always been fraught with more danger to the oppressor than to the oppressed." The National Convention was needed to reveal, "presenting it as our fathers did the question of slavery, with facts and figures, showing, as it can be shown, that where the Colored American is lynched the white American is assassinated. That ignorance and crime go hand in hand with prejudice. That schools and churches multiply where there is neither class or color distinctions in the laws. That class legislation puts a premium upon ignorance and illiteracy, in that it aids a man to think himself superior from the accident of birth, rather than by the achievements of merit and ability."

And, in Latimer's eloquent conclusion: "If our cause be made the common cause, and all our claims and demands be founded on justice and humanity, recognizing that we must wrong no man in winning *our* rights, I have faith to believe that the Nation will respond to our plea for equality before the law, security under the law, and an opportunity, by and through the maintenance of the law to enjoy with our fellow citizens of all races and complexions the blessings guaranteed us under the Constitution, of 'life, liberty and the pursuit of happiness.' "

In the waning years of the nineteenth century, Latimer corresponded regularly with Booker T. Washington and became a close friend of Richard Theodore Greener, an activist who had been the first black American to graduate from Harvard. In 1902, Latimer spearheaded a successful petition drive calling for a black representative on the Brooklyn School Board. Shortly thereafter, he volunteered to teach English and mechanical drawing to immigrants at the Henry Street Settlement House, telling the story of how the abolitionists had helped his father. He became a generous supporter of the White Rose Mission. It assisted young black women who had been lured to the city by false promises of jobs.

The granddaughter moves to another shelf and reaches for a little green book published in 1896. Its 140 pages by L. H. Latimer were part of the Van Nostrand Science Series and sold for fifty cents—"the first book," says Norman, "ever written about Edison's electric lighting." She turns to a page that describes, in clear layman's language, the marvel that opened a new technological age:

"If the electric current can be forced through a substance that is a poor conductor, it will create a degree of heat in that substance, which will be greater or less[er] according to the quality of electricity forced through it. Upon this principle of the heating effect of the electrical current, is based the operation of the incandescent lamp just described. Where copper and platinum wires readily conduct the current, the carbon filament offers a great deal of resistance to its passage, and for this reason becomes very hot, in fact is raised to white heat or incandescence, which gives its name to the lamp. You doubtless wonder why this thread of charcoal is not immediately consumed when in this state, but this is really accounted for when you remember, that without oxygen of the air, there can be no combustion and that every possible trace of air has been removed from the bulb and is so thoroughly sealed up as to prevent admission of the air about it; and yet the lamp does not last forever, for the reason that the action of the current upon the carbon has a tendency to divide up its particles and transfer them from one point to another so that, sooner or later, the filament gives way at some point."

According to Norman's research, it was Edison who urged Latimer to write the book. The year of its publication, Latimer had been named chief draftsman with a Board of Patent Control established by the General Electric and Westinghouse companies, the position in which he remained until the Board was abolished in 1911. At the age of sixty-three, Latimer had moved on to become patent consultant for the Edwin Hammer engineering firm. Failing eyesight forced his retirement in 1924, six years after he was made one of the original members of the Edison Pioneers organization. Following a stroke, he died at the age of eighty on December 11, 1928.

In the realms of education, music, and activism, the Latimer family carried on his legacy. One of Latimer's two daughters, Jeannette, became a concert pianist. "My mother was one of the first graduates from Juilliard when it was called the Institute of Musical Art," Winifred Latimer Norman recounts. "For a short period of time there was an interracial symphony orchestra in Philadelphia and she was their pianist. Later she had teaching studios in Brooklyn and at our home in Flushing. Oh, I remember those wonderful recitals people used to have—Harry Burleigh would come, and Nathaniel Dett. W. E. B. Du Bois was a close friend of the family. For a short period of time, my aunt helped him out with the NAACP publication *The Crisis.*"

Her father, Gerald F. Norman, had come to the U.S. from Jamaica when he was fourteen. Going on to graduate from New York's City College, in 1905 he became the first black to teach in a New York State high school and, over the years, instructed more than 20,000 students. Also an excellent tennis player, Norman proved instrumental in helping to enable Althea Gibson and Arthur Ashe to participate in previously segregated tournaments, through the American Tennis Association.

For many years, what the family knew of Lewis Latimer's remarkable life remained largely unknown to the world. When Middleton (Spike) Harris got in touch with the family and set out to seek verification for Latimer's contributions, he received this response in 1964 from General Electric's editorial operations consultant Neil Reynolds: "Although I have done considerable reading on the history of our industry, his [Latimer's] name is new to me."

Within a few years, however, the efforts of Harris and the family had resulted in a revived acknowledgment of Latimer's achievements.

In 1968, New York's Public School 56 was dedicated in his name; by 1971, a Con Edison exhibit would honor Latimer. In the late 1980s, the two-and-a-half story frame house where he spent his last years was saved from demolition by Latimer's descendants and a citizen's committee in Queens. In announcing plans for its conversion into a museum and educational center, Queens Borough President Claire Schulman said: "While the names of Edison and Bell are known to the everyday school child, Lewis Latimer, like many other people of color, has been denied his rightful place in history."

Now Winifred Latimer Norman is saying: "I remember being in the yard at the fiftieth wedding anniversary of my grandparents. Lewis's wife died three years before he did, and my family said they think he died of a broken heart, which is probably true. In the way of trying to cheer him up, some of his friends and family got together and went over all the poems he had written and made fifty copies of this book. Some of the *Poems of Love and Life* give you an idea of what his thinking was."

The granddaughter opens the handsomely-bound book and begins to read aloud:

> *"Though we gaze on the road behind us,*
> *We may not pause or stay,*
> *But move toward the misty distance*
> *That seems to fade away. . . .*
> *To actively cherish the present,*
> *To love to have and give,*
> *Is that which makes the living,*
> *This is indeed to live."*

FOR FURTHER READING:

McKinley Burt, Jr., *Black Inventors of America* (Portland, Oregon: National Book Co., 1989).

Sidney Kaplan, *American Studies in Black and White: Selected Essays* (essay on Jan Matzeliger) (Amherst: University of Massachussetts Press, 1991).

Kenneth R. Manning, *Black Apollo of Science: The Life of Ernest Everett Just* (New York: Oxford University Press, 1983).

Winifred Latimer Norman and Lily Patterson, *Lewis Latimer: Scientist* (New York and Philadelphia: Chelsea House Publishers, 1994).

The Laser Physicist and the Computer Wizard:
Earl and Alan Shaw

"If you look at the history of automobiles, the first ones made in Germany were essentially rich men's toys. It was not until Henry Ford put together the technology and its potential application that a real impact was made in mass transportation. Well, Earl Shaw is the Henry Ford of Free Electron Laser technology. What Earl has done is bring a light source into existence to provide answers to pretty specific questions relating to the way electrons in semiconductors work, and the way atoms and molecules in biology absorb and give off energy and how they move. There is no equivalent system like it anywhere in the world."

—DR. JOHN MADEY, Director of the
Free Electron Laboratory, Duke University

"Usually, discussions about information technology focus people's attention on how the [computer] networks can give people access to resources and people far away and not those that are nearby. The issue is usually the global village and not the local village. . . . Many of the most devastating problems people face (especially in inner-city communities) have to do with local issues. People are often afraid and alienated from their own neighbors, suffering from crime and abuses that are coming from local sources (sometimes even the kids of a neighborhood are feared). So working on these kinds of issues requires straightforward village-building at the local level, which I believe networks can help with."

—ALAN SHAW, from an abstract of his Ph.D. thesis.

"Sure, we can get together and talk," Earl Shaw was saying over the telephone. "But who you really need to see is my son Alan. He's much more important than me. He really is."

Dr. Earl Shaw, named chairman in 1996 of the physics department at Rutgers University's Newark, New Jersey campus, is a scientist whose breakthroughs in laser technology could someday earn him a Nobel Prize. Dr. Alan Shaw, now in his mid-thirties, is the creator of an unprecedented software system that may revolutionize the way we think about both computers and urban communities. Their impact upon the fields of light and communication, in the tradition of Lewis Latimer, is a story that has much to do with the flowering of their personal relationship.

Bob Birgenau, today the dean of science at MIT, describes another impact made by Earl Shaw. They had worked together at Bell Laboratories and, not long after Birgenau went to MIT as then-head of the physics department, the men had dinner together. "At that time," Birgenau says, "Earl had the view that universities were really the seat of racism in America and asked me how I could possibly take a job at MIT. He said if I was to be there, it was my responsibility to improve the situation for black students. I put a lot of energy into recruitment and development of black graduate students. My last year before I became dean of science, our department graduated half of the black physics Ph.D.s in the United States. That, in some ways, traces back to Earl, what I learned from him and my respect for him."

On a mid-summer morning, Earl Shaw is driving through the streets of Newark, pointing out revitalizations of the downtown area which the city fathers hope will attract more visitors from the outlying suburbs. He is a tall, lanky, good-looking man with close-cropped, slightly graying hair and a little beard and mustache. A set of glasses hangs from a strap around his neck. He is dressed casually in light-colored slacks and a red-and-blue T-shirt adorned with figures from African-American history. "It's a long way," he is saying, "from the cotton fields of Mississippi."

Earl Shaw was born on November 26, 1937, "in my grandparents' house on a plantation near Clarksdale, Mississippi," he begins recalling over lunch at a fashionable Spanish restaurant. "My mom married quite early and I was born on her seventeenth birthday. My dad had been raised by my grandfather, after his mother died at an early age."

Both of Shaw's parents worked as sharecroppers, and were "very spirited people. A couple of years before I was born, my father got in a hassle with the plantation owners and pulled a gun on the boss. Because my grandfather was a minister, they were able to stop the lynch party. My grandfather then turned my father in, and he was sent to the Parchman penitentiary. When he came back, they were afraid to keep him in the house. The story I've heard is that he went to Denver, Colorado, and stayed with relatives for a while. My mom has told me that the last time I saw him was when I was three. At some period he ended up going north to Chicago. That's where he and his brother were both killed in a shoot-out with the police. He was twenty-six."

When Shaw was five, his mother remarried and they moved onto a wealthy plantation called Hopson's, in the Mississippi Delta country. "I don't believe my mom ever finished the eighth grade, but she had me reading newspapers from an early age. I went to school in the plantation chapel. I always loved math, and had a wonderful teacher named Mrs. Reagan who encouraged me. After school I worked in the cotton fields. I wasn't physically strong, but I would concentrate and was always very industrious. So when I was about ten years old, I could earn as much as an adult. The men who had known my father said I looked just like him. He was revered for his spirit of rebellion, and they used to call me by his nickname, Buck.

"I believe Hopson's is where the machine cotton pickers were first utilized," Shaw continues, "which led to the decrease of manual labor on these farms. That, plus the development of the steel mills and the auto industry, precipitated the migration northward."

When his mother and stepfather fled their sharecropper status seeking a better life in Chicago in 1948, for two years Shaw stayed behind in a foster home. The Mississippi schools were segregated, but the achievement testing procedure was standardized. Still only in the sixth grade, Shaw achieved the highest scores of anyone in Coahoma County. When he skipped a grade and repeated his off-the-scales testing in the eighth, family friends and teachers encouraged his mother to bring him north. Shaw moved into a poor neighborhood on Chicago's West Side with his stepfather and mother. Armed with a letter from the plantation principal asking a high school to enroll him, Shaw was tested and accepted at Crane Technical High School. He was only twelve.

It was the early 1950s, the era that spawned the movie *Blackboard Jungle*, and the Blackstone Rangers and other gangs soon came to dominate both Shaw's neighborhood and his vocational high school. "They weren't shooting each other back then, but they were beating each other with chains," Shaw remembers. "I came out of the South with this heavy Mississippi accent, which at first got me in a lot of trouble. But then for some reason, the older guys in the Blackstone Rangers sort of adopted me. I was younger and short, and really I was protected by them. I used to go to a boys' club where a lot of the gangs played basketball. When there was going to be trouble, they would always tell me, 'You'd better go home.' I was not told, 'You are smart and you shouldn't be so smart.' I was told, 'You are smart and you shouldn't stay here.' "

At Crane Tech, Shaw found himself in the woodshop and machine shop and doing two years of mechanical drawing—"which, in the long run, served me very well, because I ended up being an experimentalist."

His interest in science also "just happened in high school, where I had some very good physics and chemistry teachers; before that, I really hadn't paid these subjects much attention." He was sixteen when he graduated in 1954, "quite young and socially immature." It was only the continual urging of a friend in his homeroom that moved him on to higher education. "If it hadn't been for that white kid," Shaw says, "I might not have gone to college."

Standing in line to register for his freshman classes at a Chicago branch of the University of Illinois, Shaw overheard two other students complaining that engineering physics was the school's most difficult major. When the registrar asked Shaw to declare his probable specialty, he answered "engineering physics" without hesitation. "I had never even heard the phrase until the minute before. But somehow, I was sure I could do it."

The ensuing undergraduate years were not easy ones for Shaw. When he moved downstate in 1957 to the main university campus at Champaign-Urbana, there were only about seventy black students enrolled on a vast campus. His professors offered him little encouragement, and he almost dropped out. "I remember looking at my record of files, which said 'This student should be discouraged from studying physics.' I ended up with a bachelor's degree not knowing what to do."

Deciding to get married as he approached graduation and his twenty-third birthday in 1960, Shaw ended up heading back to Chicago with a pregnant wife and "desperate to find a job." He was offered work as an engineer with Western Electric but, longing to get out of the city, wound up moving to Hanover, New Hampshire as a lab techician for the U.S. Army Corps of Engineers. There, Shaw decided to enroll in a math class at Dartmouth College on the side. A professor noticed his talent, resulting in a physics scholarship. Shaw returned to school full-time in 1962.

The Shaws already had twin boys when Alan was born in Hanover on January 23, 1963. But after Earl received his Master's degree and moved west with his family to pursue a Ph.D. in physics at the University of California in Berkeley, as Alan puts it, "the pressure of the student life and everything didn't work out for the marriage. My parents broke up when I was three, and my brothers and I went to live with our mother."

These were the height of the student protest years, and Earl Shaw soon found himself swept up in the movement. "I went from being a fairly conservative person to quite embittered at one point," he says. "I became president of the Black Students' Union at Berkeley and very active politically, so active that I was sort of a marked man. I knew some of the Black Panthers well—Huey Newton and his brother, and Bobby Seale—and Ron Dellums, who's now a congressman."

After Shaw's arrest in the midst of his involvement in campus turmoil—for an unpaid parking ticket—made headlines, he considered leaving the country and going to teach in Africa. "I really went into physics rebelliously," Shaw continues. "Even though I was doing well at it, I thought there must be something wrong with it. So I used to spend a lot of time in the library at Berkeley, reading papers by these old guys, particularly in thermodynamics. I wanted to see what they were thinking that allowed them to formulate things—because I figured there must be another way to do it. I ended up deciding that the fact the ideas were successful was enough. What was important was to proceed."

By the spring of 1969, when Shaw received his doctoral degree from Berkeley, he had remarried to a campus activist who worked as a counselor for students seeking to avoid being drafted into the Vietnam War. Alan Portis, his thesis adviser, aided him in connecting up with AT&T's Bell Laboratories. One of the most prestigious research institutions in the world, the Morristown, New Jersey company had never before hired an African-American research physicist.

MIT's Bob Birgenau recalls: "One of Earl's earliest experiences was walking down the hallway wearing hip clothes, and someone asked him to change the lightbulbs. He was correctly outraged. On the other hand, he was a pioneer. When you're the first person in a new role, there's a price."

The experimental group that Shaw joined in 1969 was headed by Kumar Patel, whose inventions included the carbon dioxide laser. The word laser is an acronym for Light Amplified by Stimulated Electromagnetic Radiation. Shaw offers a basic laser-related physics lesson, as he drives out of downtown Newark and toward his new lab on the Rutgers University campus.

"In nature, energy is stored in molecules and atoms. By shining a light through these, you can tell the energy levels by the color of light that is emitted or absorbed. Electrons, or subatomic charged particles, transfer between very discrete orbits, emitting or absorbing light of very distinct colors. Also in nature, light exists for a very broad range of colors, much of which is invisible to the human eye. At one end of the electromagnetic spectrum—what we physicists call light—are FM radio waves and microwaves. At the other end are X-rays and gamma rays, and in the middle range is the light we see. Both the shortest wavelengths, from ultraviolet to gamma rays, and the longest wavelengths, from infrared to radio waves, are not visible to us.

"Uncovering the mystery of how atoms absorb and emit light is really an extension of radar research in World War II. And it's led to breakthroughs in lasers, X-ray and microwave sources, and many other kinds of radiation sources. Einstein knew the physics of lasers in about 1905, but it took until 1960 to demonstrate one. Basically, laser devices filter and amplify a visible light beam by stimulating high-energy atoms. Today laser technology not only plays a role in human research, but it gives scientists laser sources for spectroscopic studies that couldn't happen with light-bulb sources."

Shaw continues: "I knew the field was underdeveloped, so I'd begun building equipment and looking for new ideas when I was at Berkeley." He found himself "at the right place at the right time" in coming to Bell. The carbon dioxide laser was then the most efficient such light amplifier in existence. It emitted the kind of infrared light that radiates from fireplaces, but its fixed wavelength had limited use. Shaw participated in an experiment to steer the light with mirrors to a synthetic crystal, which was kept in a thermos chilled to below-250 degrees centigrade. At certain power levels of the $CO2$ laser, the crystal then sent forth a light beam at a longer wavelength, which could be adjusted precisely with a magnetic field. This light-tuning system became known as the spin-flip Raman laser, and Shaw was credited as its co-inventor.

"It was the first demonstration that you could broadly change the color of one laser," he says. "So from that perspective, it had historical importance. It was a prototype and a group in Scotland at the University of Edinburgh tried to commercialize it. But it just didn't have the purity of light that you needed for spectroscopy. So it was more important in the physics culture than of any practical use."

Despite his early success, Shaw was not happy at Bell Laboratories. "I really hated it. When I first got there, Bell had an ABM [Anti-Ballistic-Missile] program. Many of the scientists around me were very opposed to this, and we ran an antiwar ad in the *New York Times*. Upper management at the time seemed afraid of bringing minorities inside. It was like, 'Earl, you're alright, but you know. . . .' So I thought I could make a better contribution at a university."

Shaw left Bell Laboratories and taught at the University of Rochester for three years, an environment where he felt he could work without compromising his beliefs. Then, in 1974, Bell beseeched him to come back, this time in a capacity beyond his laser research work. The company wanted him to recruit other minority scientists. Shaw's discoveries came to include such currently well-known physicists as Drs.

Shirley Jackson, Roosevelt Peoples, Kenneth Evans and Walter P. Lowe.

"It became a very exciting time," MIT's Birgenau remembers. "All these very bright, aggressive young people who came out of the '60s, suddenly finding themselves at a conservative institution in suburban New Jersey. What you would call consciousness-raising took place within AT&T."

As Walter Lowe has said of Shaw: "I could not imagine such a thing as a black scientific community evolving the way it has without him. When you talk of genius, generally you talk of someone who's aloof or vague or someone you can't get close to. Earl's not like that. We can walk down the hall and he'll introduce me to the president of the company, and then introduce me to the lady who cleans the floors, and have the same rapport with both."

Back inside the Bell lab, Shaw renewed his efforts on increasing the range of colors at which lasers emit. Until 1978, he notes, physicists had to depend upon the energy emitted by atoms as their only mechanism to determine the color of laser light. "If the atoms didn't want to cooperate, there was nothing you could do," Shaw says. Then a group of professors at Stanford University devised a means of taking electrons and, instead of letting them move back and forth in atoms, they began using a special magnet called an undulator to either speed up or slow down the electrons. The resulting light energy could be generated at ranges of ultraviolet (blue) or infrared (red) wavelengths or any colors desired. This was the first Free Electron Laser, and it promised new vistas for the scientific future. "It allowed scientists," Shaw adds, "to determine what color of light they want and then design an experiment to get it."

But the physicists' ability to study the far-infrared range of light still did not exist. Large molecules such as proteins and solids vibrate at frequencies in the far-infrared. Scientists wanted to study the process that controls these large molecular structures with the same precision that they were able to study atoms, which in theory are governed by rules of energy transfer described by quantum mechanics.

"Well, if you want to study anything, you want to be able to change it," Shaw is saying, as we approach the Rutgers campus. What he did was to take the Free Electron Laser technology developed in 1978, and push it further—stimulating electrons freed from their atomic orbits to generate a beam of invisible light in the far-infrared range. No Free Electron Laser had previously penetrated that end of the electromagnetic spectrum. In a 1983 book that described Shaw's laser work at Bell, Ivan Sertima wrote: "If he succeeds it is likely to have as much significance for scientific studies of solid materials as any laser yet invented." It took Shaw ten years of research at Bell Labs to come up with his new application, which he sees as requiring further development once it is fully operational at Rutgers.

The uniqueness of Shaw's one-of-a-kind machine is an ability to be "tuned" to different frequencies of the electromagnetic spectrum. "My laser," he says, "allows me to tune the wavelength by turning a knob." The difference between Shaw's and other such devices is the range. "If your radio could only work at three places, you could only hear three stations," as fellow physicist Walter Lowe puts it. "With Earl's, you could look at areas of the spectrum where you never could before."

Thus, for the first time, scientists can now "see" into the far-infrared range, where much molecular activity takes place. Shaw's Free Electron Laser provides the perfect tool to study this arena. "It's almost as if nature has chosen this application," he says. The opportunities it opens cross many disciplines. It can be utilized to study biological functions, chemical reactions, and the electronic properties of semiconductors that could prove crucial to the future development of electronic components.

We are winding down a long series of corridors in the sub-basement of Smith Hall on the Rutgers campus, heading for the inner chambers of Shaw's Free Electron Laser Laboratory. After Shaw accepted an offer to teach and conduct research at the university in 1991, Bell Laboratories agreed to donate the $1.4 million laser to accompany him. Since the court-ordered divestiture of AT&T in 1984, the company had been reorganizing and decided that the Free Electron Laser was no longer in line with its future research direction.

"What happened, unfortunately," Shaw is saying, "is that for political reasons the Free Electron Laser was represented as being capable of shooting down missiles. So a lot of money, hundreds of millions in fact, got spent on this at places like Los Alamos. When those projects failed, and the extent to which they were unrealistic to start off with became obvious, it gave the whole field a bad name. It was part of the Reagan strategy for breaking the Russians. It broke everybody, right? Including almost the whole Free Electron Laser community. It's currently a difficult technology because of the expensive equipment involved. There are probably five to ten Free Electron Laser programs in the world—and we have one of them.

"Mine is a poor man's version," Shaw continues. "But do I want a breakthrough in a different area? Well, I'm certainly looking for it. I want to shoot the works! What I want to do is study molecular and biological systems with this. What I'm really interested in is looking at human DNA."

It had taken Shaw almost three years to reassemble his ten-ton, fifty-foot-long machine beneath the Rutgers campus. First workers dug a hole two stories deep, making a seventy-foot-long trench that was lined with three-foot-thick concrete walls to absorb any radiation emitted from the device. Although the infrared light beam is itself harmless, the microtron accelerator that accelerates the electrons up to the speed of light creates radioactive byproducts in the process. (The microtron's effect is similar to that of a linear accelerator, one of whose many uses is in the treatment of cancer.)

Everything was dropped in by hand, using a motorized forklift. After the installation was completed, the area above was covered with soil and replanted with grass. At the end of what is basically an underground tunnel buried under ten feet of earth, Shaw's work area is a concrete cavern behind two padlocked doors. "Let me turn the lights on here," he says, pointing to an outer room that he calls "my little machine shop." With its scattered wires, the space looks not unlike a home handyman's garage. "I got tennis elbow from tightening things," Shaw adds. "What I've been doing these past couple years is putting in infrastructure. All of this used to be space to store monkey cages. There was water all over the floor. That transformer over there, most of this equipment, came from Bell." Behind a second locked door is the Free Electron Laser and its long metal accelerator that determines the speed of the high-energy electrons.

Walking back toward his upstairs office after the tour, Shaw goes on: "It's hard to describe exactly how difficult it is to change the color of lasers. For example, industry has tried very hard to build a blue laser—just like they have red lasers in use now at check-out counters. A blue laser would allow, for instance, the storage of more information on a smaller space on a compact disc—so you could either have a smaller CD, or more tunes, or whatever. So billions of dollars have been spent trying to develop blue lasers, and we still don't have a commercial one yet. IBM and all the big companies are trying, but they're probably still two to five years away."

Shaw himself is far more interested in seeing his laser used to study the functions of the hemoglobin molecule, or the double helix structure of DNA. When he arrived at Newark, the physics department already had researchers working with lasers in the visible light and ultraviolet ranges, including the use of laser-based instrumentation for diagnosing diseases. "The addition of Earl Shaw and his far-infrared laser," then-department chair Daniel Murnick said at the time, "gives us a national presence in applied laser science."

Since the human body is driven by biological molecular systems, understanding how these systems work requires the ability to break down the structures to their most basic elements. "I wouldn't be doing that," says Shaw, "but I would be the guy who creates the tools for doing it. I mean, how *does* the double-helix structure of DNA wind and unwind? What we're hoping for is that this laser will prove to be capable of providing measurements closer to the time frame of ten quadrillionths of a second, which is the time scale at which a great deal of atomic and molecular phenomena occur." Ultimately, Shaw hopes to show that biochemical processes could be controlled by using free electron laser light, thus opening new inroads in pharmaceutical research and other areas.

For several years after his arrival at Rutgers, Shaw was basically alone with his research. Now he has a new assistant, Dr. Hubert Burke, along with one graduate and several undergraduate students working with him. Appointed to head the Newark campus's physics department in the summer of 1996, Shaw also teaches courses in electricity and magnetism. Beyond his lab, his biggest goal is to bring more African-American students into the sciences—paralleling his successful effort at Bell Laboratories.

According to the American Institute of Physics, of the approximately 33,000 Ph.D. physicists in the United States, fewer than 400—a little more than one percent—are black. As Anthony Johnson, chairman of the American Physical Society's Committee on Minorities, has said: "There's very little encouragement, from elementary school on, for blacks to pursue the hard sciences. The stereotypes begin very early where minorities should go."

Those stereotypes, Shaw found, applied to the university which had hired him. In 1994, Rutgers president Francis Lawrence made what Shaw calls "an infamous statement about blacks' genetic heritage"— linking low test scores to heredity, in an echo of *The Bell Curve*. Shaw was one of three professors who compiled the Newark campus's outraged response. "I was worried this would hurt our recruitment of minority students," he said at the time. "The sciences are a very social field. There's no genius sitting in a room with a textbook. You need collaboration. There's no question that the isolation of any outside group in the sciences, including blacks, is an impediment."

Shaw moved quickly to do all that he could to change the equation. The initial campus reaction to the president's remarks was eventually formalized and taken to Rutgers's Board of Trustees. "Mr. Lawrence has since represented the comments he made as being totally out of character," says Shaw, "and in fact he really rallied to the response of people like myself, by getting the Board to move some resources. The result has been up to fifty more minority scholarships, probably an increase by at least a factor of two."

In 1994, Shaw also arranged for the campus to host the annual conference of the National Society of Black Physicists. Predominantly held in the South, the gathering brought together about 150 black professionals in the fields of natural science, high energy, and laser physics. Above all, Shaw wanted to get the word out that, as an urban center, Rutgers-Newark offers a solid education and viable career opportunities for the future.

Shaw was a member of the planning committee for a sixty-five-million-dollar, hands-on Liberty Science Center that has opened in Jersey City, again aimed at showing inner-city young people the wonders of the field. He also served as program leader for a campus science fair for high school students from across New Jersey. Now, with another physicist, he has plans for an interactive videoconference system that would hook grammar school and high school age students into his Rutgers department.

"We'd like to move it around monthly to attract as many students to the sciences as we possibly can," says Shaw. "Science has done so much for me. It's the social and economic vehicle that sprang me out of nothing. If I could have four or five black Ph.D. students to my credit by the end of my career, I would consider that a helluvan accomplishment. It would be as good as winning the Nobel Prize."

As a young teenager, Alan Shaw remembers going to visit his father when Earl took his first hiatus from Bell Laboratories and was teaching in Rochester, New York. "The students were just camping out at his house, they adored him. I was moved by the friendliness of my father, though he was also very intense, both about his work and his playtime. I would always visit him for a week in the summertimes. But I didn't really get a chance to learn where he stood on things, who he was personally, until I came East to go to college and began spending whole summers with him."

We are sitting in Alan Shaw's study in Dorchester, a suburb of Boston, surrounded by a large desk-top computer and considerable software. He is a lean, bespectacled, very studious-looking fellow with close-cropped hair, and it is easy to imagine him in the Media Technologies lab at MIT where he received his doctoral degree in 1995. But when Alan Shaw talks about where he's come from, and where he wants to go, the passion very much echoes the high-spiritedness that permeates his family's traditions.

"There's an old African proverb that says, 'It takes a village to raise a child,' " Shaw is saying. "And there has always been a social network of some sort to be the infrastructure for a village. However, we don't have that now. People move in and out of communities, and don't really believe in their value anymore. So we can't just focus on the global village with our technology. Computers in general are very good at keeping track of information and resources, keeping things flowing back and forth. But why does this technology always have to address the outside world? I want to see it internalize, see if we can take some ownership over what we *do* with the technology."

That is the basic philosophy behind the computer networking software that Alan Shaw has pioneered. It's called MUSIC, which stands for Multi-User Sessions in Community. It is being used to empower people in low-income communities, by providing them a new means of talking to each other. Starting in his own Dorchester neighborhood, Shaw's unique database system has since spread to Newark, Harlem, Brooklyn, and Cincinnati. And its expansion is very much tied to the relationship Alan Shaw has discovered with his scientist father.

After his parents' marriage broke up when he was small, Alan and his two older brothers were raised in Berkeley by their mother Harriet. It was she, Alan remembers, who "really pushed for education; my mother went on to get her Ph.D. in psychology." She also emphasized what Alan calls "a search for roots and identity." He studied Swahili and African dance in high school and, when his mother entered a short-lived second marriage, Alan was given an African name at the wedding ceremony. It was Abudu Watu, and it means "Here to Serve His People." All three of Shaw's young children also have African names—Yesuto, Chinua and Obasi.

Like his father, Alan loved math and science. Also like his father, he was very politically oriented. "Growing up in Berkeley, I was involved in high school in a lot of political movements, like being elected student council representative to the city's Board of Education. When I had a chance to take some computer courses at the university during my senior year, I protested the [military] draft recruitment that was going on there, and fought against funding cutbacks in the African-American Studies Department. We even took over the superintendent's office for a couple of days. Some people thought I was headed for politics, because I always loved to talk about community issues. But there was this tension because, with my father as a role model even though we didn't live together, I always considered myself more of a science person or mathematician or engineer."

Shaw's fascination with computers had begun with classes in the eighth grade, in the pre-PC era when first punch cards were used and later Basic and Pascal were the primary computer languages. As he approached graduation from Berkeley High in 1981, his father urged him to apply for the Bell Labs Engineering Scholarship Program that the company had established for women and minorities. Shaw ended up with a scholarship to Harvard, working in the summers at Bell.

"That's when I really lived with my father for the first time. At the time, I was rebelling from a lot of things that had been occurring in my family. Basically my brothers and my mother and I had grown apart, all living in different locations. So while my dad was sort of this outsider to the inner circle of my family, he was able to be there for me at a time when I wasn't really looking for anybody inside the family. He was also able to talk to me about what had happened between him and my mother, stuff I really needed to know. When they married young in 1960, he explained it was hard for a family focus to take priority in people's lives. All these social changes were going on. Everything was up for grabs, everything was a question mark. He told me they really didn't have the ability to resolve the issues among two strong-willed people on a road to self-discovery."

At Harvard, where Alan worked toward his bachelor's degree in applied mathematics, he became a committed Christian. The pentecostal Azusa Christian Church to which he first belonged placed strong emphasis not only on building community but, Shaw says, "on bringing black intellectuals back *into* the community. After the '60s, there was this big integration myth that black people should move out of the areas they were confined to. But this ended up meaning that those who could leave tended to be the more affluent and educated. So then the inner city becomes filled with people with little hope. My group was saying, move back in."

After getting his Master's in Computer Science from MIT in 1988, Shaw rented a house in a black neighborhood of Dorchester and began working with local youth. With continuing financial aid from Bell Laboratories, he also remained at MIT in pursuit of a Ph.D. in Media Technologies. There Shaw worked in the Media Lab, "a mix of computers and different kinds of video technologies," as part of a group studying means of developing new educational technologies for schools. The underlying philosophy of the "Learning and Epistomology" researchers was called constructionism. "The idea," says Shaw, "is that learning is not passive, that intellectual models are built by kids rather than given to them. In their external world, there are tools and materials that they can use to 'build constructions.' Then they can reinternalize their creations, beginning a cycle where they don't just stop after learning something."

Shaw told the Media Lab group that he wanted to move out of the classroom and "into the world outside where kids are being affected." His first project in Dorchester was helping young people shoot and edit a rap video, which was aired on a local cable TV station. "But it didn't really alter their lives. One of them got caught up in a gang war. Another ended up in jail after his brother was killed. It was tragic, and eye-opening for me. So I started looking for something that would make more lasting changes."

Shaw next tried forging informal apprenticeships between adults with skills and the local teenagers, including their learning how to bake, repair appliances, or videotape special events. "I was hoping for creating a whole other job market, kind of like a village economy," Shaw says. "But it just couldn't happen. You couldn't do enough through an informal network like this, because a steady stream of work just didn't exist in the neighborhood. There was very little economic activity in my area, and no library or YMCA. In the old villages, you had the town hall, where people could come together and talk about issues. But people no longer had these kinds of shared spaces."

So, in the end, Shaw's doctoral thesis project on social construction-ism turned toward creating a low-budget computer bulletin board system for his Dorchester neighborhood. In 1990, after a long courtship, Alan married a beautiful Harvard Law School graduate, Michelle Barnett. Leaving behind a high-paying job at a corporate law firm, she set up a neighborhood legal-aid office and also began helping Alan with his own efforts. With assistance from their church and a small foundation grant, in 1993 Shaw was able to place twelve Apple computers in people's homes.

"The idea was that someone, when they log on, sees some buildings. There's actually a visual presentation of a street. Each of the buildings represents a project that people are working on." Four local kids used the system to start a collective food stand. But the initial impetus for Shaw's first MUSIC program faded because of internal dissension in the Azusa church. When he and his wife left to join the Bethel A.M.E. congregation, the church held onto the rights to the computers.

That is where Shaw's innovative attempt might have stopped, except for a sudden fortuitous connection through his father. In 1993 at Rutgers, Earl Shaw hired a future physics graduate named Talib Morgan as his first research assistant in the Free Electron Laboratory. "I had sent my thesis proposal to my father," Alan remembers, "who showed it to Talib, and he then asked if he could take it to his mother." Pamela Morgan happened to be the computer project coordinator for the Newark Board of Education; she invited Alan to visit that November and provide a demonstration of his software. "A lot of people were interested in the idea, but she was *more* than interested. She went and wrote grant proposals to get it all going."

As Alan Shaw has written in describing the backbone of his unique networking system: "The nature of the MUSIC program is essentially that of a Graphical MUD, or 'Multi-User Dungeon.' MUDs are programs that accept network connections from multiple simultaneous users and provide access to a shared database of 'rooms,' 'exits,' and other objects. Users browse and manipulate the database from 'inside' the rooms, seeing only those objects that are in the same room and moving between rooms mostly via the exits that connect them. MUDs are thus a kind of social virtual reality, an electronically represented 'place' that users can visit. MUDs are extendable from within—MUD users can add new rooms and other objects to the database and give those objects unique virtual behavior, using an embedded programming language."

While MUDs have been around for about ten years, recently becoming prominent on the Internet, they have been used almost exclusively for recreational purposes. In Shaw's MUSIC system, "users are able to use the MUD environment to work together and provide infrastructure to their neighborhood or community organization. . . . The system is designed with a graphical user interface that has been modeled after a neighborhood with streets and buildings. The buildings represent the programs that are being organized on the system."

So it was not an on-line "Superhighway," but a kind of "information commons" that captured Pamela Morgan's attention. In the spring of 1994, she applied for a grant to enable installation of Shaw's community computer network, obtained from the Department of Commerce's Telecommunications Information Infrastructure Assistance Program. Two consecutive years of funding—a total of $206,000— brought Shaw's system booming into Newark's Central Ward. Today there are more than seventy computers in numerous homes, as well as social service offices, the public library, a local school and area church, Morgan's Board of Education office, and the New Jersey University of Medicine and Dentistry.

"If MUSIC can work in Newark, then it can work anywhere in America," Shaw feels. Indeed, for some years the city has been considered one of the nation's prime examples of an urban nightmare. Founded in 1666, Newark is America's third oldest city; but its population has fallen by almost half since peaking at 500,000 just before the Great Depression. First came more than 600 factories closing their doors, then a migration of the white middle class for the suburbs that began after World War II. In a six-year period during the 1960s, Newark went from being 65% white to 52% black and 10% Hispanic— with many of the remaining residents confined to dilapidated dwellings. The Newark riots of the summer of '67—five days of chaos that saw twenty-three people killed, damage at over ten million dollars, and the National Guard patroling the streets of the Central Ward—seemed to seal its fate. Not long after that, much of the Central Ward's housing was destroyed, primarily through arson. The rumor was, most of the fires were being set by landlords looking to take the insurance money and run.

"Every week, there was a fire," Pamela Morgan remembers. "Every week. Kids would come in and tell me stories of how they would wake up and see their ceilings burning, falling on them while they had to scramble out." A non-profit New Community Corporation was formed in the 1970s in an effort to salvage the area. Today it owns and operates some 2,500 public housing units in Newark, one third of these in low-rise buildings that encompass the Newton Street School. Right across the street is the medical and dental college, built during the '60s on 150 demolished acres. And it is these three entities, within a fifteen-block sector of the Central Ward, that became the backbone of Alan Shaw's "Making Healthy MUSIC/Linking Up Villages" prototype.

In January 1995, after children came home from the elementary school with notes seeking parental involvement, the selection of families (known as "captains") commenced to take part in MUSIC. The criteria were that they must live in New Community Housing, have a child attending the Newton school, and agree to allow at least four people from outside their immediate families access to the computer. At a weekend-long training "retreat" held at the campus across the way, Morgan recalls: "They developed a real cohesiveness. And they started caring about one another. The contract they decided upon had things that each family has to do. One is to log on daily and let the other members know they're okay.

"Approximately eighty percent of our participants had never previously used a computer," she continues. "So we ran a series of training classes for families, where parents and children worked together to learn the computer and Alan's software. Theorists have said it doesn't make sense to give poor African-Americans access to telecommunications, because what would they do once they get on-line? Well, we're dispatching that myth."

Alan Shaw sits down at his Macintosh keyboard to demonstrate the system, dialing into Newark's Central Ward through his phone modem. The backdrop that appears on his screen is a painting of Haiti, downloaded from the Worldwide Web. "This is the mailbox and these are the various community projects that are ongoing," Shaw says, pointing to the screen where a number of colored images are projected at the click of his computer mouse. "You can scroll down a street, where the neighbors or four different institutions are running projects.

To get in and see what's going on, you just click on the appropriate building. Now here's the Newton Street School that initiated everything. We can actually load on the principal's picture in his office."

A man's face appears on the screen at another click. "Everybody in the system has their own password and an icon that they choose for themselves," Shaw continues, his excitement building. "You can edit the icon to try to make it look more like you. There are 140 pictures on-line here, and basically four people can talk to each other at the same time through the four phone lines. Now inside this room, if you've got some information you want to give to the principal, you can send that. Or the principal can put information in his 'room,' or on the bulletin board."

The bulletin board is used to advance ideas or information. There are chat rooms and E-mail. People can communicate through text, graphics, or sound. Now Shaw moves to an image of a doctor's building where six physicians from the University of Medicine and Dentistry regularly field questions from local residents. Here a number of rooms are available for entry, bearing names such as "Ask the Doctor," "Pharmacology," "Family Medicine," and "Asthma/Allergy." Today's questions from network participants include: "What's the difference between a kidney stone and a gall bladder stone? . . . What's the first thing I should do in the case of insulin shock? . . . Which drugstore has the lowest price for Tylenol?" Within a day, simple answers to the queries will be sent back. The medical school also provides a directory of clinics, listing their hours and phone numbers. And people can make appointments through the system.

As Pamela Morgan says: "You name it, we have it—high rates of AIDS, tuberculosis, ambulatory care—cases that if treated when the ailment first appeared often would not have required hospital care." But, Morgan has written, "The participation of physicians, which is not meant to provide curative support, provides educational and preventative information for the participants. The desired effect is to improve the relationship between community residents and medical personnel so the residents will develop healthful lifestyles, and seek medical help in times of illness, rather than using the emergency room as the source of primary care."

The linkage has also brought a tremendous increase in parental involvement at the Newton Street School. According to its principal Willie Thomas, "Four parents elected to offices on the PTA this year have MUSIC computers in their home. Before the program, I had never seen any of these people. We've become like a big family really. One time, a group of parents reached out to another parent of a disruptive student, and brought a public apology."

Initially, Shaw's project faced potential big trouble from drug dealers operating out of the New Community Housing project. Assuming that it would be used to report on their activities, they began intimidating parents helping to set up the computer system. That is when Willie Thomas, who has been principal at Newton for more than twenty years and had known many of the drug dealers as kids, took to the streets for a personal confrontation. "I told them," he has said, "that this project was for the education of the children and had nothing to do with them. And they backed off."

The only hook-ups between Shaw's networkers and the police have centered around neighborhood Crime Watch and Security Watch programs. The MUSIC system was also used by residents to organize a meeting with the police, to talk about the unsolved murder of a twenty-two-year-old housing project resident. Shaw tells a poignant story about what happened after another slaying, of a sixteen-year-old girl.

"The New Community organization has a parade once a year. They budget money for it, and have people working on it a month in advance. As it happened, the parade was scheduled on the same day as this sixteen-year-old girl's funeral. So two days beforehand, one of the teenagers—who had been a friend of hers—posted a note on the network bulletin board. She said something like, 'I can't believe you are having this parade on the day of the funeral. Are we going to see people celebrating when we come back from it?' A couple of bulletins later came another note: the parade had been cancelled. They probably would never have heard directly from this girl, because she's not going to go knocking on doors saying, 'I don't want your parade.' But enough people in the community read the bulletin board to see what was going on. It was clear that a lot of them were concerned. In fact, for a week or two after, people were writing messages saying that they were really saddened by this situation, that they didn't know the girl who posted the message personally but they wanted her to know that they cared."

By the end of its first year of operation, the Newark network had already seen over 7,300 log-ons and more than 21,400 pieces of E-mail. MUSIC discussion groups have been organized around parenting, AIDS, women's and men's issues (Circle of Sisters and Circle of Brothers). A program called Rights of Passage offers activities for guiding young people into adulthood. Spawned by the network were a community garden and talent show, potluck dinners and bake sales, a waste recycling project, a Thanksgiving drive to feed Newark's homeless, even a collective birthday party for neighbors born in the same summer months. People log on to find out information about voter registration, or how to get high school equivalency diplomas (GEDs).

Field trips to the Newark airport and Atlantic City have been organized. A photography exhibit created by the Newton Street students has been published on the World Wide Web. There are rooms known as Poetry, Hip Hop and Kids Corner, where young users compete to see who can give the right answers to quizzes in math and history. Interactive learning has become the flip side of television.

"This is uniting a fragmented community, and providing hope for children and adults," Pamela Morgan says. "At our last retreat in September [1996], local participants requested the Mental Health Association to facilitate the gathering. In most communities, people are reluctant to admit they need help from mental health professionals, but here many have become secure enough to feel comfortable about requesting this. The Association now has its own 'room' in the system, and parents have put their children in counseling sessions. It's almost overwhelming to see the difference. One of our captains feels this was the motivational force for getting her off the welfare rolls and into productivity. People that nobody ever thought would do anything, who were basically written off, have become major influences in our community."

Alan Shaw's personal model came from Bob Moses, a community organizer in Mississippi during the civil rights days of the '60s. Shaw and his wife began working as volunteers ten years ago with Moses' Algebra Project, a pioneering effort headquartered in Cambridge, Massachusetts, which is organizing a new, experientially-based system of learning math in a number of school districts around the country.

"Bob Moses taught me the difference between a spokesman and an organizer," Shaw says. "Spokesmen are the ones acknowledged by the outside world as 'leaders,' and are often thought of as being more critical than the people who actually do the day-to-day work. But as Bob says, the college students who went to Mississippi in the '60s didn't go to promote themselves and be the leadership, but to be facilitators. So that hopefully you build up leadership with the people who have to live there, for real."

Alan Shaw has begun building his community software into Algebra Projects in Baltimore, San Francisco, and Jackson, Mississippi. At the same time, Shaw is expanding his MUSIC base into Cincinnati, in conjunction with the city's Urban League; Harlem, in tandem with a community center; and San Francisco, through the Greenlining Institute. He has begun to travel widely, running a recent workshop at a Washington conference on the new telecommunications bill. Through an Internet company he has formed called Imani Information Systems, he is also looking for ways that a for-profit corporation might help out a non-profit one.

"If we can make this model part of the economic world, and there is a profit to be made somewhere, I don't see any limits," Shaw says. "I like the idea that neighbors get the system for free, the commercial and civic districts pay for it, and then possibly they get neighbors to buy into their services. Because we're talking about doing this in backyards all over the country. I think if communities are strong, they can take on any challenge."

Shaw leans back in his chair and continues: "That's why my father wants to emphasize the work I'm doing. His dream is to apply technology to the social conditions of black people. He would have loved to do that with physics, but it's just a different overall endeavor."

As the modem rings from Newark into Dorchester, Alan Shaw concludes with this observation about fathers and sons: "I think for any young kid who didn't have a father figure when they were growing up, it's important not to leave childhood feeling negatively about it. The only way to overcome this is not to get into the cycle of being rigid and unforgiving. If you can't forgive your parents, then when you see the same things in yourself, you have to deny they're there. You then do everything you can not to address the problem. When you encounter problems in your own life, you need to be able to forgive yourself too.

"So I'm blessed really. My father and I have built a wonderful relationship, we're like best friends. I would probably have stayed with politics, had I not had a physicist for a father. Now, when there are doubts about whether what I'm dreaming of is possible to accomplish, he's always there with me. I couldn't ask for more than that."

FOR FURTHER READING:

James Michael Brodie, *Created Equal: The Lives and Ideas of Black American Innovators* (New York: William Morrow & Co., 1993).

Hattie Carewell, *Blacks in Science: Astrophysicist to Zoologist* (Hicksville, New York: Exposition Press, 1977).

Ivan van Sertima, *Blacks in Science: Ancient and Modern* (New Brunswick, N. J.: Transaction Books, 1983).

Lisa Yount, *American Profiles: Black Scientists* (New York: Facts on File, 1991).

Bob Moses and the Algebra Project

"The tradition that I came out of in the Civil Rights Movement is an organizing tradition which tries to stake out some problem around which there is consensus and to see if there is a solution to the problem. In the Sixties, the issue was the 'Right to Vote,' the question was 'Political Access,' and associated with both of these was a literacy question around reading and writing.

"In the '90s there is another issue: math and science literacy. It is associated with, not political access, but economic access. At the center of it are mathematicians and the question about algebra."

—BOB MOSES, in a speech before a national conference of mathematicians, 1993.

He was a legendary figure in the civil rights struggles of the 1960s. "In Mississippi, Bob Moses was the equivalent of Martin Luther King," as Taylor Branch, author of the civil rights period's most comprehensive history, *Parting the Waters*, has said. Without Bob Moses and the grassroots movement he inspired, there would have been no "Freedom Summer" in 1964. Nor any Voting Rights Act passed into law in 1965.

Now, more than thirty years later, Moses is devoting his life to another calling. The Algebra Project he created is spreading across the United States. It currently involves more than 45,000 junior-high-age youth in 105 schools, both in inner cities and the rural South. The revolutionary approach makes the abstractions of algebra come alive in concrete terms. As a recent study in Mississippi funded by the National Science Foundation concluded: ". . . the Project has had an extremely beneficial effect on students—particularly on their attitudes, motivation, problem solving, and ability to articulate and share mathematical ideas."

Moses was the recipient of a MacArthur Foundation "genius" award that allowed him to spread the concept beyond his own children's school in Cambridge, Massachusetts. These days, he is constantly on the move. Half of his time is spent once again in the Mississippi Delta, where his quietly charismatic presence changed the course of history. The rest is divided between his Massachusetts home base and the fifteen other states where the Algebra Project now has sites around the country.

Catching up with Moses is not easy. Early in July of 1997, we sat down together in his spartan office at the Algebra Project's national headquarters near Cambridge's Central Square. Now in his early sixties, Moses is a soft-spoken man who expresses his thoughts slowly and methodically. He is dressed casually and stands about five-feet-nine. He has short hair and a graying trimmed beard, and wears glasses. In the outer office are colorful posters depicting math learning in Mexico, Japan, and other parts of the world. There is, as well, a poster photograph of the late Ella Baker. She had been a director of the Southern Christian Leadership Conference, and Moses' mentor during the civil rights movement.

Sitting in a straight-backed chair in front of his desk, Moses is talking about the dramatic shift of recent years in American education. "The country has always had two ways of educating its students," he says. "A certain group went to elite private schools, groomed to be the leadership. Everyone else was just educated to work. That was the industrial model, which the country was comfortable with. Today you're seeing the switch to computer, information-age technology. On the one hand, this has brought the literacy question of math front-and-center along with reading and writing. On the other hand, it's brought the issue of educating by drill-and-practice to a question mark, if not a halt. And it has placed the development of what are called 'critical thinking skills' on the table. These weren't thought to be a vital part of education under the previous system. Now such skills need to be developed around information that is encoded with quantitative data.

"This is new for everybody, and the country isn't even sure what it means yet. In the meantime, school desegregation and the education of black people has paralleled the shift in emphasis. Because the old system of segregated schools was not fully dismantled until the 1970s. So it barely got off the ground before the changing technology happened. For black youngsters, you now have race and class caught up in the educational system in a devastating way."

Moses' views are corroborated by statistics from the U.S. Department of Labor: More than half of all high school graduates lack the analytic skills required for today's jobs. Blacks and Hispanics, which will comprise one third of the student population by the year 2000, lag farther behind. Only eleven percent of all high school students, Moses notes, move from algebra through calculus. And the majority of African-American and Hispanic students, if they take algebra at all, do not begin learning the subject at an early enough grade level to gain a solid footing on today's college-preparatory math track.

Literally defined, algebra means "the uniting of broken parts to re-store a whole." That is precisely what Moses is looking to do in the educational system. "The Algebra Project is trying to get the notion of mathematics *into* the concept of literacy," he continues. "What this country has done, up to now, is turn out students who basically can do enough math to negotiate the post office. The new requirement for math literacy means mastery over symbolic systems. In our educational system, algebra holds that function. So algebra has a certain mystique that a phrase like New Math or Integrated Math doesn't have. To be a citizen of the future, you must know algebra and you need to start young. The question is: How do you get there?"

How to get from here to there has always been the question for Bob Moses. His grandfather, William H. Moses, had been a prominent Southern minister, rising to the vice-presidency of the National Baptist Convention. After moving his family to New York, the minister had taken ill during the Great Depression. He was unable to educate or support the last of his many children, including Moses' father Gregory. While Gregory's two older brothers had gone through college, he had to settle for a maintenance position at a Harlem armory after high school.

Born on January 23, 1935, Bob Moses and his two older brothers were raised by their parents in the Harlem River housing projects. He remembers his father telling him: "I lost my chance at college because of the Depression. You'll have a better chance than I did, and you *have* to take it." Early on, Moses displayed a particular talent for mathematics. He would never forget struggling for two hours with a complex equation, and feeling a surge of pride when he solved it. "I never thought I could, but I did it!" It was math, Moses believes, that taught him about perseverance and thinking logically.

In the ninth grade, Moses was among a handful of black youth to pass a citywide entrance exam for admission to the elite Stuyvesant High School. There, during part-time work at the NYU Medical Library, he began reading books about Eastern philosophy. In 1952, Moses earned a scholarship to Hamilton College in upstate New York. One of only three blacks among the student body, he got interested in logic.

"Moses became a philosophy major," as Taylor Branch writes in *Parting the Waters*. "He read Camus in French, renewed his study of Eastern philosophers, and took an interest in pacifist thought on the issues of war and peace. Admiring professors placed Moses in Quaker workshops held overseas."

Moses spent one summer in France, another in Japan, where he lived for a period in the home of a Zen Buddhist monk. He went on to Harvard for his Master's and, in 1956, was accepted into the university's Ph.D. program in philosophy. All was going smoothly until February of 1958, when Moses received word that his mother had suddenly died. After attending the funeral, Moses received a call from the police. His father, who had abruptly packed his bags and left the family's residence, seemed to have had a nervous breakdown on the street. He would receive treatment for many months in a psychiatric hospital. Moses left Harvard and came home to take care of him. He took a job as a math teacher at Horace Mann High School in suburban Riverdale.

That is where Moses was in February 1960, when he read in the newspapers about sit-ins taking place at segregated lunch counters in North Carolina. "They were kids my age, and I knew this had something to do with my own life," he says. He learned that a Committee to Defend Martin Luther King had been established in New York to raise funds for the then-incarcerated civil rights leader. He joined the office as a volunteer, working under Bayard Rustin. Through Rustin's auspices, Moses was soon on a bus heading for Atlanta to help King's Southern Christian Leadership Conference (SCLC). He had just turned twenty-five.

When he arrived, Moses found the SCLC office staffed by a handful of enthusiastic young volunteers associated with a new, integrated Student Non-Violent Coordinating Committee (SNCC). He joined them on picket lines outside supermarkets that were refusing to hire black clerks. When it was suggested that Moses take a recruiting trip through Southern states not yet represented in SNCC, he received his briefing from Ella Baker. She was a remarkable woman, a civil rights activist since the 1940s.

"Coming into SNCC," Moses recalls, "it was Ella who was really our model. What she did for the students was help them carve out a space within the adult civil rights community, where they could move into and develop their own organization and leadership. After the sit-ins started in 1960, she convened a conference on April 1 in Raleigh [N.C.]. It brought together the leaders from the NAACP, SCLC, CORE, the Urban League. But she also had the network to get the students who were active in the new sit-in movement to come. And when they arrived, she had the clout to hold off the national leadership, who might otherwise have competed for the students to become their youth branches. So Ella Baker helped create an organization she never intended to lead. And SNCC then intuitively decided to organize people we would not lead, the disenfranchised voters of Mississippi. Her faith in the power of a grassroots movement provided a sharp demarcation, a boundary line."

Dispatched to Mississippi, Moses' first contact was Amzie Moore. He was a gas station owner who had gotten involved in a local voter registration effort. Across the state, some one-half million black voters were being deprived of their right to the ballot. Moore suggested that SNCC send students into the state to help, using civil rights legislation passed by Congress in 1957 as the justification.

They would become known as the Freedom Riders. After returning North for a while, in mid-summer of 1961 Moses came back to stay. Settling in McComb, Mississippi, he began holding nightly voter education classes in a Masonic Temple. He lived with various families connected to the NAACP.

"In Mississippi," Moses remembers, "you had a state government which was absolutely committed to an effective apartheid system. People were not to cross those barriers. Violence was sanctioned."

He had not been in Mississippi a month when, taking a group of blacks to register in the town of Liberty, he encountered three white men blocking the entrance to the courthouse. Suddenly, one of them struck Moses on the forehead with a knife handle. He staggered to the sidewalk as Billy Jack Caston continued to beat him. When the assault finally stopped, Moses stood up. "We've got to go on to the registrar," he said. "We can't let something like this stop us." His head and shirt covered with blood, he led his group into the courthouse. The stunned registrar abruptly closed the office.

White physicians would not treat blacks, and there was no black doctor in the county. Moses drove back to McComb to get nine stitches in three head wounds. The following day, he returned to Liberty to file a complaint. Soon, outside the little courtroom where Moses was testifying, some 100 white citizens flooded into town. Many were armed. As a jury deliberated, gunshots sent Moses' supporters running for cover. Moses received an emergency police escort to the county line. Billy Jack Caston was acquitted of the assault charge.

Writes Taylor Branch: "Already [Moses'] name, borrowed from the most famous figure in the Old Testament, was acquiring a Christlike ring within SNCC, where the story was repeated that he had clasped his hands and looked heavenward during the Caston assault, saying 'Forgive them.' This apocryphal story was within the realm of belief, as his solitary, mystical, stubborn meekness had nicked the heart of Mississippi."

Two months after the incident in Liberty, Herbert Lee, a black farmer and father of nine with whom Moses had begun working closely, was shot and killed in broad daylight. E. H. Hurst, a state representative and the father-in-law of the fellow who had beaten Moses, claimed self-defense. Moses was devastated. Each night, he sought out witnesses. One was willing to come forward. But Moses could not get a contact in the Justice Department to file an indictment ensuring the witness's protection. The murder of an unarmed man was ruled a "justifiable homicide" by a Mississippi jury.

"Lee's death became a symbolic signing-over in blood to the struggle," Moses says. "It was clear now they would have to kill us to get us out of there." Moses and 119 students were thrown into jail after a nonviolent protest. Martin Luther King sent Attorney General Robert Kennedy a telegram of protest over "an apparent reign of terror" in Mississippi. Not long thereafter, King was invited to meet privately for the first time with President Kennedy. When 100 black students who had joined the voting rights protests were not allowed to return to their high school in McComb, Moses helped set up their own Nonviolent High. Soon he was in jail again.

"It's mealtime now," Moses wrote in his cell. "We have rice and gravy in a flat pan, dry bread and a 'big town cake'; we lack eating and drinking utensils. Water comes from a faucet and goes into a hole. This is Mississippi, the middle of the iceberg."

While Moses was incarcerated, a U.S. district judge outlawed any more Freedom Rides. The Masonic Temple in McComb closed its doors to SNCC. Emerging from jail, Moses could no longer find enough local citizens willing to attend registration classes. But the movement was already spreading beyond the control of the segregationist authorities. Along with several SNCC members, Moses headed for the Mississippi Delta.

Starting in the spring of 1962, he worked on small voter registration projects in the plantation country north of Jackson. There impoverished, illiterate blacks lived in one-room shacks, sharecroppers on scattered farms. Now, in their churches, the biblical sermon "Moses and his stick" translated into the pursuit of the vote.

Looking back on these years, Bob Moses says: "You forgot about family, career, education, money. We really didn't have a source of income. We lived through a network of people who became our extended family. So you could travel down the road and knew that there was someplace there that would take you in. Unannounced. And they were going to take care of your basic needs."

Through such a support system, Moses says he learned "to live with my fear and what the fears do to you. I used to think, 'Pick one foot up and step forward, put it down and pick the next one up.' You get down to that level of reality." As one SNCC worker wrote in a letter:

"I just didn't understand what kind of guy this Bob Moses is, that he could walk into a place where a lynch mob had just left and make up a bed and prepare to go to sleep, as if the situation was normal."

Following confrontations, Moses would send reports out to the Justice Department, the FBI, the news media, and Martin Luther King. In the Delta town of Ruleville, night riders fired shots into two homes that were offering shelter to SNCC volunteers. The local authorities blamed Moses' presence. But the Kennedy Administration was finding the Mississippi madness impossible to ignore. At a news conference, President Kennedy called the shooting incident in Ruleville "cowardly as well as outrageous. I commend those who are making the effort to register every citizen. They deserve the protection of the United States government, the protection of the states. . . . And if it requires extra legislation, and extra force, we shall do that."

That fall of 1962, when James Meredith became the first black student to enroll at the University of Mississippi, the Administration sent 23,000 troops to make sure it happened.

In December, Moses issued a statement with three conditions: removal of the White Citizens Council from control of Mississippi politics; action by the Justice Department; and a mass uprising demanding the right to vote. Then, on January 1, 1963, with the endorsement of King and support from the Gandhi Society, Moses filed a lawsuit in Washington against the Justice Department and FBI. It was a demand for enforcement of six different sections of the Federal Code that made it a crime to harass or intimidate anyone trying to vote.

Mississippi officials immediately cut off the distribution of federal food surpluses to two poor Delta counties. Singer Harry Belafonte, comedian Dick Gregory, and other prominent figures issued an appeal for relief. Thirty tons of donated supplies soon arrived in Greenwood by plane and truck. Awaiting the arrival outside a chapel stood more than 6,000 people.

The backlash was swift. Four black-owned businesses in Greenwood near the local SNCC offices were struck by arson fires. Moses was riding with two coworkers when they noticed a car following them. As a Buick sped past, shots rang out. The driver was struck in the neck and slumped into Moses' lap. As their car swerved off the highway, Moses grabbed the steering wheel with one hand. He held Jimmy Travis with his other hand, desperately seeking the brake with his foot. Miraculously, Moses brought the car to a stop. The windshield and every window were shattered. Moses drove on into the night, looking for a hospital willing to treat his wounded friend.

Jimmy Travis survived. Robert Kennedy sent lawyers into Greenwood to investigate the suspension of food relief. A young folksinger named Bob Dylan arrived and sang: "The answer, my friend, is blowin' in the wind." Media descended from across the country to cover the voter registration marches. The local police attacked with dogs. Moses and others were again jailed, and convicted of disturbing the peace. At another press conference, President Kennedy endorsed their case.

Standing behind bars, Bob Moses was leading his coprisoners in song when the jailers suddenly began opening the cells. The sentences had been suspended. They were all singing *This Little Light of Mine* as they emerged to the glare of dozens of TV cameras.

Unknown to Moses at the time, the Justice Department had made a deal with Mississippi officials. The prisoners would be released if Moses' lawsuit demanding voting rights enforcement was ignored. Things seemed to reach a stalemate in Mississippi. Martin Luther King was concentrating his own efforts on Birmingham, Alabama. In June of 1963, Mississippi civil rights leader Medgar Evers was murdered. On the eve of King's March on Washington in August, Moses led an all-night vigil of picketers outside the Justice Department.

President Kennedy was assassinated. The Civil Rights Bill he had introduced in 1963, banning discrimination in public places, had gone nowhere in Congress. The voter registration drive seemed at an impasse. At a convention of SNCC, Moses stated that the only hope in Mississippi was to force a confrontation between federal and state authority. Plans commenced for what became the Freedom Summer of 1964. Hundreds of white college students from the North would be bused into backwoods Mississippi to educate and register black voters. The ultimate purpose was to form an alternative political delegation to challenge the "Dixiecrats" at the Democratic Convention and thereby, as Moses put it, "break open Mississippi as a closed society."

Among those who joined the massive effort were three students— two white, one black—named Michael Schwerner, James Chaney, and Andrew Goodman. On June 4, 1964, they disappeared. "It was reported back to us at the volunteers training session that they were missing," Moses recalls. "Those who knew the situation in Mississippi and the area that Mickey was working in [Meridian] knew that they were dead."

Moses broke the news to about 300 volunteers at the Freedom School. Standing before them in a T-shirt and bib overalls, looking down at his feet, he told them it was "very clear what the stakes were." Given that "some of your crew are already dead before you even get there," they should not feel like cowards if they chose to avoid Mississippi. He did not want to put them at risk, although they were desperately needed. "All I can say," he concluded, "is I'll be there with you."

For five minutes after Moses spoke, the room was silent. Then a black woman in the back stood up and began to sing: "They say that freedom is a constant struggle. They say that freedom is a constant struggle. Oh Lord, we've been struggling so long—that we might be free." None of the students turned back. The bodies of Goodman, Chaney and Schwerner were discovered two months later. "To give meaning to their lives," Moses said, "was to make the project actually fulfill its goals."

And so it did, inspired by this shy, bespectacled teacher. It succeeded despite 4 deaths, 80 beatings, 35 shootings, 1,000 arrests, and 67 churches, homes and businesses destroyed. The Magnolia State had armed itself against the Northern students' invasion. Yet they went door to door alongside the sharecroppers and domestic workers who took them into their homes. It was an unprecedented coming together of cultures.

That August, to the 1964 Democratic Convention came the new Mississippi Freedom Democratic Party. It had emerged from precinct, county and district meetings as the representative of the people. "The Freedom Democratic Party was organized by the young people from SNCC and CORE and some of the adults," Moses recalls. "But the idea was to set up an organization where we understood we were not going to merge ourselves as the leaders. Out of that process, Fannie Lou Hamer became a national symbol. Alongside her were a number of other people, many of them women."

On one of the buses to Atlantic City, forty-six-year-old Fannie Lou Hamer of Sunflower County sang *Go Tell It on the Mountain*. Only two years before, she had learned she had the right to vote. Now she was the chosen spokesperson to issue a clarion call to the country. Her impassioned speech on national TV called for an end to all-white convention delegations. The new President, Lyndon Johnson, was furious. He called a simultaneous press conference looking to upstage her. The networks covered it, but replayed Hamer's speech in its entirety.

The Freedom Democratic Party did not succeed in unseating Mississippi's all-white delegation. Both sides rejected a compromise proposed by the White House. But the dramatic event did mark the death knell for Mississippi's politics-as-usual. The 1965 Voting Rights Act would guarantee federally supervised elections for the first time since Reconstruction. Thousands of people were enfranchised. Today, Mississippi has more elected black officials than any other Southern state, fully one-quarter of its state legislature.

"We used the vote as a tool to organize the target population to get political access," Moses says. "We were successful in doing that, in a broad sense. The advocacy groups—civil rights organizations, churches, congressional liberals—were not themselves able to really pierce the resistance. Which, in that case, was the political system as established within the Democratic Party and the lock it had on Congress. Their basic argument was, 'You folks are trying to get these people to do something they don't want to do.' You couldn't counter that without the people themselves. Once they got involved directly, and articulated their own demands, the argument disappeared."

Moses reflects and continues: "The work I am doing today is a continuation of what we did in the '60s. The people in Mississippi were living in serfdom on plantations. They had no control over their lives. Today, we have these same serflike entities within our cities. We're a society which is permitting criminalized neighborhoods to grow.

"So the issue we are grappling with now is using math literacy as an organizing tool to achieve economic access. The political access has gained economic access for an elite of black people. Even this is being threatened. This past year, the University of Texas law school didn't admit any black students, as opposed to eighty the year before. But this does raise the ante. Out of such situations, we may be able to get the consciousness to make a demand.

"In this case, the target population are the young people and their supporters. The opposing argument is essentially the same as in the '60s: 'You're trying to force these young people to do intellectual work that they don't want to do.' Again, you can't move this country without articulation from a mass base around a major issue. And that's what the Algebra Project has set out to do, taking what we learned in the '60s and applying it to activate the young."

Bob Moses did not arrive at his new quest overnight. Over the course of Freedom Summer in 1964, he had become disillusioned with what SNCC was becoming. "That project had a double-edged sword," he says. "It marked the transition from what SNCC and the Movement had been to 'Black Power.' SNCC evolved into an organization which cultivated a national media personality. The original working style was to have autonomous field secretaries, with a clear flow of decentralized decision-making. But that summer, people who had been working together left."

The phase-out within SNCC included the white students who had come to help in the Mississippi registration drive. By the summer of 1966, pushed increasingly to the margins of the organization, Moses would leave, too. He had become active in protests against the Vietnam War. During his first year of college back in 1953, he had applied to the draft board for conscientious objector status as a pacifist. He had been granted a student deferment, which was later extended to math and science teachers. "Then when I left teaching and went South," he remembers, "the draft board called me up for a hearing and classified me 1-A. In the summer of 1966, when I was speaking out against Vietnam, they ordered me to report to the Army. I decided to leave the country."

By now, Moses had divorced from his first wife, an SNCC worker he had met in Mississippi. He journeyed alone to Montreal, Canada. Living under an assumed name, he scraped out a meager living doing odd jobs. During his two years in Canadian exile, he met and married another former SNCC activist, Janet Jemmott. Not long after the assassination of Martin Luther King in April 1968, they decided to move to Africa. They settled in a dusty Tanzanian village called Same. Moses went back to teaching high school math, Janet taught English. They remained there for eight years, beginning to raise a family of four children.

"One thing that was important," says Moses, "was being in a system which, for its own internal reasons, was absolutely dedicated to every student. Because the country needed them. So it really had a different look and feel from an educational system where the country isn't quite sure that it needs all these kids, and so treats them accordingly.

"What we also started in Tanzania was beginning to look at games [as educational tools]. And being there raised for me this question about language. The secondary school was built on the British system. So the kids spoke to each other in Ki-Swahili, but their books and instruction were in English. I walk into this situation, I don't have command of Ki-Swahili. What I would do was ask them to read stuff and then talk about it to each other. Then we would try to meet on the blackboard with symbolic representations. But it was clear to me that they needed another language besides English to get any kind of concept about what was going on underneath these symbols."

Why had he decided to come back to America after ten years? "There was a lot of romanticizing about what it would be like to live in Africa," Moses says. "But what really was the extent to which African-Americans can, in this case myself and Janet, transfer into African culture and feel comfortable? I think we learned what our boundaries are on that."

In 1976, Moses and his family moved back to Cambridge, Massachusetts. While Janet went to medical school, Moses returned to Harvard to pursue the doctoral studies in philosophy that he had abandoned fifteen years before. He became fascinated with the theories of Professor Willard Quine. According to Quine, "set theory, arithmetic, and symbolic logic are, all of them, products of the straightforward mathematization of ordinary interpreted discourse."

"He was sort of the star of the Harvard philosophy department as I was coming through," Moses says. "He made the point that the actual process of getting logic and arithmetic off the ground was what he called 'regimentation of ordinary language.' That is, you take ordinary language and straight-jacket it, so to speak. And you come out with a conceptual language which no one speaks, but which underlies the symbolic representations that appear in the logic and math. These symbolic representations really have no weight unless they are *related* to a conceptual language, which in turn is related to some natural language."

The educational ideas that had germinated in Tanzania and under Harvard's Quine were about to bear fruit. It began when Moses' daughter Maisha, then twelve, began protesting against the algebra that her father insisted on teaching her at home. After all, none of her friends were yet learning algebra. At the time, only a small percentage of students in the U.S. took the subject as early as the eighth grade. "Dad would say, 'It's important. You need to do it.' He would sit there and force answers out of me," Maisha remembers. "Finally he decided that the only way to get me to do algebra was to go into school."

The Moses children's school was King Open, named after Martin Luther King. It was an alternative facility that had been established by a group of parents in 1969, partly in response to desegregation of the Cambridge public schools. Forty percent of the 300 students were black, many from low-income families. The curriculum for the kindergarten through eighth graders was set by parent-teacher committees. Moses asked Maisha's teacher if his daughter might be allowed to sit by herself in class and do his algebra assignments. That wouldn't work, Mary Lou Mehrling replied. But would Moses be interested in coming to the school and teaching algebra to Maisha and three other students?

That was 1982. The experiment paid dividends. Under Moses' tutelage, his daughter and her classmates became the first students in King Open's history to pass a citywide algebra test that made them eligible to pursue an honors math/science curriculum in high school. The next year, with Moses' eldest son about to enter the seventh grade, he agreed to keep working with Mehrling and another teacher. By the fall of 1985, Moses and Mehrling were instructing all of the school's seventh and eighth graders in traditional algebra. Once again, Moses had "dropped out" of Harvard. The Algebra Project, as the other teachers called it, was underway.

"I think it was in the third year," Moses is saying, "when there was a young student in the class who was a friend of my son. He wanted to do algebra, but he couldn't multiply. It really helped me in working with him, to crystallize where this conceptual gap was. As he tried to do problems with integers, it became clear that he had one strict idea about numbers in his mind. It went back to what he'd learned before he ever started school, learning how to count. 'How many fingers, how many toes?' He didn't have the foggiest idea that anything else was part of the number concept. So it became clear that we needed to figure out how to put another question in his mind. I finally settled on direction: 'Which way?' Okay, well, how are we going to do this? That's when I got into looking at experiential learning: 'We'll take a trip!' "

The trip was on the Boston subway system. "At every stop, they advertise whether the train is going inbound or outbound," Moses continues. "So it's a direction issue, not a 'how many.' And, in some sense, not even a place. So we were able to use that trip to get this concept of attaching direction to numbers."

During their journey, Moses invited the students to sketch anything that caught their eye along the way. Then, back in class, they took magic markers and assigned a value of zero to the originating station. The whole route was soon transformed into a number line: positive values for inbound stops, negative for outbound. Soon Moses was asking the class: "What do you call the relationship between the location at the finish and the location at the start?" And the students were responding: "Displacement!"

Moses says: "Then the issue was, how do we work toward abstract symbols? At that point, my background in the philosophy of mathematics and Quine began to percolate through my mind. Over the next few years, we came to name the steps."

Moses' aim was to move from the natural language of "People Talk" into "Feature Talk," the conceptual language that undergirds symbolic representations. First came the experience of the event. Then drawing a picture or constructing a three-dimensional model. Then writing and talking about the trip. Finally translating these discussions into mathematical language, and developing symbols to represent it. Through this process of relating algebraic concepts to their everyday lives, as Moses and several coauthors outlined in a 1989 article for the *Harvard Educational Review*, students forged "their own platform of mathematical truths" that had content and meaning to them.

In short, math could be fun. You could use Play-Doh, jump ropes, and snap-together cubes to learn equivalence. You could order the heights of class members to understand the difference between median and average. You could build "algebra forms" making gumdrops and toothpicks into squares, cubes, and rectangles. You could have championship math tournaments between schools in the gymnasium, where sixth-graders factored numbers from one to 200 into primes and raced to tape their answers onto the hardwood floor.

All this, and more, Moses incorporated into the curriculum as the Algebra Project began to spread beyond Cambridge. Its methods closely adhere to standards developed during the 1980s by the National Council of Teachers of Mathematics. "There were no curricular models, so schools began coming to us," Moses says. After becoming a nonprofit corporation in 1991, with financial support from private foundations, corporations, and banks, the Algebra Project soon caught on in inner-city classrooms in New York, Baltimore, Chicago, Indianapolis, Milwaukee, Los Angeles, San Francisco, and Oakland. "When these kids get the privilege of creating their own [innovative approaches to] mathematics, they become independent learners," says Dorothy Strong, director of mathematics for the Chicago Public Schools. In Louisville, Kentucky, one principal credits the Algebra Project with almost doubling the number of students scoring at or above the fiftieth percentile on a national math achievement test.

For Moses personally, the most rewarding challenge has been his return to Mississippi. It began in 1988. A new film, *Mississippi Burning*, had just been released about the murders of the three students at the beginning of Freedom Summer. To Moses and others who knew the real story, the movie's glorification of the FBI's role in the investigation was an outrage. A meeting among some of the onetime civil rights activists was organized for Jackson, Mississippi. One of these was Freedom Summer's codirector Dave Dennis. He and Moses had not seen each other in twenty-four years.

Dennis had gone on to become a successful lawyer in New Orleans. But, he has said, "when I left Mississippi, I felt that there was a part of me missing. I didn't finish something." He and Moses arose at dawn and talked for hours at the edge of a motel pool. Moses spoke animatedly of the Algebra Project, drawing comparisons with the empowerment of Fannie Lou Hamer all those many years before. After Moses received an offer from the Atlanta-based Southern Regional Council to bring the Algebra Project into the Mississippi Delta, in 1992 Dennis left his law practice behind. He moved to Jackson with his wife and two youngest children to run the Project's Southern Initiative.

In some ways, time had stood still in Mississippi. The state remained the worst in the nation when it came to poverty, infant mortality, and illiteracy. When court-ordered school desegregation took place in the early 1970s, things shifted to a predominantly white-private, black-public system. So the need was as strong as ever. Today, the Algebra Project is growing faster in Mississippi than anywhere; it is in more than forty schools, reaching over 2,000 youngsters. And, in little towns like Indianola, where Moses once organized voters, since the Project's inception the students are scoring in the top twenty percent of the nation on the Scholastic Achievement Test.

At the Brinkley Middle School in Jackson, all but one of the 587 students are African-American. Here Moses spends a considerable portion of the school year. Before the Algebra Project, says Brinkley teacher Lynn Moss, "A few kids were learning, but most were stuck at third- or fourth-grade level. The learning just wasn't connected to their lives." All that has changed. Here Ben Moynihan, the son of two Freedom Summer volunteers, uses the varying rhythms of African drumming to explain math ratios.

There is no subway system for the initial take-a-trip phase. So the students go on an eight-stop bus tour. It is as much a history lesson as a math exercise. They visit the home of Medgar Evers and other sites associated with the civil rights movement. They journey to Tougaloo and Jackson State Colleges. Sometimes they stop to visit with a Freedom Rider.

"The import of Moses' discussion of the epistemology of mathematics is this: in order to reach our students, whose experience is often more concrete, more visual, and quicker-paced than ours has been, we mathematicians and mathematics educators need to work on developing multiple points of view. . . ."
—DON GOLDBERG, Associate Professor of Mathematics at Occidental College, after Moses' speech, 1993.

At the King Open School in Cambridge, Algebra Project coordinator Pam Paternoster is sitting in the library in between classes. She has recently returned from Mississippi, where she observed the classes at the Brinkley Middle School. An education major, she began working as an assistant art teacher at King Open in the late 1980s.

"I know the way math was taught when I was in school didn't make sense," Paternoster says. "I learned algorithms and how to plug numbers into formulas, but it never occurred to me that we were modeling something in real life. With that knowledge, my own learning has been exponential."

Before the Algebra Project, she notes, all the school's students were "tracked" by ability. "Math was done by the textbook. The kids were split into ability groups, and the ones in the higher group were self-propelling. Kids in the middle needed a little supervision, and the ones at the bottom level weren't getting it. If you looked at the third tier, it was mostly African-American and Latino. It's very clear to me that kids know when they're being tracked, and they were ashamed of being in this lower group. Which was evidenced by their disruptive behavior and not doing the work."

At Moses' urging, the school staff had convened to talk about student achievement. The issue of race loomed large over a three-year period of discussions. In the early 1990s, the time-honored tracking system was dropped.

"It's very easy to worship Bob," Paternoster says of Moses. "I feel fortunate to have seen many sides of him, to get to know him as a human being. I would have to say that he is one of the most devoted, thoughtful people in the world. An extremely nonjudgmental person, who feels things very deeply."

With the Algebra Project now in ten Cambridge junior highs, the Superintendent of Schools has mandated eighth-grade algebra citywide. "There is no textbook math in Cambridge," says Paternoster, "except for eighth-grade algebra, and even that is supplemented. The kinds of language that children are learning to use around mathematics will be consistent all through school."

Indeed, the Algebra Project's methods are being applied to other disciplines at King Open. Paternoster leads me to a sixth-grade classroom. The teacher is working entirely from the blackboard, engaging the children as they add pieces to a word puzzle. Their enthusiasm is infectious; rarely are fewer than twenty hands up at a time. As we depart, I ask Paternoster whether this is an English lesson. "Probably," she replies, "but not necessarily."

Bob Moses concurs that the Algebra Project's concepts are applicable across the board. "In experiential learning," he explains, "you really work your way around a circle. It's the way we go about learning most things. We do something, we think about it, we make some improvements, we practice it. Cooking, bicycle riding, learning language, everything. In this country, there has been a lot of work around experiential learning at the lower-grade levels. What you have now is a tool where higher-grade mathematics can drive an interdisciplinary process."

In the summer of 1997, teachers in language arts, social studies, science and math formed a team to try to take further a more integrated curriculum. As it was in the civil rights days, the team approach remains central to the Algebra Project. "Years ago, we stumbled upon the workshop style of meeting," Moses says. "How could meetings be structured as a tool for empowering the people, to get their *active* participation? Classrooms are just meeting places. So the central issue remains how to empower the students to learn."

This comes to involve not only training teachers, but training the trainers themselves. For this, Moses has turned to a clinical psychologist, Jim Burrus, who has worked in training everyone from Peace Corps volunteers to executives with Fortune 500 companies. "The science of this, which comes out of psychology and small group interactions, has really evolved from the '60s," says Moses. "But its application in the real world is pretty new."

Building the math literacy movement remains very much a family affair. From the beginning, Moses brought parents directly into the process. They attend weekend tutorials and get involved in math games with their children. What they themselves don't understand, the kids explain. Moses' own children have all elected to work with the Algebra Project. Since graduating from Harvard, Maisha has been at the Oakland site. The youngest daughter, Malika, began Project activities with college students in Atlanta, where she graduated from Spelman College in 1997.

"My two sons, Omo and Taba, are both working with our young people's project in Mississippi," adds Moses. "Omo, who's twenty-five now, has been involved in developing graphing calculator workshops, traveling from Jackson up to the Delta. Taba is twenty-two, working on the desktop publishing aspect. What we're trying to do is have the young people take over the task of producing the Algebra Project materials. They're running their own summer camp in Mississippi for 25 to 30 middle school students."

It is all about what's passed on between generations. So strong were the bonds formed in Mississippi in the '60s that Freedom Summer's cocoordinators are working together again. Alongside them is Charley Cobb, who thought of the Freedom School idea in 1964. After eleven years as a staff writer for *National Geographic*, now he is writing a book about the Algebra Project. Meantime, some graduates of Cambridge's King Open school have gone on to finish college—and returned to the Algebra Project that first opened them to new possibilities.

"We now have a commitment from students who have been through the process, to come back and work with the next generation," Moses says. "And these young people in their early twenties make it acceptable for the ones in middle school to deliver mathematics. This generation has grown up pushing buttons to make an image move on a screen. They spend hours doing that in various games and formats. They think such a tool is worthy of their attention, and they're proud to be able to demonstrate to their peers or to adults what they know and can do with it."

Here is where Moses' linkage with Alan Shaw's MUSIC computer software enters the picture. It's part of spreading the math culture. "Alan and [his wife] Michelle recently brought some computers down

This portrait of Nobel Prize-winning novelist Toni Morrison was taken by Pulitzer Prize-winning photographer Brian Lanker. Photo by Brian Lankar.

The young James Baldwin, a photograph taken in 1950 by Albert Murray in Antibes, a Mediterranean seaport in southeastern France. Photo by Albert Murray.

The venerable Frederick Douglass, not long before his death in 1895. Photo: Portraits, Photographs and Prints Division, Schomburg Center for Research in Black Culture, The New York Public Library, Astor, Lenox and Tilden Foundations.

The venerable James Baldwin, while living in Amherst, Massachusetts, not long before his death in 1987. Special Collections and Archives, W.E.B. Du Bois Library, University of Massachusetts at Amherst.

LEWIS LATIMER AND FAMILY

Inventor Lewis Latimer (front row, far left), with his family. His granddaughter Winifred Latimer Norman is standing at the far right. Photo: Portrait Collection, Photographs and Prints Division, Schomburg Center for Research in Black Culture, The New York Public Library, Astor, Lenox and Tilden Foundations.

Physicist Earl Shaw holds his new grandson, Obasi, standing alongside his computer pioneer son, Alan, in the backyard of the elder Shaw's home in Morristown, New Jersey. Photo by Erin Shaw, 1997.

Bob Moses in Mississippi, summer of 1964, preparing for "Freedom Summer." Photo by Steve Schapiro, Black Star.

ob Moses in 1992, back in Mississippi to spearhead his Algebra Project in the Delta region's schools.
hoto: Chester Higgins, Jr./*New York Times* Permission.

A sketch of the 18th-century almanac writer, astronomer, and surveyor Benjamin Banneker. Photo: 16th–19th Century Portraits, Photographs and Prints Division, Schomburg Center for Research in Black Culture, The New York Public Library, Astor, Lenox and Tilden Foundations.

Award-winning architect Charles McAfee, working up a new project in Atlanta with his daughter Cheryl McAfee-Mitchell (right) and Charyl McAfee-Duncan (left). Photo by Reggie. C. Mitchell Sr., 1997.

Wright's daughter, Dr. Jane Cooke Wright, Associate dean of the New York Medical College and one of the first chemotherapy researchers. Photo: Portrait Collection, Photographs and Prints Division, Schomburg Center for Research in Black Culture, The New York Public Library, Astor, Lenox and Tilden Foundations.

r. Louis Tompkins Wright, pioneering physician and civil rights activist, at the speaker's podium.
oto: Portrait Collection, Photographs and Prints Division, Schomburg Center for Research in Black Culture, The
w York Public Library, Astor, Lenox and Tilden Foundations.

Byllye Avery, founder of the National Black Women's Health Project. Photo courtesy of Byllye Avery.

One of the few photographs of the 19th-century activist/evangelist Sojourner Truth: "I sell the shadow to support the substance." Photo: Portrait Collection, Photographs and Prints Division, Schomburg Center for Research in Black Culture, The New York Public Library, Astor, Lenox and Tilden Foundations.

The religious leader Dr. Howard Thurman, during his days as dean emeritus of Marsh Chapel at Boston University. Photo: Portrait Collection, Photographs and Prints Division, schomburg Center for Research in Black Culture, The New York Public Library, Astor, Lenox and Tilden Foundations.

Morehouse College president Benjamin E. Mays, a leading mentor for Dr. Martin Luther King, Jr. Photo: Portrait Collection, Photographs and Prints Division, Schomburg Center for Research in Black Culture, The New York Public Library, Astor, Lenox and Tilden Foundations.

A rare photo of Martin Luther King standing next to Benjamin Mays, at a commencement exercise at Atlanta's Morehouse College, A. L. Adams photo studio, courtesy of Morehouse College.

to Mississippi for the math lab at Brinkley. They showed the students how to set these up, and walked them through their MUSIC system. The computer provides an opening for the active participation of both students and teachers in the ongoing process of developing materials. So it's not just receiving something, but there's a real creation back and forth."

A real creation, back and forth. . . . Since those spirited years in Mississippi, that has been Bob Moses' vision—working among communities, bringing people together, leading by example and pushing others to the fore. University of Massachusetts/Amherst professor and writer Michael Thelwell, who has known him since the early days, says: "Bob's genius is inspiring confidence in people to become enthusiastic participants in difficult projects. He may be the world's greatest organizer. Bob Moses does it in the interest of people and humanity and the progress of the race."

FOR FURTHER READING:

Taylor Branch, *Parting the Waters: America In the King Years 1954-63* (New York: Simon & Schuster, 1988).

The American Experience: Freedom on My Mind (1996 PBS documentary).

Ancestors—The Astronomer/Surveyor:
Benjamin Banneker

"The expanded spheres, amazing to the sight,
Magnificent with stars and globes of light,
The glorious orbs which heaven's bright host compose,
The imprison'd sea that restless ebbs and flows,
The fluctuating field of liquid air,
With all the curious meteors hovering there,
And the wide regions of the land, proclaim
The power Divine that rais'd the mighty frame."
—BENJAMIN BANNEKER'S ALMANAC FOR 1792.

As twilight descended, the old man could be seen silhouetted against the venerable pear tree at the edge of his orchard, alternately playing tunes on his violin and flute. With dusk he leaned on his long staff and walked back inside the single-story log house where he was born, cooking a solitary meal before wrapping himself in a great cloak and emerging again to contemplate the night sky. Often he would lie awake under the pear tree until almost dawn, listening to the murmur of a spring that issued from a massive golden willow nearby. It was a perfect spot to gaze upon any celestial phenomenon, in this tidewater Maryland valley beneath hills that swept gently toward the Patapsco River about half a mile away.

Benjamin Banneker did not seem to need that much sleep. Each morning he would explore the hills and, by afternoon, be busy cultivating the garden, trimming the fruit trees, or observing the flights of his bees. All of which Banneker then recorded in the manuscript journal or "commonplace book" that he kept on a large oval table in his study, alongside his mathematical puzzles and astronomy books. On many days, visitors would drop in, often traveling considerable distances on horseback to the farm located about ten miles outside Baltimore.

"He was very precise in conversation and exhibited deep reflection," one of these visitors, Charles Worthington Dorsey, would later write. "He seemed to be acquainted with everything of importance that was passing in the country. . . . His head was covered with a thick suit of white hair, which gave him a very venerable and dignified appearance. His dress was uniformly of super fine drab broad cloth, made in the old style of a plain coat, with straight collar and long waistcoat, and a broadbrimmed hat. . . . In size and personal appearance, the statue of [Benjamin] Franklin at the Library in Philadelphia, as seen from the street, is the perfect likeness of him."

By the time he died in 1806, Benjamin Banneker was somewhat of a legendary figure along the East Coast of a recently independent United States—a self-taught mathematician, astronomer, inventor, surveyor and almanac writer who corresponded with Thomas Jefferson in an attempt to influence his views on slavery.

Banneker's heritage went back to England as well as Africa. His white grandmother, Molly Welsh, had been a British dairymaid who, accused of stealing milk from her employer, was exiled to the Maryland colony around 1683. Upon her release from indentured servitude, she had earned enough money to buy her own land—as well as two slaves off a ship that docked in Chesapeake Bay. One was an African prince who called himself Banneka, and Molly Welsh fell in love with him. In defiance of colonial custom, she took his name for her own, and the couple carved a successful tobacco farm out of the wilderness.

An act passed in Maryland in 1681 declared free any children born of white servant women and blacks. One of the four Banneker daughters also purchased and married a slave, who was given his freedom after converting to Christianity. Robert Banneker took her name, since he did not know his own. They, too, had four children; the only son, Benjamin, was born on November 9, 1731.

As a boy he studied his grandfather's ingenious diversion of a stream to construct canals for the tobacco plants. His grandmother, with a Bible she had brought from England, taught him to read and write. For a brief period, he was the only dark-skinned youth in a nearby Quaker school, adopting many of the Quaker principles and customs, including his manner of dress. Largely teaching himself history, literature, and his particular fascination—mathematics—after the day's farm work, Benjamin Banneker is said to have attained the equivalent of an eighth-grade education by his fifteenth birthday.

The story goes that, on a trip to the Maryland coast to sell tobacco while in his late teens, Banneker encountered a traveling salesman named Josef Levi. Observing the young man's excitement as he explained the workings of a pocket watch, Levi gave it to him. For days thereafter, Banneker studied its inner workings, taking the watch apart and reassembling it again. He is said to have visited his Quaker schoolteacher, who provided him with an old English journal containing a picture of a clock, a book on geometry, and Isaac Newton's *Principia* on the laws of motion. Using these models, plus a compass and ruler to do measurements, Banneker devoted almost all his spare time over the next two years to figuring out the right mathematical ratios and hand-carving with a pocket knife every gear, movement, and chime. Around 1752, he is said to have completed the first wooden clock in colonial America. It kept perfect time, striking the hour for more than forty years, and before long people were coming from far distances to see it. Scholars also frequently came to test Banneker's capacity for solving difficult mathematical problems, in which he reportedly always succeeded, occasionally supplying his answers along with rhymed compositions.

After the deaths of his grandparents and father, one by one Banneker's sisters married and left home to settle nearby. Benjamin remained with his mother and responsibility for the farm. He was forty when, in 1772, a white family named Ellicott purchased a large adjoining tract of land. Banneker assisted them in assembling machinery and, within a few years, Ellicott's Mill had developed into a small village—complete with flour and sawmills, a general store, and iron foundry.

"Banneker often called at the post-office," wrote George W. Williams in his 1882 *History of the Negro Race in America*, "where, after overcoming his natural modesty and diffidence, he was frequently called out in conversations covering a variety of topics. His conversational powers, his inexhaustible fund of information, and his broad learning (for those times and considering his circumstances), made him the connoisseur of that section."

Around the time that his mother died, one story, perhaps apocryphal, has Banneker traveling on horseback to a meeting of the Third Continental Congress at Philadelphia in 1776. There he is said to have watched Jefferson submit the Declaration of Independence. Whether or not this actually occurred, it is known that Banneker worked with the neighboring Ellicotts in planting wheat that helped feed the Revolutionary Army.

George Ellicott, some years Banneker's junior, shared a mutual interest in science and was especially interested in astronomy. In 1788, Ellicott loaned his friend several texts by the leading astronomers of the day, some scientific instruments, and a table to study upon. A new passion, one that would last to the end of his life, was set afire in Banneker. He began teaching himself how to calculate an ephemeris, establishing the positions of the sun, moon, and other planets of the solar system in order to compute solar and lunar eclipses, rising and setting times, weather predictions and more. Within three years Banneker was ready to incorporate all this into a scientific almanac which he submitted to several printers, initially to no avail.

Then, early in 1791, came a calling that would again change the direction of Banneker's life. Major Andrew Ellicott, George's cousin, had been appointed by President Washington to survey a ten-mile square then known as the Federal Territory for the creation of a new national capital. At the time, the new U.S. government was headquartered in Philadelphia but, in 1789, Maryland and Virginia had agreed to cede portions of their states to form what would become the District of Columbia. En route from New York to begin the work, the major stopped at Ellicott Mills, informing his cousin that he was in search of a capable assistant to help with the scientific apparatus. George Ellicott told him about Banneker's abilities, specifically for recording the astronomical observations vital to such a survey.

Major Ellicott proceeded to check with Thomas Jefferson, then secretary of state, who encouraged him to bring Banneker along for the preliminary survey. As Jefferson wrote to the Marquis de Condorcet of France the following year: "I procured him [Banneker] to be employed under one of our chief directors in laying out the new Federal City on the Potomac. . . ." For Jefferson, who was on record as believing that "the blacks are inferior to the whites in the endowments of body and mind," it was quite a departure. Ironically, not long after Banneker's arrival with the surveying team, the Georgetown *Weekly Ledger* reported in March 1791 that Banneker possessed "ability as a surveyor and an astronomer [which] already prove that Mr. Jefferson's concluding that race of men were void of mental endowment was without foundation."

Banneker was approaching sixty and, in poor health at the time, was unable to participate in much of the actual field work. But he set up shop in an observatory tent, proving invaluable to Ellicott in utilizing astronomical instruments for laying out base lines and boundaries for the new capital. Banneker's methodical creation of his original wooden clock forty years before now came full circle. As biographer Silvio A. Bedini describes in *The Life of Benjamin Banneker*:

"His most important responsibility was the maintenance of the astronomical clock, which proved to be far more complicated a chore than he had imagined. The clock was an extremely well-made timepiece designed for the maximum precision that could be achieved in that period. It was housed in a simply made wooden tall-case, and Banneker eventually began to understand why Ellicott seemed to be so fretful of its operation. Remembering his own wooden clock, Banneker admired the movement in this one, which was the finest he had ever seen. It was his study to keep it wound, to check its rate by means of equal altitudes taken out of the sun at periodic intervals with the transit and equal altitude instrument, and it was necessary to keep the temperature in its vicinity constant. For this purpose he had several thermometers placed at appropriate points from which he recorded the readings several times each day."

By the end of April 1791, with the initial survey completed, Banneker returned alone to his Maryland farm. There he set to work feverishly on preparing a new almanac. Since the early colonial days, almanacs rested alongside the Bible in just about every home. In this period, clocks and watches were still rare items, and most timepieces remained simple sandglasses or sundials; so the positions of the sun and moon were crucial information to the agricultural society. With the advent of Benjamin Franklin's *Poor Richard's Almanac* in the eighteenth century, almanacs also became popular sources of homilies on various religious, literary and historical themes. But while Franklin did little original work for his publication, Banneker produced all the calculations himself, along with lists of medicines to stave off diseases, plus recipes, poems, and short essays gathered from various sources.

Through the Ellicott family, Banneker came to the attention of abolitionist groups in Maryland and Pennsylvania. On July 4, 1791, at a meeting of one such organization, a prominent physician named Dr. George Buchanan gave an oration considered courageous in a Southern state. Citing "Phillis Wheatley, who distinguished herself as a poetess" and "Banneker, the Maryland Astronomer" as two examples of distinguished blacks, Buchanan's talk was published as a pamphlet and brought increasing attention to Banneker.

His ephemeris was submitted for review to David Rittenhouse, president of the American Philosophical Society and the foremost scientist in the country. Checking out Banneker's calculations, Rittenhouse offered a favorable response and added: "Every instance of Genius amongst the Negroes is worthy of attention, because their oppressors seem to lay great stress on their supposed inferior mental abilities."

Finding himself a focus of racial debate, and desiring that his competence—not his color—be the determining factor in whether his almanac saw print, Banneker sent a manuscript copy that August to Thomas Jefferson. It was accompanied by a twelve-page letter. Some years earlier Jefferson, in his *Notes on Virginia*, had expressed strong misgivings about the slavery system, while admitting that his own livelihood as a Virginia planter was dependent upon it. Now Banneker's gesture sought not only to appeal to Jefferson's higher nature, but also chastised the secretary of state for failing to make the Declaration of Independence a reality for all Americans.

"We are a race of Beings who have long laboured under the abuse and censure of the world," Banneker wrote, "that we have been looked upon with an eye of contempt. . . ." If his hope was true that Jefferson was indeed "measurably friendly and well disposed toward us," Banneker implored that Jefferson "readily embrace every opportunity to eradicate that train of absurd and false ideas and oppinions which so generally prevail with respect to us, and that your Sentiments are concurrent with mine, which are that one universal Father hath given being to us all, and that he hath not only made us all of one flesh, but that he hath also without partiality afforded us all the same Sensations, and endued us all with the same faculties, and that however variable we may be in Society or religion, however diversified in Situation or colour, we are all of the Same Family, and Stand in the Same relation to him."

Thus it was a duty and Christian obligation to extend one's "power and influence to the relief of every part of the human race, from whatever burthen or oppression they may unjustly labour under." How, asked Banneker, could Jefferson "rest Satisfyed" in the face of such "unjustifyable cruelty and barbarism?" Then he struck to the heart of Jefferson's conscience:

"Sir, Suffer me to recall to your mind that time in which the Arms and tyranny of the British Crown were exerted with every powerful effort, in order to reduce you to a State of Servitude; look back I intreat you on the variety of dangers to which you were exposed, reflect on that time in which every human aid appeared unavailable, and in which even hope and fortitude wore the aspect of inability to the Conflict, and you cannot but be led to a Serious and grateful Sense of your miraculous and providential preservation."

Jefferson needed to acknowledge "that the present freedom and tranquillity which you enjoy you have mercifully received. . . ." Was it not, Banneker stated, Jefferson's "Just apprehension of the horrors" of slavery that led him to publicly set forth these words: "'We hold these truths to be Self evident, that all men are created equal, and that they are endowed by their creator with certain inalienable rights, that amongst these are life, liberty, and the pursuit of happiness. . . .'"

After taking Jefferson to task for continuing to own slaves himself—"guilty of that most criminal act, which you professedly detested in others"—Banneker continued his letter by quoting from the Book of Job: "Put your Soul in their Souls' stead." Then he made an offering of the almanac, reminding Jefferson of the surveying service he had performed. "This calculation, Sir, is the production of my arduous study, in this my advanced Stage of life; for having long had unbounded desires to become Acquainted with the Secrets of nature, I have had to gratify my curiosity herein thro[ugh] my own assiduous application to Astronomical Study, in which I need not to recount to you the many difficulties and disadvantages which I have had to encounter."

How did Jefferson react? Within four days of receiving Banneker's message, on August 30, 1791, Jefferson wrote back from Philadelphia: "No body wishes more than I do to see such proofs as you exhibit, that nature has given to our black brethren, talents equal to those of the other colors of men, and that the appearance of a want of them is owing merely to the degraded condition of their existence, both in Africa & America. I can add with truth, that no body wishes more ardently to see a good system commenced to raising the condition both of their body & mind to what it ought to be, as far as the imbecility of their present existence, and other circumstances which cannot be neglected, will admit.

"I have taken the liberty of sending your Almanac to Monsieur de Condorcet, Secretary of the Academy of Sciences at Paris, and member of the Philanthropic society, because I considered it as a document to which your whole colour had a right for their justification against the doubts which have been entertained of them.

"I am with great esteem, Sir your most obed[ient] humble serv[ant]. Thomas Jefferson."

In his letter to the Marquis, Jefferson described Banneker's ancestral origins, his employment in helping to lay out Washington, D.C., his almanac, and Jefferson's personal witness of Banneker's "very elegant solutions of Geometrical problems." Jefferson wrote that, through examples like Banneker, he would personally "be delighted to see these instances of moral eminence so multiplied as to prove that the want of talents observed in them is merely the effect of their degraded condition, and not proceeding from any difference in the structure of the parts on which intellect depends."

There is no record that the Marquis de Condorcet, if he received the letter, ever replied or acted upon Jefferson's request that Banneker's work be reviewed by a French Academy of Science committee. But in America, a Philadelphia printer published and distributed widely Banneker's and Jefferson's correspondence six months later as a pamphlet. And some critics would use the correspondence against Jefferson when he campaigned for the presidency in 1800. "What shall we think of a secretary of state thus fraternizing with negroes," wrote one, "writing them complimentary epistles, stiling them *his black brethren*, congratulating them on the evidence of their *genius*, and assuring them of his good wishes for their speedy emancipation?"

As Winthrop D. Jordan has said in *The White Man's Burden*, "Jefferson had been thrown into confusion by his unsettling confrontation with Banneker." The contradictions in Jefferson, which Banneker so eloquently pierced, came to the fore during his presidency when a newspaper accused him of having an ongoing liaison with a slave mistress. Contemporary historians still debate whether, after his wife's death, Jefferson did indeed have a thirty-eight-year-long intimate relationship with Sally Hemings, with whom he is said to have fathered seven children.

On October 17, 1791, Banneker penned a poem that accentuated the theme of his correspondence with Jefferson:

> *"Behold ye Christians! and in pity see*
> *Those Afric sons which Nature formed free;*
> *Behold them in a fruitful country blest,*
> *Of Nature's bounties see them rich possest,*
> *Behold them herefrom torn by cruel force.*
> *And doomed to slavery without remorse,*
> *This act, America, thy sons have known;*
> *This cruel act, relentless they have done."*

Banneker's initial almanac, published in Baltimore in 1792, was the first scientific book ever written by an African-American. It was widely read along the Eastern seaboard. Banneker's tide tables for the Chesapeake Bay proved a boon to seafaring travelers. His weather predictions are said to have been remarkably prescient—although little knowledge of the laws governing weather, and certainly no forecasting methods, yet existed. It is not known precisely how Banneker devised his system.

For the ensuing five years, at least twenty-eight known editions of Banneker's series continued to be published. The 1793 edition contained his correspondence with Jefferson and a plan for permanent peace drafted by prominent physician Dr. Benjamin Rush. According to Banneker's biographer Silvio Bedini, this made it "one of the most important publications of its time. It was distributed in great numbers and became the subject of widespread discussion at all levels."

In the 1795 Almanac, there appeared this Banneker quote: "The most sensible of those who make scientific researches, is he who believes himself the farthest from the goal, & who whatever advances he has made in his road, studies as if he yet knew nothing and marches as if he were only yet beginning to make his first advance."

As Bedini writes: "As the scientific effort of a free Negro, his almanacs provided tangible proof of the mental equality of the races, a topic which was central to the antislavery movement. By the second half of the final decade of the century, however, a strong reaction to the cause of abolition had set in." In 1797 the Maryland Society for the Abolition of Slavery closed its doors. The same year marked the final edition of Banneker's almanacs, although his increasingly failing health may have been the primary reason. Complaining in one letter of palpitations, constant headaches, and trembling hands, Banneker began selling off his land.

Until 1802, he continued calculating his yearly ephemerises. He still hunted small game occasionally in the surrounding woods, where since boyhood he had known the identification of every shrub and tree. His sisters came often to assist with his laundry and basic chores (no legitimate evidence of a love interest in Banneker's life is known to exist). In his final years, he was glimpsed at times inside a nearby Quaker meeting house, sitting on a bench toward the rear, leaning upon his staff in deep meditation.

Banneker kept up his journaling, as he had for years, writing down dreams—an encounter with "the Infernal Spirit," another with a white fawn—as well as reports on the beekeeping interest he had acquired from his father. He also recorded more than one incident of gunshots striking his house, and of break-ins. Sometimes he also wrote down religious notes. One of these was a quotation from the Book of Samuel:

"And he brought away the people that were therein and put them under Laws, and under harrows of iron, and under axes of iron, and made them pass through the brick-kiln."

A free man himself, yet haunted by those harrows and axes of iron that shackled most of his people in America, Benjamin Banneker was a month shy of his seventy-fifth birthday when he set out on an autumn Sunday for his customary walk through the hills he loved. Happening upon a neighbor, Banneker said he was suddenly feeling very ill. Both men returned to the log cabin. Banneker lay down on a couch, lost his power of speech, and died quietly on October 9, 1806.

In the throes of a previous sickness, Banneker had asked his sisters to make sure that all the books and instruments loaned to him years before by George Ellicott be returned upon his death. In addition, Banneker asked that Ellicott receive all of his manuscripts, including the almanacs and the correspondence with Jefferson. His sisters immediately took care of his request.

Then, two days later, just as Banneker was being placed in his grave, his old wooden house mysteriously caught fire. It burned so quickly that nothing inside could be salvaged, including his prized old wooden striking clock. As Silvio Bedini writes: "It seemed almost as if an act of fate was determined to destroy every earthly vestige of the Negro sage with the extinction of his life."

For some years thereafter, Banneker was all but forgotten. When the abolitionist movement renewed itself, the first relatively comprehensive account of his accomplishments appeared in print in 1844. The following year, a group set out to try to locate his gravesite, but could not place it. His memory, however, received regular revival in the years leading up to the Civil War. It included the establishment in Philadelphia in 1853 of a Banneker Institute, a large library and instruction society for young African-Americans.

Not long before the turn of the twentieth century, Anne Tyson Kirk began editing a biography of Banneker based upon notes that her mother, Martha Ellicott Tyson, had compiled years before. She wrote seeking advice from Frederick Douglass on three occasions. Her letters have not survived, but Douglass's replies did.

". . . I believe that a full narrative of the life of so exceptional a character as Bannecker [sic] will find a ready sale both in the North and in the South among colored and among white readers. The country needs it today. It will, I believe help my race immensely both as an incentive and a vindication. I remember your family as friendly to the enslaved in my early childhood—and have no doubt you have been just to Bannecker."

After several more years of editing, Anne Kirk submitted for publication the last depiction of Banneker to be based upon original materials. When she died suddenly, relatively little distribution of the biography ever occurred. Once again, the decades rolled past with Banneker lost to American history. Finally, in the embryonic years of the civil rights movement, the State Roads Commission of Maryland put up a memorial marker. The location of the Banneker homestead was derived from an old deed of partition made with the Ellicott family. And so, in 1954—the year of the Supreme Court's landmark integration decision—these words were incribed on the premises of a grade school in Oella, Maryland.

BENJAMIN BANNEKER
1731-1806

SELF-EDUCATED NEGRO
MATHEMATICIAN-ASTRONOMER
HE MADE THE FIRST MARYLAND ALMANAC IN 1792.
ASSISTED IN SURVEY OF DISTRICT OF COLUMBIA.
HIS ACHIEVEMENTS RECOGNIZED
BY THOMAS JEFFERSON.

WAS BORN, LIVED HIS ENTIRE LIFE, AND
DIED NEAR HERE.

From Banneker's Almanac, 1794: "Presumption should never make us neglect that which appears easy to us, nor despair make us lose courage at the sight of difficulties."

FOR FURTHER READING:

Silvio A. Bedini, *The Life of Benjamin Banneker* (New York: Scribners, 1972).

The Architects:
Charles and Cheryl McAfee

"Minority design professionals—by their very nature, by their history, by their culture—are sensitive to the needs of people who interact within the spaces we create and to the impressions of attitudes on future generations. We cannot build buildings that are only necessary to house a piece of machinery, that do not affect the lifestyle of a neighborhood.

"It is necessary that minority professionals succeed; we are the moralists of the construction industry."

—CHARLES F. McAFEE, *Faia.*

Seated behind a large desk covered with bluelines, surrounded by walls of photographs of friends such as photographer/filmmaker Gordon Parks and former U.S. Ambassador to the United Nations Andrew Young, Charles McAfee remembers the first house he designed in his hometown of Wichita, Kansas. The year was 1963, and his architectural project had won one of the seven national design awards that the Federal Housing Administration gave that year.

"Three others who got awards were I. M. Pei, Mies van der Rohe, and Skidmore, Owings & Merrill," McAfee recalls. "At this lavish ceremony in Washington, all these huge projects other people did were displayed right along with this little single-family house I did. When the name Charles McAfee was announced, all eighteen hundred people in the audience wondered who I was. Then I. M. Pei asked me how old I was. I said 'I'm twenty-nine.' He smiled and said, 'Yes, I remember those days.' And I thought to myself, Did he have to borrow the money from his father to come here to Washington like I did?"

Thirty-five years and countless awards later, Charles McAfee is considered by many of his peers to be the leading African-American architect in the United States. A tall, husky man in his mid-sixties, McAfee's architectural firm is headquartered in Wichita and has offices in Atlanta, Dallas, and Oklahoma City. He helped assemble the joint venture that oversaw the program, design and construction of all thirty-three competition sites for the 1996 Summer Olympics. A modular housing system he developed for inner-city residents with limited incomes has been lauded nationally as an answer to urban decay.

"There's no question about his leadership in the African-American architects' community," notes Cecil Steward, a past president of the American Institute of Architects (AIA) and dean of the College of Architecture at McAfee's alma mater, the University of Nebraska. "His practice has reflected his social conscience, working on projects that many architects shy away from in the central city."

In a profession where more than ninety percent of the members are white males, Charles McAfee and two of his three children are opening new frontiers. Oldest daughter Cheryl McAfee-Mitchell, who led the Olympics project team, manages the Atlanta office. Youngest daughter Charyl McAfee-Duncan runs the family offices in Dallas and Oklahoma City. Both women hold graduate degrees in architecture and are two of only eighty African-American women among the approximately 1,065 licensed female architects in the United States. Cheryl was featured in a 1995 *Ebony* article, "America's Top Women Architects."

"Charles McAfee has been an important mentor not only to his daughters, but also to many other young African-Americans who have gone into the field," says Eugene Kremer, former president of the Association of Collegiate Schools of Architecture while dean of the department at Kansas State University. "It's quite an accomplishment that, from a base in Kansas, Charles has managed to get work in major metropolitan areas like Washington, Boston, and Atlanta against tough competition from other firms that operate in those cities."

Gordon Parks first met McAfee in the late 1970s, over a tennis game in New Orleans. At dinner that evening, after Parks informed McAfee that he had no desire to return to his native Kansas since filming *The Learning Tree*, McAfee excused himself from the table and placed a call to Wichita State University. "An exhibition of my photographs became the first retrospective at the art gallery Charles designed on the campus," Parks recalls. Now McAfee is working behind the scenes to establish a Gordon Parks multidisciplinary center at the university. "Charley's become very close to what's left of my family in Wichita," Parks says. "He's struggled to become a top-rank architect, with a conscience about the problems of black people in Kansas. Even though he's been denied certain things, he still feels this is the place that ought to recognize his talent and promote it. And well they should."

I first encountered Charles McAfee in 1994 at the annual AIA convention in Chicago. The theme of this gathering was sustainability; in a controversial speech, McAfee took his colleagues to task for what he called "architectural genocide." Now, in his Wichita office, the man who designed Andrew Young's house and Spike Lee's clothing store pulls no punches as he elaborates:

"It's a disaster that there are one million substandard houses between Washington, D.C., and the Texas/Louisiana border. Poor folks are living in horrible conditions in this country. When a doctor makes a mistake, you bury it. When an architect makes a mistake, you live with it." To illustrate his point, McAfee criticizes a housing project in Chicago, which was designed with elevators on the outside of the buildings. "Anybody in his right mind knows better than to run exterior elevators twenty stories down in Chicago, where the temperature can drop forty degrees in an hour. The elevators aren't going to work. When I said we commit architectural genocide, that's exactly what we do."

So McAfee Manufacturing Company, a new outgrowth of Charles F. McAfee Architects and Planners, is setting out to alter that equation. As the only builder in the nation of modular homes designed especially for urban use, his high-quality product is assembled in a factory, transported onto vacant lots, and erected in a fraction of the time required for conventional housing. The homes are designed to sell for $45,000, which is far below the median price of $129,000 for a new home. As the *Wichita Eagle* described in a lead editorial in 1994:

"Never let it be said that Wichitan Charles McAfee is shy. He's not reserved in his fight for racial equality. . . . He isn't timid about criticizing his hometown. . . . He's training unskilled workers to build homes. He's purchasing supplies, materials and services from near-northeast [Wichita] neighborhood businesses. In other words, he's putting his money, his business and architectural know-how—and his dedication to making the world a better place for folks who are struggling to make it—where his mouth is."

Life for the McAfee family in a rural state where African-Americans comprise only four percent of the population was an uphill fight. McAfee's great-grandfather, Jacob, who was wounded while fighting for the Union Army during the Civil War, migrated with his family from Ohio to Wichita in a covered wagon in early 1865. Jacob was an aggressive and resourceful entrepreneur who built the first high-rise building in Wichita. During the Great Depression, McAfee's parents, Arthur and Willie Anna, left Kansas's largest city temporarily to find work in Los Angeles. There Charles was born on Christmas 1932. After six months, his parents returned to Wichita with their three young children.

"My father was a redcap. He carried bags at the Union Station, and also worked awhile as a sleeping car porter," McAfee recalls. "I remember watching him walking up a long ramp carrying four bags at once—one under each arm and one in each hand. I tried it once and almost killed myself!"

The youngest of seven children, Arthur McAfee had dropped out of high school to care for his mother when she became ill. That experience cemented in him a determination to ensure that his own children receive an education. He told his children that he wanted them to study rather than work. He never bought a car, choosing instead to walk to work every day to earn enough money to take care of his family. Ultimately, the three McAfee children collectively earned five undergraduate and graduate degrees. Arthur's daughter, Gwen, became head of the hematology outpatient clinic at the renowned UCLA Medical School, and his son Arthur, Jr. became athletic director and basketball coach at the prestigious Morehouse College in Atlanta. Strolling together across the University of Nebraska campus on Charles's graduation day, Arthur told his youngest child, "Now I've done what I wanted to do in life."

"My father was the most honest man I ever met," says Charles. "He used to say, 'When you wake up in the morning and look in the mirror, you want to know who you're looking at.' He basically set standards for us that I don't think I could ever meet, and I once told him the only thing I could leave him was a reputation." An emphasis on education has passed down two generations: Arthur McAfee's six grandchildren have earned collectively ten college degrees.

Charles's interest in building began with model airplanes he designed as a child during World War II. He took his first mechanical drawing course in seventh grade. He had completed so many projects by the time he reached high school that he was assigned to small projects for local contractors.

Also a talented basketball player, McAfee became the first African-American to play on the University of Nebraska's team in 1950. But Nebraska's coach left McAfee at home when the team traveled to the universities of Arkansas, Tennessee, and Texas, because McAfee was shut out of the hotels and arenas in Fayetteville, Knoxville, and Austin.

A member of the Reserve Officers Training Corps program during the Korean War, McAfee was turned in to the draft board after his second year of college. He had learned from his brother that black ROTC officers were not respected, so he notified the ROTC office that he did not want to enter the advanced program. By March 1953 McAfee was drafted into the Army and sent to Germany. This blessing—disguised as mean-spirited bad luck—allowed him to see sites he had studied in his architecture, government, and history of art classes at Nebraska. "When I came back to school, I had a perspective about what it meant to talk about St. Peter's or the Arc de Triomphe," McAfee explains. He learned that popes and kings commissioned architects to design buildings. "When people referred to 'my architect,' they meant someone who was almost in servitude. The Pope referred to Michelangelo as 'my architect.' Understanding the client base and the inequality of the process probably saddened me the most," laments McAfee.

After returning to Nebraska, McAfee married Gloria Myrth Winston, whom he had known since childhood. A talented soprano and Marian Anderson scholar, Gloria studied music at Howard University and the University of Indiana, yet chose to forgo a promising career in opera to marry McAfee and raise a family. She later received her Master's degree in elementary education at Wichita State University, and ultimately became principal of several schools in Wichita, including the one she and Charles attended as children. Gloria maintained her singing voice throughout her teaching career, and was invited to perform at then-Kansas governor Robert Docking's two inaugurations as well as for Presidents Truman and Eisenhower, and Illinois governor Adlai Stevenson. On October 24, 1956, Gloria gave birth to the McAfees' first child, Cheryl.

Two years later McAfee received his bachelor of architecture degree from Nebraska and began to ponder his future. He stayed in Kansas because of a bet he made with an African-American man who had gone into architecture after World War II. The man claimed he could not get a job in Kansas because he was black, and challenged McAfee to find work in the state. When McAfee interviewed with a local firm, one of the partners told him, "Your work is really good; my partner and I often wondered what we'd do if a colored fellow came in to apply for a job." Impressed with McAfee's work, the man arranged for Charles to meet his partner.

During the second interview, the partner told McAfee, "Yep, your work really is good; we often wondered what would happen if a colored fellow ever came in looking for a job. But I'm worried about my partner." McAfee asked him why. "Because he's from Oklahoma." Thinking over his answer, McAfee asked where the man was raised. Arrogantly he exclaimed, "I'm from Texas!"—as though racism did not exist in his home state.

Nevertheless, McAfee won the bet and worked at the firm until its work ran out a year later. He completed his three-year internship with other firms in Kansas, and even did design work. But he was forbidden to meet with the clients.

McAfee did not lack for offers on either coast. One came from Paul Revere Williams. In 1923 Williams became the first African-American member of the AIA, and in 1957 was honored as its first black Fellow. Author Michael Webb described him: "Most of all he impressed everyone he met with his dignified bearing, impeccable dress, and courtly manners." During the 1930s, Williams was commissioned to create three Los Angeles landmarks: the mansion of automaker Errett Cord, interiors for Beverly Hills' new Saks Fifth Avenue, and the offices of the Music Corporation of America. He also designed the theme building at Los Angeles International Airport, which has a restaurant in the middle and resembles a large spider.

Williams's talent was legendary among residential designers in Los Angeles. His clientele included Desi Arnaz and Lucille Ball, Barbara Stanwyck, Tyrone Power, Lon Chaney, and Frank Sinatra. McAfee says: "He was an extremely talented man, but also fortunate enough to be in a part of the country where the clientele had sufficient arrogance—and sufficient money—to hire whomever they wanted to be their architect. Who was going to tell Frank Sinatra whom he could hire?"

McAfee considered Williams his mentor, and had been invited to work for Williams's firm when he first graduated from college. But Charles did not think he was good enough. In 1963, McAfee called to tell Williams he was interested in coming to the West Coast. The Architects Collaborative in Boston had also offered McAfee an overseas position at its Rome or Ankara offices. These stellar opportunities placed McAfee in a serious quandary. He explained all his offers to his father, who watched his son's face as he listened. Arthur McAfee knew nothing about architecture but certainly understood his children. Finally the elder McAfee asked, "What's wrong? You're not happy. What do you *really* want to do?"

Charles responded, "Daddy, I want to open my own office."

"Let's do it," his father replied simply.

Father and son found an office on the second floor above a grocery store in an old building across from the Wichita courthouse, where McAfee's great-grandfather had built the first high-rise in the city. Later that year McAfee earned a national design award for his first solo-designed home.

The job that helped to spawn his architectural career was, ironically, a mortuary. Val and Gene Jackson, twin brothers with whom McAfee had grown up, hired him to design their new facilities. That project won him yet another design award.

Asked to describe his architectural style, McAfee responds that the designer he admires most is Mies van der Rohe, "because he was so disciplined about what he did." McAfee has no preconceived ideas about how something should look; he develops that impression only after carefully studying the culture of the building and the factors that affect it. "The direction I've gone is simply to approach whatever materials I'm using with great respect. If it's wood," McAfee illustrates, "I don't expect it to function like concrete."

Driving through downtown Wichita, McAfee points toward the offices of the town newspaper, a block-long glass and concrete structure. In 1969 Britt Brown, then publisher of the *Wichita Eagle-Beacon*, selected McAfee over a host of architects to design a large annex to his newspaper. Now retired, Brown recalls the experience:

"I was more of the old traditional type, and when Charles came up with the drawings, I thought, 'Oh no, that's just too modern.' I wanted it to blend in with our existing building. He said, It's not really an addition, so it should look separate. I let him talk me into it and when it was all done, he was quite right." This project too earned McAfee a design award.

Brown endured great criticism from his friends when he hired McAfee. One day he invited McAfee to lunch at his club, "You know, the one you can't belong to," Brown goaded McAfee. McAfee mused that the progressively-minded Brown was "on a roll today." Brown was angry as they began to eat. He recounted an incident that had happened at the Wichita Country Club—another place McAfee could not join. Some of the city leaders confronted Brown and asked what he was trying to prove by having a "nigger" do his work. Indignantly Brown responded, "First of all, it's my money. Second, the 'nigger' as you call him is the best architect in this town."

"Not many people had the guts this guy had. I have huge respect for him," acknowledges McAfee.

After the *Wichita Eagle-Beacon* building, however, McAfee had difficulty procuring other work in the Wichita area. One of his white competitors, the son of a managing executive at one of the city's major aerospace manufacturers, had an inside track on most of the architectural projects. "Charles had a double uphill road to hoe but he has done it," reflects Brown. "He's never stuck in any one mode, and his work today is as valid as it was thirty years ago."

While driving throughout the city, McAfee points out more of his projects: the multi-award-winning McKnight Art Center on the Wichita State University campus, Calvary Baptist Church, and McAdams Park in near-northeast Wichita, where he played as a child. He notes that beyond Wichita's urban center, most of his clients are based outside Kansas. Yet he remained in Wichita not only because it is home, but also because it is halfway between New York and Los Angeles and also allows easy access to most of the other cities where the firm works.

In his typically definitive manner, McAfee shares his disappointment in much of postmodern architecture. He finds it "crude, disproportionate, and rude." He thinks today's work seems to have been created by people who grew up with no personal responsibility. By contrast, most of the work McAfee has done has tight budget constraints. One of his basic design philosophies is to ensure that a building sustains itself over the long term with the least amount of maintenance.

In 1974, McAfee opened a third office in Atlanta, where his first task was to plan a thirty-five million dollar rapid-rail station. He has since programmed a similar transit system for Miami, and designed seventy buildings all across the country for the Federal Aviation Administration. Indeed, McAfee projects can now be found in all fifty states. In 1981 he was named a Fellow of the AIA, the organization's second-highest honor.

The concept for McAfee's dream house, a modular system that he pioneered, originated many years ago. During the first Nixon Administration, Secretary of Housing George Romney challenged the profession to develop affordable housing. A veteran of the automobile industry, Romney reasoned that if cars could be manufactured, then so could houses. McAfee chuckles, "A few of us were young enough, idealistic enough, and crazy enough to believe that was true."

McAfee invested a significant portion of his savings to develop the modular system. Working in a Quonset hut at a lumberyard, he and four others built Wichita's first modular home, transported it across town on a truck, hoisted it with a crane, and set it in place near the banks of the Arkansas River. Two days later the home was finished, five thousand people visited it during a one-day open house, and the AIA bestowed McAfee with another design award.

Encouraged by the initial success, McAfee opened a manufacturing plant and hired more than 100 people from surrounding communities. They built many homes during the 1970s, but not one bank in Wichita would support McAfee's efforts. Eventually the plant closed down, forcing McAfee to lay off many employees. "It really hurt me, I mean hurt me to my heart," McAfee soberly recalls. "I swore I'd never bring it back—until housing in this country got so bad that I felt it was the only solution."

Steering the car into the parking lot in front of the new McAfee Manufacturing Company, McAfee shares his concern that he waited too long to resurrect the company. About five years ago, the mayor of Wadley, Georgia, called McAfee to discuss the town's housing needs.

McAfee paid a visit, and was shown a factory that manufactured high-quality garments that ultimately sold in retail giants such as Saks and Macy's. The mayor then drove him to the neighborhood where the factory workers lived. The factory owner also owned the properties, and charged two hundred dollars a month in rent for dilapidated mobile homes set on concrete blocks. After witnessing such greed and inhumanity, McAfee thought, "My God, I've *got* to bring back what I started to do twenty years ago."

When McAfee ran into the same obstacles while seeking financial support, he turned again to his boyhood friends, the Jackson brothers whose mortuary he had built. Pooling their resources, the three formed a partnership, purchased a twenty-acre site from the city, obtained a line of credit from Wichita's American Bank to finance construction and installation, and set up McAfee Manufacturing for production by April 1994.

"We now have almost eighty employees," McAfee states as we enter the vast warehouselike space lined with rows of building materials and assembly-line work spaces. Only about ten percent of the staff are trained as journeymen carpenters, along with one journeyman electrician and one plumber. Most of the other employees had no experience or skills related to the construction industry, and lived in economically depressed neighborhoods surrounding the plant. Through a special training and counseling program, these unskilled workers learn a trade and the few who had seen tougher times—such as welfare, prison, or substance abuse—have been able to improve their lives. In addition to strengthening the human resources in the area, the manufacturing plant also purchases most of the materials and equipment it uses from local, minority-owned suppliers, which further boosts the community economically.

McAfee negotiated a contract with Wichita's AFL-CIO, the Unified Brotherhood of Carpenters Union, whereby each employee becomes a union member at a starting salary of at least seven dollars and fifty cents per hour plus full health insurance coverage. When then-Secretary of Housing and Urban Development Henry Cisneros asked McAfee how he pulled it off, McAfee explained simply, "We had something they wanted, and they had something we wanted." The average union member and carpenter in Wichita was more than fifty years old, and the union had only one African-American member. Now more than fifty percent of the union membership is employed at McAfee Manufacturing, including the local union president. The issue of health care coverage was particularly sensitive. The large insurance companies in town resisted providing coverage because of the community in which the plant was located, among other issues.

Today is a holiday, and the usual din of pounding hammers and buzzing electric saws is absent as McAfee continues the plant tour. He explains that the modules can be assembled in more than 100 ways using eight basic designs. The factory can build anything from a 600-square-foot apartment to a 2,500-square-foot custom home. Up to two modular units can be assembled per day. "Once they're bolted together," says McAfee, "these homes are structurally stronger than 'stick-built' homes because they're made to withstand being lifted by crane onto the flatbed trailers and transported to the home site." The modularity is not just in the individual pieces, it is in the system, which allows McAfee to create a sophisticated method of building blocks.

McAfee and his partners have now bought 150 vacant lots in the predominantly black northeastern sector of Wichita, where they grew up. This is an area that had seen no new construction in decades. We pull up to a 1,200-square-foot, two-story single-family townhouse unit that features three bedrooms, two bathrooms, vinyl siding, full carpeting and appliances, centralized climate control system, and detached garage. Twelve more townhomes and forty units of varying style are also planned for the twenty-acre site.

McAfee bemoans that the majority of Americans cannot afford moderately priced homes. "Banks are interested in providing mortgage loans, yet the reason neighborhoods deteriorate is that people with fixed or low incomes simply do not have enough money to make repairs and perform basic upkeep," he says. McAfee's manufactured homes are designed to be as maintenance-free as possible.

Within walking distance of the townhouse is an assisted-living care community with thirty-one units. Approximately 100 modular homes will be erected for senior citizens, due to a joint venture with the Kansas City-based Minority Enterprise Financial Acquisition Corporation. The complex of 600-square-foot units, designed according to accessibility standards for physically challenged people, will offer dining, housekeeping, lawn maintenance, and grocery shopping assistance services.

McAfee has his sights set on taking the modular housing concept to many other cities in the United States. Inquiries about his revitalization efforts have also come from Mexico, Japan, South Africa, the former Soviet Union, and some Caribbean nations. McAfee notes that Chicago alone has clear title to some 52,000 empty inner-city lots, all of which must be maintained while taxpayers foot the bill. With more than five million American families either living in substandard dwellings or spending more than half their income on housing, the need could not be more obvious.

With justifiable pride McAfee remembers the Reverend Jesse Jackson's recent visit to the factory, where he suggested at a press conference that President Clinton would do well to take a look at McAfee Manufacturing. Jackson walked through the plant, chatting with workers. Two weeks later Jackson's son, Jesse Jackson, Jr., called McAfee and asked, "What did you to do my father in Wichita? He's the kind of person who's always focused on the next place; he never has time to talk about someplace he's been. But he hasn't stopped talking about Wichita since he got back." McAfee compassionately explained that what the elder Jackson saw in Wichita was what people of his and McAfee's generation have been saying for a long time: all people are looking for is an honest chance.

To McAfee, life ultimately derives from a sense of family, in a network that radiates from his lifelong neighborhood. Over lunch at a fashionable restaurant across from the newspaper headquarters he designed, he is continually interrupted by well-wishers. After a middle-aged African-American woman stops briefly by the table, McAfee quietly tells a story about her son. The young man had been both an outstanding student and star basketball player at a Wichita high school, and later was arrested for selling drugs during his first semester at a junior college. McAfee knew nothing about the incident when the mother came to see him and ask if he would prepare a recommendation for the young man to submit to Morehouse College, where McAfee's brother, Arthur Jr., served as basketball coach. McAfee later learned the entire story from the young man's high school coach.

"We were old friends and he told me that the fellow was really intelligent but throwing his life away," McAfee reminisces. "I asked, 'Would you recommend him if we can get him into Morehouse?' The coach said he absolutely would because the kid, who just got off on the wrong track, was one of the finest players he had ever coached." Arthur McAfee agreed to help his brother with the situation. The young man was admitted to Morehouse, won Conference Newcomer-of-the-Year honors, and graduated with almost straight As.

In October 1995, the *Wichita Eagle* ran a story headlined "In Sickness and in Health." It described how complications from diabetes forced Gloria McAfee to undergo kidney dialysis for nine months. She had been placed on the list to receive a transplant but her kidneys were deteriorating too quickly for a donor to be identified. Her condition escalated into an emergency. Something had to be done quickly. The obvious potential donors were the couple's daughters. Until that point, Gloria had been taking the situation well. She choked up and said she did not want to put any of her children through that ordeal. Charles looked at the doctor and said, "Don't worry. I'm going to do it." The physicians were highly skeptical. At sixty-two, McAfee was two years older than the oldest previous donor. But McAfee had considerable persuasive powers. "The doctor claims I threw him on the ground and told him to start making preparations. Well, I didn't do *that*."

Following a long series of tests, McAfee underwent a four-hour transplant operation alongside his wife at the St. Francis Regional Medical Center. During his recovery McAfee watched the progress on one of his modular homes that was being erected near the hospital. When the story went out over the Associated Press wire services, flowers poured in from all over the country.

Within a week, McAfee was back at work. "Looking back over my life," he says, "destiny says that the reason I never drank or smoked or did drugs is so that my kidneys would be as healthy as they were. Everything else I've ever accomplished takes a very minimal place compared to this." He considers himself blessed fourfold—once for being able to help Gloria, and three more times for having been able to spare all of his daughters from surgery.

Cheryl McAfee-Mitchell, Charles and Gloria's eldest daughter, is sitting behind a large desk in her office in downtown Atlanta's Candler Building. Visible from the picture window is her father's first project in Atlanta in 1974, the Midtown Station rail terminal, which was a major stop for spectators en route to the 1996 Summer Olympics. Citations noting Cheryl's service as a deputy director of the Program Services Group for the Games adorn the walls. The Atlanta office has continued to manage the conversion of thirty-three venues to post-Games use, including transforming the Olympic Stadium into Turner Field, home of the Atlanta Braves baseball team.

The phone rings, and the stunningly attractive woman picks it up. "That was my sister Charyl," she explains afterwards. "She's on her way from Dallas to Oklahoma City, where the firm is renovating nineteen school buildings." Cheryl adds that while her sister always wanted to be an architect, Cheryl at one time searched for a reason not to pursue the field. Yet she continued to find beauty in her father's works—and eventually discovered it for herself.

Growing up in Wichita, Cheryl remembers her father's mother as a strong influence during her formative years. "Grandma Willie was always teaching me about things. I would ask questions like, 'Well, how do you know there's a God?' She would say, 'Look out the window. See those trees? Who else could have done that?'" Such moments spawned a love and deep respect for nature and animals, as well as a sense of faith that Cheryl would need when she was selected along with a handful of other black children to integrate Wichita's all-white Murdock Elementary School in the early 1960s.

The children were separated so that no more than one would be in any classroom. Cheryl had no idea she was "different" until she was placed in an environment where other children did not talk to her and teachers ignored her or gave her a low grade because of a "label." She once memorized the lines for the lead role in a school play but was told the only part she could play was a maid.

Amused, Cheryl relates an ironic incident from her childhood. "We had a spelling bee at school and I was one of the two finalists. The teacher asked me to spell 'architect' since my father was one, even though it wasn't part of the word pool," she laughs. "I spelled it correctly but the teacher didn't know how to spell it and told me I was wrong. After that, for a while I wasn't allowed to sit in the classroom."

Urged by her father to pursue her talent for drawing, Cheryl went on to attend a private school in Wichita. She also had a strong aptitude for math and science and received several college scholarships. She chose Kansas State University, which many of her friends attended and which had strong programs in architecture and her other fascination, veterinary medicine. Ultimately she opted for architecture, and later completed an internship with the Boston-based Architect's Collaborative. With their encouragement, she soon entered graduate school at Harvard University, where she studied architectural history, took courses in policy and law, and achieved a Master of Architecture degree in urban design and planning policy in 1981. "It was brain overload, but I soaked it up like a sponge," she says. She returned to work at the Collaborative, which was undertaking the redevelopment of Boston's landmark Copley Square.

"They took my love for architecture to a whole new level," McAfee says. She produced several presentation drawings for the Copley Square project and started to understand some of the issues her father sometimes discussed, such as the rhythm of buildings and phoniness versus realism. "From him I learned about how materials continue to change and you have to research what a material can do in terms of strength, texture, or color to make the expression of a building more interesting. Now it all began to make sense."

McAfee was in the midst of a design project in Baghdad when the telephone calls from her father and other family members became more persistent. "You have to come back, you must return home," Cheryl imitates her father in her best Godfather impression. "So, that's what I did."

Cheryl became the first African-American woman in Kansas's history to receive an architect's license. Again she encountered obstacles, but then-attorney general of Kansas Bob Stephan was in her corner. "Now when I'm facing a challenge, I always hear his voice saying, 'Your greatest revenge will be your success,' " she reflects.

For eleven years she worked for her father's firm in Wichita. Then in 1992, the Atlanta Committee for the Olympic Games selected the joint venture PSG from a field of sixteen competitors to build the infrastructure for the 1996 Games. The McAfee company had been successful in Atlanta for seventeen years, and former mayor Andrew Young, cochairman of the committee, was an advocate for the firm. Almost overnight Cheryl moved to the South's largest city and commenced planning for a billion-dollar effort. The Games, then more than four years away, would bring together more than 10,000 athletes from 200 countries—nearly twice the size of the 1984 Summer Games in Los Angeles.

To prepare for the project Cheryl embarked upon fact-finding missions, the first one financed out of the firm's pocket. She traveled to Barcelona to observe the 1992 Summer Games, and to Munich to learn how that city used its limited space to put on the 1972 event. She also visited Oklahoma City, to study the equestrian facilities at the famed Remington Park racetrack.

"I wanted to learn the language of the architecture," she recalls. Phrases such as "Olympic family" and "seating requirements" carried different connotations. She visited the library and ensconced herself in publications about various types of Olympics and sports facilities, because she would have to communicate with other architects and needed to make certain the facilities were programmed properly.

As a girl, Cheryl had dreamed of competing in the Olympics. The coach of her synchronized swimming team had been an Olympic athlete. Winter morning practices left Cheryl numb, with ice hanging from her hair. Eventually the team disbanded when she entered high school, "and I figured that was the end of my dream," she shrugs.

Faced with tremendous time pressures, McAfee's pace was every bit as grueling as an athlete's in training. The first project her team developed was the largest: the 85,000-seat Olympic Stadium in Atlanta. "We were thrown into the deep end!" she exclaimed. She worked out of the Olympic Committee headquarters at the Inforum building downtown. Spring and summer had come and gone the first year before she realized she had missed the seasons completely. She sometimes left the office at one or two o'clock in the morning, taking work home with her, only to return to the office two or three hours later. She and her team members were dedicated to building a superior facility.

By February of 1993, McAfee became ill and could not recover. Her father, who flew to Atlanta from Wichita each week, told her she needed a break. Manifesting the same drive and determination as her father, she refused to rest and instead changed to a healthier diet, which provided no relief. One day in her office she suddenly began shaking uncontrollably. She rushed home, called the doctor, and then her father. "He said he didn't care about the project if I was going to kill myself over it," she recalls. Laden with antibiotics, at her father's orders she flew to the Cayman Islands. When her hotel room was not ready, she lay down in a chair on the beach and immediately fell asleep. McAfee awoke four hours later to the tide lapping at the winter clothes she was wearing. Four days of rest, coupled with a fortuitous blizzard that kept her home as soon as she returned from Atlanta, brought a complete recovery.

Cheryl McAfee became an ombudswoman, bringing together various groups such as architects, media, logistical staff, and volunteers to discuss their needs. She ended up being one of the point people for the rest of the Olympic Committee, because members of other departments had difficulty communicating with each other. McAfee also worked closely with the broadcast group. "A man named Ralph Mellanby kept saying he was going to match me up with one of the broadcast journalists," said McAfee. "I said, 'I doubt it; you guys have crazy careers.' Then my friend Carol Miller introduced me to a handsome man named Reg who worked in broadcasting."

Reg is Reginald Mitchell, Sr., an Emmy-winning camera operator who had worked with CBS News in Los Angeles, often alongside Connie Chung. He had taken a job as manager of electronic field production for the Games' broadcasting division. McAfee and Mitchell were married in 1994, and Mitchell now holds a professorship at Atlanta's Clark University and is director of broadcast training.

The pace of preparing for the Olympics reached a feverish level, and many people worked around the clock. When people inquired about the McAfee team's progress, Charles McAfee's response was, "Every morning we're right on schedule, and every night we're behind schedule." Although he would not assess the structures as "great pieces of architecture," it was distinguished as a great public works project because it was functional and got finished on time.

As the July 1996 opening approached, Bill Rathburn, the Olympic Committee's director of security, asked Cheryl to comanage the main security operations center during the event. According to Cheryl, he explained that the teams of police officers from around the country, the Department of Defense, the Secret Service, and antiterrorism units knew their field but were not as familiar with the many venues as she was. She found herself at a desk alongside a Presidential communications liaison to the Secret Service, the man who carried the little red telephone.

Looking back on the experience, Cheryl says, "Working with so many people was an incredible challenge. We differed not only in race and gender but also in our philosophies. There was a reason I was given this opportunity. I was supposed to grow from the experience." Typically a fighter who confronted issues head-on, she learned something new about integrity and patience, and why God is essential to her life.

Following the Games, McAfee's architectural staff in Atlanta continued to convert the Olympic structures for post-use. Many venues, including the aquatics center, and gymnastics and field hockey facilities, were turned over to the universities. Other locations were given to surrounding counties, and those that had no post-Olympic use were restored to their original condition, such as wildlife habitats.

There was another aspect to the Atlanta Games, which concerned housing—and the direction that Cheryl McAfee wants to go, again in her father's footsteps. The Atlanta Housing Authority demolished blighted areas of the city prior to the Games. McAfee believes that the people who were displaced should not be returned to the same level of poverty and untenable conditions; they need to live in better homes, which is considered replacement housing. "The city needs thousands of replacement homes, and that's a niche for us," McAfee explains. "Our firm wants to be a part of uplifting America. We've already started it in a big way with the modular housing factory in Wichita." She is committed to getting significantly involved in creating affordable housing in the Atlanta area, and the business community has expressed strong support.

As the first female president of the National Organization of Minority Architects, a title her father once held, Cheryl certainly is in the position to make such a difference. She still contemplates writing a book about the concept of walled cities, which she first considered while at Harvard. She explained that walled cities—communities designed to keep some people out and others in—continue to exist, only differently now than during earlier periods in world history. "Redlining that existed in the '60s and '70s is now illegal, but I see it happening in other forms," she laments. "We have to lower our national obsession with race and start to deal with people on a human level. What are we going to do to bring humanity to the place where God intended us to be?"

We are having breakfast together inside Atlanta's chic 191 Club when I ask Cheryl McAfee-Mitchell whose architectural work she most admires. "Honestly, it's my father's and Eero Saarinen. They both express architecture with elegance, detail, and simplicity," she replies. "I have watched dad develop perfect solutions to a complicated design problem. They're incredible in their aesthetics and functionality yet completely different as to alternative solutions to the same project. I don't understand how he is so systematically disciplined." She feels Charles McAfee has yet to express all of his ability and hopes one day he will have the financial freedom to do anything he wants.

Charyl McAfee-Duncan, who aspired to be an architect like her father when she was seven years old, adds this observation about his influence on the field and his family. "He came out of school with a lot of ideas, hopes, and dreams. Some people tried to douse that flame because of his race. But he had incredible drive to persevere." She feels his vision and designs are extremely functional and have a timeless style. "Since the day my second-grade teacher invited him to speak to our class, I wanted to be just like my dad," she says proudly.

Charyl, who earned her Bachelor of Architecture degree at the University of Nebraska, her father's alma mater, and a Master of Architecture degree at the University of Texas at Austin, worked with several architectural firms in Dallas before joining the family business. She opened the Dallas office in 1994. Now she is drawing up a business plan for modular housing to be presented to the city.

As for Charles McAfee—who has not only watched two daughters follow him into architecture but also daughter Pam excel in the health care field as director of occupational therapy for a major hospital near Dallas—his legacy is what counts. He remembers, many years ago now, sitting with his daughters in the living room to compare drawings from their school days. "Beginning drafting has been the same for years. You draw a wheel and a cube and a sphere on funny little sheets of yellow paper," he points out. The three students splayed their works out on the living room floor. "Two or three projects were almost identical, and Cheryl, Pam and Charyl made better grades on them than I did. All of a sudden, daddy the giant got to be the right size."

Recently the firm was interviewed to design a library in Oklahoma City. Cheryl was listed as the principal in charge, Charyl was the project manager, and Charles was the designer. Still constantly on the go, Charles visited a city in which he had invested thirty years building a reputation. He met a young woman who introduced herself and added the title "architect" before he could ask what she did. He in turn introduced himself as "Charles McAfee, architect." Immediately, she responded, "I know who you are, you're Cheryl's father."

"So that's my reputation," Charles McAfee concludes. "Gloria's husband, Cheryl, Pam, and Charyl's father. I have no problem with that at all. Because I don't just belong to myself. Everything I've done in architecture is about the way I try to live my life."

FOR FURTHER READING:
Paul R. Williams, Architect: A Legacy of Style, by Karen E. Hudson (Rizzoli Books, New York, 1993).

Part 4

HEALERS OF BODY AND SPIRIT

"In the individual accomplishments of each man lies the success or failure of the group as a whole. The success of the group as a whole is the basis for any tradition which we many create. In such traditions lies the sense of discipleship and the inspiration which serves as a guide for those who come after, so that each man's job is not just his job alone but a part of a greater job whose horizons we at present can only dimly imagine for they are beyond our view."

—DR. CHARLES DREW

"The church has been and must continue to be the great gateway to these spiritual influences which lead us to the realization of the Fatherhood of God and the brotherhood of Man. But this influence can be willed only by a living, breathing church that puts this concept into practice, whatever its denomination or the power of its affiliation."

—MARY McLEOD BETHUNE

Ancestors—The Physicians:
Louis Tompkins Wright and Jane Cooke Wright

"I've seen changes I never expected in my life. And I'd like to see a continuation of the growth of this kind of human amity, continuation to the point where it's not race that counts, but where ability and character are the only measure of a man's dignity."

—DR. LOUIS TOMPKINS WRIGHT, 1952

"As far as I know, my sister Jane was the first female pursuing clinical cancer chemotherapy in this country—first with our father and then on her own."

—DR. BARBARA WRIGHT PIERCE

Chicago, 1893: It was a sweltering summer afternoon when a young black man who had been stabbed in the chest was brought into the Provident Hospital and Training School. Only two years before, America's first interracial private hospital had been founded on the city's South Side by Daniel Hale Williams, or "Dr. Dan," as his patients called him. Now, as Provident's chief surgeon, Williams was called in to examine this latest victim. At first, the stab wound did not appear that serious; it was about an inch long, and not bleeding badly. But when young James Cornish's face grew pale and he began coughing sharply and painfully, Williams speculated that there must be internal bleeding. He decided to operate.

This was long before the advent of X-rays or blood transfusions and, for fear of infection or collapsed lungs should air enter the chest cavity, surgeons almost never opened a patient's chest. Daniel Hale Williams made a small incision, enabling him to see into the chest cavity. He tied off a large blood vessel that had been hit by the assailant's knife. The weapon, Williams saw, had also torn into a sac surrounding the heart called the pericardium. This was, as author Lisa Yount recounts in her book *Black Scientists*, "fluttering like a wounded bird, moving up and down with every heartbeat—130 times a minute." After using a salt solution to cleanse the wound, Williams brought the pericardium's edges together and sewed them closed with a thin catgut suture. Then the outer incisions were stitched.

For most of the next three days, the surgeon remained close to the patient's bedside. No infection set in. Released from the hospital fifty-one days afterwards, James Cornish made a complete recovery. Dr. Daniel Hale Williams, who would go on to become the first black member of the American College of Surgeons, had performed the world's first successful open-heart surgery.

New York, 1938: All through his earlier years at Canada's McGill University Medical School, a onetime star athlete named Charles Drew had long been fascinated with the problem of how to preserve and store blood. He had watched patients die for lack of a transfusion, because whole blood taken from donors spoiled quickly or became easily contaminated. Red blood cells simply broke down too quickly to allow storage for longer than a few days. The freezing of blood had been attempted without success.

Now, as a resident surgeon at Columbia's Presbyterian Hospital, Charles Drew spent long hours experimenting to find some means of changing this equation. Eventually he settled on isolating the yellowish plasma, which constituted the blood's liquid portion minus the cells. Drew's crucial discovery was that recombining red blood with plasma was not always necessary in transfusions. Pure plasma could work by itself. Not only could plasma be stored for a considerable time without spoiling, its use did not require a cross matching of blood type. Anyone's plasma could be given to someone else.

On the battlefield, time was essential to save the lives of wounded soldiers. With the outbreak of World War II, Drew's revolutionary discovery would ensure the survival of thousands. In beleaguered Great Britain, blood banks were implemented based upon Drew's research. Shortly before America's entry into the war in 1941, Drew was named director of the American Red Cross's blood donor project. He resigned in a fury the same year, after the War Department issued a decree that the "mix [of] Caucasian and Negro blood indiscriminately for later administration to the military forces" was "not deemed advisable." In a bitter irony, the man whose pathbreaking blood work would allow so many American soldiers to survive would now have found his own blood rejected by the Red Cross.

Drew called a press conference and left the Red Cross with these pointed words: "The blood of individuals may differ by blood groupings, but there is absolutely no scientific basis to indicate any difference in human blood from race to race." He returned, as medical director, to the Howard University Freedmen's Hospital where he had formerly interned.

At this same hospital, one world war before, another doctor had initiated his own medical breakthroughs—and begun his own lifelong battle against discrimination.

In her spacious New York apartment across the street from the American Museum of Natural History, Dr. Barbara Wright Pierce sits surrounded by numerous boxes containing memorabilia about her father, Dr. Louis Tompkins Wright. Both she and her sister, Dr. Jane Cooke Wright, had carried forward a family tradition in medicine that went back three generations. It was a trailblazing heritage.

During World War I, Louis Wright had come up with a new method for vaccinating American troops against smallpox. In the mid-1930s, he developed a special brace for neck fractures that still remains in use. In 1948, he was the first to conduct clinical trials of aureomycin, the forerunner of today's leading antibiotics. The director of surgery at Harlem Hospital, Wright also served for seventeen years as board chairman of the NAACP.

His daughter Jane, who worked alongside her father on cancer studies during the three years preceding his death in 1952, went on to become the nation's leading researcher in the new field of treating cancers with chemotherapy and the first black woman ever named associate dean of a medical school. Barbara, best known as the wife of Samuel Pierce—Secretary of Housing and Urban Development under President Reagan—concentrated on occupational medicine during her own nearly forty-year career.

Now in her late seventies, Barbara Wright Pierce speaks passionately and eloquently about the father she calls "a benevolent presence" in her formative years. Framed by a sweeping vista of Central Park outside her picture window, she closes her eyes as she remembers: "Medicine, and the movement [for civil rights], was really his whole life. Poppa was very different than today's specialists, because his mind roamed all over the place. He was a wonderfully skilled surgeon. But he was also so versatile in other areas, coming up with creative solutions to both scientific and social problems. He knew how to organize and get things done. And he didn't let anything go by. If he saw that someone was not behaving as a physician should in his eyes, believe me, he let them know about it!"

Louis Wright's penchant for medicine began in his youth. Born in LaGrange, Georgia, on July 22, 1891, he was the second son of a physician who had ended up becoming a minister. Dr. Ceah Ketcham was district supervisor of the American Methodist Church in Atlanta when he died suddenly, when Wright was four. After the death of Wright's brother not long thereafter, his mother, Lula Tompkins Wright, married Dr. William Fletcher Penn. The first black student to graduate from Yale Medical School, Penn had come to Atlanta to teach at Clark University and practice medicine. "I saw him sew up a man's hand," Wright would say years later, "and then and there decided to be a surgeon."

Wright's daughter remembers: "Dr. Penn truly adored my father, treated him like his own son, and was a great inspiration to him. He was a very courtly gentleman, tall and handsome. And he was uncompromising when it came to racial matters. When the Atlanta riots broke out [in 1906], Poppa was about fifteen or sixteen. Dr. Penn put a gun in his hand, and faced him at the living room window, and told him that if anybody came up the walkway he was to shoot."

In the rough draft of an autobiography that Wright never completed, he further outlined what transpired on that terrifying night. "It was a moonlit night. . . . I was placed with a loaded Winchester rifle at a window . . . and we saw hordes of white men passing going to South Atlanta where we had heard the discharge of firearms. . . . All night long white men passed our house . . . and in the morning a group of white men came in the front gate of our home led by a white man who lived two doors above us and whose wife my father had delivered of three children. . . . My father stated, 'What are you doing here? Do you know?' He said, 'No, I don't know. Well, there's trouble.' My father said, 'Yes, there's trouble and you come to my house.' The white men left after that. We learned indirectly that several white men had been killed by Negroes in South Atlanta and that martial law had been declared. Finally a Mr. O'Neil, a white man, came and took myself and my family away to another section of the city because of the threat of mob violence."

Other incidents seared the young man's conscience. Wright witnessed black prisoners being brutally treated on the chain gangs building Atlanta's roads. When he entered Clark University not long after the Atlanta riots, he and a group of classmates stumbled upon a black man hanging from a tree in the adjoining woods. The afternoon newspaper merely reported that a man had been found dead on the campus. It was what was known as a "quiet lynching," and Wright did not forget it.

At the age of twenty, Wright graduated from Clark as class valedictorian. His stepfather then packed him off to Boston to seek admittance to the Harvard Medical School. As Wright later recounted, the director of admissions found it bizarre that someone from "one of these funny schools" would attempt to enter Harvard without even having taken an entrance exam in chemistry. He passed Wright along to an internationally renowned biochemist, Dr. Otto Folin, who asked at the end of a heated interview: "Mr. Wright, have you any sporting blood in your veins?" When Wright responded affirmatively, Folin went on: "Will you agree if I ask you a few questions here today that I will never be bothered with you again in life?" Wright agreed to an oral inquisition. "I think Poppa had been reading his father's medical books," says Barbara Pierce. Wright, Dr. Folin quickly concluded, "has had adequate chemistry for admission to this school."

His daughter adds that "there were not many black students up there at that time. During the summers, he would work as a porter on the railroad to earn money." An outstanding student at Harvard, one day Wright was told by an assistant professor of obstetrics that he would not be permitted to deliver babies at the Boston Lying-In Hospital because of his race. Instead, he would have to work apart from the rest of his class, under a black physician in private practice. But the Harvard catalogue said otherwise, Wright insisted upon his rights, and his classmates rallied to his support. The time-honored "separate-but-equal" Harvard policy was abolished. Then, during Wright's senior year, the D. W. Griffith silent film *Birth of a Nation* debuted in Boston—with its blatantly racist depictions of hooded Klansmen hunting down and lynching blacks. Wright left school for three weeks to join protests against its showing.

In 1915, despite ranking fourth in his Harvard class, Wright was denied election to the honorary Alpha Omega Alpha medical fraternity. "That's the medical Phi Beta Kappa, but one person from the South blackballed him," says Barbara Pierce. "This stayed with him awhile, I must say. He didn't live to see his fiftieth class reunion, where he was voted by his classmates as the member who had made the greatest contribution to medicine."

Although he had graduated cum laude, Wright found himself unable to land an internship at any of the leading Boston hospitals. At his stepfather's suggestion, he went on to the Freedmen's Hospital in Washington, where Dr. Penn had also interned. There Wright was outraged when he read an article in the current medical literature. It stated that the Schick test for determining immunity to diphtheria did not apply to blacks due to their "heavy" skin pigmentation. (Diphtheria was a communicable bacterial disease, often fatal prior to the successful development of a vaccine.) Wright decided to carry out a laboratory study. When the National Vaccine and Antitoxin Institute did not want to provide him with the necessary diphtheria toxin, Wright's supervisors came to his defense. His research proved there was absolutely no basis for the "scientific" allegation.

When his internship ended, Wright learned that his stepfather's financial situation was grave, and he went home to Atlanta to open an office with Dr. Penn. His return coincided with the arrival of James Weldon Johnson, who was organizing a branch there of the recently formed NAACP. Walter White was named secretary, and Wright the treasurer; this marked the beginning of an association that would later carry both men to the top of the nation's most influential black organization. In Atlanta, too, Wright published the first of his eighty-nine scientific papers ("The Effect of Alcohol on the Rate of Discharge from the Stomach," an article based upon work he had done while in medical school).

Then came the First World War. Wright applied for a commission immediately after the U.S. declared war against Germany in 1917, and was soon a first lieutenant in the Army Medical Corps. Before he shipped overseas, Wright met and married an attractive and vivacious young schoolteacher named Corinne Cooke. "My mother was with a group that was giving a benefit for the NAACP, and some of the men who were already in the Army were there," Barbara Pierce remembers. "That's where they met. My maternal grandmother had come to America from a little town in Germany, seeking better opportunities. She wound up with a family that went to Saratoga [New York], for the summer. That's where she met my grandfather, who was a steward on the Vanderbilts' private car. They moved into an apartment in the Bronx, in an area where there were other white ladies married to black gentlemen. That's where my mother and her two brothers were born."

From one of her memorabilia boxes, Pierce brings out a rubber-banded collection of postcards sent by Wright to her mother from "Les Vosges" in France in the summer of 1918. On the frontlines there, Wright and his battalion suffered an attack of phosgene—a colorless, poisonous gas that the Germans had formed from chlorine and carbon monoxide. After three weeks of hospitalization, he had returned to active duty. But the consequences of Wright's being gassed would be permanent lung damage.

"What I remember him most mentioning to me," Pierce continues, "was that a very prejudiced Southern colonel was in charge of his batallion who didn't like him at all. At the end, the colonel came over to Poppa and said, 'You know, Wright, I didn't expect you to do what you've done, and I've developed a great respect for you.' For those days, that was something!"

Wright had become the youngest American surgeon to be placed in charge of a base hospital in France. He also developed a new means of intradermal vaccination against smallpox, adopted by the U.S. Army Medical Corps because it had fewer side effects than the customary "scratch" method. At war's end, Wright was discharged a captain and, says his daughter, "he always wore a tiny pin on his lapel—his Purple Heart."

Soon after returning from France, Wright opened his first medical offices in his wife's home city of New York. Around the time that their first child, Jane, was born on November 30, 1919, Wright learned that Harlem Hospital was short on physicians. Despite its location in a predominantly black sector, the hospital was then staffed completely by white doctors. Although he entered at the lowest possible level as a clinical assistant for outpatients, Wright became the first black physician ever appointed to any New York hospital. The superintendent who hired him was immediately transferred; four Harlem Hospital physicians resigned in protest.

"When I first started here," Wright would later recall, "no one would talk to me. I'd make the rounds with one doctor, and he never said good morning." Wright was undaunted. He quickly made influential white friends who, at his urging, pressed the mayor for an investigation of the city's hospital system. An agreement was reached to reorganize the Harlem facility, forcing it to admit more black physicians and interns.

Barbara Wright, born a year after her sister, remembers of her early years in the '20s and '30s: "We lived between Seventh and Eighth Avenue on 139th Street. All we heard over the dinner table was about the NAACP, the movement. I remember letting [W. E. B.] Du Bois into the house one day, with his goatee and very proper—I didn't know he was important. A lot of people from different walks of life would just come up and ring the doorbell, coming for Poppa's advice and insights. For some reason the artists liked to talk to him—'Spinky' [Charles] Allston and 'Romie' [Romare] Bearden were the two I remember most. Poppa was very fond of Paul Robeson and [his wife] Essie, he had great admiration for Paul."

In 1929, New York mayor James Walker carried forward a complete reorganization of the municipal hospitals, bringing more black doctors into Harlem's. Walker also appointed Wright the first black surgeon of the city's police department, a position he would hold until his death. "The joy in our household! This meant a steady income as the Depression years arrived," says his daughter. "My father would always say that Walker was really straight. Poppa's feeling was that, if you were straight on the race question, you could count on someone for a lot of other things being right."

Then the backlash came. After the Harlem Hospital reorganization in 1930, the Julius Rosenwald Fund came in with a proposal to establish a separate, all-black hospital. The Rosenwald Fund was known for its building of black schools and hospitals in the segregated South. Wright was adamant that the same philosophy did not need transplanting to New York. After forming the Manhattan Medical Society to oppose the plan, Wright stated: "Segregated hospitals represent a duality of citizenship in a democratic government that is wrong. Whenever colored hospitals are established, other hospitals in the community which have been admitting Negroes immediately begin to refuse admission to them, referring them only to the colored hospital, which in many cases is rather small. Thus the Negro doctor would not be a physician to minister to the needs of all mankind irrespective of color, but he would be trained and taught that he is a Negro doctor—one who can treat only Negroes."

The Rosenwald Fund backed down. In Wright's unpublished memoir, he recalled his simultaneous clash with Dr. John Fox Connors, the president of Harlem Hospital's Medical Board: ". . . there came up a question in the Medical Board of a promotion of a colored man who had rendered good service in the field of gynecology, Dr. Peter Marshall Murray. The whites had a candidate that they wanted [and] they gave it to a less competent white doctor." In response, Wright's Medical Society blitzed city and hospital officials with telegrams.

"These telegrams were timed so that they would arrive at two o'clock in the morning and get all the respective gentlemen out of bed. When I arrived at the hospital the next morning Dr. John F. Connors, [also] the director of surgery, said, 'Look at this. I was awakened at two in the morning. What about it?' I said, 'Well, it seems that the Medical Board of Harlem Hospital went back on a gentlemen's agreement. . . . Men were to be promoted according to merit. . . . Therefore, the Medical Board is not to be respected.' He said, 'Do you think I am going to take orders from these Negro doctors up here?' I said, 'I don't know what you're going to do. All I know is that when you are right, we'll hold your hands up and when you're wrong we'll give you hell and you no longer have the right to be called gentlemen.' He berated me for one hour. The next day he called a meeting of the Medical Board which reversed their decision and promoted Dr. Murray and three days later he got on a boat and went to Europe and I did not see him for three months.

"I expected that when he [Connors] did get back he would give me the works. When he arrived he had his whole staff in front of him, numbering about twenty surgeons, internes and others. I stood on the edge of the crowd. He pushed his way through the crowd and said,

'Wright, I am god damn glad to see you.' From that day on we were friends until his death."

All through the turbulent 1930s, Wright's surgical reputation grew, particularly around his heart and brain surgery in accident cases. His ongoing clinical research included, Barbara Pierce recounts, "inventing a special brace for people who had sustained head and neck injuries in accidents, so the neck would stay in the proper position while you got them to a hospital. He did this on his own, paying to have the brace made up." Wright also designed new kinds of plates for fixing thigh, femur, and shin bone fractures; another plate for repair of recurrent hernias, and a splint for cervical fractures.

In 1934, he became the second black doctor named as a Fellow in the American College of Surgeons (pioneering heart specialist Daniel Hale Williams was the first). In 1937, he organized the Harlem Surgical Society as a scientific medium for black surgeons. His chapter on "Head Injuries" in *The Treatment of Fractures* challenged traditional theories, and marked the first such contribution by an African-American to an authoritative medical text.

At the same time, Wright became chairman of the NAACP's Board of Directors in 1935. His leadership as a "bare-knuckle fighter," as Roy Wilkins would say in a Memorial Lecture in 1963, "enabled the NAACP to spearhead a greatly accelerated drive for first class citizenship. . . . As the Rooseveltians dashed about, carrying out the task of re-building a nation that had crashed almost to the ground, Negro citizens clamored for inclusion in the New Deal on a new basis of equality. . . . It was evident to Louis Wright that if no new national consciousness of the Negro as a citizen were to develop in these years of common suffering, the inclusion of the Negro in the period of recovery would be an almost insuperable task. . . .

"The Wright-led NAACP fought for opportunities for Negro youth," Wilkins went on. "It banged away at the organized labor movement and threw a picket line around the AFL convention in San Francisco protesting the color line in labor. . . . As for jobs in industry, that came to a head in 1939–41 with the slow burn of Negroes over the flat refusal of defense industries to hire them while filling war material contracts at enormous profits. The March on Washington project, conceived and initiated by A. Philip Randolph, had the close cooperation and support of the Wright-[Walter] White NAACP."

Then, in 1939, disaster struck the Wright family. Barbara, whose older sister Jane was beginning her sophomore year at Smith College, was about to start at Mount Holyoke College and remembers: "Poppa had developed a cavity in his chest the size of an egg. He finally coughed blood one morning, and a diagnosis of tuberculosis was made."

It had apparently been brought on by the phosgene gas attack he had suffered in World War I. Wright would spend the next three years in a hospital, mostly in upstate New York. "I never thought I'd practice medicine again," Wright later told a newspaper columnist. "But we borrowed some, and prayed more, and even sent two daughters through school."

With money short, Corinne Wright borrowed on her husband's life insurance while struggling to keep up with his business affairs. "It was very hard for my mother in those years, very hard," says Barbara Pierce. "They wanted to operate on him, do something with his ribs and collapse that lung, but Poppa said no. He went through the whole process of letting nature heal it. No one knew what was going to happen really. But he was remarkably cheerful, and had good friends who kept him apprised of what was going on at the hospital and at the NAACP. It was while he was still flat on his back that Harlem Hospital appointed him director of surgery!"

When that happened in 1943, it was still a predominantly white Medical Board that recognized Wright's accomplishments. Not long thereafter, Wright finished his recovery at home and went back to work. His last ten years proved, in fact, the most productive of his life. As Roy Wilkins put it, "The magnificent fight for the desegregation of public education gathered momentum under Louis Wright. With Louis at the policy level, Walter [White] at the administrative level and with Charles Houston and Thurgood Marshall in the courtroom, something was bound to give."

Barbara Pierce recalls: "Charley Houston was a very dear friend of my father. You don't hear many people speak about Charley Houston today, but his was really the grand master plan. It was his vision of the constitutional factors that started the fight. Thurgood Marshall was one of his students, worked with him, and carried on after Houston's early death."

In 1948 Wright was named president of the Harlem Hospital Medical Board, and directed a team of doctors that conducted successful clinical trials on a new "wonder drug" called Aureomycin. For some time Wright had been looking for a cure for a little-known and baffling venereal disease called *lymphogranuloma venereum*, which turned its victims into lifelong invalids. Finally Wright turned to an Indian physician, Dr. Yellapragada Subbarow, whom he had known since his long-ago internship days at Howard University's Freedmen's Hospital. As research director at Lederle Laboratories, Subbarow had come up with a new antibiotic then known only as A-377. It had been tested for two years with no ill effects on laboratory animals. Wright wondered if it might be his answer.

"Poppa did what a lot of doctors in the olden days did," says Barbara Pierce. "He said, 'I won't give it to anybody unless I first take it myself.' Well, they later ended up doing trials on twenty-five patients who had this venereal disease, and it was an unbelievable success. Before Aureomycin, there were the sulfa drugs and then penicillin. But Aureomycin was the first of the new broad-spectrum antibiotics that followed—like Terramycin and Tetracycline, which my father also tested clinically."

As *Industrial Trends* magazine described the Wright team's results with Aureomycin in 1949: "Since the first Harlem experiments, the doctors there and in hospitals throughout the land have found that the newest of wonder drugs is particularly successful against rickettsial diseases like typhus, parrot fever and lymphogranuloma venereum. . . . In general doctors feel that Aureomycin has probably the widest range of activity of any known antibacterial substances. . . . it works with amazing speed. One 68-year-old woman at Harlem Hospital, suffering from peritonitis from a ruptured appendix, was symptom-free inside of 7 days after taking Aureomycin capsules."

By now, both of Wright's daughters had followed him into the medical profession. In their undergraduate days, Jane was a championship swimmer who considered becoming an artist. Barbara says she herself "wanted to explore until, all of a sudden during my third year, I said: 'What am I doing here? I enjoy science more than anything, but don't want to sit in a lab all my life. I want to be involved with people.' So what does one do? Become a doctor.

"Poppa was ill when Jane and I came to our decisions separately. Our parents in no way pressed us to become physicians or not, they both always let us know they would support us in anything we wanted to do." Jane Wright, who now lives in retirement in New York and no longer gives interviews, has spoken similarly, saying that her father "warned her how hard becoming a doctor would be."

The sisters had each finished their courses in three years—Jane receiving her MD with honors from New York Medical College in 1945, Barbara following a year later as one of only four women in a class of 120 at Columbia University's College of Physicians and Surgeons. Both interned at New York's large Bellevue Hospital. Both soon married lawyers. And, after their father established a Cancer Research Foundation at Harlem Hospital in 1948, Jane became part of his team, with Barbara filling in for six months after her sister became pregnant.

Initially the chief resident in internal medicine at Harlem Hospital,

Jane Wright was a stunningly attractive woman whom a newspaper columnist once listed among the ten most beautiful black women in America. Now, working alongside her father on cancer research, she quickly became mesmerized by the possibilities of new drug treatments. The treatment of cancer with chemicals, now commonly called chemotherapy, was in its infancy in the 1940s. Ironically for Louis Wright, it was nitrogen mustard—a relative of the poisonous mustard gas widely used in World War I—which was the standard chemical treatment of the time. He and Jane experimented with this and other new alkylating agents, which were found to work on the reproductive mechanisms of the cancer cells and often kill them.

This work preoccupied Wright during the last four years of his life, as he secured support from the U.S. Public Health Service and published fourteen papers on chemotherapy. At a dinner dedicating the Louis T. Wright Library at Harlem Hospital on April 30, 1952, more than 1,000 people, including Eleanor Roosevelt, assembled to honor the physician. That night, Wright looked back and said: "Harlem Hospital represents, to my mind, the finest example of democracy at work in the field of medicine. Its policy of complete integration throughout the institution has stood the test of time, having now been in practice for over twenty years. . . . Merit alone, in the light of the highest standards, governs the selection of professional personnel. Patients of all races are admitted and treated by doctors of many races. . . . No one can any longer question the wisdom of total integration in the operation of large institutions. It has served as a basis of ennobling growth and strength for all of us."

Less than six months later, after suffering a heart attack at the age of sixty-one, Wright died in his home on October 8, 1952. Jane was named his successor as director of his hospital's Cancer Research Foundation. In 1955 she joined the New York University Medical Center, as director of cancer chemotherapy. All through the '50s and '60s, Jane Wright treated cancer patients with a broad array of drugs. One of these, an antibiotic produced out of a soil mold, called Mithramycin, proved particularly effective in treating a brain tumor known as glioblastoma.

In 1967 Wright returned to her alma mater, the New York Medical College, as professor of surgery, associate dean, and director of its new cancer research laboratory. She would remain there until her retirement in 1987, also continuing clinical work at other city hospitals. During her long career, as described by author Lisa Yount in a profile in *Black Scientists*: ". . . between 1953 and 1975, Wright worked out ways to use pieces of a patient's own tumor, removed by surgery and grown in nutrient culture medium in the laboratory, as a 'guinea pig' for testing drugs. . . . Wright developed a 'philosophy' or general approach to treating cancer patients with these drugs." She would adjust the dosages, depending upon a patient's tolerance and the response of tumors.

Today, a combination drug therapy approach, which goes after tumor cells along several pathways, has supplanted the original hope that a single chemical cure could be found. With over fifty anticancer drugs now available, those that Jane Wright helped pioneer in testing have saved or extended thousands of lives.

In her New York apartment, Louis Wright's daughter Barbara speaks with equal pride of her sister's accomplishments. "Jane pursued clinical chemical chemotherapy, first with her father and later on her own. She is a very remarkable person. She had to face obstacles alone and many problems from those who had other agendas. But she never stopped pursuing it—all of this with a husband and two children at home."

For her part, Barbara Wright Pierce led a very different kind of life. She and Jane practiced internal medicine for five years after their residences, and were on the attending staff at their father's Harlem Hospital. It was at this time that Barbara's husband accepted his first appointment in Washington. Upon returning to New York, she chose not to reopen an office for private practice. This proved to be a wise decision because of subsequent Washington appointments, and the difficulties involved in opening and closing offices for private practice.

Instead, Barbara pursued occupational medicine, which allowed her greater time flexibility. Always involved with the patients themselves, she worked on Teacher's Health for the New York Board of Education and for the Metropolitan Life Insurance Company, dealing with employee health and doing clinical medicine at the home office. For a while she worked with a team researching the company's experience with "biochemical profiling"; at another juncture, with a group analyzing the company's experience with employees who had been accepted with a history of treatment for cancer. Occasionally she traveled and presented their papers at medical meetings. All this, she says, "provided diversity and clinical medicine, with scheduling that permitted time for both my work and my family."

For many years, while raising a daughter, Victoria, Barbara regularly traveled back and forth to Washington. Her attorney husband, Samuel Pierce, Jr., served in three Republican Administrations—as an assistant to the undersecretary of labor under Eisenhower, as general counsel to the treasury department under Nixon, and finally as secretary of housing and urban development under Reagan. Her sister Jane's late husband, David D. Jones, Jr., had risen to become New York City's commissioner of corrections.

"In one way or another, medicine still seems to dominate my family," Pierce says. "My brother-in-law is a psychiatrist at Harvard, my niece practices psychiatry in New Jersey. A cousin is also, a physician. Of course, it really goes back to my two grandfathers. My father, I feel, has a place in history as a warrior against segregation, a pioneering researcher in so many different fields—and a wonderfully skilled surgeon whose patients would get up and go home."

Walking over to a box of papers in a corner, she brings out a brochure from the National Portrait Gallery in Washington. It contains sculptured busts of many of America's most prominent. "Now who do you see there?" she asks. "There's Henry Ford, Ralph Waldo Emerson, Woodrow Wilson. And there is a terra-cotta of Louis Tompkins Wright." Barbara Wright Pierce closes her eyes, musing quietly on the legacy of her father that she and her sister have done their utmost to carry forward.

FOR FURTHER READING:

James Michael Brodie, *Created Equal: The Lives and Ideas of Black American Innovators* (New York: William Morrow & Co., 1993).

Louis Haber, *Black Pioneers of Science and Invention* (New York: Harcourt, Brace & World, 1970).

Spencie Love, *One Blood: The Death and Resurrection of Charles R. Drew* (Chapel Hill and London: University of North Carolina Press, 1996).

Aubre de L. Maynard, *Surgeons to the Poor: The Harlem Hospital Story* (New York: Appleton-Century-Crofts, 1978).

Alma Smith Payne, *Partners in Science* (Cleveland and New York: World Publishing Co., 1968).

Lisa Yount, *American Profiles: Black Scientists* (New York: Facts on File, 1991).

21

Byllye Avery and the National Black Women's Health Project

"There is clear evidence that many of the most severe health problems facing African-American women are primarily caused by poverty, racism, and lack of opportunity. . . . To redefine our status, African-American women will require opportunities and safe settings, and social supports (including child care) in steps toward enhanced health. Before African-American women will be able to take these steps in large numbers, we will require vocal and committed leadership from our own community. But we are not waiting for that commitment before beginning to organize for needed health opportunities."
—Byllye Y. Avery, *The Health Status of Black Women*

In her office in downtown Atlanta, the director of maternal and child health for the state of Georgia is sitting comfortably on the floor, talking about a woman who changed her life. "You know," Dr. Virginia Davis Floyd is saying, "if you saw Byllye [pronounced Billie] Avery standing at a bus stop, you probably wouldn't even notice her. That's one of her beauties. But you're almost mesmerized by this woman if you're not careful. Luckily for us, Byllye started the National Black Women's Health Project instead of a cult!"

Dr. Floyd, who prefers to be called Ginger, laughs and continues: "The vision that she inspires other people to see becomes such a part of your life, it's almost like it was always there. There's a part of Harriet Tubman that's Byllye, the part that says you're gonna get on this train and you're not gonna turn back. Byllye says that—your life is too important, I'm not gonna *let* you mess it up. Byllye taught me that for education and life changes to occur, all of this is in the self-help movement. I mean, she'll turn the airport, or McDonald's, or your bedroom into a self-help group! Because the theory is, you only need two women to make a start."

Ginger Floyd had been a practicing physician and professor at the Morehouse School of Medicine when she first met Byllye Avery, not long after Avery came to Atlanta in 1981. The Health Project was then a one-woman operation, with Avery working out of a cramped little space in her home. By the end of the decade, Avery would have an office with twenty-one employees and be giving speeches all across America. Today, the nonprofit National Black Women's Health Project is headquartered in Washington, D.C., with a $1.5 million annual budget and some 150 affiliated groups around the country. Byllye Avery, now sixty, serves as an adviser for the organization from Swarthmore, Pennsylvania, completing a book titled *An Altar of Words: Wisdom, Comfort and Inspiration for African-American Women.*

Dr. Louis W. Sullivan, former Secretary of Health and Human Services and now president of the Morehouse School of Medicine in Atlanta, has called Avery "a national treasure and a national resource because of what she is doing . . . to empower black and low-income women with knowledge about health issues so they can improve their health and maintain a sense of independence and self-sufficiency."

The figures assembled by the National Black Women's Health Project are startling. Compared to white women, black women are twice as likely to die from diabetes between the ages of forty-five and sixty-four. They die from cervical cancer at three times the white women's rate. In their first year of life, black infant mortality is twice that of white babies.

Dr. Ginger Floyd elaborates: "If the problems that plague black women were just part of a medical model, we would have solved them a long time ago. But it really comes down to how a woman feels about herself and her life, and about taking control of it. You name the parameter and I can give you the statistic that shows we are dying of it at higher levels than anyone else. But it's Byllye's belief that it doesn't have to be that way. We can change it."

Some years ago now, the doctor remembers making a trip with Avery to colecture on black infant mortality at the University of North Carolina. "We're sharing a hotel room, trying to save the state money, and after the speech I'm real tired and starving. So I go out to get something to eat and then get some sleep. I come back—I'll never forget it—and there are forty women in my bedroom! I say, 'What is this?!' Byllye says, 'We gotta start a self-help group up here.' The word got out that Avery was in town, and we sat up all night talking. That's what I'm saying, she lives it, breathes it. There's no such thing to Byllye Avery as a dream that's not dreamable."

Norma Swenson, founder of the Boston Women's Health Book Collective, recalls being at a conference in 1979 where Byllye Avery was giving one of her first speeches. "She couldn't find her glasses, and finally gave up trying to read her notes and just started talking. It was so powerful that I told Byllye afterwards she should never worry about giving a prepared speech again." Swenson calls Avery's mesmeric speaking ability "an art form. Something happens in the connection that she makes with an audience that can't be explained."

Now, at the convention center in downtown Philadelphia, several hundred people are waiting to hear the final speaker at a regional conference of the Maternity Care Coalition. The 1997 theme is "Blueprint for a Village: Families and Communities Building the Future." The woman introducing Byllye Avery is listing off some of her accolades: the 1989 recipient of a "genius" award for social contribution from the MacArthur Foundation; honored by the Academy of Science Institute of Medicine with the 1994 Gustav O. Leinhard Award for the Advancement of Health Care, and getting the 1995 Dorothy I. Height Lifetime Achievement Award.

Her head bowed, Avery advances toward the stage. She is wearing an African necklace and colorful hoop earings, dressed completely in purple from an attractive three-piece outfit all the way to her shoes. At first glance, with her short-cropped hair and a diminutive frame, she seems hardly an imposing figure. Then, as Avery takes the hand-held microphone and walks out among the gathering, her fiery eyes survey the room. Her presence indeed suggests someone who, as she was introduced, "reminds us of some of the wise sages we used to read about." She begins, impromptu:

"I don't think we can talk about a village without all of us making a little trip into the past. Because that makes it so you can really realize what we don't *have* now. When the past was our present, we didn't even know that we *had* a village. That was just the way it was."

Avery describes growing up in the black section then known as "Africa" in Deland, Florida. A place where the janitor at the bank came by every morning in the wintertime, to light the family's heaters in the café that her father ran next door—"so by the time we got over there to cook breakfast, the restaurant was always warm." A place where the midwife came "running downstairs barefooted to tell me that I had a baby brother." A place where a neighbor lady always dropped in for breakfast and drove the kids to school. A place where, if you got stranded somewhere, "we could call the taxi driver and he'd say, 'I'll be right there, baby, to get you.'"

Avery continues: "This was how people lived. I went to Bethel A.M.E. Church, and every adult in the community, black or white, was your parent. They felt it was their duty to correct you—any way they saw you acting out! Somebody was watching you all the time. So that whenever we finished high school, or college, or got married, everybody felt that *they* raised us. You belonged to everybody. It did some of us pretty good, didn't it? We made it, and we're making it.

"Now that's not the way I raised my children. Things started to change just a few years after that, and they've been changing rapidly. So we have to figure out, how do we cope with what's going on? . . . It's never gonna be like that again. But that doesn't mean there isn't something we can do in the future. One of the first things is, we need to have a change of consciousness about how we treat human beings."

The home of Byllye Avery is a spacious residence filled with artifacts brought back from trips to Africa. There are combs from Tanzania; dolls from South Africa; masks from Ghana, Nigeria, Zimbabwe, the Cameroons. Along one wall is another collection: nineteenth-century photographs of African-Americans, including one of Avery's grandfather. "He was a supervisor for people who gathered turpentine from the pine trees," Avery is saying as we tour the house. "That's what he did his whole life. He was a very religious man. If there was nobody else in the church, he'd have church by himself!"

Nearly all of her relatives came from the vicinity of little Waynesville, Georgia, where Avery was born on October 20, 1937. How did she get the name Byllye? "Billie Holiday was big at the time, so that gave my mother permission." Before she was a year old, her family moved to Deland, a central Florida town of about 5,000 people. There her stepfather ran the next-door café, while her mother went on to attain a degree at Bethune-Cookman College and become an elementary schoolteacher. Avery's extended family included a third "brother," whom her mother adopted after her brother-in-law's wife died.

"My mother being a teacher, nothing was more important than education," Avery is remembering, sitting on a rocking chair in the living room. "Summertimes were full. School would end and then my mother would start my assignments—so many poems I had to learn, so many books I had to read. My mother talked all the time about Mary McLeod Bethune. When I was a senior in high school, I met her once while I was walking with my mother on the campus. Miss Bethune asked me where was I going to school, 'Are you coming to Cookman?' I said, 'No, I'm going to Talladega College.' I'd read about Talladega in a big spread in *Ebony* magazine when I was in seventh grade, and never changed my mind. She said, 'Oh, that's fine, just go somewhere.' When she died in 1955, I remember traveling over to Daytona and going to her funeral.

"I knew Mary McLeod Bethune was a great lady. Not only as an educator, but working the whole political scene—the moral rearmament movement that she started at Bethune-Cookman College, and the National Council of Negro Women. It's sixty-some years old and going strong. Just the concept of bringing together all of these black women's organizations to have one central place that they could work out of The faith she had to do what she did!''

Avery speaks softly, strikingly different from her dynamic stage presence. Yet during the course of our long afternoon together, her face is constantly changing, as though taking on the character of something ancient and nameless. As she describes Bethune's impact upon her, I am reminded of what Dr. Ginger Floyd had said: "Byllye talks a lot about standing on the shoulders of people. She told me once, she prays she lives long enough to become an elder. That doesn't mean getting old. It then takes you to be an ancestor.''

After graduating from Euclid High School in 1955, Avery had gone on to Talladega College in Alabama. "It was a hard school," she remembers, "and special for us. Because they really took us and let us know that we could make a contribution to the world. It was in its heyday, at that time ninety percent of its graduates went on to graduate school. The school has a rich history, being a part of that American Missionary Association where white teachers came to the South to teach, and some of them lost their lives. A lot of my teachers were white. On our campus for a while they hid out Authurine Lucy, who was the first black to integrate the University of Alabama, when riots broke out over there. Martin Luther King came to speak while I was at Talladega. He talked about three kinds of love: erotic, platonic, and redemptive love.''

Avery took her degree in psychology in 1959, and soon married her college sweetheart. "Wesley Avery was a year ahead of me, and I'd met him my very first day at Talladega. We ended up working side by side in occupational therapy at the new North Florida State Mental Hospital that had just opened about thirty miles outside Jacksonville. It was really wonderful. We taught ourselves how to weave and played games with the patients. I worked there for about six years, then came home to have a baby.''

While she was pregnant, Avery also gained a teacher's certificate from Edward Waters College in Jacksonville. After working for several years in a school program for emotionally disturbed children, she received a scholarship to pursue a Master's in Special Education at the University of Florida in Gainesville. By now, the couple had two small children; her husband stayed home to care for them while Avery commuted. After a year, Wesley Avery was awarded a fellowship at the same school in educational research. They moved into two-bedroom college housing, with Byllye becoming the first black teacher at an elementary school in nearby Waldo. In October of 1970, she took an opening at the university-based children's mental health unit. One month later, tragedy struck.

Painfully, she remembers: "Wesley was thirty-three when he died from a massive heart attack. He was about four months away from getting his Ph.D., and he'd never been sick a day in his life. He was what we in the black community call 'in the picture of health.' It was really a picture of death. He was hypertensive and we didn't know it. Because he grew up in a poor rural community in Alabama, where everybody had high blood pressure or bad nerves. His family respected education, but they were strapped by their poverty and culture. So they ate all the wrong things—like too much fat and too much salt. I hadn't thought much about health until my man was taken from me, much too soon.

"I spent the first two years being so mad at Wesley for dying and leaving me to parent our two children. There were many days when all I wanted to do was get in bed and pull the covers up over my head. You sit around trying to think about how could this happen? How could I not have known that he had high blood pressure, that the butter he always insisted on having on the table was bad for him? Then I realized that nobody had put the information to us in a way it made sense. This was before the big campaign about high blood pressure being the silent killer.

"So when people I knew started talking about women's health, I came with all these questions. It was a way for me to start to work out my grief, and also to make a commitment to not have this kind of thing happen to someone else."

When Avery resumes her story, she says she quickly realized that it was impossible to raise her son and daughter in isolation. She and two women friends who also worked on the University of Florida's child psychiatry unit began sharing their kids and cooking together several times a week. After school, their children would walk over to the unit and play with the autistic ones. "I organized a whole self-help group around the needs I felt as a young mother," Avery says, "though I didn't really know that's what I was doing."

The director of the child psychiatry unit was a radical Quaker named Paul Adams, who "supported our looking at the women's health movement, which was just beginning at that time. I grew up politically with that unit." In the wake of the Supreme Court's ruling which legalized abortion in 1973, "we knew there was a need for abortion services, because every Saturday we'd be driving someone seventy miles down to a clinic in Jacksonville." Over long talks at the kitchen table, Avery and her friends began envisioning the creation of a local place that would focus on reproductive issues. "We dreamed: how would we want to be treated?" The result, in 1974, was their founding of the Gainesville Women's Health Center.

"We used whatever resources we had, borrowed up to the neck to buy the equipment that was needed. We found a building right across from the Shand Teaching Hospital, which reluctantly provided our back-up doctors. Our main ones were residents from the university. It was a first-trimester abortion cinic with other gynecological services. But we didn't just open the facility, we created a philosophy and a way to deliver services. We had the walls painted in colors. There was blue shag carpet on the floor—which was the in thing at that time— and denim furniture and pictures on the walls and plants everywhere. Even in the examination rooms, we had posters on the ceilings so women could look at something when they were lying down. See, all this was unheard of in medical facilities then. They'd usually have as-phalt floors and completely sterile surroundings.

"Then we would have the doctor come in and meet the woman while she was still dressed. This is regular procedure today, but back then customarily she'd already be lying there on the table. And we wanted the women to understand every single thing that's happening to their bodies, gave them access to their charts. Which has all become part of the fabric of care, but again it wasn't during that time. Today, the Gainesville clinic is over twenty-some years old, and still going."

Norma Swenson, a coauthor of the best-selling book *Our Bodies, Ourselves*, twice visited Avery in Gainesville after they met at a con-ference of the National Women's Health Network in 1975. "Byllye invited me to talk about women's issues," Swenson remembers, "and it took my breath away that the meeting took place in a church. Ba-sically I—a white woman from the Northeast—was being asked by Byllye to 'preach' to all these Southern black women. It was a very hot night, I think I still have the dress I wore. And it was so inspiring to be there, to begin learning how to make these connections."

One night, Avery convened a meeting to find out if people in Gaines-ville might be interested in an alternative birthing environment. An overflow crowd showed up. In November of 1978, after receiving per-mission from Florida's Medical Society and raising money from local supporters, Avery and her friends opened "Birthplace" in a large, two-story, turn-of-the-century house. As they had with their clinic, the women set about creating a decor "so that when families walked in that door, the environment said yes." There were family education and private breakfast rooms, filled with antiques, carpeting, pictures and huge pillows.

At the moment of birth, often several generations of families came to witness. All of the services were performed by nurse midwives, most of whom worked at the university. Avery herself assisted the midwives in more than one hundred births, an experience she looks back upon as "miraculous in so many ways. I really came to understand both birth and death. There's something about the beginning of life that makes you understand when it's no longer there. I remember one birth—it was like our fourth baby—when Nancy Redfern, the midwife, went into the next room to take a short nap. When she woke up, she said, 'I had a dream that this baby was born with no neck.' When the baby arrived, the [umbilical] cord was wrapped around its neck. So because she'd had this dream, she reached down and pulled the cord from around the baby's neck. From then on, seeing if this might be happening became part of our regular routine.

"Other times, I would be down in my office and all of a sudden I'd get up, start vacuuming and straightening everything. Nancy came in and said, 'Oh, I guess we're gonna have a baby tonight.' I said, 'Why?' She said, 'You're nesting.' Sure enough, sometimes it might not be till five in the morning, but there would be a birth that night.

"We reached the point where we didn't need words to communicate around some events. Another time we were having an emergency we'd never had before, and Nancy needed something and just looked at me. I handed her this instrument. I think it was called a Gelpi [perineal] retractor, but I had never used it or even seen it being used. All this was very much a spiritual experience, it changed my life."

In those years, Avery recalls, it cost about $3,000 for someone to get prenatal care and have her baby in a hospital. "Birthplace" charged $1,800. "Support and childbirth education during pregnancy was key, since the women would go home three hours after they had their babies. We made sure they had support at home, someone to take care of them, and then our nurses went out and saw them the next day. Which was much more cost-effective than keeping them at the center."

The regular Tuesday night orientation sessions marked Avery's debut as a motivational speaker—something for which, to her surprise, she possessed considerable talent. "My goal was to get every person who came in to sign up," she says, "and most of them did." Then, when "Birthplace" needed an extra midwife whom its budget couldn't afford, Avery decided "they needed that more than another talking type like me." So she moved over to Gainesville's Santa Fe Community College, taking charge of a new federally funded project surrounding educational training in women's health issues.

"I'd always looked at myself as a woman, but when I went there I started looking at myself as a black woman. I started noticing that these young black women, who were being paid to come to the school, were out so much with illnesses. When I started questioning them, it was surprising to me how many had high blood pressure or lupus or other diseases that I didn't think you got until you were much older. So I started researching."

In Washington for a meeting, Avery tracked down a book put out by the National Center for Health Statistics in 1979. "The figure that really caught my eye," Avery remembers, "had to do with psychological well-being. Over half of the black women whom they'd surveyed between the ages of eighteen to twenty-five rated themselves as living in psychological distress. They rated that distress as greater than white women of the same ages who had been diagnosed as mental patients! It became clear that I had to figure out a way to organize black women and bring them together to talk about what's going on. You couldn't start discussing the physical illnesses until you got into talking about psychological distress."

By then a board member of the Washington-based National Women's Health Network, Avery felt, according to Swenson, "dissatisfied with what it was becoming, in a continual combat posture with the government regulatory apparatus. It was too far away from the thousands of black women who really needed something very different. She believed something more decentralized was crucial, and initially launched the National Black Women's Health Project as an arm of our Network."

Avery first established her Project in Gainesville, but found it difficult to get women to become engaged in the work. With the Gainesville Women's Health Center and "Birthplace" running smoothly, and feeling that she had done all she could there, in 1981 Avery took a friend's advice and moved to Atlanta with her high-school-age daughter Sonja (Wesley, Jr., remained in Gainesville attending a community college). It was in Atlanta that her vision took root—in a way that Byllye Avery never anticipated.

Starting out on a shoestring budget in her new home, before long Avery had raised enough money to rent an office at the Martin Luther King Center. "I had no strategic plan, I was just flying by the seat of my pants," she says. "Here I'd been talking about women's health all these years with white women. But no wonder black women were absent from the discussions, because they didn't include our perspective, just didn't talk our talk. Well, I didn't know what our talk was either, because we hadn't come together. That's what the self-help groups and the task force meetings I started organizing were about: the realities of our lives, how are we feeling, how are we coping.

"White women were talking about reproductive health issues, but white women were twice healthier than black women. So what's number one on the white women's list might be number six on our list. Long before CDC [the federal Centers for Disease Control] declared violence to be a public health issue, that's what black women were saying was their most important concern. I'd had some idea that domestic violence was pretty rampant, but I didn't know how bad it really was. Psychological and sexual abuse are also pressing issues for black women.

"People just have no idea of the devastating effects these have on women's lives. Why do you think our babies are dying? Because their mommas are dying. They're in dead relationships and they feel empty. If someone is in a relationship with a man who's beating them, do you think they're going to remember to get their Pap smear? These are things women had struggled with in silence. What the Health Project did was give people permission to discuss matters that had been totally taboo. To say, There's no shame in being afraid, come hold my hand. By putting it in the air, this helped change the psyche and the climate. We watched women grow. When they would first come to us, they'd have their heads down. Asked what do you love about yourself, they couldn't tell you a thing. In less than a year, you watched them move to a whole different level. There's nothing like the validation that you get from your peers. I've seen lots of people turn their lives around."

The self-help groups that Avery organized did not try to do actual therapy. In some instances, women were guided to psychiatrists, or to another group that dealt with such specifically difficult topics as incest. Some were encouraged by their peers to leave abusive relationships or apply for a different job. An entire piece of the Project focused on reproductive health, because Avery observed that women were willing to talk about miscarriages but reluctant to speak of their abortions. Dr. Ginger Floyd says, "It's through the telling of stories that Byllye has brought people together."

Early in 1983, Avery assembled twenty-one women to plan the first National Conference on Black Women's Health Issues. When it took place that June at Spelman College in Atlanta, Avery expected perhaps 200 women to attend. More than 2,000 showed up. "It was remarkable," recalled Sybil Shainwald, then president of the National Women's Health Network. "Black women came by bus, by car, however they could get there." Avery began the event by pouring libations to honor the ancestors, evoking their knowledge and permission to speak.

The National Black Women's Health Project began to spread rapidly across the South, a region where, as Dr. Floyd describes: "If you put your hand on a map, started in Texas and worked around to Virginia, you would outline what we call the infant mortality belt of the nation. It's also the poverty belt and the minority belt—all those variables that impact upon why babies live or die."

As Avery says, "Sometimes I felt like I opened Pandora's box. Raising money through foundations and other sources wasn't easy. We kept getting bigger and bigger, and couldn't meet the demand. I remember how awful I felt the day I realized I was not gonna know everybody's name. But whenever a new group would want to organize, somehow we'd send people down to help get it going."

Dr. Floyd remembers: "Byllye talked to me about how it takes both the right message and the right messenger. Old black women can't come into the neighborhood and talk to young black teenagers. So how do you build a team? How do we get the black churches involved? How do we get mothers in the projects involved? That's what these self-help groups were all about. Byllye's not a Mother Teresa. *You* gotta participate in this."

As the organization grew, it was not without enemies. "We got beat up pretty bad because we tackled the gender issues, the racism issues, all the 'isms,' you know," adds Dr. Floyd. "Byllye also created a lot of controversy in my world, because the Health Project taught women how to do their own gynecological self-examinations."

Avery was also involved in an effort by the National Women's Health Network to take on the Upjohn company. That Network initiated a class action lawsuit in Atlanta against the use of Depo Provera—a long-term injectable contraceptive—without informed consent on women at the city's Grady Hospital. "It was a drug that then caused various problems," Avery explains, "causing your hair to fall out and excessive weight gain. If you think about African-American women putting on weight—and some gained as much as 150 pounds!—that speeds up their predisposition to high blood pressure or diabetes. Hundreds and hundreds of calls came into our hotline. But the suit never was never allowed to proceed in court—because, although women suffered, no one died from Depo Provera." (An altered form of Depo Provera remains in use today.)

Dr. Floyd remembers: "Byllye was my conscience. She'd walk into my office and say, 'This ain't about helping Miss Jones, Ginger. This is about bureaucracy, this rule is in the way. Now are you gonna help us change it or what?' Her vision, and the belief system that she has inculcated in many of us, has clearly shifted policy in this state."

Avery not only altered public policy, but changed individual attitudes. Floyd recalls the anger that permeated the black women's gatherings in the early years, which often targeted whites. "Basically, we didn't want white women to participate. But Byllye said, 'No, the world ain't like that.' After all, she had come to this project *through* the white women's movement. So she developed what she called a Council of Allies. What is the role that white women can play in the movement of black women as they make this journey? Byllye clearly defined this concept of space. Sometimes, that space needs to be for women of color only, so that we can talk openly among ourselves and heal. Sometimes, that space can be shared. Unbelievably, it worked."

At the same time, links were forged with new Latina and Native American women's health organizations. An international program called Sister Reach was formed, extending itself to help create self-help groups in Africa and the Caribbean. Avery's efforts inspired the creation of a National Black Men's Health Project, which functioned for several years in Atlanta. Her organization moved into a two-story Victorian house in Atlanta and began publishing a membership magazine, *Vital Signs*. It also raised $40,000 to produce a teen-pregnancy prevention film titled *On Becoming a Woman: Mothers and Daughters Talking Together*. Using footage from evening meetings of mothers and their teenagers discussing menstruation, sex, birth control, love, and why it is so hard for them to talk, the 104-minute-long documentary also featured an engaging and explicit animated sex-education section.

"I've tried to look back and ask, what have I really done that's so significant?" Avery says. "When women started looking at health, all I did was say, let's look at black women within that. This started Latina, Asian, and Native American women looking at themselves. Then the whole healthcare education arena started viewing the role of ethnicity in terms of health. It opened up a whole new field."

In July of 1989, Avery's landmark work was recognized by Chicago's MacArthur Foundation. She received a five-year, $310,000 "genius" award which, as the American Medical Association's magazine described in an article about Avery, "is designed to allow exceptional individuals the freedom to develop new ideas without the pressure of having to account for how their time and money are spent. Fellowship winners are nominated without their knowledge by members of a national panel and are selected after a lengthy and confidential evaluation process." Although Avery says she used the money to pay some debts and travel, Dr. Floyd maintains that Avery "put all her money back into the cause. She basically took the MacArthur and underwrote this organization."

Avery's innovations continued unabated. "I walk, and I noticed that a lot of black women walk," she says. "So in 1991, we got some initial funding and I created this Walking for Wellness idea." A friend at the Women's Sports Foundation put Avery in touch with former Olympic track star Wilma Rudolph, who agreed to become the spokesperson. The following summer, the program was launched in Eatonville, Florida, "one of only two or three black towns left in the country, from the home of [novelist] Zora Neale Hurston. We all had buttons on— Walk With Wilma—and walked all through the town. I'll never forget Wilma taking the hand of this little child who had go to the bathroom, leading him into somebody's house. That's just the kind of person she was."

Rudolph came to subsequent events in Detroit and then Atlanta. The latter coincided with the tenth anniversary conference of the National Black Women's Health Project, which drew 2,500 people. But on the morning of the walk, Rudolph suffered a terrible headache and failed to show up. At the breakfast where she was the featured speaker, the Olympic sprinter began repeating the same phrases over and over.

The 1994 Walking for Wellness event proved to be Wilma Rudolph's last public appearance. Diagnosed with a brain tumor, she was given five weeks to live; she survived for five months. What Rudolph helped to inspire has been carried on by Avery's Project. A partnership was formed with the American Heart Association and the walks have continued. "We had over 300 people in Baltimore, in the worst rain you've ever seen," Avery says. "I know Wilma was there in spirit." Then, at a June 1997 walk in Detroit, more than 2,000 people from the very young to the very old took part.

In recent years, the National Black Women's Health Project has undergone a major transition. In 1992, Avery ceased day-to-day management and accepted an offer to spend two years as a visiting fellow at the Harvard School of Public Health. In Boston, she collaborated with Norma Swenson and others on a policy paper concerning how to reform maternity care. After that, Avery moved to Swarthmore, Pennsylvania, to concentrate more on her speaking and writing. There she currently serves on the National Institutes of Health's Advisory Committee for the Office of Research on Women's Health. She also continues to meet regularly with a self-help group in a public housing project in nearby Chester.

Her children are now in their thirties—Wesley, Jr., having recently married and working as a UPS driver in Gainesville, and Sonja having followed her mother's footsteps to work at the Feminist Women's Health Center in Atlanta. The National Black Women's Health Project has named a new executive director and moved in 1996 to Washington, looking to affect the national agenda on health issues. Recently, the office announced a new program to work on substance abuse prevention at a number of black college campuses.

"Part of the reason I stepped down," Avery says, "was so that the organization could figure out how to institutionalize without my being at the center. It was hard for me, because the National Black Women's Health Project is my heart and my soul. But it had to evolve and develop a life of its own."

So, in Atlanta, the women whom she served as counselor and friend raised $150,000 to form a spin-off organization, the Center for Black Women's Wellness. Located in a housing project, its atmosphere is in the customary Avery style. "You walk in and it's full of pictures of African-American women, with the right kind of music," says Dr. Floyd. "It's using the self-help model integrated with a medical model. There is a female physician's assistant on staff, and the Center works with our state agency on our infant mortality and teen pregnancy prevention projects. It's an example of how public agencies can work with community-based organizations."

Avery also lent her assistance to what Floyd calls "an attempt to bring traditional medicine into public health." In the summer of 1996, spiritual healers from five Native American tribes came together with counterparts from Senegal and Nigeria for an eight-day meeting on South Carolina's St. Helena Island. Cosponsored by the Morehouse School of Medicine, the ceremony drew over 650 people from twenty states and five foreign countries.

Having now made seven trips to the African continent, its ways and means have become increasingly important to Avery. "At our conferences, we always start off with a ritual. The drummers get your heart flowing and your spirits up, and it clears out your mind. We decorate our stages with African cloths and sculptures, to cleanse the air and open us up to be receptive. You need ceremony. It just seems unreal to start off a meeting with somebody standing up front and saying good morning."

Avery draws strength, too, from her African-American ancestors. "I have a funny little ritual I do. Whenever I'm having problems, I put a committee together before I go to sleep. I've got Harriet Tubman, Sojourner Truth, and Mary McLeod Bethune as regulars. If there's somebody who's special to whatever the problem area is, I throw them onto the committee. Then I give *them* the problem, and invariably I wake up the next morning and know what to do."

At the same time, Avery remains intensely practical—as well as visionary—concerning what is needed in American medicine. "I really want a single-payer health care system, so that everybody has access. Community health centers should have local boards, who talk specifically about health care delivery as it relates to a certain area's needs. I'd like to see small medical facilities and many, many more of them. I would also have lay health workers, people who go into homes and be someone's guide. Do the follow-up, hold their hand, and make sure they're taking their medications properly. You don't necessarily need a physician or even a nurse to do these things. The system needs to take in the whole individual, to make sure we have adequate playgrounds and safe bicycle paths. And some way to ensure that certain communities have fresh vegetables that don't cost an arm and a leg. Of course, the mental well-being of people has to be taken into account."

Avery's primary means of support derives from the thirty-or-so paid lectures per year that she continues to give across the U.S. She addresses Seattle physicians about diversity, Denver scholars about ethics, Texas university students about "compassionate medicine." Like Harvard's Cornel West, with whom she has shared platforms, Avery's speaking style is not only stunningly charismatic but deeply personal. Also like West, she never uses a prepared text. And, as West is never seen publicly in anything but a dark three-piece suit, Avery goes nowhere in anything but purple.

"It's just my color, I guess," she says. "I started wearing purple about ten years ago, and it makes me feel good. Sometimes I mix it up with a little black or turquoise. But if I don't wear purple, people seem to get very upset. One day I went into Harvard and had on black, and I had to go back home and change. They were havin' a fit!"

She considers her speaking ability "truly a gift from the Creator. There are certain cardinal principles that I hold true to, and I will never talk about anything I don't know about. But basically I just stand up and deliver. I always get there a few hours early, collect myself and hear what other people are talking about, and see what comes to me. I kinda fill in the spaces. Since I've been working on this book about spirituality, I've asked people in the audience for words I should include. I'm so glad somebody gave me 'water,' because I wouldn't have thought to write about that."

When I ask Avery to define her concept of leadership, she thinks for a long time and then says: "Oh, that's a hard one. It's got to do with making a commitment. And it's lonely. But I really see myself as standing not in front of people, but behind them."

Now, standing among the Maternal Care Coalition audience in Philadelphia, Byllye Avery is talking about the next generation. "We are not a culture that thinks about children," she is saying. "I remember when Marian Edelman went to Japan and told people about her Children's Defense Fund, they wondered, why do you need a defense fund for children? Think about it. I'm talking about collective caring. It's—not—there."

Her voice rises as she continues, impassioned: "Infant mortality is not only a medical problem, but it has a very important social dimension. The health care system that's the most advanced in the world can't get the care to the people. . . . You go into a neighborhood, you see ten liquor stores. Well, put in ten health care centers! We don't have the political will to make these things happen. . . .

"Now how do we start to do the personal work? We have to be willing to clean the cobwebs out of our own mind. We got a lotta hurt and a lotta pain. . . . Some of us are broken and some of us are bent— but that doesn't mean we can't be repaired. You've got to have people who know who they are, people who are willing to deal with their own stuff. . . ."

Avery talks for a time to the men, "[who are] saddled with . . . you ain't supposed to feel nothin', you ain't supposed to show no emotion. . . . What happens is, it ends up coming out in awful ways, in ways that are not deserving of the fine creatures you are. You have to figure out what is the 'man thing' in you and confront it, so that it's a human thing, a respecting thing. And then you've gotta reach out to the other brothers, because they are your natural allies. . . . Speak up on my behalf! When you do that, you are also speaking up for yourself."

She moves on to talk about students who now pass through metal detectors in their schools, to the deleterious influence of bad TV, to the necessity of "somebody in the village driving the kids to ballet or football or some after-school activity." She describes the self-help groups that brought family members together to delve into sex education. In all of this, Avery addresses the realities of our times, offering no panaceas.

"Now I want to talk about welfare, people who are affected around welfare reform." As Avery tells the story of what she was told on a trip she made to Milwaukee in 1997, at several junctures there are stunned gasps from the audience. It is about a young mother who had managed to get off welfare and find her first job. Ordinarily a neighbor kept her one-year-old child while the woman was at work. On this particular day, the neighbor had to go to the doctor.

"So the woman called in and told her boss, 'I can't come to work today because I don't have child care.' Her boss told her she'd better come in. So she brought her baby and left him in the car with the windows cracked. It wasn't real hot that day. Every hour up until noon, she went out to check on the baby. She took him to lunch with her at McDonald's and went back to work. Two o'clock, she looked in on the baby again. She didn't go back anymore until five and, when she got there, the baby was not breathing. She ran with it into the medical facility where she worked. They pronounced the baby dead. Now she's in jail, charged with manslaughter.

"So I said to the women of Milwaukee, what are you all going to do about this? There needs to be a network of people who can talk to folks who've come off welfare. Somebody she could call, who could either help with child care or give her some advice. If she'd called up that morning and said, 'I got the flu,' it would've been fine. But she doesn't know that, she tried to be a good citizen."

There is a pained silence in the auditorium. Finally Avery continues: "When you look at building the village, start with what is needed around the most vulnerable element. Talk to the people who have families that need support. This concept calls for all people to be involved. . . . Know that you can't change the world, but the person you can change is you. . . . You have to be connected to the part of you that is spiritual. Because when it gets hard and you want to throw up your hands, sometimes all you can do is say, 'Lord, have mercy, help me, help me.'

"We have a job to do in the United States. We have a challenge. We have the most diverse country in the world. The main job we have to learn is how to walk the high road with each other, how to give each other the benefit of the doubt. To learn how to trust. We ultimately only have one job to do here on earth. That is, to learn how to live and work and play and protect each other, together. It's up to us."

FOR FURTHER READING:

Boston Women's Health Book Collective, *The New Our Bodies, Ourselves: A Book by and for Women* (New York: Simon & Schuster, 1992).

22

Ancestors—Sojourner Truth and the
Nineteenth-Century Visionaries

"I talk to God and God talks to me. . . . [He] is a great ocean of love; and we live and move in Him as fishes in the sea, filled with his love and spirit, and his throne is in the hearts of his people. . . . [People] would never get to heaven by lifting themselves up in a basket, but they must lift those up below them. . . . We shall never see God only as we see Him in one another."
—SOJOURNER TRUTH

"More than anything else she did or said in her life, this ability to act with the support of a powerful supernatural force and to mine its extraordinary resources made Sojourner Truth a representative African-American woman."
—NELL PAINTER, *Sojourner Truth: A Life, a Symbol*

In the spring of 1844, near the western Massachusetts town of Northampton, an apocalyptic religious group known as the Millerites was holding an outdoor camp meeting. Among the attendees was a woman then approaching her late forties, an escaped slave who a year earlier had changed her name from Isabella to Sojourner Truth. The name derived from her belief that God had called upon her to travel and "declare the truth to the people." Already, she had developed quite a reputation as a mesmerizing speaker.

On this particular evening, as often occurred at such unorthodox Millerite gatherings, a mob of young people invaded the services. Hooting and hollering, they announced their purpose to burn down the tents which had been set up in an open field. Sojourner Truth cowered behind a trunk inside one of these. "I am the only colored person here," she later recalled thinking, "and on me, probably, their wicked mischief will fall first, and perhaps fatally."

Then, as the youths proceeded to shake the tent, Truth described herself wondering: "Have I not faith enough to go out and quell that mob, when I know it is written—'One shall chase a thousand and two put ten thousand to flight'? I know there are not a thousand here; and

I know I am a servant of the living God. I'll go to the rescue, and the Lord shall go with and protect me."

Failing to enlist any support from the frightened Millerite leaders, Truth nonetheless emerged from the tent. "I felt as if I had *three hearts*! And that they were so large, my body could hardly hold them!" She walked over to a small hill, this very tall, bespectacled, rather gaunt-looking pied piper. Followed by some of the unruly crowd, she began to sing one of her favorite hymns. It was a "home-made" resurrection song, one that she would also sing on her deathbed some forty years later.

> *"It was early in the morning—it was early in the morning,*
>   *Just at the break of day—*
> *When he rose—when he rose—when he rose,*
>   *And went to heaven on a cloud."*

The powerful voice of Sojourner Truth pierced the surrounding countryside. "Why do you come about me with clubs and sticks?" she paused and asked. "I am not doing harm to anyone."

"We aren't going to hurt you, old woman," one of the youths replied. Others asked her to continue. Some called upon her to speak. The crowd grew as Truth began to preach. Her sermon started with these words:

"Well, there are two congregations on this ground. It is written that there shall be a separation, and the sheep shall be separated from the goats. The other preachers have the sheep, *I* have the goats. And I have a few sheep among my goats, but they are *very* ragged."

The young people laughed, and asked that she move to a nearby wagon so that they could see her better. "If I step up on it, will you tip it over?" she asked. A response came that should anyone attempt such, they would be knocked down. Truth was helped onto the wagon. For more than an hour, she sang and talked, calling them "children," pausing periodically for questions and answers. When she got tired and wanted to stop, they would not let her.

Finally, Truth said: "I have talked and sung to you, as you asked me; and now I have a request to make of you; will you grant it?" If she performed one more song, would they go away and leave the camp meeting alone? Three times she asked, until satisfied with a gathering crescendo of positive response. Then she sang:

> *"I bless the Lord I've got my seal—to-day and to-day—*
>   *To slay Goliath in the field—to-day and to-day*

The good old way is a righteous way,
I mean to take the kingdom in the good old way."

Sojourner Truth's "children" dispersed, moving rapidly toward the main road, their leaders disciplining the ones who still held back.

She was a legendary figure in nineteenth-century America, an illiterate woman who not only influenced her own time but presaged social movements of a century later. Sojourner Truth was a feminist leader, a civil rights activist whose "ride-ins" altered segregated transportation practices, and a resident of several intentional communities (the first one run by a doomsday-awaiting messianic figure). She met with Abraham Lincoln and challenged Frederick Douglass. In building bridges to white America, she became a symbol who forged her own myth. Above all, she was deeply spiritual—and, in this, among her people Truth was far from alone.

Slaves had never seen the Christian Bible before their forced removal to this country. It turned out to be the primary source from which thousands of them drew strength. Indeed, in many cases they took "The Word" to levels far beyond the pious self-righteousness of white churchgoers, who often used the Bible to justify the practice of slavery. The leaders of the first three slave rebellions—Gabriel Prosser, Denmark Vesey, and Nat Turner—all cited biblical passages to inspire their followers. Nat Turner was known as "The Prophet." He seemed able to foresee the momentous conflict between North and South that would result in his people's freedom from slavery.

One day, as author Lerone Bennett, Jr., describes in *Before the Mayflower*: "He saw black and white spirits wrestling in the sky; the sun grew dark and blood gushed forth in streams." Thirty years before the outbreak of the Civil War, the peculiar color of the sun provided Turner's "sign" that the day of revolt was about to arrive. With seventy men, Turner set out across Southampton, Virginia, killing at least fifty-seven whites before he was captured. He was hung on November 11, 1831. That day, Turner is said to have prophesied that it would grow dark and rain. It did. His insurrection is seen by historians as having initiated the gathering storm of debate and ultimately war over the issue of slavery.

"The drum was outlawed with Nat Turner, so then the spiritual came on—as a liberating tune," as Dr. Joseph Roberts, current pastor of Atlanta's Ebenezer Baptist Church where Martin Luther King presided, explained to me. "Where are we going to meet? 'Down by the riverside.' That didn't have a thing to do with going to heaven. 'Oh Lord, have mercy, if you please'—*don't* let them catch me! White people are thinking it's a great communion hymn. But it was a revolutionary, political hymn, telling you when the next group was going to leave on the Underground Railroad. 'Wade in the water'—because they've got the *dogs* after you! 'God's gonna trouble the water'—and He'll throw off the dog's scent. This was very widespread. A number of black preachers gave these codes, Harriet Tubman wasn't the only one."

Tubman was known by the code name of Moses. An escaped slave herself, she returned nineteen times to the South and helped more than 300 others to escape. In her later years, Tubman spoke to several interviewers about having used the spirituals as a message system where "the uninitiated knew not the hidden meaning of the words." *Go Down Moses* was her anthem, and it was filled with allegories. Egyptland was the South. Pharaoh signified the slaveholders, the Israelites the slaves, and Moses the whites who might assist their escape. Canaan was Canada, the goal of their flight. The Jordan River marked the distance from their point of embarkation to the "Promised Land" of freedom. The "year of Jubilee" harkened to their eventual emancipation.

While Tubman is not known to have been a churchgoing Christian during her years in slavery, she spoke to two interviewers about having prayed for and received divine intervention while rescuing slaves. She ascribed this spiritual gift as an inheritance from her father, who "could always predict the weather" and "foretold the Mexican War." Through prayer, dreams, and waking visions, she said "she always knows when there is danger near her."

Jean Humez, a professor of women's studies at the University of Massachusetts, elaborates: "Because she never wrote them down herself, we don't know exactly what Harriet Tubman's trance states and predictive dreams were like. One story is told about how, as a young child, she was in the path of an object hurled by her slave-master at someone else. It hit her on the head. From then on, she would often drop off during the day in what appeared to be sleep. But various of her interviewers said, 'She can tell you afterwards what's been happening.' In one source, there is an indication that she had visionary experiences during these mysterious states."

The surviving writings of Rebecca Cox Jackson offer the most complete record of these kinds of illuminations. Covering the years between 1830 and 1864, Jackson's detailed accounts of her dreams and visions were edited by Humez into a book called *Gifts of Power*. Like Sojourner Truth, Jackson was a wandering preacher, abolitionist and women's rights advocate, as well as a spellbinding orator. Shortly before the Civil War, she founded a predominantly black women's Shaker community in Philadelphia that survived her death by twenty-five years.

"Rebecca Jackson's writings describe an inner world to which few of us, with modern, secularized consciousness, have sustained or frequent access," Humez writes in her introduction. "She was able to capture states of consciousness in which waking personality, with all its quirks and defenses, drops away. Laws of nature are violated with ease, particularly in her accounts of visionary dreams. She soars, lifts, leaps easily into the sky, flies through the air, looks down from a great height, and can see things never visible from such a perspective before."

A free black woman and seamstress, Jackson described having received her religious awakening during a severe thunderstorm in July of 1830. The following year, this formerly unlettered woman recounts suddenly being given the "gift of reading." In 1833 Jackson set out across Pennsylvania by stagecoach, steamboat, and on foot as a Methodist preacher, arousing revivalist fervor among both blacks and whites wherever she went. In "A Dream of Three Books," set down three years later, she wrote of a white man who appeared at her back door as an instructor. He showed her three books covering "the beginning of creation to the end of time," and was still present when she awoke. Over the ensuing thirty-five years before her death in 1871, Jackson wrote of the man's periodic returns.

The woman had, according to Humez, an "ability to embed religious mystery squarely in the recognizable, commonplace reality in which we all live." Jackson, too, may have worked with "some kind of esoteric 'code' or private language to convey a message that she did not want 'outsiders' such as whites to understand—in the manner of coded references to slavery and white oppression that linger in black folklore and folksong." The points of the compass seemed essential in many of her dream accounts. In the years leading up to the Civil War, Jackson wrote, "I dreamed that I was going south to feed the people. . . . I was brought into deep tribulation of soul about my people, and their present condition, seeing the awful event that is at hand."

Like Rebecca Jackson in coming to the Shakers, Sojourner Truth would cast aside conventional religion in search of an ideal spiritual community. Truth's own moment of revelation had come in 1827, when she was about to return to a slaveholding family to which she had belonged for sixteen years and from which she had recently escaped. After God showed himself "in the twinkling of an eye, that He was all over"—a conversion she also described as akin to a flash of lightning—Truth changed her mind about going back to the Dumont clan.

Born sometime around 1797 in the Hudson River country of upstate

New York, Truth's original language was the Dutch that her first owners spoke. Before she was half-grown, she had lost both parents and ten siblings—most of the latter having been sold to other slave-masters. Truth was auctioned off on several occasions before ending up with the Dumonts. She married a fellow slave in 1815.

Only nine months before legislation to release all remaining slaves was to take effect in New York, Truth decided in 1827 to flee the Dumont household after the owner went back on a promise to provide her and her husband early freedom and a log cabin. She left behind three children, all except for a baby. She took refuge with a white family that had known her since childhood, which paid off Dumont to prevent his taking her back. Then, when Truth learned that her five-year-old son Peter had been illegally sold into slavery in the South, she took her case before a grand jury. Such boldness was unheard of. "I felt so tall within," she would say later, "I felt as if the power of a nation was within me!"

Truth made the five-mile trip to the courthouse barefooted, and offered a persuasive case. Peter was returned from Alabama, reinforcing her faith in her recent evangelical conversion. Bringing the boy along, Truth decided to move 100 miles south to New York City, where she found work as a domestic. There, a white Methodist leader termed "the influence of her speaking . . . miraculous."

Early in the 1830s, she fell under the sway of a cult leader who called himself the Prophet Matthias. It was an abusive environment similar to those Truth had known all her life. Joining the white "apostles" in the New York village of Sing Sing as a housekeeper, she kept her growing doubts about Matthias's "Kingdom" to herself. After the group fell apart following a member's mysterious murder in 1834, Truth found herself scandalized in the press. Once again, she went to court, this time to sue a former cult member for slander. Once again, she won. According to the *Narrative* she dictated for publication in the late 1840s, she resolved "not to be thus deluded again" into submissively trusting any authoritarian figure.

For some fourteen years, Truth lived in or around New York. She ultimately came to feel it was a "wicked city" where "the rich rob the poor, and the poor rob one another" and that she herself had been "unfeeling, selfish and wicked." With her son Peter having been imprisoned several times for theft (he finally shipped off as a seaman and disappeared), in middle age she changed her name from Isabella. She packed a few pieces of clothing in a pillow case and, with scarcely a cent, began walking west. She was determined to repudiate "the house of bondage"—and to preach God's word. It was June 1, 1843.

For a time, Truth hooked up with the Millerite sect on Long Island, which foresaw the imminent arrival of famine, war, pestilence, and tempest. If the end came, Truth told one audience filled with ministers and citizens, "I am going to stay here and *stand the fire*, like Shadrach, Meshach, and Abednego." Moving on to reside with whomever might offer food and lodging, Truth soon arrived at western Massachusetts's Northampton Association. This was a utopian community of some 130 people, whose specialty was the manufacture of silk thread for industry. Founded by two antislavery advocates, it had already taken in some blacks as members. One of these was David Ruggles, who had been a principal agent for the Underground Railroad in New York.

The Northampton Association is considered to have been a haven for fugitive slaves. Abolitionist spokesman William Lloyd Garrison was a frequent visitor. Frederick Douglass, who would meet Sojourner Truth here for the first time, had already stayed at Northampton briefly in 1843. "The place and the people struck me as the most democratic I had ever met," Douglass recounted. "It was a place to extinguish all aristocratic pretensions. There was no high, no low, no masters, no servants, no white, no black. I, however, felt myself in very high society."

Although the community dissolved for lack of finances in 1846, it had a considerable impact on Truth's thinking and future. Here she met the woman, Olive Gilbert, who would assemble the first version of her life; Garrison would arrange for the initial printing of Truth's *Narrative* in 1850. Another Northampton member built a house for her in a mostly white neighborhood, the first she ever owned. And, the same year her book came out, Truth began speaking publicly on the issues that would dominate the rest of her life: the rights of blacks and women.

She sometimes shared podiums on both matters with Douglass and Garrison. "Woman set the world wrong by eating the forbidden fruit, and now she's going to set it right," Truth told one of the first national women's rights conventions ever held, in Worcester, Massachusetts. At an antislavery convention in 1851, she reportedly said that while others "had been talking about the poor slave . . . she was going to talk about the poor slaveholder. She wanted to know what would become of him; she feared he would go down to perdition, unless he could be reformed."

Audiences watched her stride toward the stage in a gray dress and white turban, "with the air of a queen," according to one account. Truth had such a deep, robust voice that some accused her of being a man in disguise. It was a combination of a guttural Dutch accent, black dialect, and broken and standard English—which extemporaneously came across, as one Chicago journalist wrote, like that of "the most learned college professor." Douglass said that "she seemed to please herself and others best when she put her ideas in the oddest forms," a free association of metaphor, poetry, and parable. Said Truth herself: "I go to hear myself as much as anyone else comes to hear me."

In her middle years, Truth did make an attempt at learning to read, but "the letters got all mixed up and I couldn't straighten them out." Yet, as she told the increasingly large crowds that came to hear her, "I can't read a book, but I can read the people." On one occasion, she even chastised her audience: "With all your opportunities for readin' and writin,' you don't take hold and do anything."

She was on a mission, certain she was in the hands of a higher power. The story is told that, en route to a speaking engagement in Ohio, Truth rode alone in a horse-drawn buggy loaned her by a friend. Whenever she came to a fork in the road, unable to read the signs, she would stop and say, "God, you drive." The Lord would take the reins, Truth believed, to the best spot for another evangelical meeting.

It was in Salem, Ohio, on August 22, 1852, that one of those "moments of Truth" took place which have resounded ever since. A Friends [Quaker] meeting house was reportedly jammed to capacity of about 1,000 people. Shortly before, President James Buchanan had proposed to amend the Constitution, to make clear that it supported legalized slavery. Frederick Douglass, who preceded Truth on the podium, was in a justifiable rage. He declared that the time had come for slaves to take up arms against their oppressors. "What is the use of moral suasion to a people thus trampled to the dust?" he cried. Then the voice of Truth suddenly boomed out:

"Frederick! Is God gone?"*

As Douglass later recalled, "We were all for a moment brought to a stand-still, just as we should have been if someone had thrown a brick through the window." The hour was not right; Truth's was a call for faith. A personal, accessible God would eventually and actively intervene for justice. This was not the last time she would seek to shift Douglass's thinking. He would call hers a "strange compound of wit and wisdom, of wild enthusiasm and flint-like common sense."

Until the mid-1850s, Truth kept residence in Northampton, where her lecturing and book sales provided enough income to pay off the mortgage on a house that also came to contain all three of her daughters.

---

*Many early accounts, based upon Harriet Beecher Stowe's 1863 *Atlantic Monthly* article about Truth, had her asking Douglass, "Is God dead?"—the words that were in fact engraved upon Truth's tombstone. Recent scholarship, however, reveals that this and certain other phrases attributed to Truth were inaccurate.

Then, on a visit to Battle Creek, Michigan, she encountered another utopian group called Harmonia, a small Spiritualist community founded by former Quakers. It was loosely structured, with no common property or rules, and separate families living in proximity of about a dozen houses. She sometimes attended seances, where her reaction seems to have been a mixture of fascination and humor. "Come spirit, hop up here on the table, and see if you can make a louder noise," Truth reportedly said. By the time this community, too, fell apart because of internal dissension, Truth had moved into another home in Battle Creek.

That was where she was living when the Civil War broke out in 1861. Now she became an ardent supporter of the Union cause. That June, she traveled across the state line into Indiana, to address a large pro-Union rally. There, her white friends "thought I should be dressed in uniform. . . . So they put upon me a red, white, and blue shawl, a sash and apron to match, a cap on my head with a star in front, and a star on each shoulder. When I was dressed I looked in the glass and was fairly frightened. [I said,] 'It seems I am going to battle.' My friends advised me to take a sword or pistol. I replied, 'I carry no weapon: the Lord will reserve [sic: preserve] me without weapons."

Driven to the event at the Steuben County Courthouse in a lovely carriage, Truth and her entourage marched in between two rows of soldiers to *The Star-Spangled Banner*. Trouble awaited. If she was ten years younger, said Truth, she "would fly to the battle-field, and nurse and cook for the Massachusetts troops, brave boys! and if it came to the pinch, put in a blow, now and then." At that point, the meeting was mobbed by agitators—Northern "Copperheads" who supported the Southern Confederacy. "It seems that it takes *my* black face to bring out *your* black hearts," Truth is said to have told them, "so it's well I came."

She was placed under arrest, under pretext of having broken a rarely enforced Indiana law that prohibited those of African descent from entering the state. For the next ten days, Truth was held while angry supporters and detractors gathered outside the jail. Eventually, she was set free and returned to Michigan.

During the year of the Emancipation Proclamation, Harriet Beecher Stowe's article about Truth appeared, based upon an interview conducted ten years earlier. It brought Truth national attention as "the Libyan Sibyl." That was the name of a new statue by the renowned sculptor William Wetmore Story, unveiled at the London World's Fair in 1862. Stowe contended it was based upon Truth as an "imaginary model." This remains a questionable assumption, and one that Truth herself seems not to have been particularly enamored of. She didn't like having Stowe's article read to her, saying: "I don't want to hear about that old symbol; read me something that is going on now."

One of Truth's grandsons had volunteered to serve with the all-black Massachusetts 54th Regiment. When Michigan organized a similar contingent in the autumn of 1863, Truth collected contributions for a Thanksgiving dinner and delivered these personally to the soldiers. She had composed a song for black troops and, visiting the camp in Detroit, Truth sang it to them. To the tune of *John Brown's Body*, one of its verses went like this:

"Look there above the center, where the flag is waving bright;
We are going out of slavery, we are bound for freedom's light;
We mean to show Jeff Davis how the Africans can fight,
As we go marching on."

John Brown's Body was the theme song of black soldiers during the Civil War. According to one veteran's account to a historian years later, Truth's verses were also sung as one group of them moved into battle.

Early in 1864, Truth announced that the Lord intended her to go to Washington and meet "the first Antislavery President." Accompanied by her fourteen-year-old grandson Samuel to assist her with reading and writing, Truth set out that summer for a lengthy trip. Stopping in Boston, she met Harriet Tubman for the first time. Tubman had continued her work in the South, as a spy for the Union Army behind Confederate lines. Truth's biographer Nell Painter has noted that the two women had much in common: "in adventurous pasts, intimate connection with God, singing, and ways of knowing independent of literacy." Truth was a generation older than Tubman, and dwarfed her in height. Little is known of what they talked about, except for an unresolved disagreement. Tubman was skeptical about President Lincoln, because he permitted white soldiers to receive more money than blacks. Truth insisted that Lincoln was their friend.

Truth moved on, giving speeches on behalf of Lincoln's reelection. When she arrived in the nation's capital, she began working among recently freed slaves. Then, on October 29, 1864, with entree provided by the Lincolns' housekeepr Elizabeth Keckley, Truth and a white female companion met with the President. While there are different versions of what transpired—some not as laudatory as Truth's herself—here is some of what she set down in a dictated letter published not long thereafter in the antislavery press. After Lincoln rose from his desk, he extended his hand and greeted her with a bow:

I said to him, "Mr. President, when you first took your seat I feared you would be torn to pieces, for I likened you unto Daniel, who was thrown into the lions' den; and if the lions did not tear you into pieces, I knew that it would be God that had saved you; and I said if He spared me I would see you before the four years expired, and He has done so, and now I am here to see you for myself."

He then congratulated me on my having been spared. Then I said: "I appreciate you, for you are the best President who has ever taken the seat." He replied thus: "I expect you have reference to my having emancipated the slaves in my proclamation. But," said he, mentioning the names of several of his predecessors (and among them emphatically that of Washington), "they were all just as good, and would have done just as he had done if the time had come. If the people over the river (pointing across the Potomac) had behaved themselves, I could not have done what I have; but they did not, and I was compelled to these things." I then said: "I thank God that you were the instrument selected by him and the people to do it."

He then showed me the Bible presented to him by the colored people of Baltimore. . . . After I had looked it over, I said to him: "This is beautiful indeed; the colored people have given this to the Head of the government, and that government once sanctioned laws that would not permit its people to learn enough to enable them to read this Book. And for what? Let them answer who can."

I must say, and I am proud to say, that I never was treated by any one with more kindness and cordiality than were shown to me by that great and good man. . . . He took my little book, and with the same hand that signed the death-warrant of slavery, he wrote as follows:

"For Aunty Sojourner Truth,
Oct. 29, 1864 A. Lincoln."

As I was taking my leave, he arose and took my hand, and said he would be pleased to have me call again. I felt that I was in the presence of a friend, and I now thank God from the bottom of my heart that I always have advocated his cause, and have done it openly and boldly. I shall feel still more in duty bound to do so in time to come. May God assist me. . . .

Truth stayed on in Washington, exhorting the former slaves in the Freedmen's Village to know and defend their rights. She was appalled by the refugee-camp conditions in which they lived. She pushed government officials to provide jobs, and prodded her people to "take care of themselves." Asked by a sympathetic visitor what she was doing in Washington, Truth replied: "Fighting the devil."

In 1865, as the Civil War drew to a close, Congress passed a law that forbade Washington's streetcar companies to exclude anyone because of their color. Now Truth took it upon herself to fight for the law's implementation. She began running after the streetcars that failed to stop for her. In one incident, after two conductors had ignored her, she shouted at a third: "I want to ride! I want to ride! I WANT TO RIDE!" Truth's booming voice so startled nearby horses, drivers, and pedestrians that all traffic came to a halt. She climbed onto the blocked streetcar as the other passengers laughed: "She has beaten him." The enraged conductor told Truth to "go forward where the horses are, or I will throw you out." She dared him, saying that she "knew the laws as well as he did." Truth rode on, journeying farther than she had intended. When she disembarked, she cried: "Bless God! I have had a ride."

A few weeks later, Truth took a seat alongside a white woman friend who was visiting from Michigan. The conductor, trying to force Truth out, twisted her arm. Her friend, Laura Haviland, stepped in and pulled the conductor away. "Does she belong to you?" he asked. Haviland replied: "She does not belong to me, but she belongs to Humanity." Truth had injured her shoulder and needed to go to a hospital. But the two women had taken the conductor's number, and their complaint successfully resulted in his dismissal. Truth also had the man arrested for assault and battery. For the third time in her life, Truth took her case to court—and won. When the widely reported trial was over, Truth's action had inspired numerous other black citizens to follow her lead in what became known as "ride-ins."

As she approached seventy, Truth served as a counselor to patients at the Freedmen's Hospital and worked with the government's new Freedmen's Bureau to help people find jobs. She assisted some in resettling in Rochester, New York. Frustrated when the Bureau ran short of funds, in 1867 Truth returned to Battle Creek almost penniless; she had given what little funds she had to the freed slaves.

Back in Michigan, Truth turned increasingly toward championing women's rights. Here she found herself at odds with such white feminists as Susan B. Anthony and Elizabeth Cady Stanton, who rejected the Fourteenth Amendment granting full citizenship to blacks—because it introduced the word "male" into the Constitution for the first time. Stanton also supported education and property qualifications for voting, while Truth was adamant that such barriers did not reflect the Fifteenth Amendment. She often spoke at more than one gathering daily, "kept a strenuous schedule and addressed crowds that numbered in the thousands." Women, Truth asserted, deserved their "God-given right, and be the equal of men, for she was the resurrection of them."

Unlike other feminists, the majority of whom were white middle-class women, Truth refused to wear the then-fashionable bloomers (short, loosely-fit dresses worn over pants). That style, she said, was too akin to her slave garb. Instead, she dressed modestly in long full dark dresses and occasional shawls. In other respects, she could be outrageous when pressed. At one convention, when a heckler accused her of being a man and suggested she prove her femininity by baring her breast, Truth retorted that her "breasts had suckled many a white babe; that some of these babies had grown to man's estate, and that they were far more manly than they [her persecutors] appeared to be." Then she allowed she'd take the man up on his offer. Two young fellows came forward. Truth quietly opened her dress. "Do you wish to suck?" she asked.

At a women's rights convention in 1878, Truth spoke of her own life's trials and tribulations. Women needed to be "something better than mere toys," she said, yet took to task their "vanity and love of dress." They should receive equal pay, and children needed to be brought into "the ranks of reform. . . . I tell you if you want great men, you must have great mothers." In advocating social reform, Truth spoke of the necessity for women lawyers, judges and politicians. Her logic went like this: "Who ever saw a man clean up a house? Men can make dirt, but can't clean it up. It will never be done till women get into government. . . . As men have been endeavoring for years to govern alone, and have not yet succeeded in perfecting any system, it is about time the women should take the matter in hand."

The last great matter that Truth took in hand was a plan she said had come to her through divine command. With freed blacks continuing to arrive in Washington in huge numbers by the 1870s and finding jobs scarce, she wanted the federal government to set aside portions of plentiful Western land for resettlement "and erect buildings thereon for the aged and infirm." In Massachusetts, Truth initiated a petition drive. For nine months in 1870-71, she journeyed with her grandson Samuel across the New England and Mid-Atlantic states gathering signatures. Eventually, she was offered an all-expenses-paid trip to Kansas, where the pair traveled and met with officials there. But, when Truth went again to Washington in 1874 with her petition, there seemed little enthusiasm in Congress. Her grandson became gravely ill, and would soon die in Battle Creek at the age of twenty-four from an aneurism in his neck. Truth mortgaged her house and went several hundred dollars into debt, in order to cover the costs of Samuel's medical care and burial.

Suddenly, in 1879, what Truth had inspired conceptually became a reality. A great migration of blacks began from the South, traveling primarily to rural Kansas by wagon, train, steamboat, and on foot. They were called "The Exodusters." In Michigan, Truth heard about the events and decided to head for Kansas herself. There, now in her early eighties, she remained for several months, counseling refugees and speaking in churches. "God still lives," she said, "and means to see the black people in full possession of all their rights."

During her last years, Truth was cared for in Battle Creek by two of her daughters. A reporter from a Grand Rapids newspaper was the last outsider to pay her a visit. He described Sojourner Truth as short of breath and no longer able to speak distinctly, yet her eyes remained bright and her mind sharp. She spoke of hoping to see the Western resettlement project continued. And she sang the resurrection song that she had delivered so long ago to the unruly boys on the Massachusetts campground.

"If we can laugh and sing a little as we fight the good fight of freedom," Truth said, "it makes it all go easier." As late as 1877, one newspaper account described her voice as "still like a trumpet." Her singing before about 600 people at the age of seventy-one was said to fall "like a sacred baptism upon all hearts present."

Truth was critical of conventional religion, which she wrote was as "empty as the barren fig-tree," and of Sunday churchgoers whom she once described as "like the door that swings in and out—they don't know any more when they go out than they do when they go in." So many preachers, she felt, talked about "what happened thousands of years ago, but quite forgot that the living present around them teemed with the sternest realities." Don't be waiting for Christ to return, she urged her listeners: "He is with you now, all the time, and what more can you want?" God "was to be worshipped at all times and in all places."

Sojourner Truth died, "early in the morning" as in her resurrection hymn, on November 26, 1883. A thousand people came to her funeral. The following day, Frederick Douglass eulogized her in Washington: "Venerable for age, distinguished for insight into human nature, remarkable for independence and courageous self-assertion, devoted to the welfare of her race, she has been for the last forty years an object of respect and admiration to social reformers everywhere."

The time would come, Truth prophesied, when women would stand alongside men as legislators and make their "power" felt. The time would come when blacks would hold "prominent offices" in the United States. In 1972, America's first black Congresswoman, Shirley Chisholm, would inaugurate her campaign for the presidency at the Michigan gravesite of Sojourner Truth.

In 1997, when the first American space vehicle set down on Mars, the rover that explored the planet's surface was dubbed the Sojourner—after Sojourner Truth.

> *"While I bear upon my body*
> *The scars of many a gash,*
> *I am pleading for my people*
> *Who groan beneath the lash. . . ."*

> *"We are going home, we have visions bright*
> *Of that holy land, that world of light*
> *Where the long dark night is past,*
> *And the morning of eternity has come at last. . . ."*
> —from the Hymns of Sojourner Truth

FOR FURTHER READING:

Jean McMahon Humez, ed., *Gifts of Power: The Writings of Rebecca Jackson, Black Visionary, Shaker Eldress* (Amherst: University of Massachusetts Press, 1981).

Carleton Mabee with Susan Mabee Newhouse, *Sojourner Truth: Slave, Prophet, Legend* (New York and London: New York University Press, 1993).

Nell Painter, *Sojourner Truth: A Life, A Symbol* (New York and London: W. W. Norton & Co., 1996).

Sojourner Truth, *Narrative of Sojourner Truth* (Salem, N.H.: Ayer Co., 1990).

23

Howard Thurman, Benjamin Mays, and the Martin Luther King Legacy

"It must be borne in mind that the tragedy in life doesn't lie in not reaching your goal. The tragedy lies in having no goal to reach. It isn't a calamity to die with dreams unfulfilled, but it is a calamity not to dream. It is not a disaster to be unable to capture your ideal, but it is a disaster to have no ideal to capture. It is not a disgrace not to reach the stars, but it is a disgrace to have no stars to reach for. Not failure, but low aim is sin."
—BENJAMIN MAYS, inscription on his tomb at Morehouse College.

"As a result of a series of fortuitous circumstances there appeared on the horizon of the common life a young man who for a swift, staggering, and startling moment met the demands of the hero. He was young. He was well-educated with the full credentials of academic excellence in accordance with ideals found in white society. He was a son of the South. He was steeped in and nurtured by familiar religious tradition. He had charisma, that intangible quality of personality that gathers up in its magic the power to lift people out of themselves without diminishing them. In him the 'outsider' and the 'insider' came together in a triumphant synthesis. Here at last was a man who affirmed the oneness of black and white under a transcendent unity, for whom community meant the profoundest sharing in the common life. And his name was Martin Luther King, Jr."
—HOWARD THURMAN, *The Search for Common Ground*

It is a windy spring afternoon in 1997 on the campus of Morehouse College in Atlanta. Outside the Martin Luther King, Jr., International Center, his widow, Coretta Scott King, is sitting next to her friend Johnetta Cole, president of Spelman College, as both women await their turn to speak. About 100 feet behind Coretta King is a statue of her husband, which depicts him with one hand outstretched to the world. In marble at the base is inscribed: "From Morehouse College he launched his humanitarian pilgrimage to create the beloved community, and for that purpose he moved out from the classroom and his pulpit to march his way into immortality."

Directly in front of Mrs. King is another monument—a towering obelisk which terminates in a pyramid at its apex. It was built to memorialize an earlier Morehouse graduate, Reverend Howard Thurman. Today, the ashes of his wife, Sue Bailey Thurman, will be interred here alongside his. From all across the country, black scholars and theologians have gathered to pay their tributes.

Near the beginning of the program, Martin Luther King's sister, Christine King Farris, offers a reading from the 139th Psalm. Now Coretta King approaches the microphone. "There is no doubt in my mind," she says, "that the marriage and partnership of Sue and Howard Thurman were divinely inspired and guided. I first met the Thurmans while I was a student at the New England Conservatory of Music in Boston, and Dr. Thurman was serving as dean of Marsh Chapel at Boston University. Of course I had heard from Momma King and Martin how beautiful, intelligent, and talented Sue Thurman was. But when I first met her, and all the years since when I was in her presence, I was keenly aware that I was in the presence of a great spirit.

"We all knew that Dr. Howard Thurman was deeply spiritual and God-centered, but I don't believe many people realized that Sue Thurman was also endowed with the same gifts. To be in her presence was uplifting, and her quiet penetrating spirit always made you feel special."

Then she turns to the Thurmans' three children and says: "I want you to know that your mother was chosen by God to be the helpmate for your father. What a great privilege it is to be chosen." Mrs. King's voice cracks and she pauses briefly. "Together they were instruments of God's will and purpose, and did a mighty work and kingdom building here on earth. Personally she was my spiritual mentor. I'm sure she was not aware of this. Although we didn't often see each other, I always felt her and your father's prayers and support. . . . Her example was that of the finest in womanhood."

As Coretta King returns to her seat, her quiet dignity—and the pain that is written in her eyes—brings a hush over the assembly. The wind is blowing and birds are singing and I am sitting a few rows behind her, remembering the words of an unknown African poet:

> "Those who are dead are never gone,
> they are there in the thickening shadow.
> The dead are not under the earth;
> they are in the tree that rustles. . . ."

A few months before I journeyed to Atlanta to learn more about Martin Luther King's spiritual forbears—Howard Thurman and Benjamin Mays—I was talking with Reverend Anthony Campbell at his Boston University office. That particular afternoon marked the beginning of my education about the remarkable impact of the black Baptist Church. Campbell, a professor of homiletics [preaching] at the B.U. School of Theology, commutes to Detroit on weekends. There, he serves as senior pastor—like his father before him—at the historic Russell Street Baptist Church. Over the past thirty years, Campbell has been invited to give sermons in twenty-seven countries; his most recent sojourn to England's Westminster Abbey made him the first Baptist and one of the first African-Americans ever to preach there. He had known them all—Thurman, Mays, and King.

"Preaching," Campbell is saying, "is that art of presentation which moves people to action. Now if you're going to write about these great Baptist preachers, you've got to start with the fellow who founded the First Baptist Church of Yamacraw. That's in Savannah, Georgia, and there are two African-American churches there. One is called First African Baptist, and one is called First Brian.

"Brian was a slave, who every Sunday afternoon would preach under a tree in this swampy area called Yamacraw. It was against the law for slaves to preach. The state of Georgia had passed legislation saying nobody could be ordained to the Christian ministry without three current preachers laying hands on him—that is to say, three white guys giving their blessing. So every time Brian got through, his master would come out and beat him with a whip. One day the master was drunk and dropped the whip. Big crowd was watching. Brian picked it up and gave it back to him. The man hit him a few more times. Same thing happened. The third time he dropped the whip and Brian tried putting it back in his hand, the master fell on his knees and said, 'I'd like to be baptized by you.' Huge scandal! If slaves go around baptizing their masters, it's going to lead to rebellion and trouble, right? So Brian was absolutely forbidden to preach again. But by this time, he had already organized the First African Baptist Church."

Campbell walks over to his teeming bookshelf, and pulls down two ancient works. "There are two different histories here," he explains. "A white and a black version. You see, after these events transpired, the white Georgia Convention organized a First African Baptist Church—because they didn't want *Brian's* First Baptist to be *the* established church. They had the fellow who was heading their church write to the church they were now calling First Brian, saying please dismiss all your members to our legitimate church. What does the slave Brian write back? 'Dear sir, if we are no church, how did you write us? And if we are a church, how is it that you want us to dismiss our members to you? You should join us.' "

Both churches, Brian's original and the one his opponents started, continued to function. A Baptist church became whatever its congregation said it was, its pastor whomever the congregation wished to elect. The Georgia law that decreed the need for an outside authority was noted to be unconstitutional. "So this became the basic foundation of the black Baptist Church," Campbell adds, "from which all its legitimacy flows."

A bear of a man with an engaging smile, Campbell moves on to speak of two men who emerged from these Baptist traditions—and are today considered the leading icons of the twentieth-century black ministry. "I came to greatly admire Benjamin Mays, who taught both myself and, earlier, Martin Luther King at Morehouse College. Because Mays was a man who had a poetic eye. I remember Mays once saying in class that 'God was subtle, but never malicious.' I didn't know until later that he had stolen that from [J. Robert] Oppenheimer, who in turn had stolen it from Einstein. Then I realized that you had to read *everything* in order to know how to preach effectively."

In the early 1960s, Campbell was a student pursuing his Master's degree in divinity at Boston University when Howard Thurman was the school's dean of chapel. "Howard Thurman taught me how to use silences," Campbell is saying. "He had a way of speaking that could appear to be very dangerous. He would say, 'Everywhere' "—Campbell pauses—" 'I go' "—another pause—" 'I see' "—yet another pause—" 'Jes—us.' You'd almost think he forgot his lines. One day I was imitating to my girlfriend this way he had of talking. Tap on the shoulder—Thurman's caught me making fun of him in the pulpit!

"He said to me, 'You've got it all wrong. I don't pause. I use silences like other people use words.' He said, 'Secondly, I always preach standing on one foot. So when my leg gets tired, I know it's time for me to end that sermon.' Then he told me, 'Now get up on one foot, crouch your body and create tension, and act is if what you *don't* say is as important as what you do say.' "

Campbell continues: "Howard Thurman recognized that the highest reaches of philosophy and theology and physics are really poetry. He was a mystic, and was not well understood here. Some people took umbrage when he did an Easter service one year and never mentioned Jesus. He was always a revered hero of my father's, because he had done things that no Negro man had ever done in those times. He had gone from a black chapel at Howard University to an interracial church in San Francisco. Thurman had the ability to make magical things happen to people who had given up on the church, who were no longer able to affirm Catholic theology and wanted something better than Pentecostal emotionalism. All the loose pieces, as it were, in town were swept up into his chapel. What he did was legitimize the hearing of his poetics, in ways that made it possible for Martin King—and people like me."

Howard Washington Thurman was born on November 18, 1900, in Daytona Beach, Florida—the same vicinity where Mary McLeod Bethune would soon form her first school, and where years later Byllye Avery would come of age. "As a boy in Florida," Thurman would remember, "I walked along the beach of the Atlantic in the quiet stillness. . . . I held my breath against the night and watched the stars etch their brightness on the face of the darkened canopy of the heavens. I had the sense that all things, the sand, the sea, the night, and I, were one lung through which all of life breathed."

Both his father and then a stepfather died when Thurman was young, and he found a sense of family in the Baptist Church. Often Mary McLeod Bethune came to services there, sang a solo, and "would talk of her dreams for Negro youth. . . . [She] gave boys like me a view of possibilities to be realized in some distant future." When Bethune died in 1955, it would be Thurman who delivered her eulogy.

Through childhood poverty he had managed to finish high school in Jacksonville. Then he had gone on to Morehouse College, founded in 1867 as one of America's first black colleges. One of his classmates was Martin Luther King's father. Thurman's debate coach was Benjamin Elijah Mays; five years older than Thurman, this was Mays's first teaching job. "I found a special, intangible something at Morehouse in 1921," Mays would remember, "which sent men out into life with a sense of mission, believing that they could accomplish whatever they set out to do." It was Mays, Thurman has said, who "first awakened in me a keen interest in philosophy."

Mays, born on August 18, 1895, in rural Epworth, South Carolina, was the youngest of eight children of formerly enslaved parents. Where Thurman's earliest memories already bore metaphysical overtones, Mays's own emanated from a stark reality that was to fuel his particular religious activism. He was four when "a crowd of white men rode up on horseback with rifles on their shoulders. I was with my father . . . and I remember starting to cry. They cursed my father, drew their guns and made him take off his hat, bow down and salute them several times. Then they rode off."

As a youth, Mays plowed, chopped cotton, and "prayed myself into an education." Recognized early for particular brilliance in mathematics and oratory, he was twenty-one before he was finally able to complete high school, as class valedictorian. Then Mays told his mother he needed "to seek a new world" beyond South Carolina. He worked his way through Maine's Bates College as a waiter, furnace tender, and Pullman porter. By the time he graduated with a Phi Beta Kappa key in 1920, Mays had decided to enter the ministry. Recruited by Morehouse College to teach higher mathematics and coach the debating team, Mays was simultaneously ordained and pastored the congregation at the nearby Shiloh Baptist Church. He moved on to attain his Master's degree at the University of Chicago, with a thesis on "Pagan Survivals in Christianity."

Both Mays and Thurman lost their first wives. Mays's college sweetheart died early in 1923, only three years after their marriage, following an operation in an Atlanta hospital. Thurman's wife was diagnosed with tuberculosis soon after he graduated from seminary and began his first full-time pastorate at Mount Zion Baptist Church in Oberlin, Ohio. She died in December of 1930; Thurman had just accepted a joint teaching position at Morehouse and the men's sister college, Spelman, across the street.

It was not long thereafter that Sue Bailey reentered Thurman's life. They had been casual friends nearly ten years earlier, when Thurman was studying at Morehouse and she was briefly at Spelman. Sue was originally from Arkansas, a minister's daughter whose grandfather "was supposedly related to Frederick Douglass." She and Thurman would encounter one another again when he ended up a pastor in Oberlin and she became the first African-American to earn a music degree from Oberlin College. By the late 1920s, Sue Bailey had been named the YWCA's national secretary for colleges in the southern region. Her counterpart at the YMCA was none other than Benjamin Mays, with whom she worked closely. "We have a great history; we have a greater future," Mays said in a 1926 speech. "We have a rendezvous with America."

Some months after Howard Thurman returned to Atlanta to teach and lost his first wife, Sue Bailey enlisted him to fill a speaking engagement that she had been scheduled to deliver at Spelman College. "I remember Howard seemed bored during the program," she recalled, "yet I noticed he was writing something. And sure enough, he passed me a note, asking me to join him for breakfast the next day." Thus began a year-and-a-half-long courtship, culminating in marriage in the summer of 1932.

As the Depression years dawned, the destinies of Howard Thurman and Benjamin Mays would become increasingly intertwined—in ways that eventually had a profound impact upon Martin Luther King. Thurman moved with his new bride to join the faculty of Howard University's School of Religion. Soon thereafter, Mays was appointed the School's Dean. He, too, had remarried. Now Mays enlisted Thurman to assist him in researching two major theological works: *The Negro's Church* and *The Negro's God*.

Mays transcribed hundreds of long-forgotten black preachers' sermons by hand. The picture that emerged in these studies was of a deeply personal God in African-American religion. "The Negro's ideas of God," Mays wrote, "grew out of the social situation in which he finds himself," the very "hardness of life" providing understanding. The liberated personality, Mays concluded, was God's "most successful force" for revolutionizing the social order. Years later, King would speak of the "cosmic companionship" inherent in his civil rights campaign. He believed in "metaphysical and philosophical grounding for the idea of a personal God"—taking the ideas that Mays (with Thurman's aid) had set forth in the 1930s and making them his daily reality.

This was not the only precursor of the King philosophy. In the autumn of 1935, Howard and Sue Thurman departed with another couple for a lengthy "pilgrimage of friendship" to universities in Burma, Ceylon (now Sri Lanka) and India. The following February, they held a private three-hour conference with India's Mahatma Gandhi. The Thurmans were the first African-Americans to meet with Gandhi to discuss the question of nonviolence.

Howard Thurman called this journey "a watershed experience in my life." In an essay titled *The Centering Moment*, he would write: "Occasionally there comes into view on the horizon of the age a solitary figure who, in his life, anticipates the harmony of which he speaks. No one dreamed that Mahatma Gandhi would be able to introduce into the very center of a great modern empire such as Britain a principle contrary to empire, and abide. For Gandhi to have come out of the womb of a religion outside the Christian faith and address himself to an empire whose roots were nurtured by that faith is the most eloquent testimony of the timeless, universal character of what was working in him. It is as though there were at work in this little man an Intent by which he was caught up, and of which in some way he became the living embodiment. The moving finger of God in human history points ever in the same direction. There must be community. Always, in the collective conscience and in the private will, this intent appears and reappears like some fleeting ghost."

In his autobiography, *With Head and Heart*, Thurman described Gandhi emerging from a tent to greet them. They sat down on the floor of a rather large room in the center. "He had questions," Thurman wrote. "Never in my life have I been a part of that kind of examination: persistent, pragmatic questions about American Negroes, about the course of slavery, and how we had survived it. . . . He wanted to know about voting rights, lynching, discrimination, public school education, the churches and how they functioned. His questions covered the entire sweep of our experience in American society."

Sue Thurman recalled: "I asked him, 'If you are using nonviolence against prejudice and hatred, how do you apply this to places where prejudice runs very deep? Where there are guns and lynching at the end of every trial, and there are no real trials anyway, and no courts to protect people?—often the scene in America in the 1930s."

She remembered the Hindu leader considering her questions thoughtfully before responding: "Suppose someone lynches your brother. Then every one of your people in your community must protest peacefully, walking out on their jobs and refusing to work for those people who did that to her brother."

Knowing that Gandhi's advice would be difficult for impoverished African-Americans, she encouraged Gandhi to visit the United States and explain the use of nonviolence in the struggle for freedom. "I'll come," he said, "but not until we get rid of the [segregation of] 'Untouchables' in my society."

As their meeting drew to a close, Gandhi asked Howard Thurman: "Will you do me a favor? Will you sing one of your songs for me? Will you sing *Were You There When They Crucified My Lord?* I feel that this song gets to the root of the experience of the entire human race under the spread of the healing wings of suffering." Thurman said that his wife was a musician, and that the others would join her.

"Under the tent in Bardoli in a strange land we three joined in music as one heartbeat," Thurman would remember. "When it was over there was a long silence and there may have been a few words that Gandhi used in prayer." After the Thurmans returned home in April 1936, a cloth arrived—woven for them by Mahatma Gandhi.

Howard Thurman delivered a report on the visit to Howard University's president Mordecai Johnson, another Morehouse graduate. Johnson was so impressed with the Gandhi philosophy that he brought the entire faculty together for an unscheduled meeting. In the Andrew Rankin Chapel where Thurman had just been named to preside, he spoke eloquently of Gandhi's struggle and methods. Benjamin Mays was in attendance. Two years earlier, during convalescence from a serious illness at the Mayo Clinic, Mays had heard Thurman preach over the radio from the Rockefeller Memorial Chapel at the University of Chicago. It was, Mays felt, "one of the greatest sermons to which I have ever listened."

Now Thurman was opening Mays's eyes to a whole new potential approach to the problems of segregation and discrimination. Mays remained no stranger to racism. In 1923, he had been forced out of a

Pullman car with a pistol at his back. "One has to rebel against indignities in some fashion in order to maintain the integrity of his soul," he believed. When Thurman urged him to go to India and meet Gandhi, Mays did.

Twice during the late 1930s, Mays journeyed with several other black leaders to discuss with Gandhi the feasibility of applying his nonviolent principles to the African-American fight for civil rights. Late in 1946, the two men met privately again at a world conference of the YMCA in India. Mays had to decide between seeing Gandhi and seeing the Taj Mahal. "You made a wise choice," he recalled Gandhi telling him. "When you visit India again, the Taj Mahal will still be here, I may not."

Mays later wrote: "He was right. He was emphatic in stating that nonviolence is an active force. Nonviolence is three-fourths invisible, and the results are spiritual and largely invisible. Nonviolence, he made clear, is not a technique or strategy that one uses because he is too weak to use force. It is a way of life. It must be practiced in absolute love and without hate. In a nonviolent campaign, the welfare of your opponent must be taken into consideration. If the campaign destroys your opponent, it must be called off."

When Howard Thurman first began spreading the word about Gandhi, among the student body at Howard University were two young men who would become pillars of the civil rights movement. One was James Farmer, future founder of the Congress of Racial Equality and organizer of the first sit-ins in Chicago. Another was Samuel Woodrow Wilson, whom Mays would hire in 1945 to teach philosophy at Morehouse. There, Wilson used Thoreau's essay on *Civil Disobedience* in a class that included Martin Luther King, Jr. King read the essay three times; it was his introduction to strategies for dealing with unjust governments.

After Mahatma Gandhi was assassinated on January 30, 1948, Mays delivered an address in the Morehouse chapel on "Gandhi and Nonviolence." Sitting directly in front of the pulpit, by then in his senior year, was Martin King.

King had grown up steeped in the Baptist tradition. His maternal grandfather, A. D. Williams, had become pastor of Atlanta's Ebenezer Baptist Church in 1894. He was the first president of the city's NAACP chapter, instrumental in pushing for the erection of Atlanta's first black high school. When Williams died suddenly in 1931, he was succeeded at Ebenezer by his son-in-law, Martin Luther King, Sr. Later affectionately known as "Daddy King," he had graduated from Morehouse four years earlier. His wife Alberta became the church organist. Their son Martin had been born in his parents' bedroom in grandpa Williams's home, on January 15, 1929.

Young M. L., as he was then called, first came to the Morehouse campus as a seventh-grader, riding a segregated bus to the Atlanta University Laboratory School. The year was 1940, and Benjamin Mays had just been appointed president of the college. By now, Mays had achieved his doctorate and a theological reputation so towering that he was included in a private "brain trust" created by Reinhold Niebuhr and Paul Tillich. King's father, as a Morehouse trustee, had known Mays for some time. Daddy King often took Martin and his two other children to Mays's lectures.

"Mays was a tall and extremely handsome man," Anthony Campbell, a later student of Mays, remembers. "He looked like he was carved out of ebony, but his features were sharp almost to the point of being caucasian. He'd get up to speak without notes and would kill you dead! He always made it look so easy and extemporaneous. But he said, 'Oh no, like Winston Churchill, even my mistakes are practiced.' "

Dr. Hugh Gloster, a 1931 Morehouse graduate who was the first teacher Mays hired there and who later succeeded Mays as college president in 1967, recalls: "He was a motivator, a challenger. That was his great strength. He could take a group of ordinary high school graduates and inspire them to be somebody—to try to do everything possible to eliminate segregation, to try to establish close ties with people in other countries, especially Africa. His addresses were sermons, you see. He really felt that his mission was to build men. That's what we used to call him, a builder of men."

Although conservative in his social mores—Gloster notes that Mays frowned upon any smoking or drinking among his faculty and students—Mays did not shy from public challenges. In 1943, at a time when Paul Robeson was already being shunned by many for his Communist sympathies, Morehouse became the first black college to award him an honorary degree. In introducing Robeson, Mays said: "You represent in your person, in your integrity, and in your ideals the things for which this college stands and for which it shall continue to stand."

M. L. King entered Morehouse the following year, at the age of fifteen. "There was a freer atmosphere at Morehouse, and it was there that I had my first frank discussions on race," King would write in his autobiography, *Stride toward Freedom*. "For the first time in my life, I realized that nobody was afraid."

Chapel was compulsory, and King took notes on Mays's call for "honest men . . . who are sensitive to the wrongs, the sufferings, and the injustices of society and who are willing to accept responsibility for correcting those ills." Blacks, Mays said, could be "segregated and discriminated against, but still be free in their minds and soul." He was adamant. "Every year I talked to my students and told them that I did not want them to go up in the 'buzzard's roost' to see anybody's . . . theatrical performances. And I made it very strong. I said . . . I would not go to a segregated theater to see Jesus Christ, Himself . . . I would rather go to hell by choice than to stumble into heaven following the crowd."

Mays later said of his association with the young King: "There we began a real friendship which was strengthened by [my] visits to [his] home and by fairly frequent informal chats on campus and in my office. Many times during his four years at Morehouse, he would linger after my Tuesday morning address to discuss some point I had made— usually with approval, but sometimes questioning or disagreeing."

During King's time at Morehouse, he observed Mays take on the powers that be. Back in 1942, Mays had been riding the Southern Railroad between Atlanta and Washington, when he refused to sit at a segregated table and was forced out of the dining car. He decided to sue the railroad over its segregated dining practices and, in the spring of 1947, he won. Often in his later years, King would refer to Mays as his "spiritual mentor."

When King first came to Morehouse, he was considering a career as a doctor or lawyer. He majored in sociology, sang in the glee club, and won the school's annual debate contest in his sophomore year. He was not enamored of what he considered the "emotionalism" of the Black Church. But at Morehouse, where Mays also brought such speakers as Howard Thurman, W. E. B. Du Bois, and Mary McLeod Bethune to his chapel, something new was awakened in King.

As Coretta Scott King wrote in her autobiography, "From first to last Dr. Mays took a great interest in Martin. It was not that he deliberately guided him towards the ministry as that he influenced Martin by his example. For although Dr. Mays was brilliant, he was not removed from the heart of the people. In the pulpit . . . you might say he preached a social gospel. This conformed exactly with Martin's views, and it helped to form them. . . . At Morehouse listening to Dr. Mays preach. . . . Martin came to see that the ministry could be intellectually respectable as well as emotionally satisfying. When he accepted this fact, it opened the way for him to go into the church."

One evening, King made the surprising and welcome announcement to his mother that he had decided to become a minister. His trial sermon at Ebenezer Baptist was a huge success. In February of 1947, with Mays among the members of his ordination council, King was ordained. At the age of eighteen, he became assistant pastor at his father's church.

Dr. Samuel D. Cook, a King classmate and student body president who went on to head Dillard University, recalled the senior sermon that M. L. King delivered at Morehouse's Sale Hall Chapel in 1948: "I remember, as if it were yesterday, M. L.'s great oratorical flourish. He asserted that there are moral laws in the universe that we cannot violate with impunity. He electrified us." As for Mays, Cook added, he understood that "the heart of the ethical consciousness is the cry of the human heart and soul for something better, nobler, higher, and richer."

The Mays connection did not fade when King moved on to Crozer Seminary in Chester, Pennsylvania. The seminary was run by a man who had taught Mays at the University of Chicago. Mordecai Johnson, still president of Howard University, came to Crozer to describe a trip that he, too, had made to India at the urging of Thurman and Mays. "His message was so profound and electrifying," King said, "that I left the meeting and bought a half-dozen books on Gandhi's life and works." When King left Crozer in 1951, he was student body president and at the top of his class. Entering Boston University for his Ph.D., he was introduced to Coretta Scott by Mary Powell, a classmate of Coretta's at the New England Conservatory of Music, who was married to a nephew of Mays. Martin and Coretta wed in June of 1953. It was at Boston University that King would briefly enter the circle of Howard Thurman.

During the life-changing voyage to India in the mid-1930s, Thurman had had a vision while overlooking the Khyber Pass—of a religious fellowship open to people of all colors and creeds. Back at Howard University, as the school's current dean of chapel Dr. Bernard Richardson described to the 1997 gathering at Morehouse, Thurman and his wife "kept the doors of their home unlocked [and] gave to students a way to feel at home—not only with the Thurmans, but within themselves and with others." In 1940, Sue Thurman approached her old friend Mary McLeod Bethune with an idea for a new publication that would document the achievements of Bethune's National Council of Negro Women. Sue Thurman founded the *Aframerican Women's Journal*, which laid the groundwork for the creation of the Negro Women's Archives, its purpose being "to collect and preserve documents of historical value. . . ."

Then, as the Second World War raged on, in 1943 Howard Thurman suddenly received an offer to fulfill the mission he had foreseen at the Khyber Pass. It came from a Presbyterian minister, Alfred Fisk, who had assembled a loose congregation in San Francisco from various cultures and ethnicities. Sue Thurman journeyed to meet Fisk, insisting that her husband would only accept if the church did not come under the umbrella of any particular denomination. In the autumn of 1944, Howard became copastor of the new Church for the Fellowship of All Peoples. The Thurmans spent nine years developing their interfaith effort in San Francisco, and Howard began publishing his first poetic meditations.

As I sat with Hugh Gloster beneath the photographs of Thurman, Mays, King and others that line the walls of the Morehouse chapel's conference room, the retired college president described Thurman's impact like this: "He was the most inspiring individual that I ever met in my life, anywhere. He was not a black speaker, in the sense that Mays was. Mays was most effective with black youth, but Thurman was a colorless speaker. His message went across racial lines, and could lift anybody. The church was his means of unifying humanity."

During Martin Luther King's final year pursuing his doctorate in theological studies at Boston University, Thurman accepted an offer to become dean of the University's Marsh Chapel and a professor in the School of Theology. "In 1953," as Thurman scholar Vincent Harding has written, "that was an unheard-of position for a black man." As always, the Thurmans kept an open door for students. King was among their frequent visitors.

Howard had known King's father, and Sue had been friendly with Martin's mother, since their respective days at Morehouse and Spelman colleges. Young Martin, now twenty-four, spent some afternoons watching televised baseball games with Howard, betting on their favorite teams. "When Martin graduated," Sue Thurman recalled, "I said to him, 'Martin, you know that when we left Fellowship Church, we left a vacuum in leadership. How would you like to go there and serve as pastor?' King politely said no, explaining that he planned to return South and take a ministership at the Dexter Avenue Baptist Church in Montgomery, Alabama. "I do believe in fate," Sue Thurman added. "It certainly has a hand in the road you take. I often imagine what would have happened to the civil rights movement—or if there would have been one at the time—if Martin had accepted my offer."

But King did take with him something else from his friendship with the Thurmans. It was a copy of Howard Thurman's 1949 book, *Jesus and the Disinherited*, a book initially inspired by his experiences in India. During the ensuing years of the civil rights crusade, King was never without a copy. The book began with these words: "Many and varied are the interpretations dealing with the teachings and the life of Jesus of Nazareth. But few of these interpretations deal with what the teachings and the life of Jesus have to say to those who stand, at a moment in human history, with their backs against the wall."

The Christ that Thurman described was an impoverished Jew, "a member of a minority group in the midst of a larger dominant and controlling group. . . . His message focused on the urgency of a radical change in the inner attitude of the people." While Christianity had itself become "a religion of the powerful and the dominant, used sometimes as an instrument of possession," such was not the reality of Jesus. Comparing Jesus' social position in Palestine to "that of the vast majority of American Negroes," Thurman outlined the various means of resistance among the disinherited. He discussed segregation and how Jesus overcame fear. He discussed deception, with "a complete and devastating sincerity" as its only alternative. Here he quoted a portion of a letter from Gandhi:

"Speak the truth, without fear and without exception, and see everyone whose work is related to your purpose. You are in God's work, so you need not fear man's scorn. If they listen to your requests and grant them, you will be satisfied. If they reject them, then you must make their rejection your strength."

Thurman wrote about hatred, which "provides for the weak a basis for moral justification," and which Jesus rejected as "the great denial." In his epilogue, Thurman added: "When a solitary individual is able to mingle his strength with the forces of history and emerge with a name, a character, a personality, it is no ordinary achievement. . . . It means that against the background of anonymity he has emerged articulate, and particular."

Martin Luther King also read these words of Howard Thurman: "Living in a climate of deep insecurity, Jesus, faced with so narrow a margin of civil guarantees, had to find some other basis upon which to establish a sense of well-being. He knew that the goals of religion as he understood them could never be worked out within the then-established order. Deep from within that order he projected a dream."

King's predecessor at his first pastorate in Montgomery was Vernon Johns, who had once courted Sue Bailey before she elected to marry Howard Thurman. Johns was a maverick who assailed his own black congregation for being status-conscious and took on white Alabama officials for their segregated transportation policies. "There was a restless genius about him," says Anthony Campbell, whose brother dated one of Johns's daughters. "If Vernon Johns were alive today, they'd probably medicate him heavily and calm him down and he'd be mediocre. When I was at Howard University, he showed up to speak one day driving an old pick-up truck. He put on his academic gown, damn near killed everybody with his Latin, Greek and French. Then we found him after he left the chapel, in bib overalls, selling watermelons and hams off the back of that truck!"

So, in a Southern enclave already engraved with the consciousness of Vernon Johns, King embarked on his great crusade. On December 1, 1955, Rosa Parks refused to move to the back of a segregated Montgomery bus and was arrested. That was the beginning. "I want it to be known that we're going to work with grim and bold determination to gain justice on the buses in this city," King told his congregation. "If we are wrong—Jesus of Nazareth was merely a utopian dreamer and never came down to earth! If we are wrong—justice is a lie!"

The Montgomery bus boycott King organized along Gandhian principles would soon result in court indictments of himself and eighty-eight others. He and his family were away when the edict came down, visiting his parents in Atlanta. His home in Montgomery had just been bombed. King's father feared for his son's life if he returned. Daddy King assembled Atlanta's leading black citizens in his living room, hoping they would convince Martin to remain far from Montgomery. Benjamin Mays was among them.

"My friends and associates are being arrested," Martin recounted having told them. "It would be the height of cowardice for me to stay away. I would rather be in jail ten years than desert my people. . . . I have reached the point of no return. In the moment of silence, I heard my father break into tears. I looked at Dr. Mays, one of the great influences in my life. Perhaps he heard my unspoken plea. At any rate he was soon defending my position. The others joined him in supporting me."

Mays later told him that, when King uttered the phrase about rather being in jail, "At the moment my heart, mind and soul stood up erect and saluted. I knew then that you were called to leadership for such a time as this."

Mays offered to pay for King's legal counsel if necessary. The next morning, King's father drove the family back to Montgomery, where Martin was placed under arrest for the first time. In November of 1956, the U.S. Supreme Court upheld a lower court ruling declaring racial segregation on city bus lines unconstitutional; that December, the Montgomery buses were integrated.

In June of 1957, Morehouse College bestowed an honorary degree upon King. Mays said: "You are mature beyond your years, wiser at twenty-eight than most men at sixty; more courageous in the righteous struggle than most men can ever be; living faith that most men preach about but never experience. Significant indeed is the fact that you did not seek the leadership in the Montgomery controversy. It was thrust upon you by the people. You did not betray the trust of leadership. You led the people with great dignity, Christian grace, and determined purpose."

It was mid-August of 1958 when the chairman of the Gandhi Memorial Trust and several other prominent Indians made a pilgrimage to Montgomery to see King. They warned him of imminent danger. As Taylor Branch describes the scene in his Pulitzer Prize-winning book *Parting the Waters*: "Pointing to lessons from Gandhi, he [chairman R. R. Diwakar] advised King to prepare not just to talk about suffering but to endure physical sacrifice himself. The path of his life dictated such a course. King said he was ready."

Slightly more than a month later, three days after publication of King's account of the Montgomery events (*Stride toward Freedom*), he was signing copies in a Harlem bookstore when a mentally deranged woman stabbed him in the chest. For a time, he was in near-critical condition. Howard Thurman was still at the Boston University chapel, and recounted:

Only one time during the phenomenal dynamism of the civil rights movement did we meet personally for serious talk. It was while he was recovering in the Harlem hospital after the stabbing that nearly cost him his life. His wife, Coretta, and aides had come up from Atlanta to be with him. Many times through the years I have had strange visitations in which there emerges at the center of my consciousness a face, a sense of urgency, a vibrant sensation involving some particular person. On a certain Friday afternoon, Martin emerged in my awareness and would not leave. When I came home I said to Sue, "Tomorrow morning I am going down to New York to see Martin. I am not sure why, but I must talk to him personally if the doctors will permit."

When we were alone, I asked, "What do the doctors say about the length of your convalescence before they will okay the resumption of your work?"

When he told me I urged him to ask them to extend the period by an additional two weeks. This would give him time away from the immediate pressure of the movement to reassess himself in relation to the cause, to rest his body and mind with healing detachment, and to take a long look that only solitary brooding can provide. The movement had become more than an organization; it had become an organism with a life of its own to which he must relate in fresh and extraordinary ways or be swallowed up by it.

In June of 1959, King delivered a commencement address at Morehouse titled "Remaining Awake through a Great Revolution." Predicting correctly that African peoples would sever their colonialist ties over the next decade, King told the students: "You are graduating at a time when the world is experiencing one of the greatest revolutions ever known, a worldwide revolution."

In 1960, King settled again in Atlanta as copastor of his father's church. During the 1961-62 academic year, Benjamin Mays enlisted him to teach a Morehouse seminar in social philosophy. When President Kennedy nominated Mays to the U.S. Commission on Civil Rights, Georgia's two senators strenuously objected. King sent a telegram to Kennedy, saying: "It would be a tragedy if such a distinguished American were deprived of the opportunity to serve his country in a unique position merely because of unwarranted and false accusations made by two senators from Georgia. It seems obvious that the objections the senators have to Dr. Mays is that he has not been an accomodating ultra-conservative leader."

Although Kennedy acceded to the Georgians and withdrew Mays's nomination, the President did name him a member of the advisory council of the Peace Corps. In August of 1963, Howard Thurman was "a fellow pilgrim" at the March on Washington. It was Mays who gave the benediction after King's momentous "I Have a Dream" speech. That winter, after the Kennedy assassination, Mays wrote to King: "President Kennedy's death was almost more than I could take. If they hated him, you know they love you less. I hope that you will take every precaution as you move around." Following King's receiving of the 1964 Nobel Peace Prize, Mays organized tributes to him at Morehouse and in Atlanta. Three years later, when King began speaking out against the Vietnam War, Mays offered his unequivocal support.

Upon retiring from Boston University in 1965, Howard Thurman had returned with his wife to San Francisco and work with an educational trust they had established there. Early on the terrible evening of April 4, 1968, a radio station called and asked Thurman to prepare a statement about Martin Luther King's assassination in Memphis, which could be played throughout the night. In his testament, Thurman said:

"There are no words with which to eulogize this man. Martin Luther King was the living epitome of a way of life that rejected physical violence as the life-style of a morally responsible people. His assassination reveals the cleft deep in the psyche of the American people, the profound ambivalence and ambiguity of our way of life. Something deep within us rejects nonviolent direct action as a dependable procedure for effecting social change. And yet, against this rejection something always struggles, pushing, pushing, always pushing with another imperative, another demand. It was King's fact that gave to this rejection flesh and blood, courage and vision, hope and enthusiasm. For indeed, in him the informed conscience of the country became articulate. And tonight what many of us are feeling is that we all of us must be that conscience wherever we are living, functioning, and behaving. . . .

"Always he spoke from within the context of his religious experience, giving voice to an ethical insight which sprang out of his profound brooding over the meaning of his Judeo-Christian heritage. And this indeed is his great contribution to our times. He was able to put at the center of his own personal religious experience a searching ethical awareness. Thus organized religion as we know it in our society found itself with its back against the wall. To condemn him, to reject him, was to reject the ethical insight of the faith it proclaimed. And this was new. . . .

"He was killed in one sense because mankind is not quite human yet. May he live because all of us in America are closer to becoming human than we ever were before. . . ."

Several days later, as some 150,000 people gathered on the Morehouse campus for his funeral, it was Benjamin Mays who delivered the eulogy.

"To be honored by being requested to give the Eulogy at the funeral of Dr. Martin Luther King, Jr., is like asking one to eulogize his deceased son—so close and so dear was he to me," Mays began. "It is not an easy task; nevertheless, I accept it with heavy heart and with full knowledge of my inadequacy to do justice to this man. He would pay tribute to me on my final day. It was his wish that if he predeceased me, I would do the homily at his funeral. Fate has decreed that I eulogize him. I wish it might have been otherwise, for, after all, I am three score and ten and Martin is dead at 39. . . .

"Too bad, you say, that Martin Luther King died, so young. I feel that way, too. But as I have said so many times before, it isn't how long one lives, but how well. It's what one accomplishes for mankind that matters. No! He was not ahead of his time. Every man is within his own star, each in his own time. . . .

"I close by saying to you what Martin Luther King, Jr., believed: if physical death was the price he had to pay to rid America of injustice, nothing could be more redemptive."

Having retired as Morehouse's president in 1967, Benjamin Mays became the first black to serve as vice-president of the Federal (now National) Council of Churches. In 1977, he began working closely with President Jimmy Carter, the native Georgian who described Mays as "my personal friend, my constructive critic and my close adviser." Mays felt that Carter, who appointed forty-one blacks to judgeships in the federal courts, did more for civil rights than any other President.

Mays spent twelve of his remaining years as chairman of the Atlanta School Board, until retiring at eighty-seven as the nation's oldest such official. Saying "I plan to die in the harness," he began working on the last of his nine books. Mays died just short of his eighty-ninth birthday, on March 28, 1984; he is interred in a marble memorial on the Morehouse campus.

Howard Thurman had died in San Francisco, at the age of eighty, on April 10, 1981. His wife lived to see the completion of the obelisk in his honor at Morehouse, before her death on Christmas Day of 1996. On the campus, the spacing of the memorials to Howard Thurman, Benjamin Mays, and Martin Luther King forms a triangle.

James H. Cone, a professor of systematic theology at the Union Theological Seminary in New York and the author of *Martin & Malcolm & America*, offers this evaluation of those two black leaders' influence on his life: "Malcolm X taught me how to accept my blackness, to affirm my own culture and history as a gift. King taught me the depths of my spiritual commitment as a Christian, the importance of embracing other human beings. I think all black people have something inside them of what they each represent and symbolize. It's that double consciousness that Du Bois spoke about. Malcolm is about being African, King is about being American. I don't know of any Christian that lived its meaning better than Martin King."

Inside his Boston University office, where photographs of King, Mays, and Malcolm X appear on the entryway, Anthony Campbell also reflects on the legacy. "Preaching in a real sense is a mystery," he says. "Because it's not what you say at all, it's what people hear. King legitimized the hearing of African-American preachers. Martin was a profound and arresting figure, the same way Jesus was. The gospels, after all, come out of people who were quoting Jesus thirty and forty years later—which means his sermons made a *real* impression. Now King had this way of making memorable phrases, his voice, his cadence. You know, the 'I Have a Dream' part was not in his original notes for that speech. He felt the sermon dying, and pulled that phrase forward, and saved it. It becomes a great sermon because it resonates beyond the moment in which it was given."

Campbell's brother had been at Morehouse with King, and "I've never known a time when I didn't know Martin Luther King. It was a small world then. My father and his father were friends. When I first met Daddy King, I'll never forget walking into the King Library when it was temporarily housed on the Morehouse campus and introducing myself. He said, 'Your father's Dynamo'—that was his nickname— 'your mother's Pauline.' And it was off to the races. To this day, I can't meet a pastor over fifty or sixty years old who didn't know my father."

His father, Reverend Stephen Campbell, had been born in the same state, South Carolina, in the same year (1895) as Benjamin Mays. They knew one another as young men. Indeed, says Campbell, "it was when Mays laughed at my father, and told him he sounded like a cartoon character, that my father embarked on a 30,000-book, sixty-year quest *not* to sound like a cartoon character." Campbell inherited his father's massive library. He describes the entire family as "bookaholics," including one brother who is now a Unitarian minister.

Had his father's style of preaching been a strong influence on Campbell? I wondered. "No, because my father was very much a preacher of the rural South. There are genres in black preaching. Particular regions had certain distinct styles—depending on whether you were from Mississippi, or Georgia, or Alabama, or South Carolina. South Carolina preachers tended to be melodious, which was called tuning. And tuning was different from hooping, and hooping was different from hacking.

"Some writers about black preaching have emphasized how ungrammatical it was, without understanding its poetics. Well, you could say that Chaucer in writing in old English was writing ungrammatically— but it now feels to us like it's classical. The object in rural preaching was to build rhythm and cadence with your voice. Because you didn't have instruments then—organs or drums—you had to beat out the sermon. Call-and-response, which is the way it's said simplistically, was a way of doing that. To give you an example, since you didn't have a musician, whoever would get up to sing would begin to kick the floor and clap their hands."

Here Campbell begins to act out what he means, then continues: "I saw Ralph Abernathy do that once in a church where I was preaching. People forget Abernathy was an Alabama rural preacher before he moved to the city. He started kicking the floor and clapping, singing— 'This joy I haaa-ve, the world didn't give it to me.' Then people joined him: 'The world didn't give it and the world can't take it away.' Now I was carried right from 1984 to the rural South of 1954 and my father, because I'd seen him do the same thing."

Campbell goes on: "There was an old man when I was growing up named Reverend Timberlake. This was my second year in Morehouse College. He said, 'Campbell, can you write a sermon?' Then he threw his arm into the air and said, 'Write this!' I said, 'But Dr. Timberlake, you haven't said anything.' He cried out again, 'Write this!' and threw his arm up a second time. I said, 'Dr. Timberlake, that's a gesture.' He said, 'The day will come when that will be all you have.' Oh, boy! He said, 'You must not have a hoop better than your swoop. If they cannot see the sermon being lived out, in your life, in your face, then your words and your acrobatics will not matter at all.' The guy never went through the third grade—genius!"

There were three things, Campbell said, that his father had taught him about preaching. "Number one, you prepare a sermon every week whether you use it or not, to get into the discipline of thinking about preaching. You must always be looking for how to make the sermon come alive. The second thing he said was, use the same text but don't preach the same manuscript. In other words, if what the Bible says about something was successful for you before, throw that away and look at it fresh. As you get older and go through more experiences, the text will reveal itself to you as more complicated than you could see before. The third point was, do not deny yourself to preach anywhere. If you get an invitation, go. If it's really the gospel, it oughta work on Roxbury's Blue Hill Avenue—or in Westminster Abbey."

Campbell has heeded the advice. He has delivered some 6,000 sermons in twenty-seven countries on four continents over the last four decades. These have included sermons in about thirty cathedrals, and one before 50,000 people at the 1984 World Baptist Alliance Conference in Rio de Janeiro. Still, Campbell considers his father, who had a Detroit congregation that numbered 4,000 before his death in 1974, "a much better preacher than me, I've just had more opportunities than he had." He equates his profession to that of both a musician and a historian, and believes that "every preacher has the particular time when he will say the right word to your spirit."

By way of example, Campbell tells a story that transpired during the legendary Boston blizzard of 1978, when the entire city shut down for days. He was then pastor at Eliot Congregational, "kind of a silk-stocking church where the highbrow black folks of Boston belonged." The minister of a far less prestigious church found himself stranded and, Campbell says, "As a courtesy, I let him preach. We called him Big Stevenson, and this man was frankly as common as pig iron. But he got up and said the following: 'Last night, the Lord brought the city of Boston to its knees, one snowflake at a time. It's the gentlest thing in nature—melts in your hand, blown away with one puff, wade through it, roll in it. But, one snowflake at a time, the prostitutes stopped working and the dope dealers stopped dealing, crime went to zero, the city became silent.'

"I'm remembering it almost word for word, so you know it was pretty damn good. Twelve years later, I was reading Lefebre's history of Napoleon's wars in Russia, when I came across this passage: General Winter conspired with General Weather and brought Napoleon to his knees—one snowflake at a time. Now how did Big Stevenson know *that*? Or did he simply have a poet's eye, to recognize what had happened?

"I tell my students all the time, look around the room, nothing is unimportant. Jesus was a gifted preacher because he could look at what everyone else saw, and make a story out of it. There's no theology in the Bible, not a single argument between Genesis and Revelation. It is basically people telling their stories of how God met them somewhere and interacted with them.

"Look, I'm a damn radical! I think there's no greater oxymoron than a conservative Christian. I mean, anybody who believes that God so loved the world that he made the word flesh and sent Jesus to dwell among us to save the world—that automatically is a crazy notion! These people who say God's agenda is to make everybody heterosexual—ain't no 'family values' in the Bible. The Good Book is filled with a bunch of gangsters and thugs and scurvy individuals! Yet God saw in them values, and took out of David's miserable family some things that could be useful for the Kingdom of God here on earth.

"I said in my sermon at Westminster Abbey, preaching is dangerous work that needs to be done in dangerous places, not in beautiful subtle rooms like this." It had taken Campbell perhaps 100 hours of research over a six-month period, he estimates, to organize a sermon that he was required to give within ten minutes at London's 900-year-old cathedral. His chosen topic was "Only Speak the Word," from a passage in the Book of Matthew where a Roman centurion comes to Christ and informs him that his servant is sick, asking Jesus to "only speak the word and my servant will be healed." Campbell's approach was to "shepardize the text, to ask, What's not said there? In every sermon, I must ask what does the culture say about this moment? What is missing in our understanding? What would a first-century Jew have seen and known that we do not see and know?" His historical probing took him from religious works to classics to fiction. Eventually, the sermon took shape with "about ten hours of massaging, and three or four hours to hone it.

"The question was, how do you end a sermon at the Abbey? Because in the African-American church, it would end high. I would have talked about how every time Jesus spoke the word, something happened. At the Abbey I couldn't do that. I didn't have time, and it would have taken me to a genre. So what I decided to do was slow down my delivery. I said, 'Speak' "—and here Campbell makes the silence pregnant, as Howard Thurman once taught him—'the—Word.' "

Anthony Campbell grows quiet for a time. Then he returns to another favorite theme of Thurman, the spiritual. "Ever notice that there's not a single hateful line in a Negro spiritual? Nobody ever says something like, 'Blessed is he who crashes the honky's head against the stone.' Or 'Oh, you white people all goin' to hell.' In fact, [theologian] James Cone made a statement that black music is the only music he knew that went from oppression to salvation with no transition. 'Nobody knows the trouble I've seen, nobody knows but Jesus—Glory, hallelujah!' Now tell me this, how do you go from trouble to glory just like that?"

As Campbell speaks, I am drawn back to these poignant lines that Howard Thurman had expressed in his book about the spirituals, *Deep River*. "The existence of these songs is in itself a monument to one of the most striking instances on record in which a people forged a weapon of offense and defense out of a psychological shackle. By some amazing but vastly creative spiritual insight the slave undertook the redemption of a religion that the master had profaned in his midst."

Now Campbell is saying: "Well, bring it up to Martin Luther King. He would take a term like 'redemptive love' and make it sound like something you *had* to do. I don't think you can tell the Bible story without telling the story of liberation, of the radical discontinuity of oppression with the coming world—and what will happen when God takes charge of this mess."

Where was it all going? What had become of the legacy of Martin Luther King and his remarkable predecessors? On a warm spring afternoon in Atlanta, the day after the interment service for the Thurmans at Morehouse College, I am standing in front of the Ebenezer Baptist Church on Auburn Avenue. It is an inauspicious brick building. A simple bulletin posted outside under glass lists the coming Sunday's services. Across the street on Jackson Avenue, there is a smaller National Divine Spiritual Church and a soul food restaurant at the edge of a little mall. The downtown skyline—Equitable, Marriott, Georgia Power—looms on the horizon.

Although an estimated 750,000 tourists a year visit the Ebenezer church, it seats only 750 people. Inside the Heritage Sanctuary, I join a small group of visitors to watch a videotape about the church's history. After its founding in 1886, it outgrew four sanctuaries under King's grandfather, A. D. Williams. This one dates back to 1922, and soon there will be a new Horizon Sanctuary across the street with a seating capacity of 1,700. King, the videotape notes, preached both his first and last sermons here. Between 1960 and his death in 1968, he had presided at least once a month over Sunday services. "This would be his oasis in the desert. This would be the place where he would be fortified to carry on his fight," the voice of Reverend Joseph Roberts, Jr., informs.

Since 1975, when King's father stepped down, Roberts has been the senior pastor here. He was the elder King's handpicked successor, although Roberts was not a Baptist but a Presbyterian. Raised in the Midwest, where his father was an A.M.E. Episcopal minister, Roberts had attained his Master's in theology from Princeton in 1968. When the call came from Ebenezer, he had been two years in Atlanta as the director of corporate and social mission for the Presbyterian Church U.S.—the highest position ever held by a black in its organization. Roberts had returned to the region where his grandparents were once Georgia sharecroppers.

Now, in a conference room where he meets with visitors, Roberts sits down for an interview about the ongoing mission of Ebenezer Baptist. He is a tall, good-looking, bespectacled man with a deep voice. He came here, Roberts tells me, "sort of by accident. Congressman William Gray, who used to be the House Budget chairman, knew me when we were going to Princeton together. When I came from a pastorate in New Jersey to a desk job with the Presbyterians, he told the Kings that I was a pretty good preacher."

After Martin's mother, Alberta, was shot and killed at the organ by a deranged gunman during a Sunday service in 1974, Roberts says "it took the bottom out of Dr. King [Sr.]. It was just too much. He wanted to retire, and it just so happened I was here—with ecumenical and social action portfolios. I had no singular gifts that I brought, there were many other people who could have come. I accepted because of the kinds of things Dr. King believed in, and the kinds of things I felt were needed."

Roberts explains that there is an ideological debate going on in theological circles, "an attempt on the part of some to divide Martin Luther King's civil rights work from his work as a religious leader. In other words, they are claiming that his church involvement was secondary. There are others of us who say that what he did, though it may not always be clearly seen, grew out of this understanding of the gospel as an incarnational act. And because it fleshes itself out in social scenes, it is very much the Word among us."

Roberts proceeds to set the church's history in historical context. It arose in the post-Reconstruction era, amid the dispute between Booker T. Washington and W. E. B. Du Bois over the future direction for blacks. King's father and grandfather stood more in the Washington tradition than Du Bois's activist mode; they urged their parishioners to obtain property, build their own businesses and schools. When Martin, Jr., came along, "he was an eclectic amalgam. But he was also able to do a twist on it all, in that he was so steeped in the classical traditions that he could be the bridge builder. I think that's how he was able to bring white people in."

When King rose to international renown, Roberts continues, "this church was a surprised mother of a genius. It wasn't quite ready for the influx of attention that came during his life, or at his death. This is a small conservative evangelical Baptist church, which loved him and said 'He's our boy, even though we don't know everything he's doing or why he's doing it.' I do think this church understood Dr. King's belief that you had to be political and theological at the same time. That has always been the genius of the Black Church."

Roberts has sought to carry on King's quest for such a synthesis. From the pulpit, he speaks about the burning of black churches in America and the refugees of Rwanda. The church's brand of late '90s activism sends parishioners acting as mentors to schools in the immediate communities. "We feed 300 people here every Sunday, homeless folks, and we're seeing a growing number of women and children in those lines. That's deplorable! We have a food co-op, and seventy-one senior citizens in our day-care center. The co-op allows them to buy groceries at wholesale prices. There's a visiting physician and nurse, and a tutoring program. Now this isn't cutting-edge stuff. But it's about the best one can do, when foundations and corporations are not terribly willing to give too much support."

There is much that disturbs Roberts about contemporary society—from how the balanced budget agreement will affect people, to the public education problem, to the impact of welfare reform. "One of the things that Dr. King fought for was the Voting Rights Act. So now the enemy is us. We've got enough people of goodwill in elected office, and it's a new Easter egg hunt. On the one hand here at Ebenezer, we're for social change and on the other hand we're involved in social service. We keep them in creative tension. Because if we simply go with social service, we baptize the status quo and we'll remain in the same mess."

Roberts minces no words about another of his greatest fears—the evangelists, both white and black. "We used to teach around great themes—creation, redemption, sanctification, and doctrinal statements—which presupposed a knowledge of the scriptures. But these Christian Right evangelists don't know the scriptures. They come in and say we're not preaching, we're teaching—but they're not reading the Bible contextually, they're giving a truncated version. If a preacher doesn't know what a metaphor is, and the people don't, you're off and running. I have people who come in here and tell me, 'But it says it in the Bible.' All of a sudden they're going to change their behavior and bring it back into the first-century ethos. These questions of fornication, which are important, pale into significance when you realize that when that was written, people married at thirteen!"

It is refreshing to listen to Joseph Roberts's viewpoints. But there is also visible frustration in the minister, as he confronts the gap between societal realities and the King vision he clearly desires so much to keep alive. So he harkens back to his ancestors, not only Martin King but men like Benjamin Mays and Howard Thurman.

"People don't want to admit it," Roberts is saying, "but there are correlations between the better side of the Nation of Islam and all of the things that positive blacks have said. People get all bent out of shape with Farrakhan, but he's got guys learning how to read. Sure, they sell his *Final Call* on the street. But they're respectable-looking people and they take care of their own neighborhoods. And that's sort of what Benny Mays used to say at Sage Hall. Every time he had chapel—Get yourself together!

"It's interesting, people have been called the sons of Mays and he had no natural children. But he was so instrumental, and I think he helps us address the problem of the black male. There's a church in Detroit that's started a school called the Benjamin E. Mays Elementary School for Boys. I may do something like that here. We'll run it ourselves, like the old sixteenth-century reformers ran them. Comply to our rules, wear uniforms. With a parent-child emphasis, I think that could work pretty well."

When I follow by asking Roberts about Howard Thurman, he shakes his head and looks up at the ceiling. "Now *that's* a religious experience. He is the mentor of whole bunches of us. He's a black Niebuhr with poetry, a mystic on the order of Meister Eckhart in the Middle Ages. I've preached thousands of sermons based on ideas I got from Howard Thurman."

Roberts recalls a moment long ago, when Thurman "was preaching before a group of people who laughed at him, because he was short like [the apostle] Paul and not too attractive. There were maybe 5,000 people in that audience. Well, he turned his back on them. He turned it across and preached it across, brought the house down! And when he got through, he walked out the back door. Never looked at them again."

Then, as one of Thurman's illuminations comes back to him, sitting there in a conference room of the unpretentious Baptist church whose leadership shook the world, Joseph Roberts cannot help but begin to preach. "Howard Thurman talks about the fact that there is within all of us a seed, a tiny organism of life. Within that seed is everything you need for life. And life is like that seed. We are caught up on the wind, blown here there and yonder, but when we are able to land, we can bring forth fruit. In every individual, there is that precious undetermined potential for growth and development, given the proper nutrients. You don't know me until you get inside that seed, where you can see who I really am."

I walk outside into the spring breezes of Atlanta. Across the street is the Martin Luther King museum, where ground has been broken for the new Ebenezer Baptist Church site. I gaze upon a bronze sculpture of a man holding a small baby in the air. Just down the block from the existing church is the Chapel of All Faiths, adjoining the King Center for Nonviolent Social Change. The Freedom Walk connecting the two buildings is lined with a courtyard fountain. The monument to King lists simply his date of birth and death, above the words: "Free at last, free at last, thank God almighty I'm free at last."

On the way across town for one last look at the Morehouse College campus, I read the words of Benjamin Mays: "If God does not make men love more, hate less and do justice toward men, he is not there. God is truly dead. . . . The Christian cannot excuse himself by saying, 'I cannot go against tradition; I cannot buck the mores; I cannot jeopardize my political, social, or economic future.' The true Christian is a citizen of two worlds. Not only must he answer to the mores, but he must give an account to God. And with God's help he can be loyal to the highest and to the best he knows."

The crowd that had gathered on the campus to pay homage to the Thurmans is long dispersed. A few students pass along the walkway of the Morehouse monuments. There is silence here. I stand between the outstretched hand of Martin Luther King and the obelisk that honors Howard Thurman. I swim in a sea of faces. Some I have met along the course of this journey. Some I have discovered only in books. Many through the eyes of others. All are a living presence within.

I walk around the obelisk. Passages from Thurman's writings and sermons are engraved in stone on all four sides. One speaks of the dream as "the quiet persistence of the heart that enables us to ride out the storms of our churning experiences . . . the ever-recurring melody in the midst of the broken harmonies of human conflict. . . . Keep alive the dream."

The sea of faces is ever more tangible. Will Cook and Duke Ellington and Louis Armstrong and Wynton Marsalis. . . . Albert Murray and Ralph Ellison and Romare Bearden. . . . Meta Warrick Fuller and Loïs

Mailou Jones and Jacob Lawrence. . . . Ira Aldridge and Paul Robeson and Gordon Parks. . . . Mary McLeod Bethune and Elma Lewis. . . . W. E. B. Du Bois and Alain Locke and Cornel West. . . . Frederick Douglass and James Baldwin and Toni Morrison. . . . Lewis Latimer and Earl and Alan Shaw and Bob Moses. . . . Benjamin Banneker and Charles McAfee and his daughters. . . . Louis and Jane Wright and Byllye Avery. . . . Sojourner Truth and Benjamin Mays and Howard Thurman. . . . Martin Luther King.

The faces merge with a passage on the obelisk. I read:

"We who seek community within our own spirit, who search for it in our experiences with the literal facts of the external world, who make this our formal intent as we seek to bring order out of the chaos of the collective life, are not going against life but will be sustained and supported by life. In the conflicts between individuals, between group and group, between nation and nation, the loneliness of the seeker for community is sometimes unendurable. Yet the radical tension between good and evil, as we see and feel it, does not have the last word about the meaning of life and the nature of existence. There is a spirit in us and in the world working against the thing that destroys and lays waste. Always we must know that the contradictions of life are not final or ultimate, we must distinguish between failure and a many-sided awareness so that we will not mistake conformity for harmony, uniformity for synthesis. We must know that for all to be alike is the death of life in all, and yet perceive the harmony that transcends diversities and in which diversity finds its richness and significance."
                                                              —HOWARD THURMAN

FOR FURTHER READING:

Taylor Branch, *Parting the Waters: America in the King Years 1954-63* (New York: Touchstone/Simon & Schuster, 1988).

Lawrence Edward Carter, Sr., ed., *Walking Integrity: Benjamin Elijah Mays, Mentor to Generations* (Atlanta: Morehouse College, 1996).

Martin Luther King, Jr., *Stride toward Freedom: A Leader of His People Tells the Montgomery Story* (New York: Harper Bros., 1958).

———, *Why We Can't Wait* (New York: Harper & Row, 1964; Signet, 1964).

———, *Strength to Love* (New York: Harper & Row, 1982; Fortress Press, 1982).

Benjamin E. Mays, *Born to Rebel, An Autobiography* (Athens, Ga.: University of Georgia Press, 1971).

Anne Spencer Thurman, ed., *For the Inward Journey: The Writings of Howard Thurman* (New York: Harcourt Brace Jovanovich, 1984).

Howard Thurman, *With Head and Heart: An Autobiography* (New York: Harcourt Brace Jovanovich, 1979).

————, *Jesus and the Disinherited* (Richmond, Ind: Friends United Press, reprint, 1981).

Afterword

In the little more than a decade that has passed since this book was first published, many of the individuals profiled have gone on to yet greater achievements. Four others have since died, and one has turned ninety. Here is an update on what has transpired for these remarkable individuals:

ALBERT MURRAY: Still residing in Harlem with his wife Michelle, he turned ninety in 2006. His book, *Trading Twelves: Selected Letters of Ralph Ellison and Albert Murray*, was published in 2000. A collection of his essays and book reviews, *From the Briarpatch File*, and a volume of poetry, *Conjugations and Reiterations*, followed the next year. His papers were purchased by the Houghton Library at Harvard University. In June 2007, Murray was presented Harvard's W. E. B. Du Bois Medal at Lincoln Center by his protégé, Wynton Marsalis.

WYNTON MARSALIS: Some five million copies of his recordings have been sold worldwide. He has served as artistic director and co-producer of Ken Burns' documentary series, *Jazz*, and his epic composition *All Rise* for gospel choir, big band, and symphony was presented soon after the millennium dawned. Following the devastation of Hurricane Katrina, Marsalis organized a large benefit concert and became a leader in the effort to rebuild New Orleans. He was awarded the National Medal of Arts by President Bush in 2005.

LOIS MAILOU JONES: Following an artistic career that spanned nearly seventy years, she died at her home in Washington in June 1998, at the age of ninety-two.

JACOB LAWRENCE: Now considered one of the great figurative painters of the twentieth century, he died in June 2000 at his home in Seattle, at the age of eighty-two.

PAUL ROBESON: The first volume of Paul Robeson's biography by his son, Paul Robeson, Jr., *The Undiscovered Paul Robeson: An Artist's Journey, 1898–1939*, was published in 2001.

GORDON PARKS: The world-renowned photographer, filmmaker, writer, and composer died at his home in New York City in March 2006, at the age of ninety-three.

ELMA LEWIS: The mentor to generations of young music students, she died from complications of diabetes at her home in Boston, on New Year's Day 2004, at the age of eighty-two.

CORNEL WEST: Leaving Harvard in 2002, West returned to Princeton to teach courses in religion and philosophy. *The Cornel West Reader* was published in 2000 and *Democracy Matters* in 2004. West also played a role in developing storylines for the *Matrix* movie trilogy and played a recurring role in two of the films. His latest CD, *Never Forget: A Journey of Revelations*, offers a collection of "socially conscious music" and collaborations with Prince, Outkast, Jill Scott, and Talib Kweli.

TONI MORRISON: The Nobel Prize-winning author retired in 2006 as the Robert F. Goheen Professor in the Council of Humanities at Princeton. That same year her book, *Beloved*, was named the best American novel published in the last 25 years by a *New York Times* poll of critics. Morrison's eighth novel, *Love*, was published in 2003, and her latest, *Mercy*, in 2008.

EARL AND ALAN SHAW: Earl continues to teach and conduct research at Rutgers, while his son Alan continues to use technology to address issues surrounding social justice, education, and community building. He currently teaches computer science at Kennesaw State University.

ROBERT MOSES: His book, *Radical Equations: Civil Rights from Mississippi to the Algebra Project*, was published in 2001 and described by Cornel West as "the definitive book on one of the most important projects of youth empowerment and citizenship of our times." Moses received the Heinz Award in the Human Condition for developing the Algebra Project, which continues to thrive in a number of locations. Moses was named a Frank H.T. Rhodes Class of '56 Professor at Cornell University in 2006.

THE MCAFEES: Charles McAfee and his two daughters, Cheryl McAfee-Mitchell and Charyl McAfee-Duncan, continue their architectural partnership (CFM) in Wichita, Atlanta, and Dallas. Cheryl was named to a Fellowship with the American Institute of Architects in 2003, and Charyl has been recognized as one of the eight outstanding African-American men and women in Dallas.

BYLLYE AVERY: The women's health activist is today a clinical professor at Columbia University's Mallman School of Public Health, and an advisor to the National Institutes of Health.

Acknowledgments

This book has been a group effort in so many ways. It could not have been written without the help of dozens of people: offering advice on the structure, suggestions for the extremely difficult task of deciding whom to profile, editing and photographic assistance, and entree to others.

In the cases of most of the living individuals whom I chose to profile, I decided to send each of them a manuscript copy of the chapters where they appeared. In return, I received not only certain factual corrections and suggested new turns of phrase, but often invaluable additional material. My deepest thanks to the many people who took the time to help me better tell their stories and make their voices ring as true as I could.

Richard Newman, of Harvard's W. E. B. Du Bois Institute, assisted greatly in the book's conception and framework, as well as providing advice and encouragement as he read through a number of the chapters. My thanks also to his Institute colleagues, Andre Willis and Michael Vorenberg.

Especially helpful in critiquing my early chapters and encouraging my direction was my writer friend Ross Gelbspan. UMass/Amherst professor and author Michael Thelwell's probing honesty proved invaluable when I was still grasping at straws, as well as his continuing support in reading several of the chapters. Albert Murray, while a primary subject in this book, also took the time to raise crucial questions about the overall content and gave me a number of wonderful photographs to include from his personal collection.

Also providing important thoughts for the book's outline and difficult introductory chapter were: Edmund Barry Gaither of the National Center of Afro-American Artists; scholars Cornel West, Marilyn Richardson and Jean Humez; Boston University's Dr. Adelaide Cromwell; author Mel Watkins; James H. Cone of the Union Theological Seminary; Massachusetts state representative Byron Rushing, and Jacqueline Bruzio.

My friends Jesse Given, Tom Langman, John Andrew Ross, Abby Rockefeller and Bob Carey were instrumental in leading me to certain interviews, as were publisher Howard Kessinger, writers Jack Newfield and David Hacker, and Emory University's Richard Long. Author David Leeming and Princeton scholar David Carrasco read pertinent chapters and responded with helpful comments. Paul Robeson, Jr., was always available for clarification about his father's remarkable life and times. Scholars/educators Hugh Gloster (Morehouse College), David Blight and Asa Davis (UMass/Amherst) and Kenneth Manning (MIT) offered fascinating insights into their subjects of expertise.

For giving me important background materials, I thank my neighbor Joan Stanley, my friend Scott Schwartz, poet Michael Harper, and Colin Rock of *Emerge* magazine. Librarians Alice Adamczyk and Betty Obadashian of the Schomburg Center for Research in Black Culture graciously helped in my research-gathering, as did Jim Huffman and Anthony Toussaint of the Schomburg's Photo and Prints Division. Archivists at many other institutions, including the Morland-Spingarn Library, Morehouse College, Columbus College, and the W. E. B. Du Bois Library at UMass/Amherst, also offered their kind assistance. So did professional assistants Abby Moore (for Byllye Avery), Rene Shepherd (for Toni Morrison), Johanna Fiore (for Gordon Parks), and particularly Ronnie Veals (for her astute "edits" concerning Charles McAfee and his daughters).

I am grateful, too, to my photographer friends Lou Jones and Brian Lanker for providing me with their outstanding pictures; to David Parks for the memorable shots he sent along from my interview with his father; to painter Jacob Lawrence for sending a number of fine photographs from which to select, and to photographer Frank Stewart. Thanks, too, to Robert A. Clark of the Rutgers Newark Office of Campus Communications; Laurie Jakobsen for arranging my interviews with Wynton Marsalis; and Barbara Washkowitz for sharing her son Andy's fine paper on Benjamin Banneker.

My appreciation to my literary agent Sara Jane Freymann for her ongoing encouragement, my editor Kent Carroll for his careful work on the manuscript, his colleague Herman Graf for his enthusiastic belief in this project, and their partner Richard Gallen for his conceptual assistance.

My thanks, too, to my writer friends Amy and Alan for their reading and thoughtful responses, Michael Fosberg for sharing his observations and personal experiences, and Marianne Shenafield for her everintriguing "overviews."

Within my family, it was Alice who provided first-draft criticism and editing, and consistent moral support, and who made the suggestion that I send the chapters out for prepublication review by the subjects. A number of Alice's and my closest friends were there at what can only be described as "difficulty at the beginning." In forcing me to do some soul-searching about myself and my limitations, my friends initiated what became a challenging and wonderful journey. Especially Jessie, Devora, Laura, Eben, David and Etta pushed me in a new direction, away from a standard (and flat) chronological history toward a focus on relationships, and eventually my meeting people through whom I might offer fresh insights. I also thank Jonny Gube and Patty, Daria and Irene, Gale and Rosesharon for their research assistance; Randy, Mark, Terry, Geoffrey and Kurt for their insights; George and Padrick for their encouragement, and Faith for being there.

Finally, my gratitude to my father Clarence Russell and my late mother Olive Nelson Russell, who raised me in a household filled with their beautiful music.

Notes on Sources

All of the in-person interviews conducted by the author were tape-recorded with permission of the interviewees.

The majority of the articles cited were found at Harlem's Schomburg Center for Research in Black Culture.

INTRODUCTION

The author's conversation with Edmund Barry Gaither took place on February 29, 1996, in Roxbury, Massachusetts.

The author's interview with Cornel West took place on April 9, 1996, in Cambridge, Massachusetts.

PART ONE: A CERTAIN HERITAGE

CHAPTER ONE: ANCESTORS—ELLINGTON'S MENTOR: WILL MARION COOK.

The author's interview about Cook with Albert Murray took place in New York on July 4, 1997.

Background material on the life of Will Marion Cook was drawn from the following books and articles:

The Music of Black Americans: A History, by Eileen Southern (2nd ed., New York: W. W. Norton & Co., 1983).

Frederick Douglass, by William McFeely (New York: W. W. Norton & Co., 1991).

100 Years of the Negro in Show Business: The Tom Fletcher Story, by Tom Fletcher (Schomburg collection).

Dictionary of American Negro Biography, vol. C,

Dictionary of Afro-American Performers.

Duke: A Portrait of Duke Ellington, by Derek Jewell (New York: W. W. Norton & Co., 1977).

The Making of Jazz: A Comprehensive History, by James Lincoln Collier (New York: Delta Books, 1978).

"Will Marion Cook on Negro Music," by Will Marion Cook, *New York Age*, September 21, 1918.

Cook letter, "Noted Musician Assails White Authors Works," *New York News*, October 29, 1927.

"Will Marion Cook: He Helped Them All," by Mercer Cook, *Crisis*, October 1944.

"Clorindy, the Origin of the Cakewalk," by Will Marion Cook, *Theatre Arts*, September 1947.

Background on African-American music and history of jazz is derived from:

"Jazz at Home," by J. A. Rogers, in *The New Negro: Voices of the Harlem Renaissance*, edited by Alain Locke (New York: Atheneum Books, 1992).

The Music of Black Americans, by Eileen Southern.

The Making of Jazz: A Comprehensive History, James Lincoln Collier.

Paul Laurence Dunbar: *The World's Great Men of Color*, vol. 2, by J. A. Rogers (New York: MacMillan, 1972).

CHAPTER TWO: ALBERT MURRAY AND LOUIS ARMSTRONG

The author's interviews with Albert Murray took place in New York on March 25, 1996; August 22, 1996; and July 4, 1997.

The author's interviews with Wynton Marsalis took place in New York on April 16, 1996 and August 22, 1996.

The author's interviews with Stanley Crouch took place in New York on December 21, 1995, and April 17, 1996.

The author's interview with John Edgar Wideman took place in Amherst, Massachusetts, on February 11, 1997.

Background on Albert Murray was derived from:

"The Omni-American," An interview by Tony Scherman, *American Heritage*, September 1996.

"The Unsquarest Person Duke Ellington Ever Met," by Mark Feeney, *Boston Globe Magazine*, August 1, 1993.

"King of Cats," by Henry Louis Gates, Jr., *New Yorker*, April 8, 1996.

"Renaissance Riffs," by Malcolm Jones, Jr., *Newsweek*, February 5, 1996. '

Dictionary of Literary Biography no. 38, pp. 214–24.

"Albert Murray at 80," by Gene Seymour, *The Nation*, March 25, 1996.

"The Soloist: Albert Murray's Blues People," by Joe Wood, *Voice Literary Supplement*, February 1996.

Conversations with Albert Murray, University Press of Mississippi (collection of interviews), 1997.

Background on Louis Armstrong was derived from:

Louis Armstrong, An American Genius, by James Lincoln Collier (New York: Oxford University Press, 1983).

Swing That Music, by Louis Armstrong (Longmans, Green & Co., 1936, Da Capo, 1993).

American Masters: Louis Armstrong, PBS-TV documentary, 1996.

The Making of Jazz: A Comprehensive History, by James Lincoln Collier.

The Blue Devils of Nada, by Albert Murray (Pantheon, New York, 1996).

Stomping the Blues, by Albert Murray (New York: McGraw-Hill, 1976).

Early Jazz: Its Roots and Musical Development, by Gunther Schuller (Oxford University Press, New York, 1968; reprint 1986).

"An Encore for Pops," by Gene Seymour, *New York Newsday*, December 13, 1994.

Background on Stanley Crouch was derived from:

"The Professor of Connection," by Robert S. Boynton, *New Yorker*, November 6, 1995.

CHAPTER THREE: THE CRAFT OF RALPH ELLISON

In addition to the author's interviews about Ellison with Albert Murray, Wynton Marsalis, Stanley Crouch, and John Edgar Wideman (dates cited above), the interview with Michael S. Harper took place in Providence, Rhode Island, on February 15, 1997. The author's discussion about Ellison's family background with Cornel West took place in Cambridge, Massachusetts, on July 8, 1997.

Considerable background material on Ellison, and quotes from his work, were derived from his essays, as they appear in *The Collected Essays of Ralph Ellison* ed. John F. Callahan (New York: Modern Library, 1995).

The Murray quote on the blues appears in his *The Blue Devils of Nada*. The Murray quote on Ellison appears in his *The Omni-Americans* (New York: Outerbridge & Dienstfrey, 1970). Murray also discusses Ellison in the *New Yorker*'s "King of Cats" and in *Conversations with Albert Murray* (cited above).

Stanley Crouch writes about Ellison in his *The All-American Skin Game, Or, The Decoy of Race* (New York: Pantheon, 1995).

Other background on Ellison was derived from: "Visible Man," by David Remnick, *The New Yorker*, March 14, 1994; Talk of the Town: "Seeing Ralph Ellison," *The New Yorker*, May 2, 1994; "Ralph Ellison, Author of 'Invisible Man,' Is Dead at 80," by Richard D. Lyons, *New York Times*, April 17, 1994; and "The Singular Vision of Ralph Ellison," by Charles Johnson, *Washington Post*, April 18, 1994.

CHAPTER FOUR: FROM DUKE ELLINGTON TO WYNTON MARSALIS

The majority of background on Duke Ellington, including many quotes from him, was derived from John Edward Haase's *Beyond Category: The Life and Genius of Duke Ellington* (New York: Simon & Schuster, 1993). Ralph Ellison's reminiscences and quotes about Ellington were found in the *Collected Essays*, and Albert Murray's, in his *Blue Devils of Nada*.

Other Ellington sources include his autobiography, *Music Is My Mistress* (New York: Da Capo, 1976), *The Duke Ellington Reader* (New York: Oxford University Press, 1993), Southern's *The Music of Black Americans*, Collier's *The Making of Jazz*, and the article "Duke," by Mark Feeney, *Boston Globe Magazine*, December 19, 1993.

In addition to the author's interviews with Marsalis, Murray and Crouch (cited earlier), background material on Marsalis was derived from the following:

"Wynton Marsalis: Blow on This," by Greg Tate, *Village Voice*, July 25, 1989.

"Marsalis Explores Jazz's Past in a Fresh Way," by Bo Emerson, *Atlanta Constitution*, July 30, 1989.

"Miles of Heart," by Playthell Benjamin, *Village Voice*, November 6, 1990.

"The New York Newsday Interview with Wynton Marsalis: What Is It That Makes an Artist Heroic?", *New York Newsday*, February 11, 1991.

"Jazz: Wynton Looks Back," by Whitney Balliett, *The New Yorker*, October 14, 1991.

"The Young Lions' Roar," by Richard Guilliatt, *Los Angeles Times Calendar*, September 13, 1992.

"Going a Round with Wynton Marsalis," by Don Heckman, *Los Angeles Times*, October 13, 1994.

"Medium Cool," by Jervis Anderson, *The New Yorker*, [December 12, 1994]

"Lincoln Center Elevates Status of Jazz," by Peter Watrous, *New York Times*, December 19, 1995.

"Marsalis' class," by Bob Blumenthal, *Boston Globe*, January 5, 1996.

"The Music of Democracy," by Tony Scherman for *American Heritage*, reprinted in *Utne Reader*, March–April, 1996.

"From Duke Ellington, Themes for the Movies," by Peter Watrous, *New York Times*, May 13, 1996.

"Horns of Plenty," by Thomas Sanction, *Time*, June 17, 1996.

"Wynton Marsalis: Speaking from the Melody," by Antonio J. Garcia, *Jazz Educators Journal*, July 1996.

"Jelly Roll and the Duke Join Wolfgang and Ludwig," by Jon Pareles, *New York Times*, July 2, 1996.

"The Jazz Zinger: Wynton Marsalis," by Anthony DeCurtis, *Men's Journal*, August 1996.

"For Marsalis, the Poison of Slavery Bends to Love," by Peter Watrous, *New York Times*, January 30, 1997.

"The Marsalis Masterpiece," by Bob Blumenthal, *Boston Globe*, February 7, 1997.

"Wynton Marsalis oversees majestic 'Fields,' " by Bob Blumenthal, *Boston Globe*, February 10, 1997.

"Songs of Slavery Lifted by a Chorus of Horns," by Theodore Rosengarten, *New York Times*, February 23, 1997.

"20 Pulitzer Prizes Are Announced with a Theme of Personal Impact on Lives," by Iver Peterson, *New York Times*, April 8, 1997.

"Jazz at the Center," *The Nation*, May 12, 1997.

"Wynton Marsalis," by Touré, *Icon Thoughtstyle Magazine*, August 1997.

Biographical press releases from Shore Fire Media, March 11, 1996; June 27, 1996; July 15, 1996; April 7, 1997.

CHAPTER FIVE: VARIATIONS ON A THEME: ROMARE BEARDEN, ARTIST

The quotes about Romare Bearden from Albert Murray appear in his *Blue Devils of Nada*; the quotes about Bearden from Ralph Ellison appear in "The Art of Romare Bearden" in Ellison's *Collected Essays*. The author also discussed Bearden in the interviews with Murray and Marsalis.

Jacob Lawrence discussed Bearden with the author during an interview in Scowhegan, Maine, on August 6, 1996. Richard Long discussed Bearden with the author in a telephone interview on May 7, 1997. Photographer Lou Jones's story about Bearden comes from an interview with the author on July 2, 1997.

Several quotes from Bearden are taken from the transcript of a 1978 conversation between Bearden, Alvin Ailey, James Baldwin, and Murray, which first appeared in *Callaloo*, vol. 12, no. 3 (Summer 1989), pp. 431–52 and again in *Conversations with Albert Murray* (Jackson: University Press of Mississippi, 1997).

Background on Bearden, including quotations, was also drawn from the following books and articles:

African American Art and Artists, by Samella Lewis (Berkeley: University of California Press, 1990).

"Romare Bearden, Collagist and Painter, Dies at 75," by C. Gerald Fraser, *New York Times*, March 13, 1988.

"The Saints Make Room for Romare Bearden," by Amei Wallach, *Newsday/Fanfare*, April 28, 1991.

"Visual Jazz from a Sharp Eye," by Robert Hughes, *Time*, June 10, 1991.

"Romare Bearden: Integrating Scholarship and Soul," by Paul Richard, *Washington Post*, October 4, 1992.

"King of Cats," by Henry Louis Gates, Jr., *New Yorker*, April 8, 1996.

PART TWO: CREATION UNDER FIRE

CHAPTER SIX: ANCESTORS—META WARRICK FULLER, SCULPTOR

The story of Fuller was derived primarily from the following sources:
· *African American Art and Artists*, Lewis.

"Meta Warrick Fuller" by Dolores Nicholson, in *Notable Black American Women*, edited by Jessie Carney Smith (Detroit: Gale Research Inc.)

"Meta Warrick Fuller: Her Life and Art," by Velma J. Hoover, *Negro History Bulletin*, no. 40, March–April 1977.

"Meta Vaux Warrick Fuller," by Robert C. Hayden, *Dictionary of American Negro Biography* (New York: W. W. Norton, 1982).

"Meta Vaux Warrick Fuller," by Judith N. Kerr, *Black Women in America: An Historical Encyclopedia*, edited by Darlene Clark Hine (Brooklyn, N.Y.: Carlson Publishing, 1993).

CHAPTER SEVEN: THE PAINTERS: LOÏS MAILOU JONES AND JACOB LAWRENCE

The author's interview with Jacob Lawrence took place in Scowhegan, Maine, on August 6–7, 1996.

The author's interview with Loïs Jones took place in Washington, D.C., on January 17, 1997.

The author's interview with Rae Alexander-Minter took place in Rutgers, New Jersey, on May 8, 1996.

Additional background material was derived from:

Jacob Lawrence: American Painter, by Ellen Harkins Wheat, (Seattle, University of Washington Press in association with Seattle Art Museum, 1986).

The Life and Art of Loïs Mailou Jones, by Tritobia Hayes Benjamin (San Francisco: Pomegranate Artbooks, 1994).

African American Art and Artists, by Samella Lewis.

"Loïs Mailou Jones," by Tritobia Hayes Benjamin in *Black Women in America.*

"Presidential Visit Honors Loïs Mailou Jones," by Virginia Poole, *Vineyard Gazette,* September 24, 1993.

"An Invigorating Homecoming," by Michael Kimmelman (profile of Lawrence), *New York Times,* April 12, 1996.

"The Tanner Family: A Grandniece's Chronicle," by Rae Alexander-Minter, in *Henry Ossawa Tanner* (catalogue of Philadelphia Museum of Art).

CHAPTER EIGHT: ALL THE WORLD'S THEIR STAGE: PAUL ROBESON AND IRA ALDRIDGE

The author's interviews with Paul Robeson, Jr., took place in New York, on March 25, 1996 and April 16, 1996. Additional telephone interviews were conducted on May 8, 1997, and July 29, 1997.

The author's interview with Pete Seeger took place at his home on March 27, 1996.

Additional background on Robeson was derived from:

Paul Robeson Speaks, Edited by Philip S. Foner (New York: Citadel Press/Carol Publishing, 1978).

Here I Stand, by Paul Robeson (Boston: Beacon Press, 1988).

The Whole World in His Hands: A Pictorial Biography of Paul Robeson, by Susan Robeson (New York: Carol Publishing, 1990).

Paul Robeson: A Biography, by Martin Bauml Duberman (New York: Ballantine, 1989).

"The Robeson File," *The Nation,* February 3, 1997.

The primary source for the Ira Aldridge story was *Ira Aldridge: The Negro Tragedian,* by Herbert Marshall and Mildred Stock (Carbondale, Ill.: Southern Illinois University Press, 1968).

Other source material on Aldridge included:

"Ira Aldridge: Greatest of the Othellos," by J. A. Rogers in *World's Great Men of Color,* vol. 2 (New York: Collier Books/Macmillan, 1972).

"Ira Aldridge, American Negro Tragedian and Taras Shevchenko, Poet of the Ukraine: Story of a Friendship," by Marie Trommer (pamphlet published in 1939).

"Daughter of Great Negro Actor Dies," by David Platt, *Daily Worker,* March 22, 1956.

"Ira Aldridge vs. Paul Robeson," by Frank Griffin, *New York Amsterdam News*, November 20, 1943.

"Aldridge," *The New Yorker*, January 22, 1944.

"Century of Negro Drama," by Archibald Haddon, *Crisis*, February 1934.

"Ira Aldridge, Shakespearean Actor," by Owen Mortimer, *The Crisis*, April 1955.

"Ira Aldridge," *National Anti-Slavery Standard*, January 21, 1865.

CHAPTER NINE: GORDON PARKS: A LENS ON HUMANITY

The author's interview with Gordon Parks was conducted in New York on July 4, 1997; with Toni Parks, in New York on June 7, 1997.

Background material on Parks was derived from two of his autobiographies, primarily *Voices in the Mirror* (New York: Doubleday, 1990) as well as *To Smile in Autumn* (New York: W. W. Norton, 1979), and the following sources:

"A passionate vision, a precious talent: Gordon Parks," by Susan L. Rife, special reprint section of *The Wichita Eagle*, 1994.

"Gordon Parks," in *Current Biography Yearbook 1992*.

"Gordon Parks: A True Renaissance Man," by David Hacker, *Prime Time News & Observer*, May 1997.

CHAPTER TEN: ANCESTORS: MARY MCLEOD BETHUNE, EDUCATOR

Background for the Bethune story was derived primarily from: *Mary McLeod Bethune*, by Catherine Owens Peare (New York: Vanguard Press, 1951). Also from a chapter on Bethune in *13 Against The Odds* by Edwin R. Embree (New York: Viking Press, 1946), Bethune's writings in *Black Women in White America: A Documentary History*, edited by Gerda Lerner (New York: Vintage Books, 1972); "Mary McLeod Bethune" by Elaine M. Smith in *Black Women in America*; "Mary McLeod Bethune and the National Youth Administration: A Case Study of Power Relationships in the Black Cabinet of Franklin D. Roosevelt," by B. Joyce Ross, *Journal of Negro History*, no. 60, January 1975.

CHAPTER ELEVEN: A TEACHER'S MISSION: ELMA LEWIS

The author's interviews with Elma Lewis were conducted in Roxbury, Massachusetts, on September 30, 1995, and June 15, 1997; telephone interviews took place on February 29, 1997 and April 6, 1997.

The author's interview with John Andrew Ross was conducted primarily on September 29, 1995.

Numerous interviews, including Kamal Scott, Reverend George Thomas, and Senator Edward Brooke, were conducted by the author at the Elma Lewis Tribute and Symposium in Boston, September 20–22, 1996.

Additional background material on Elma Lewis was derived from the following sources:

"Elma Lewis," by Ruth Edmonds Hill, in *Notable Black American Women*.

"Black Boston's Miss Lewis: Art Czarina with a Needle," *Boston Globe*, April 18, 1968.

" 'There Aren't Enough Elma Lewises,' " by Joan B. Cass, *Boston Herald Traveler*, April 28, 1968.

"Lewis Arts School Will Enroll 500," by Samuel Hirsch, *Boston Herald Traveler*, August 18, 1968.

"600 Salute Elma Lewis, Art Plans," by Jim Droney, *Boston Herald Traveler*, October 14, 1968.

"Black America's Barnum, Hurok and Guthrie," by Caryl Rivers, *New York Times*, November 17, 1968.

"A Spark for the Dance in Boston," by Joan B. Cass, *Boston Herald Traveler*, December 15, 1968.

"Black Art's Amazing Fund-Raiser," by Peter Bailey, *Ebony*, June 1970.

"The Undeferred Dream of Elma Lewis," by Suzanne Bailey, *Essence*, July 1973.

"Center for Black Culture Thriving Now in Boston," by Robert Reinhold, *New York Times*, June 24, 1974.

"Elma Lewis School of Fine Arts," by Zarine Merchant, *Black Enterprise*, August 1975.

"Big Boom in Black Arts and Culture," by Perry Garfinkel, *Sepia*, September 1976.

"Elma Lewis: A Champion of Black Artistic Expression," *Bostonia*, December/January, 1985.

"Tuning Up 'Black Nativity,' " by Elijah Wald, *Boston Globe*, December 30, 1995.

"The Lioness in Winter," by Joseph P. Kahn, *Boston Globe*, September 12, 1996.

"Widening of the Spirit," by Mary Jo Palumbo, *Boston Herald*, September 19, 1996.

"A Spiritual Awakening: The Restoration of Our Memories—Celebrate Elma Lewis," program of the Museum of Science, Boston, September 21, 1996.

"Elma Lewis: Up You Might People!," by Rosesharon Oates, term paper at Boston University, December 3, 1996.

"The Spirit Behind 'Black Nativity,' " by Cate McQuaid, *Boston Globe*, December 5, 1996.

"The Miracle of 'Black Nativity,' " by Derrick Z. Jackson, *Boston Globe*, December 20, 1996.

CHAPTER TWELVE: THE PHILOSOPHERS: CORNEL WEST AND THE DU BOIS/LOCKE LEGACY

The author's interviews with Cornel West were conducted in Cambridge, Massachusetts, on April 9, 1996, and July 8, 1997. The author attended lectures by West at the Harvard Students Forum on "The Future of Black Leadership," April 13, 1996, and at the William Barton Rogers Middle School in Hyde Park, Massachusetts, on May 20, 1996. The author also attended Harvard class lectures by West on April 1, 1996, and April 22, 1996.

Background material and quotes from West were also found in his books: *Race Matters* (New York: Vintage, 1994); *The Future of the Race*, (co-authored by Henry Louis Gates, Jr., New York: Alfred A. Knopf, 1996); *Breaking Bread: Insurgent Black Intellectual Life* (co-authored with bell hooks, Boston: South End Press, 1991); *Keeping Faith: Philosophy and Race in America* (New York: Routledge, 1994), and *Jews & Blacks: A Dialogue on Race, Religion, and Culture in America* (co-authored with Michael Lerner, New York: Plume/Penguin, 1996).

Additional background on West was derived from the following:

"The Public Intellectual," by Jervis Anderson, *New Yorker*, January 17, 1994.

"Can Harvard's Powerhouse Alter the Course of Black Studies?", by Peter Applebome, *New York Times*, November 3, 1996.

"Cornel Matters," by Sylvester Monroe, *Emerge*, September 1996.

"Cornel West: Seeking to Expand America's 'Public' Conversation," by Janet Clayton, *Los Angeles Times*, May 9, 1993.

"Skip Gates Has a Dream," by Sally Jacobs, *Boston Globe*, March 7, 1996.

"Why I'm Marching in Washington," by Cornel West, *New York Times* (Op-Ed), October 14, 1995.

"Cornel West," interview with Algia Benjamin, *Spare Change*, November 16–30, 1996.

"Philosopher with a Mission," by Jackie White, *Time*, June 7, 1993.

"Voice of Reason," by Chris Bohjalian, *Boston Globe Magazine*, September 24, 1995.

In addition to Gates/West's *The Future of the Race*, background on W. E. B. Du Bois was derived primarily from *The Oxford W. E. B. Du*

Bois Reader, edited by Eric J. Sundquist (1996). Other source material on Du Bois included: *Paul Robeson Speaks; W. E. B. Du Bois: Biography of a Race*, by David Levering Lewis (1993); J. A. Rogers's *World's Great Men of Color*, vol. 2; "Lewis's Du Bois: The Race Man as All Too Human Genius," by David W. Blight, *Massachusetts Review*, Summer 1994; "W. E. B. Du Bois and the Struggle for American Historical Memory," by David W. Blight, in *History and Memory in African-American Culture*, edited by Genevieve Fabre and Robert O'Meally (New York: Oxford University Press, 1994); "The True Legacy of W. E. B. Du Bois," by Robert Paul Wolff, *Boston Globe* (Op-ed), April 1, 1996.

The author's interview about Alain Locke with Professor Richard Long was conducted by telephone on May 7, 1997. Ralph Ellison's essay "Alain Locke" appears in the *Collected Essays*. Considerable material was drawn from the Locke-edited *The New Negro: Voices of the Harlem Renaissance* (1992). Other source material on Locke included his essays in *Voices from the Harlem Renaissance*, edited by Nathan Irvin Huggins (1976); his "The American Temperament," *North American Review 1914*, later appearing in the anthology, *The Critical Temper of Alain Locke*, edited by Jeffrey C. Stewart (1983); his "The Negro in American Culture," January 18, 1944 (Schomburg Center source unlisted); Locke's biography in the *Dictionary of American Negro Biography*; a Locke profile in *The Black 100*, by Columbus Salley (1993); "Locke Was the Herald of the 'New Negro,' " by D. A. Wilkerson, *The Worker*, June 27, 1954; *When Harlem Was in Vogue*, by David Levering Lewis (1979).

CHAPTER THIRTEEN: TONI MORRISON: NOBEL PRIZE FOR LITERATURE

The author's interview with Cornel West about Morrison took place in Cambridge, Massachusetts, on July 8, 1997. The author's telephone interviews about Morrison were conducted with Davíd Carrasco on June 23, 1997; Albert Raboteau, on July 14, 1997; Erroll McDonald, on July 14, 1997; Wahneena Lubiano on July 22, 1997; and Michael Thelwell on July 16, 1997. The Thelwell quotes come from his letter to the author of July 30, 1997.

Background information on Morrison and quotes from her work were derived from a number of her books: *Playing in the Dark: Whiteness and the Literary Imagination* (1992); *The Bluest Eye* (1994); *Song of Solomon* (1987); *Sula* (1993), and *Beloved* (1988). Her eulogy to James Baldwin appears in *James Baldwin: The Legacy*, edited by Quincy Troupe (1989). Her Nobel Prize lecture, copyright 1993 by the Nobel Foundation, appears in *Humanities*, March/April 1996.

Other source material on Morrison was derived from:

"Toni Morrison's Black Magic," by Jean Strouse, *Newsweek*, March 30, 1981.

"The Pain of Being Black," interview with Bonnie Angelo, *Time*, May 22, 1989.

"Rooms of Their Own: Toni Morrison," by Paul Gray, *Time*, October 18, 1993.

"Toni Morrison's Manuscripts Spared in Christmas Fire at Home," by Robert D. McFadden, *New York Times*, December 28, 1993.

"Howard's Beloved Graduate," by David Streitfeld, *Washington Post*, March 4, 1994.

"Chloe Wofford about Toni Morrison," by Claudia Dreifus, *New York Times Magazine*, September 11, 1994.

" 'I Come From People Who Sang All the Time'—A Conversation with Toni Morrison," with Sheldon Hackney, *Humanities*, March/April 1996.

"Toni Morrison: Writing above Ground," by Claudia Brodsky Lacour, *Humanities*, March/April 1996.

"Healer in the Village: An Appreciation," by Maryemma Graham, *Humanities*, March/April 1996.

Biography and press release about *Paradise* from Alfred A. Knopf Publishers, 1997.

CHAPTER FOURTEEN: TIMELESS VOICES, PARALLEL REALITIES: JAMES BALDWIN AND FREDERICK DOUGLASS

The author's interviews about James Baldwin were conducted with Mel Watkins in New York on November 30, 1995; Norman Mailer, in Brooklyn on December 21, 1995; William Styron, in Edgartown, Massachusetts, on September 1, 1996; Michael Thelwell, in Amherst, Massachusetts, on September 4, 1996; John Edgar Wideman, in Amherst, Massachusetts, on February 11, 1997; by phone with David Leeming on April 13, 1997. The author discussed the Robert Kennedy relationship with Jack Newfield in New York in April 1996, and received a fax from Harry Belafonte about the same subject on June 13, 1997.

The author's interviews about Frederick Douglass were conducted with Michael Vorenberg in Cambridge, Massachusetts, on April 3, 1996, and with David Blight in Cambridge on October 5, 1996.

The majority of quotations from the writings of Baldwin and Douglass were found in two sources: *Price of the Ticket: Collected Nonfiction 1948–1985*, by James Baldwin (1985) and *Life and Times of Frederick Douglass, Written by Himself: His Early Life as a Slave, His*

Escape from Bondage, and His Complete History (1962, reprinted from revised edition of 1892).

Additional background on the lives of Baldwin and Douglass came from the following books: *James Baldwin: A Biography*, by David Leeming (1994); *James Baldwin: Artist on Fire*, by W. J. Weatherby (1989); *James Baldwin: The Legacy*, edited by Quincy Troupe (1989); *Robert Kennedy and His Times*, by Arthur Schlesinger, Jr. (1978); *Parting the Waters: America in the King Years 1954–63*, by Taylor Branch (1988); *Duties, Pleasures, and Conflicts: Essays in Struggle*, by Michael Thelwell (1987); *Living Our Stories, Telling Our Truths*, by V. P. Franklin (1995); *Advertisements for Myself*, by Norman Mailer (1959); *Frederick Douglass*, by William S. McFeely (1991); *Frederick Douglass' Civil War: Keeping Faith in Jubilee*, by David W. Blight (1989); *Frederick Douglass: New Literary and Historical Essays*, edited by Eric J. Sundquist (1990); *The Life and Writings of Frederick Douglass*, by Philip S. Foner (1950–75); *World's Great Men of Color*, vol. 2, by J. A. Rogers; *Lincoln and the Negro*, by Benjamin Quarles (1962); *Reminiscences of Abraham Lincoln by Distinguished Men of His Time*, collected and edited by Allen Thorndike Rice (1889).

Source articles on Baldwin: "A Prophet Is Not without Honor," by Ekewueme Michael Thelwell, *Transition*, no. 58; "Jimmy: Remembrances of James Baldwin," by Ekewueme Michael Thelwell, *The Valley Advocate*, May 26–June 1, 1994; "Letters from a Journey," by James Baldwin, *Harper's*, May 1963; " 'Go the Way Your Blood Beats': An Interview with James Baldwin," by Richard Goldstein, *Village Voice*, June 26, 1984; "The Black Situation Now: An Interview with James Baldwin," *Washington Post/Outlook*, July 21, 1974; "Dialog in Black and White," by James Baldwin and Budd Schulberg, *Playboy*, December 1966.

Source articles/papers on Douglass: "A Dangerous Literacy: The Legacy of Frederick Douglass," by Henry Louis Gates Jr., *New York Times Book Review*, May 28, 1995; "Lincoln and Douglass: Dismantling the Peculiar Institution," by Dorothy Wickenden, *Wilson Quarterly*, Autumn 1990; "Lincoln and Frederick Douglass: Another Debate," by Christopher N. Breiseth, *Journal of the Illinois State Historical Society*, February 1975; "Frederick Douglass in Baltimore," *National Anti-Slavery Standard*, December 10, 1864; "Beyond the 'New Birth of Freedom': Abraham Lincoln and the Nation's Vision of the African American Future," paper by Michael Vorenberg presented at the Lincoln and Gettysburg Symposium, Gettysburg, Pennsylvania, November 20, 1993; "Frederick Douglass and Abraham Lincoln: Same Struggle, Different Policies," term paper by Jesse Given, Kansas State University, November 20, 1995.

PART THREE: BUILDERS OF AMERICA

CHAPTER FIFTEEN: ANCESTORS: LEWIS LATIMER AND THE EARLY BLACK INVENTORS

The author's interview with Asa Davis took place in Amherst, Massachusetts, on September 4, 1996; with Winifred Latimer Norman, in New York on July 17, 1996; by telephone with Bayla Singer on July 14, 1996.

Additional background on Lewis Latimer was derived from: *Lewis Latimer: Scientist*, by Winifred Latimer Norman and Lily Patterson (1994); *Blueprint for Change: The Life and Times of Lewis H. Latimer*, edited by Janet M. Schneider and Bayla Singer with essays by Asa J. Davis, Kenneth R. Manning and Bayla Singer (1995); *Created Equal: The Lives and Ideas of Black American Innovators*, by James Michael Brodie (1993); *Black Inventors of America*, by McKinley Burt, Jr. (1989); *Black Pioneers of Science and Invention*, by Louis Haber (1970); *Life and Writings of Frederick Douglass*, by Philip Foner; Latimer's unpublished autobiographical writings and other materials in the Latimer collection of the Schomburg Center for Research in Black Culture; *Lewis Howard Latimer, a Black Inventor: A Biography and Related Experiments You Can Do,* produced by Thomas Alva Edison Foundation, 1973; "Lewis H. Latimer, Edison's Assistant, Dies at Age of 81," by Aubrey Bowser, *Amsterdam News*, December 19, 1928; "Late Lewis H. Latimer, Electrical Inventor, Is Paid Tribute at the 'Light's Golden Jubilee' Program," *New York Age*, November 9, 1929; "Gerald F. Norman—Teacher and Role Model," by Jeff Gottlieb, *New York Voice*, June 20–26, 1996.

Background on Elijah McCoy was derived from: "Elijah McCoy: 1844–1929, Inventor," *Contemporary Black Biography*, vol. 8, edited by L. Mpho Mabunda (1995); "Elijah McCoy," by Mae P. Claytor, *Dictionary of American Negro Biography; Black Inventors of America*, by McKinley Burt, *Created Equal*, by James Michael Brody. Background on Norbert Rilieux comes primarily from *Created Equal*. Background on Jan Matzeliger was derived from: *American Studies in Black and White: Selected Essays*, by Sidney Kaplan (1991); *World's Great Men of Color*, vol. 2; *Black Pioneers of Science and Invention; Created Equal*; "Jan Earnest Matzeliger and the Lasting Machine," by Robert Alexander Smith, in *No Race of Imitators: Lynn And Her People: An Anthology*, edited by Elizabeth Hope Cushing. Sources on Granville Woods: *Black Pioneers of Science and Invention; Created Equal*; "65 Years Later, He's Remembered," *New York Daily News*, April 24, 1975; *Men of Mark*, by William J. Simmons, 1887.

CHAPTER SIXTEEN: THE LASER PHYSICIST AND THE COMPUTER WIZARD: EARL AND ALAN SHAW

The author's interview with Earl Shaw took place in Newark, New Jersey, on July 17, 1996; with Alan Shaw in Boston, on May 18, 1996; follow-up telephone interviews with Earl Shaw on May 5 and May 18, 1997, and Alan Shaw on May 5, 1997, and July 2, 1997. The author also conducted telephone interviews with Pamela Morgan on May 1, 1997, and Bob Birgenau on June 18, 1997, and discussed Alan Shaw's work with Bob Moses on July 3, 1997, in Cambridge, Massachusetts.

Additional background on Earl Shaw was derived from: *Created Equal*, by Brodie; "In Line for a Nobel?" by Patricia Alex, *Bergen County (New Jersey) Record*, September 5, 1995; "The Genius of Earl Shaw," by James Michael Brodie, *Black Issues in Higher Education*, February 27, 1992; "Spectrum Revealed," by Kathleen Brunet, *Rutgers Magazine*, Summer 1993; "Top Researcher and New Laser to Light Up Physics at Rutgers-Newark," by Kitta MacPherson, [Newark] *Star-Ledger*, August 14, 1992; "Laser Beams Down to R-N," by David Scull, *Rutgers Observer*, September 14, 1992.

Additional background on Alan Shaw was derived from: "Making Healthy MUSIC: Technology as a Tool for Social Revitalization," by Pamela Morgan, *The Journal of Urban Technology* vol. 3, no. 1, 1995; "The MUSIC Networking System," paper by Alan and Michelle Shaw; "Newark on Line," by Karrie Jacobs, *Metropolis*, June 1995; "MUSIC, a Poor Man's Internet," by Ronald Roach, *Focus*, October/November 1995; "Community Empowerment through Technology: Alan Shaw's Computer MUSIC," by Heather Davis, *Community Jobs*, November 1995; "Inner City Computer Link Is MUSIC to Their Ears," by Kevin Coughlin, *Star-Ledger*.

CHAPTER SEVENTEEN: BOB MOSES AND THE ALGEBRA PROJECT

The author's interview with Bob Moses took place in Cambridge, Massachusetts, on July 3, 1997. The author interviewed Pam Paternoster, in Cambridge, in June 1997, and Michael Thelwell by telephone on June 1, 1997.

Considerable detail about Moses' early years was drawn from *Parting the Waters* by Taylor Branch, as well as the 1996 Public Television documentary "The American Experience: Freedom on My Mind." Background about Moses and the Algebra Project was derived from: "Mississippi Learning: Algebra as Political Curriculum," by Bell Gale Chevigny, *The Nation*, March 4, 1996; "Freedom," interview with

Moses by Jimmie Briggs, *Emerge*, June 1994; "Bob Moses's Crusade," by Peter Michelmore, *Reader's Digest*, March 1995; "A Luncheon Talk for SUMMAC Given by Bob Moses," *SUMMAC Forum*, February 1994; "Mississippi Learning," by Alexis Jetter, *New York Times Magazine*, February 21, 1993; "A Freedom Summer Activist Becomes a Math Revolutionary," by Bruce Watson, *Smithsonian*, February 1996; "Make Math Matter!," by Nancy-Jo Hereford, *Middle Years*, April/May 1995; "The Algebra Project: Organizing in the Spirit of Ella," by Robert P. Moses, Mieko Kamii, Susan McAllister Swap and Jeffrey Howard, *Harvard Educational Review*, November 1989; "The Vertical Hand Span: Nonstandard Units, Expressions, and Symbols in the Classroom," by Lynne Godfrey and Mary Catherine O'Connor, *Journal of Mathematical Behavior,* no. 14, 1995; "Remarks on the Struggle for Citizenship and Math/Science Literacy," by Robert P. Moses, *Journal of Mathematical Behavior,* no. 13, 1994; "The Algebra Project in Mississippi: An Evaluation, Report Highlights," National Science Foundation, 1994, and publications of the Algebra Project Inc., Cambridge, Massachusetts.

CHAPTER EIGHTEEN: ANCESTORS: THE ASTRONOMER/ SURVEYOR: BENJAMIN BANNEKER

Primary source material on Banneker was derived from *The Life of Benjamin Banneker*, by Silvio A. Bedini (1972). Additional sources were: *Created Equal*, by James Michael Brodie; *Black Pioneers in Science and Invention*, by Louis Haber; "In the Nation: Meet Benjamin Banneker," by Tom Wicker, *New York Times*, March 26, 1968; "Benjamin Banneker: Unschooled Wizard," by Saul K. Padover, *New Republic*, February 2, 1948; obituary in Boston's *Columbia Centinel*, November 12, 1806; " 'Discipline to the Mind': Philadelphia's Banneker Institute," by Emma Jones Lapsansky, *The Pennsylvania Magazine of History and Biography*, January/April 1993; *History of the Negro Race in America, 1619–1880*, by George W. Williams (1883).

CHAPTER NINETEEN: THE ARCHITECTS: CHARLES AND CHERYL MCAFEE

The author's interview with Charles McAfee took place in Wichita, Kansas, on December 30, 1996; with Cheryl McAfee in Atlanta on May 14/15, 1997; by phone with Charyl McAfee on May 27, 1997, and a follow-up telephone interview with Charles McAfee on May 21, 1997. Telephone interviews about the McAfee family were conducted with Cecil Steward on May 28, 1997; Eugene Kremer on May 23, 1997; Britt Brown on May 20, 1997; and Gordon Parks on May 27, 1997.

Background source material on the McAfees was derived from: "Trying to Make a Difference in Wichita, Kansas," by Susan Bady, *Professional Builder*, March 1995; "Atlanta's '96 Olymic Plans Overseen by McAfee firm," by David Dinell, *Wichita Business Journal,* July 29, 1994; "Wichita Firm Takes Lead in '96 Olympics," *Kansas State Globe*, June 6–13, 1996; "McAfee Mfg.—'Not Just Building Homes, We're Building Futures and Communities,' " by Gail Finney, *Automated Builder*, January 1995; "Friends Now Partners in Modular Home Plant That Also Produces Opportunities," by Irene Clepper, *Automated Builder*, July 1996; "Rebuilding the Inner City, One Home at a Time," by Ann Scott Tyson, *Christian Science Monitor*, November 14, 1994; "The Old Neighborhood's Needs Good Fit for McAfee's Business," by Anita Schrodt, *The Wichita Eagle*, November 7, 1994; "McAfee Manufacturing Eyes Plant in Fort Worth," by Roz Hutchinson, *Wichita Business Journal*, October 7, 1994; "Charles McAfee: Venture Helps Neighborhood," editorial, *The Wichita Eagle*, August 25, 1994; "Company Builds More Than Houses," by Jim Cross, *The Wichita Eagle*, August 23, 1994; "King's Words of Understanding Linger," by Charles F. McAfee, *Wichita Eagle-Beacon*, January 18, 1986; "In Sickness and in Health," by Karen Shideler, *The Wichita Eagle*, October 10, 1995; "Wichita Native Achieves Her Own Olympic Glory," by Stan Finger, *The Wichita Eagle*, July 14, 1996; "Top Women Architects," *Ebony*, August 1995; "Cheryl McAfee: Urban Designer," by Kate Watson, *Wichita Women*, March 1990.

Source material on Paul R. Williams: "An Architect Who Beat the Odds," by Michael Webb, *American Legacy*, Winter 1997.

PART FOUR: HEALERS OF BODY AND SPIRIT

CHAPTER TWENTY: ANCESTORS: THE PHYSICIANS: LOUIS TOMPKINS WRIGHT AND JANE COOKE WRIGHT

The author's interview with Dr. Barbara Wright Pierce took place in New York on June 6, 1997, with a follow-up by telephone on June 9, 1997.

Background material on the Wright family was derived from: *Black Pioneers of Science and Invention*, by Louis Haber; "Louis Tompkins Wright, 1891–1952," by Dr. W. Montague Cobb, *Journal of the National Medical Association*, March 1953; transcript of speech by Roy Wilkins at Louis T. Wright Memorial Lecture Series, Harlem Hospital, New York, March 6, 1963; "The Louis T. Wright Library of Harlem Hospital," reprinted from *Journal of the National Medical Association*, July 1952; *Surgeons to the Poor: The Harlem Hospital Story*, by Dr. Aubre de L. Maynard (1978); "The Wright Way," column in *New*

York Daily Mirror, May 29, 1952; chapter on Wrights in *Partners in Science*, by Alma Smith Payne (1968); "Louis Tompkins Wright, 1891–1952," by Dr. W. Montague Cobb, *Negro History Bulletin*, May 1953; biography of Wright by Rayford W. Logan in *Dictionary of American Negro Biography*; "Dr. L. T. Wright Dies; Surgeon, Negro Leader," *New York Herald Tribune*, October 9, 1952; "Honor Surgeon Who Broke the Ban on Negro Doctors," *New York World Telegram*, April 29, 1952; "Wonder Drug," *Industrial Trends*, October 1949; profile of Jane Wright in *Black Scientists*, by Lisa Yount (1991); "The Doctor Is Here: A Profile of Barbara Penn Wright, M.D.," by Glenda Mattox, *Intercom* newsletter.

Background material on Dr. Daniel Hale Williams and Dr. Charles Drew was also derived from *Black Scientists*. Other sources on Drew included: *Created Equal*, by James Michael Brodie; *Black Pioneers of Science and Invention*, by Haber; "Charles Richard Drew—1904–1950," by Dr. W. Montague Cobb, *Negro History Bulletin*, June 1950; biography by Rayford W. Logan in *Dictionary of American Negro Biography*, and *One Blood: The Death and Resurrection of Charles R. Drew*, by Spencie Love (1996).

CHAPTER TWENTY-ONE: BYLLYE AVERY AND THE NATIONAL BLACK WOMEN'S HEALTH PROJECT

The author's interview with Avery took place in Swarthmore, Pennsylvania, on June 4, 1997; with Dr. Virginia Davis-Floyd in Atlanta on May 14, 1997; by telephone with Norma Swenson on July 18, 1997. The author attended Avery's speech before the Maternity Care Coalition Conference in Philadelphia on June 5, 1997.

Background sources on Avery were: "The Health Status of Black Women," paper by Byllye Y. Avery; "Visionary: Byllye Avery's Healthy Example Serves to Inspire Others," by Deborah S. Pinkney, *Chicago Tribune*, June 24, 1990, reprinted from *American Medical News*; *Vital Signs*, vol. 12, no. 1, 1996, and vol. 10, no. 2, April–May, 1994; Avery biography in "Blueprint for the Village: Families & Communities Building the Future," program of Maternity Care Coalition Annual Conference, June 5, 1997; "Racism, Sexism, and Social Class: Implications for Studies of Health, Disease, and Well-Being," by Nancy Krieger, Diane L. Rowley, Allen A. Herman, Byllye Avery, and Monta T. Phillips in *Racial Differences in Preterm Delivery: Developing a New Research Paradigm*, edited by Diane Rowley and Heather Tosteson, *American Journal of Preventive Medicine Supplement* to vol. 9, no. 6, November/December 1993; "Coumba Lamba, USA: An African Traditional Healing Ceremony," Penn Center of St. Helena Island, South Carolina, program booklet, August 11–19, 1996.

CHAPTER TWENTY-TWO: ANCESTORS: SOJOURNER TRUTH AND THE NINETEENTH-CENTURY VISIONARIES

The story of Sojourner Truth was derived primarily from two biographies: *Sojourner Truth: Slave, Prophet, Legend*, by Carleton Mabee with Susan Mabee Newhouse (1993), and *Sojourner Truth: A Life, A Symbol*, by Nell Painter (1996). The author's interview with Jean Humez about Truth and Harriet Tubman took place in Boston on February 1, 1996. The author's discussion of the spirituals with Dr. Joseph Roberts took place in Atlanta on May 16, 1997.

Background on Rebecca Cox Jackson was derived from *Gifts of Power: The Writings of Rebecca Jackson, Black Visionary, Shaker Eldress*, edited with an introduction by Jean McMahon Humez (1981). Additional background on Tubman and other nineteenth-century leaders of slave resistance movements came from: "In Search of Harriet Tubman's Spiritual Autobiography," by Jean M. Humez, *NWSA Journal*, Summer 1993, and *Before the Mayflower: A History of Black America*, by Lerone Bennett, Jr. (1993).

CHAPTER TWENTY-THREE: HOWARD THURMAN, BENJAMIN MAYS, AND THE MARTIN LUTHER KING LEGACY

The author's interviews took place with Rev. Anthony Campbell in Boston on February 4, 1997; Dr. Hugh Gloster in Atlanta on May 15, 1997; Rev. Joseph Roberts in Atlanta on May 16, 1997; Dr. James Cone in New York on April 18, 1996. The author attended the interment service for Sue Bailey Thurman at Atlanta's Morehouse College on May 15, 1997.

Background information on Mays and his relationship with King was derived primarily from *Walking Integrity: Benjamin Elijah Mays, Mentor to Generations*, edited by Lawrence Edward Carter, Sr. (1996); also from *Parting The Waters*, Branch; *Stride Toward Freedom*, by Martin Luther King, Jr. (1958); *Born to Rebel, An Autobiography*, by Benjamin E. Mays (1971); Mays's profile in *The Biographical Dictionary of Black Americans* by Rachel C. Kranz (1991); "Tribute to Dr. Benjamin E. Mays," speech by Hugh M. Gloster, King International Chapel, Morehouse College, March 31, 1984.

Background on Howard and Sue Thurman was derived from: *With Head and Heart: An Autobiography*, by Howard Thurman (1979); *For the Inward Journey: The Writings of Howard Thurman*, selected by Anne Spencer Thurman (1984); *Jesus and the Disinherited*, by Howard Thurman (1981); "Sue Bailey Thurman: Building Bridges to Common Ground," by Trudi Smith (pamphlet, 1995); "Tribute to Dr. Howard

Thurman," by Hugh M. Gloster, *Morehouse College Bulletin,* Summer 1981; Thurman biography in *Black Writers: A Selection of Sketches from Contemporary Authors,* edited by Linda Metzger et al. (1989).

Background on Anthony Campbell was derived from: "Spreading the word: Anthony Campbell to preach at Westminster Abbey," by Jim Graves, clipping from "B.U. Public Relations"; "The Interview: Anthony C. Campbell," by John Koch, *Boston Globe Magazine,* January 19, 1997; Boston University biography of "Reverend Doctor Anthony Cordova Campbell."

Background on the King family and history of the Ebenezer Baptist Church was found in *Parting the Waters,* by Taylor Branch. Background on pastor Joseph Roberts was derived from: church biography; "Ground Breaking: New Horizon Sanctuary," *Spotlight on Ebenezer* newsletter, April/May 1977; "Historic Old Church to Get New Sanctuary," by Gayle White, *Atlanta Journal/Constitution,* March 23, 1997.

Selected Bibliography

Armstrong, Louis. *Swing That Music*. New York: Longmans, Green and Co., 1936.

Baldwin, James. *The Price of the Ticket: Collected Nonfiction 1948–1985*. New York: St. Martin's/Marek, 1985.

———. *Go Tell It on the Mountain*. New York: Alfred A. Knopf, 1953.

———. *Giovanni's Room*. New York: Dial, 1956.

———. *Another Country*. New York: Dial, 1962.

Bedini, Silvio. *The Life of Benjamin Banneker*. New York: Scribner, 1972.

Benjamin, Tritobia Hayes. *The Life and Art of Loïs Mailou Jones*. San Francisco: Pomegranate Artbooks, 1994.

Bennett, Lerone, Jr. *Before the Mayflower: A History of Black America*. New York: Penguin Books 6th revised ed., 1993.

Blight, David W. *Frederick Douglass' Civil War: Keeping Faith in Jubilee*. Baton Rouge: Louisiana State University Press, 1991.

Bradford, Sarah. *Harriet Tubman: The Moses of Her People*. Bedford, Mass.: Applewood Books, 1993.

Branch, Taylor. *Parting the Waters: America in the King Years 1954–63*. New York: Simon & Schuster/Touchstone, 1988.

Brawley, Benjamin. *The Negro in Literature and Art in the United States*. New York: Duffield & Co., 1930.

Brodie, James Michael. *Created Equal: The Lives and Ideas of Black American Innovators*. New York: William Morrow & Co., 1993.

Burt, McKinley, Jr. *Black Inventors of America*. Portland, Oregon: National Book Company, 1989.

Carleton Miscellany: A Review of Literature of the Liberal Arts. *A Ralph Ellison Festival*. Vol. XVIII, No. 3, Winter 1980.

Carter, Lawrence Edward, Sr., ed. *Walking Integrity: Benjamin Elijah Mays, Mentor to Generations*. Produced by Scholars Press on behalf of Morehouse College, 1996.

Charters, Ann. *Nobody: The story of Bert Williams*. New York: Macmillan, 1970.

Collier, James Lincoln. *The Making of Jazz: A Comprehensive History*. New York: A Delta Book, 1978.

———. *Louis Armstrong, An American Genius*. New York: Oxford University Press, 1983.

Cone, James H. *Martin & Malcolm & America: A Dream or a Nightmare*. Maryknoll, N.Y.: Orbis Books, 1991.

Crouch, Stanley. *The All-American Skin Game, or, The Decoy of Race: The Long and the Short of It 1990–1994*. New York: Pantheon Books, 1995.

Contemporary Black Biography, Vol. 8. Edited by L. Mpho Mabunda. Detroit: Gale Research, Inc., 1995.

Current Biography Yearbook 1992. Bronx, N.Y.: H. W. Wilson.

Dictionary of Literary Biography. Detroit: Gale Research, Inc.

Douglass, Frederick. *Life and Times of Frederick Douglass Written by Himself: His Early Life as a Slave, His Escape from Bondage, and his Complete History*. New York: Bonanza, 1962.

Duberman, Martin Bauml. *Paul Robeson: A Biography*. New York: Ballantine Books, 1989.

Ellington, Duke. *Music Is My Mistress*. New York: Da Capo, 1976 (reprint).

Ellison, Ralph. *The Collected Essays of Ralph Ellison*. Edited, with an introduction by John F. Callahan. New York: The Modern Library, 1995.

———. *Invisible Man*. New York: Second Vintage International Edition, 1995.

Embree, Edwin R. *13 Against the Odds*. New York: Viking Press, 1946.

Febre, Genevieve and Robert O'Meally, Ed. *History and Memory in African-American Culture*. New York: Oxford University Press, 1994.

Fletcher, Tom. *100 Years of the Negro in Show Business: The Tom Fletcher Story*. New York: Burdge, 1954.

Foner, Philip S. *The Life and Writings of Frederick Douglass*, Vols. 1–5. International Publishers, 1950–75.

———, ed. with an introduction by. *Paul Robeson Speaks*. New York: Citadel Press/ Carol Publishing, 1978.

Franklin, V. P. *Living Our Stories, Telling Our Truths: Autobiography and the Making of the African-American Intellectual Tradition*. New York: Oxford University Press, 1995.

Fraser, Steven, ed. *The Bell Curve Wars: Race, Intelligence, and the Future of America*. New York: Basic Books, 1995.

Gates, Henry Louis, Jr. *Figures in Black: Words, Signs, and the "Racial" Self*. New York: Oxford University Press, 1987.

Gates, Henry Louis, Jr., and Cornel West. *The Future of the Race*. New York: Alfred A. Knopf, 1996.

Giddings, Paula. *When and Where I Enter: The Impact of Black Women on Race and Sex in America*. New York: Bantam Books, 1985.

Goldman, Roger, with David Gallen. *Thurgood Marshall: Justice for All*. New York: Carroll & Graf, 1993.

Green, Jeffrey P. *Edmund Thornton Jenkins: The Life and Times of an American Black Composer, 1894–1926*. Westport, Ct.: Greenwood Press, 1982.

Haber, Louis. *Black Pioneers of Science and Invention*. New York: Harcourt, Brace & World, 1970.

Harper, Michael S. *Healing Song for the Inner Ear: Poems by Michael S. Harper*. Urbana & Chicago: University of Illinois Press, 1985.

——— and Robert B. Stepto, eds. *Chant of Saints: A Gathering of Afro-American Literature, Art, and Scholarship*. Urbana/Chicago: University of Illinois Press, 1979.

Hasse, John Edward. *Beyond Category: The Life and Genius of Duke Ellington*. New York: Simon & Schuster, 1993.

Higginbotham, Evelyn Brooks. *Righteous Discontent: The Women's Movement in the Black Baptist Church, 1880–1920*. Cambridge, Mass.: Harvard University Press, 1993.

Hine, Darlene Clark, ed. *Black Women in America: An Historical Encyclopedia*. Brooklyn, N.Y.: Carlson Publishing, 1993.

hooks, bell, and Cornel West. *Breaking Bread: Insurgent Black Intellectual Life*. Boston: South End Press, 1991.

Huggins, Nathan Irvin, ed. *Voices From the Harlem Renaissance*. New York: Oxford University Press, 1976.

———. *Revelations: American History, American Myths*. New York: Oxford University Press, 1995.

Hughes, Langston. *Famous American Negroes*. New York: Dodd, Mead, 1961.

————. Milton Meltzer, and C. Eric Lincoln. *A Pictorial History of Black Americans*. New York: Crown Publishers, 1983.

———— and Arna Bontemps, ed. *The Poetry of the Negro 1746–1949: A Definitive Anthology*. Garden City, N.Y.: Doubleday & Co., 1949.

Humez, Jean McMahon, ed. with an introduction by. *Gifts of Power: The Writings of Rebecca Jackson, Black Visionary, Shaker Eldress*. Amherst: University of Massachusetts Press, 1981.

Jackson, Blyden. *A History of Afro-American Literature*, vol. 1: *The Long Beginning, 1746–1895*. Baton Rouge: Louisiana State University Press, 1989.

Jewell, Derek. *Duke: A Portrait of Duke Ellington*. New York: W. W. Norton & Co., 1977.

Jordan, Winthrop D. *The White Man's Burden: Historical Origins of Racism in the United States*. New York: Oxford University Press, 1974.

Kafka, Phillipa. *The Great White Way: African American Women Writers and American Success Mythologies*. New York: Garland Publishing, 1993.

Kaplan, Sidney. *American Studies in Black and White: Selected Essays*. Amherst: University of Massachusetts Press, 1991.

Keckley, Elizabeth. *Behind the Scenes or Thirty Years a Slave and Four Years in the White House*. New York: Oxford University Press, 1988.

Keepnews, Orrin and Bill Grauer, Jr. *A Pictorial History of Jazz: People and Places from New Orleans to Modern Jazz*. New York: Crown Publishers, 1955.

Kent, George E. *A Life of Gwendolyn Brooks*. Lexington: The University Press of Kentucky, 1990.

King, Coretta Scott, selected and introduced by. *The Words of Martin Luther King, Jr.* New York: Newmarket Press, 1987.

King, Martin Luther, Jr. *Stride Toward Freedom: A Leader of His People Tells the Montgomery Story*. New York: Harper & Bros., 1958.

King, The Rev. Martin Luther, Sr., with Clayton Riley. *Daddy King: An Autobiography*. New York: William Morrow & Co., 1980.

Kranz, Rachel C. *Biographical Dictionary of Black Americans*. New York: Facts On File, 1991.

Leeming, David. *James Baldwin: A Biography*. New York: Alfred A. Knopf, 1994.

Lerner, Gerda, ed. *Black Women in White America: A Documentary History*. New York: Vintage Books, November 1992.

Lerner, Michael, and Cornel West. *Jews & Blacks: A Dialogue on Race, Religion, and Culture in America*. New York: Plume, 1996.

Lewis, David Levering. *When Harlem Was in Vogue*. New York: Oxford University Press, 1989 (paperback).

————. *W. E. B. Du Bois: Biography of a Race, 1869–1919*. New York: Henry Holt, 1993.

Lewis, Samella. *African American Art and Artists*. Berkeley: University of California Press, 1990.

Locke, Alain Leroy. *The Critical Temper of Alain Locke: A Selection of His Essays on Art and Culture*. Ed. Jeffrey C. Stewart. New York: Garland Pub., 1983.

————, ed. *The New Negro: Voices of the Harlem Renaissance*. New York: Atheneum, 1992.

Logan, Rayford Whittingham. *Dictionary of American Negro Biography*. New York: W. W. Norton & Co., 1982.

Love, Spencie. *One Blood: The Death and Resurrection of Charles R. Drew*. Chapel Hill: University of North Carolina Press, 1996.

Mabee, Carleton with Susan Mabee Newhouse. *Sojourner Truth: Slave, Prophet, Legend*. New York: New York University Press, 1993.

McFeely, William S. *Frederick Douglass*. New York: W. W. Norton & Co., 1995.

Mailer, Norman. *Advertisements for Myself*. New York: Signet, 1959 (paperback).

Manning, Kenneth R. *Black Apollo of Science: The Life of Ernest Everett Just*. New York: Oxford University Press, 1983.

Marshall, Herbert, and Mildred Stock. *Ira Aldridge: The Negro Tragedian*. Carbondale/Edwardsville: Southern Illinois University Press, Arcturus Books, April 1968.

Maynard, Dr. Aubre de L. *Surgeons to the Poor: The Harlem Hospital Story*. New York: Appleton-Century-Crofts, 1978.

Mays, Benjamin E. *The Negro's God: As Reflected in His Literature*. New York: Atheneum, 1968.

———. *Born to Rebel, An Autobiography*. Athens: University of Georgia Press, 1971.

Metzger, Linda, Senior Editor. *Black Writers: A Selection of Sketches from Contemporary Authors*. Detroit: Gale Research, Inc., 1989.

Miller, John Chester. *The Wolf by the Ears: Thomas Jefferson and Slavery*. Charlottesville: University Press of Virginia, 1991.

Morrison, Toni. *The Bluest Eye*. New York: Plume, 1994.

———. *Song of Solomon*. New York: Plume, 1987.

———. *Sula*. New York: New American Library, 1993.

———. *Jazz*. New York: Plume, 1993.

———. *Beloved*. New York: Plume, 1988.

———. *Playing in the Dark: Whiteness and the Literary Imagination*. Cambridge, Mass.: Harvard University Press, 1992.

Murray, Albert. *The Omni-Americans: Some Alternatives to the Folklore of White Supremacy*. New York: Outerbridge & Dienstfrey, 1970.

———. *South to a Very Old Place*. New York: McGraw-Hill, 1974.

———. *Stomping the Blues*. New York: McGraw-Hill, 1976.

———. *The Hero and the Blues*. New York: Vintage Books, 1995.

———. *The Blue Devils of Nada: A Contemporary American Approach to Aesthetic Statement*. New York: Pantheon Books, 1996.

———. *The Seven League Boots*. New York: Pantheon Books, 1996.

Newman, Richard, and Marcia Sawyer. *Everybody Say Freedom: Everything You Need to Know About African-American History*. New York: Plume, 1996.

Norman, Winifred Latimer, and Lily Patterson. *Lewis Latimer: Scientist*. New York/Philadelphia: Chelsea House Publishers, 1994.

O'Reilly, Kenneth. *Nixon's Piano: Presidents and Racial Politics from Washington to Clinton*. New York: The Free Press, 1995.

Painter, Nell Irvin. *Sojourner Truth: A Life, a Symbol*. New York: W. W. Norton & Co., 1996.

Parks, Gordon. *Gordon Parks: Whispers of Intimate Things*. New York: Viking Press, 1971.

———. *To Smile in Autumn*. New York: W. W. Norton & Co., 1979.

———. *Voices in the Mirror*. New York: Doubleday, 1990.

Payne, Alma Smith. *Partners in Science*. Cleveland/New York: World Publishing Co., 1968.

Peare, Catherine Owens. *Mary McLeod Bethune*. New York: Vanguard Press, 1951.

Prenshaw, Peggy Whitman, General Editor, Literary Conversations Series. *Conversations with Albert Murray*. Oxford: University Press of Mississippi, 1997.

Quarles, Benjamin. *Lincoln and the Negro*. New York: Da Capo Paperback 1991.

Rice, Allen Thorndike, collected and ed. *Reminiscences of Abraham Lincoln by Distinguished Men of His Time*. New York: New American Review, 1889.

Robeson, Paul, with Lloyd L. Brown. *Here I Stand*. Boston: Beacon Press, 1988.

Robeson, Paul, Jr. *Paul Robeson, Jr. Speaks To America: The Politics of Multiculturalism*. New Brunswick, N.J.: Rutgers University Press, 1993.

Robeson, Susan. *The Whole World in His Hands: A Pictorial Biography of Paul Robeson*. New York: Citadel Press/Carol Publishing, 1990.

Rogers, J. A. *World's Great Men of Color, Vol. 2*. New York: Collier Books/Macmillan, 1972.

Salley, Columbus. *The Black 100: A Ranking of the Most Influential African-Americans, Past and Present*. New York: Citadel Press/Carol Publishing Group, 1994.

Schlesinger, Arthur, Jr. *Robert Kennedy and His Times*. New York: Houghton-Mifflin, 1978.

Schneider, Janet M. and Bayla Singer, ed. *Blueprint for Change: The Life and Times of Lewis H. Latimer*. New York: Queens Borough Public Library, 1995.

Schuller, Gunther. *Early Jazz: Its Roots and Musical Development*. New York: Oxford University Press, 1968.

———. *The Swing Era: The Development of Jazz, 1930–1945*. New York: Oxford University Press, 1989.

Smith, Jessie Carney, ed. *Notable Black American Women*, Vols. 1 and 2. Detroit: Gale Research, Inc., 1991 and 1995.

Southern, Eileen. *The Music of Black Americans: A History*. 2nd ed. New York: W. W. Norton & Co., 1983.

Sundquist, Eric J., ed. *Frederick Douglass: New Literary and Historical Essays*. Cambridge, England: Cambridge University Press, 1993 (paperback).

———. *The Oxford W. E. B. Du Bois Reader*. New York: Oxford University Press, 1996.

Thelwell, Michael. *Duties, Pleasures, and Conflicts: Essays in Struggle*. Amherst: University of Massachusetts Press, 1987.

Thurman, Anne Spencer, selected by. *For the Inward Journey: The Writings of Howard Thurman*. New York: Harcourt Brace Jovanovich, 1979.

Thurman, Howard. *Jesus and the Disinherited*. Reprint edition. Richmond, Ind.: Friends University Press, 1981.

———. *With Head and Heart: An Autobiography*. New York: Harcourt Brace Jovanovich, 1979.

———. *Deep River and the Negro Spiritual Speaks of Life and Death*. Richmond, Ind.: Friends United Press, 1975.

Troupe, Quincy, ed. *James Baldwin: The Legacy*. New York: Simon and Schuster/Touchstone, 1989.

Tucker, Mark, ed. *The Duke Ellington Reader*. New York: Oxford University Press, 1993.

Turner, Patricia. *Dictionary of Afro-American Performers*. New York: Garland Publishing, 1990.

Watts, Jerry Gafio. *Heroism & The Black Intellectual: Ralph Ellison, Politics, and Afro-American Intellectual Life*. Chapel Hill: University of North Carolina Press, 1994.

Weatherby, W. J. *James Baldwin: Artist On Fire*. New York: Laurel, 1989.

Weisenfeld, Judith and Richard Newman, ed. *This Far by Faith: Readings in African-American Women's Religious Biography*. New York: Routledge, 1996.

Wells, Diana, compiled by. *We Have a Dream: African-American Visions of Freedom*. New York: Carroll & Graf Publishers/Richard Gallen, 1993.

West, Cornel. *Keeping Faith: Philosophy and Race in America*. New York: Routledge, 1993.

———. *Race Matters*. New York: Vintage Books, 1994.

Wheat, Ellen Harkins. *Jacob Lawrence: American Painter*. Seattle: University of Washington Press, 1986.

Wideman, John Edgar. *Fatheralong: A Meditation on Fathers and Sons, Race and Society*. New York: Vintage Books, 1995.

Williams, George Washington. *History of the Negro Race in America, 1619–1880*. New York: Arno Press, 1968 (reprint of 1883 edition).

Wolfe, Charles, and Kip Lornell. *The Life & Legend of Leadbelly*. New York: First HarperPerennial Edition 1994.

Yount, Lisa. *American Profiles: Black Scientists*. New York: Facts On File, 1991.

Index